D0548798

The American History Cookbook

The American History Cookbook

Mark H. Zanger

An Oryx Book

GREENWOOD PRESS
Westport, Connecticut • London

Library of Congress Cataloging-in-Publication Data

Zanger, Mark.
   The American history cookbook / Mark H. Zanger.
      p.   cm.
   Includes bibliographical references and index.
   ISBN 1–57356–376–5 (alk. paper)
   1. Cookery, American—History.   I. Title.
TX715.Z36   2003
641.5973—dc21   2002069608

British Library Cataloguing in Publication Data is available.

Copyright © 2003 by Mark H. Zanger

All rights reserved. No portion of this book may be
reproduced, by any process or technique, without the
express written consent of the publisher.

Library of Congress Catalog Card Number: 2002069608
ISBN: 1–57356–376–5

First published in 2003

Greenwood Press, 88 Post Road West, Westport, CT 06881
An imprint of Greenwood Publishing Group, Inc.
www.greenwood.com

Printed in the United States of America

The paper used in this book complies with the
Permanent Paper Standard issued by the National
Information Standards Organization (Z39.48–1984).

10 9 8 7 6 5 4 3

Copyright Acknowledgments

The author and publisher gratefully acknowledge permission for use of the following material:

"Dualism: In Ralph Ellison's *Invisible Man*," from *Conjure*, copyright 1971 by Ishmael Reed, reprinted with permission.

Translation for recipes for "Rebanadas O Tajadas de Queso Fresco Que Es Fruta de Sarten" and for "Potaje de Fideos," copyright 2001 by Robin Carroll-Mann, reprinted with permission.

Recipes for "Cocoa Nut Pudding" and "Eve's Pudding" from Francis B. Smith Recipe Book, with permission of the Smith-Townshend Family Papers and Papers II, Massachusetts Historical Society.

Recipe for "Custards & Ices" from Mary Channing Eustis Recipe Book, with permission of the Pemberton Collection, Massachusetts Historical Society.

To Ginny

CONTENTS

PREFACE

The *American History Cookbook* is a book of recipes used in the United States, some from very long before it was called the United States, some still followed today. Some of the recipes make delicious dishes. Some were never very good. Some recipes document actual dishes cooked and eaten by soldiers, pioneers, or other "bad cooks." But I haven't improved them because this is not a book about the best cooking in American history. The recipes were picked because they tell people's stories. In particular, this book is about people becoming part of American history—whether they knew it or not. Even though she was a woman. Even though he was only a common soldier. Even though they were slaves. Even though he was a Spaniard living in the distant province of New Mexico. Even though she was an Indian, and we know about her only in what was written by colonists. Even though her father's work was secret, and she only knew it would help win the war. Even though historians are still arguing about his presidency. Even though we may *never* know her name.

This book has more than 350 recipes, exactly as written down between 1524 and 1977. For example, the recipe for **sofkee** (a thin porridge of grits) was submitted by mail for a church cookbook in 1900 by Nancy Osceola. She was the surviving sister-in-law of the great Seminole war chief, Osceola, who made the same sofkee in the 1830s while he was outwitting federal troops. But sofkee was used for thousands of years before that, from present-day Arizona in the west to present-day Georgia in the east.

The written recipes are doors into history. To cook and taste historic foods is to glimpse through those doors. When we cook and taste sofkee in the twenty-first century, it helps us see a thousand years back to the ancestors of the Creek and Seminole Indians, taking a refreshing sofkee break in the work of building the huge earth structures we now call "mounds." We can almost hear the shipwrecked Spanish explorer Cabeza de Vaca thanking Indian hosts for a hot cup of sofkee during his many years of wandering back to Mexico. We can feel how Osceola and his warriors, many of them escaped African slaves, might have warmed their hands around a secret campfire in the Everglades. We can imagine the voice of Nancy Osceola, telling the old stories to her grandchildren as she pours them a cup of sofkee. We can imagine the Louisville church ladies of 1900 tasting the sofkee and deciding "it is not a very tempt-

WEST HILLS COLLEGE
LEMOORE LIBRARY/LRC

ing dish . . . nothing but real hunger inducing one to touch it." We can try to imagine that hunger. And we can imagine the hunger for connection that makes plain sofkee a rich cup of memories for Native American families today.

The *Cookbook* is divided into fifty chronologically overlapping chapters, running from pre-Columbian times to the mid-1970s. Some chapters are about specific periods of time, such as World War I, but most chapters are about such topics as the "Temperance and Prohibition Recipes" or "The Civil Rights Movement and Its Opponents." The recipes come from all fifty states and the District of Columbia, and from every decade from the 1710s to the 1970s.

Most recipes are reprinted verbatim. The recipe is then presented in modern format, but without alterations—except as necessary to reproduce the original dish using supermarket ingredients and contemporary kitchen equipment. Many of the recipes are among the earliest published versions of the dish. Some are drawn from since-published kitchen manuscripts; seven are published here for the first time. About fifty recipes are from before 1800. Four core chapters cover seasonal meals from the early American period between the American Revolution and the Civil War, a period when distinctively American food fully emerged yet still reflected the seasonal struggles to farm and store foods in the North American climate.

The recipes were collected as a resource for understanding American history and for research in local history, social studies, food history, and culinary arts. The recipes illustrate the development of foods eaten today in the United States, foods associated with specific historic figures or events, foods widely referred to in American literature, and foods associated with political campaigns and social movements. Recipes are given for many of the most popular dishes of different eras and also for dishes that rep-resent how individuals adapted to historic circumstances. A secondary theme of the book is showing the various techniques culinary historians use to re-create historic foods.

Three to seventeen recipes are provided in each chapter. The introduction offers some comments on the processes of historic cooking and some advice on doing local food history. Although the *Cookbook* is broadly chronological, the chronological index will help users to pinpoint the recipes from any historical period. The index by states demonstrates that American history has happened in every state. The subject and recipe index has some fun listings. You can find recipes associated with Ernest Hemingway, Louisa May Alcott, and Emily Dickinson; recipes written by men; no-cook recipes; and recipes associated with Democrats, Republicans, Federalists, Whigs, and third-party presidential candidates. You can also follow vegetarian recipes, ethnic recipes, or chocolate recipes as they developed through American history.

The American History Cookbook was planned to accompany my previous work, *The American Ethnic Cookbook for Students*, which in turn is part of a series with *The Multicultural Cookbook for Students* by Carol Lisa Albyn and Lois Sinaiko Webb, and two succeeding multicultural cookbooks by Ms. Webb. In this *Cookbook*, recipes of special interest to students are followed through history in chapters on "Camping Out" and "School Lunch," in three chapters about cooking for and by children in American history, and in many individual recipes for sweets and snacks. The author's own indulgence has been to follow the development of American chocolate recipes with special attention. No recipe in this book requires the use of alcoholic beverages, although this was almost universal in colonial and early American times. We are fortunate that the early temperance movement published alcohol-free recipes for syllabub, mince pie, and plum pudding. In a few cases, substitutions recommended during the period by temperance activists have been suggested.

Food history has developed greatly improved standards since Karen and John Hess published *The Taste of America* twenty-six years ago. This book draws upon the works of previous food historians over many periods. You hold in your hands the largest assembly of American historical recipes to date, covering the broadest sweep of history. The book is necessarily thin in places, and some interpretations are new, especially on the exchanges of corn dishes among Indians, colonists, and "African slaves"; on the political meanings of named cakes before and after the Civil War; and on the nature of abolitionist and suffragist recipes. There is still much to learn and discover in American food history, and I hope readers will correct any errors in this book for many years to come.

As I completed this book in the winter of 2001–2002, the United States was again in crisis. At such times, we turn to history for a sense of meaning. It seemed to fit as I read how Americans named foods after skyscrapers as a symbol of hope during the Great Depression, and how red-white-and-blue desserts were popular at the height of World War II. I remembered again the words of Ishmael Reed:

i am outside of
history. i wish
i had some peanuts, it
looks hungry there in
its cage.

i am inside of
history. its
hungrier than i
thot.

ACKNOWLEDGMENTS

The first historical American recipe that I cooked was a baked bean recipe written by Lydia Maria Child in 1827. Child gave up food writing a few years later to dedicate herself and her writing to the abolition of slavery. This year is the two-hundredth anniversary of her birth, and I thank her for recording many old New England foods; the nation acknowledges her help in righting one of the great wrongs of our history.

I got Child's baked bean recipe twenty-six years ago, reading *The Taste of America* by Karen and John Hess. That book opened the idea of connecting food history with populist food politics and conservative good taste, a combination that solves many riddles. This book was enriched by conversation and correspondence with the Hesses and with food historians Andrew Smith, Stephen Schmidt, and Sandra L. Oliver. Manuscript collector Karen Hicks has been an e-mail companion, and I am especially grateful to her for access to her 1832 New England manuscript and for sending me a copy of *Jennie June's Cook Book*. My family inspired much rewriting, especially when called upon to eat the early tries at Apisas, Whigs, Lafayette Gingerbread, Preble Cake, Brownies, Hermits, and Bean Bread. The book owes much to discussions with Dr. Judith A. Birnbaum; Christopher Kimball; my late grandmother, Malvina Kurtz; Dr. Carmen Judith Nine-Curt; John Thorne; and my late father, Martin Zanger. I am also grateful for briefer clarifications over the years from Joan Avant, Jessica Harris, Annie Parker, and Tubby Torrez. This is not to imply that any of these people approve of the consequences but only that debate is the way that history digests information.

And we know now that it is always hungry.

INTRODUCTION

HANDS-ON HISTORY

Many things in history can be understood more deeply by reenacting them. I had an experience of this a week before I signed the contract to write this book. I was coming out from a swim on Cape Cod when I found an Indian artifact in the sand. I had seen grooved stones like this in books and museums, and remembered one that was described as a "side-notched fishing weight." Since I was near the low-tide line, and the stone had been worn down in the surf, "fishing weight" stayed in my mind for at least ten minutes. New England Indians had constructed very

Figure 1 *Source: Author's collection.*

large fish traps and weirs. One found by archeologists in Boston Harbor was several miles long. They might have needed many weights to control their nets.

But by the time I had dried off from my swim, I had turned the stone all over in my hands, and found that it fit my hand perfectly as a hand-hammer or crushing stone, perhaps as a mortar to grind corn. I could also see that this stone was granite, a very hard rock with no natural layering or grain. The groove around it could not have developed in any natural way, and that groove was not easy to cut in granite. Someone had worked for many hours to peck or rasp what was originally a clean notch (as I had seen in the museum specimens) all the way around this egg-shaped piece of granite. After spending that much time, they would not have risked such a valuable tool as a fishing weight. No Indian ever threw this stone into the sea, even at the end of a fishing line or net. It must have been lost in some sudden accident or conflict, or been buried with its owner many centuries ago, in a place that is now under the sea. I tried pecking out a notch in another piece of granite, using a pointed quartz (a harder stone) to see how long it would take to work up a grooved stone like this. Based on what I could do in half an hour, my guess is that at least twenty hours of tedious work would go into making this tool. As I pecked away, I realized that there was a somewhat faster way to cut a groove in granite, by rubbing it against an exposed vein of quartz on a large boulder. However, there are very few large boulders on the sandy part of Cape Cod where I found the stone. A couple of the bigger ones have grooves cut in them that the Indians used to straighten arrows, but they don't have the right kind of exposed quartz. This stone was probably made somewhere else and carried or traded to where I found it, perhaps over several generations.

Handling the stone, I thought about how it might have been used. Shelling nuts came to mind, or breaking deer bones for soup. You could crack corn with it, or pulverize red stone to make body paint. If it was tied around the groove to a stick, the stone could be a handy hammer, even a weapon.

It was several months before I found a description of the same kind of stone as used by modern Plains Indians in the book, *The Cheyennes; Indians of the Great Plains*, by E. Adamson Hoebel, published in 1960 but based on field work done among the Northern Cheyennes in Montana and Wyoming in 1935–1936. Hoebel had interviewed elderly people who remembered the old way of life and reconstructed the life of Cheyennes in the period 1840–1860:

> The basic household item of the woman is her stone maul—an oval river stone with pecked out grooves on the short sides around which is fixed a supple willow withe firmly fastened with green rawhide. When dried out, the rawhide shrinks and holds the maul within the handle with the grip of a vise. With the maul she breaks up fuel, drives tipi pegs, and crushes large bones to be cooked in soup. With smaller handstones the housewife crushes her chokecherries and pulverizes her dried meat.

This book gives the original versions of many historical recipes. At the same time, it provides ways to use modern kitchen tools to produce the closest possible result. Without spending an hour beating eggs with a kitchen knife, as housewives or their slaves did before the Civil War, you can still taste the cakes enjoyed by early American families. But there is another kind of understanding you can gain by using some of the old techniques, such as creaming the butter and sugar for a pie crust with your hands, or by kneading bread without a bread machine, or even baking a Jonny-cake in your fireplace.

No one is proposing that the dishes taste very differently if you make them "the hard way." And no one should be re-enacting slavery without supervision. But some early techniques will be explored as activities in the next book in this series, *The American History Cookbook Reference Companion*. In this book, you can re-enact the lengthy process mothers went through to make the first peanut butter and jelly sandwiches in the 1890s. You can learn how to make an Early American chicken pie inside a Dutch oven in a large fireplace. Or you can use a food processor to make Cherokee **Bean Bread** that actually sticks together. Sometimes.

AMERICAN HUNGER

One of the harder things to reenact is the hunger and thirst of early Americans. They were hungry all the time because they did everything by hand, walked everywhere, and barely heated their houses. This was true of Native Americans, colonists, and early Americans, and remained true for many families well into the twentieth century. When possible, they ate lots of fats and meat as energy foods. They ate on various schedules, but all of them—men, women, and children—ate a lot. Early American recipes are generally twice as large as recipes today, and smaller families is only part of the story. People filled up by eating the pudding first, had meat at every meal when they could, and probably consumed twice the calories many healthy, athletic people now consume. (By the way, neither the Indians nor the American-born colonists were much smaller than their descendants are today. They just had smaller beds.)

Farmers' families and farm workers spent most of their time producing, storing, and cooking food. Until early in the twentieth century, city dwellers spent more than half of their income on food. (The figure now is between 10 and 11 percent, in spite of restaurant meals.)

Even as hungry as they were, their food always meant more than stalling their hunger. Native Americans had more than a hundred recipes for corn alone, some reserved for certain ceremonies, or secret societies, or events like weddings and funerals. They savored the earliest corn and the last corn. They had recipes for the side shoots they weeded out of the corn patch, and the animals they caught trying to steal the corn. The earliest colonists had their starving times, but still treasured certain foods that reminded them of European homes and quickly invented others to celebrate their new identity as American colonists. People also have a hunger to belong, and eating certain foods was part of belonging—to a church, to an ethnic group, to a social class, to a region, to a vision of social reform, to a moment in history. Colonial New England men belonged with their fellow citizens when they ate election cake and voted for local officers. Confederate widows belonged to their society when they baked cakes named after Robert E. Lee or pies named for Jefferson Davis. Civil rights activists belonged to their movement by demonstrating racial integration in public, but also by eating southern African-American dishes in private meetings.

Cooking these recipes now doesn't commit you to the point of view of historical actors, but it may help you see into their personalities. The wives of the Tories enjoyed good English food as part of being Royal Subjects. William Paca, a signer of the Declaration of Independence, wore a wig to court, but loved a rich oyster stew he might not have been able to afford as an English barrister.

You cannot go back in time, but you can go back in taste.

You can taste the hominy spoon-fed to a French missionary priest at an Illinois Indian village in 1673. You can taste the pancakes made by pioneer wife Mattie V. Oblinger on the Nebraska prairie one day in 1873 when she didn't have any eggs. You can taste the meat loaf sandwiches fifteen-year-old Sara Rowan made for her parents and brothers and sisters during World War II, when the family had moved to the secret city of Oak Ridge, Tennessee, and four of her family members took those sandwiches into the plants extracting nuclear material for a weapon that might end the war. You can taste the delicious beef noodle soup nervously prepared by the first Vietnamese refugees in 1975, as they took English lessons at a Florida airbase.

We do not have the recipes for foods cooked by Harriet Tubman while guiding slaves north to freedom, not those she used in her hospital for African-American soldiers during the Civil War, but you can share the cornbread she enjoyed with the family of her pastor in her eighties and nineties. You can share an after-hours gizzard stew with African-American abolitionists of the 1840s working as hotel waiters. You can taste the kind of granola the hippies actually ate.

HUNGER WE CHOOSE NOT TO SHARE

Some parts of American food history cannot or should not be re-enacted. As a child born into slavery, Frederick Douglass was sometimes fed with other slave children from an animal trough. It is sufficient to read about this humiliating experience without re-enacting it, and no recipe will be given.

Over much of American history, alcoholic beverages were widely used by people of all ages and included in many recipes. However, the temperance movement began even before Independence, as a response to the extraordinary public abuse of alcohol in eighteenth-century London and the many problems in the British colonies. In Early America, as a result, many baked goods began to be made without alcoholic ingredients, and alcohol-free recipes were developed for such staples as mincemeat, desserts,

and beverages. To give examples of these important foods, temperance cooking has been included in this book out of proportion to its early influence. Temperance recipes are also included because they were part of a grouping of reform issues that initially included the abolition of slavery, women's rights, religious revival, and social reform. After the Civil War, reformers split and reformed around these issues.

Indians, early colonists, and early Americans hunted and gathered many wild species, which are now endangered or otherwise unavailable in typical supermarkets. If you study foraging or work with experienced local hunters, fishermen, or foragers, you may be able to reproduce some early recipes for your region. This is especially important in the history of Native American cooking, but wild foods have remained part of American food history from the venison at the so-called "First Thanksgiving" to the many game recipes in the 1977 book *Cooking On Extended Benefits; The Unemployed Cookbook*, collected by unemployed steel workers in Pennsylvania. Some popular early American recipes, for pigeons or chestnuts, actually refer to the now extinct passenger pigeon and the endangered American chestnut, and thus cannot be accurately reproduced today.

The book also underplays the elaborate (and often French) cuisine of some very wealthy Americans. This kind of food was served on some historic occasions and was the daily diet of colonial leaders and some of the "founding fathers." However, it is generally more difficult than popular cooking and often features luxury ingredients that are still quite expensive. Some of this food was valued precisely because ordinary citizens could not afford it. If you want to put together some historically accurate "millionaire's dinners," they are generally better recorded than the meals of average citizens, and the bibliography mentions some reprinted cookbooks that describe how to produce the meals of very wealthy families from the 1820s until now.

Perhaps surprisingly, some foods that were very inexpensive one hundred years ago are now expensive luxuries. Maple sugar was originally the cheapest available form of sugar and quietly substituted for sugar in many recipes by farm families short on cash. As late as the 1960s, fish was much cheaper than steak. When rice was widely grown in the Carolinas it was fed to slaves in preference to corn. (But stories about Colonial servants refusing to eat lobster or salmon more than once a week cannot be substantiated. Eastern Salmon stocks were already declining in the early nineteenth century.) Veal was seasonably the cheapest meat in the market, and nineteenth-century thrift recipes tried to disguise it as chicken or pork.

GETTING STARTED IN FOOD HISTORY

This book is only a beginning of collecting recipes that illustrate American history. Readers should begin their own collections and someday publish their own books. You can start with family history, local history, or today's newspaper.

This book ends in the 1970s, but history didn't end then. What recipes will people in the future use to re-create our period? What is happening around us that will be studied in American history class in 2102? My previous book has many recipes from the *Roots* ethnic revival of the 1980s, and I've carefully set aside the dueling chocolate chip cookie recipes published by Hillary Rodham Clinton and Barbara Bush during the 1992 presidential election. But what else will bring recent history back to life? Wraps? Blueberry bagels? Pineapple on pizza? Do these dishes signal an end to ethnic politics in American life, or an acceptance of a multicultural society, or both, or neither? If the 2001–2002 revival of meat loaf and mashed potatoes continues, will that indicate a return to the Cold War caution of the 1950s, or an end to the health food fads of the 1970s, or just that people were sick of the creative cheflike cooking of the 1990s? If your family has been eating meat loaf all along, does that mean you missed something?

Some readers are thinking that the cooking in their family is so dull or even so bad that no one will ever want to know about it. And they may be right. But there was a lot of dull and bad food promoted by food writers around the turn of the twentieth century, and in 1986 Laura Shapiro wrote a completely fascinating 237-page book about it, called *Perfection Salad*. She could have doubled the length of her book by including recipes. Ms. Shapiro's research unearthed the reasons why home economists thought dull and bad food was good for society and how they persuaded portions of their audience (perhaps your ancestors). So in addition to collecting recipes, you have to interview the cooks in your family about why they make the food that way.

Resources in local food history are larger than anyone knows. You can begin with "oral histories" with senior cooks in the community, some of whom have old handwritten recipe books that have passed down to them, or antique cookbooks used by their ancestors. Historical societies and local libraries have those kitchen manuscripts, too, as well as church and community cookbooks from even earlier times. They may also have a few general antique cookbooks, or bound copies of *Godey's Lady's Book* or other nineteenth-century women's magazines that had recipes.

You can also work with early accounts of pioneer or farm life in your area, or reports on factory conditions, or old files of the local newspaper, or court records of the estates of prominent citizens. These materials may have no recipes but will indicate what foods were available, market prices, or what kitchen equipment people owned. Even though it means guesswork, concentrating on one historic person or building or town has been a useful method for food historians. Sandra L. Oliver's great book, *Saltwater Foodways*, is an outcome of her work as a costumed interpreter and supervisor of interpretation for four buildings and two ships at the Mystic Seaport Museum. These are real buildings and ships, although they have been moved to the museum. There are historical records of who lived in the houses and some of what was sold at the store, but all the recipes had to come from New England cookbooks, cooking manuscripts, and the kitchens and galleys of contemporary New Englanders.

Family history and genealogy often turn up old recipes, as well as reminiscences of favorite dishes where the recipe has been lost. Sometimes these old recipes can be reconstructed. Although some family history is only interesting to the family (and some of it is embarrassing), the history in books is just the summary of the history of families. Mrs. Robert E. Lee kept a kitchen notebook, much of which was published in 1997 as *The Robert E. Lee Family Cooking and Housekeeping Book*. This would be of historical interest in any case, but in this case we are fortunate that the book was edited by Anne Carter Zimmer, who is the great-granddaughter of Robert E. Lee. Ms. Zimmer was able to use family connections to check the handwriting on recipes written into the book and track relationships with other family members who had written or published similar recipes in the nineteenth century.

GETTING STARTED IN THE KITCHEN

This book is written with beginning cooks in mind, but experienced cooks should read through this section anyway. You can always learn something new. The recipes in this book assume that you are cooking in a kitchen with measuring cups, measuring spoons, salt, pepper, water, a set of saucepans with lids, one or more frying pans, a stove, an oven, knives, work surfaces, a cutting board, and a few other basics. Nevertheless, you should begin by reading the recipe all the way through several times to make sure you have everything you need and know what you have to do. Because this book includes many unfamiliar ways of cooking, you should assemble all the equipment and ingredients in plain sight before you begin.

Before we begin the safety warnings, I want to emphasize that you should relax and have fun in the kitchen. It's only food. If the dish doesn't come out right the first time, this is not a historic catastrophe. Cooks in American history burned many dishes and others came out badly. Bad food is part of history. You might have made a mistake. The book might have a mistake in it. The oven temperature might be off. The dish may just be like that. The good news is, because our ancestors survived their historic food failures, we can go out for fast-food later.

You should cook with other people. The contemporary nuclear family with one-cook kitchens was not the norm over most of American history. Indian cooks, army cooks, slave cooks, and most other cooks worked alongside other people. In farm families, two and three generations of women worked together in the kitchen even when neighbors and visitors weren't around. Not only do professional cooking students always cook with an experienced professional to answer questions, but many expert cooks like to work in a group, since they can compare techniques and discuss problems (and gossip and have a good time). If the recipe contains a warning, or if any step is new to you, go over your plans with an experienced cook. I have tried to avoid difficult and dangerous steps as much as possible, but some important historical dishes involve deep-fat frying or candy making, and inexperienced cooks should be supervised.

FIRE SAFETY

Always have a fire extinguisher rated A, B, and C handy. Grease fires can actually be spread by water. In an emergency where you do not have a fire extinguisher, do not hesitate to call the fire department. With fire, a few minutes can make a big difference. To prevent kitchen fires, be most careful with hot oil—it can flash up. Never turn your back on a pan of hot oil. Never try to move a pan with hot oil in it. Turn off the heat and let it cool down. This book attempts to minimize deep-fat frying and generally suggests doing so in saucepans with high sides. It is much safer to deep-fry chicken in a soup pot than in a "frying pan." Don't answer the telephone while cooking. Don't leave wooden or plastic utensils on or near the stovetop.

BURN SAFETY

Besides avoiding kitchen fires, you can avoid burning yourself by being extra careful with hot oil, hot sugar mixtures, boiling soup, and when opening covered pots of steaming food. Keep dry oven mitts or pot holders handy. Don't adjust the shelves in hot ovens, or reach into a hot oven when you can use tongs or a wooden pothook instead. Fireplace recipes should be supervised, as they were in Early American times when everyone grew up with fireplace cooking.

KNIFE SAFETY

Keep knives sharp so they don't slip on hard foods. If you find yourself sawing or forcing a knife through food, stop to sharpen the knife or ask for help. The most common cutting accidents involve round foods like bagels, onions, winter squash, crusty loaves of bread, and carrots. The food rolls under the knife and the knife comes down on a finger. Stabilize round foods by cutting a slice from one side and setting them on that flat side. All other knife rules are based on keeping the cutting edge foremost in your mind: Don't push foods under a moving knife; only move the knife. Don't put down a knife anywhere near the edge of a working surface. Don't put anything else on top of a knife, ever. Don't carry a knife and anything else at the same time. When you finish a cutting step, wash the knife and put it back in a block. If you drop a knife, move your feet—don't try to catch it.

HOT PEPPER SAFETY

Hot peppers carry most of their heat in oils that are hard to remove from hands and easy to transfer to eyes and other sensitive parts. You can avoid many problems by wearing gloves or plastic bags over your hands while handling hot peppers, even just one small one. Washing hands after working with hot peppers does not remove all the burning oils, but it does remove some. If you do touch your eyes, splash with a lot of cold running water.

FOOD-BORNE ILLNESS

Don't cook for other people when you are sick. Wash your hands frequently. Most food poisoning is caused by bacteria on the surface of uncooked protein foods *that are transferred* to cooked protein foods—which are then held at room temperature. So the key is to clean up right away after working with raw chicken or other meats or uncooked sausages. Wash your hands before working with other foods, especially foods that aren't going to be cooked through for at least five minutes. If you are unsure how to handle any food, or if you think the food has spoiled, ask an experienced cook.

BURNT FOOD

This isn't usually dangerous, just frustrating. The most common pots of burned food belong to cooks who were distracted. As a beginner, don't answer the telephone or leave the kitchen while cooking. Food burns because too much heat is being transferred too rapidly across too small an area. Too much food in a small pot doesn't circulate well, so only a little of it is getting all the heat. Once it starts to burn on the inside of the pot, the food will stick and circulate less, and burn more. Use a larger pot, so the heat is spread across a larger bottom, and the food can be stirred around more easily. Pots that are not covered cool off on top, but burn on the bottom. A covered pot with lower heat is more efficient and cooks more uniformly. (Sometimes instructions are not to cover a pot so a food will become more concentrated, or so that it simmers at a slightly lower temperature.) Heavier pots transfer heat more evenly than light-gauge pots. Stickier foods are more likely to burn: clear soups simmer for hours while starchy porridges have to be stirred constantly. Sugared foods burn quickly.

If your food does burn on the bottom, you can save most of a soup or stew by pouring it into another pot without stirring. Usually the burned food and the burned taste will stay stuck to the pot.

Burnt food was an even bigger problem in fireplace cooking. Cooks began with a big fire and generated enough hot coals to make small piles of embers like the burners on a stove. Some dishes could be cooked in pots within the piles of hot coals or with hot coals on the lids of the pots to make an oven effect. Pots left open for any amount of time usually were contaminated by soot or a few ashes. Covered pots would burn without anyone noticing. Children or servants or slaves who were supposed to be watching the food were beaten if it burned. Sometimes the natural consequence was meat without bread, or pudding without meat, or not much for supper.

PERSONAL DISTASTE

Because the object of this book is to increase understanding, you should try to taste at least a little bit of anything you make. I have not searched out weird and disgusting foods, but we each have our own ideas of taste. The recipes in this book are exactly as made by historic American cooks so that you can get as close as possible to their food experiences. If your culture or region is not one that uses a lot of pepper, and the recipe is very spicy, try to make at least a sample of the highly spiced dish to get an idea of the difference between cultural norms. In general, you should avoid substituting ingredients even when you think it would taste better with something different. In fact, you should especially avoid trying to make the recipes taste better, because this almost always means using the taste rules of our own historical period.

RELIGIOUS AND OTHER TABOOS

No one using this book should feel under any pressure to eat something that would normally break a food rule from his or her own background. Observant Jews and Muslims should feel free to substitute for pork products. Point-cut corned beef brisket substitutes well for salt pork in many recipes and was used in just that way by colonial and Early American cooks, and possibly by early Jewish Americans. You may get into historical cooking very effectively by keeping your taboos with you and imagining how people of your background would have adjusted to the available foods of different periods in American history. It is known that a group of Turkish weavers were sent to Virginia in the seventeenth century and that some African slaves were Muslims. Although we have not recovered any recipes from these early American Muslims, we can imagine how they tried to eat around the foods on the colonial Virginia table. Ask experienced cooks in your group how they might make such a "foreign" recipe, and they may have good suggestions.

Vegetarians may have to do some research outside the book, although they will meet fellow vegetarians of the 1830s and since in the health food and communal experiments chapters. The book has generally avoided recipes with alcohol or caffeine. Again, committed Mormons, Christian Scientists, and recovering alcoholics will get the best advice from experienced cooks in their own group on how to substitute vanilla sugar for vanilla extract and so on.

A WARNING FOR "GOOD COOKS"

Since the object of most projects with this book is to understand historic cooking as it was, you should try to make the recipe exactly as written, even if you know a better way. The results of the original technique may be a pleasant surprise (they sometimes surprised me), but in any case, they are what the original cooks intended to serve. This is actually a more serious warning than the one about changing the ingredients, because it is so easy to impose our own lifestyles on the very different context of historic recipes. For example, **To Make a Frykecy,** from the seventeenth century, makes a rich sauce out of stewed chicken with egg yolks and amounts of butter that seem grossly unhealthful. A modern "Good Cook" will almost automatically cut back on the egg yolks and butter, and thicken the sauce with corn starch or flour-butter paste. That makes the flavor much less intense, but the dish *changes*

function as well. As this chicken fricassee was understood in England and Colonial America, no one ate more than a little bit of it. It was one of many dishes set out on a mid-day table, of which the main items were an unsauced roast and a boiled ham or fish, all to be eaten with a lot of bread, salads, and vegetables as well. This is not to say that sixteenth-century Carolina planters ate health food. But the rich fricassee could be balanced with leaner meats and carbohydrate foods. The lightened fricassee is a dish that fits our meat-potato-vegetable supper, but it wouldn't get much attention on the Colonial Virginia table next to the boiled turkey or roast leg of lamb. (Some people in Colonial times tried to go on a diet by eating only one meat dish at each meal. Two such people were William Byrd of Westover and George Washington. Ironically, Byrd's sister-in-law owned the manuscript from which the fricassee recipe comes, but was not very interested in food. Martha Washington owned the manuscript for many years, but by then fashions were changing.)

FOR INTERNET USERS:
WWW.HISTORYCOOK.COM

This book has a website, where you can find additional recipes. You can also leave questions, comments, or corrections for the author. The website has links to other sources of historic recipes and American historic food information. There is a link to www.ethnicook.com, the site for my previous book, *The American Ethnic Cookbook for Students*, and a sneak preview of my next book, the *American History Cookbook Reference Companion*.

1

FIRST NATIONS AND EARLY SETTLERS (1200–1674)

American food did not begin with European settlement. Just because we haven't yet found written recipes from before Columbus, it doesn't mean that people didn't have recipes. Ten years after the conquest of Mexico, a friar named Bernardino de Sahagún wrote down information on hundreds of Aztec dishes. Many of these dishes were known to Native Americans in what is now the United States, and some are still used, if only occasionally, by more than one million living Native Americans. This chapter looks at some of the Indian foods that were offered to European explorers and settlers in what is now the United States and discusses which were adapted and how.

It is useful to remember that Native American food also had a continuing history. Some of the dishes in this book, such as **Sofkee**, were already thousands of years old when the first cup was offered to Spanish explorers of what is now the United States, such as Alvar Nunez Cabeza de Vaca in the 1520s and 1530s. Other foods, such as the **Leatherbritches Beans** that begin this chapter, may have reached the eastern Indians only a few hundred years before their first contact with European explorers. Contrary to some histories, Native Americans

domesticated plants and animals in what became the United States, and probably de-emphasized some of the earlier crops (such as sunflowers and jerusalem artichokes), to specialize in the corn, beans, and squash they were growing when European visitors began arriving in the early 1500s. The visitors were mostly here to fish but also to trade copper pots and iron tools for beaver skins. Although corn was probably first domesticated in what is now Mexico, Indians may have domesticated tepary beans in what is now Arizona. It is likely that the ancestors of acorn and butternut squash were domesticated in the southeastern states. Native Hawaiians had built up a considerable cuisine in Hawaii prior to its English "discovery" in 1788 and the possible Spanish visit hundreds of years earlier. Native Alaskans and Eskimos had found ways to eat well in environments in which it was difficult or impossible to farm.

Many of the written comments on Native dishes are sketchy, because all of the European explorers and most of the early colonists were men. Men did not cook much in European society (although sailors and soldiers did some cooking), and the explorers of what became the United States were not as curious as Sahagún and not very interested in food technology. Even when hungry, an English explorer who saw Indian women molding breads to be cooked in boiling water, didn't usually stop to find out whether they had started with mashed fresh corn, cornmeal, corn flour, ground parched corn, ground lye hominy, or ground pearl hominy. When women did arrive as colonists, they investigated American foods and food technology, but they didn't write a lot about it. The first American cookbook was published in 1796. Surviving colonial cooking manuscripts and notebooks contain mostly British recipes for preserves, medicinal foods, or fancy desserts that were used a few times a year. Everyday cooking didn't have to be written down. We have to guess about was learned from Indians by what dishes were retained in general use and how they were changed.

Relations between Colonial housewives and their Indian and African-American slaves and neighbors were complicated and often painful. But they were extensive. Settlers, slaves, and Indians all faced problems of survival at times and often helped each other. A trade in foodstuffs started immediately and has never ended to this day. I've bought wild rice, corn-meal, dried berries, and restaurant meals from Native enterprises. And so did Puritan housewives, Spanish missionaries, Mormon wagon train leaders, and Montana pioneers.

The case of corn cuisine is the most interesting, because the colonists had to adapt some corn dishes or die. Their staple grains of wheat and barley didn't grow well in the American colonies for more than a hundred years. Of the dishes we know about, **Roasting Ears** were an immediate hit with the colonists, but were eventually replaced by the quicker and easier boiled sweet corn we still enjoy. Hominy/ **Sagamité**/Samp/Suppawn is still a popular food, but the more liquid Sofkee never became popular in the eastern colonies and

was only locally popular much later in the old west (under its Mexican/Aztec names of Atolé, Pinole, and Champurado). Soups of corn, beans, and meat were used by colonists and early Americans in the north, but southern versions such as Brunswick Stew and Burgoo only developed in the nineteenth century, possibly via the Indian ancestors of African-American slaves. The Native southwestern style of hominy stew, Pozole, became a national fad food only in the 1980s.

Lye Hominy became a southern staple. Colonists had used ash lye to make soap in Europe and could figure out how the Indians were using ashes to remove the skins of corn. Parched corn was appreciated by colonists who tasted it, but was too much trouble to make in any quantity. European settlers ultimately preferred to treat corn the way they used other grains, by drying it for storage, grinding it into meal and flour, and trying to make porridges and puddings (which worked) and bread (which was quite difficult). **Hasty Pudding**, a cornmeal porridge similar to Indian dishes, was accepted by some Indian families, even with added milk, within a few generations. Indian [meal, the Colonial name for cornmeal] Pudding, which was similar to some forms of Sagamité that had been sweetened with dried berries, eventually became a dish Indians ate as well—almost every Native cookbook of the twentieth century has a recipe for it.

On the other hand, native tamales like **Broadswords**, and cornmeal dumplings like **Indian Bread** or **Bean Bread** were almost never used by colonist families even though they often boiled other foods. Mexican-style tamales became popular in the late nineteenth century. Tortillas and similar flatbreads used by Southwestern tribes had to wait until the end of the twentieth century to reach every American supermarket. But leafbreads and ash breads made of cornmeal were close enough to British Isles griddle breads that they were renamed as **Jonny-Cake, Hoe Cake**, or corn dodgers. Again, the transmission may have been from Indian slaves to African-American slaves to Anglo-American tables. The Indian technique of scalding the cornmeal with hot water was retained, but the cooking process moved onto cast-iron griddles or frying pans, possibly via broad hoes in the fields, from the Indian use of flat rocks or ash baking.

The Indians also picked up new foods from settlers, sometimes so rapidly that it confused European writers, who thought that watermelons and peach trees used by remote tribes might be native species.

Indian cooking did not begin in 1492, and it did not end then either. Food historians are fortunate that so many Native American cooks have been family food historians and have kept alive traditional dishes as they invented new ones. Just as it took a long time for archeologists in Mexico to accept that the Mayan hieroglyphic carvings recorded a language similar to the home language of Mayan laborers on their crews, so it may not occur to most Americans that the Virginia tamales described in 1618—"they lap yt in rowlls within the leaves of the corne, and so boyle yt for a deyntie"—are quite similar to the Kneel-Down Bread enjoyed by many Navajo families today, and a great variety of tamales cooked by immigrants from Mexico and Central America.

Some Indian dishes are all but lost today because they were based on passenger pigeons, which are extinct, or American chestnuts (which are almost extinct), or endangered species such as whales, wild striped bass, or wild salmon. As I write this, buffalo meat is becoming more available, but Atlantic codfish stocks are dangerously low. (For more dishes used by native Americans and native Hawaiians before contact with Europeans, see my *The American Ethnic Cookbook for Students*.)

A-Ni-Ka-Yo-Sv-Hi Tsu-Ya, or Leatherbritches Beans, or Shuckey Beans (1200)

Dried string beans reconstituted with preserved meat was healthful winter food for many Native American groups, in some places from the beginnings of corn-bean-squash agriculture. Beans are widely recorded in archeological sites across the northern United States from 6–500 B.C.E., and from sites in the American southwest as early as 2300 B.C.E., but may not have reached the eastern coastal tribes until a few centuries before Colombus. (If so, they very quickly were working with six to eight varieties, as reported by the first colonists.) This dish using dried green beans is still used by Eastern Cherokee and quickly passed into use by Appalachian settlers. The version below is taken primarily from a pamphlet, *Old Timey Recipes*, collected by Phyllis Connor of Bluefield, West Virginia, in 1969. The only difference between her recipe and the Native original is the substitution of salt pork or a ham hock where the Indians would have used dried or smoked game. (Although most Native Americans did not use salt to preserve meat, there is some evidence of an early salt trade from Gulf-Coast tribes reaching as far as the Cherokee trail system. The name "Shuckey Beans" is still used in Kentucky.)

NOTE: RECIPE TAKES AT LEAST A WEEK TO MAKE.

Yield: Serves 6–8

2 pounds fresh green beans
1 ham hock or slice of lean salt pork

Equipment: Dehydrator (optional), darning needle and heavy thread (optional), colander

1. Wash and drain beans.

2. Pinch off ends and pull out "strings."

3. Slit each bean the long way, leaving a half inch or so to hold it together. This step makes the beans dry faster. The slit parts curl away from each other to make the "britches."

4. If using dehydrator, dry at the lowest temperature according to directions. (My dehydrator suggests 140 degrees for two hours, then dry until crisp at 130 degrees.) If using the Native American method, sew the beans onto the thread, leaving them slightly spaced apart. Stagger the beans so that they point out in different directions. Hang to dry. Appalachian settlers hung them in many rows inside and under the porch roofs of their cabins and also used this method to dry apples.

5. When beans are shriveled up and greenish gray, you can take them off the strings and store them in a jar.

6. "To cook in the winter time, as the pioneers did, cover with water and soak overnight."

7. Drain, cover with fresh water, and bring to a boil.

8. Simmer ½ hour, and again drain off the water.

9. Add the ham hock or salt pork to the beans and cover with fresh water. Bring to a boil and simmer until tender, as much as two more hours.

*Serve with Hoe Cakes or **Sagamité**, or Indian bread for an Indian meal; or with cornbread for a settler meal.*

HERB TEA (1584)

Early explorers and colonists were surprised to see Indians drinking water from lakes and streams. In Europe, people who did that got sick. Colonists took most of their water in soup or beer, both of which were boiled in the making. Herbal teas were used as medicine in Europe, but Native Americans served them at meals, including the substantial feast served to Captain Arthur Barlow on Roanoke Island in July 1584. Barlow was exploring for Sir Walter Raleigh and on the hunt for valuable spices like sassafras, which was then thought to cure syphilis. He may have tasted teas made from wild ginger, spicebush, bayberry, or sassafras. He reported to Raleigh: "their drinke is commonly water . . . but it is sodden [boiled] with Ginger in it, and blacke Sinamon, and sometimes Sassaphras, and divers other wholesome, and medicinable hearbes and trees." Mint is probably the most widely available herb used by early settlers and Indians (who got similar flavors from wintergreen leaves, black birch, and wild mints). If you know wild plants well, or can get some help from a wild plant collector, some other popular Indian teas were (and are) made from pine, spruce, hemlock or juniper needles; the leaves of wild berries and currants; sagebrush; and many others.

Yield: 5 6-ounce cups

½ cup wild leaves or herbs (or 2 tablespoons dried mint)

Equipment: Saucepan, strainer

1. Bring 1 quart of water to a boil. Add leaves or mint.

2. Steep 5–10 minutes.

3. Strain into tea cups (or wooden bowls, or birchbark cups).

Serve with hominy, "sodden [boiled] Venison, and roasted, fish sodden, boyled and roasted, Melons [squash] rawe, and sodden, rootes of diuers [diverse] kindes and diuers fruites."

INDIAN BREAD OR BEAN BREAD (1607)

The Indians made several kinds of corn into boiled dumplings. The dumplings could be cooked in boiling water, soup, or stew, or wrapped in leaves to make **Broadswords**. They were often combined with beans, the sweet American chestnuts, or chunks of pumpkin, and seasonally with berries to make a boiled version of **Strawberry Bread** (or blueberry or chokecherry bread). In addition, the boiled dumplings could be dried out by the side of the fire, and stored as an instant porridge mix for traveling or winter. One of the earliest notes is by George Archer, a Jamestown colonist, as quoted by Captain John Smith:

> I saw Bread made by their women, who doe all their drugerie. . . . The manner of baking of bread is thus. After they pound their wheat into flowre, with hote water they make it into paste, and worke it into round balls and Cakes; then they put it into a pot of seething water; when it is sod [boiled] thoroughly, they lay it on a smooth stone, there they harden it as well as in an Oven.

This kind of boiled bread did not become popular with the colonists, although Early Americans did eventually make **Corn Dumplings**. It is not clear that Archer is correct about what kind of corn to use. Today's degerminated cornmeal will not hold together well enough to make dumplings. Stone-ground cornmeal is better, and the fine cornflower that could be sifted out of the samp mills would be better still. But the Wampanoag interpreters at Plimoth Plantation today use parched corn to make boiled breads, and the most detailed Cherokee recipe uses fresh lye hominy. It is by Aggie Ross Losiah (1880–1966) in the 1951 *Cherokee Cooklore*, edited by Mary Ulmer and Samuel E. Beck. I have also taken some details from the 1980 *Hopi Cookery*, by Juanita Tiger Kavena, a number of recipes in the 1933 *Indian Cook Book*, published by the Indian Women's Club of Tulsa, Oklahoma, and an old New England recipe for hulled corn in Mrs. Lincoln's 1883 *The Boston Cookbook*. Cherokee bean breads are often demonstrated as **Broadswords** wrapped in cornmeal, because they tend to fall apart. This problem is alluded to in the *Indian Cook Book*. Indian recipes often warn that using salt will make bean breads fall apart, but I think the secret is to use so little liquid in mixing that the breads barely hold together in your hand.

Lye hominy was made by all corn-growing Native Americans and did become popular with settlers. It is still made by Appalachian mountaineers and by Native American cooks from the southwest, to New York and Canada. Most tribes also have a recipe for hominy soup with beans and meat.

Any kind of dried whole corn will work for this recipe, except popcorn (which the Indians did not have until the 1800s) and dried sweet corn. You can get Indian corn by saving the ears that people hang up on their doorways in the autumn. Check that it hasn't been treated with fungicide, however. A feed store (ask a horse owner) often has whole corn.

Yield: 20 breads or bean breads

2 cups dried red beans or 2 16-ounce cans

4 cups whole corn (about 8 ears of "Indian corn"), or 5 cans white hominy

1 cup sifted hardwood ashes or 2 tablespoons baking soda

2 quarts water—10 cups

Equipment: Stainless steel, iron, or enamel soup pot, sieve

1. If using dried beans, bring to a boil in 3 cups of water. Reduce heat to a simmer and cook until tender, about 2 hours. If using canned hominy, go to Step 10. If using Indian corn, shell the kernels off the husks. Usually you can start them with a can opener (the Indians used a deer jaw). Once you get a row going, you can push off the kernels with your fingers, and roll the ear in your hands to push off other rows into the empty area.

2. Bring 2 quarts of water to boil in an enamel or cast-iron pot.

3. Strain the ashes to get a cup of sifted ashes. Use the fireplace ashes from a hardwood fire that had no painted wood in it. (The Hopi use the ash of the wild chamisa shrub.)

4. Add the ashes or baking soda to the water. It will turn slate gray if you are using ashes.

5. Add the corn and bring back to a simmer.

6. "Stir once in a while and let cook until the bubbles come up."

7. "Take out a grain to test it with the fingers to see if the skin is ready to slip. That is the way we tell if it has been in the lye water long enough." This might be anywhere from 20 minutes to several hours, depending on the corn and the strength of the ashes. Be patient, or add some baking soda.

8. When *all* the hulls have started to slip, stir the corn hard with a wooden spoon to loosen them some more, then drain off the lye water. Cover with water, stir, and drain 5 or 6 times. (Aggie Losiah did this in a hulling basket in a flowing stream.) I've tried pounding the corn around in batches in a food processor with the plastic blade, and skimming off the hulls with a fine strainer. This works, although the processor gets stuck every so often.

9. When the corn is well washed, rub off the remaining skins with your hands, and pick out any black "eyes" in the swollen white grains of corn. You now have lye hominy, which can be simmered two to four hours for **sagamité**, or boiled with beans and meat for a typical Indian corn soup or **Plymouth Succotash**.

10. To make bean bread, Aggie Losiah lets the hominy drain thoroughly, then beats the hominy in a wooden tree-stump mortar with the small end of a heavy carved wooden pestle. For a food processor method, put ¼ of the corn at a time in the bowl with the steel cutting blade, and process for several minutes. Stop and scrape down the sides a few times. The corn is ready when the consistency is almost down to cornmeal, and the dough sticks together and rides up above the rotating knife. (If the corn is still in bigger pieces, add a *very little* boiling water or bean liquid and keep processing.) Another trick is to set one side of the food processor on a book so the bowl is tilted.

11. Lay out several sheets of waxed paper. Bring 5–6 inches of water to a rolling boil in a soup pot.

12. When the dough is ready, wet your hands, and make breads by working it into 2-inch balls. Or make bean breads by putting all the dough in a bowl with the beans, mixing well, and forming 3-inch balls.

13. Arrange the balls on the waxed paper.

14. When the boiling water is ready, lower in the breads with a slotted spoon. They will rise to the top of the water in a few minutes. Boil 20–40 minutes for breads, 30–60 minutes for

bean breads. If they fall apart, do what Mrs. Victoria Martin Rogers of Tulsa did, and call the thickened water "Sequoyah Sauce."

15. The breads could be dried for winter use or as an instant soup on the trail. The bean breads were not dried.

ROASTING EARS (1618)

The first form of corn that Europeans really took to was green corn roasted in the husk. This is still popular in corn-growing areas, and at Indian pow-wows. It was the first method described by William Strachey, the secretary and recorder of the Jamestown colony, in his 1618 *The Historie of Travaile in Virginia Britannia*:

> Their corne they eat in the ears greene, roasted, and sometyme bruising yt in a mortar of wood with a little pestle; they lap yt in rowlls within the leaves of the corne, and so boyle yt for a deyntie; they also reserve that corne late planted that will not ripe, by roasting yt in hott ashes, the which in wynter (being boyled with beans) they esteeme for a rare dish, calling yt pausarawmena.

The only problem is to find sweet corn that tastes like the Indian flour corn of Virginia. You can grow multicolored Indian corn in the garden, but the Indian corn sold for autumn decorations is already too dry. The Indians had sweet corn, but it wasn't as sweet as corn today. Probably the best you can do is somewhat tired supermarket corn, but watch out for supersweet Florida corn— no Indian sweet corn was ever that sweet, and it doesn't get starchier if you leave it around. The oven method is based on suggestions collected by the late Paula Giese (Ojibwe) and posted on the Internet at ⟨www.kstrom.net/isk/food/f_corn.html⟩.

Yield: Serves 12

12 ears of sweet corn in husk
1 stick salted butter (optional)

Equipment: Fireplace or campfire and shovel (optional), aluminum foil (optional)

1. Peel back husks to remove corn silk. Put back inner husks and tie shut with one of the outer husks.

2. If using fireplace or campfire, burn it down to a good bed of coals. Move coals to one side, and make a neat row of roasting ears. Shovel a little dirt or cool ashes onto the corn to protect it, then put the hot coals back on top of the roasting ears. Add dried sticks to make a short, hot fire. After about 45 minutes, corn will be done. Remove fire, ashes, and dirt, and cool ears until ready to handle. (Indians and settlers also roasted individual ears of corn on sharpened sticks, and large lots by building a fire in a long trench and leaning ears of corn against a long branch or sapling set up a little above the top of the trench.)

3. If using home oven, bake at 450 degrees for 20 minutes, or wrap in aluminum foil and bake 25 minutes.

Indians mostly ate roasting ears without salt, or oil. Settlers probably started using butter as soon as they had enough dairy cattle, likely by 1628.

BROADSWORDS (1618)

Strachey's second corn dish did not become popular among non-Indians for another 250 years, when "hot tamales" were viewed as "Mexican food." Almost all Native Americans made boiled leaf breads from green corn. The Cherokee version came to be known as "Broadswords," probably from the shape of the corn husks or the tamales; or "Dog heads," which were wrapped balls. Cherokees and Appalachian settlers both changed to grating the corn on homemade metal graters, later used loaf pans to bake "Gritted Bread" from the same recipe. I have combined two Cherokee recipes ("Broadsodes" from Mrs. Annie Presley in the 1980 *Seems Like I Done It This A-Way*, by Cleo Stiles Bryan and one for "Dogheads" by Betsey Schrimsher Lewis in the 1933 *Indian Cook Book*, published by the Indian Women's Club of Tulsa, Oklahoma), an Iroquois recipe in the 1910 *Iroquois Uses of Maize and Other Food Plants*, by A.C. Parker, and one for Navajo "Kneel Down Bread" (which is baked).

Yield: 12–14 servings

10 ears of corn, ideally flour corn a little too dry for roasting ears

3 dozen white oak leaves (optional)

Kitchen string (optional)

Equipment: Blender, sharp knife or corn cutter

1. Peel the corn, saving the husks and discarding the silks. Tear the smaller husks into thin ribbons for tying. Put the husks in a plastic bag while you work to keep them from drying out.
2. Cut the corn off the ears with a sharp knife or corn cutter. "Milk" the germs of the kernels off the cobs with the back of the knife.
3. Grind the kernels into a mush in a food grinder, blender, or food processor. (The Iroquois used a mortar.) If the kernels are too dry, add a little boiling water. (This won't be necessary with supermarket corn.)
4. To make broadswords, take one large piece of corn husk, or overlap two smaller pieces. Face the pointed end of the husk. (You can also use oak leaves.)

5. Put two or three tablespoons of the corn mixture toward the top and one side of the corn husk(s).
6. Roll into a long tube to enclose the mush. The Cherokee method was to roll a long corn leaf around the tube.
7. Fold up the bottom (pointed) side of the husk in half, but entirely over the mush.
8. Tie three times around the tamale, closing the open ends, and once the long way. You can use kitchen string without affecting the flavor.
9. When all the broadswords are made, bring a large pot, half full of water, to a boil.
10. Add broadswords and boil 30 minutes or more, depending on thickness.

Eastern Indians also dried these leaf breads near campfires for winter use.

PAUSARAWMENA (1618)

Strachey's third corn dish, parched green corn reconstituted with beans, remains a popular dish among the Iroquois, under the names "Ogonsa" (for the corn) and "Onahn-dah" (the soup). (Most Iroquois recipes for onahn-dah use lye hominy, see above.) The oven method given here was described by Hazel Dean-John (Seneca) for the 1979 book, *Cooking with a Harvard Accent*, by Melanie Marcus. Ms. Dean-John uses the parched corn with canned or roasted corn in her onahn-dah. Parched green corn was an Indian favorite for its sweet flavor and concentrated nutrition. Europeans who tasted it generally liked it, and sometimes took it on explorations or military excursions. But it did not become a colonial staple, probably because the Europeans preferred to treat corn like one of their own grains, storing it as dried kernels, grinding it on mill wheels and making it into breads and porridges like **Hasty Pudding**.

This was only one of the varieties of parched corn used as travel rations by Native Americans and some early settlers. Kernels of ripe corn could be worked off the cobs and parched in hot ashes, or mixed with hot sand and a fire built on top. The sand or ashes would be washed off, and then the kernels would be pounded in a mortar. Whole cobs of flour corn could be parched by drying them and cooking them like roasting ears, only more slowly. Pounded parched corn was could be mixed with hot or cold water for an instant meal, or two or three tablespoons could be taken directly on the march. It was very filling. The Iroquois were mixing it with maple sugar by the 1750s and may have done so before contact. The result was a lot like the "Indian Sagamite" in the civil war section, which has nothing to do with **sagamité** but is a lot like parched corn.

The salt pork in this recipe must have been added by a colonial cook, to replace smoke-dried fish or game in the original recipe. Because the Indians did not use salt as a preservative, there is no real substitute in the supermarket, until someone markets a salt-free jerky. The salt pork has been accepted by the Iroquois as the standard recipe, although some people use bacon or chicken.

Yield: 24 1-cup servings

12 ears corn

2 cups dried red beans

1 pound salt pork (optional)

Equipment: Lasagna pan or sheet-cake pan or heavy roasting pan, pancake turner or dough scraper

1. Cut the corn off the cobs in three steps. Begin by cutting off the tops of the kernels with a sharp knife.

2. Take another pass, cutting off the kernels at the bottom.

3. "Milk" the germs of the kernels off each ear with the flat back of the knife.

4. Spread the corn evenly in the baking dish and mash the larger pieces to release their juice.

5. Bake at 350 degrees for 45 minutes to an hour, or until corn is dried and brown.

6. Scrape corn from pan, let it cool, and keep in glass jars with tight tops.

7. For the soup, bring the dried beans to a boil with 4 quarts of water. Reduce heat to a simmer and cook 30–40 minutes, or until beans are almost tender.

8. Dice salt pork, if using. (It is easier to do this if it is partially frozen.) Add to the soup.

9. After an hour, add the parched corn and stir well.

10. Simmer another 30–60 minutes.

Serve Indian-style as a mid-morning family meal, and as a standing dish when someone is hungry the rest of the time. Among New England settlers, a similar bean porridge or succotash was a winter dish, preserved by freezing, and carried to reheat as a hot lunch when cutting firewood.

NASAŨMP (1643)

One Indian corn dish that Europeans took over immediately was a thick porridge of cracked corn. The Indians cracked the corn in large wooden mortars, often with a heavy pestle tied to an overhanging branch as a balance. They enriched it with nut oils and animal fats, smoke-dried meat or fish, and sometimes fresh game. (For a Colonial version of that kind of Nasaũmp, see

Plymouth Succotash.) The settlers used the same kind of "samp mills" until they refined their own grinding-stone milling to accommodate the larger and oilier kernels of corn. They sifted out the fine flour, used the wind to blow away the hulls, and used the larger pieces of cracked corn to make hominy (a word we now apply to corn treated with alkali, but which was applied by early writers to a variety of hulled corn dishes) or porridge. This was called "samp" (from Narragansett "Nasaümp") or "hulled corn" in New England (Jossylyn mentions both names as mushes eaten with milk), "big hominy" in the southern English colonies, **Sagamité** by the French, and "suppawn" by the Dutch. The basic version (see **Sagamité**) was probably the "some wheat like furmentie" served to Barlow in 1584. The variety of terms shows that Indians and settlers exchanged this dish several times in different places. The settlers very quickly replaced the bear fat or nut oil with goat milk, and then, by the 1650s with cow's milk. The clam broth in this Narrangansett recipe was probably used by other coastal Indians during shellfishing seasons, but was not taken up by the settlers.

This Narragansett Indian recipe was published by Roger Williams (1603–1683) in London in 1643, in his book *A Key into the Language of America*. He probably observed the dish after his banishment to Rhode Island in 1643, but possibly as early as his arrival in Boston in 1631. A recent Native American version can be found in the pamphlet, "Narragansett Indian Recipes Traditional and Contemporary" by Ella Thomas Sekatu. In New England, cracked corn is sold as "samp" in the Portuguese section of the supermarket. Elsewhere you may have to go to a health food store or a feed store. In the feed store, make sure the grain has not been treated with fungicide.

Sickissuog. *Clams*. *Obs*. This is a sweet kind of shelfish, which all Indians generally over the Countrey, Winter and Summer delight in; at low water the women dig for them: this fish, and the natural liquor of it, they boile, and it makes their broth and the *Nasaümp* (which is a kind of thickened broth) and their bread seasonable and savory, instead of Salt.

Yield: Serves 4–6

1 cup white cracked corn
3 cups clam juice or the broth from steamed clams or mussels

Equipment: Stew pot, wooden spoon

1. Combine corn and clam juice with a cup of water in stew pot.
2. Bring to a boil, reduce heat to a simmer, and simmer 2 hours.
3. Stir often as it cooks down so that it does not stick to the pot and burn. Stirring also breaks up some of the starch so that it can absorb water and thicken the stew.
4. Nasaümp is done when the corn is easily chewed and the surrounding stew is thick and creamy.

Serve in wooden bowls with horn or wooden spoons.

STRAWBERRY BREAD (1643)

This recipe was published by Roger Williams (1603–1683) in London in 1643, in his book *A Key into the Language of America*. Williams was aware that the Indians used controlled forest fires to clear their fields, drive game, and reduce insects. What he didn't notice or write down was that these fires were also intended to produce forest-edge habitat favorable to berries and large game animals. As English-style cleared fields took over New England, the large crops of wild strawberries diminished, and strawberry bread was no longer made by Indians or colonists. The American wild strawberry plant, however, was crossed with European alpine strawberries to produce the strawberries we now enjoy. The adapted recipe makes pink flatbreads with a strawberry aroma.

Wuttáhimneash Strawberries

Obs. This Berry is the wonder of all Fruits growing naturally in these parts: It is of it selfe excellent: so that one of the chiefest Doctors of *England* was wont to say, that God could have made, but God never did make a better Berry: In some parts where the Natives have planted, I have many times seen as many as would fill a good ship within few miles compasse: The Indians bruise them in a Mortar, and mixe them with meale and make Strawberry bread.

Yield: 6 hamburger-shaped flatbreads

1 cup sliced strawberries

1¼ cups white corn meal

Shortening to grease a baking sheet (Indians would have used bear fat, pigeon oil, or nonstick soapstone griddles; seventeenth-century colonists used salted butter or an ungreased wooden plank.)

Equipment: Food processor or blender, baking sheet, long-handled spatula to turn hot breads

1. Unless you can get stone-ground white cornmeal or Rhode Island "Johnny Cake Corn Meal," whirl it for a few minutes in a food processor or blender to get a finer grind.

2. Empty the cornmeal into a bowl.

3. Hull the strawberries, and cut them or process them to small pieces, but don't purée them.

4. Add one cup of cornmeal to the strawberries and process to form a soft dough. You may need to add more cornmeal to get a firmer dough. If you don't have a food processor, mix the blended strawberries with the cornmeal in a bowl and mash in more cornmeal as needed.

5. Pat out the cornmeal into patties about the size of hamburgers.

6. Grease a baking sheet and slide on the pink patties.

7. Bake in a 350-degree oven for 30 minutes, turning once. To avoid burns, don't reach into the oven to turn the breads. Use a long-handled spatula. (You can also use any of the methods for cooking **Hoe Cake**. The Indians might have cooked the breads wrapped in leaves and covered with hot ashes, or on flat stones over the fire. By the time Williams observed them, they had traded for European pots and pans, and sometimes fried the breads like pancakes.)

Serve with boiled fish. Colonists might have eaten these broken into a bowl with fresh milk.

THE ANCIENT NEW-ENGLAND STANDING DISH (1672)

This early recipe for pumpkin appeared in *New-England's Rarities Discovered . . .* by John Josselyn, published in London in 1672. Josselyn had lived in the Massachusetts Bay Colony in 1638 for a year, and from 1663 to 1671, mostly in what is now coastal Maine.

There are several explanations for why this was a "standing dish." It was a dish that stood at the back of the fireplace, always warm; or a dish that was thicker than a "running pottage," (thus, a "standing pottage"); or it was a dish that was "in good standing." In any case, the long cooking process and the mentions of spice tell us that native pumpkins in the 1670s were just as watery and bland as our Halloween pumpkins are now. Early settlers were quite mixed about pumpkins as food. They were used, especially in hard times, to stretch out the cornmeal in breads and dried to last through the winter.

Having a pot constantly on slow heat, and adding to an ongoing dish are Native American practices that probably influenced the English settlers as they coped with an unfamiliar vegetable. Native Americans also roasted pumpkins whole in the ashes, or dried them for winter soups. Both processes concentrate the flavor. Notice that Josselyn makes an analogy to apples. The next step for pumpkin was to be enriched with custard and used as a pie filling, exactly as apples are used in the English recipe for **Marlborough Pudding** that also became a popular Early American pie.

Some historical interpreters substitute butternut squash for the pumpkin because it tastes better and because an ancestor of butternut squash was known as "crookneck pumpkin" in colonial Pennsylvania. I suggest trying it with a contemporary pumpkin or a mixture and using a crock pot to simulate the "back burner" of a colonial fireplace. The crock pot won't burn, but it does keep in the moisture, which makes the pumpkin very soupy. You can also start with cooked, unspiced pumpkin or squash. The proportions and spice are those used at Plimoth Plantation by food interpreter Kathleen Curtin, based on seventeenth-century British recipes.

> *Pompions*, there be of several kinds, some proper to the Country, they are dryer than our *English* Pompions [the English pompion was a large gourd], and better tasted; you may eat them green.
> But the Housewives' manner is to slice them when ripe, and cut them into dice, and to fill a pot with them of two or three Gallons, and stew them upon a gentle fire a whole day, and as they sink, they fill again with fresh Pompions, not putting any liquor to them; and when it is stew'd enough, it will look like bak'd Apples; this they Dish, putting Butter to it, and a little Vinegar, (with some Spice, as Ginger, &c.) which makes it tart like an Apple, and so serve it up to be eaten with Fish or Flesh; It provokes Urin extreamly and is very windy.

Yield: Serves 15–20 as a side dish

5-pound pumpkin (or ten cups cooked)
5 tablespoons butter
2½ tablespoons cider vinegar
1–2 tablespoons ground ginger (or nutmeg, cloves, or pepper)
Rounded teaspoon salt

Equipment: Crock-Pot or heavy kettle, carrot peeler, strainer (Crock-Pot method only)

1. If using cooked pumpkin, go to Step 8. Quarter the pumpkin, peel, and remove seeds. (You can leave on some of the peel where it is clean.)
2. Cut into quarter-inch slices. They ought to look a little like apple sections.
3. Fill the Crock-Pot or kettle with about ⅔ of pumpkin slices. Add ¼ cup water and turn the Crock-Pot on "high." Put a regular kettle on very low heat.
4. Cover and cook 2 hours, stirring occasionally.
5. Add half the remaining pumpkin, and cook another 2 hours.
6. Add the rest of the pumpkin, and cook for an additional hour or more.
7. If using the Crock-Pot, about 20 minutes before serving you should

ladle off the extra juice (about a cup), and strain it into a small saucepan. Bring this juice to a boil and reduce it to ¼ of its original volume. Be careful not to let it burn as it concentrates. This step duplicates some of the evaporation that would have occurred in slow fireplace cooking.

8. About 10 minutes before serving, add butter, vinegar, and spices, and stir well.

Serve as a side vegetable with roast meat or grilled fish.

SAGAMITÉ (1674)

Of the various names for cracked-corn porridge or hominy, the word "sagamité" came through French (possibly from Abenaki 'sôgmôipi'—"repast of chiefs"), because there were French fishing camps in Eastern Canada and what is now the United States from the early 1500s, with settlements in Eastern Canada and Maine in the early 1600s, and extensive French exploration of what we now call the Midwestern states and Mississippi Valley. This kind of hominy was know as "Saccamité" in New Orleans well into the twentieth century.

We'll place this dish of **Sagamité** with Marquette and Joliet's canoe trip down the Mississippi, at a June 25, 1673, four-course dinner hosted by Illinois Indians at a village in Eastern Iowa, southern Illinois or northeastern Missouri. Marquette reported:

The Council was followed by a great feast, Consisting of four dishes, which had to be partaken of in accordance with all their fashions. The first course was a great wooden platter of full of sagamité,—that is to say, meal of indian corn boiled in water, and seasoned with fat. The Master of Ceremonies filled a Spoon with sagamité three or our times, and put it in my mouth As if I were a little Child. He did The same to Monsieur Jollyet. As a second course, he caused a second platter to be brought, on which were three fish. He took some pieces of them, removed them therefrom, and, after blowing upon them, to cool Then he put them in our mouths As one would give food to a bird. For the third course, they brought a large dog, that had just been killed; but when they learned that we did not eat this meat, they removed it from before us. Finally, the 4th course was a piece of wild ox [buffalo], The fattest morsels of which were placed in our mouths. (Source: *Jesuit Relations*, edited by Edna Kenton, NY: The Vanguard Press, 1954, page 292.)

Sagamité could be enriched with a variety of oils. The Illinois probably used bison fat, but other native groups used nut oils, sunflower seed oil, or bear fat. In June it might have included a few green beans or dried squash, and later in the year might have included shell beans and fresh squash, making it more of a succotash. In fall and winter, it might have included fresh game or dried fish. Europeans quickly switched to milk, cream, and butter as enrichments, as Roger Williams wrote of New England as early as 1643, "There be diverse sorts of this Corne, and of the colours: yet all of it either boild in milke, or buttered." By the eighteenth century, some groups of settled Indians were keeping cows and doing the same. (Josselyn mentions one such Indian in Maine in the 1670s.) I have taken proportions from an Iroquois recipe for Onondäät in the 1910 paper, *Iroquois Uses of Maize and Other Food Plants*, by Arthur C. Parker.

The optional sunflower seeds were noted by Pehr Kalm, the Swedish botanist who visited the Iroquois and Hurons in Quebec in 1749: "They plant our common sunflower in their maize fields, and mix the seeds of it into the sagamite, or maise-soup."

Yield: Serves 8–12

2 cups white cracked corn

2 quarts whole milk (optional)

½–1 cup hulled sunflower seeds (optional)

1 cup sunflower or walnut oil (optional) or butter (for English "loblolly," French "sagamité," or Dutch "suppawn")

Equipment: Stew pot, wooden spoon

1. Bring corn to a boil in 2 quarts of water (Indian version) or the milk and 2 teaspoons salt (colonist or settled Indian version).

2. Add oil to the Indian version.

3. When it comes back to a boil, reduce heat to a simmer, and simmer 2 hours, stirring more frequently as it thickens so the porridge doesn't stick to the pot and burn.

Serve as an Indian post-Council feast in one large wooden bowl, feeding each other by hand, followed by courses of catfish, dog, and bison. Serve as a settler staple by ladling onto wooden plates shared by two people. Make a depression in the mush for each diner, and put butter in it to melt. Eat with wooden horn, or shell spoons.

2

EARLY COLONIAL DISHES (1524–1674)

This chapter focuses on some dishes used by early colonists when they *weren't* adapting the foodstuffs and food technologies pioneered by Native Americans. Some of these dishes became everyday foods as the colonies adjusted to American agriculture, but others were rare treats, or restricted to a few leading colonists with the means to live like European aristocrats. Colonists arrived with a supply of familiar foods, and were resupplied with European staples including cheeses, spices, and flour. Most of the colonies were intended to provide export goods for their owners and soon were part of an Atlantic trade network that also provided sugar and fruit from the Caribbean, slaves and new foods from Africa. Thus hot chocolate, the royal drink of Mexico, reached England first from Spain, but became more widely available in England after the British takeover of Jamaica in 1655. Important English colonists like the governor of Massachusetts were serving it in the 1690s, and it was a popular breakfast among Virginia planters by the early eighteenth century.

The early colonists came from many countries in Europe and settled among hundreds of Indian nations. (The loose Indian confederations were not like modern nations, but they were not so different from seventeenth-century Italy or Germany, which were not unitary countries. Some of the areas controlled by the Iroquois, the Creek Federation, the Ojibwe, and the Cherokee were larger than most European countries.) In addition to the various English colonies and the Dutch New Netherlands, there were French outposts in Maine, in what are now the Midwestern states, and down the Mississippi River. Refugee French Protestants settled in their own towns in the Dutch and English colonies. The Spanish set up a permanent settlement in St. Augustine in 1565, with outposts in the Carolinas, and settled in Texas, New Mexico, and Arizona by the end of the seventeenth century. Spanish explorers claimed the Pacific Coast and may have visited Hawaii. Settlers made and broke alliances with Indian nations in a complicated political landscape that was more like the fragmented Europe of the Thirty Years' War than the bipolar world of the Cold War. In only one region, the Great Lakes "Beaver Wars," which historians now date from about 1630–1690 involved Indians from New England to Minnesota, with dealings and double dealings by French, English, and Dutch colonists, often pressing their Indian allies to attack other Europeans.

Although the period is not very well documented in written recipes, food historians have a number of ways of reconstructing the foods that were eaten. One way is to use cookbooks printed in England during the time period and pick out the recipes that use ingredients the colonists are known to have had, such as butter, dried peas, and barley and rye flour. The English colonists probably attempted to eat familiar English dishes whenever they could get the ingredients, and this chapter uses a chicken recipe from a British cooking manuscript that was brought to the American colonies, and probably used in this period. The chapter does use two Spanish recipes from the 1500s that are still used (in modified form) in some of the early Spanish colonial areas of the United States, a salad recipe from a Dutch cookbook that belonged to a New Netherlands family, and a 1650 recipe from Sweden as a possible dish for the New Jersey Swedish colony, which left no culinary records.

Food historians also work with the few documented American recipes from this period, and with diaries and letters about food, as well as indirect evidence about the foods and cooking tools in estate inventories and court cases. In recent years, costumed interpreters in historic houses and restored villages have begun demonstrating historic cooking. These hands-on interpreters have learned a lot in the process and brought food history to life. (In Chapter 1 similar insights from Native American tradition-keepers proved useful.)

Recent food historians have undermined many myths about foods eaten by the settlers. Neither settlers nor Indians ate popcorn until the early nineteenth century, and they did grow and eat tomatoes and potatoes much earlier than that. Work has also begun on defining the African contribution to the settler's table, beginning with foods that Africans brought to America or knew better than European cooks, such as rice, eggplant, okra, cowpeas, and sesame seeds.

REBANADAS O TAJADAS DE QUESO FRESCO (1565)

This recipe for cheese fritters was published in Spain in the 1529 *Libro de Guisados* by Ruperto de Nola, a work republished in Spain for more than two hundred years. The recipe, somewhat modified over time, is still in use in St. Augustine, Florida, where the pastries are now baked and called "Fromajadas." Since the St. Augustine colony was supplied with cooking oil by sea, and supplies were often short, it is possible that the fried pastries had to be baked in the early life of the colony. Or they may have been influenced by baked English cheese tarts during the period of British rule at St. Augustine. Fromajadas are usually attributed to the Minorcan community that arrived in Florida in 1765, after a British takeover had driven the original Spanish colonists off to Cuba. The Spanish returned to Florida in 1783, as part of the international settlement of American Independence. The United States did not annex all of Florida until 1821. However the presence of this recipe in an upper-class Spanish cookbook of 1529 suggests that these cheesecakes were known to Ponce de León and might well have been an Easter treat for the earlier Spanish settlers of Florida. I have taken proportions from recipes in modern St. Augustine cookbooks.

The translation of *Libro de Guisados* is by Robin Carroll-Mann, with her permission. You can read the entire book on the Internet site <www.florilegium.org>.

Take new cheese, and make slices as thick as your finger; and take dough which is well-leavened and is from good flour, and let it be kneaded very thin and take some egg yolks, and mix them well with the dough, and [wrap] the slices of cheese above and below, and then put them to fry in a pan with very good lard, and turn it promptly so that it cannot burn. But if you cook it with grease, like fritters, it will be much better. And when they are cooked, cast sugar on top of them, and eat them hot, because this dish is worthless in any other manner.

Yield: 16 fried or baked cakes

½ pound mild cheese such as Monterey Jack

6 large eggs

2 cups flour

½ cup whole wheat flour

¼ cup wheat germ

1 teaspoon dry yeast

¼ cup sugar

2 pounds lard or olive oil for frying (optional)

Equipment: Large mixing bowl, rolling pin and board, baking sheet or heavy pot with high sides and deep-fry thermometer, waxed paper, grater or food processor with grating disk (optional), wire racks

1. Dissolve yeast in a little water with a pinch of sugar.

2. Mix together flour, whole wheat flour, and wheat germ in a large mixing bowl.

3. Separate eggs by pouring from shell to shell over a cup, and reserve whites for another use.

4. Beat egg yolks briefly.

5. Heat a cup of water to lukewarm.

6. Once the yeast has a foam of bubbles on top, make a well in the middle of the flour mixture. Put in the yeast and half the water, and stir into the flour.

7. Mix the egg yolks into the flour. If you are going to bake the cheesecakes, you want to get a fairly stiff dough, even by adding a little more flour. If you are going to fry them, you need a softer dough, and may need more of the water.

8. Flour your hands and the board, and knead the dough 15 or 20 times to mix it. Work the dough into a ball, and let it rise, covered, until doubled in bulk, about two hours.

9. For the fried cheesecakes, cut the cheese into sixteen slices, each about ⅜ of an inch thick. For the baked cheesecakes, grate the cheese.

10. When dough has risen, "punch down" to break up the large bubbles, and give it three or four kneads.

11. For the baked cheesecakes, flour the rolling pin and board, and roll out dough about ¼-inch thick. Cut 5-inch rounds (or press them out with a saucer). Put spoonfuls of the grated cheese in the center of each round. Pull opposite sides to the center and pinch to hold. Then pull up the opposing open ends and do it again, forming a purse shape. The filling should show through the four folds.

12. For the fried cheesecakes, roll dough into a long sausage shape, and divide into 16 pieces. Flour the rolling pin and board, and roll out each piece to a rectangular or square shape like the cheese slices, but more than twice as large. Put a slice of cheese in one side of each pastry, fold over to enclose the cheese completely, work out any trapped air, and crimp the edges closed.

13. Arrange the completed pastries on waxed paper. Cover with another sheet of wax paper, and let rise 10–20 minutes.

14. For baked cheesecakes, preheat oven to 375 degrees. Grease baking sheet and arrange cakes. Bake 15–20 minutes, or until light brown with cheese bubbling up through folds.

15. For fried cheesecakes, heat up 2 inches of olive oil or lard to 370 degrees in a heavy pot with high sides. Drop a slotted spoon or skimmer in the hot oil, place a cake on it, and lower carefully into the hot oil. Turn over to brown on both sides. Remove promptly and cool on wire racks.

16. Sprinkle sugar on hot cheesecakes.

Serve to carolers at Easter, or as a banquet dish anytime. People who serve this around Christmas might be secret Jews.

POTAJE DE FIDEOS (1601)

The Spanish presence in New Mexico is usually dated from the 1601 establishment of Santa Fe, although there were many previous visits and military incursions along the Rio Grande Valley. This recipe for noodle soup is from the 1529 *Libro de Guisados* by Ruperto de Nola, but the dish is still popular in Mexico and among old Hispanic families in New Mexico. It was noted under the name, "Sopa de Vermicelli," by a Santa Fe Trail traveler of 1847. Noodles would have been a rare treat in the earliest New Mexico colony, which was supplied by seizing corn from Pueblo Indians and infrequent mule trains from Mexico City. Noodles became more available as missionaries and settlers began planting wheat and as Pueblo Indians acquired the new crop. Noodles would have been shipped by sea to early Florida, California, and Texas settlers. The sweetened and spiced versions in the original recipe were more in the medieval style of upper-class cooking and probably for Lenten use. The chef's admission at the end of the recipe that cheese was really better in a meat-broth soup foretells the modern style. I have taken quantities and added details and how to make the noodles at home from a traditional New Mexico recipe in *The Genuine New Mexico Tasty Recipes* by Cleofas M. Jaramillo, first published in 1939. Sra. Jaramillo's garnish is slices of hard-boiled egg instead of the grated cheese, but I have followed her cooking directions as being more likely for early settlers. The translation of *Libro de Guisados* is by Robin Carroll-Mann, and reprinted with her permission. You can read the entire translation on the Internet site, ⟨www.florilegium.org⟩. You may be able to buy dry fideos rolled into nests in a Latino grocery. Thin egg noodles are a possible substitute. You want to end up with a soupy noodle dish, what Mexican cooks call a "dry soup" (*sopa seca*) rather than a thin soup.

Clean the fideos of their filth, and when they are well-cleaned put a very clean pot on the fire with good fatty hen's broth or mutton broth that is well-salted; and when the broth begins to boil, cast the fideos into the pot with a piece of sugar; and when they are more than half cooked, cast goat or sheep milk into the pot with the hen's broth or mutton broth; or instead of that, almond milk, for that can never be lacking; and cook everything well together, and when the fideos are cooked, remove the pot from the fire and let it rest a little while; and prepare dishes, casting sugar and cinnamon upon them; but as I have said in the chapter on rice, many say that with pottages of this kind which are cooked with meat broth that one should not cast in either sugar or milk, but this is according to each one's appetite; and in truth, with fideos or rice cooked in meat broth, it is better to cast good grated cheese upon the dishes.

NOTE: HOMEMADE NOODLES TAKE TWO DAYS.

Yield: Serves 4 as a side dish

½ pound fideos or other egg noodles, or the following 5 ingredients:

    1 cup flour

    1 large egg

    1 teaspoon olive oil, plus more to oil hands

    1 pinch dried mint

    1 pinch saffron

1 quart chicken stock, unsalted if canned

1 tablespoon lard

1 small onion

¼ cup grated Parmesan cheese

Equipment: To make noodles: sieve, board, rolling pin, spatula or dough scraper, pasta dryer, or mounted twigs or baking sheets, with prepared dry noodles, soup pot

1. If you have fideos or egg noodles, go to Step 8. To make noodles from flour, boil a little water and measure 2 tablespoons of hot water into a Pyrex measuring cup.

2. Stir in saffron and let it steep until the water is red-orange.

3. Beat 1 egg with the olive oil.

4. Mix the flour and ½ teaspoon salt.

5. Strain the saffron water into the egg mixture.

6. Stir the liquid ingredients into the solid ingredients to make a firm dough.

7. When dough is sticking together well, oil your hands and turn the dough out onto a wooden board. Work the dough until it isn't sticky.

8. Sra. Jaramillo's method was to "roll the dough into long shoe strings." I would suggest oiling the rolling pin and rolling out dough into thin sheets. You can stretch the sheets a little by pulling from the edges. You can then cut thin noodles from the sheets. Or let them dry about an hour on the backs of chairs, or a pasta drier, or on the bare wire racks of an oven set to the lowest possible heat. Don't let them get hard and brittle. When the sheets are dry, roll them short side to short side to make a loose scroll. Cut thin slices out of the scroll to make the noodles. You can cut on the bias to get longer noodles. Dry the long noodles for several hours in the sun or in a dry room or the oven.

9. Bring stock to a boil in a large soup pot.

10. Halve, peel, and chop the onion.

11. Heat lard in a heavy skillet, and put in the dried noodles. Stir them around to brown without burning. If you are using the nests of fideos, turn the nests to brown as much as possible. You can break some of the longer noodles to fit.

12. Add the onions to the skillet and stir around to brown somewhat.

13. Put noodles and onions into boiling stock and cook uncovered until noodles are tender and most of the stock has boiled away.

14. Grate the cheese if necessary.

Serve in shallow bowls with grated cheese spooned onto each serving.

En Lökesoppa (An Onion Soup) (1650)

Although there were no American-written cookbooks until 1796, there were printed cookbooks in Europe during the early era of European settlement in the United States. Culinary historians can use these to guess at what early settlers might have cooked given the foodstuffs at hand. The settlers were citizens of the European mother countries and would prefer that food to American food.

The Swedish colony of New Sweden was founded in Delaware in 1638, and was conquered by the Dutch colony of New Netherlands (New York) in 1655. The Swedes remained as farmers, but their culture gradually disappeared. When the Swedish naturalist Pehr Kalm visited around 1750, he found little food he recognized, other than the large rye cracker breads (*knäckebröd*) in the homes of a few of the clergy.

The Wasa company in Sweden exports such cracker breads to U.S. supermarkets, if you want to set a Delaware Swedish-American table of the eighteenth century. For the seventeenth-century Swedish colony, we have to use sources like the 1750 book, *Een Lijten Kockebook*, as translated by Martin Skjöldebrand for the Swedish historical food website "The Olde Cookery Book" ⟨http://www.bahnhof.se/~chimbis/⟩. Although "soppa" is translated as soup, this is served like a Welsh Rabbit and could also be a sauce for roast meat. If the settlers in New Sweden knew this recipe, they would usually have had to use stale cornbread and fresh farmer's cheese, or precious supplies of flour and cheeses from Sweden.

> Take peeled onion, slice it and let it simmer. Take cheese, which isn't too old, and slice it thin. Mix it together and add some butter and give it a boil again. Slice a bun [Swedish *vetesemla*], put in a tray and then pour this over it.

Yield: Serves 2 homesick farmers

1 onion
¼ pound semi-soft cheese such as fresh Gouda
4 tablespoons salted butter
2 soft rolls (or 2 squares of cornbread)

Equipment: Saucepan, cheese slicer (optional)

1. Halve, peel, and slice the onion.
2. Simmer the onion in a saucepan with two cups of water until the onion is transparent.
3. Slice the cheese as thinly as possible. Stir the slices and the butter into the onion soup.
4. Slice up the rolls or cornbread, and place in a large bowl.
5. As soon as the cheese is melted, pour over the bread and serve.

The early settlers ate this with spoons, often two diners to a bowl or wooden trencher.

TO PREPARE SALAD FROM CELERY (1667)

We imagine the early settlers as eating plain, dull, overcooked food—but in fact that sort of cooking did not fully develop until late in the nineteenth century. Seventeenth-century Europeans liked elaborate spices, and American colonists began shipping and smuggling them as soon as they could build ships. Settlers also ate salads, as shown in this recipe from *The Sensible Cook*, a Dutch cookbook known to have been used by some colonists in New Netherlands and New York, as translated by Peter A. Rose. English settlers ate similar salads, except that they didn't have as good connections to the Mediterranean olive oil trade, so were more likely to use the butter dressing, taken from another recipe in the same Dutch book. By 1750, the visiting Swedish scientist Pehr Kalm found Dutch settlers in upstate New York still eating a large salad at every afternoon dinner, but with much more vinegar and less oil.

> Take Celery, clean it, and pull the tip of the knife through the heads, then place it in cold water. It will curl nicely. Eat with Oil, Pepper, and Salt.

Some take Vinegar or press out a fresh Lemon over it.

Yield: Serves 8

3 heads celery

6 tablespoons olive oil or butter

2 tablespoons red wine vinegar, or 1 small lemon (optional)

Equipment: Paring knife, large punch bowl or soup pot, saucepan (for butter sauce)

1. Break off a stalk of celery to check for sand. Cut off the ends. If celery is reasonably clean, cut long slits in each stalk from just above the base to the end. Bend back the stalks carefully to get to the ones inside, and the heads of celery will open up like giant flowers after they soak. (If celery has a lot of sand at the base, break off stalks and wash them, then slit individually several times each.)

2. Soak the celery in very cold water 20 minutes. For whole heads you will need a large punch bowl or soup pot.

3. Remove celery from water and shake dry.

4. Dribble on the oil, and sprinkle salt and pepper. Sprinkle on the vinegar or half the lemon and squeeze it. (If no ship from Holland has landed recently, melt butter in a small saucepan with vinegar, and sprinkle hot sauce over the celery along with salt and pepper.)

Serve with meats, fish, and bread. Kalm found many families dining on bread and salty butter, salad, and buttermilk, "one mouthful after another."

To Make a Frykecy
(1669–1691)

Chicken Fricassee is still popular in many areas of the United States, and was known in French cooking from the late Middle Ages and in English cooking manuscripts from the 1500s. We know that the dish was popular in Virginia in 1709–1712, from the diaries of William Byrd, who wrote down almost everything he ate. However, being a man, Byrd did not cook nor record recipes. If food historians wanted to reconstruct Byrd's fricassee, we would have to start with an English cookbook of the time.

However, there is a recipe for chicken fricassee in a very famous cooking manuscript that belonged to Byrd's sister-in-law, Frances Parke Custis, and eventually passed down to Martha Custis Washington, wife of President Washington. (This style of fricassee would not have seemed old-fashioned by George Washington's time, but Washington was known not to like such fancy dishes, so it is unlikely that Martha Washington used the recipe.) Byrd's wife, Lucy, had written her name in the manuscript as a child. However, neither Lucy nor Frances was known for her cooking (or, to be fully accurate, for the cooking of her slaves). And Byrd's diary does not mention eating fricassee at home or at the Custis home.

So, if this English recipe was ever used in America, it was probably by an earlier owner of the manuscript, such as Lucy and Frances's mother, Jane Ludwell Parke (1688?–1708). However, the editor of *Martha Washington's Booke of Cookery,* Karen Hess, deduces that the manuscript was copied from an earlier family manuscript by someone with handwriting very different from that of Jane Ludwell Parke. Hess suggests that that copyist may have been Jane Ludwell Parke's stepmother, Frances Culpepper Berkeley Ludwell (1634–1691), who had come to America between 1649 and 1669. As Lady Berkeley, she was the wife of the governor of Virginia, and as Mrs. Ludwell, wife of the governor of Carolina. She would have been in charge of a well-equipped kitchen with a budget for frequent entertaining of leading planters. (One of the guests who might have eaten the "Frykecy" was Lady Berkeley's cousin Nathaniel Bacon, who left the inner circle to lead a rebellion in 1676, burned Jamestown, and threatened to shoot the seventy-year-old governor. Lord Berkeley coolly turned away, but compromised by letting Bacon continue his unauthorized Indian fighting.)

The details of breaking the bones to enrich the sauce, and thickening at the end with egg yolks survived almost into the nineteenth century, and the seasoning with parsley, thyme, onion, and lemon suggest that this recipe was first written after the medieval use of fruit and sweet spices in chicken dishes had faded. I think this dish would fit onto the dinner menu of any affluent Colonial home from the 1640s to the American Revolution. For cutting up the chickens, I have relied on Mary Randolph's *Virginia House-Wife* (1824). Some quantities are as suggested by Karen Hess.

> Take 2 Chicken, or a hare, kill & flaw [skin] them hot, take out theyr intrills & wipe them within, cut them in pieces & break theyr bones with A pestle. Thn put halfe a pound of butter into the frying pan, & fry it till it be browne, thn put in the Chiken & give it a walme [bubble] or two. Thn put in halfe a pinte of faire water well seasoned with pepper, & salt, & a little after put in a handfull of parsley, & time [thyme], & an ounion shread all smal. Fry all these together till they be enough, & when it is ready to be dished up, put into the pan the youlks of 5 or 6 eggs, well beaten & mixed wth A little wine vinegar or juice of leamons, stir thes[e] well together least it Curdle, thn dish it up without any more frying.

Yield: Serves 16 as 1 dish at a plantation midday dinner

2 broiler-fryer chickens, or 6 pounds cut-up broiler-fryer, free range preferred

½ pound salted butter

1 cup homemade chicken broth (optional, suggested by Karen Hess to compensate for today's less flavorful chickens)

A bunch parsley

10–15 sprigs of fresh thyme or 2 teaspoons dried thyme

1 onion

2–3 eggs

1 lemon or 2 teaspoons wine vinegar

Equipment: Chef's knife or mallet and cleaver to cut up chicken, kitchen mallet or brass pestle to crush bones, heavy soup pot with tight lid, large ovenproof platter, tongs, lemon juicer

1. If using cut chicken, go on to Step 2. With whole chickens, remove bag of giblets, wash chickens, and drain. Cut off wings and drumsticks. Remove thighs, cutting off the leg bones near the backbone. Cut breasts off the backbone. Cut across or break the backs in half.

2. With a pestle or kitchen mallet, break up the backbone, the ends of the drumsticks and thighbones, and crush the wing tips and some of the ribs.

3. Melt the butter in the soup pot over medium heat and let it foam until starting to brown.

4. Increase heat and add chicken backs, necks, and giblets to pot, followed by legs and thighs, with the breasts and wings on top. Allow to brown for a few minutes before stirring.

5. Add a teaspoon of salt and some fresh ground pepper to a cup of water.

6. Pour water into the soup pot, stir once, and cover tightly. Reduce heat to a simmer.

7. Halve, peel, and chop the onion.

8. Take a handful of parsley. Tie it up into a bundle with one of the parsley stems.

9. If using fresh thyme, tie it up into a bundle with another parsley stem.

10. Open the soup pot and add the onion, parsley, and thyme. Stir to get the herbs under the surface.

11. Again cover tightly, and cook until chicken is just beginning to fall off the bones, about 30–40 minutes.

12. Heat a platter in a warm (150 degrees) oven.

13. Remove chicken from pot to the platter and keep warm in the oven. Discard the bundles of herbs.

14. Scrape any browned bits into the remaining pan juices. There should be about 1 to 1½ cups. If there is much more, increase heat to boil off some of the water and concentrate the juices. If there is much less, add a little water or chicken broth.

15. Break 1 egg for every ½ cup of juices over an empty cup and separate by pouring the yolks from shell to shell. Save the whites for another use, such as **To Make Chocolet Puffs**. Put the yolks into a bowl.

16. Stir the eggs to a golden yellow. Remove the soup pot from the heat.

17. Juice half a lemon and add a tablespoon of lemon juice (or 2 teaspoons of vinegar) to the egg mixture, stirring well.

18. Stirring rapidly, add a little of the hot pan juices into the eggs to warm them.

19. Stirring the remaining pan juices rapidly, add the eggs and whip to a light creamy texture.

20. Quickly add the chicken pieces, stirring to coat them with the sauce.

Serve in a typical Colonial Virginia dinner at 2 P.M. with at least three other meat or fish dishes and numerous side dishes including seasonal vegetables, sweet potatoes, and green salad. Remove the tablecloth for an equally elaborate course of desserts. Seventeenth-century Englishmen ate many foods with small bones, and would not necessarily prefer the drumsticks to the necks or backs, although the gizzards might be saved for servants. The egg-bound sauce cannot be reheated without curdling, so spoon it onto any leftover pieces of chicken to make a pretty glaze, and serve cold for a Virginia supper or breakfast.

ANOTHER STANDING DISH IN NEW-ENGLAND (1672)

This recipe for an oatmeal pudding appeared in *New-England's Rarities Discovered* by John Josselyn. Josselyn was a physician who recorded plant lore carefully, and this would appear to be the first Colonial recipe with exact directions. However two problems arise right away. How big is a "spoonful?" And what was the grain, "silpee?"

Spoonfuls were rounded in the seventeenth century, but spoons came in many sizes. There were very large spoons for stirring pots, and ladlelike spoons for eating soup and porridge. If you look at old pewter spoons in a historical museum, you will see that their size varied, and some might have held a rounded amount of as much as four tablespoons. We have a clue in the comparison to "White-pot," a sort of custard bread pudding. There are English recipes for white-pot we can make, and they come out like modern pudding. So the spoonfuls should be enough to thicken the milk substantially. And twelve of today's tablespoons do a pretty good job with today's oatmeal and homogenized milk. But this takes us back to the problem of "silpee" and how much thickening power it might have had.

Oats were grown in New England as early as 1602, and naked oats (meaning that they matured without an outer husk) were being grown in the colder parts of England. Because the New England climate was colder and damper in the seventeenth and eighteenth centuries than it is now, oats were the first European grain that grew well there. We know that naked oats have much smaller seeds than ordinary oats. This implies that they had proportionately more seed coat and germ and less starch. So silpee might have had less thickening power than oats do now, and Josselyn's spoons might have been larger. (We could also question whether Maine milk was richer or thinner in the 1660s.)

We can guess that silpee didn't taste *a lot better* than ordinary oats, or it would still be grown. It probably didn't taste very different, or Josselyn would have mentioned that. So we can't know exactly what silpee tasted like, but we can work with the guess that it was similar to the oats we have now. The New England taste for oatmeal has continued to the present, but the name "Silpee" has never appeared in print before or since. (It may be related to the Latin *siligo*, a farmer's term used in early English for wheat or rye that had degenerated in quality over generations of planting. Or, it may be related to a southern American rice bread called "philpy.")

With imported sugar and spice, this "standing dish" was a winter treat for the upper class of the colony. Note that the preliminary toasting and beating make this a "fast food" for supper or guests. To modern tastes, it is a bland pap, and you can see why sick people might tolerate it. The indentured servants (and Josselyn had at least one African slave and may have had Native American slaves) got the water version, or maybe a gruel based on the cooking liquid of boiled salt meat. Most servants, slaves, and poorer farmers ate rough cornmeal mush at every meal. I have guessed at the spices used in the 1670s; the use of sugar reminds us that the colony was already focus-ing on trade with the West Indies and might also have used Jamaican allspice.

> Naked Oats, there called Silpee, an excellent grain used instead of Oat Meal, they dry it in an Oven, or in a Pan upon the fire, then beat it small in a Mortar.
>
> And when the Milk is ready to boil, they put into a pottle [2 quarts] of Milk about ten or twelve spoonfuls of this Meal, so boil it leasurely, stirring of it every foot [constantly], least it burn too; when it is almost boiled enough, they hang the Kettle up higher, and let it stew only, in short time it will thicken like a Custard; they season it with a little Sugar and Spice, and to serve it to the Table in deep Basons [bowls], and it is altogether as good as a White-pot [a custard thickened with bread crumbs].
>
> For people weakened with long Sickness.
>
> It exceedingly nourisheth and strengthens people weakened with long Sickness.
>
> Some times they make Water Gruel with it, and sometimes thicken their Flesh Broth with this or Homminey [cracked corn, as Josselyn uses the term], if it be for Servants.

Yield: Serves 10

12 rounded tablespoons of oat flour (from about 1 cup oatmeal)

2 quarts whole milk

½ teaspoon cinnamon

½ teaspoon nutmeg

2 tablespoons sugar

Equipment: Food processor or blender, medium saucepan, cake pan in toasting oatmeal, flat whisk, rubber spatula, custard cups or small coffee cups, nutmeg grater (optional)

1. If you cannot find oat flour, whirl 1 cup oatmeal in a blender for 2 minutes to make a meal with some powdery flour. Toast flour in a 350-degree oven for 25 minutes (optional).

2. Put milk in the saucepan, and whisk in the oat flour. (Because today's milk is pasteurized by heating, you don't need to heat the milk before adding the flour.)

3. Heat the mixture slowly to boiling, whisking often to keep it from sticking to the pot.

4. Boil until the mixture is about the consistency of pancake batter, about 10 minutes, stirring almost constantly.

5. Reduce heat and simmer 15–30 minutes more.

6. If you have a nutmeg grater, you can grate whole nutmegs and cinnamon sticks for a fresher flavor.

7. Divide the porridge into 10 coffee cups or custard cups.

8. Mix the sugar, nutmeg, and cinnamon in another cup and sprinkle on top of the porridge.

Serve as a breakfast or light supper.

VIRGINIA HAM (1674)

While European grains and vegetables were not easy to grow in America, some of the animals, such as honeybees, pigs, and horses thrived and sometimes established wild populations. The pigs fattened nicely on wild American chestnuts, and colonists soon learned to feed them corn and peanuts as well. William Byrd the elder, a leading planter, thought enough of this ham recipe to write it on the flyleaf of the family Bible, as quoted in the 1939 *The Williamsburg Art of Cookery* by Mrs. Helen Bullock. In the recipe we can see the ready availability of milk at this early date and also that hams were already close to their present size, since the simmering time still works. Pots were bigger, however, so I have taken the suggestion to saw off the hock from "How to Cook a Country Ham," by Sarah Fritschner and Joe Castro, in *Cook's Illustrated*, November/December 1996. Their directions suggest thirty-six hours soaking for a fourteen to fifteen pound ham six to twelve months aged. Adjust soaking times for more or less age and size.

> To eat the Ham in Perfection steep it in half Milk and half Water for 36 Hours, and then having brought the Water to a Boil, put the Ham therein and let it simmer, not boil, for 4 or 5 Hours according to Size of the Ham— for simmering brings the Salt out and boiling drives it in.

Yield: Serves 30

1 country ham
1 gallon whole milk
1 quart whole milk yogurt (optional)

Equipment: Oversize stock pot, hacksaw with clean blade, vegetable scrubbing brush, instant-read meat thermometer

1. Scrub any mold off ham with the brush under cold running water.

2. Saw the hock off the ham so it fits into the stock pot well. (Reserve for another recipe.)

3. Fit ham into the stock pot and cover with a mixture of milk and water.

4. Soak 36 hours. Over that time, Byrd's milk almost certainly soured, possibly helping to tenderize the ham. Modern milk won't sour as easily, so you can try to duplicate the effect with the optional yogurt, stirred into the mix.

5. Drain off soaking mixture and wash off ham.

6. Return the ham to the pot and cover with cold water.

7. Bring to a boil over high heat, reduce heat to a slight simmer. Cook 4–5 hours, or until meat thermometer registers 140–160 degrees. (You will then see if early Virginians cooked their hams less and saltier, or more and firmer, than we do.)

8. Remove ham from pot and cool slightly before carving. Reserve the stock for boiling greens, perhaps with the hock.

Serve in a Virginia dinner at one end of the table, balanced by a roast beef or turkey at the other. The hostess carved and served the ham; the host carved the other dish.

3

The Twenty-One Colonies (1710s–1790s)

The title is arbitrary, but the point is clear. There were more than thirteen colonies in what is now the United States during the eighteenth century. Bands of Native Americans lived independently in every colony, and powerful Indian confederations controlled much of the continent. France claimed parts of New England and colonized areas of the Mississippi River basin, including what is now the Midwest and Deep South. The west coast and Alaska were colonized by Spain and Russia. Spain also held Florida for most of the century, and all of French North America for a time. During the period of Spanish rule in Louisiana, the French community was reinforced by refugees deported by the English from Canadian "Acadie," now known as "cajuns." Within the English colonies, about 10 percent of the residents were German-speaking immigrants, another 10 to 15 percent were "Scotch-Irish" Protestants with little loyalty to England; there was a strong French-speaking community in South Carolina, and African slaves were developing a widespread English dialect of their own.

Even after the American Revolution, parts of what is now the United States were still the colonial domains of England, France, Spain, and Russia. Hawaii was an independent kingdom. After the Revolution, some leaders of the original states imagined that the areas west of the Appalachians would be treated as colonies of the individual states. You can find maps in which Virginia, the Carolinas, and Pennsylvania extend westward toward the Mississippi, and Connecticut claims a "Western Reserve" in northeast Ohio.

Although documentation remains poor, American food was settling down in the eighteenth century. Leading citizens continued to use British cookbooks and imported foods to create an English lifestyle, but they were also developing fancy versions of local foods and participating in a global British Empire that delivered cheap sugar, exotic spices and condiments, and tropical fruits to American cities. In French areas and the back country, settlers were sometimes trading food with Indians, but more and more often consuming and storing large crops. African slavery was evident in the kitchens of every colony.

Yet the sheer size of the country left many pockets of old-fashioned cooking, a completely German-speaking food culture in and around rural Pennsylvania, and an elaborate Native American cuisine among

Figure 2 Pueblo Indians baking in a Spanish-style outdoor oven, 1940. *Source: Bettmann/Corbis.*

the Iroquois and other settled tribes. A fusion cuisine was developing among the Spanish settlers and Pueblo Indians of New Mexico, and another in French and Spanish New Orleans and Mobile. The end of the century marked the extension of Spanish missions into California and the creation of another fusion cuisine among Native American servants, Spanish colonists who were arriving with Mexican recipes, and the very different agricultural possibilities of California.

Gisado de Trigo (Whole Wheat Stew) (1700s)

Spanish settlers had been driven out of New Mexico and Western Texas by the Pueblo Revolt of 1680 and were not able to return until 1700. In many ways, the events were parallel to King Philip's War in New England at about the same time, except that in New Mexico the Indian coalition was victorious. Subsequent hostility, especially with the plains Apaches, kept the Spanish settlers from effectively colonizing the plains north of New Mexico throughout the eighteenth century. In New Mexico and Arizona, the colonists had more stable relationships with Eastern Pueblo Indians and traded with Navajo and Apaches. It is easy to imagine the early Spanish settlers hungrily making this stew with the first wheat berries harvested, not even waiting to grind the grain into flour. But settlers would have stored their wheat as whole grain and ground flour as needed over the course of a year. So this stew could be made through the winter and into the spring lamb season in good years. The stew is quite similar to southwestern Indian dishes of posole, made from hulled corn, and may have been influenced by them. Where the Indians began growing wheat (quite early in the Pueblos and among the settled Hopi, Zuni, and Pima Indians of Arizona), they made similar wheat stews. These wheat stews continued in both Indian and Hispanic communities and are still made as traditional dishes. (There is a Hopi version in *The American Ethnic Cookbook for Students*.) This is a dish that may have gone back and forth several times between settlers and Indians. The general recipe is like a Mediterranean rice pilaf, but the hint of chile added at the end is very much in the style of Native southwestern cooking, where strong peppers are an occasional treat rather than the usual spice. This recipe is from 1939, from *The Genuine New Mexico Tasty Recipes* by Cleofas M. Jaramillo, a descendant of Spanish pioneers at Arroyo Hondo, north of Taos.

> Wash ½ cup dry wheat; dry & toast slightly in frying pan greased with lard. Pour the wheat into a pot of hot water. Add a pound of lamb loin cut in small pieces as for hash. Cook until tender and almost dry like hash. Add chopped onion, salt, & a little ground red chile, like adding pepper.

Yield: Serves 6

½ cup whole wheat berries (substitute cracked wheat)

1 tablespoon lard

1 pound boneless stew lamb

1 small onion

Ground red chile (not chili con carne powder, which has other spices mixed in)

Equipment: Heavy skillet (cast iron preferred), large soup pot, wooden spoon

1. Bring a quart of water to boil in the large soup pot.

2. Meanwhile, melt the lard in the heavy skillet.

3. Add the wheat berries or cracked wheat to the lard and stir well.

4. Increase the heat under the wheat to medium and stir it around as it toasts so that it browns and pops a little without burning.

5. When wheat is ready, pour it into the pot of hot water.

6. Cut the lamb meat into ½-inch cubes, cutting off any fat (although early Spanish settlers would have relished the fat; their animals were leaner and tougher than ours, even as lamb).

7. Add the lamb to the pot and bring back to a boil.

8. Return heat to a slow boil and cook uncovered until wheat and lamb are tender.

9. Halve, peel, and chop the onion.

10. If the water level falls below the meat before the stew is ready, heat more water in a teakettle and add boiling water to the stew. If there is too much water when the stew is done, turn up the heat and boil it off until the stew looks "almost dry like hash."

Serve on plates with onion and chile sprinkled on top, with a small bowl of coarse salt on the table.

TO MAKE A SOUPE MEAGRE (1723)

This is the third recipe in the Ashfield family recipe manuscript begun by Isabella Morris Ashfield (1705–1741) around the time of her marriage. She probably copied it from another manuscript. It is for a no-meat vegetable soup for the end of Lent, when early peas and lettuce might be ready. The manuscript was published in 1982 by the New Jersey Historical Society as *The Pleasures of Colonial Cooking*. It's not hard to guess that her half peck of peas (one gallon) is intended to measure peas still in the pod.

> Take three quarts of water. Set it boyling in a pipkin [saucepan with legs for fireplace use] or Els Something that is well Tin'd. Take three larg handfulls of Sorrill, one handfull of parsley, a Cabbige lettice, two larg Onions, pepir and salt, three cloves, two french roals cut into Eight Pieces. Dry your Bread before the fire, put in your Soupe with half a pound of butter. Let it all boyle together two hours and a Slow fire. Sieve it up. In the season you may put half a peck of Pease.

Yield: Serves 12 as a main dish, could be sampled for 36

3 bunches sorrel (or 8 ounces spinach and ¼ cup lemon juice)

1 bunch parsley

1 iceberg lettuce

2 large onions

3 cloves

2 large sandwich rolls

2 sticks salted butter

6 cups shelled peas (optional)

Equipment: Large soup pot, food mill or "chinoise" (pointed sieve with wooden pestle), blender (optional)

1. Put 12 cups of water in the soup pot and bring to a boil.

2. Halve, peel, and slice onions into half-rounds. (Use swim goggles to avoid tears). Add to soup.

3. Roughly chop the sorrel, lettuce, and parsley and add to soup.

4. Add 2 teaspoons of salt and 1 teaspoon of black pepper, and the cloves. Add peas if using.

5. Cut rolls into 4 diagonal slices, and toast them in an oven or toaster oven. Brown them nicely but do not burn.

6. Add toasts and butter to the soup. Return to a boil, then cover with the lid ajar, and reduce heat to a simmer for 2 hours. Stir occasionally so that it will cook evenly and not burn.

7. When ready to serve, pour batches in a blender, food mill, or chinoise and puree. If you use the blender, you should use a sieve, food mill, or chinoise to remove any large fibers or chunks.

Serve hot. Soupe Meagre was sometimes thickened with eggs or garnished with hard-boiled eggs. But in early Colonial times, hens may not have resumed laying in time.

Cocoa Nut Pudding (1738)

I found this recipe in a manuscript cookbook of the Boston Smith family begun in 1738, now at the Massachusetts Historical Society. This is a later copy of a faded version in the original handwriting. The continuing use of coconuts and rosewater shows that Boston's largest business at this time was trading Caribbean products to Europe and that this affluent merchant family enjoyed a global cuisine over many generations. This is another Anglo-American recipe for pudding that was probably intended to be baked with a crust, making what we now call a pie, but you can try it in buttered pie tins to make a kind of macaroon/pudding. This recipe looks like a custard pie filling but when we correct for the small size of eighteenth-century eggs, we get something looser, like shoo-fly pie, richer and spicier than it is sweet.

Take 2 large cocoa nuts, peel and grate them, 12 yolks of eggs, 2 whites well beaten, half a pound of butter melted in a gill of rose water, half a pint of thin cream, one nutmeg, sweeten to your taste with loaf sugar, bake it in a quick oven.

Yield: Serves 12–16 as a dessert

2 fresh coconuts, or 6 cups (1¼ pounds) shredded unsweetened coconut, or 1-½ pounds sweetened

12 small eggs or 8 extra-large eggs

2 sticks salted butter, plus some for pie plates (optional)

½ cup rosewater

1 cup light cream

2 teaspoons nutmeg

1½ cups sugar

2 nine-inch pie shells (optional)

Equipment: Coconut grater, or vegetable peeler and food processor with grating disk, whisk or handheld electric beater, two 9-inch pie plates, spatula

1. To open coconuts, bake at 350 degrees for 20 minutes. Let cool. Tap around the shell with a hammer or heavy cleaver, and open over a sink to drain off liquid. The hard part is levering the meat out of the shell. If you can find a coconut grater, perhaps in an Asian or Caribbean grocery, it is easier to scoop or grate coconut directly out of the shell. One kind looks like a curved vegetable peeler, another kind like a small ice cream scoop with metal teeth. If you lever the meat off with a spoon, you still have to peel off the brown layer with the vegetable peeler. You can then grate it with a food processor but should also process it with the blade to the texture of meal.

2. Separate eggs by pouring from shell to shell. Reserve all but two of the whites for another recipe, such as **Chocolet Puffs**.

3. Beat yolks until creamy and light.

4. Melt butter in a small saucepan or microwave oven.

5. Mix rosewater and cream.

6. Mix sugar and nutmeg with coconut. (If using sweetened coconut, reduce the sugar by 1 cup).

7. In a mixing bowl, combine coconut mixture with butter. Mix in egg yolks and cream mixture.

8. Beat egg whites until they form soft peaks.

9. Stir whites into coconut-cream mixture with a spatula.

10. Divide the coconut mixture between the pie shells, or buttered pie plates.

11. Bake 15 minutes at 375 degrees, then reduce heat to 300 degrees and bake until the pudding is firm throughout and knife inserted at the center comes back almost clean, about an hour. A soft spot at the center will finish cooking after the pie is removed from the oven.

12. Cool on wire racks.

Serve in wide slices either before the meat or, at a more formal midday dinner with candied fruits and dried nuts, after the tablecloth has been removed.

APPLE DUMPLINGS (1749)

Apples grew well in much of Colonial America. The Swedish botanist Pehr Kalm found apple dumplings a popular dish over much of the English colonies. He visited the old Swedish colony in New Jersey, spent some time in Philadelphia, traveled to upstate New York, living in Albany and noting Dutch-American food customs, and went through Iroquois country to Quebec, noting Indian foods on the way. This kind of boiled dumpling remained popular until more accurate ovens encouraged a switch to easier baked dumplings in the 1870s.

> . . . [T]ake an apple and pare it, make a dough of water, flour, and butter. Roll it thin and enclose the apple in it. This is then bound in a clean linen cloth, put in a pot and boiled. When it is done it is taken out, placed on table and served. While it is warm, the crust is cut on one side. Thereupon they mix butter and sugar, which is added to the apples and the dish is ready.

Yield: Serves 8

8 small–medium apples (not Macintosh)

2 cups flour, plus more to knead, roll, and flour the pudding cloth

¼ cup whole wheat flour

2 tablespoons wheat germ

3 sticks butter

¼ cup sugar or brown sugar

Equipment: Food processor, clean old pillowcase or sheet, kitchen string, soup pot, vegetable peeler, breadboard, and rolling pin

1. Cut 2 sticks of the butter into small pieces.
2. Mix flour, whole wheat flour, and wheat germ in a mixing bowl.
3. Put half the flour mixture and half the butter into the work bowl of the food processor. (Don't worry too much about measurements.)
4. Process with the steel blade in short bursts until the mixture looks like small kernels of corn.
5. Put ½ cup of cold water in a measuring cup. Open the feed tube of the food processor. Turn on the processor, and pour a thin stream of water into the feed tube until the pastry comes together in a ball and rides up on top of the rotating knife.
6. Flour your hands and the board, and knead the ball of pastry for a few minutes, then wrap in a plastic bag and refrigerate.
7. Repeat with the other half of the butter and flour mixture.
8. Peel the apples.
9. Start a large pot of water boiling.
10. Tear the sheet or pillow case into pieces big enough to make a nice purse around one of the apples, or leave it as one large piece.
11. Bring out half the pastry, flour the board and rolling pin, and divide pastry into 4 pieces.
12. Roll out the largest piece of pastry from the center into a circle big enough to enclose an apple and seal it up. Do that. If you have way too much pastry, roll the next piece out a little thicker. If you don't have enough pastry to lap the ends and seal, try a smaller apple, or re-roll it thinner.
13. Repeat until all the apples are done. (You can refrigerate the completed apple dumplings.)
14. Wet down the cloth or cloths in the hot water. Wring it (them) out, and arrange on the countertop.
15. If you are using one large cloth, the technique is to flour a circular area a little larger than your circles of dough, and tie one apple dumpling snugly into that area with kitchen string, then flour another area and repeat. So you end up with a cloth and eight bulb shapes coming out of it. If using single cloths, just flour them well, put on an apple dumpling, and tie into a snug purse.
16. Turn up the heat so the water is at a rolling boil, and add the apple

dumplings. When pot returns to a boil, you can reduce heat, but keep it boiling well with a cover on top. Boil 45 minutes.

17. Melt the remaining stick of butter with the sugar.

18. When apples are done, cut the strings with a scissors, and unmold the apples into serving bowls. (You can serve the individual ones in the bags.)

19. Cut open the top of the pastry and pour in a little of the butter-sugar mixture.

Serve for dessert or with meats.

COLE SLAW (1749)

In Albany Kalm watched his Dutch landlady make a cabbage salad of the kind that became an all-American food in the next century. The hot butter dressing was actually more typical in Colonial times. I have taken the passage as quoted by Peter Rose in *Foods of the Hudson*, but added some proportions from recipes in the 1843 *Every Lady's Cook Book* by Mrs. T. J. Crowin.

She took the inner leaves of a head of cabbage, namely the leaves which usually remain when the outermost leaves have been removed, and cut them in long, thin strips about $1/12$ to $1/6$ of an inch wide, seldom more. . . . She put them upon a platter, poured oil and vinegar upon them, added salt and some pepper while mixing the shredded cabbage, so that the oil etc, might be evenly distributed, as is the custom when making salads. Then it was ready. In place of oil, melted butter is frequently used. This is kept in a warm pot or crock and poured over the salad after it has been served.

Yield: Serves 8–10 as a side dish

1 small green cabbage

1 stick of salted butter, or ½ cup pure olive oil

3 tablespoons cider vinegar

Equipment: Saucepan, sharp knife

1. Wash the cabbage well and break off the outer leaves for another recipe or soup stock.

2. Cut the cabbage in half with a sharp knife.

3. Cut very thin shreds across the halved cabbage. (If your knife is not very, very sharp, it is somewhat safer to quarter the cabbage.) Mix vinegar with 1 tablespoon water.

4. Melt butter (if using) with vinegar in a small sauce pan.

5. Put shredded cabbage in a bowl. If using oil, add and toss well to coat the leaves. Grind on fresh pepper and toss again.

6. If using butter mixture, stir it very thoroughly and pour over the cabbage, toss with salt and pepper. If you have added oil in Step 5, now sprinkle on the vinegar mixture and salt, and toss once more.

Serve for midday dinner with roasted meat, bread and butter with grated cheese, and buttermilk, which Kalm found at most summer meals in Albany.

TO MAKE CHOCOLET PUFFS (1750s)

This recipe for macaroons (also known as "kisses") comes from an apparently English cooking manuscript that was brought to the American colonies and is now at the historical Tryon Place, home of Governor Thomas Tryon of North Carolina in the 1770s. I have picked the 1750s because most of the recipes seem similar to those of E. Smith's *Compleat Housewife*, first published in 1727 and reprinted in Williamsburg in 1742; and even closer to Hannah Glasse's *The Art of Cookery Made Plain and Easy*, first published in 1747 and one of the most popular English cookbooks in the American colonies. If the date is right, this is one of the first recipes in English for any use of chocolate other than drinking, but there is no reason that this recipe might not have been tried out in an American plantation. There is a somewhat similar 1733 English recipe for "Chocolate-Puffs" in the book *Mrs. Mary Eale's Receipts*. E. Smith had a crude chocolate candy, and four other kinds of puffs, not chocolate. Glasse had no mention of chocolate or puffs at all. Chocolate had become more available in the British Empire after the conquest of Jamaica in 1655, and the recipe probably was designed for spiced and sweetened cakes of chocolate, somewhat as Mexican chocolate is still made. You can get rosewater and sometimes orange flower water in Middle East groceries. The unbaked material is sticky, so plan your moves carefully in advance. We can substitute a food processor for the laborious pounding in a mortar and sieving necessary for any eighteenth-century recipe using sugar or nuts.

> Take a pound of Loaf Suger beat and Sifted very fine, 2 Ounce of Almonds blancht and beat very fine with a little Oring Flower water or any other, to keep them Oyling, but not make the same too thin, take 2 ounces of Chocolet and grate it, then mix it well together, then take the white of an Egg and beat it to a froth, if one be not Enough take a little more, then beat it well to a past & Squert it, and do it on Slight paper and Set the same in an oven after Bread, for Chocolett Ditt [heat] it up a while but not for White ones, for fear of makeing them too Brown.

Yield: 12 macaroons

1 pound sugar

2 ounces blanched almonds (½ cup slivered)

1 tablespoon rosewater or orange-flower water

2 ounces of chocolate (semi-sweet, or 1⅓ cakes of Mexican chocolate)

Pinch cinnamon (if not using Mexican chocolate)

1 egg or equivalent egg white product

Butter for parchment paper

Equipment: Food processor, pastry bag and tube tip, parchment paper, baking sheets (nonstick preferred), whisk, rubber spatulas

1. Preheat oven to 300 degrees.
2. Grate chocolate with food processor grating disk. With Mexican chocolate you may have to break it up into pieces and pulse with the steel blade.
3. Remove chocolate to a mixing bowl.
4. Process almonds and rosewater or orange-flower water with the steel blade. Make a fine paste, but don't let the oil separate (the waters were added to the mortar to help prevent separating the oil).
5. Add the grated chocolate and cinnamon (if using) to the mixing bowl, and pulse a few times to mix well.
6. Whisk the egg white until it forms soft peaks when you remove the beater. (If you think this is boring, imagine trying to get your slave to whip egg whites with a spoon or butter knife, as was often used in eighteenth century. That took an hour.)
7. Add the egg whites to the almond paste and process another few seconds to mix well.
8. Cut parchment paper to fit baking sheet.

9. Butter parchment paper on both sides.

10. Scrape all the paste into the pastry bag, work out any bubbles, and fold down the sides so you are ready to "squert."

11. Squeeze out thick chocolate-kiss shapes a little less than an inch in diameter, lifting the bag to get the pointy top. If they aren't just right, don't fuss with them, they're too sticky! You can also try this with two teaspoons.

12. Bake 30–40 minutes.

13. Cool by pulling the paper onto the wire racks.

14. Remove puffs from paper after cooling. You may need to wet the paper a little for it to peel off.

15. Keep in a sealed container.

Serve with many other desserts, cookies, candied fruits, and nuts on the second course at midday dinner. The dessert course was called a "remove" because the tablecloth (on which people wiped their knives) was removed and dessert served on a bare table.

"DIRECTIONS FOR MAKING A CHOUDER" (1751)

The earliest American recipe for chowder is a poem, but it is otherwise a typical early chowder composed of fresh fish and shipboard supplies and layered like a casserole. Clams, milk, and potatoes did not enter chouders until the 1830s and 1840s. The recipe appeared in the *Boston Evening Post* and is quoted in 1978 *The Book of Chowder* by Richard J. Hooker, still the definitive work on the subject. The recipe does not specify fish, but chowders were typically made with cod and haddock, and sometimes striped bass. Halibut steaks would be a reasonable substitute. Colonial-era diners did not mind picking through fish bones. You can use boneless pieces of fish, but the chowder will not be as good. Later chowder recipes include a codfish head for richer broth. You may be surprised by the use of herbs and spices. They wouldn't have been part of a chowder for sailors but show the typical eighteenth-century English taste for lots of seasoning. Note the error in the first line—one should first fry some of the *salt pork* to keep the *onions* from burning. Either the poet or the painter was a man who had not actually cooked chowder.

First lay some Onions to keep the Pork from burning,

Because in Chouder there can be no turning;

Then lay some Pork in slices very thin,

Thus you in Chouder always must begin.

Next lay some Fish, cut crossways very nice

Then season well with Pepper, Salt and Spice;

Parsley, Sweet-Marjoram, Savory and Thyme,

Then Biscuit next which must be soak'd some Time,

Thus your Foundation laid, you will be able

To raise a Chouder, high as Tower of Babel;

For by repeating o're the same again,

You may make Chouder for a thousand Men,

Last Bottle of Claret, with Water eno' to smother 'em,

You'll have a Mess which some call *Omnium gather 'em.*

Yield: Serves 12–16

4 pounds cod steaks

1 pound lean salt pork

4 onions

10–12 **Hardtacks**, or a box of Crown
Pilot Crackers

½ teaspoon mace

4 sprigs parsley

½ teaspoon marjoram

½ teaspoon summer savory

½ teaspoon thyme

1 cup red wine (optional)

Equipment: Tall soup pot, another soup pot

1. Slice pork into thin slices. Heat half
   a pot of water in the other soup pot.
2. Put 4 or 5 of the thickest slices of the
   salt pork in the bottom of the soup pot
   and heat slowly.
3. Halve, peel, and slice the onions.
   (Wear swim goggles to avoid tears.)
4. Break up the hardtacks (if using) and
   soak in water to begin softening them.
5. When the salt pork is frying nicely,
   add a layer of onions, then put in some
   of the fish steaks.
6. Put on a sprig of parsley and sprinkle
   on some of the spices and a little salt
   and pepper.
7. Top with some of the crackers or
   hardtacks.
8. Now start again with a few slices of
   salt pork; a layer of onions; more fish
   steaks; another round of herbs, spices,
   salt and pepper; and more crackers or
   hardtacks.
9. It's better to end with salt pork or
   fish.
10. When you get to the top, add the
    cup of wine, if using. Then fill the pot
    with hot water to cover all the layers
    by an inch.
11. Bring (back) to a boil, then reduce
    heat so it barely simmers. You may need
    to add more hot water if the hardtacks

are very dry and absorb it. Simmer
about 30 minutes. The idea is to cook
all the fish steaks so they don't entirely
fall apart, while giving the broth a
chance to develop flavors and thicken.

*Serve in bowls making sure each person gets
some good hunks of fish and a slice of salt pork.
Because there is no milk, this kind of chowder
was seasoned at the table with lemon juice, or
sharp sauces like Worcestershire sauce.*

YAM PUDING (1758)

This may be the first written American
recipe for sweet potato pie; significantly, it
uses the African term "yam," which was also
used in the Caribbean. It was written by
Eliza Lucas Pinckney (1722–1792) in her
"Rect. Book No. 2," published by the South
Carolina Society of Colonial Dames as
Recipe Book Eliza Lucas Pinckney, 1756. Mrs.
Pinckney had grown up in the Carolinas as
an independent planter and begun this
recipe book in 1756 while living briefly in
England. She may have acquired this recipe
back in South Carolina as a widow, once
more managing a large plantation. Her
daughter, Harriott Pinckney Horry, copied
the recipe into her recipe book in 1770,
adding that the wine was to be *stewed* with
spice. Although the dish does not specify
that it be baked in a crust, the precise measurements assure that it was supposed to be
made in a particular dish, almost certainly
lined with pie crust.

Take a pound of yams boil'd dry, beat
it fine in a mortar with a pound Butter
till it Puffs, take ten eggs, half the
whites, beat them with a pound sugar
and half a pint of wine with Spice, the
juice of a lemon with a little of the
rine, and some slices of citron laid on
the Top.—

Yield: Serves 6–10

1 lemon

3 medium sweet potatoes or yams

1 pound salted butter

2 cups sugar or granulated brown sugar

1 cup wine or apple juice

1 teaspoon cinnamon

1 teaspoon nutmeg

10 small eggs, 8 large eggs, or 6 jumbo eggs

Candied citron

9-inch pie shell (optional)

Equipment: Lemon zester or vegetable peeler, juicer, potato masher or ricer, whisk, ovenproof casserole or deep-dish pie plate if not using pie shell

1. Bring sweet potatoes or yams to a boil in water to cover. Cook 25 minutes, then drain well.

2. Peel sweet potatoes, and mash or put through potato ricer. Cut butter into small pieces and whisk into hot sweet potatoes. Beat hard to trap some air and lighten the mixture.

3. Separate eggs and reserve half the whites for another recipe, such as **To Make Chocolet Puffs**.

4. Beat eggs until creamy and light.

5. Preheat oven to 425 degrees. Mix spices with sugar and beat into the eggs.

6. Zest or peel off the yellow part of the lemon peel, and mince fine.

7. Juice the lemon.

8. Beat the wine or apple juice into the egg mixture, followed by the lemon zest and lemon juice.

9. Whisk sweet potato mixture with egg mixture, and fill pie crust or pie plate.

10. Bake 10–12 minutes, and reduce heat to 300 degrees.

11. Bake another hour.

Serve hot as part of the first course of a large midday meal.

"To make Chocolate Cream" (1760s)

Also from the Ashfield manuscript (see **Soupe Meagre** above), this may be the first American recipe for chocolate ice cream, since the usual procedure for a cream was to cool it by stirring it in a metal bowl sunk into cold water or ice. The relatively small number of eggs and the omission of any form of gelatin also suggest that this cream was to be frozen. The recipe is very similar to the first printed American recipe for chocolate ice cream, also called "Chocolate Cream," in the 1824 *The Virginia House-Wife* by Mary Randolph.

By the time this recipe was written in, it was probably by the granddaughter, Euphemia Ashfield Brinckerhoff (1752–1849). She might have begun writing in the manuscript in the mid-1760s. By the time of her marriage in the 1790s, chocolate was being manufactured in the United States. These are clearly English-style recipes, but by Euphemia's section of the manuscript they have become more exact and simplified, perhaps as a result of simpler Colonial living. Or it may be that Euphemia personally preferred simple food, or omitted to write down flavorings she habitually used. The affluent Ashfield family was split by the American Revolution. A brother left for Barbados, two sisters married Tories and moved to Nova Scotia, while Euphemia and another sister retained some of the Ashfield land holdings in New Jersey.

Take a quart of good Sweet Cream. Grate 4 ounces of Chocolate in it, and thicken it with the yolks of 6 eggs. Take it off from the Fire and sweeten it to your Taste. Stir it Till its cold. So serve it up to the Table.

Yield: Serves 8–12

4 cups heavy cream

4 ounces unsweetened chocolate

1–2 cups sugar

6 small eggs or 4 extra large eggs

2 bags crushed ice (one optional)

1 bag rock salt (optional)

Equipment: Heavy saucepan, whisk, box grater or food processor, mortar and pestle (optional), large metal mixing bowl and a larger bowl with room for ice and the metal bowl

1. Bring cream to a rolling boil over medium heat, stirring occasionally.

2. Let cream boil and reduce while you prepare chocolate and eggs. Grate chocolate with food processor grating disk or on a box grater. (Careful not to grate your fingers.) If you are using the Mexican chocolate, which is harder, break it into pieces and pulverize with the steel blade of the food processor, or in a mortar and pestle.

3. Separate eggs by pouring the yolks from shell to shell over a cup. Reserve whites for another use, such as **To Make Chocolet Puffs**.

4. Stir the grated chocolate into the boiling cream so that it melts.

5. Beat egg yolks.

6. Reduce heat so that cream just simmers.

7. Beat a thin stream of hot cream into the egg yolks to warm them, then beat a thin stream of egg yolks into the hot cream.

8. Continue stirring until the cream mixture thickens, then remove from heat.

9. Beat in 1 cup of sugar (less if using Mexican chocolate), and cool a spoonful to taste. Because sugar is harder to taste in cold food, it will need to taste very sweet when warm. Two cups of sugar is a modern proportion, but in the Colonial era people were not so accustomed to sweets and probably used a cup or less.

10. Fill the larger bowl with crushed ice, and sink the metal mixing bowl into the ice. Pour in the cream mixture and whisk it until it cools and thickens.

11. For ice cream, discard the melted water and add the second bag of crushed ice, layered with $\frac{1}{4}$ part of rock salt. Sink the basin of cream back in the large bowl and stir until you can't stir anymore. Chill in freezer until ready to serve. (In Colonial times, the bowls would be covered with toweling and stored in a cool place.)

Serve from the freezing bowl in scoops, with candied fruits and cookies.

To Pickle Salmon (1763–1769)

This recipe "To Pickle Salmon the Newcastle Way, according to a Receipt procured from England, as is said by the infamous Governour, Sir Francis Bernard" is from the manuscript cookbook of Anne Gibbons Gardiner (1712–1771), published privately in 1938, and in 1982 as *Mrs. Gardiner's Family Receipts from 1763*. The "infamous" Bernard was British governor of Massachusetts and Maine from 1760 to 1769 and was strongly disliked by the pro-Independence Americans for his efforts to enforce taxes and reduce smuggling, notably the Stamp Act of 1765. The Gardiners were loyalists, and the family left for England in 1776. Mrs. Gardiner's husband, a physician and importer of druggists' supplies, owned land in

Maine. Her son-in-law was the customs collector at the time of the Stamp Act. His house was attacked by protesters in 1765, and he was injured in a fight over inspecting a ship of John Hancock's in 1768. Thus Mrs. Gardiner would have had the social position to trade recipes with Bernard, and both families would have had access to large seasonal hauls of salmon and possibly owned clocks. (Notice the direction to poach the salmon for twenty-three minutes!)

The word "infamous," was taken by the 1982 editor, Gail Weesner, as evidence that the manuscript was compiled by a descendant of Mrs. Gardiner. (The family returned to the United States in the 1790s.) However, Mrs. Gardiner may have used the word as a bitter joke, or she may not have approved of Governor Bernard's tactics while agreeing with his politics and trading recipes. In any case, the recipe was a good way to preserve a large catch of salmon back before refrigeration and still tastes good. I have reduced the quantities to one-fourth and adjusted for today's stronger vinegar. Wild salmon is leaner than today's farmed salmon, but this doesn't affect the recipe. You can use ground spices in about the same volume, loosely packed (Mrs. Gardiner doesn't specify), but then you should eat the salmon after a day or two.

To Pickle Salmon the Newcastle Way, according to a Receipt procured from England, as is said by the infamous Governour, Sir Francis Bernard

Scale your salmon, split it down the back, and take out the back bone; then, with a Cloth, wipe off all the Blood, and then cut it into Junks [chunks] of about four or five inches thick. Put on your Pot of Water, making it sharp with Salt, and when it boils put in your junks of Salmon, and let them boil for twenty three Minutes. Then take it off the Fire and let it cool.

Make a Pickle with two ounces of Allspice, two ounces of black Pepper and one Gallon of Vinegar, which boil, and into which, when cold, put an handfull of Salt. Place the Salmon in a Keg, and, when the salt is dissolved, pour the Pickle upon the Salmon. After it has stood one night in this manner, strain off the Oyl that may have arisen to the Top, to prevent its acquiring a strong taste, then head up the Keg.

NOTE: RECIPE TAKES TWO OR MORE DAYS.

Yield: Serves 4

2 boneless, skin-on salmon steaks

¾ cup kosher salt

½ ounce allspice berries (3 tablespoons)

½ ounce black peppercorns (4 teaspoons)

1 quart red wine vinegar

Equipment: 2-quart pottery or plastic bowl, stainless steel or enamel kettle skimmer

1. Mix ½ cup of salt with 2 quarts of water. (This amount should have a fresh egg floating with a spot the diameter of a 25-cent coin above the water.) Bring salt water to a boil.

2. Lower in salmon steaks with the skimmer so that they are covered. Reduce heat to simmer 12–13 minutes for a 1½ -inch steak. (The idea is to firm up the salmon but not overcook it so it starts to fall apart. Ten minutes per inch of the thickest part is a useful rule.)

3. Remove from heat and let cool.

4. Add 2 cups water to the vinegar and bring to a boil with the spices.

5. When vinegar and salmon are cool, lay out salmon steaks in a deep, nonreactive pottery or plastic bowl.

6. Pour on vinegar. You may need a smaller bowl to weight salmon steaks under the surface of the brine.

7. Leave out overnight.

8. The next day, skim off bubbles of oil from surface of brine.

9. Cover and refrigerate for at least another day.

Serve the next day for a mild flavor like pickled herring; as it ages it gets sharper. This dish would have been served among many carefully arranged at a large table, probably in the first course with larger dishes of fresh fish and boiled meats. The New England Cookery, compiled by Lucy Emerson and published in Montpelier, Vermont, in 1808, has a similar recipe, probably from an English source, with the direction: "[W]hen you want to use it, put it into a dish, with a little of the pickle, and garnish it with green fennel." Another early American cookbook suggests curly parsley.

MINORCAN PILAU (1768–1783)

Ethnic communities can preserve recipes over long periods of time. For the culinary historian, this is the equivalent of oral history. Although we have no cookbooks from the early settlers brought from Minorca to Northern Florida in the 1768, several of their dishes have survived in St. Augustine. They arrived after the British had taken over (1763) and most of the original Spanish settlers had left for Havana. The Minorcans originally came to New Smyrna to work for a Scottish speculator, Andrew Turnbull, but the colony failed in 1777, and they marched sixty miles to St. Augustine. The Spanish were returned to power in St. Augustine in the settlement of the American Revolution in 1783. The United States did not annex all of Florida until 1821.

Pilau in the American southeast is usually attributed to African slaves and French Huguenot planters in South Carolina. It may have been introduced in part by Minorcans, although this dish would not be called "pilau" but rather "arroz" on Minorca today. The recipe was submitted by Betty Gooch Gaster of West Palm Beach, Florida, to *The Panhellenic Cookbook, Meats*, published in 1968. Mrs. Gaster notes, "This is an authentic Minorcan recipe handed down four generations in my mother's family, who were among the early settlers in historic St. Augustine, Florida." The datil pepper is a very, very hot pepper native to St. Augustine. The appropriate substitute would be a habanero or scotch bonnet chile, but you can use milder peppers or a little hot sauce.

CAUTION: HOT CHILE PEPPER USED, HANDLE WITH GLOVES OR WASH HANDS REPEATEDLY BEFORE TOUCHING EYES OR SENSITIVE PARTS.

Yield: 10–12 servings

1 5–6 pound hen

4 stalks celery

2 onions

2 tablespoons oil

1 to 1½ cans tomatoes

1 tablespoon sugar

1 teaspoon dried or fresh thyme leaves

3 cups long grain rice

1 native datil fresh pepper (or other fresh chile pepper)

Equipment: 2 soup pots with covers, skillet, wooden spoon

1. Cut up hen into serving pieces. You can also cook the boney parts and giblets other than the liver.

2. Cover with water in a large pot, add a teaspoon of salt and some black pepper, and bring to a quick boil.

3. Cut celery into half-inch pieces. Halve, peel, and quarter 1 onion.

4. Add celery and onion to the soup pot, and reduce heat to simmer. Cook until tender but not falling apart or off the bone.

5. Meanwhile, halve, peel, and chop second onion.

6. In the skillet, brown the onion in oil.

7. Add tomatoes, thyme leaves, sugar, and some salt to the onions.

8. Chop tomatoes further with cooking spoon. Cook until bubbly.

9. Reduce heat on tomatoes and allow to fry until liquid is reduced and mixture is beginning to brown and stick.

10. Mash onion-tomato mixture to a pulp. Add 2 tablespoons of water, and cook until liquid is again absorbed.

11. Scrape mixture into second soup pot, add rice and 3 cups of the chicken broth. Season with more salt and pepper. Place on high heat and bring to a boil.

12. Stir rice well, then place chicken parts on top. Don't stir again. Cover and reduce heat to a simmer.

13. Halve datil pepper and scrape out seeds and pith with a spoon. Open pot and place halves of datil pepper (or other fresh chile) on rice.

14. After 20 minutes, open the top and lift some chicken with a fork to check the rice. Dish is done when the rice is ready. Remove peppers before serving and reserve them for hot pepper lovers.

Serve as a one-pot supper.

PLYMOUTH SUCCOTASH (1769)

This recipe was obtained from Mrs. Barnabas Churchill of Plymouth, Massachusetts, by Mrs. Evelyn Lincoln for the first edition of her *Boston Cooking School Cookbook* in 1883. Mrs. Churchill had been making this dish for about fifty years, and there is no reason to doubt that this recipe is much, much older. Plymouth tradition holds that this was the same succotash served as part of a nine-course dinner on Forefathers' Day, December 21, 1769, the anniversary of the landing of the Pilgrims at Plymouth, celebrated by the Old Colony Club in "commemoration of the landing of their worthy ancestors in this place." The event had some independentist overtones, and the group subsequently split over the issue. Despite this impeccable Yankee pedigree, the recipe is very close to traditional Wampanoag Indian succotash, and the Wampanoag town of Mashpee was not far. The 1769 dinner was one of the first recorded examples of self-consciously historical cooking in what had not yet become the United States, and also a very early case of Native American food being used as a symbol of national solidarity by Anglo-Americans, a practice we continue with succotash, turkey, squash, cranberries, and green beans on the Thanksgiving table.

Even in 1769 there was still some exchange of cooking techniques between Indian and Anglo-American families in Southern New England, and the English beef, chicken, turnip and white potato were pretty accurate substitutes for the dried meat, fresh game birds, and native tubers that would have flavored a late fall Native stew of corn and beans before contact with Europeans. Probably this dish had developed in both communities for many decades. We can't be sure whether an Indian cook or an English cook first made it with corned beef instead of dried venison, or first tried turnips instead of "Indian Potatoes." It is, however, quite certain, that no English cook knew how to make hominy or succotash—or any other dish with corn or haricot beans—before the 1600s. Native cooks had cast-iron pots from the early 1500s; they were coveted trade goods obtained for beaver skins and food from any of hundreds of European ships on exploratory and fishing expeditions before the Pilgrim settlement, and from the English settlers thereafter. Prior to the 1500s, stews could be made in clay or birch bark pots or hollowed logs by heating stones in a campfire and lifting them into the liquid.

The only obstacle to making this recipe today is that most homes don't have the large wash-boiler pots used before washing machines. (The 1769 dinner was held at an inn.) You can reduce the size of the recipe keeping the proportions. Use part of the fowl, however, rather than switch to a smaller chicken.

NOTE: RECIPE TAKES TWO DAYS.

Yield: Serves 25 hungry Pilgrims

1 quart "large white beans (not the pea beans)" (or 6 1-pound cans of beans)

6 quarts white hominy (12 16-ounce cans)

6–8 pounds corned beef

1 pound lean salt pork

4–6 pound fowl

1 "large white French turnip" (or 4 smaller purple-top turnips)

8–10 medium potatoes

Equipment: 2 oversized soup kettles, meat thermometer (optional)

1. To make hominy from scratch, see the recipe for Indian Bread or Bean Bread in Chapter 1. Soak beans overnight in cold water. If using canned beans, go on to Step 4.

2. In the morning, drain the beans and bring to a boil in fresh water to cover.

3. When beans have boiled a few minutes, pour off the water, and again bring them to a boil in water about an inch over the beans. Let simmer until

beans are soft enough to mash to a pulp.

4. About 4 hours before the stew is to be served, put corned beef and salt pork on to boil in a lot of water in another large kettle.

5. "Two hours before dinner time, put the beans, mashed to a pulp, and the hulled corn [hominy] into another kettle, with some of the fat from the meat in the bottom to keep them from sticking. Take out enough of the liquor from the meat to cover the corn and beans, and let them simmer where they will not burn."

6. "Clean and truss the chicken as for boiling, and put it with the meat about an hour and a quarter before dinner time."

7. Peel the turnip and cut into inch-thick slices, add it to the meat pot about an hour before serving.

8. Peel and sliced the potatoes, and add them to the meat pot about half an hour later.

9. Remove the chicken as soon as it is tender (or a meat thermometer in the thigh indicates 170 degrees.)

10. In Mrs. Churchill's time, the chicken was served from a platter, with another platter for the meats and vegetables. The beans and corn were served from a soup tureen, so succotash was both a thick soup, and a boiled dinner. The next day, leftovers were reheated in the meat broth. Colonials probably put everything together, at least by the second day, and ate it with a spoon. The Native American stewpot was a standing dish in which ingredients were replenished and more water added for days. The salt meats usually provided enough salt, and Native Americans in New

England did not use salt other than clam broth until the seventeenth century.

Serve with some of the other dishes of the 1769 dinner: "a large baked Indian Whortleberry Pudding, a dish of Clamms, a dish of Oysters & a dish of Codfish, a haunch of Venison . . . , a dish of seafowl, a ditto of frostfish & Eels, an Apple Pye, a course of Cranberry Tarts & Cheese made in the Old Colony."

ALBONDIGAS (1769)

San Diego was the first real Spanish settlement in California, with a fort and mission in 1769. This was burned by the Indians six years later but restored in 1776. These meatballs were described by Julia Flynn DeFrate for the 1950 *Favorite Recipes of the Navy and Marine Corps San Diego Area; including a Collection of Mexican and Old San Diego Dishes Contributed by Descendants of Early Settlers of San Diego County.* Mrs. DeFrate was 1898 graduate of San Diego High School. However, the recipe is very old and would have been used in the early missions, barracks, and ranchos. Albondigas recipes remained popular throughout the Spanish southwest and were picked up by Anglo-American soldiers and settlers after the 1845 Mexican War.

First make a kettle (3 qts.) of rich beef soup. The old-fashioned soup-bone type. When done, remove bone and all solids. Season this clear soup with salt, peppercorns and chopped parsley. Grind on the metate [Aztecan grinding stone with stone roller] 1½ pounds of good fresh beef, venison, or jack rabbit meat until reduced to a pasty consistency and all the sinewy, fibrous matter is separated so that it can be removed from the mass.

Yield: Serves 6

2 pounds beef shin with marrow bone

12 peppercorns

1 bunch parsley

1 small Spanish onion

1 clove garlic

1½ pounds beef round

1 cup yellow cornmeal

1 large red bell pepper

½ teaspoon oregano

3 leaves fresh or dried sage

2 teaspoons ground coriander seed

1 bunch chives

Equipment: Large soup pot, colander, 2 mixing bowls, food processor, food mill, teakettle

1. Bring the beef shin to a boil with 4 quarts of water in a large pot. Add peppercorns and a teaspoon of salt. Reduce heat and simmer with lid ajar for 2 hours.

2. Halve and peel onion. Peel garlic. Cut beef round into 1-inch cubes.

3. Core bell pepper and cut into small pieces.

4. Process bell pepper in food processor until finely minced.

5. Put onion, garlic, and beef in food processor and process until it is a fine paste. (Early Spanish missionaries and soldiers had captive Indians do this on a lava-rock mortar with a lava-rock pestle.)

6. Put meat paste through food mill or force through colander to get rid of fibrous material.

7. Bring a teakettle of water to a boil.

8. Put cornmeal in a small mixing bowl. "Mix with scalding water until wet but not sloppy." Stir well and set aside to cool.

9. Chop chives.

10. Add chives, oregano, sage, and cornmeal to meat paste. Blend well. You can refrigerate mixture until the soup is ready.

11. Chop parsley.

12. Strain soup through colander. You may skim off fat with a soup spoon. (Early Spanish settlers would have left the fat in the soup and probably cut off any soup meat and added it back to the soup.)

13. Add parsley to soup.

14. Wet your hands and mold meat mixture "into balls the size of pigeon eggs." That would be a little smaller than a golf ball. Drop them one at a time into the simmering soup.

15. Cook slowly until all the meatballs are well cooked.

Serve as a main-dish soup.

OLY COOKS (1770S)

These fruitcake doughnuts were a treat that hung on well into the twentieth century among some Dutch descendants. The older recipes make one hundred or more, because these treats were shared with invited guests over Christmas—a holiday that was not widely celebrated in New England or among the Quakers of Pennsylvania. This recipe is from the manuscript notebook of Maria Van Rensselaer (1749–1830), part of a grand Albany family, published with others in *On the Score of Hospitality*, compiled and edited by Jane Carpenter Kellar, Ellen Miller, and Paul Stambach for publication by Historic Cherry Hill, the house Mrs. Van Rensselaer moved into in 1785. I believe that the recipe omits typical quantities of raisins, apples, and spice as being familiar and obvious parts of the dish, so I have restored them according to recipes in *The Sen-*

sible Cook, a seventeenth-century Dutch cookbook translated and edited with additions from later Dutch-American recipes by Peter A. Rose. (Canola oil is actually specified in the Dutch book, although colonists probably switched to lard.) If you think that *olie koeks* (another early spelling) had become simpler as the old families became more Anglicized, you can omit the stuffings.

To make Oly Cooks 4 lb flour, 1 lb butter, 1 lb sugar, 12 eggs, some yeast & as much milk as you like

CAUTION: HOT OIL USED.
NOTE: RECIPE REQUIRES TWO DAYS.

Yield: About 120 fried balls.

4 quarts sifted flour

1 quart sifted whole wheat flour

1 cup raw wheat germ

1 pound salted butter

1 pound sugar, plus 2 cups to coat finished koeks

2 pounds raisins (optional)

6 large tart apples (optional)

1½ teaspoons mixed spice—cinnamon, ginger, and cloves (optional)

5–6 cups whole milk or half-and-half

12 small eggs, or 8 large eggs

1 tablespoon dry yeast

½ gallon canola oil

Equipment: Pastry blender, 2 large mixing bowls, heavy soup pot or large kettle for frying, deep-fry thermometer, wire skimmer or slotted spoon, paper towels or clean newspapers, wire racks

1. An hour before beginning, remove butter from refrigerator to soften.

2. Dissolve yeast in ½ cup warm water with a few pinches of the sugar. Wait until a bubbly foam forms on top.

3. Combine flour, whole wheat flour, and wheat germ.

4. Crack eggs and whisk several minutes until light and creamy. Blend in 4 cups of the milk or half-and-half.

5. Cream butter and sugar together.

6. Add yeast to butter-sugar mixture.

7. Add flour mixture and eggs alternately to make a stiff batter or very soft dough. If using spices, sprinkle on as you do this. You may not need all the flour, or you may need more of the milk.

8. When you have all the dough mixed, cover with kitchen towels and let rise until light and airy and double in bulk. This may take 4–6 hours or overnight.

9. If you let it rise overnight, and it gets too spongy and floppy, stir it down to get rid of the overlarge bubbles, and let rise again. If using apples and raisins, plump raisins in a little warm water or cider for 10 minutes. Peel apples and cut into small dice. Drain raisins.

10. When dough is ready, heat 2 inches of the oil to 350 degrees in the heavy kettle. Scoop up the dough with a tablespoon, round into egg-size balls, and slide into the hot oil with a second spoon. If stuffing the cooks, take somewhat larger balls, perhaps 2 inches in diameter, and poke a hole in the dough with your thumb. Put a few raisins and a little apple in the whole, and seal it off.

11. Turn balls in the oil to brown on all sides. Remove promptly when brown and let drain on wire racks over clean newspaper or paper towels.

12. As the oil runs down, you will have to add more oil and wait for the temperature to come back up to 350 degrees.

13. When cooks are well dried, roll in sugar.

Serve with other sweets at Christmas or New Year's, or store in airtight containers for a few days. Peter A. Rose reports that they can be frozen, but I don't think New York colonists did that. I think they sent extra oly koeks to each other in baskets.

DOED KOEKS (1780S)

English and Dutch colonists had a custom of making large molded cookies for funerals. The cookies were baked quite hard so they could be kept for years as a memento of the dead person and the occasion. (The old New England custom was to hand out gloves, rings, or commemorative poems or booklets.) This is the only recipe I have found specifically for a funeral cake, and its history is uncertain. It is described as a 1680 Douw family recipe in a group of recipes printed in the 1927 and 1933 editions of the *Congressional Club Cook Book*, as submitted by Mrs. Louis C. Crampton, whose husband was a U.S. representative from Michigan. Mrs. Crampton attributed the recipes to a privately published collection by Mrs. Morris P. Ferris of Westfield, New York. I think that Mrs. Ferris probably obtained the recipe from an Albany manuscript described by food historian Peter A. Rose as written by Anne Douw Stevenson (1774–1821) with some contributions from her mother, Magdalena Douw (1750–1817). I am therefore more comfortable with the 1780s date. It would have been an old-fashioned recipe by then, but the mention of pearl ash (potassium carbonate baking powder derived from wood ashes) suggests that it had been "improved" toward the end of the eighteenth century, not the seventeenth. This recipe makes about thirty large cookies, as one might expect for this prominent family.

Yield: About 30 large cookies

2 pounds flour (6 cups flour, 1½ cups whole wheat flour, and ½ cup wheat germ)

1 pound sugar (2 cups)

½ pound salted butter, plus more to grease baking sheets

1½ "teacupfuls" milk (1½ cups whole milk or half-and-half)

½ teaspoon pearl ash (substitute baking soda)

1 ounce caraway seeds (about 4 tablespoons)

Equipment: Pastry blender, 2 baking sheets, large round cookie mold (optional), rolling pin and bread board

1. An hour before beginning, remove butter from refrigerator to soften.

2. Cream together butter and sugar with a pastry blender or a large fork.

3. Dissolve baking soda in milk.

4. Combine flour ingredients to make the equivalent of eighteenth-century fine flour. Stir in the caraway seeds.

5. Stir in the milk and flour alternately to make a stiff dough. Divide into half and refrigerate.

6. Grease or flour baking sheets. Preheat oven to 375 degrees.

7. Flour the rolling pin and board.

8. Roll half the dough out ⅜ to ½ inch thick.

9. If you have a large cookie mold that isn't too cheerful, rinse it in cold water, and press in dough to make a distinct form. (It won't do to make funeral cakes for Santa Claus!) If the dough sticks you need to work in more flour. You can also cut out the cookies around the outline of a 4-inch round

or small saucer. You could then inscribe a funeral design, such as the 3 white plumes that decorated horses in a funeral procession, and/or the initials of the dead person.

10. Arrange completed cookies on the baking sheets.

11. Put cookies in oven and immediately reduce temperature to 325 degrees. Bake 12–15 minutes.

Serve to each person at the funeral. Don't eat them. Keep them.

RASPBERRY VINEGAR (1782)

This was a way to preserve the sudden summer harvest of raspberries. The syrupy vinegar was pretty stable and could be kept in a cool cellar for a year, if it didn't mold. A spoonful or two in a glass of water was a refreshing drink, and suitable for temperance families or temperate visitors. The straight vinegar was also recommended as cough medicine! The source is a Savannah, Georgia, manuscript begun in 1782 by Dorothea Schmidt, born in Stuttgart, Germany. It was translated for the 1994 edition of *The Backcountry Housewife; A Study of Eighteenth-Century Foods*, by Kay Moss and Kathryn Hoffman, published by the Schiele Museum in Gastonia, North Carolina.

Take a quart of raspberry and a pint of wine vinegar, the raspberries have to [illegible] before. Then add the vinegar and leave it for 4–5 days. Then press them as you do when you make juice. For half a pint of juice, add a quarter of sugar. Then put it into a pot and let it boil until it becomes thick. You have to cook it for about an hour. (2 quarts of raspberries and 1 quart of vinegar yield 3.5 pints of juice.)

Yield: Serves 12–18

2 pints fresh raspberries

2 cups wine vinegar

1¾ cups sugar

Equipment: Recycled mayonnaise jar or 1-quart glass canning jar, jelly bag or very fine strainer

1. Fill jar with raspberries, pour on vinegar. You can add a few tablespoons of water.

2. Cover jar and shake well. Let raspberries steep 4–5 days, shaking once in a while.

3. Strain berries through the jelly bag or fine strainer, pressing to get all the juice. (The leftover pulp, mixed an equal amount of sugar, made a rough "raspberry cheese" that could be mixed into cakes and cookies.)

4. Boil the juice with the sugar very slowly for one hour, stirring so that it doesn't stick and burn.

5. Bottle tightly.

Serve a few spoonfuls in a glass, with cold water stirred in.

Ejotes (1790s)

As the Colonial era was ending in the eastern states, Spanish colonists were dividing California into vast ranches—a process accelerated by the Mexican Revolution of 1821, which secularized the land holdings of the large missions. This dish shows the combination of Spanish, Mexican, and Native American elements that were already defining a California style of cooking and eating. This recipe is from the 1938 *Early California Hospitality; the Cookery Customs of Spanish California,* by Ana Begué de Packman.

Yield: Serves 10 as a side dish

2 pounds green beans

3 tablespoons olive oil

2 ripe tomatoes

1 onion

2 green chile peppers

1 small clove garlic

1 teaspoon vinegar

Equipment: Frying pan or saucepan with tight lid, teakettle

1. Wash beans, snap off the ends and pull out any strings.

2. Halve, peel, and slice the onion into half-rounds about as wide as the beans.

3. Peel and mince garlic.

4. Cut the stem-end core out of the tomatoes and chop into small pieces.

5. Cut off the tops of the chiles and slit down one side. Use a teaspoon to scrape out seeds and pith.

6. Chop chiles into fine pieces, and wash your hands several times before touching eyes or sensitive parts.

7. Heat up olive oil in the pan, add beans, and stir to coat with oil.

8. Add remaining ingredients, a teaspoon of salt, and ¼ teaspoon of pepper.

9. Cover pan tightly and let simmer on reduced heat for 20 minutes.

10. Heat up some water in a teakettle in case you need to add a little boiling water to the beans.

11. Lift the top of the pan a few times and stir things around, and check if you need more water.

Serve at an 8 P.M. supper including tortillas and beans and roast beef or stew. The ranchers and cowboys ate an even bigger meal at noon, followed by a siesta.

4

THE AMERICAN
REVOLUTION (1776–1784)

There are few written recipes from the years of the American Revolution and surprisingly few attached to the period in later memoirs. As food historian Clarissa Dillon has written, "Too little is known about large-scale cookery in the eighteenth century. Not one book, for instance, has been found which deals with cooking for the Army or Navy because, perhaps, food for both services was funded out of allowances made to the regimental or ship's commanders, whose paymasters or pursers were keen to show a 'profit' out of those allowances, and did not wish to publicize the sort of economies in catering which made such profits possible." This section must therefore be composed primarily of reconstructions and provides an opportunity to look at some of the strategies food historians use to reconstruct dishes of particular historical periods.

Our first reconstruction was actually made during the Revolution, as Benjamin Franklin (a non-cook) attempted to explain to his French hosts how Americans made cornbread. The next two recipes were recorded shortly after the Revolution, by men intent on publicizing exactly the economies in catering to the military that could be used. The first of these is in fact the oldest precisely

written recipe for hasty pudding or cornmeal mush, a staple of Native American food for thousands of years, and perhaps the most frequent dish on Colonial and American tables. It was reconstructed in London in 1794 by a former American Tory, Benjamin Thompson (later Count Rumford), in a scientific paper promoting a number of American corn recipes for volume feeding of the poor and the military in Europe. The second of these was collected by a Philadelphia physician named J.B. Bordley from a military officer for a 1799 book, and two hundred years later matched by a food historian to actual foodstuffs appropriated by the British army around Brandywine in 1777.

Two more recipes were developed in the 1990s by Bernadette Noe, a site interpreter at Knox's Headquarters in Vail's Gate, New York, using soldier's memoirs, Continental army documents, and experience with printed eighteenth-century recipes.

Of these reconstructions, we can have confidence only that the **Hasty Pudding** and cornbread were actually eaten by participants in the American Revolution. They would have recognized the **Hard Bread** and **Peas Porridge**, but we cannot be sure that the recipes we are using will produce exactly the dishes of that time. With the **Pottages** by Col. Paynter, the 1799 recipe we make would not have been thought unusual fifteen to twenty-five years earlier, and the ingredients were in the possession of British army quartermasters at the end of 1777, but we have as yet no documentation that this dish was actually cooked and consumed at that time.

To Make Bread with Maize Flour Mixed with Wheat Flour (1785)

Benjamin Franklin was not a cook and seldom included recipes in his early almanacs, but he did experiment with varieties of corn and collected information about Indian cooking techniques. In 1785 he wrote a pamphlet about the advantages of corn with some recipes for his French hosts. (Franklin spent almost the entire Revolutionary period, October 1776 to 1785, as minister to France.) This recipe for what would later be called "mush bread" is typical of many American everyday recipes that had already been in use for more than a hundred years and didn't have to be written down because no one forgot them from weekly baking to weekly baking. (John Josselyn described a similar mush bread in Maine in 1672.) Revolutionary-era farm wives might have made this bread by using their usual recipe for **Hasty Pudding** (see below) and pouring some or all of that into a large flour bin then adding sourdough yeast. They could mix with their hands until the dough felt right and then take it out of the flour bin and make as many free-form loaves in whatever size they wanted—to be baked on the floor of a brick oven. So proportions were not too important and would not have been too important to French cooks of the era, either. I have taken some rough proportions from an 1830 Long Island manuscript cornbread recipe posted on the website of food historian Alice Ross ⟨www.aross.binome.com/recipes.htm⟩.

Maize Flour takes longer to bake well than Wheat Flour; so that if mixed together cold, then fermented and cooked, the Wheat part will be well baked whilst the Maize Part will remain uncooked.

To remedy this inconvenience, We boil one Pot of Water with a little Salt added and whilst the Water boils with one Hand we throw into it a little Maize Flour and with the other Hand stir it into the boiling Water that must be kept on the Fire, and this Operations shall be repeated with a little Flour each time, until the Mush is so thick it can hardly be stirred with the Stick. Then, after leaving it a little longer on the Fire, until the last Handful has done boiling, it is taken off, then the Mush is poured into the Kneading Trough where it must be thoroughly mixed and kneaded with a Quantity of Wheat Flour sufficient to make a Dough thick enough to make Bread, and some Yeast, or Leaven, to make it rise; and after the necessary Time it is shaped into Loaves, and then put into the Oven.

Yield: Serves 10–12

3 cups yellow cornmeal (stone ground preferred)

1½ cups all purpose flour (or 1⅓ cups flour, ¼ cup whole wheat flour, and a heaping tablespoon wheat germ), plus more for kneading.

2 teaspoons dry yeast

Equipment: Oven mitt, deep pot, wooden spoon or pudding stick (a thinner-bowled spoon), large bowl or wooden "kneading trough," wooden cutting board, kitchen towel, 2 loaf pans or round cake pans, wooden toothpick or wire cake tester

1. Bring 4 cups water to a boil in a large pot.

2. Add 1 teaspoon salt to the boiling water.

3. Stirring with one hand, add the cornmeal a little bit at a time from the other hand.

4. When all the cornmeal is added, continue cooking and stirring the mush for another 15 minutes. Put an oven mitt on your stirring hand to avoid burns from sputtering mush.

5. Turn cooked mush into a large mixing bowl and let it cool somewhat, stirring occasionally. It will continue to thicken.

6. Dissolve yeast in a half cup of water. You can add a little sugar and wait until it bubbles up to "proof the yeast." You can also use a half cup or more of the **Potato Yeast** from Chapter 6.

7. If you are using the optional flour mixture, measure it out and sift well. As the mush cools, begin working in the flour. Depending on the dryness of the original cornmeal, the dough will take more or less flour.

8. When the dough is lukewarm, add the yeast and remaining flour. Work with your hands (remove rings) or a wooden spoon until the dough will stick together in one ball. You may need a little more water or liquid yeast to get all the flour into the ball.

9. Flour a wooden board. Turn the dough out onto the board.

10. Flour your hands and knead (See Appendix I in *The American Ethnic Cookbook for Students*), flouring the dough until the dough is well mixed and less sticky. It will be heavier and stickier than white bread dough, but should hold together well.

11. Return dough to the bowl and cover with a kitchen towel. Let rise in a warm place for an hour or more, or until visibly larger and easily dented with the finger poke. (Cornbread will not "double in bulk.")

12. When dough has risen, "punch down" to eliminate large bubbles and knead briefly.

13. Butter loaf pans or round cake pans. (Revolutionary-era farmers might have baked this bread in a free-form round loaf in brick ovens, or in very large loaf pans.)

14. Divide dough in half, and press each half into a bread pan.

15. Cover bread pans with a kitchen towel and let rise a second time, 45 minutes or more.

16. Bake in a 425-degree oven for 15 minutes. Reduce heat to 350 degrees and bake 10 minutes longer, then begin testing with a toothpick or wire cake tester. You can turn loaves out of the pans and finish cooking them on the wire racks of the oven. Breads are done when a tester in the highest part of the cake comes out clean, or when the loaves are turned out of the pans and sound hollow when tapped.

17. Remove breads from oven and cool on wire racks.

Serve hot with salted butter.

HASTY PUDDING (1795)

Hasty pudding was the typical breakfast and supper dish for most of two hundred years (1640–1840) in New England and popular among poor farmers in much of the rest of the American colonies and United States. Revolutionary soldiers made hasty pudding when they could get cornmeal and were offered some by sympathetic farmers. John Greenwood, a young fifer who finished his enlistment at the end of December 1776, was on his way home to Boston from General Washington's army when he spotted a farmhouse in the woods. "In I went and the people were very glad to see me, for they had a son in the army and were delighted with my description of the battle of Trenton, where we had but two or three men killed in the whole affray, and took upward of 900 prisoners. I was given a good supper of mush and milk, and a blanket to lie down by the fireside." (Source: *The Wartime Services of John Greenwood, 1775–1783*.)

We associate the name pudding with dessert, but in Colonial and Early American times, puddings were eaten before the meat (to fill up) and were not necessarily sweet. Hasty pudding was an unsweetened cornmeal mush that was taken directly from Native American dishes like **Nassaŭmp**. Mush is probably the oldest form of cooked grains and would have been equally familiar to Indians, African slaves, and colonists. The colonists knew old country forms like Scottish oatmeal porridge, English frumenty, or "hasty pudding" (an English dish of oat or rye flour).

What made the pudding hasty was that it was hastier than puddings boiled in a bag for eight to ten hours. British colonists often found that corn worked well in oat recipes. In coastal Africa, corn was introduced early by Spanish and Portuguese slave traders and replaced sorghums and millets in very similar mushes (as it later did in European mushes like polenta and mamaliga). Many African slaves arrived in the Americans already familiar with cornmeal mush. No one needed to write down the recipe for a food made nearly every day, and descriptions like "thick as hasty pudding" in the song "Yankee Doodle" were obvious to everyone.

However, we are fortunate to have this lengthy and precise recipe written down in 1795 by the scientist Benjamin Thompson (later Count Rumford, 1753–1814). Thompson was an American-born Tory who left his New Hampshire home and worked in the British foreign office during the war. His interest in corn cookery was to find cheaper ways to feed armies and the urban poor in Europe, but he wrote down quite a lot about how corn dishes were eaten in New England. He also invented several stoves. Thompson notes that hasty pudding could also be made of a mixture of rye and corn meal, rye meal alone, or a mixture of rye and wheat. One thing we learn from cooking with Thompson's recipe is how different cornmeal was in 1795. Cornmeal was much heavier and moister. Today's drier cornmeal absorbs almost twice as much water to make mush as was recorded in Thompson's careful experiment! In the spirit of this early American scientist, measure carefully and see how much meal you have left when your mush will hold up a spoon. Meal then was all stone ground, with the germ and bran left in, and it was much moister and more prone to lumps. When fresh it had a lot more flavor, but also could turn rancid in storage.

Yield: Serves 6 as a side dish; Thompson suggested ⅔ of this recipe as one 1795 dinner

"58 grains or 1/120 pound" salt (⅜ teaspoon)

"Half a pound of Indian meal" (2½ cups yellow cornmeal, but you may use as little as 1¼ cups)

1½ tablespoons salted butter

2 tablespoons molasses

¼ teaspoon vinegar, or a little less

Equipment: Saucepan, wooden spoon with a long handle to avoid droplets of boiling mush (or a pudding stick—a flatter, thinner spoon)

1. Measure a quart of water into a saucepan. Add salt, and heat to boiling.

2. As the water heats, add handfuls of the cornmeal little by little, "sifting it

slowly through the fingers of the left hand, and stirring the water about very briskly at the same time with the wooden spoon with the right hand, to mix the meal with the water in such a manner as to prevent lumps being formed."

3. Simmer 1 half hour, adding as much of the cornmeal as you need in the same way and stirring frequently. "The wooden spoon used for stirring it being placed upright in the middle of the kettle, if it falls down more meal must be added; but, if the pudding is sufficiently thick and adhesive to support it in the vertical position, it is declared to be *proof*, and no more meal is added."

4. "If the boiling . . . be prolonged to three quarters of an hour or an hour, the pudding will be considerably improved by this prolongation."

Serve at the beginning of the meal, spread out upon a wooden plate. Make an "indentation" with your spoon, and put in a pat of butter, then a "spoonful of brown sugar, or more commonly of molasses," and a dash of vinegar. Each spoonful of pudding is dipped in this sauce. Thompson notes that many Americans dipped their hasty pudding in a bowl of milk, and that leftover pudding could be sliced and toasted, eaten cold in hot milk, or fried in a chopped hash with leftover cabbage and boiled beef. He does not mention fried slices of mush, which were already popular in the southern states.

HARD BREAD (1782–1783)

This and the following recipe are reconstructions by Bernadette Noe, then a site interpreter at Knox's Headquarters in Vail's Gate, New York, published in the 1995 *Foods of the Hudson* by Peter G. Rose. No actual recipes survive from any encamp-

ments of the Continental Army, but Noe could use records of rations, soldiers' letters, and memoirs to reconstruct the unleavened bread they were able to bake in camp ovens at their final winter camp, the New Windsor Cantonment. In this case, a pound of flour or bread was the official ration of the Continental Army, and by 1782–1783 the soldiers would have usually been getting it. Note the lack of salt, a problem for Continental soldiers throughout the Revolution. The added bran would approximate the very rough unbolted flour issued to soldiers, and you could add a little wheat germ as well. The Valley Forge encampment five years earlier had been selected because it had a gristmill and some supplies of flour, but shortages soon forced the soldiers to cook similar flat breads on campfire griddles or in the ashes. These were remembered as "fire cakes," cynical humor since "cakes" were what we would now call cookies. If kept dry, such hard breads could be kept for long periods of time without spoiling.

Yield: A 1-pound loaf (You will need 3 of these for the **Peas Porridge** recipe following.)

2 cups whole wheat flour, plus some to flour a board
½ cup wheat bran

Equipment: Mixing bowl, baking sheet, wood board for kneading

1. Preheat the oven to 375 degrees.
2. In a bowl, stir together the bran and flour.
3. Make a well in the middle, and pour in one cup of warm water.
4. Mix thoroughly.
5. Flour the board. Turn out the dough, and knead "into a uniform loaf." (For how to knead, see Appendix I of *The*

American Ethnic Cookbook for Students.) You should have a very stiff dough.

6. Shape into a round, flat bread.

7. Take any leftover flour from the board and put on the baking sheet. Put on the bread. (The flour will keep it from sticking.)

8. Bake for 4½ hours.

Serving such hard breads was a problem. They were most often soaked in hot water or coffee or some kind of soup, sometimes enriched with bacon fat or meat, or made into a kind of stew as in the following recipe.

PEAS PORRIDGE (1782–1783)

This is Bernadette Noe's reconstruction of another universal army dish of the Revolutionary period and indeed hundreds of years before and since. Dried peas were a staple for British and American navy ships, and peas were planted out by the Pilgrims the first year in Plymouth. The amount given here was the daily ration for six Continental soldiers, so it is reasonable to imagine six recruits sharing a day's peas and half a day's hard bread and salt meat to make a palatable stew. Without the peas, the dish might have been called "lobscouse." Again, the soldiers had little salt and would have had to obtain vinegar from nearby farmers.

Yield: Serves 6 hungry soldiers

  3 loaves hard bread (see above)

  3 pounds corned beef or lean salt pork

  3 cups dried split peas

  3 tablespoons vinegar

Equipment: Iron kettle or large pot

1. Cut the meat into ½-inch cubes and brown them in the bottom of the pot.

2. Stir in peas.

3. Stack the whole breads on top if the pot is big enough. If not, break them in halves or quarters to fit. Remember that the six of you will want to divide everything evenly at the end.

4. Fill the pot with water and bring to a boil. Boil briskly until the water reduces down to the bottom of the bread, but still covers the meat and peas.

5. Refill the pot with water and simmer until the peas are almost dissolved into the broth, and the meat and bread chunks are tender.

Serve divided carefully into six portions, hot or cold, sometimes even undercooked.

POTAGES, BY COL. PAYNTER (1799)

This early soup for volume feeding was recorded by J.B. Bordley in a book called *Essays and Notes on Husbandry and Rural Affairs.* It was reprinted by Clarissa Dillon in her 1999 *So Serve It Up; Eighteenth-Century English Foodways in Eastern Pennsylvania.* Ms. Dillon began with a list of supplies commandeered by British units in the countryside around Philadelphia in September 1777 and later claimed as damages by the farmers. She then suggests the Bordley recipe, among others, as what the British might have done with the foods they had. That Bordley attributes the recipe to Colonel Paynter and reports that the recipe was tried out on twenty soldiers, adds to the sense that this recipe would have fit in with military thinking twenty years later when Bordley's book was published. Unfortunately, the likeliest author—Lt. Col. Lemuel Paynter of the Pennsylvania militia, later a state legislator and U.S. representative—did not serve during the Revolution, although he did serve in the War of 1812.

Three pounds of the sticking piece of beef [lower neck], or a part of the shin, or any coarse piece. Boil it in 11 quarts of water, two hours. Then add a pound of Scotch barley, and boil it four hours more in which time add potatoes six pounds, onions half a pound, and some parsley, thyme or savory, pepper and salt; with other vegetables, and half a pound of bacon may be added, the bacon cut into small bits. It gives three gallons of pottage. Boil it over a slow fire to be thick. It satisfied 20 soldiers, without bread; the nature of the food not requiring any. Col. Paynter adds that the men in the barracks like it very much; and the officers introduced it into their mess, and found it excellent. Its cost would be 30 cents; or 1½ cents a man.

Yield: Served 20 soldiers in the 1790s

3-pound piece of beef shin

16 ounces pearl barley

6 pounds potatoes

2 medium onions

1 bunch parsley

1 teaspoon dried thyme

½ pound lean bacon (optional)

Equipment: Oversize soup pot or 2 standard spaghetti pots

1. Put beef and 11 quarts of water into pot or pots. Bring to a boil.

2. Reduce heat to a simmer. Cook 2 hours.

3. Add barley and again bring to a simmer.

4. After 2 more hours, peel potatoes, slice and add to pot.

5. Halve, peel, and slice onions into half rounds and add to pot.

6. Chop parsley and add to pot.

7. Season with thyme, salt, and pepper to taste. (Potatoes will absorb some salt, so check again before serving.)

8. If using bacon, cut into inch squares (or smaller cubes if using slab bacon). Add to pot.

Serve in tin mess cups. Early American soldiers liked fat on top of the soup, so do not skim.

5

PATRIOTIC CAKES
(1795–1860)

This chapter collects a number of recipes for cakes and other baked goods that were named or renamed to express patriotism in the new nation. Prior to the Civil War, cakes named after politicians did not express partisan politics but a patriotic respect for national leaders. In my research for this book I found cakes named after eight elected officials in thirteen published cookbooks. Almost one third of all these recipes were named for George Washington. Many are similar to pound cake or queen's cake and perhaps are part of a renaming process that started right after the Revolution in which roads called "King's Highway" were often renamed "Washington Street." Two cakes were named for James Madison, or possibly for his widow Dolly Madison, who was a popular Washington hostess until her death in 1849. President Madison was quite highly regarded after the War of 1812. The most successful general of the War of 1812, Andrew Jackson, provided the name for **Jackson Jumbles. Harrison Cake**, described in four of the cookbooks, commemorated the first presidential candidate to campaign for the office. Harrison was elected in 1840, but he died a month after his inauguration.

Zachary Taylor, the only other president commemorated in a cake before the Civil War, also died early in his term. I believe that these cakes patriotically commemorate fallen leaders and were not understood as cheering on their Whig Party or particular positions. Two other Whig presidential candidates, Henry Clay and Daniel Webster, had cakes named after them around the time of their deaths in 1852. When the cakes appeared both men had been national leaders for a long time and had recently set aside the political positions of their respective regions in attempts to preserve the union with the Compromise of 1850.

Local and statewide election campaigns before the Civil War could be bitter, and while they often involved food and drink, the food was more in the nature of barbecues, chowders, Brunswick stews, and other large, hearty dishes served to unruly groups of male voters. Two cookie recipes for the early 1840s, **Whig Cakes** and **Democratic Tea Cakes**, commemorate the first mass political parties and possibly the Harrison-Van Buren campaign of 1840, but the recipes were not intended to favor either party and more likely expressed a patriotic regard for free elections. I have placed them in Chapter 16 with other recipes that reference the growing diversity of ideas in the United States in the 1830s and 1840s.

The other elected official for whom published cake recipes were named was Governor Caleb Strong, a Massachusetts federalist who is now remembered mainly as an opponent of the War of 1812. The recipes for "Governor Strong's Cake" or "Granny Strong's Cake" that appeared in the 1850s are large, old-fashioned cakes similar to **Election Cake**. So the reference to Caleb Strong may simply be a patriotic expression of nostalgia for Early American times. It is also possible that by the 1850s patriotic cakes had a political bias for keeping the country together and avoiding war, as Caleb Strong had tried to keep Massachusetts out of the nearly disastrous War of 1812. If so, that was a transition to the openly political cakes published from 1865 to 1900 and sampled in Chapter 26.

The first American cookbook, *American Cookery* by "Amelia Simmons, an American Orphan" emphasized the newness of the just orphaned ex-colonies with recipes for "Election Cake," "Independence Cake," and **"Federal Pan Cake."** Election cakes were a local colonial custom that continued into the nineteenth century. The other two were invented or renamed by Simmons and were followed in other books by more Federal Cakes, Ratification Cake, Union Pudding with the word "Union" spelled out in frosting, Franklin Cake, Columbian Pudding, and a variety of Washington cakes. Washington was the one-man symbol of the new nation and also the name of its capital. Recipes for Queen's Cake (similar to pound cake) were often renamed "Washington Cake." By the 1840s, pound cakes were going out of style as wedding cakes but had a solid, nostalgic quality that kept them associated with George Washington. Patriotism was increasingly expressed with smaller cakes for family gatherings, often for July 4

or Washington's Birthday, which remained the main national secular holidays until Thanksgiving was so proclaimed during the Civil War.

As a technical note, Early American cakes are among the most difficult historical recipes to reproduce today because so many ingredients have changed. Don't be surprised that these are dense coffee cakes with strong spice flavors. Although we think of Early American cooking as bland, many people still liked the heavy spice flavors of the Middle Ages, and reformers like Sylvester Graham were only beginning to argue that spices were overstimulating—a view that became more popular in the 1880s and 1890s. It is also possible that spices may not have been so fresh as the ones we buy, and you may want to reduce some quantities, but try them as written first. Flour was lower in protein and even the whitest cake flour had some bran and germ in it. Flour changed somewhat in the 1820s, when the Erie Canal brought higher-protein Midwestern flour to market, but did not really take its modern form until the development of roller mills in the 1880s made possible the production of cheap white flour. Early American flour and cornmeal were stone ground and stored under moister conditions than today's flour; they were therefore heavier and required less liquid (or more flour for the same liquid) in recipes. Butter was often very highly salted, so recipes had no salt, and some suggested washing the salt out of the butter before cooking. Milk was richer than today's homogenized milk, unpasteurized, and naturally often went sour within a day. The cream rose to the top and was used in cooking and baking where the recipe specified "rich milk," "top milk," and sometimes just "milk." Buttermilk was a little richer and less sour than the "cultured buttermilk" we can buy now. Yeast was cultured in various ways, and often worked more slowly. Eggs were much smaller and more variable in size. Baking powders used different chemicals. In addition, teaspoons were two-third their present size; "spoonfuls" had no standard size and were usually heaped up. Cups and pans were not of standard sizes. Baking pans were made of pottery or cast iron, with sheet-metal pans coming into wide use later in the nineteenth century. Last, ovens had no thermostats and cooked differently than ovens do now. Wood-fired brick ovens stored a great deal of heat; radiated it from top, bottom, and all sides; and the temperature gradually fell over a matter of hours. Today's gas ovens heat from the bottom only and maintain constant temperatures. Today's electric ovens heat from top and bottom. Convection ovens are unlike any earlier design. Some historic cooks use pizza stones or tiles to reproduce some of the characteristics of brick ovens.

In the recipes below I have generally followed the recommendations of food historian Karen Hess about modifying flour, estimated the eggs along lines suggested by Sandra L. Oliver in *Food History News*, and followed the recommendations of early cookbook writers on substitutions for sour milk. The right proportions of flour and liquid are still highly variable, so you will have to ask experienced cooks to make sure that you have something like cake batter, soft dough, stiff dough, or whatever. You may need to add more flour or more liquid.

Don't worry too much, though. Early American cooks were people like ourselves, often young and inexperienced, and took several tries to get a recipe right, especially with a cake they might only make once or twice a year. Not everyone owned a clock; there were many distractions even without telephones or televisions; and mistakes often led to ruined food at best, house fires at worst. Everything in the early American kitchen came out smelling of smoke, including the cook. People ate burnt or undercooked cake; they were hungrier and ate and worked off food with up to double as many calories as we need now.

ELECTION CAKE (1795)

Election cakes date from well before the American Revolution. They were very large, enriched yeast cakes, tasting like modern coffee cakes or Hot Cross Buns. In England such cakes were called "great cake" and made for local festivals. The Puritan election cakes were made for Election Day, Muster Day, or Training Day. These were spring and September (a second training day) regional gatherings to elect local officials (by vote of adult male property owners belonging to the established church), drill in military tactics, and do a little marketing and gossip. The custom persisted into the 1820s, but by then the larger cakes were, in Lydia Maria Child's cookbook, "old-fashioned."

These two recipes are from a Salem, Massachusetts, manuscript begun in 1795 by Mrs. Dalrymple and now in the Essex Institute there, but reprinted in 1992 in *The Compleat New England Huswife* by Elizabeth Stuart Gibson. The first is almost exactly the same as one quoted from an 1828 manuscript in *Food, Drink, and Recipes of Early New England* (Sturbridge Village, 1963) by Jane Whitehill. It is possible that Whitehill dated the same manuscript more conservatively or that two early American cooks copied out the recipe from an early almanac or newspaper. I have added some details from the 1827 recipe for "old-fashioned" Election Cake in *The Frugal Housewife*, by Lydia Maria Child, and an 1846 recipe for "Old Hartford Election Cake (One Hundred Years Old)" in *Miss Beecher's Domestic Receipt-Book* by Catherine E. Beecher. Unlike many early recipes for Election Cake, Dalrymple's and Child's do not use wine or brandy. This is probably not because of temperance, since the early temperance movement permitted alcoholic beverages in cooking and as medicine. In all likelihood they were being frugal with these enormous coffee cakes made for mass consumption. I have also used some other early recipes for techniques and cut the size of the smaller recipe in half to fit a modern home oven. If you have a bigger oven, you can double or triple the recipe. You can divide the work for a team project.

> I—7 lb. flour, 2 butter, 2½ sugar, 18 eggs, 1 qt [yeast] ½ pt milk spice to your taste.
>
> II—10 lb. flour, 8 butter, 4 sugar, 29 eggs, 3 pts yeast, 1½ pint new milk, cinnamon, nutmeg, few cloves.

NOTE: RECIPE TAKES TWO DAYS.

Yield: 40–50 modern servings

8–10 cups flour, plus some for kneading

2 cups whole wheat flour

½ cup wheat germ

1 pound salted butter, plus some to grease pans

1¼ pounds sugar (3 cups)

9 small eggs (6 large eggs)

1 cup half-and-half

1 quart **Potato Yeast** (from Chapter 7), or 1 tablespoon dry yeast and 1 quart whole milk

1 pound currants or raisins (optional)

2 nutmegs or 2 rounded teaspoons nutmeg

2 rounded teaspoons cinnamon

½ teaspoon cloves

Equipment: 9-by-13-inch sheet-cake pans or 7 large loaf pans, pastry blender or large fork, standing mixer or large food processor (optional), very large mixing bowl, breadboard

1. An hour before starting, remove butter from refrigerator to soften.

2. In the large mixing bowl, mix flour, whole wheat flour, and wheat germ to make something like "well-bolted" Early American flour. Use a higher proportion of whole wheat flour or even some wheat bran to approximate cheaper flour that might have been used in poorer towns or hard times.

3. "Rub the butter very fine into the flour" (Beecher). In 1795 this would have been done by hand, which would mean removing any rings and wading right in. Some experienced bakers might have used a food chopper or a knife or two to cut the butter into the flour. You can approximate this with a pastry blender or a large fork, although these tools were not widely available. If you use a standing mixer or food processor, work the mixture down to the consistency of sand.

4. Mix with half the sugar.

5. Stir in the yeast or yeast mixture and half the cream.

6. Beat the eggs until creamy and light and mix with the flour mixture.

7. Work in the rest of the cream to make a soft dough. Mrs. Child says, "Wet it with milk as wet as it can be, and still be moulded on a board." You may need to add more milk or more flour.

8. Mix the spices with the other half of the sugar and the raisins or currants if using.

9. Work the sugar mixture into the dough.

10. Flour board and your hands, and turn out dough onto the board. Knead it a dozen times or so, and cut into 2 or 7 pieces, depending on what pans you are using.

11. Grease pans with butter.

12. Press dough evenly into pans. "Set to rise over night in winter; in warm

weather, three hours is usually enough for it to rise" (Child). Beecher let the dough rise overnight in the mixing bowl, worked in the sugar and spice, and had a second rising of three hours. The difficulty is that yeast cultures varied so much (and none of these authors then knew that yeast was a living culture of microorganisms). Modern yeast also varies, so my suggestion is to let the bread rise all night in the pans.

13. If the cake has doubled in bulk, bake away. If it hasn't doubled in bulk, or has risen too much, "punch down" any large bubbles, take the cakes out of the pans and knead a little on the board, then return them to the pans, cover them and let rise until doubled in bulk.

14. Bake at 375 degrees for 15 minutes, then turn down the oven to 350 degrees for another 30–45 minutes, depending on the pans. "A loaf, the size of common flour bread, should bake three quarters of an hour" (Child).

Serve in thick slices.

FEDERAL PAN CAKE (1796)

This recipe from Amelia Simmons's *American Cookery* makes a heavy flatbread with a crispy crust—a quick-fried **Jonnycake** or **Hoe Cake** of the kind Americans continued to eat well into the nineteenth century. The mixture of rye and cornmeal is surprisingly good, and it was inexpensive. Often corn and rye were all poor farmers had, because wheat grew poorly in New England. In better times, wheat flour would be mixed in. The meal and flour would have been stone ground and much moister than what we have now, but even so there doesn't seem to be enough liquid in this recipe, and we would use about two table-

spoons of baking powder to lighten the pancakes. I have reduced the measures of flour and cornmeal to compensate, but it is more difficult to restore the flavor of stone-ground grains. If you can find fresh stone-ground cornmeal and rye flour, decrease the milk.

> Take one quart of boulted [bran sifted out] rye flour, one quart of boulted Indian meal, mix it well, and stir it with a little salt into three pints milk, to the proper consistence of pancakes; fry in lard, and serve up warm.

Yield: 30–60 4-inch pancakes

3 cups rye flour or whole rye flour

3 cups yellow cornmeal

6 cups whole milk or half-and-half

2 teaspoons salt

½ cup lard

Equipment: Heavy skillet or griddle, pancake turner, small ladle

1. Mix dry ingredients in a mixing bowl.

2. Stir in milk or half-and-half.

3. Heat 2 tablespoons of the lard in the skillet.

4. When the oil is hot but not yet smoking, ladle in enough pancake batter to make a 4-inch pancake a little more than ¼ inch thick. If you have to flatten out the batter with the ladle, add a little more milk. (The flour and meal absorb liquid as they stand, so you may have to do this a few times. If you get too much milk, it will rise to the top and you will need to stir the batter.)

5. When a few holes appear in the sides of the pancakes, and they appear to be browning, turn once to brown the other side. Depending on how thick

they are, this may take only 2 or 3 minutes per side.

6. Add more lard as needed, but keep the pan hot so the cakes don't absorb too much of it.

Serve hot with maple syrup or molasses, and plenty of salted butter.

PREBLE CAKE (1832)

This recipe is unique to an 1832 manuscript recipe book from northern New Hampshire or Southern Maine. (I am indebted to the owner, Karen Hicks, for letting me study this manuscript.) The proportions are similar to the pound cake (a pound each of flour, butter, sugar, and eggs) and "Queen's Cake" recipes of published cookbooks of that time, so it appears that this patriotic family had renamed Queen's Cake. The most likely Preble was Senator William Pitt Preble of Maine, who was quite popular at that time for pressing a border settlement in Northern New Hampshire against British Canada. Another possibility is Revolutionary War hero Commodore Edward Preble (1761–1807), a Portland native who led the capture of an anchored British ship at the Tory stronghold of Castine, Maine.

Although the recipe does not include many instructions, we can guess how this cake was made and typically spiced from the instructions for similar cakes in *75 Receipts for Cooking* by Eliza Leslie and *The American Frugal Housewife*, by Lydia Maria Child. The author of the manuscript copied at least twenty-seven of her eighty-five recipes from the Leslie book, and another ten or so from the Child book. However, she did not copy the recipes in either book for Pound Cake or Queen's Cake.

An eighteenth-century feature of Preble Cake is creaming the butter with flour (not the sugar), and whipping the eggs with the sugar. What results is a rather dense pound cake with the flavor of today's spice cakes, a useful reminder that the old English taste for a lot of spices persisted in the United States to at least the mid-nineteenth century. If you want to make an early American pound cake, increase the sugar and butter to a full pound, add another large egg (or two small eggs), and bake the cake in large loaf pans. For a typical "Washington Cake," add half a pound of raisins or currants. If you want to make an early American version of Queen's Cake, get some mini loaf pans or muffin tins and use the recipe below, but reduce the baking time.

I have taken the spices from Eliza Leslie's recipe and some other details from "The Best Pound Cake" by Stephen Schmidt (*Cook's Illustrated*, May–June 1994). Kitchen temperatures of the 1830s (no refrigerators) were ideal for making pound cakes, which may help explain why the cakes became less popular in urban areas as iceboxes and home refrigerators became more common. Pound cakes remained popular in pioneering zones and isolated areas such as Appalachia well into the twentieth century; the recipe is easy to remember and the cake works without refrigerators, yeast, or baking powder.

1 pound of flour, ¾ of sugar, ¾ of butter, 8 eggs, spice as you please, or lemon, haff the flour whisked with the butter to a froth, beat the sugar and eggs together.

Yield: Serves 18–20

2½ cups flour (not sifted)

½ cup whole wheat flour

¼ cup wheat germ

¾ pound salted butter (3 sticks)

¾ pound sugar

8 small eggs (or 6 large eggs, or 4 jumbo eggs)

1 rounded teaspoon nutmeg

1 level teaspoon mace

1 level teaspoon cinnamon

12 drops lemon extract (optional)

Equipment: 2 small loaf pans, parchment paper, pastry blender or food processor, whisk, toothpick or wire cake tester, wire rack

1. An hour before beginning, remove eggs and butter from refrigerator to soften.

2. Cut out parchment paper to fit the bottom and 2 sides of the loaf pans. Cut the next piece to fit the bottom and the other 2 sides.

3. Butter pans and put paper in pans.

4. Butter paper.

5. Preheat oven to 325 degrees.

6. Mix flour, whole wheat flour, wheat germ, and spices.

7. Beat eggs until creamy and light. Stir in the sugar.

8. Cream the butter and flour together, or process in the food processor until it has the texture of fine sand.

9. Beat the egg mixture into the flour mixture.

10. Divide the batter between the 2 pans.

11. Bake an hour and test by putting a wooden toothpick or wire cake tester into the deepest part. When the tester comes out clean, the cake is done. It may need another 10 minutes.

12. Cool the completed cakes in the pans for a few minutes, then turn out of the pans and cool on a wire rack. If not using immediately, wrap tightly with plastic wrap or aluminum foil, or freeze.

Serve with butter or jam.

HARRISON CAKE (1850)

Harrison Cake seems to be the most popular of the patriotic cakes, perhaps because it was easy and quick to assemble and keeps very well. Published and manuscript recipes continued to appear almost until President Harrison's grandson Benjamin Harrison was elected president in 1888. This recipe, from *The Young Housekeeper's Friend*, by Mary Cornelius, may have appeared as early as 1846. I have only been able to trace it back to the 1850 edition. It is interesting in that Ms. Cornelius makes the cake in "cup cake pans," which we now call muffin tins. This is a very large recipe, from the era of brick ovens where you only got one baking out of building a fire to heat the oven, then removing the coals for the actual baking. The instant rise of the molasses-baking soda reaction made it possible to get these muffins ready in a hurry when the oven was nice and hot. You can halve or quarter the recipe.

To two cups of molasses, put one of brown sugar, one of butter, one of sour cream, or milk, a cup of raisins, and one of currants, a teaspoonful of powdered clove, and two, rather small of saleratus [potassium bicarbonate].

To mix it, cut the butter in little pieces, and put into a saucepan with the molasses, to melt. When the molasses boils up, pour it immediately upon three or four cups of flour, and add the sugar and half the cream. Stir it well, then add the saleratus, the rest of the cream, the spice, and flour enough to make it of the consistence of cup cake, and last, the fruit. Bake in cup-cake pans, rather slowly. All cake containing molasses is more liable to burn than that which has none.

CAUTION: BOILING MOLASSES STICKS AND BURNS.

Yield: 50–56 2-inch muffins

2 cups molasses

1 cup brown sugar

1 cup butter (2 sticks)

1 cup sour cream

1 cup raisins

1 cup currants

1 rounded teaspoon cloves

2 level teaspoons baking soda

3–3½ cups flour

Equipment: 5 muffin tins, 56 paper or foil muffin cups (optional), toothpick or wire cake tester

1. Butter muffin tins, or set paper or foil cups in them. Preheat oven to 375 degrees.
2. Cut the butter in small pieces and put in a saucepan with the molasses.
3. Slowly heat the molasses to boiling, watching carefully so that it doesn't boil up suddenly.
4. Put the 4 cups of the flour and sugar in a metal mixing bowl.
5. When the molasses boils, pour it over the flour and sugar, and stir in half a cup of the sour cream.
6. Sprinkle on the baking soda, the spices, and the rest of the sour cream.
7. Stir together quickly and then put in the raisins and currants to make a thick batter. You may need a little more flour.
8. Fill each muffin mold or paper about halfway. If you run out of batter, half fill the empty molds with hot tap water.
9. Bake 20–25 minutes. Because there is so much molasses in the mixture, the cake tester may not come out completely clean when the muffins are done.

Serve for dessert.

WASHINGTON PIE (1856)

Washington Pie is a cake, and became the Washington's Birthday cake that survived the longest, from just before the Civil War into the early twentieth century, probably because it was made as a layer cake at the beginning of the fashion for layer cakes. This layer cake may have been called "pie" because it was an early layer cake with thin layers that could be baked in pie pans. With the thick filling suggested by Mrs. Putnam, a slice looks more like pie than cake. As layer cakes got taller after the Civil War, Washington Pie looked less like pie, but kept the name. The idea is similar to **Laura Keene's Jelly Cake**. The recipe is from *Mrs. Putnam's Receipt Book and Young Housekeeper's Assistant*. It was first published in Boston in 1849, but my copy is from 1856. (The recipe is near the end of the pastry chapter, suggesting that it was added in one of the enlargements of Mrs. Putnam's book. Perhaps a library or historical society near you has an older edition of this popular book that will help us pinpoint when the Washington Pie recipe was added.)

By the 1870s Washington Pie was being served all winter. The earlier Washington Cakes (see above) were pound cakes with raisins or simplified election cakes. When someone, possibly at the Parker House Hotel in Boston, changed from jam filling to custard filling and chocolate icing, Washington Pie became "Boston Cream Pie," which is still made and still has us wondering why a cake is called "pie." Mrs. Putnam also had a Lafayette Pie that was a cake. She suggested a lemon buttercream filling as well as the marmalade or jelly. Jelly or applesauce became the usual filling for Washington Pie, sometimes with frosting on top. Mrs. Putnam's book has a recipe for apple marmalade as well as quince and lemon, and for raspberry, blackberry, and apple jellies.

Three-quarters of a pound of sugar; half a pound of butter beat to a cream; add a cup of cream, half a tea–spoonful of saleratus, six eggs beat up well; flavor it with lemon; add a pound of flour; bake it in round tin pans, or a wooden box-cover, about 15 or twenty minutes; when cold, lay one on a plate, and spread over it marmalade, or any other jelly, as thick as the cake; then cover it with another cake. Frost it, or not, as you please.

Yield: 10–12 slices

2 sticks salted butter, plus some to butter cake pans

3 cups sugar

1 cup heavy cream

½ teaspoon baking soda

1 lemon

6 medium eggs or 5 large eggs

3¾ cups all-purpose flour

1 ½-ounce jar marmalade (or apple butter, or blackberry or raspberry jam or jelly, or canned prepared lemon frosting)

Equipment: 2 8-inch round layer cake pans, waxed paper, pastry blender or large fork, lemon zester (optional) lemon juicer, spatula, toothpick or wire cake tester, wire racks to cool cakes

1. An hour before beginning, remove butter from refrigerator to soften.

2. Use bottom of cake pans to trace pattern onto waxed paper. Cut out two circles waxed paper to fit bottom of cake pans.

3. Butter pans and waxed paper and put paper in pans.

4. Dissolve baking soda in cream.

5. Break eggs into a cup 1 at a time. Remove any bits of shell and move to a large bowl. Whip until creamy and light.

6. Zest lemon and chop zest fine (optional).

7. Halve and juice lemon and reserve juice. Preheat oven to 375 degrees.

8. With pastry blender or large fork, cream together butter and sugar in a large mixing bowl.

9. Quickly stir in the cream, and alternately add flour and eggs.

10. Whisk in lemon juice and minced zest if using.

11. Pour batter into cake pans. Level with spatula from middle to edge so that it goes into the oven slightly lower in the middle, which will rise to make an even layer.

12. Bake 15 minutes and test with toothpick or wire cake tester. Cake is done when the tester comes out clean. It may need longer if layers are thick.

13. After removing cakes from oven, cool in the pans a few minutes.

14. The edges should pull away from the sides of the pans, but cut once around with the spatula to free any catches.

15. Invert the cakes onto wire racks.

16. Put the more uneven cake on a cake plate, good side down. You can trim it a little on top with the spatula.

17. Cover with a thick layer of your selected filling, though probably not quite "as thick as the cake."

18. Put on the better of the 2 cake layers, good side up.

Serve cut into thin wedges.

6

EARLY AMERICAN MEALS— SPRING (1792–1852)

The Early American period from the Revolution to the Civil War is where we can document a full range of seasonal menus. Printed cookbooks and surviving kitchen manuscripts give a clear picture of seasonal cooking, as recipes used only once a year had to be written down. Seasonal lines had blurred, as settlers and colonists became more efficient farmers and preservers and as transportation improved. But seasons were still very important for average Americans. (And, incidentally, the unusually cool climate of 1645–1825, sometimes called "the little ice age," also exaggerated the effect of seasons upon early settlers. It was somewhat abating by the Early American period, except for the famous "year without a summer," 1816.)

Most calendars of Early American life begin in winter, the season that defined the activities of the other three. In terms of food, however, early spring was the time of simple meals and scarcity, as stored supplies ran out and natural refrigerators began to fail. Hens stopped laying eggs in the dark of winter, but eggs could be stored for a while. Most farmers stopped milking in late fall or early winter, and slaughtered surplus cattle, so that the remaining cows could be kept more economically. By spring, stored butter

and cheese had run out, or were of very poor quality.

Pigs were the easiest animals to keep through the winter and were slaughtered in midwinter for Christmas roasts. So salt pork or pickled pork were the basis of early spring meals, with the last of the beans and cornmeal. Hunting and trapping supplied what fresh meat could be had. The other activity in rural areas was tapping maple trees for syrup and sugar. Because the climate was colder in Early American times, maple syrup was still being produced in the southern states.

The first spring greens, onions, and asparagus were eagerly awaited, and sometimes eaten in omelets with the first eggs and butter. Americans were beginning to grow rhubarb for spring pies. In coastal areas, fishing and shellfishing resumed once the worst winter storms were over, and spring runs of spawning fish such as smelt, shad, and salmon were still important. By late spring, the salt pork could be stretched around meals of veal and lamb, as farmers culled male calves from dairy herds and male lambs from wool flocks. Veal was one of the cheapest meats and considered food for the poor.

(A very ingenious study of stored foods listed in estate inventories from 1711 to

1835 by Sarah F. McMahon shows numerically how seasons gradually extended. It's in " 'All Things in Their Proper Season': Seasonal Rhythms of Diet in Nineteenth Century New England," in Vol. 63, No. 2, Spring 1989 *Agricultural History* magazine.)

ANN'S INDIAN BAKED PUDDING (1822–1852)

Indian pudding is one of the best-remembered early American foods, but a lot of mythology has grown up around it. For one thing, the name derives from the "Indian meal" (cornmeal) used in a simplified English pudding. Although Native Americans had long made enriched and sweetened cornmeal mushes, this kind of baked pudding was not thought of as Indian food by most early Americans. (The most obvious Indian retention in this recipe is the step of scalding the meal before assembling the pudding.) Settled Native Americans ate this kind of pudding in the Early American period, but probably did not begin thinking of it as an ethnic food until the early twentieth century. It's also important to remember that early American puddings were not very sweet and were not usually eaten as desserts. Indian pudding in particular was often eaten first, before the meats, to fill up on. Many early Indian puddings were boiled in cloth bags, as home ovens were not common in some regions.

This particular recipe is from the manuscript cookbook of Elizabeth C. Kane, a member of a prominent Philadelphia family. The Kanes could afford sugar (possibly brown sugar) in this pudding, where most people used molasses, and farmers might use their own maple or sorghum. The recipe was published by food historian Jan Longone in an article in the Spring-Summer 1986 issue of *The American Magazine and Historical Chronicle*. I have guessed at the quantities of sugar and spice from other early recipes. The "whey method" is from Lydia Maria Child's *American Frugal Housewife*, and you may need the extra milk to compensate for the dryness of modern cornmeal. If you increase the recipe, increase the baking time.

> One cup of meal, with one quart of Milk, a pint of which make hot and scald the meal, the other half add cold, three eggs, a lump of butter the size of a large walnut, sugar Cinnamon and nutmeg to your taste bake it one hour: you may add a little ginger if you like it—Either Wine sauce or butter and sugar mixed together.

Yield: Serves 8

1 cup yellow cornmeal (stone ground preferred)

1 quart whole milk or half-and-half, plus 2 cups more for optional whey method

3 small eggs or 2 extra large eggs

3 tablespoons salted butter, plus 1 stick for sauce, and some to grease baking dish

3 ounces white or light brown sugar, plus ½ cup for sauce

1 tablespoon mixed cinnamon and nutmeg

½ teaspoon ginger (optional)

Equipment: 2- or 3-quart baking dish

1. Bring 2 cups of the milk or half-and-half almost to a boil in a pot or microwave oven.

2. Stir hot milk carefully into the cornmeal.

3. Stir in 3 tablespoons butter and let cool.

4. Break eggs and mix with spices and the 3 ounces of sugar.

5. Mix 2 more cups of milk with the egg mixture, and then work everything into the cornmeal.

6. Grease baking dish.

7. Fill baking dish with pudding mixture. (To make "whey," a sweet clear liquid that would be used as a sauce, add another cup or two of cold milk on top of the pudding before it goes into the oven.)

8. Bake 1 hour at 350 degrees.

9. For sauce, blend a stick of softened butter with ½ cup sugar or brown sugar.

Serve before or with the meat at a large afternoon "dinner." The butter-sugar sauce would be melted onto a mound of pudding, or the whey ladled over it in a bowl.

A GOOD PICKLE FOR BEEF AND PORK, CALLED THE "KNICKERBOCKER PICKLE" (1825)

This recipe would have been used in the fall and winter slaughter of cattle and pigs respectively, but I place it here so you can make your own pickled beef and pork for the bean recipes that would have been more important in early spring. In winter some cuts could be frozen or refrigerated in a barrel of snow, but most beef and pork, and some mutton and fish, were preserved by salting or pickling and brought out for daily use. Even in cities, salt pork and corned beef were cheaper than fresh meat and more widely used.

This pickle recipe is from the 1825 *The Family Receipt Book, containing Thirty Valuable and Simple Receipts . . .* , by "A Long-Island Farmer." The quantities given would cure a barrel of meat, so I have a given a one-twelfth-size recipe, suitable for a full brisket of beef or five pounds of country spareribs. Knickerbocker pickle shows the developing American sweet tooth, later expressed in sugar-cured hams and sweet glazes for baked corned beef or ham. The "Long-Island Farmer" is among the first American

authors to print a list of ingredients in a column as we do today.

The following Receipt is making pickle for beef or pork, is strongly recommended to the adoption of those who pickle beef and pork for family use. Persons in the trade who adopt it will find a ready sale. It has been used by many families in this city and always approved.
Receipt,—

6 gallons water,

9 lbs. salt, coarse and fine mixed,

3 lbs, Brown Sugar,

3 oz. salt petre [sodium nitrate, optional],

1 oz. pearl-ash [substitute baking soda],

1 gallon molasses.

In making a larger or smaller quantity of pickle, the above proportions are to be observed. Boil and skim these ingredients well, and when cold, put them over the beef or pork.

Yield: Enough for a full brisket of beef or 5 pounds of spareribs

2½ cups (¾ pound) kosher salt or pickling salt

1 cup lightly packed down (¼ pound) brown sugar

1½ teaspoons (¼ ounce) sodium nitrite (optional)

½ teaspoon (1/12 ounce) baking soda

1⅓ cups molasses

2–3 pound flat-cut brisket, or 12 country spareribs

Equipment: Deep plastic or enamel or pottery bowl or bucket, clean stones to weight meat, refrigerator space

1. Put 2 quarts of water into a soup pot and measure in the other ingredients.

2. Heat the water to boiling, stirring to dissolve the other ingredients.

3. Remove from heat.

4. Wash off meat, arrange in bowl, pour the pickle over it. Weight down the meat with stones as necessary to keep it submerged.

5. Store in refrigerator. After a week, meats will be quite salty.

Use in recipe for **Boiled Dish** *or* **Baked Beans***, below, or other recipes calling for corned beef or salt pork.*

BOILED DISH—MEAT (1844)

This recipe, from the 1844 *The New England Economical Housekeeper, and Family Receipt Book*, by Mrs. E.A. Howland, seems to be the first for what we now call "New England Boiled Dinner," or at least the first to describe it as made in one pot by timing the vegetables. However, by 1845 boiled corned beef and salt pork had probably been eaten almost every day for more than 150 years in the United States, north and south. Mrs. Howland's boiling times suggest either that she was working with very dried-out early spring vegetables, or that Americans were beginning in the 1840s to overcook vegetables. Lydia Maria Child's *American Frugal Housewife*, fifteen years earlier, had much shorter boiling times for beets and potatoes, although longer for parsnips. Because we have much smaller pots today, I have given a recipe with boiling times suitable to modern vegetables, and suggest cutting them into four-ounce pieces to cook faster. Unlike most modern cooks, Mrs. Howland cooked her beets along with everything, often staining the meat and cut vegetables pink, except when she had white beets or yellow beets (which you may still find in farmer's markets). Her turnips may have been larger than ours, and she probably cooked the cabbage whole.

Corned beef should be boiled three hours, pork two hours. Beets need as much boiling as the beef in winter; one hour will do in the summer, when they are more tender; carrots, cabbage and turnips, each an hour, parsnips forty-five minutes, potatoes twenty to thirty minutes.

Later recipes mention other vegetables, such as summer or winter squash, corn, and rutabagas. I have not found a reference to boiled corned beef with onions in the nineteenth century. There is also some record of cooking an Indian pudding in a muslin bag along with the beef and vegetables, or adding dumplings like the **Corn Dumplings** below.

Yield: Serves 6

1 flat-cut corned beef brisket (2–3 pounds)

lean salt pork (optional)

6 2-inch beets

6 potatoes (red or waxy preferred)

6 parsnips

6 large carrots

Large head green cabbage

6 2–3-inch, white-topped turnips (or one large rutabaga)

Equipment: 1 oversized soup pot, or 2 spaghetti pots, long tongs

1. About 3½ hours before you are planning to eat, put the meat in a large pot, and cover with water up to about half the pot (4 quarts). Bring to a boil.

2. Remove top of pot and reduce heat until water just simmers.

3. Turn up the heat and a bagged pudding, if using. Reduce heat again to a bare simmer. Make a time chart for when the dish is to be served, and plan to add beets an hour before serving,

depending on size; potatoes 10 minutes later; turnips 10 minutes after that; parsnips and carrots 25 minutes before serving for the biggest pieces, 15 minutes for smaller ones; and cabbage 7–10 minutes. If your pot isn't big enough, plan either a second pot with salted water, or start the beets and potatoes earlier and plan to remove them to make room.

4. Trim off tops and roots of beets. When it is time to add them to the pot, increase heat so that it does not stop simmering, then reduce heat to keep them at just a simmer.

5. Wash potatoes and peel off any green areas on potatoes. Add to pot.

6. If using rutabaga, scrub; peel off wax, if any; trim; and cut in half at the equator. Quarter each half. If using turnips, scrub and trim off any roots or sprouts. Add to pot on schedule.

7. Peel parsnips and carrots and cut into 1-inch lengths. Separate all the pieces an inch or more in diameter into one pile, to add about 25 minutes before serving.

8. Check corn beef for doneness (It will have lost some of its stiffness). If done, you can remove from the pot and weight between 2 plates for cleaner slices. This makes more room for vegetables. Check the beets for doneness by poking with a fork (it should go all the way in). Check the potatoes and rutabaga or turnip by halving the largest one or piece. Potatoes should be cooked all the way through; turnip or rutabaga could have a small granular area at the center. Remove vegetables that are done.

9. Add the large chunks of carrot and parsnip 25 minutes before serving.

10. Add the smaller chunks of carrot and parsnip 15 minutes before serving.

11. Cut the cabbage the long way into 6–8 wedges, each with some of the stem to hold it together. Add to the pot about 7–10 minutes before serving and cover tightly so the cabbage steams.

12. Slice corned beef (and/or salt pork, if using) in thin slices. Arrange on a platter with vegetables surrounding the meat.

Serve with melted butter.

Corn Dumplings (1845)

Boiled dinners were in favor because the physics of boiling water guarantee a constant temperature with relatively little tending of the open fireplace. The large pot of boiling water invited the addition of storage vegetables and also bagged puddings or simple dumplings like these from *Domestic Cookery*, by Marylander Elizabeth Lea, first published in 1845. Notice the similarity of these dumplings to the **Indian Bread** in Chapter 1. Mrs. Lea's cornmeal would have been stone ground with the germ and some of the bran still in it. It was moister and stickier than ours, and may have cooked faster.

> When you boil corned beef, new bacon, or pork, you can make dumplings by taking some grease out of the pot with some of the water, and pouring it hot on a quart of Indian meal, mix and work it well, (it will not require salt), make it into little round cakes (they should be stiff, or they will boil to pieces); take out the meat when it is done, and boil the dumplings in the same water for half an hour. They may be eaten with molasses and make a good common dessert.

Yield: About 48 dumplings

4 cups yellow cornmeal (stone ground preferred)

1 recipe **Boiled Dish** (above)

1 cup molasses or maple syrup

Equipment: Food processor or blender, mixing bowl, wooden spoon or pudding stick, ladle, waxed paper, skimmer or slotted spoon

1. If using modern cornmeal, as boiled dinner is cooking, whirl half the cornmeal for 5 minutes in a blender or food processor with one side propped up with a thin book.

2. Put all the cornmeal in a mixing bowl and skim the grease and some of the broth out of the boiled dinner, starting with about 2 cups. Add little by little to the cornmeal, stirring hard to get a crumbly-looking "pre-dough" that will stick together when compressed.

3. Wet hands and form patties smaller than your palm.

4. Set out patties on waxed paper.

5. When boiled dinner is served, turn up heat on broth, and put in corn cakes with skimmer or slotted spoon, a few at a time. Cover pot and reduce heat to a simmer.

6. Cook 30 minutes.

Serve two dumplings as a dessert, striped with a little molasses or maple syrup.

CORNED BEEF HASH (1861)

Boiled dinner was almost always followed by a hash of the leftover meats and potatoes. This was so obvious, and so variable, that early writers did not write down a detailed recipe. The name "hash" comes from the French verb to slice or chop. Older English and French hashes were sliced meat reheated in gravy. The chopped and fried hash with potatoes we still enjoy is a somewhat later development, and this 1861 recipe, from *The Housekeeper's Encyclopedia* by Mrs.

E.F. Haskell, suggests that some people still did not accept fried hash at that date.

The best hash is made from boiled corned beef. It should be boiled very tender, and chopped fine when entirely cold. The potatoes for hash made of corned beef are the better for being boiled in the pot liquor. When taken from the pot, remove the skins from the potatoes, and when entirely cold chop them fine. To a coffee-cup of chopped meat allow four of chopped potatoes, stir the potatoes gradually into the meat, until the whole is mixed. Do this at evening and, if warm, set the hash in a cool place. In the morning put the spider [frying pan with legs] on the fire with a lump of butter as large as the bowl of a table-spoon, add a dust of pepper, and if not sufficiently salt, add a little; usually none is needed. When the butter has melted, put the hash in the spider, add four table-spoons of water, and stir the whole together. After it has become really hot, stir it from the bottom, cover a plate over it, and set the spider where it will merely stew. This is a moist hash, and preferred by some to a dry or browned hash.

Yield: Serves two hungry farmers, but can be multiplied according to available leftovers

1 cup corned beef

4 cups boiled potatoes and other vegetables from boiled dinner, such as beets, carrots, parsnips

2 tablespoons butter

Equipment: Heavy frying pan with loose lid

1. Cut up and measure corned beef. Rub skins off potatoes and vegetables before cutting up and measuring them.

2. Heat up butter in skillet, add a little pepper. If you are working with left-

overs of the boiled dinner above, you should not need more salt.

3. Mix meat and vegetables together and add to frying pan with 1/4 cup water.

4. When water begins to bubble, stir once to turn it over, reduce heat and simmer until hash is warmed thoroughly.

Serve for breakfast with eggs and hot biscuits or mush.

Baked Beans (1829)

This is the first historical recipe I ever cooked, and I still make it. "Boston Baked Beans" became associated with so much sweetening by the end of the nineteenth century that it is quite a surprise to try them with no sugar or molasses at all!

This is apparently the first written recipe for pork and beans, although written sources mention it as a common food for more than a hundred years, and folklore associates it with Puritan Sabbath observance. This recipe appears in the 1829 *The Frugal Housewife*, by Lydia Maria Child. Mrs. Child learned to cook in Maine as a teenage housekeeper for her married older sister, but wrote the book as a resident of Boston. Native Americans stewed beans with fat or smoked meat (and often with dried corn), and there are dishes of fava beans with pork or bacon in English and French cooking traditions.

Home baking ovens were most common in New England and Pennsylvania, and thus much of the country would have used something more like the boiled **Stewed Beans and Pork**. Mrs. Child does not specify what kind of beans to use, and the use of small white beans in "Boston Baked Beans" seems to have developed over the eighteenth century. Probably early Americans used whatever dried beans were available, including spotted and yellow-eye beans like the multicolored Indian beans. Mrs. Child's recipe is very close to the method currently recommended by the California Bean Board to soak out many of the bean sugars now known to cause intestinal gas. I have added a corned beef option mentioned in other early recipes. You can half this recipe for a small pot.

Baked beans are a very simple dish, yet few cook them well. They should be put in cold water, and hung over the fire, the night before they are baked. In the morning, they should be put in a colander, and rinsed two or three times; then again place in a kettle, with the pork you intend to bake, covered with water, and kept scalding hot, an hour or more. A pound of pork is quite enough for a quart of beans, and that is a large dinner for a common family. The rind of the pork should be slashed. Pieces of pork alternately fat and lean are most suitable; the cheeks are the best. A little pepper sprinkled among the beans, when they are placed in the bean-pot, will render them less unhealthy. They should be just covered with water, when put into the oven; and the pork should be sunk a little below the surface of the beans. Bake three or four hours.

NOTE: RECIPE REQUIRES TWO DAYS.

Yield: Serves 6–8

2 pounds dried beans, small white or yellow-eye preferred

1 pound lean salt pork, or point-cut corned beef brisket

Black pepper

Equipment: Large soup pot, bean pot or covered casserole, colander

1. The night before serving, wash beans carefully in the colander and pick over

to remove any dirt, small stones, or spoiled beans.

2. Put beans in a large soup pot and cover with a lot of water.

3. Cover pot and bring to a boil for 4 minutes. Remove from heat and let soak overnight.

4. Drain beans in colander. Rinse with fresh water a few times.

5. Slash rind of salt pork, if using. Return beans to pot, add meat, and cover with water.

6. Bring pot to a boil, but immediately reduce heat to simmer 1 hour without cover.

7. Again drain beans and meat in colander.

8. Bring 6 cups of water to a boil. Preheat the oven to 250 degrees.

9. Put about ⅔ of the beans into the bean pot or covered casserole, sprinkle on some pepper. Add the meat, then the rest of the beans, and another sprinkling of black pepper.

10. If using a rounded bean pot, use just enough water to cover (about 4 cups). In any other covered casserole, add another cup of water.

11. Cover pot and place in the oven. Reduce heat to 200 degrees and cook 3–7 hours. Check once or twice to see if you need to add a little water, and for doneness.

Serve as simple supper or with brown bread, **Thirded Bread,** *or codfish cakes. Leftover beans were reheated, made into a soup with added water, or spread on bread to make baked-bean sandwiches.*

STEWED BEANS AND PORK (1841)

Home brick bake ovens were most characteristic of the northern colonies and states prior to the wide acceptance of cooking stoves from 1840 to 1870. Thus pork and beans in the middle and southern colonies were more likely to be boiled over the fire. Because the dried beans and salt pork represented concentrated and easily transported food energy, this form of pork and beans was widely used on sailing ships, army camps, and wagon trains. The recipe is from the 1841 *The Good Housekeeper*, by Sarah Josepha Hale. Mrs. Hale was editor of *Godey's Lady's Book* (magazine) from 1837 to 1877 and seems to be the first to specify white beans. Her recipe largely copies Mrs. Child's and again does not use sweetening.

"Stewed beans and pork are prepared in the same way [as her previous baked bean recipe, similar to Child's, above], only they are kept over the fire, and the pork in them, three or four hours instead of being in the oven. The beans will not be white or pleasant to the taste unless they are well soaked and washed, nor are they healthy without this process."

Yield: Serves 6–8

2 pounds dried white beans (pea, navy, or small white preferred)

1 pound lean salt pork, or point-cut corned beef brisket (the fattier, front part)

Black pepper

Equipment: Large soup pot, bean pot or covered casserole, colander

1. The night before serving, wash beans carefully in the colander and pick over to remove any dirt, small stones, or spoiled beans.

2. Put beans in a large soup pot and cover with 2 quarts of water.

3. Cover pot and bring to a boil for 4 minutes. Remove from heat and let soak overnight.

4. Drain beans in colander. Rinse with fresh water a few times.

5. "Score the rind" of salt pork, if using. Return beans to pot, add meat, and water, just to cover.

6. Bring pot to a boil, but immediately reduce heat to simmer 1 hour without cover.

7. Again drain beans and meat in colander.

8. Return beans to pot, add meat, and water to cover, "one tea-spoonful of salt," and "a little pepper."

9. Bring to a boil, then reduce heat to simmer 3–4 hours. Beans are done when floury clear through.

THIRDED BREAD (1833)

New Englanders especially were apt to make puddinglike breads of rye and corn-meal, or this thirded bread of wheat, corn, and rye flours. They later evolved into the steamed brown bread that some people still like with baked beans. The recipe is from Lydia Maria Child's *The American Frugal Housewife*, with some quantities from a version tested by Sandra L. Oliver in *Saltwater Foodways*.

Some people like one third Indian [cornmeal] in their flour. Others like one third rye; and some think the nicest of all bread is one third Indian, one third rye, and one third flour, made according to the directions for flour bread. When Indian is used, it should be salted, and scalded, before the other meal is put in. A mixture of other grains is economical when flour is too high.

Flour bread should have a sponge set the night before. The sponge should be soft enough to pour; mixed with water, warm or cold, according to the temperature of the weather. One gill of lively yeast is enough to put into sponge for two loaves. . . . About an hour before your oven is ready, stir in flour into your sponge till it is stiff enough to lay on a well floured board or table. Knead it up pretty stiff, and put it into well greased pans. . . . Common sized loaves will bake in three quarters of an hour. If they slip easily in the pans it is a sign they are done.

NOTE: RECIPE TAKES TWO DAYS.

Yield: 30–36 slices

3 cups rye flour (stone ground preferred)

3 cups yellow cornmeal (stone ground preferred)

3 cups whole wheat flour, plus 1–2 cups more to knead

1 tablespoon yeast

Butter to grease loaf pans

Equipment: 3 loaf pans or 2 large loaf pans, board for kneading, 2 mixing bowls (1 large), kitchen towels

1. Heat 3 cups water to boiling.

2. In a mixing bowl, stir boiling water into cornmeal and 1 tablespoon salt.

3. Mix yeast with a little water and a pinch of sugar in a small cup. When a foam of bubbles forms on top, you know the yeast is active and can proceed to make the "sponge."

4. Blend the yeast with the rye flour and enough water to make a pourable batter, 2–3 cups.

5. Cover the two mixing bowls and let sit overnight.

6. In the morning, combine the corn-meal and the rye sponge, and mix well.

7. Work in the whole wheat flour to make a stiff dough. It will be fairly sticky.

8. Flour the board and your hands, remove rings, and knead the dough until it is somewhat elastic and smooth. It will remain more sticky than bread dough.

9. Roll the dough up into a ball, and return to the large mixing bowl. Cover with a kitchen towel and let rise until at least half-again larger.

10. "Punch down" dough to remove large air bubbles, and divide into 3 parts.

11. Grease loaf pans. You may sprinkle a little cornmeal in the bottom of each pan.

12. Knead each portion of dough a few times, then shape into loaves and put them in the pans. Let rise until about half-again as large.

13. Preheat oven to 375 degrees. Bake loaves 10 minutes, then reduce heat to 325 degrees and bake another 40–50 minutes, or until the loaves come out of the pans easily, and the bottom sounds hollow when tapped. (If the loaves come out, but the bottom doesn't sound done, put the loaves directly on the wire racks of the oven, upside down, for another 5–10 minutes.)

Serve hot with butter, often with baked beans. Early American health food enthusiasts would not eat hot bread, so they would bake a day ahead. Leftover crusts were broken into crumbs for puddings, or stewed with milk to make "brewis."

OYSTER SOUP MR. PACA'S WAY (1799)

Shellfish beds could be raked in early spring, and oysters were already being packed into barrels of ice and shipped inland on rivers and canals in Early American times. Railroads made them a popular luxury food over much of America. This recipe is from a Maryland cooking manuscript of Miss Ann Chase, begun in May 1811. The recipe is reprinted in the book, *Maryland's Way*, published by the Hammond-Harwood House Association in 1964. William Paca, a signer of the Declaration of Independence, died in 1799, so we can assume that this recipe dates from his lifetime. Miss Chase's father, Justice Samuel Chase, was a colleague of Mr. Paca and also a signer of the Declaration. Mr. Paca liked a very thick oyster stew. This was a rich soup course served in the home of the chief magistrate of Maryland, but probably only the richness and spice would have been lacking on the tables of more ordinary city dwellers. Since oysters were larger in his time, I have changed around the directions slightly to thicken the soup before adding the oysters.

Take half a gallon of oysters opened new with their liquor and stew them: when half done take a piece of butter the bigness of a teacup and rub in with as much flour as will thicken them. Season with pepper, salt and mace. Just before you take them up add half a pint of cream.

Yield: Serves 12

2 quarts of oysters and juice (from about 6 dozen whole oysters)

6 ounces salted butter (1½ sticks)

½ cup flour

1 tablespoon wheat germ (optional)

1 cup heavy cream

½ teaspoon mace

½ teaspoon pepper

Equipment: Large soup pot, mixing bowl, fine sieve

1. About an hour before starting, remove butter from refrigerator to soften.

2. If you are starting from whole oysters, scrub off the shells and put them

in a large pot with a tight lid. Add a few tablespoonfuls of water and steam the oysters for a few seconds until all the shells open slightly. Now cut the oyster meats into a mixing bowl and discard shells. Save juices with meats. When you are finished, pour the steaming liquid carefully into the mixing bowl, so you don't get the sand or shells into the soup. (Mr. Paca's cook, who may have been a slave, might have had extra help to open the oysters, or might have been authorized to pay a peddler to shuck the oysters.)

3. Cream butter and flour together. Cut mixture into small pieces.

4. Pour oyster liquor off oysters into a soup pot, and heat it to a simmer.

5. Add mace and pepper, and the flour-butter mixture. Stir to dissolve all the flour and cook until it thickens.

6. Add oyster meats and simmer 5–10 minutes, stirring to mix well.

7. Remove from heat and mix in cream. Taste and add salt if needed.

Serve hot with hard crackers.

TO BROIL COD, SALMON, WHITING, OR HADDOCK (1792)

This recipe is from a London cookbook published in Boston, *The Frugal Housewife*, by Susannah Carter. We know this book was widely used, in part because sections of it were borrowed for *American Cookery* by Amelia Simmons four years later. Right now, cod and haddock are somewhat endangered species, and hake (the American version of whiting) is not usually sold whole or in steaks. On the other hand, farmed salmon are now widely available, so we can make this Early American spring dish much as it was eaten along many rivers as the salmon came up to spawn in the spring

months. The main difference is that the farmed salmon of today are fattier than wild salmon, but this makes them even better when broiled or grilled. Early American broiling was done over burned-down wood coals, on a gridiron. We can use a charcoal grill, a gas grill, or the oven broiler on any stove. The lobster-butter sauce was typically English and does not seem to have been popular in the United States, where lobsters were spit-roasted or boiled and eaten as a separate dish.

Flour them and have a quick clear fire; set your gridiron high; broil them of a fine brown; lay them in a dish and for sauce have good melted butter. Take a lobster, bruise the body in the butter, cut the meat small, put all together into the melted butter, make it hot and pour it into the dish, or into basons. Garnish with horseradish and lemon.

Yield: Serves 6

3–4 pound section of salmon, or salmon steaks

Shortening to grease grill

½ cup flour

1 lemon

Prepared horseradish

Equipment: Paper towels, charcoal or gas grill (optional), fish cage for grill (optional), broiler pan, stoneware dish, hardwood chips (optional), pancake turner

1. Before cooking, wash fish in cold water and dry with paper towels. If using charcoal grill, make a smaller fire than usual, mostly on one side, and let it burn down to coals. If using oven broiler, set up pan as far from the heating element as possible. If you grill outdoors with wood chips for added flavor, it may surprise you to know that

Amelia Simmons suggested this for grilling fish in 1796: "[M]ake a smoke with small chips while broiling."

2. Spread out flour on a plate or in a paper bag, and mix with salt and pepper. Dredge fish in flour.

3. Grease grill or cage with shortening. (Early American recipes call for rubbing the gridiron with a piece of suet.) Set fish in cage (if using) or "flesh side down" (if using split or filleted fish) on the grill or skin-side down in a broiler pan.

4. Grill or broil inch-thick salmon steaks or fillets about 4 minutes before turning. Try to keep them quite far from the coals. With larger pieces, start at about 5 minutes per inch.

5. Turn fish by sliding onto the stoneware plate. Turn over on the plate, and slide back onto the grill or broiler pan.

6. Cook steaks or fillets about 3 more minutes, larger pieces another 5 minutes per inch. Early American cooks considered fish done when it flaked down to the bone at the thickest part. (Some people now consider this overdone.) A large fish will cook a little more after removed from heat.

7. Remove fish from grill back onto plate. A sauce of drawn butter (see **To Melt Butter**, Chapter 8) or **Common Egg Sauce** (see below) would be poured on.

8. Slice lemons and spoon up horseradish for garnishes. On the Colonial table, they would have been put in small dishes and arranged symmetrically in a line, or at 4 corners.

Serve as early Americans did, by placing the fish platter centered on the table at one end. The host or hostess would carve the main dish and serve to each diner.

COMMON EGG SAUCE (1852)

Egg sauce remained the typical New England sauce for salmon well into the twentieth century. This recipe is from *Mrs. Hale's New Cook Book*, by Sarah Josepha Hale. Her "Very Good Egg Sauce" has a little more butter and two extra egg yolks.

Yield: Serves 6

2 medium eggs
½ cup (1 stick) salted butter

Equipment: Small tureen or large gravy boat

1. Boil eggs 15 minutes, then cool in cold water.

2. "Break the shells by rolling them on the table, take them off and, separate the whites from the yolks, and divide all of the latter into quarter-inch dice."

3. Mince the whites "tolerably small."

4. Rinse out gravy boat in hot tap water to warm it, and dry off with a paper towel.

5. Mix egg whites and yolks in the gravy boat.

6. Pour hot butter over the eggs and stir.
Serve immediately.

DELIGHTFUL CAKES (ABOUT 1830)

This recipe for cookies topped with meringue and a bit of candied fruit or jam became known as "Marguerites," because the resulting cookies looked a little like daisies. In the mid-twentieth century, marguerites were being made with marshmallows (which are a sort of meringue), and thus may have been an ancestor of **S'mores**.

The recipe occurs toward the end of a manuscript cookbook belonging to the

Ohio State Historical Society and acquired with a group of Quaker manuscripts from Selma, Ohio. A transcription was published in *Mississippi Valley Historical Review* in 1948. The author, who may have had the initials F.B.E. or H.B.B., had probably moved to Ohio from Virginia, as the book begins with about twenty recipes similar to recipes in *The Virginia Housewife*, by Martha Randolph, first published in 1824. She then copied almost twenty recipes exactly from the Randolph book, among some others. In the middle of this part of the manuscript she wrote down a non-Randolph recipe with a date of February 1828. However, the last twenty-five recipes in the book show influences of the Ohio settlers, a "Yankee" gingerbread, a sweetened custard cheese that may derive from Pennsylvania Dutch settlers, and this Virginia-style recipe for "small cakes." I have added some details from an 1847 recipe for Marguerites in *The Southern Gardener and Receipt Book*.

> To one and half lbs of Flour add one lb of Sugar one lb of butter six Eggs leaving out four whites Spice to your taste Mace or Nutmeg Roll these cakes out thin put in the oven and bake nearly done—then take them out and lay them on a dish to cool—Whip the four whites to a froth and make them thick with powdered sugar, adding a few drops of Essence of lemon put Sweetmeats of stiff Jelly on the top of each Cake and with a spoon fill the Icing up high on the Cakes return them to the oven and bake them of a light brown.

Yield: 50–60 cookies

4½ cups sifted white flour, plus more to flour board

1 cup whole wheat flour

6 tablespoons wheat germ

4 cups sugar

6 medium eggs or 4 extra large eggs

1 pound butter

1 tablespoon nutmeg or mace

¼ teaspoon lemon extract

4 cups confectioner's sugar

Quart jar strawberry jam or currant jelly

Equipment: Pastry blender or large fork, rolling pin and wood board, 2 or more baking sheets, wire racks, wire whip or hand beater, spatulas

1. An hour before beginning, remove butter from refrigerator to soften.
2. Separate eggs by pouring from shell to shell over a cup. Put the first 4 whites in a medium bowl, and the first 4 yolks into a small bowl. Crack the last 2 eggs into the cup, and add to the yolks. (If using extra large eggs, separate the first 3, and use the 4th with the yolks.)
3. Beat egg yolks until light and creamy.
4. Measure out the flour, whole wheat flour, wheat germ, and spice, and sift together.
5. Cream butter and sugar together with pastry blender or large fork.
6. Combine butter mixture and egg yolks in a large bowl with a wooden spoon.
7. Stir in flour mixture until you have a lump of dough.
8. Use remaining flour mixture (or just flour) to flour board and rolling pin.
9. Turn dough out onto board, and work a little until smooth. Roll out ½-inch thick and cut rounds with a drinking glass or biscuit cutter.
10. Flour baking sheets, and arrange biscuits so as not to touch.
11. Preheat oven to 425 degrees.

12. When you have covered both baking sheets, bake biscuits 5 minutes. Combine scraps and re-roll until all the dough is used up. You may need to bake a second batch.

13. Cool half-baked cookies on wire racks.

14. Beat egg whites with a wire whip or hand mixer until they form soft peaks.

15. Add lemon extract and whip in enough sugar to form a stiff but spreadable icing.

16. Put a lump of jam or jelly at the center of each cookie, and spoon a pile of icing over that. (It will flatten out in the baking.)

17. Turn the oven down to 300 degrees and bake until icing is browned at the edges.

Serve as dessert, or with ice cream as part of the dinner of a wealthy family.

ELIZA COOKEES (1849)

This recipe is from a collection of recipes dated from 1829 to 1849 and probably made by Anna Moore Hubbell (1790–1861) of Bennington, Vermont. Mrs. Hubbell's husband was born in upstate New York, and the word "cookie" came into American use from the Dutch language. The first printed recipe for cookies is quite similar, although not so rich, and was published by Amelia Simmons in the 1796 *American Cookery*. This manuscript recipe shows that Simmons's book was read and used, or perhaps reinforces the theory that Simmons lived near Albany, where the second and much-corrected version of her book was published. We know that Mrs. Hubbell made these cookies in the spring, because she dated the recipe. Since she gives no method, I have taken the directions from Simmons.

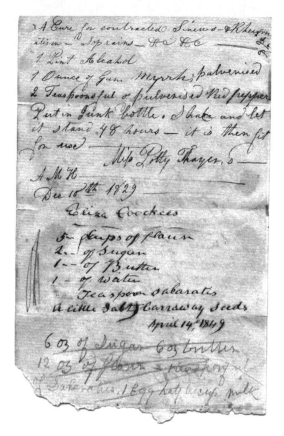

Figure 3 Manuscript of recipe for "Eliza Cookees." *Source: Hubbell manuscript, author's collection.*

5 cups of flour

2 [cups] of Sugar

1 [cup] of Butter

1 [cup] of Water

Teaspoon salaratis [potassium bicarbonate]

a little Salt Carraway Seeds

April 14, 1849

Yield: 50–60 cookies

5 cups flour

2 cups sugar

1 cup butter (2 sticks), plus some to grease baking sheets

1 teaspoon baking soda

1 tablespoon whole milk

2 tablespoons coriander

Equipment: Pastry blender or food processor, small saucepan, 2 baking sheets, wood board and rolling pin, cookie cutters (optional), cookie jar

1. Remove butter from refrigerator 1 hour before using to soften. Grease baking sheets.

2. In a small saucepan, mix sugar with a cup of water and bring to a boil, stirring to dissolve sugar.

3. When syrup is cool, dissolve 1 teaspoon salt and baking soda in a little milk, and add to syrup.

4. Measure flour into a large mixing and bowl and stir in the coriander.

5. If using food processor, cut the butter into small cubes and process with most of the flour until it has the consistency of cornmeal, then blend with the rest of the flour. If using pastry blender, cut the butter into the flour until it is evenly distributed. (Mrs. Hubbell may have "rubbed" the butter into the flour with her hands.)

6. Work syrup into the butter-flour mixture to make a stiff, or even a little crumbly, dough.

7. At this point, Simmons writes, "Make rolls half an inch thick and cut to the shape you please." This probably means to roll out the dough on a board ½-inch thick, and then cut into shapes such as rounds, hearts, or diamonds. If your dough doesn't roll well, thin with a little more water, or add a little flour. Gather scraps of dough and re-roll to make as many cookies as possible.

8. Bake 25 minutes in a 325-degree oven.

9. Leave in cookie jar overnight to soften.

Serve as a snack for up to three weeks.

7

EARLY AMERICAN MEALS— SUMMER (1800s–1856)

Summer in Early America brought a succession of minor harvests, along with running out of some staples that would not be available again until fall. A number of summer dishes from Early American tables depended on wild fish and game that are now extinct or endangered. Passenger pigeons, already in decline, were killed in tremendous numbers when they roosted. Sea and land turtles were important feast dishes. Striped bass and bluefish, now protected species, were collected in large coastal runs, and bison were killed as needed for overland travel.

Early American summer food was less monotonous but somewhat less reliable than at other times of the year. Food storage improved radically over the course of the Early American period, as icehouse technology and improved refrigeration gave some city dwellers year-round refrigeration. A growing network of railroads and canals also made some crops available over longer seasons, although freshness suffered. Wheat flour from what are now the Midwestern states became cheaper and more widely available. In hard years, farmers on the frontiers ran out of cornmeal and money in the summer, and had to borrow or eat game and vegetables until fall.

One food strongly associated with summer was chicken. The spring-born chickens were still tender enough for frying or relatively quick stewing. The salt pork and salt beef were apt to run out. This was high season for dairy products and eggs, however, so we see a number of rich desserts associated with summer occasions, such as the Fourth of July.

In the northern states, fish runs in the rivers continued into early summer. Salmon, already declining in some of the large rivers, were the New England favorite for the Fourth. Terrapin stew was the celebratory meal in the middle and southern states. Shellfishing and freshwater fishing ran down in the summer, although ocean fishing was easier and safer. Raspberries and blueberries were the first summer fruit, along with currants, gooseberries, a few cherries, and then peaches and plums.

Fresh peas and lettuce were welcome arrivals, with green beans in July. There was plenty of hard work in the summer, improving farmland and beginning to store butter, preserves, and beans for the winter.

This chapter includes some chicken dishes, some fancy desserts, and some Early American bread that would have been on the table at most meals. Although summer patterns varied somewhat with the long days, Early Americans could eat most foods at any meal. Breakfasts were huge and featured a lot of meat and hot breads. The big meal of the day was eaten in the middle of the afternoon, and many people ate about the same foods for supper as they did for breakfast. Sunday dinner was the best meal of the week, and Sunday night supper was often a hash or reheated leftovers. Monday was washday, with the kitchen full of huge pots of boiling clothes, and a stew or soup on a corner of the fire. If the family had an oven, baking day was often Friday or Saturday. Because the wood-fired oven was hard to manage, there was a lot of preparation of breads and cookies for the hottest oven at the beginning, with pies, cakes, and perhaps a casserole or bean pot as the heat wound down.

CHICKEN PYE (1800S)

This recipe is from a manuscript of the Tucker family of East Virginia begun around 1800, now at the College of William and Mary, and published in *Hearthside Cooking* by Nancy Carter Crump, in 1986. This recipe is very unusual in giving detailed directions for baking a pie in a Dutch oven. The lack of brick ovens in private homes in the southern states during the Colonial and Early American periods led to a lot of Dutch oven baking, and also to the invention of the chicken pot pie, in which top and side crusts could be cooked directly in the iron pot. The punctuation and capitalization suggest to me that this recipe was written much later than 1800, but by an older person. We know this is a summer recipe because there are specific directions for how to make the crust in the summer, and because it calls for small chickens, which would have been born in the spring and would still be tender (not requiring long stewing before going into the pie) by summer.

One immediate difficulty with this recipe is that either chickens were a lot smaller in the early 1800s, or pie dishes were a lot bigger. In fact, both things were the case. I have specified Rock Cornish game hens, because some "spring chickens" were that size in the 1800s, and because Early American diners did not mind bony pieces in their chicken pie or the game-bird pies they had in the fall. Although this recipe doesn't specify the pie crust recipe, it implies a butter-rich puff pastry, which was typical for the period. This is very hard to make, but you can sometimes buy frozen puff pastry in the supermarket, and roll it out. If not, use the food-processor recipe here. If you want to make this in the fireplace, you need a camper-style Dutch oven with a rimmed lid to hold hot coals on top.

Put your paste in the dish (in the winter make it with full weight of Butter, and in the summer with as much Butter as the flour will take in) Lay in two large or three small Chickens cut up strew between the Layers and at Top a double handful of bits of lean Bacon boiled or raw (if boiled your pie will require less salt—Lay at top several lumps of Butter about ¼ pound strew over a heaped Table spoonful of salt and an even one of fine pepper *black*, Fill last of all with cold water—Put into a dutch oven first laying in the bottom a little warm ashes and let it bake gradually with the top of very moderate heat and put coals under from time to time when nearly done increase the fire on the top to brown the paste—It will take near two hours baking.

Yield: Serves 12

3 Rock Cornish game hens
½ cup cubed slab bacon
¼ pound butter (1 stick)

1 tablespoon black pepper

Frozen puff pastry for 3 or 4 pies, or:

$2\frac{1}{2}$ cups flour

$\frac{1}{2}$ cup whole wheat flour

$\frac{3}{4}$ pound unsalted butter (3 sticks)

Equipment: Ovenproof deep-dish pie dish or casserole, cast-iron Dutch oven larger than the pie dish or casserole and 3 small stones or fire bricks (optional), fireplace tools (optional), food processor (optional), breadboard and rolling pin, parchment paper

1. If using frozen puff pastry, follow package directions to line casserole or deep dish. If using fireplace method, have a large fire burning down to hot coals.

2. Cut slab bacon into small pieces to make up $\frac{1}{2}$ cup.

3. If using food-processor pastry, put 2 ice cubes in a cup measure and fill with cold water. Cut cold butter into small dice. Pulse flour with 1 teaspoon salt. Add butter and process until the mixture looks like kernels of corn. Run the processor, pouring in ice water until the dough forms a ball. Flour the board and your hands and work the pastry until it sticks together well. Divide in 2 and put half of the pastry in the refrigerator. Flour board again and flour rolling pin. Roll out pastry from center to form a pie crust. Lift crust to line casserole or deep dish. Cut off the ends of the pastry $\frac{1}{2}$-inch past the edges of the dish. Use the extra pieces to patch any holes or weak spots.

4. Cut the stick of butter into small pieces. If using fireplace method, preheat top and bottom of Dutch oven. If not, preheat oven to 425 degrees.

5. Cut the game hens into leg and breast quarters.

6. Put a layer of hen pieces into the casserole or deep dish, topped with half the bacon.

7. Put the rest of the hen pieces into the dish, topped with the rest of the bacon.

8. Scatter the pieces of butter on top of that.

9. Sprinkle on the pepper and 1 tablespoon salt, if you have used unsalted butter.

10. Wash your hands well after handling raw chicken.

11. Roll out the rest of the frozen puff pastry, or the other half of the food processor pie pastry.

12. Pour a little water into the dish so you can see it, but it shouldn't cover the hens completely.

13. Put on the top crust, and trim the edges to match the bottom crust. Crimp edges together, and roll them into the pie to make a seal. Cut slits in the top of the pie to let steam escape.

14. If using fireplace method, arrange Dutch oven on 3 small stones or firebricks, over a few hot coals. Shovel cold or warm (but not smoking) ashes into the bottom of the Dutch oven to make an insulating cushion for the pie dish. Place the pie dish in the Dutch oven, and cover with the lid. Use fireplace tongs to set about as many hot coals on top of the oven as are underneath. Bake 2 hours, adding more hot coals under the oven, and a few more on top from time to time.

15. Bake in stove oven 15 minutes, then reduce heat to 325 degrees and bake another hour and 45 minutes. If top of pie is getting too brown, cover with buttered parchment paper.

16. If baking in Dutch oven, add many more hot coals in the final 15 minutes.

(If your fireplace isn't big enough for a separate fire to generate more hot coals, you may have to finish the pie in the stove oven.)

Serve as part of the second course of an enormous Virginia mid-afternoon dinner. I hope I'm on that side of the table!

To Make a Cooling Cinnamon Water (1809)

Most summer drinks were somewhat alcoholic, with families using up the last of the hard cider, and brewing weak ale as necessary. However, this kind of slightly sweetened refresher would have been used in the fields by temperate families, as well as medicinally for fevers. With a pinch of salt, it would resemble a modern sports drink. The recipe was first published in *Valuable Secrets in Arts, Trades, & c.*, by Evert Duyckinck of New York, and reprinted in *The Backcountry Housewife* by Kay Moss and Kathryn Hoffman(1985). We know that Duyckinck considered this a summer drink from his recipe for raspberry, strawberry, cherry or other such waters, which are to be cooled in a pail of ice and make "a fine cooling draught in summer."

> "Boil one quart of water. . . . Take it off, and put in two or three cloves, and about half an ounce of whole cinnamon. . . . When the water is cold put half a pint of it in two quarts of water with sugar to your palate, a quarter of a pound is the proper quantity."

Yield: Serves 4 hardworking farmhands; whole recipe makes 4 pails or 36 8-ounce cups

2–3 cloves

4 3-inch cinnamon sticks

2 cups sugar or 2¼ cups light brown sugar

Equipment: Pail and dipper, soup pot, measuring cups

1. Bring a quart of water to a boil. Add the cinnamon and cloves, and remove from heat. Cover and let cool. It will look like weak tea.
2. To make up a pail for one farmer or hand, take a cup of the essence, and add 2 quarts of cold water. Dissolve ½ cup of sugar or ½ cup plus a tablespoon of brown sugar in the mixture.
3. To make the entire recipe, remove the spices, and add 2 gallons of water and 2 cups of sugar (or 2¼ cups of brown sugar).

Serve from a wooden pail with a tin dipper.

Waffles (1851)

Waffles were introduced by Dutch colonists of New York and New Jersey, although old English "Wafers" are closely related. This recipe is from the *Farmer's Almanac and Housekeeper's Receipt Book*, published by John Simon of Philadelphia, as reprinted in the *1970 America and Her Almanacs*, by Robb Sagendorph.

> Milk, 1 quart; eggs, 5; flour, 1¼ pound; butter ½ pound; yeast, 1 spoonful. When baked, sift sugar and powdered cassia [cinnamon] on them.

NOTE: RECIPE TAKES TWO DAYS.

Yield: 12 large waffles

1 quart whole milk or half-and-half

5 small eggs or 4 medium or large eggs

4 cups flour

½ pound salted butter (two sticks), plus some to grease waffle iron

¼ cup **Potato Yeast** (below), or 2 teaspoons dry yeast

½ cup sugar

2 teaspoons cinnamon

Equipment: Waffle iron, whisk, clean kitchen towel, large mixing bowl, pastry brush

1. If using dry yeast, dissolve in a little water with a pinch of sugar.
2. Melt butter over low heat.
3. Warm milk to lukewarm in a saucepan or microwave oven.
4. Mix milk, yeast, butter, and flour to make a medium batter.
5. Cover batter with a clean kitchen towel and leave overnight (or all day) in a warm place to bubble and rise.
6. In the morning, or 6–8 hours later, beat eggs until creamy and light.
7. Combine eggs and batter, but do not stir too much.
8. Heat waffle iron and brush with butter.
9. Spoon in waffle mixture, but not too much since it spreads when the waffle iron is closed.
10. Waffles are done when they are puffed up, stop steaming, and come easily off the irons.
11. Mix cinnamon and sugar thoroughly.

*Serve with cinnamon sugar, or maple syrup, or **Stewed Golden Pippins**—for breakfast or dessert.*

POTATO YEAST (1854)

City dwellers could obtain a little active yeast from a brewer or baker. Farm wives had to keep up a sourdough starter. Because it was not yet understood that yeast was a microorganism, the starter itself was called yeast. Most recipes used hops as a preservative, but Catherine Beecher's *Domestic Receipt Book* spread the word about potato-based starter:

> By those who use potato yeast, it is regarded as much the best, as it raises bread quicker than common home-brewed yeast, and, best of all, it never imparts the sharp, disagreeable yeast taste to bread or cake, often given by hop yeast.
>
> Mash half a dozen peeled boiled potatoes, and mix in a handful of wheat flour, and two teaspoonfuls of salt, and after putting it through a colander, add hot water till it is a batter. When blood warm, put in half a teacup of distillery yeast, or twice as much potato, or other home-brewed. When raised, keep it corked tight, and make it new very often in hot weather. If made with hop water, it will keep much longer.

Yield: Enough for 8–10 loaves of bread

6 medium potatoes

¼ cup flour

1 teaspoon dry yeast

Equipment: Potato masher; potato ricer, colander, or food mill; instant-read thermometer (optional), clean kitchen towel

1. Peel potatoes. Dissolve dry yeast in a little water, and sprinkle on a pinch of sugar.
2. Put potatoes in a pot with water to cover, and bring to a boil.
3. Cook until a fork meets no resistance, about 20 minutes.
4. Drain potatoes and mash.
5. Push mashed potatoes through a colander with a wooden spoon, or use a potato ricer or food mill.
6. Mix in the flour, and dilute with cold water to make a batter.

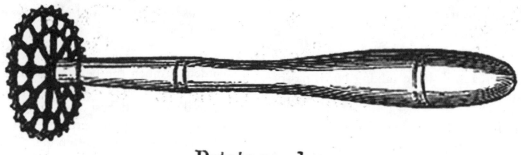

Potato-masher.

Figure 4 A potato masher. *Source: Miss Parloa's Kitchen Companion, 1887.*

7. Let cool to skin temperature (about 90 degrees).

8. When yeast is covered with a foam of bubbles, stir into the batter.

9. Cover with a clean kitchen towel and leave out overnight, or until bubbly and smelling strongly of yeast.

10. You can transfer it to a jar in the refrigerator for quite a long time. When you want to use it, stir it up and take some out to warm. Mix in a little more flour to "feed" it. To start a new batch, use ¾ cup of the old batch.

WHEAT BREAD OF POTATO YEAST (1854)

According to Miss Beecher, "This made like bread with home brewed-yeast, except that you may put in almost any quantity of the potato yeast without injury. . . . The only objection to it is, that in summer it must be made often, as it will not keep sweet long. But it is very easily renewed." On the other hand, "In winter, it is best to put the bread in sponge over night, when it must be kept warm all night. In summer it can be put in sponge early in the morning, for if made over night, it would become sour." Miss Beecher's basic bread recipe required thirty-two cups of flour, so I have reduced it

to ⅛ size. You can also make it in two small loaf pans, which bake about ten minutes faster. Like most American breads, it was made with milk instead of water. This enrichment added to the health of early American farm families, and also led to the softer, moister bread we still prefer. If you want to test Miss Beecher's proposition above, substitute **Potato Yeast** for the milk. I've used food historian Karen Hess's formula for Early American flour because it makes wonderful bread.

Yield: 1 large loaf

3 cups flour plus more for kneading
¾ cup whole wheat flour
¼ cup wheat germ
1 teaspoon dry yeast or ¼ cup **Potato Yeast**
1½ cups whole milk
Butter to grease pan

Equipment: Large loaf pan, breadboard, large mixing bowl, clean kitchen towel

1. If using powdered yeast, dissolve in a little water with a pinch of sugar. Wait until yeast has a foam of bubbles on top before proceeding.

2. Mix flour, wheat germ, and whole wheat flour in a large mixing bowl.

3. Make a well in the mixing bowl, and put in the yeast and $\frac{1}{4}$ cup lukewarm water (for potato yeast) or $\frac{1}{2}$ cup lukewarm water (for powdered yeast).

4. Stir in enough flour to make a "thick batter." You will have a pool of batter surrounded by flour.

5. "Then scatter a handful of flour over this batter, lay a warm cloth over the whole, and set it in a warm place. This is called sponge."

6. "When the sponge is risen so as to make cracks in the flour over it (which will be in from three to five hours)," heat the milk to lukewarm in a saucepan or microwave oven. Sprinkle 2 teaspoons salt over the sponge, and put in a cup of the milk. Stir the milk into the sponge, then work in all the flour to make a firm dough. Because modern flour is much drier than Miss Beecher's, you will probably need the other half cup of milk, or even a little more.

7. Flour the board and your hands (removing any rings).

8. "Knead the whole thoroughly for as much as half an hour, then form it into a round mass, scatter a little flour over it, cover it, and set it to rise in a warm place." Because we are making $\frac{1}{8}$ the recipe, it won't take as long to knead the dough into a smooth, elastic mass that isn't sticky.

9. Grease loaf pan.

10. When bread has doubled in bulk, "punch down" to get rid of the large bubbles, and knead a few times to smooth it out.

11. Form back into a loaf shape and place in the pan, covered, to rise again until doubled in bulk.

12. Preheat oven to 425 degrees. (Miss Beecher's readers had to build a fire in the oven, sweep out the embers, and time the bread rising to have it ready when the oven was ready! If the oven wasn't ready in time, they would punch down the bread again and set it to rise, which you can do if your bread rises too much and overflows.)

13. Bake 15 minutes, and reduce heat to 375 degrees for another 15 minutes.

14. Reduce heat to 325 degrees for another 15–20 minutes. Bread is done when it sounds hollow when tapped on the bottom. For more crust, you can take it out of the pan for the last 15–20 minutes, and bake it on its side. Miss Beecher's readers did not want too much crust.

CREAM TARTAR BREAD (1846)

If your yeast died for any reason, you had several choices. You could get some from a neighbor. You could start some from the bottom of the family ale or cider keg. You could make **Salt Rising Bread**. Or, increasingly, you could use chemical leavens. These quick and handy powders had been developed in Europe, but were more widely available in Colonial America because pearlash (potassium carbonate) was a major export industry. Farmers burned thousands and thousands of acres of virgin forest to clear fields and sold the ashes to factories that refined pearlash and shipped it to Europe for industrial use. We imagine early America as heavily forested, but in fact there were fewer trees in 1800 in most of the Eastern States than there are today. Pearlash didn't lighten cakes much, and it left a metallic aftertaste that was barely tolerable in gingerbread. Saleratus (potassium bicarbonate) was better, but both were replaced by baking soda (sometimes sold as saleratus) before the Civil War. Even so, the new baking powders worked better when the aftertaste could be disguised by sugar. After the Civil War, baking powder cakes became more and more popular as they became sweeter and sweeter.

This early recipe uses the baking powder mixture of saleratus and acidic cream of tartar to make plain bread. This kind of bread wasn't ever very popular, even though you could assemble it when the oven was already hot. It may have appealed to temperance activists who knew that yeast made a little alcohol as it worked in bread dough. The recipe is from *The Family Companion; Containing Many Hundred Rare and Useful Receipts On Every Branch of Domestic Economy*, by J.R. Wells, M.D., printed in Boston "for the author" in 1846.

One quart of flour two tea-spoonfuls of cream tartar one of saleratus, two and a half cups of milk; bake 20 minutes.

Yield: 14–16 slices

4 cups flour

2 teaspoons cream of tartar

1 teaspoon baking soda

2½ cups milk or half-and-half

Butter to grease bread pans

Equipment: Baking sheet or 2 small bread pans

1. Preheat oven to 450 degrees.
2. Stir dry ingredients thoroughly in a large mixing bowl.
3. Butter bread pans or baking sheet.
4. Add milk to make a firm dough.
5. Flour board and your hands and knead quickly, perhaps 20 times.
6. Divide dough and form into loaves.
7. If using bread pans, put each loaf into a bread pan and cut a shallow slash on the top. If not using bread pans, form flatter loaves, and arrange on baking sheets.
8. Bake 15 minutes, and reduce heat to 375 degrees.
9. Bake free-form loaves another 5–10 minutes and check for doneness by tapping the bottom of a loaf. If they're not done, take off baking sheet and finish on the oven grates, upside down. If using bread pans, bake another 10–15 minutes and check. If they aren't done, you can also turn them out of the pans and finish on the grates.

Serve with butter and jam.

CHICKEN DRESSED AS TERRAPINS (1856)

Large land and sea turtles were the summer feasting dishes of Early American cities. Philadelphia caterers, many of them African American, were especially renowned for their turtle feasts, and leading families competed to serve large parties for the Fourth of July. It took several days to get everything down to a rich stew. Terrapin was already expensive and difficult enough that Early American cookbooks had substitutes, usually involving a calf's head. Finally the Widdifield family, prominent caterers, suggested a chicken version, in *Widdifield's New Cookbook*. The wine was an important flavoring, but some Maryland gourmets always kept it out of real terrapin, so I have made it optional.

Boil a fine, large, tender chicken; when done, and while yet warm, cut it from the bones into small pieces, as for chicken salad; put it into a stew-pan with one gill of boiling water; then stir together, until perfectly smooth, one quarter of a pound of butter, one teaspoonful of flour, and the yolk of one egg; which add to the chicken, half at a time, stirring all well together; then season with salt and pepper. After letting it simmer about ten minutes, add half a gill of Madeira wine, and send to table hot.

This is very nice, and much liked by those who are not fond of terrapins.

Yield: Serves 6–8

1 roaster chicken or capon
¼ pound butter (1 stick)
1 teaspoon flour
1 medium egg
¼ cup Madeira [or sherry] (optional)

Equipment: Large soup pot, 2 saucepans, serving dish with metal cover (optional)

1. Wash off chicken, remove fat, and place in soup pot.
2. Add water to cover and remove chicken. Bring water to a boil.
3. When water is boiling, put chicken in pot, and add 1 teaspoon salt.
4. Reduce heat to a simmer and cook until tender, but not falling off the bone, 2–3 hours.
5. Remove chicken from broth and let cool. (Save broth for a soup.)
6. When chicken is cool, remove skin and cut meat off the bones. Cut meat into bite-sized pieces.
7. Bring half a cup of water to a boil in a large saucepan.
8. Add the chicken and reduce heat to a simmer.
9. In a smaller saucepan, melt the butter over low heat, and stir in the flour.
10. Separate the egg by pouring between the shells.
11. Reserve the egg white for another use. Remove the butter mixture from the fire and let cool.
12. Beat the egg yolk into the melted butter.
13. Beat half of the butter mixture into the simmering chicken, then the other half.

14. Taste and add salt if needed. Grind on fresh pepper or sprinkle white pepper.
15. Simmer another 10 minutes, then add wine if using.

To serve like terrapins, bring to the table in a tureen or deep dish with a metal cover. Terrapins were sometimes garnished with slices of hard-boiled egg.

ANOTHER WAY OF DRESSING TOMATOES AT TABLE (1852)

The food historian Andrew Smith has written three books to refute the myth that Early Americans thought tomatoes were poisonous. They were in fact grown in the Carolinas in the late 1680s, and there are Colonial-era recipes for tomato soup, ketchup, and various cooked dishes. Another myth is that Early Americans didn't eat salad. But salads have been part of English and Anglo-American food all along. Only for a few decades at the end of the nineteenth century did anyone think that raw vegetables were bad for you. The tomatoes are slightly cooked in this early tomato salad, in order to skin them, as described in the other three tomato recipes, also in *Home Cookery*, by Mrs. J. Chadwick.

Scald and slice them, sprinkle over salt, pepper, and mustard. Cover with vinegar.

Yield: Serves 6

6 ripe tomatoes
½ teaspoon powdered mustard
⅓ cup vinegar

Equipment: Soup pot, large platter

1. Bring ⅓ pot of water to a boil in the soup pot.
2. Add the tomatoes for 1 minute, then wash under cold running water.

3. Cut out the stem end of each tomato and peel off the skins. If any parts stick, cut them away with a sharp paring knife.

4. Slice tomatoes across the equator and arrange on a large platter.

5. Sprinkle on salt, fresh-ground pepper, and the mustard powder.

6. Measure the vinegar and add enough cold water to make ½ cup.

7. Pour the vinegar over the tomatoes, and let rest or chill for a few minutes—no longer or the tomatoes will get mushy.

Serve with bread and butter.

RASPBERRY FOOL (1835)

This is a rather simplified fruit fool, with the modern touch of whipped cream, from the kitchen recipe book of Mrs. T. Loockerman, as reprinted (and probably adapted) in *Maryland's Way*, by Mrs. Lewis R. Andrews and Mrs. J. Reaney Kelly, published in 1963 by the Hammond-Harwood House Association of Annapolis, Maryland. The fools in *The Art of Domestic Cookery Made Plain and Easy*, by Hannah Glasse, the most popular eighteenth-century English cookbook in the American Colonies (Martha Washington owned the 1763 London edition), were thickened with unwhipped cream, or a simple custard, but flavored with rosewater or orange flower water.

Yield: Serves 6

2 cups raspberries

½ cup sugar

½ pint heavy cream

Equipment: Sieve or food mill, whisk or handheld electric beater, metal mixing bowl

1. Clean raspberries, removing any bits of stem or immature berries.

2. Add sugar to fruit in a saucepan and let stand to start juices flowing.

3. Mash berries slightly with a spoon, and heat up mixture over low heat.

4. Bring to a boil, and boil a few minutes to soften all berries. (Black raspberries take longer than red raspberries.)

5. Pass the fruit through a sieve by mashing with a wooden spoon, or use a food mill.

6. Chill raspberry mixture.

7. Whip or beat cream until it forms soft peaks. (Early Americans sometimes did this with a spoon or a knife!)

8. Combine fruit and whipped cream, and chill 2 hours.

"Serve with wafers or sweet biscuits."

CUSTARDS & ICES (1830s–1840s)

These two recipes come from a very detailed recipe manuscript belonging to Mary Channing Eustis (1818–1891) and now at the Massachusetts Historical Society in Boston. From glued-in clippings, it appears that the book was underway in the late 1830s. The first recipe is in the old-fashioned handwriting (for the 1830s) of an older person, while the second reads as though copied from an older source. I have worked out the first recipe, for a lemon flavor, with the techniques of the second. Either makes an already old-fashioned ice cream, but clearly based on English creams such as **To Make Chocolate Cream.**

Although much is made of Thomas Jefferson's interest in French ice cream, it is clear that ice cream was served by wealthy American Colonials as early as the 1730s. What changed in the early nineteenth century was the availability of lake ice in the summertime, mined mechanically and stored in sawdust by the Boston-based ice companies of Frederic Tudor and Nathaniel Wyeth. They revolutionized production, locked up the rights to New England lakes and ponds, and merchandised the ice all over the world with fast clipper ships. Mrs. Eustis also had some kind of special ice cream freezer, but from the directions we gather that it did not have paddles to keep the ice cream from icing up on the sides.

Custards & Ices

To make a Custard for an Ice Creams 1 qt of milk ½ pt cream 6 eggs half the whites 3 lemons the peel of 2 added when cold.

Ice creams

To a quart of cream add five eggs—½ pound fine sugar Boil yr cream with Vanilla, Season to yr taste—Stir all the time the Vanilla is in that it may not burn add your eggs & sugar beaten together, then let it simmer together stirring one way all the time. When cool, put it into the freezer & stir round it with ice & shake it at least half an hour, not leaving it after having commenced—during the freezing it should be opened & beaten up by a strong hand with a large scoop—It is better to put it into a dry [?] mould [?] when nearly frozen Sink [?] in the ice, if covered with a double flannel where it can remain [?] two hours.

Yield: Serves 16

1 quart light cream

1 cup heavy cream

6 small eggs or four extra large eggs

½ pound sugar

3 lemons

2 bags crushed ice

1 bag rock salt

Equipment: Heavy saucepan, whisk, box grater or lemon zester, juicer, ice cream freezer, or large metal mixing bowl and a larger bowl with room for ice and the metal bowl, pudding mold (optional)

1. Grate or zest off the yellow rind of 2 lemons, and reserve.

2. Juice the lemons.

3. Mix the 2 creams, and bring to a boil over medium heat, stirring all the time.

4. Separate half the eggs and reserve the whites for another recipe.

5. Beat the yolks and whole eggs together until creamy and light, and beat in the sugar.

6. Reduce heat so that cream just simmers.

7. Beat a thin stream of hot cream into the egg yolks to warm them, then beat a thin stream of egg yolks into the hot cream.

8. Continue stirring "one way all the time" until the cream mixture thickens, then remove from heat.

9. If you have a modern ice cream freezer, add lemon peel and follow the directions to complete ice cream. If you are using early American methods, fill the larger bowl with crushed ice, and sink the metal mixing bowl into the ice. Pour in the cream mixture and whisk it until it cools and thickens. Shake the bowl to keep ice cream from sticking to the walls and insulating the rest of the mixture.

10. Add lemon peel.

11. Discard the melted water and add the second bag of crushed ice, layered with ¼ part of rock salt. Sink the basin of cream back in the large bowl, and stir until you can't stir anymore.

12. Let ice cream condition for 30 minutes, then get someone with a "strong

Whisk.

Figure 5 Egg-beater or whisk. *Source:* Miss Parloa's Kitchen Companion, *1887.*

hand" to scoop into the ice cream, break up any icy parts, and repack. If you have a pudding mold such as the oval "melon" mold, you can repack the ice cream into the mold, and sink the mold into fresh ice without salt. If not, repack into the same bowl, cover with a clean kitchen towel (or a "double flannel"), and let rest up to 2 more hours. (Or you can put it into the freezer, which Mrs. Eustis could not do.)

Serve at parties with cookies and wafers. Ice cream for the Fourth of July!

FLOATING ISLAND (1828)

Floating island was one of the most popular desserts of the eighteenth and nineteenth centuries in England, the American Colonies, and the United States. This recipe from *Seventy-Five Receipts,* the first book by Eliza Leslie, is one of the simplest, with an island of tinted meringue floating in a lake of unsweetened cream. Over the next thirty years Miss Leslie came back to the dish at least twice, eventually tinting the lake of cream green with spinach juice, supporting the island with a two-pound sponge cake or jelly cake, and mounting a cloud of whipped cream on top. Others made a custard for the lake, and floated clouds of meringue.

This is also a rather small recipe for the 1820s. Small evening dinner parties of the modern type did not develop until much later in the century, but households often had unrelated adults or houseguests to the mid-afternoon dinner where fancy desserts were the third course. Households with servants (and large henhouses and dairy barns) would be able to multiply this dish for large-scale entertaining. Miss Leslie was one of the first writers to list the ingredients before the directions, but gave up this format in her later books. The only tricky part is that egg whites are very sticky.

Six whites of eggs.

Six large table-spoonfuls of jelly.

A pint of cream.

Put the jelly and white of egg into a pan, and beat it together with a whisk, till it becomes a stiff froth, and stands alone.

Have ready the cream, in a broad shallow dish. Just before you send it to table, pile up the froth in the center of the cream.

Yield: Serves 4

5 egg whites' worth of refrigerated or powdered egg whites

1¼ cups jelly (currant preferred, or raspberry)

1 pint heavy cream

Equipment: Whisk or handheld electric beater or standing mixer, large shallow soup dish (glass or cut glass preferred)

1. Remove jelly and egg white product from refrigerator 1 hour before starting recipe. Put the serving dish in the refrigerator.

2. Measure egg whites (or add water to egg white powder according to package directions) into a round-bottomed metal pan or bowl.

3. Beat egg whites until they form soft peaks, then add jelly and beat until the mixture forms stiff peaks and is a tinted color.

4. Pour the pint of cream into the serving dish, and float the jelly-tinted egg whites in the middle.

Serve by spooning some of the cream into individual bowls, and adding some of the egg whites. Use a second spoon to get the egg whites off the first spoon.

8

EARLY AMERICAN MEALS— FALL (1803–1855)

Autumn is the easiest Early American season for us to imagine, because we have memorialized it in the holiday of Thanksgiving. Not all Early Americans celebrated Thanksgiving, which did not become a national holiday until 1863. Those who did often celebrated Thanksgiving in early or mid-December and did not celebrate Christmas, which had been questioned by Anglo-American Puritans and Quakers.

Autumn meals began with a harvest of vegetables, and some of the hardest farm labor of the year was harvesting hay and grains. The stored salt pork and grain of the previous year were gone, and this was a time of hardship in 1816—"the year without a summer." School was often delayed until after harvest time so that children could work alongside their families and hired help. In remote areas, families traded labor, so that work was almost continuous. Evenings later in the fall meant more labor traded but more fun with indoor gatherings to husk corn or pare apples for drying, good opportunities for young people to meet. With the first cold weather, beef cattle were slaughtered so the meat could be salted and stored, and so some of the large animals would not have to be fed from stored grain and hay.

Fresh meat would be eaten in the fall, with corned beef and sausages put away for winter. In some areas, families arranged to trade labor and fresh beef to extend the season. Thus four families each with one surplus ox might slaughter on successive Fridays and take home a quarter of each animal on a rotating basis.

All this work and the cool weather required hearty meals and refreshing drinks. Because there was so much fresh food in the fall, many of the dishes are more familiar today, such as roast beef, pot roast, corn on the cob (then less sweet), baked winter squash, pumpkin pie, mashed potatoes and turnips, beets, and cabbage dishes. In addition, migrating game was more available in the fall, and shellfishing increased as fin fishing declined. As the network of canals and early railroads improved transportation, oysters became a popular luxury food in the 1840s and 1850s. Apples and pears were harvested and made into cider and "perry" (pear cider) for the year.

This section does not provide full meals but a number of Early American dishes associated with Thanksgiving, the apple harvest, and fall foods. You can make them into meals with roast or boiled meats, vegetables, and lots of bread or **Hasty Pudding**.

NEW-ENGLAND PANCAKES
(1823)

These rich pancakes took full advantage of plentiful eggs and cream and might have been part of a breakfast with meat or a relatively quick dish for supper after a hard day's work. The recipe appears in the 1823 edition of *The Experienced American Housekeeper* published in New York City. Despite the name, this book is mostly taken from an English book by Maria Rundell, with some anonymous American recipes added by the publisher. Because the recipe specifies fresh [not salted] butter, we know it was not intended for the winter or early spring when all butter was heavily salted.

Yield: Serves 6

Mix a pint of cream, five spoonfuls of fine flour, seven yolks, and four whites of eggs, and a very little salt. Fry them very thin in fresh butter, and between each strew sugar and cinnamon. Send up seven or eight at once.

1 pint heavy cream

1½ cups flour (sifted)

7 small eggs (or 5 large eggs)

6 tablespoons unsalted butter

1 cup sugar

1 tablespoon cinnamon

Equipment: Whisk, skillet, pancake turner

1. Separate first 3 small eggs (or the first 2 large eggs) by pouring from shell to shell over a cup. Reserve the first 3 whites for another recipe, such as **Delightful Cakes**.

2. Beat the egg yolks and whites until light and creamy.

3. Blend cream and beaten eggs.

4. Whisk in flour and 1 teaspoon salt. (If you measured without sifting, re-move a few tablespoons of flour.) You should have a very thin batter.

5. Mix cinnamon and sugar thoroughly.

6. Melt a tablespoon of butter in a heavy skillet. Spread it around, and spoon in 4 or 5 small pancakes. They should be quite thin, like crepes. (If the pancakes are more than ¼ inch thick, thin the batter with a little water.)

7. Turn the pancakes quickly, as they cook rapidly.

8. When pancakes are done, spoon a sprinkle of cinnamon-sugar on each one, and stack another on top, again sprinkling sugar, until you have 7 or 8.

Serve with steaks or **Winter Sausage**.

MARY HUNTER'S STEWED BEEF
(1809)

The late fall slaughter of beef cattle went substantially toward the barrel of corned beef for the winter. Some organs and choice steaks were broiled on the spot, and some parts might have been chopped for **Winter Sausage** or, in the mid-Atlantic states, smoked for what is now called Lebanon Bologna. Bony parts went for soup stock, perhaps boiled down to **Portable Soup**. Relatively simple beef stews like this one must have been fairly common, but weren't often written down. This recipe is from the papers of Mary Robinson Morton (1781–1828) at the Rhode Island Historical society, as reprinted in 1975 *The Thirteen Colonies Cookbook*, by Mary Donovan, Amy Hatrak, Frances Mills, and Elizabeth Shull. This recipe is also interesting in that it calls for what today would be a fairly tender sirloin steak, to be stewed for one and one-quarter hours! I'm suggesting the cheapest cut of shoulder steak or London broil you can find.

Note also the strong flavoring. Only much later in the nineteenth century did Americans give up herbs and spices.

> Take two or three pounds of rump steaks, cut thick in square pieces as big as your hand. Put a stewpot on some hot coals with three pints of water, a bunch of sweet herbs, three or four onions chopped fine, a little allspice, a dozen cloves, a teaspoon of cayenne pepper, one of black pepper, and salt to your taste. Cover this close, and let it boil one hour very hard—then put in the beef with half a tumbler of claret or port wine, and teaspoonful of good ketchup—and boil it altogether an hour longer—thicken the gravy with butter and flour mixed together—let it boil a quarter of an hour after this last is added.

Yield: Serves 12

3 pounds shoulder steak or London Broil

1–2 sprigs thyme (or a ¼ teaspoon of powdered thyme)

2 sprigs marjoram (or a ½ teaspoon of powdered marjoram)

3–6 sprigs parsley

1 bay leaf

4 medium onions

¼ teaspoon allspice

12 whole cloves

1 teaspoon cayenne (red pepper)

½ cup red wine or port wine (optional)

1 teaspoon Worcestershire sauce or 1 tablespoon tomato ketchup

¼ cup butter (½ stick)

¼ cup flour

Equipment: Soup pot with tight cover

1. Remove butter from refrigerator.
2. Cut steaks into squares 4–5 inches on a side.
3. Halve, peel, and chop onions. (Use swim goggles to avoid tears.)
4. Tie herbs together with one of the parsley stems.
5. Bring 6 cups of water to a boil in the soup pot.
6. Add the onions, the herbs and spices, and 1 teaspoon of black pepper to the boiling water. Cover and boil for an hour.
7. After the hour, remove the bunch of herbs, the cloves, and the bay leaf. Put the beef in the pot, the wine if using, and the Worcestershire sauce or ketchup (or perhaps both, if not using wine). Add 1 teaspoon salt, cover again, and reduce heat to a simmer for another hour.
8. With a fork or your hands, work together the butter and flour into a dough like pie crust.
9. Break this dough in little bits.
10. When beef has cooked an hour, add the bits of butter and flour, and stir to thicken the soup.
11. Cook another 15 minutes, stirring frequently as the stew thickens.

Serve with bread or cornbread and a boiled vegetable at a weekday dinner or supper. Stews were not ranked with roasts or large boiled pieces of meat or fish.

TO MAKE CRANBERRY TARTS (1803)

Here's a Thanksgiving food that actually was eaten by Puritans, as recorded in Maine by John Josselyn in the 1670s: "The *Indians* and *English* use them much, boyling them with Sugar for Sauce to eat with their Meat;

and it is a delicate Sauce, especially for roasted Mutton: Some make Tarts with them, as with Goose Berries." We've kept the cranberry sauce, but forgotten the tarts. This recipe was printed in an appendix of twenty-nine American recipes to the 1803 New York edition of an English cookbook, *The Frugal Housewife*, and in 1805 was attached to another English cookbook, *The Art of Cookery Made Plain and Easy*, published in Virginia. Food historian Karen Hess has speculated that this appendix may have originally appeared in an almanac. The recipe makes four pies, which reminds us that early Americans used pies over several days between weekly bakings and ate pie at all three meals. There would have been several bakings in the days before Thanksgiving to have many pies of several kinds. I have suggested a modern amount of sugar for these tarts—1803 cooks might have used half as much. If you use the food processor method, you have to divide the dough recipe in half or thirds.

> To one pound of flour three quarters of a pound of butter, then stew your cranberry's to a jelly, putting good brown sugar in to sweeten them, strain the cranberry's and then put them in your patty pans for baking in a moderate oven for half an hour.

Yield: 4 pies or 24 4-inch tarts

3 cups sifted white flour (plus more to roll out crusts)

¾ cup whole wheat flour

4 tablespoons wheat germ

3 sticks salted butter

4 pounds cranberries

8 cups brown sugar

Equipment: Large soup pot, aluminum foil, food processor or pastry blender, dough scraper or spatula, 4 pie pans or 16 4-inch tart pans, rolling pin, and wood board

1. If not using food processor, take butter out of refrigerator ½ hour before making crusts to soften it slightly.

2. Put cranberries in large soup pot with 1 cup water and bring to a boil, covered, until skins break and berries soften a little, about 5 minutes.

3. Add sugar and stew 5 minutes longer.

4. Combine dry ingredients in large mixing bowl and stir well.

5. Fill a large glass or 2-cup measure with ice and add cold water to make ice water.

6. For food processor method, put 2 cups of the flour in work bowl. Cut half the butter into cubes, and add to work bowl. Pulse motor a few times to reduce butter to lumps the size of corn kernels. Turn on processor and pour ice water slowly down the feed tube until the dough gathers in a ball. Remove dough and repeat to make the other 2 crusts. Refrigerate dough balls until ready to roll out crusts.

7. If not using food processor, cut slightly softened butter into dry ingredients with pastry blender, large fork, or clean fingers. When lumps of butter are a little bigger than corn kernels, work into a stiff dough with ice water, starting with about ⅔ cup. Divide dough into 4 parts and refrigerate until ready to roll out dough.

8. Flour board and rolling pin. Starting with ¼ of the dough, roll from the center to all sides until it is larger than your pie pans. (If using tart shells, roll out about ⅛-inch thick.)

9. Fold circle of dough loosely in half and lift into pie pans with dough scraper or spatula. Press into edges and make a few holes in the dough with a fork. Crimp to sides of pans with fork,

and cut off excess dough. You can patch any weak spots or holes with these scraps, or gather them up and refrigerate for reuse. Skilled pie makers cut decorations out of extra dough. For tart pans, cut shapes an inch larger than the pans. Repeat until pie pans or tart shells are ready. (You can refrigerate or freeze leftover dough, or cut it into shapes and bake it on sheets with the pies, making a few cookies.)

10. Fill shells with cranberry sauce.

11. Preheat oven to 400 degrees.

12. Bake 15 minutes, and reduce heat to 350 degrees.

13. Bake 15–25 minutes more.

Serve with meat course at any meal, or as one of several pies at Thanksgiving.

Nannie Pinkney's Comical Pudding (1811)

Why comical? Perhaps because it always comes out right in the end, or perhaps in the British sense of tricky or difficult. Maybe Ms. Pinkney had a *conical* mold, which was a funny contrast to the usual round puddings. In any case, this is a basic Anglo-American steamed suet pudding of the kind usually called plum pudding, or Christmas pudding, but often eaten at Thanksgiving by Christmas-shy Quakers and Congregationalists in early American times. The suet is another product of the fall beef slaughter. The recipe is from Miss Ann Chase's kitchen book, begun in 1811, as reprinted in the 1963 *Maryland's Way*, by Mrs. Lewis R. Andrews and Mrs. J. Reaney Kelly. Nannie Pinkney was probably the wife or daughter of Senator William Pinkney, a protege of Ann Chase's father, who was then a United States Supreme Court judge.

Yield: Serves 24

2 cups flour

¾ cups whole wheat flour

¼ cup wheat germ

1 teaspoon cinnamon

½ teaspoon ginger

½ teaspoon nutmeg

½ teaspoon cloves

½ pound suet

1 cup molasses

1 cup whole milk or half-and-half

1 teaspoon baking soda

1 cup seeded raisins

Butter to grease pudding mold.

Equipment: Food processor (optional), pudding mold with tight lid, pressure cooker large enough to hold pudding mold with trivet (optional), large pot with tight lid, trivet or steamer insert for pot or pressure cooker, second large pot, oven mitts

1. Chop the suet as finely as possible, or cut into small pieces and then pulse in a food processor.

2. Grease pudding mold. Bring a large pot of water to a boil.

3. Mix flour thoroughly with the whole wheat flour, wheat germ, 1 teaspoon of salt, the baking soda, and all the spices.

4. Take out a little of the mixture to flour the raisins.

5. Mix molasses and milk.

6. Blend the suet with the flour. (You can use a large food processor for this.)

7. Mix in the molasses and milk to make a stiff batter. You may need a little more milk or flour.

8. Now stir in the raisins.

9. Fill pudding mold ½ to ⅔ full, and clamp down lid.

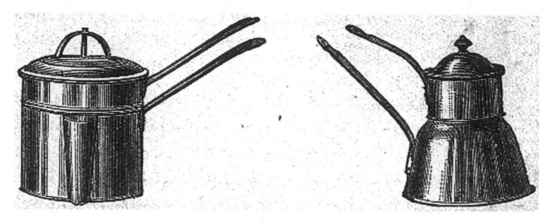

Figure 6 Two kinds of double boilers. *Source:* The Latest and Best Cookbook, *1884.*

10. Place pudding mold on trivet or steamer insert in pot or pressure cooker.

11. With large pot, add 2 inches of boiling water and cover tightly. Return to a boil and steam 3 hours, replenishing boiling water as needed with more boiling water maintained in the second pot. (With pressure cooker method, add boiling water to halfway up the sides of the pudding mold. Steam with lid on, but without pressure locked or jiggle weight in place for 30 minutes. Bring up to 15 pounds pressure for 50 minutes. Remove pot from heat and let pressure escape slowly.)

12. When pudding is done, remove mold from pot with oven mitts or tongs.

13. Release top of mold carefully so you aren't scalded by a burst of rising steam.

14. Remove top of mold and allow pudding to rest and steam to escape.

15. Unmold pudding onto a serving dish.

*Serve with drawn butter (**To Melt Butter**, below) or the sauce from **An Innocent Plum Pudding**.*

TO MELT BUTTER (1839)

Butter was the most common American sauce from early Colonial times. Thriving dairy herds had been one reason for the health and longevity and height of British colonials. And butter was an easier way to store some of the production than cheese. This very detailed recipe for drawn butter, from *The Kentucky Housewife*, by Mrs. Lettice Bryan, forms the basis for other Early American sauces such as **Common Egg Sauce** for fish, bread sauce for poultry and meats, and butters laced with lemon or vinegar-based sauces, such as the lemon butter we still use with boiled lobsters. For a warm pudding sauce, the butter might have added cream, wine, molasses, sugar, nutmeg, or lemon.

To melt or draw butter in the best manner, it should be weighed, and to each ounce allow a table-spoonful of water and a small tea-spoonful of flour. Rub the flour into the butter till it is completely saturated; then put it into a covered sauce-pan with water; set it in an [Dutch] oven of hot water, which should be placed over a bed of coals; stir it slowly and constantly till it melts; and as soon as it begins to boil, it is enough; then remove it from the fire. . . .

Melted or drawn butter is the basis of a great many delicious sauces. In repairing your sauces, if you wish to add a very thick condiment or seasoning to melted butter, such as chopped herbs, fish, &c., you had best omit half of the flour and double the quantity of water: but if it is to be seasoned with wine, &c. melt it as first directed.

Yield: 1 cup or 16 1-tablespoon servings

½ cup (1 stick) salted butter

3 teaspoons flour

Equipment: Double boiler, or nesting pots and a trivet to improvise a double boiler

1. Remove butter from refrigerator 1 hour before starting.
2. Bring hot tap water to a boil in the bottom of the double boiler or larger pot of the improvised double boiler.
3. Cream together butter and flour with a fork or your hands.
4. Place butter-flour mixture in the top of the double boiler with 4 tablespoons of cold water.
5. Stir constantly until mixture is melted.
6. Skim off any skin that forms on top.
7. When mixture is well heated through, add sauce ingredients, or serve as is.

Serve with fish, meats, vegetables, and breakfast foods.

EVE'S PUDDING (1790S–1831)

This recipe in rhyme was copied into a manuscript of the Smith family begun in 1738, now at the Massachusetts Historical Society. The rhyme seems to have been popular in England and Scotland from the 1790s, and so probably was given to this merchant family by a visitor, but is attributed to "Mrs. Smith," presumably the mother-in-law of this keeper of the book. The ultimate owner of the book was Frances Bernard Smith (1804–1888), who thus might have gotten the recipe from her mother-in-law, Hannah Carter Smith (1764–1838). Measuring the ingredients in sixes was an old memory trick, and the rhyme made the recipe even easier to remember. It makes a good baked apple pudding and was probably also baked in a crust like **Marlborough Pie**. The recipe appears in printed American cookbooks, sometimes without the rhyme, to the end of the nineteenth century. Check the packages of sliced bread to get slices about one ounce each. You can also use the pressure cooker method from **Nannie Pinkney's Comical Pudding**.

If you like a good pudding, mind what you are taught

First take six eggs when they are bought for a groat

Next take of the fruit that Eve did once cozen,

Well pared and well chopped, at least half a dozen,

Six ounces of bread, let Moll cut the crust,

And let it be crumbled as small as the dust,

Six ounces of currants from the stems you must sort,

Lest they break out your teeth and spoil all your sport,

Six ounces of sugar will not be too sweet

Some salt and some nutmeg, the whole will complete

Three hours let it boil without any flutter,

Nor is it quite finished without wine and butter.

Yield: Serves 12

6 small eggs or 4 extra large eggs

6 baking apples

5 slices white bread

1 slice whole wheat bread

1 cup currants

¾ cup sugar

2 teaspoons nutmeg

½ teaspoon salt

Butter to grease pudding mold

Equipment: Pudding mold with tight top or heat-proof bowl and aluminum foil, trivet or steamer insert, large soup pot with cover, teakettle, oven mitts or tongs

1. Grease pudding mold or heat-proof bowl.
2. Put steamer insert in pot, put in empty pudding mold or bowl, and fill with water to more than halfway up the side of the mold. Remove mold or bowl and bring water to a boil.
3. Break bread into small crumbs with 2 forks.
4. Beat eggs.
5. Peel and quarter apples, discarding cores.
6. Chop apples into small pieces.
7. Mix nutmeg and salt with sugar.
8. Stir up all ingredients.
9. Fill mold or bowl with ingredients, level the top with a spoon, and cover tightly with the lid or, in the case of a bowl, with 2 thicknesses of aluminum foil.
10. Lower mold into boiling water, and cover pot tightly. Steam 3 hours.
11. Bring a teakettle of water to a boil. Replenish large pot with boiling water as needed.
12. When pudding is done, remove mold from pot with oven mitts or tongs.
13. Release top of mold or aluminum foil carefully so you aren't scalded by a burst of rising steam.
14. Remove top of mold and allow pudding to rest and steam to escape.
15. Unmold pudding onto a serving dish.

*Serve with drawn butter (**To Melt Butter**), the sauce from **An Innocent Plum Pudding**, or sweetened heavy cream.*

HARVEST DRINK (1855)

This is the "Haymaker's Switchel," a cheap, nonalcoholic punch served to work crews cutting, drying, and baling hay. This was the some of the hardest and hottest work of harvest from the first arrival of European settlers, when they began cutting salt-marsh hay they hadn't planted. Hay was cut in clear, hot weather, so it would dry in the fields and could be stacked or baled for storage. The word "switchel" is recorded from 1800, and there are many recipes from the Colonial Revival period of the late eighteenth century, but few from Early American times. This is possibly because this informal farm drink was not made in any precise way. But it is more likely that switchel became more important as the influence of temperance increased. This recipe is from the 1855 *Practical American Cookery*, by Elizabeth Hall, rediscovered and republished in the 1995 *Saltwater Foodways*, by Sandra L. Oliver, where it stands in for a similar sailors' refreshment called Swanky. If you find a one and three-quarter-ounce jar of ginger in the spice section, that's about right, since both ginger and vinegar were not so strong 150 years ago as they are now.

Mix with five gallons of good water, half a gallon of molasses, one quart of vinegar, and two ounces of powdered ginger. This will make not only a very pleasant beverage, but one highly invigorating.

Yield: About 90 8-ounce servings, or a day's liquid for about 10 workers

2 quarts molasses
1 quart cider vinegar
2 ounces ginger

Equipment: 6-gallon soup pot or milk can, 8-ounce dipper, long wooden spoon

1. Combine molasses, ginger, and vinegar with a quart of cold tap water. Stir well to dissolve molasses and break up any lumps of ginger. (You can add another quart of water.)
2. Fill up with 4½ or 4¾ gallons cold water.
3. A later Rhode Island recipe advises, "Keep can covered with wet blanket and keep in shade if possible."

Serve with a common dipper. See if you can get the trick of pouring a mouthful without actually touching the dipper to your lips.

9

Early American Meals—
Winter (1780s–1866)

Winter is the most commonly pictured Early American season, typically with Thanksgiving or Christmas scenes. It was also the season that organized the food-related work of the other seasons. As Colonial farm families learned better methods of food storage and planning, the winter table improved, and the late-winter/early-spring "starving times" became rare.

Houses were still poorly heated, so winter food was hearty, and people ate a lot of it. Most fresh green vegetables ran out, but storage of cabbages and root vegetables lightened the heavy meals. Fresh milk and eggs became scarce, but stored butter and cheese were available. Beef cattle were mostly slaughtered in the fall (but see **Winter Sausage** in Chapter 12), but pigs were easier to keep over the winter, so fresh and salt pork joined salt beef as main courses, with game and poultry loading down the table in early winter. Fishing was hazardous in winter storm season, but stocks of oysters and clams near the shore could still be harvested and shipped inland in cold weather. Salt cod was the most common form of winter fish in areas where the English Protestant custom of fish on Saturday was still remembered.

The winter was the time for sweet desserts and puddings. Poor farmers used dried fruit and traded for cheap molasses. Winter storage of apples had improved to where some whole apples might last until early spring. In Early American times, Christmas was not yet a major celebration in New England or the Quaker parts of Pennsylvania. In those states families gathered at Thanksgiving (which was not yet a national holiday) and held open houses with sweets at New Year's. The Pennsylvania Dutch areas and the old Dutch families of New York celebrated Christmas with some foods that became part of the general culture, and the southern states generally had a week of celebration enfolding Christmas and New Year's.

An increasingly popular snack on winter evenings from the 1840s was popcorn, served initially with butter and salt or sugar, and already being stuck together with candy for popcorn balls by 1861.

Codfish Toast (1852)

The only reliable winter fish was salt cod, a durable commodity exported around the world from New England. This recipe, from *The Skillful Housewife's Book* by Mrs. L.G.

Abell, is one of surprisingly few published recipes for salt cod. Most of the rest are for codfish hash, fried codfish balls, or codfish cakes—all made from leftover codfish. This leaves the question: How did people eat the salt cod the first time? In all likelihood, they simply soaked it and simmered it and served it with melted butter alongside boiled winter vegetables such as potatoes, cabbage, onions, and beets. In 1887, *Miss Parloa's Kitchen Companion* had a special article on New England salt fish dinners, which added a garnish of fried salt pork and a sauce made from hard-boiled eggs.

Shred it in fine pieces and soak it in cold water until sufficiently fresh, then drain it well and stir into it a tablespoonful of flour, half a tea-cupful of sweet cream, and two thirds of a tea-cup of milk, and one egg, if convenient. Season it well with pepper, and let it scald slow, stirring it well. Make a nice moist toast, well-seasoned, and lay it on the platter, with the fish over it, and it is ready for the table, and is a fine dish. Made as above, without toast, is also good; with vegetables, butter may be used instead of cream.

Yield: Serves 4

1 pound salt cod

1 heaping tablespoon flour

⅓ cup heavy cream

½ cup whole milk

1 medium egg (optional)

4 tablespoons butter

4 thick slices bread

Equipment: Large platter, saucepan with cover

1. Shred or break salt cod into small pieces.
2. Soak overnight in cold water.

3. Drain fish, and put in a saucepan with the flour, cream, and milk. Turn on low heat and cover pot.
4. When pot begins to simmer, grind on plenty of pepper, reduce heat a little, and do not cover. Stir to cook evenly without boiling.
5. Toast bread in a 350-degree oven. (Mrs. Abell's readers toasted bread on long forks in front of a fire.)
6. When bread is nicely browned on both sides, butter each piece, and arrange on a large platter.
7. Beat egg, if using. (Eggs became scarce in the winter months.)
8. Stir egg into codfish mixture and cook for a minute or two to thicken.
9. Pour codfish mixture over toasts.

Serve for breakfast or Sunday night supper with baked beans. If you really hate it, mix it with mashed potatoes, form patties or balls, and fry them to make codfish cakes.

CARROT SOUP (1850S)

This is a typical winter soup for a weeknight supper, of a kind that wasn't usually written down. This one was written down apparently out of nostalgia by Rosa Ann Mason Grosvenor (1817–1872) in a handwritten collection called "My Mother's Recipes," quoted in the 1975 *A Cooking Legacy; Over 200 Recipes Inspired by Early American Cooks*, by Virginia T. Elverson and Mary Ann McLanahan. Mrs. Grosvenor did not note spices or salt and pepper. The 1975 authors reasonably suggest one quarter teaspoon mace.

To 3 Pints of strong broth, a quart of carrots sliced and stewed in butter 2 oz. till they are tender. then rub them through a sieve, add a cup of full cream and stir all together.

Yield: Serves 10

1½ quarts beef broth

2 pounds carrots

2 ounces (½ stick) salted butter

1 cup heavy cream

¼ teaspoon mace (optional)

Equipment: Vegetable peeler, food mill or large sieve, large soup pot

1. Peel and slice carrots into thin rounds.
2. Melt butter in soup pot, and add carrots, mace if using, and fresh ground pepper.
3. Cook over low heat with the pot covered so the carrots steam and stew more than fry.
4. When carrots are tender, 10–25 minutes later depending on how thick you sliced them, put them through a food mill, or push them through a colander or a large sieve.
5. Mix carrots with broth and bring to a boil.
6. Reduce heat to a simmer and stir in the cream.

Serve hot with stale bread or **Hasty Pudding**.

PORK AND PARSNIP HASH (1861)

The fresh meat of midwinter was pork. Pigs were easier to keep into the winter, but increasingly tempting as other foods and game disappeared. As with the fall beef slaughter, much of the meat was salted and/or smoked for later in the year, but a fresh roast was likely. The leftovers went into this hash with parsnips, and probably potatoes and beets in many homes. As farmers learned that parsnips allowed to freeze in the fields became even sweeter by spring, spring-dug parsnips were combined with

ham. This recipe is from *The Housekeeper's Encyclopedia* by Mrs. E.F. Haskell.

> Boil the parsnips and let them cool; to four parts of parsnip allow one of pork; make the hash into cakes fry brown. The whole should be chopped very fine. If mashed, so much the better.

Yield: Serves 4 as a main dish

2 pounds parsnips

1 cup leftover pork roast, or pork chops to make that much meat

2 ounces lard

Equipment: Vegetable peeler, frying pan, soup pot, pancake turner

1. Peel parsnips and cut into ½-inch slices.
2. Cover parsnips with cold water in a soup pot and bring to a boil.
3. Reduce heat to simmer until parsnips are tender through, about 30 minutes.
4. Cut pork into small dice. (If using pork chops, broil well done.)
5. Drain parsnips and cut into smaller pieces.
6. Mix parsnips with pork. Sprinkle on quite a lot of salt and pepper.
7. Heat up 2 tablespoons of the lard.
8. Form the pork and parsnip mixture into cakes the size of large hamburgers. You may need to mash the parsnips a little to get them to hold together.
9. Fry parsnip cakes brown on both sides over medium heat. Add more lard to the pan as needed.

Serve with **Tomato Ketchup** *for breakfast or supper.*

SNITZ AND KNEP (1866)

This recipe appeared in *Godey's Lady's Book* in 1866, according to *Civil War*

Recipes: Receipts from Godey's Lady's Book, edited by Lily May Spaulding and John Spaulding. It is an old Pennsylvania Dutch dish, originally eaten without the ham for Lent and still enjoyed as *"Schnitz un Gnepp."* For many poor Appalachian farm families, dried apples were the only winter sweet until maple syrup making.

Take of sweet dried applies (dried with the skins on if you can get them) about one quart. Put them in the bottom of a porcelain or tin-lined boiler with a cover. Take a nice piece of smoked ham washed very clean, and lay on top; add enough water to cook them nicely. About twenty minutes before dishing up, add the following dumplings.

Dumplings: Mix a cup of warm milk with one egg, a little salt, and a little yeast, and enough flour to make a sponge. When light, work into a loaf. Let stand until about twenty minutes before dinner, then cut off slices or lumps, and lay on the apples, and let steam through.

Yield: Serves 6–10

4 cups dried apples

Inch-thick ham steak or 2 to make an inch of thickness

1 cup whole milk

1 medium egg

3 cups flour

2 teaspoons dry yeast, or $\frac{1}{4}$ cup **Potato Yeast**

Equipment: Breadboard, tall soup pot with cover

1. If using dry yeast, dissolve in a little warm water with a pinch of sugar.
2. Warm the milk to lukewarm.
3. Beat the egg, and stir into the milk.
4. Add $\frac{1}{2}$ teaspoon salt to milk. When the yeast has a foam of bubbles on top, add the yeast and one cup of the flour to the milk.
5. Stir the batter well and cover with a kitchen towel until bubbly and light throughout.
6. Put apples in soup pot with water to cover.
7. Arrange ham steaks on top.
8. Bring water to a boil, but reduce heat to a bare simmer.
9. Warm more water in a teakettle. The dried apples will absorb water, and must be kept moist so they do not burn.
10. Stir the rest of the flour into the batter, to make a soft dough. You may need a little more flour or water.
11. Form dough into a loaf shape, and allow to rise until about 20 minutes before serving dinner.
12. With a very sharp knife, cut $\frac{1}{2}$ inch "slices" from the dough and arrange on top of the ham.
13. Cover pot tightly to steam dumpling slices.

Serve as a one-pot supper.

APISAS (1780S)

These cookies are still made under the name of A.P.s or Apees with a story that an early cook, perhaps named Ann Page, put her initials on each one. Food historian William Woys Weaver reports that they are now used in the Pennsylvania Dutch community on Epiphany, or Twelfth Night, with the name Epieskuchen. However, this early name in a Pennsylvania Quaker cooking manuscript suggests that the name may come from the English term "piece" for large-denomination gold coins, which survives in the expression "Pieces of Eight" applied to Spanish gold coins in pirate movies. It is possible that all three stories are true.

This recipe appears in the manuscript of Jane Paxon Parry (1767–1826) as transcribed by her great-granddaughter Jane Parry (1872–1897) and published as *A Quaker Lady's Cookbook; Recipes from the Parry Mansion*, by the New Hope [Pennsylvania] Historical Society in 1998. We cannot easily date this recipe, but there is no reason to doubt that it comes from during or just after the American Revolution. I have filled out some details from the recipe for Apees in Eliza Leslie's book, *75 Receipts* (1827), her later *Miss Leslie's New Cookery Book* (1857), and *Widdifield's New Cook Book* (1856).

> Take 1 lb. of flour (¼ left out to make them up with) ½ lb. of butter, ½ wineglass of rose water, 1 wineglass of clear water, ½ lb. of sugar and some cinnamon.

Yield: 40–60 cookies

3 cups sifted white flour

¾ cup whole wheat flour

2 tablespoons wheat germ

½ pound salted butter (2 sticks), plus some to butter baking sheets

½ pound sugar

⅓ cup rosewater

1 teaspoon cinnamon

Equipment: Pastry blender or food processor, breadboard and rolling pin, baking sheets, biscuit cutter or drinking glass, pancake turner or metal spatula, wire racks, waxed paper.

1. An hour before beginning, remove butter from refrigerator to soften.

2. Preheat oven to 350 degrees. Mix flour, whole wheat flour, wheat germ, and cinnamon.

3. Cream butter and sugar with pastry blender or food processor. (Mrs. Parry may have used her hands or a butter knife.)

4. Alternately add rosewater, flour, and up to ¾ cup water to make a very stiff dough.

5. Flour rolling pin and board, and roll out dough from the center "the thickness of a [silver] dollar" (Widdifield), that is, as thin as possible. If you make them thicker, they will take a little longer to bake and will come out chewier and less crisp. That was probably an acceptable cookie in the 1780s also.

6. Cut cookies with a biscuit cutter or drinking glass dipped in flour.

7. Arrange cookies on baking sheets.

8. Bake 10 minutes. (This kind of cookie doesn't brown much, except underneath and on the edges.)

9. Cool on baking sheets for 5 or 10 minutes so cookies harden.

10. Remove with pancake turner or metal spatula, and finish cooling on racks or waxed paper.

Serve for dessert with puddings and perhaps ice cream.

AMERICAN BLANCMANGE (1832)

Quick and easy cornstarch puddings were the staple dessert of the boardinghouses set up to accommodate the increasingly mobile American workers from the beginnings of the factory system into the 1960s. Few remembered that blancmange had been an elaborate medieval entree of meats, custard, fruit, and ground almonds. By the early nineteenth century it was a gelatin dessert based on calves-foot jelly or isinglass (a dried, purified fish gelatin). This recipe is from *The Cook's Own Book* (1832) by Mrs. N.K.M. Lee with some details from Sara Josepha Hale's 1839 book, *The Good Housekeeper*, and from the 1849 manuscript recipe book of Charles Elderfield as published by collector Byron Reece in *Grandma's Handwritten Recipes* (PageWise.com). These recipes mark a transition from almond milk or gelatin to arrowroot, a purified starch you can still find in the baking section. After the Civil War, commercial millers began to promote cornstarch heavily, and blancmange got thicker and duller in flavor. Twentieth-century recipes used twice as much starch or more to accomplish the same work of thickening a quart of milk—a testimony about the declining richness of milk and increasing taste for starch. Almond, lemon, and vanilla were the classic flavors. Chocolate seemed to come on only at the turn of the twentieth century.

> Mix half a pint of cold water with two ounces [¼ cup] of arrowroot, let it settle for fifteen minutes, pour off the water, and add a table-spoonful of laurel water, and a little sugar; sweeten a quart of new milk, boil it with a little cinnamon, and half the peel of a lemon; pick out the cinnamon and the lemon, and pour the boiling milk on the arrowroot, stirring it all the time. Pour it into a mould, and turn it out the following day. 1832

Yield: 6 large or 12 small servings

¼ cup arrowroot (or cornstarch)

1 quart whole milk or half-and-half

1 small cinnamon stick

1 lemon

3 laurel (bay) leaves

½ cup granulated sugar

Equipment: 1-quart pudding mold, or large muffin pan and baking sheet, or 12 small oven-safe cups, lemon zester or box grater, sieve, whisk

1. In a large mixing bowl, dissolve arrowroot or cornstarch in a little cold water. Set aside.

2. Zest half the lemon peel from stem end to blossom end, or by grating on a box grater.

3. Combine sugar, cinnamon, bay leaves, and lemon peel with milk, and bring to a boil.

4. After 3 minutes, add sugar and boil for 10 minutes.

5. Strain cream mixture into bowl with starch mixture and whisk as it cools. It should thicken rapidly.

6. When mixture is lukewarm, rinse mold or muffin pan or cups, and pour in pudding.

7. Refrigerate to congeal.

8. When ready to serve, rinse a butter knife and run around the outside of the mold, to unstick the edge of the pudding.

9. Invert a clean plate on top of the mold (or a clean baking sheet on top of muffin tin). Turn both upside down in one motion. Tap on the mold and lift it off.

Serve as dessert.

STEWED GOLDEN PIPPINS (1829)

This recipe is from a collection of recipes dated from 1829 to 1849, and possibly made by Anna Moore Hubbell (1790–1861) of Bennington, Vermont. It is an old English recipe, almost identical to one written in a manuscript cookbook of Katherine Bradford of Devon in the mid-eighteenth century, and now in the possession of her descendent, Richard Wright. The handwriting of this recipe is similar to others in a connected sequence, the last one dated December 10, 1829. The Golden Pippin is a large, sweet apple still grown in New York state. Golden Delicious apples are a possible substitute. The reference to using the dish for "a corner" suggests that the Hubbell

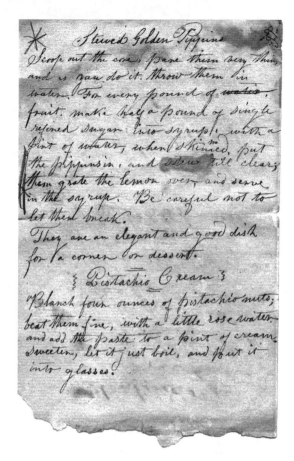

Figure 7 Manuscript of recipe for "Stewed Golden Pippins." *Source: Hubbell manuscript, author's collection.*

family was sometimes still setting a Colonial-style table with meats at the center and a symmetrical arrangement of what we still call "side dishes." The result is similar to canned pears in syrup, except that the apples are kept whole.

> Scoop out the core, pare them very thin, and as you do it, throw them in water. For every pound of fruit, make half a pound of single refined sugar into syrup with a pint of water, when skinned, put the pippins in, and stew till clear; then grate the lemon over and serve in the syrup. Be careful not to let them break.
>
> They are an elegant and good dish for a corner or dessert.

Yield: Serves 24 as a sauce or part of a dessert

- 5 pounds apples
- 2½ pounds sugar
- 1 large lemon

Equipment: Apple corer, vegetable peeler, lemon zester or box grater

1. Dissolve sugar in 10 cups water over medium-high heat.
2. Half fill a large bowl with cold water and add a little lemon juice.
3. Core apples, then peel. As you finish each one, place in the bowl of cold water to keep it from turning brown.
4. When all the apples are done, put them in the hot syrup and bring it to a bare simmer, uncovered.
5. Cook slowly until the apples are translucent and soft. Don't stir, or you will break up the apples.
6. Zest the lemon peel with the lemon zester, or by grating on the fine holes of the box grater.

Serve hot or cold with some of the syrup and the lemon zest sprinkled on top, as a side dish with roast or boiled meat, or as a dessert, perhaps over cake.

APPLE SNOW (1843)

This was a popular party dessert in Early American times, along with other kinds of "Snow Pudding" made from gelatin, and even **Potato Snow**. The recipe is from *The Improved Housewife*, by Mrs. A.L. Webster, and was reprinted verbatim in the 1850 in *The New Family Book, or The Ladies' Indispensable Companion*. If you don't want to serve uncooked egg whites, substitute refrigerated pasteurized egg whites or powdered egg whites from the bakery section of the supermarket.

> Put twelve good tart apples in cold water, and set them over a slow fire:

when soft, drain off the water, strip the skins off the apples, core them, and lay them in a deep dish. Beat the whites of twelve eggs to a stiff froth; put half a pound of powdered white sugar to the apples, beat them to a stiff froth, and add the beaten eggs. Beat the whole to a stiff snow, then turn it into a dessert dish, and ornament it with myrtle or box.

Yield: Serves 12–16

12 tart apples such as Granny Smith (not MacIntosh)

12 small eggs or 9 large eggs or 8 extra large eggs (or substitutes see above)

1 cup sugar

Evergreen leaves for decoration, from a box hedge

Equipment: Soup pot, whisk or handheld electric beater or standing mixer, food mill (optional)

1. Wash apples and place in soup pot.
2. Cover apples with cold water, bring to a boil but reduce heat immediately to simmer until apples are soft, and fork inserted to the center meets no resistance.
3. Separate eggs, or measure egg white product according to package directions.
4. Beat egg whites until they form stiff peaks, but are not dry. (In Early American times, some people did this with a knife, or a whisk of sticks like a miniature straw broom.)
5. Drain apples, cut off cores, and peel off skins. (If you are having a hard time, a food mill does this quickly.)
6. Whisk sugar into apples to make applesauce.
7. Whisk applesauce and egg whites together to make a white or pink snowy foam.
8. Set this in a large dish. It is too sticky to get it neat.
9. Decorate with evergreens.

Serve as a dessert with cake, fruit, and nuts.

10

THE WORLD OF MASTERS AND SLAVES (1800–1862)

The paradox at the core of American history is what was first debated as "African slavery." Given the prominence of African-American cooks during slavery times and since, there is a lot of evidence about the food history of slaves and slavery. But the evidence is hard to interpret without considering the full influence that slaves and slave owners had upon each other. These influences are painful to acknowledge even today and were never simple.

One of the first questions asked by my editors about *The American History Cookbook* was whether there are recorded recipes cooked by slaves. On one level, the answer is an easy yes, since slave cooks in plantation houses cooked every recipe in a number of published cookbooks known to have been owned by their mistresses. After it became forbidden to teach slaves to read in the 1830s, mistresses would read the recipes for complicated cakes and pickles, and the slave cooks would make them. You can try this team approach with the **Omelette Soufflé** below. Some slave cooks learned the recipes well enough to earn extra money by cooking and sometimes their freedom.

Food historians have traced African-American cooking to its African roots by following specific foodstuffs known to have been introduced to the United States from Africa, such as okra, eggplant, and sesame seeds. Certain styles of African cooking are evident in African-American dishes such as gumbo and greens. Sweet potatoes are known to have been adopted by slave cooks as substitutes for African yams.

More recently, food historians have expanded this list to include foods from other continents, including the Americas, that were established in Africa before much of the slave trade. It is now documented that much of American rice cookery and some of our uses of peanuts, chile peppers, tomatoes, and even corn came via Africa. Rice pilaus, jambalaya, and many fried dishes may also have African recipe ancestors. The versions as recorded by white cookbook authors may not be how the dishes were made in the slave quarters or in the homes of free people of color.

The slave trade was a multinational business and spread some African food culture that was needed to keep the slaves alive in transit. Captive Africans acquired a few food customs from the various cultures of Europe in transit and a mixture of others while held in the Caribbean before reaching the American colonies and the United

WEST HILLS COLLEGE
LEMOORE LIBRARY/LRC

States. African ethnic foods were traded among American slaves and with more recent arrivals. Some slaves continued to arrive from Africa and the Caribbean after the end of the legal slave trade in January 1808.

This history will be further complicated as we restudy the early involvement of Native American slaves and the strong association of "African slaves" with Native American recipes for corn cakes and hominy-based stews. I believe that these techniques passed directly from Native American women held as slaves to their African-American co-slaves and descendants. The late African-American historian Carter Woodson estimated that one-third of African-Americans have Indian ancestors. These relationships arose when African-American slaves ran away and joined Indian bands, but also as African slaves were sold to southern Indian tribes and as captive Indians—especially women and children—were forced into slavery in European settlements. Mixed-race and tri-racial people were thrown together at the edges of Colonial society, a process that continued into the twentieth century.

In this chapter are gathered recipes for dishes eaten by both slaves and masters. Many were also eaten before the Civil War by white southerners who did not own slaves. There is a spectrum of recipes from the English-style muffins developed by a highly educated slave of Thomas Jefferson, to the hoe cakes and stews that major slave owners tasted only on hunting expeditions. Four recipes explore the range of cornbreads and cakes produced by slave cooks for themselves and for white masters and customers.

A handful of recipes in white-authored cookbooks are attributed directly to slave cooks. In addition, some former slaves went on to write cookbooks. Mrs. Abby Fisher, born in 1832 in South Carolina, dictated *What Mrs. Fisher Knows About Old Southern Cooking* for publication in 1888. There is no documentation that Mrs. Fisher had been a slave, although it is likely. There were "free Negroes" in South Carolina and Alabama, where she lived. In any case, she learned to cook in the south during slavery times, and her recipes for "Plantation Hoe Cake" and other dishes known to be eaten by field slaves are probably the most authentic we have. A former slave who wrote a cookbook was Rufus Estes, was born in 1857 in Tennesee. He learned to cook from his widowed mother and went on to become a leading railroad chef by the time he wrote *Good Things to Eat as Recommended by Rufus* in 1911.

A general picture of what field slaves ate is recorded in interviews with former slaves, many collected by the federal government as a make-work product for writers in the 1930s. The rations for field slaves were recorded by overseers and audited by owners, and there was also a lively discussion of what to feed field slaves by owners in southern newspapers. (You can read this grisly literature in Chapter 7 of *Advice Among Masters; The Ideal in Slave Management in the Old South*, edited by James O. Breeden, Greenwood Press, 1980.)

As a generality, field slaves in the Colonial periods of slavery had more opportunities to garden, fish, hunt game, and gather wild foods than they did during the later stages of slavery in the United States. Some slaves were able to earn money at cooking or catering jobs in their spare time or obtaining tips when lent out to work at barbecues or balls. Some slaves were able to purchase their freedom through these enterprises and then earn a living selling seafood and snacks or working as waiters. Slave revolts and the evolution of larger plantations brought slaves under tighter control. In addition, the end of the legal slave trade and the demand for slave labor on cotton plantations tended to make slave labor more valuable, so profit-minded owners reduced free time and set up kitchens in the fields. Full-time cooks were designated for work crews and sometimes for nurseries on large plantations.

Rations for slaves might be given out weekly or monthly and consisted primarily of cornmeal or hominy and salt pork, bacon, or pickled pork. By the 1850s, most plantations had settled upon a weekly ration of three to four pounds of pork and a peck (two gallons) of cornmeal with seasonal fruits and vegetables (which meant little of either over the three or four winter months). Sweet potatoes and rice were added regionally or in season, and small amounts of salt and molasses were given as seasoning. In the later stages of slavery, children were kept separate from their working mothers in nurseries and fed as a group, usually on cornmeal mush. Frederick Douglass reported on this in his 1845 autobiography, describing experiences in Maryland as early as the late 1820s: "It [mush] was put in a large wooden tray or trough, and set upon the ground. The children were then called, like so many pigs, and like so many pigs they would come and devour the mush; some with oyster shells, others with pieces of shingle, some with naked hands, and none with spoons. He that ate fastest got most; he that was strongest secured the best place; and few left the trough satisfied." That this practice continued to the end of slavery, especially in Virginia, is confirmed by the reports of surviving ex-slaves collected by interviewers in the 1930s.

Modern "soul food" preserves some of the dishes of slavery times—indeed, some culinary historians trace such dishes to African foodways. It is possible to reconstruct widely recorded slave dishes from surviving soul-food dishes by subtracting ingredients and equipment that field slaves would not have had.

The food history of American slavery is still being written. New evidence continues to emerge and must be compared with emerging knowledge about the history of African food, Native American food, the cuisines of all the countries that participated in the slave trade, African-American cooking from elsewhere in the hemisphere, and the still developing social history of slavery. Our understanding of the important contributions of African slaves to rice culture and rice cookery in American have only emerged in the past twenty-five years with the historical work of Peter H. Wood and Daniel C. Littlefield and the food history of John Martin Taylor and Karen Hess.

There is still much to be done with fragments of evidence like this: in 1867 Mrs. Annabella P. Hill of Georgia published a typical Anglo-American recipe for "Pease Pudding" boiled in a bag but she specified "nice white peas (of the kind called Cornfield)." Those are cowpeas or black-eyed peas (or pigeon peas or crowder peas), which had been brought from Africa by slaves and were widely planted in their gardens. Cowpeas were a food that slaves remembered and preferred whenever they were available. Mrs. Hill may have used field peas because they grew better in North Georgia, or she may have started using them during the Civil War, because of shortages of dried English peas. However, her dish may also have been inspired by slave cooks making some of the cowpea puddings, dumplings, or tamales that are still popular in West Africa, such as Nigerian Moyen Moyen. We know that Moyen Moyen was brought to Brazil, where it is known as Abará. Could Mrs. Hill or one of her slaves or one of her friend's slaves have learned about Moyen Moyen from a slave cook of Yoruban or Igbo descent? Someone in Georgia knew about it, because twenty-five years later another white Georgian, Mrs. Frank Orme of Atlanta, contributed a recipe to the *Atlanta Exposition Cookbook* for "Ground-Pea Soup" with these distinctly

African directions, "Rub off the dry, brown skin carefully, pound the nuts to a smooth paste in a mortar."

Monticello Muffins (circa 1800)

These aren't American muffins in the modern sense, but what we now call English muffins. (See **Indian Cup Cakes** for what we would now call muffins.) The recipe illustrates some of the difficulties in recording the contributions of slave cooks to American food history. It was recorded under this name by President Jefferson's granddaughter, Septimia Anne Randolph Meikleham, in a manuscript recipe book that she kept from 1849 to 1864. If she obtained the recipe from the cook at Monticello when she visited as a child, that would have been Edith "Edy" Fossett, who was trained at the White House in 1802 and moved back to Monticello after President Jefferson left office. After Jefferson died on July 4, 1827, Septimia moved to Boston with her mother, and Edy was sold at auction (although Edy's husband, Joe Fossett, was one of the five slaves freed by Jefferson at his death).

However, the recipe for Monticello Muffins had been fixed much earlier, since we know that President Jefferson had written from the White House to Septemia's mother, "Pray enable yourself to direct us here how to make muffins in Peter's method. My cook here cannot succeed at all in them, and they are a great luxury to me." The cook mentioned as "Peter" was Peter Hemings, a slave who had been the Monticello chef since 1795. (He had been trained by his brother James Hemings, who was trained as a chef and pastry maker while he and his master were in France (1784–1789) and was the Monticello cook from 1789 until he was set free in 1795.)

Thus the "method" was probably developed by Peter Hemings between 1795 and 1801, but of more than six hundred recipes

written by the Jefferson family and edited by Karen Hess for a forthcoming book, "only four [were] attributed [by Jefferson family members] to an African-American cook. And those four are attributed to James Hemings." [The four recipes, recorded by granddaughter Virginia Randolph Trist, are for desserts, and have yet to be published in their original form.] Information from the Monticello web site (Thomas Jefferson Memorial Foundation, Inc., "Breakfast: A Child's View" September 19, 1996 ⟨http://www.monticello.org/jefferson/breakfast/fun.html⟩ Sept. 12, 2001); "Mr. Jefferson's Table: The Culinary Legacy of Monticello" (unpublished work in progress by Karen Hess); and *Thomas Jefferson; An Intimate History*, by Fawn Brodie (New York: Norton, 1974).

To a quart of flour put two table spoons full of yeast. Mix [crossed out] the flour up with water so thin that the dough will stick to the table. Our cook takes it—up and throws it down until it will no longer stick [to the table?] she then puts it to rise until Morning. In the morning she works the dough over the first thing and makes it into little cakes like biscuit and sets them aside until it is time to back them. You know Muffins are backed in a gridle [before?] in the [fire?] hearth of the stove not inside. They bake very quickly. The second plate full is put on the fire when breakfast is sent in and they are ready by the time the first are eaten.

NOTE: RECIPE TAKES TWO DAYS.

Yield: 20–24 English muffins

3¼ cups all purpose flour (plus more for working the dough)

½ cup whole wheat flour

¼ cup wheat germ

1 teaspoon dry yeast (or 2 tablespoons **Potato Yeast**)

1 stick salted butter

Equipment: Griddle or large frying pan, pancake turner, breadboard, dough scraper, 3-inch round cookie cutter or drinking glass, waxed paper, two clean kitchen towels

1. Mix dry ingredients to make 4 cups of flour resembling well-screened Early Virginia flour.

2. If using dry yeast, dissolve in 2 tablespoons water with a pinch of sugar. If it does not form a foam of bubbles in 10–15 minutes, check the expiration date.

3. Warm a cup of cold water to lukewarm and stir in the yeast.

4. Stir the water-yeast mixture into the flour mixture to make a sticky dough, but one that holds together. You will probably need a little more water.

5. Flour the board and knead the dough a few times. You can then pick it up and throw it down a few times, scraping it off with the dough scraper if necessary and flouring the board again. It will become smoother, firmer, and less sticky. (This throwing, like kneading or the hitting in **Apoquiniminc Cakes**, below, develops glutinous proteins that make the muffins rise. They also make the muffins tougher. Early Virginia flour was much lower in protein, so the cooks had to throw or beat the dough quite a lot to get a good rise and still didn't have tough muffins. If your muffins come out tough, throw the dough less the next time, or replace a little of the flour with cornstarch.)

6. Cover the dough with a kitchen towel and leave overnight to rise.

7. By morning the dough should have doubled in bulk, but may have grown much larger and spongier. In any case, stir down the large bubbles, flour the board, and knead a few times.

8. Pat the dough out to about ½ inch thick, and cut into 3-inch rounds with a cookie cutter or a drinking glass dipped in flour. Or you can just cut off parts of the dough and shape it with your hands.

9. Arrange cut-out muffins on the board on some waxed paper, cover, and let rise but not until fully doubled in bulk.

10. Melt a little of the butter on the griddle over low heat. Push it around with the pancake turner to coat the surface. Now take up the largest-looking muffins and slide them onto the griddle. You can use the pancake turner to nudge them back into shape a little, but don't handle too much.

11. Cook the muffins slowly, 10–15 minutes on each side. They should be well browned on the ends and white around the middles. You can hold them in a 150-degree oven while you do the rest, but at Monticello and at the Jefferson White House, slave cooks sent out muffins as soon as they were done, with later batches going out as they were ready. The cooks might eat a burned one while no one was looking.

Serve hot with butter. Septimia's little brother, Benjamin Franklin Randolph, seated next to Dolley Madison at one Monticello breakfast, explained that it was not done to cut an English muffin with a knife, " . . . you must tear him open, and put butter inside and stick holes in his back! And then pat him and squeeze him and the juice will run out!"

JONNY CAKE (1805–1882)

This recipe is attributed to Phillis, in the 1880 book, *The Jonny-Cake Letters*, by Thomas Robinson "Shepherd Tom" Hazzard (1797–1886). Hazzard does not say that Phillis was a slave, but does say that she was born in Senegambia and was his grandfather's cook. Hazzard's grandfather was the largest slaveholder in Rhode Island, which was the major slave state in New England and in which slavery was not outlawed until 1805. At that time, children of slaves were born free, but it was a few more years before pre-existing slaves were also freed. We sometimes forget that slavery was legal in all American states at the time of the American Revolution, and house slaves were quite fashionable throughout the northern cities. Slavery was legal in New York until 1820. President John Adams was unusual among the Boston elite in never owning a slave. Hazzard's father had refused a gift of slaves at his wedding, and "Shepherd Tom" Hazzard himself was a long-time stalwart of colonization, a plan in which slaves would be freed but returned to Africa rather than made American citizens. This was seen as a form of moderate antislavery activity, although generally rejected by free African-Americans after the 1840s. (Hazzard was such a common name in Rhode Island that all the male first names were used many times, and Hazzards all had nicknames like "Shephard Tom," "Harvard Tom," "Preacher Tom," etc.)

By the time Hazzard published his book, Phillis was already a legend used as a brand name on Rhode Island cornmeal, a real-life predecessor of Aunt Jemima, who was an invented character. A fanciful passage in Hazzard's book has her appearing to him in a dream and joking about the inaccurate picture of herself on the label of the cornmeal. If you want to try the fireplace method, be sure to get stone-ground white cornmeal. (One source is ⟨www.kenyonsgristmill.com⟩.) You also need a somewhat rough board to approximate the barrel ends used by early cooks and avoid the experience of author Betty Fussell: "Forget the coarse thread; the problem was to keep the batter on the board. The first cake slid off whole into the ashes, The next cake stuck to the board in patches, some burned,

some gummily raw. Choked with smoke, front red with heat and back blue with cold and stiff from bending, I had new respect for my ancestral grandmothers and sympathy for their corn complaints." I have had some luck with the bottom of a wooden case of wine, sanded a little smoother. I have given an oven method for supermarket cornmeal.

Phillis after taking from the chest her modicum of meal, proceeded to bolt it through her finest sieve, reserving the first teacupful for the special purpose of powdering fish before being fried. After sifting the meal, she proceeded to carefully knead it in a wooden tray, having first scalded it with boiling water, and added sufficient fluid, sometimes new milk, at other times pure water, to make it a proper consistency. It was then placed on a jonny-cake board about three-quarters of an inch in thickness, and well dressed on the surface with rich sweet cream to keep it from blistering when placed before the fire. The cake was next placed upright on the hearth before a bright, green hardwood fire supported by a heart-shaped flat-iron. First the flats' front smooth surface was placed immediately against the back of the jonny-cake board to hold it in a perpendicular position before the fire until the main part of the cake was sufficiently baked, then a slanting side of the flat-iron was turned so as to support the board in a reclining position until the bottom and top extremities of the cake were in turn baked, and lastly the board was slewed round and rested partly against the handle of the flat-iron. After a time it was discovered that the flatiron, first invented as a jonny-cake holder, was a convenient thing to iron clothes with, and has since been used for that purpose very extensively. When the jonny cake was sufficiently done on the first side, a knife was passed between it and the board, and it was dexterously turned and anointed, as before with sweet, golden-tinged cream, previous to being again placed before the fire. Such as I have described was the process of making and baking the best article of farinaceous food that was ever partaken of by mortal man, to wit, an old-fashioned jonny cake made of white Rhode Island cornmeal, carefully and slowly ground with Rhode Island fine-grained granite stones, and baked and conscientiously turned before glowing coals of a quick green hardwood fire, on a red-oak barrelhead supported by a flat-iron.

Yield: 12 flat corn cakes

2 cups white cornmeal (stone ground preferred)

$\frac{1}{2}$–1 cup milk

$\frac{1}{2}$ cup heavy cream

$\frac{1}{2}$ stick salted butter (oven method)

Equipment: Pastry brush, baking sheet or broiler pan with aluminum foil or fireplace and thin ($\frac{1}{4}$-inch to $\frac{3}{8}$-inch) flat piece of hardwood (not pine or plywood) at least 1 foot wide and bricks or antique flatirons to prop it up, pancake turner, unwaxed cotton dental floss or pancake turner

1. Heat at least 2 cups of water to boiling in a teakettle or small saucepan.

2. If using stone-ground cornmeal, pour $\frac{3}{4}$ cup of boiling water into the cornmeal, stir well, and let it cool. With supermarket cornmeal, use $1\frac{1}{2}$ cups and mix in a tablespoon of the butter to make up for the loss of corn oil in modern cornmeal.

3. As the cornmeal cools, it absorbs water, so you need to add a little milk.

Stir the meal to keep it fairly dry and stiff, but fluffy as well as sticky. For the oven method, this is not so crucial.

4. For oven method, go to Step 11. For the fireplace method, have a lively fire with small seasoned sticks of wood. A "green fire" in the recipe means new and bright, not green, freshly cut, wood. Prop the board up a few feet from the fire to warm.

5. Remove the board and slap on a $\frac{3}{4}$-inch cake of the cornmeal in the middle of the board. Start with just one, so you can adjust the batter if it slides off. Smooth the top and brush on a coating of cream, and set the board back before the fire as close to vertical as you can get it.

6. Roast the corn cake for 5 minutes, then rearrange the board slanting back from the fire to cook the bottom half another 5 minutes. Turn upside down to finish the other half.

7. Take down the board and away from the fire, and remove the corn cake with a flexible spatula or pancake turner. There should be enough cornmeal stuck to the wood to hold on the cooked surface. If this doesn't work, carefully cut and peel off the cooked surface to expose stickier dough underneath. The crispy skins of the corn cakes would be saved up and served in a basket as a special treat in southern plantation houses. The stickier dough will stick to the board better.

8. Brush the uncooked side with cream and set up before the fire at an angle for 5–10 minutes.

9. Turn the board upside down to cook the other side of the corn cake, which should be getting done through.

10. Cut off with a spatula or pancake turner. Once you have the dough at

the right amount of stickiness, you can make more than one corn cake at a time, depending on how long your board is.

11. To cook in the oven, cover baking sheet or broiler pan with aluminum foil, and butter well. Mold a ¾-inch corn cake, smooth the top, and brush with cream. Bake at 375 degrees 15 minutes. Turn over corn cake and brush the other side with cream. Bake another 10 minutes or so. Coat with cream again and broil each side for a few minutes to get the crispy crust.

Serve hot.

PLANTATION CORN BREAD OR HOE CAKE (1840s)

Hoe cake is the single dish most often mentioned as eaten by field slaves in the American south. Most accounts refer to the cakes being cooked on hoeing tools in the fields in *former times*, so I always wondered if the name did not have some other source. The garden hoes I've used are too small to bake a proper hoe cake. The name made more sense when I saw an eighteenth-century hoe, with its shorter handle and larger blade. The recipe also could be made with a New England Indian hoe, which was a sea clam shell tied to a stick. Several early explorers and settlers noticed Indians making similar flat breads of maize cooked on flat stones or in the ashes, if not on clam shells. The Native American technique of scalding the cornmeal with hot water before baking was noted by Jamestown colonists in Virginia and by John Winthrop Jr. in Connecticut. Although there were similar flat-breads in Europe and Africa, I believe that the retention of the scalding-water technique indicates a direct transmission from Indian slaves to African-American slaves, many of whom were descended from Indian slaves. The baking soda is the only ingredi-

ent that neither slaves nor Indians would have had, but it may be a replacement for the use of ashes from certain plants—a Native American practice that added flavor, nutrition, and sometimes color to corn cakes. (Although it is possible that corn-meal flatbreads developed in Africa very early in the slave trade, I haven't found the scalding-water technique in contemporary African cookbooks.)

By the time of printed cookbooks in the nineteenth century, hoe cakes were considered the specialty of African slaves, although many poor white farmers and Appalachian pioneers also made them. Slaves who did not have frying pans or griddles cooked them in the ashes on the hot hearth, or wrapped in leaves. The art of making them well does not come through in written recipes, since you have to decide how much water to add—to make anything from a crumbly dough to a semiliquid pancake batter—and how long to cook them (when you might be very hungry and impatient.) An even larger problem is that today's degerminated cornmeal stores better than stone-ground, but has much less flavor and doesn't stick together as well.

This recipe was dictated in 1888 by Mrs. Abby Fisher, for *What Mrs. Fisher Knows About Old Southern Cooking.* By that time, there had been many similar printed recipes for hoe cake, but Mrs. Fisher did not copy them. By the testimony of nine of her San Francisco customers who sponsored her book, she was an excellent cook and successful businesswoman, but she had never learned to read. Census data gives Mrs. Fisher a birth date in 1832, which means she was either a slave or a free person of color for more than thirty-three years in South Carolina and Alabama, and thus hers is the best firsthand account of hoe cakes under slavery that we have. The recipes uses one-sixteenth of the typical slave ration of cornmeal, so when hoe cakes were eaten at every meal, working adult slaves got nine or ten. This is enough calories to sustain hard work, but nutritionally unbalanced. The interviews with ex-slaves, however, report dangerous hunger with at least one former owner. Slave rations were widely reduced during the Civil War.

> Half tablespoonful of lard to a pint of meal, one teacup of boiling water; stir well and bake on a hot griddle. Sift in meal one teaspoonful of soda.—*What Mrs. Fisher Knows About Old Southern Cooking.*

Yield: 12–15 hoe cakes

½ tablespoon lard

2 cups white cornmeal (stone ground preferred)

1 teaspoon baking soda

Salt pork to grease griddle

Equipment: Cast-iron or nonstick griddle or frying pan, pancake turner

1. Heat at least 2 cups of water to boiling in a teakettle or small saucepan.

2. Stir the baking soda into the cornmeal. Rub the lard into the corn meal with your fingers or a fork until there are no lumps.

3. If using stone-ground cornmeal, start with ¾ cup of boiling water. You may need to add more water to get a dough that sticks together when pressed. You may want to add much more water to get a thick batter. With supermarket cornmeal, start with 1½ cups (yes, double Mrs. Fisher's recipe) of boiling water.

4. Heat up griddle or nonstick frying pan to medium heat. Slaves would have greased an iron griddle once in a while with a piece of solid fat salt pork. (They also made hoe cakes on a stone hearth with ashes piled on top, on a plate inside a cast-iron Dutch oven, slapped onto a board in front of the fire like the **Jonny Cakes** above, sometimes with a cabbage leaf or inverted pot over the hoe cakes, and sometimes on hoe blades over a campfire in the fields, although this would tend to soften the hoe blades.)

5. If you have a crumbly or soft dough, pat into round or oval shapes about ⅜ of an inch thick, and bake on the pan 7–10 minutes before turning. If you have something like a pancake batter, spoon out cakes about the same width or thinner, about 4 inches in diameter. Bake 5–7 minutes before turning.

6. Now, here is the hard part. These hoe cakes ought to cook about half an hour (turning occasionally) before they lose the raw cornmeal taste at the center. But you are tired and hungry. The good news is, undercooked hoe cakes sit heavily in the stomach, so you won't feel hungry for a while.

Serve with fried salt pork or stewed greens. On some plantations slaves were given milk or buttermilk, and molasses was a bonus during harvest time. When hoe cakes were eaten by white farmers, they used quite a lot of butter.

APOQUINIMINC CAKES (1824)

This is the earliest printed recipe for what became known as "Maryland Beaten Biscuits." The technique of kneading by beating the dough with a blunt object had been used in England and Norman France, but was especially useful with low-protein flour from the Southern states. There was also slave labor to beat the biscuits, and no Anglo-American food is more associated with slave cooks than beaten biscuits. The beating, with a wooden pestle, a hand hatchet, or a small bat, was often assigned to a young boy. After the Civil War, an invention called a "biscuit brake" like a pasta machine with corrugated rollers kept beaten biscuits on the table for another fifty years. The recipe is from *The Virginia House-Wife*, by Mary Randolph. Mrs. Randolph (1762–1828) was a prominent Virginia hostess until her Federalist husband lost the office of U.S. marshall under President Jefferson. Randolph later ran a boardinghouse in Richmond, and moved to Washington, D.C., where she wrote her book. Despite the history, her younger brother married Jefferson's daughter, and Mary Randolph sent a copy of her cookbook to Monticello dedicated to Thomas Jefferson, who wrote several recipes into it. Mrs. Randolph had owned slaves and probably instructed them in cooking, and certainly acquired recipes that use African-American ingredients and techniques. Abby Fisher (see **Plantation Corn Bread**) gave essentially the same recipe as "Maryland Beat Biscuits." I have some added details from other early recipes.

> Put a little salt, one egg beaten, and four ounces of butter, in a quart of flour; make it into a paste with new milk, beat it for half an hour with a pestle, roll the paste thin, and cut it into round cakes; bake them on a gridiron and be careful not to burn them.

Yield: 30–40 biscuits

1 stick salted butter

3¼ cups all purpose flour (plus more for working the dough)

½ cup whole wheat flour

¼ cup wheat germ

½ teaspoon salt

1 small or medium egg

1 cup whole milk

1 cup half-and-half or light cream

Equipment: Pastry blender or food processor, dough scraper, griddle or large frying pan; pancake turner; breadboard and rolling pin; large wood pestle, hammer handle, or small one-piece rolling pin; 2-inch round biscuit or cookie cutter, waxed paper, 2 clean kitchen towels

1. One hour before starting, remove butter from refrigerator to soften.

2. Mix dry ingredients to make 4 cups of flour resembling well-screened Early Virginia flour.

3. Beat egg.

4. Cut butter into small pieces.

5. Work butter into flour with a pastry blender or food processor (or a large fork, or your hands).

6. Stir in the egg and cream to make a stiff dough. You may need to add some of the milk, but more stirring and less liquid is the key to beaten biscuits.

7. Flour the board and beating tool.

8. Put the dough on the board and knead a few times.

9. Flatten out the dough and sprinkle a little flour on top.

10. Pound slowly, but steadily for 20–40 minutes, stopping to fold the dough back up and sprinkle on a little more flour until the dough becomes less sticky. The dough will get smoother and tougher. When it is done, it will blister and snap like bubble gum. All this beating and folding traps air and butter between the layers of gluten, making for a flaky biscuit without baking powder.

11. When dough is ready to roll, flour board and rolling pin, and roll out from the center ¼-inch thick.

12. Cut into 2-inch rounds with a biscuit cutter. Prick each one twice with a fork. (Six holes is the standard, because Early American forks had 3 round tines.)

13. Heat up a griddle or several frying pans on medium heat, and slide on

biscuits. Cook slowly, turning to brown them on both sides. You shouldn't need to butter the griddle, but you may need to cook them for 20–25 minutes. This dough does not brown too quickly. You can also bake them on ungreased baking sheets at 400 degrees for 25–30 minutes.

Serve with butter. They were split like Monticello Muffins, and sometimes filled with a piece of country ham.

OMELETTE SOUFFLÉ (1824–1850)

In a letter of February 21, 1850, Emily Wharton Sinkler wrote her sister in Philadelphia, "Rachel made the dessert entirely, and we had the best omelette soufflee we ever had, owning I suppose to our new oven." Rachel was her slave cook, and made a specialty of the omelet soufflé, but Mrs.

Sinkler did not record the recipe in her kitchen manuscript. Probably, this was because Mrs. Sinkler read Rachel the recipe from a copy of *The Virginia House-Wife*, by Mary Randolph, first published in 1824. The Sinkler manuscript refers to Mrs. Randolph in other contexts.

Try making this recipe as a team, one reading the instructions, the other doing all the work. At the time, Mrs. Sinkler had been supervising for six years, but Rachel had only been cooking for a year or two. Also, they were using a new oven (probably a new cast-iron Dutch oven in the fireplace), roasting a turkey and cooking other meats and two other desserts at the same time!

If you want to experience cooking process as it originally was, you will need a fireplace with fire burned down to coals and a cast-iron Dutch oven with an iron lid that will hold coals. You also will have to use a

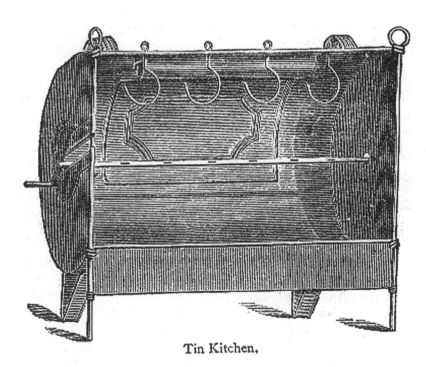

Tin Kitchen.

Figure 8 Tin kitchen reflector oven, also sometimes called a Dutch oven. *Source:* Miss Parloa's New Cook Book and Marketing Guide, *Boston, 1880.*

hand whisk, since even mechanical egg-beaters did not appear until well after the Civil War. The recipe will taste about the same as it did to Mrs. Sinkler and her guests, if you use an electric hand mixer and modern oven. Rachel would only have tasted it if some was left over, or if a little could be salvaged from a burned failure.

> Break six eggs, beat the yelks and whites separately till very light, then mix them, add four table spoonsful of powdered sugar and a little grated lemon peel, put a quarter of a pound of butter in a pan, when melted, pour in the eggs and stir them; When they have absorbed the butter, turn it on a plate previously buttered, sprinkle some powdered sugar, set it in a hot Dutch oven, and when a little brown, serve it up for dessert.

Yield: Serves 6

6 medium eggs or 5 large eggs

4 rounded tablespoons sugar, plus a sprinkle for the baking

1 lemon

¼ pound (1 stick) salted butter

Equipment: Lemon zester or box grater, ovenproof plate, 2 mixing bowls, saucepan or skillet a little smaller than the plate, large cast-iron Dutch oven with metal lid designed to hold hot coals and 3 small stones (optional for fireplace method), charcoal briquettes (optional), 2 good oven mitts, whisk or handheld mixer (optional)

1. If you are using the fireplace method, build a hardwood fire, and let it burn down to coals. (In the larger fireplace of Mrs. Sinkler's kitchen, coals could be borrowed from the roasting fire.) If your fireplace is safe with a charcoal fire, you can use a small fire of 15–20 briquettes, likewise at the red-coal stage where the briquettes appear white. Make sure there is enough room in the Dutch oven to remove your plate without burning your hands.

2. Grate or zest about a tablespoon of finely curled lemon peel. Mix well into the sugar.

3. Separate eggs by pouring them between halves of shell over a cup. Collect yolks in a small mixing bowl and whites in a larger one.

4. Beat the yolks until they are light and creamy, several minutes at least.

5. Wash the whisk or beaters carefully, and beat the whites until they form and hold soft peaks.

6. Fold the yolks into the whites with the whisk or using one of the beaters with your hand.

7. Mix in the sugar mixture.

8. If using the fireplace method, get 3 small coals (or 5 briquettes) under your Dutch oven so it begins to heat up. Put 3 small stones in the bottom to hold your plate above the hot bottom of the pot. If using a modern stove, preheat the oven to 350 degrees.

9. Melt the butter in the skillet over medium-low heat.

10. When the butter is all melted, pour in the egg mixture and stir slowly so it all heats up and absorbs the butter.

11. When the egg mixture begins to set, stop stirring and let it form a round cake.

12. When the omelet is half done, run around the edge with the spatula, and slide the entire omelet onto the ovenproof plate. Sprinkle with a little sugar.

13. Finish in the modern oven about 5 minutes. It should be browned and puffed up. For the fireplace method, put the plate onto the 3 stones, and

cover the Dutch oven. Using fireplace tongs, put 5 coals (or 7 briquettes) on top of the iron lid. Let bake 5 minutes. Remove coals from top of lid, remove lid, and remove omelet. If omelet is still not set, you can try another 5-minute bake.

Serve immediately, before omelet collapses. Cut it into pie-shaped wedges.

HANSON'S MODE OF MAKING CHICKEN BROTH; THE BEST IN THE WORLD (1834)

One slave owner who seems to have written down a number of recipes developed by slaves was Nellie Custis Lewis (1779–1852), the granddaughter of Martha Washington and adopted daughter of President Washington. She kept a household book from about 1830 into the 1840s, which was published in 1982. She grew up at Mount Vernon and had seen her adoptive father's slaves freed and educated under his will, and her mother and grandmother's efforts to educate their slaves even after it became against the law. She raised funds, like Thomas Hazzard, to help freed slaves colonize West Africa. This recipe makes a medicinal chicken soup, as recommended by Dr. D.T. Jennifer of Maryland. Since we now know cholera to be caused by water-borne bacteria, chicken soup would be both nourishing and rehydrating, and the boiling would kill any bacteria. The method is attributed to "Hanson," who was almost certainly a male slave cook, since his other recipes in Nellie Custis Lewis's book are for labor-intensive breakfast biscuits. Mrs. Lewis may have written the recipe down for her oldest daughter Frances, who had just married and moved to Louisiana. The technique of breaking the chicken's bones to add to the richness of the broth reminds us that Nellie Custis Lewis inherited the seventeenth-century English cookery man-

uscript in which we found the recipe **To Make a Frykecy** printed in Chapter 2.

Take a large chicken, kill, scald, pick, clean & skin it. put it into a pot of cold water, let it simmer slowly, in half an hour put in a little Thyme. half an hour after, a tablespoon of flour & water mixed smooth & stirred in when the bones come thro' it is done. it must never boil, only simmer slowly. If a small chicken, 1 quart of water is enough. If you wish it very nourishing—break the bones with a rolling pin before put it into the pot. Chicken water is the best remedy for cholera morbus. first warm water or weak chamomile tea, then chicken water. So tho't Dr. Jenifer who was celebrated for the cure of that disease.

Yield: Serves 6, or 1 sick person for 2 days

1 4–6 pound fowl

½ teaspoon ground thyme

1 tablespoon flour

Equipment: Soup pot with cover, one-piece rolling pin or heavy meat cleaver and cutting board (optional), colander or large sieve

1. Remove skin and large patches of fat from chicken.

2. For a richer soup, cut chicken into quarters, and break leg and thigh bones with the back of a cleaver or with a one-piece rolling pin. You can also crush the wing bones.

3. Put the chicken into the soup pot and cover with about 8 cups of cold water. Bring almost to a boil and reduce heat so that the soup just simmers with the pot lid ajar.

4. After an hour of simmering, add the thyme.

5. Half an hour after that, mix the flour with half a cup of water and stir the mixture into the hot soup.

6. When the chicken begins to break up, the soup is done. Strain it through a colander or large sieve into a second soup pot or soup tureen.

7. You can skim off some or all of the fat, although many early Americans liked a dappling of fat on their soups. You can also refrigerate the broth. In Mrs. Lewis's kitchen, Hanson probably kept leftover broth covered to reheat for the next meal or as the basis of sauces and gravies or richer soups.

Serve with toast until the digestion is more settled and the fever abates.

OLD LETTY'S PEACH CHIPS (1840s)

This is a later recipe in *Nellie Custis Lewis's Household Book*, probably acquired from the slave of one of her two daughters who married Louisiana sugar planters. The detailed directions show that Mrs. Lewis was not familiar with this method of making crystallized dried fruit, and she may have taken notes in the kitchen rather than copied a recipe out of another notebook—probably because her Virginia-bred daughters knew less about sugar cookery than "Old Letty."

As used by Mrs. Lewis, a "skillet" would have been not a frying pan but something the shape of our saucepans, probably with a longer handle, a round bottom, and legs to go over the coals of a wood fire. I have kept the original quantities although they are about six times too large for our ovens or home dehydrators. This was a seasonal effort to put away a year's supply of crystallized peach slices, and, after all, slaves did all the hard work.

Pare & slice moderately thin your peaches Fill your skillet with them, sprinkle over half a pound of sugar, just boil them stirring well until scalded through—then take them out with your skimmer & fill your skillet with more peaches scald those thro' well & fill again sprinkle in half a pint of sugar and as often as your syrup is sour add half a pint of sugar until all your peaches are scalded. As they are taken out of the skillet spread them on pewter dishes, & put them into the Sun; as you turn them over sprinkle them with sugar every day until perfectly dry, then put them in your pot with sugar sprinkled between the layers—tie up for use. a peck of peaches will scald one pound of sugar—not soft peaches or too ripe. If liquor is left, you can add more sugar or fresh peaches.

Yield: About 400 pieces of candied fruit

1 peck firm peaches (2 gallons, 12.5 pounds, or about 50 medium peaches)

2 pounds sugar

Vegetable oil for baking sheets or dehydrator trays

Equipment: Skimmer, home dehydrator or oven that goes down to 140 degrees and oven thermometer, or clean screening to cover outdoor drying; 2–12 baking sheets, vegetable peeler, tongs or chopsticks

1. The recipe calls for peeling the peaches with a vegetable parer. A more typical modern method is to dip them in boiling water for a bit less than a minute, then cooling in cold water so the skins slip right off.

2. Slice 8–10 peaches about ¼-inch thick, discarding pits. Very lightly oil the baking sheets or dehydrator trays. If you have several people to work with, have one continue to slice peaches.

3. Put peaches in a saucepan with a cup of sugar and slowly bring to a boil, so that the sugar dissolves into a syrup with the peach juices. Boil 3–5 min-

utes and remove with a skimmer. Using tongs or chopsticks, set pieces on oiled baking sheets or dehydrator trays.

4. Refill the saucepan with enough peach slices to use up all the syrup, and again boil for 3–5 minutes. Remove with a skimmer.

5. When you run out of baking sheets and/or dehydrator trays, stop boiling more peaches! You can hold the rest of the peaches in the refrigerator until the first batch is dried. With the third batch into the skillet, add another cup of sugar. If you make all the peaches, and they are very juicy, you may need another cup of sugar when the syrup gets too thin. When you are done, the leftover syrup will be delicious on pancakes, or you can add more sugar to make a jelly, or sugar and fruit to make peach preserves.

6. If using dehydrator, fill 4–8 trays with fruit, sprinkle on more sugar, and dry at 150 degrees for 2 hours, then at 130 degrees until leathery. If using oven, preheat to 140 degrees (check with oven thermometer). You may have to leave the oven door ajar or open to get a consistent 140 degrees. Put in as many baking sheets as will fit. After 2 hours, turn pieces over with tongs or chopsticks, sprinkle on a little more sugar, and continue drying until a cooled peach chip is leathery. If you have sunny, dry weather, rig up a tent of clean screening material to keep off the flies and bees, and dry your peach chips in the sun. Every few hours turn them over and sprinkle on a little more sugar. Bring them in before the sun goes down. It may take several days to dry them to the right, leathery consistency.

7. When peach chips are dry, you can store them in jars or stoneware pots or

casseroles, sprinkling more sugar between layers of fruit.

Serve as a sweetmeat on the dessert table after a large midday dinner, along with fresh fruit, cakes, cookies, and perhaps an impressive dish of ice cream or pudding.

GROUND-NUT SOUP (1847)

The peanut was developed in South America, but was introduced from Brazil to Africa in the early 1500s. It quickly replaced a native African groundnut in seasoning pastes, stews, and soups like this one. Slaves brought the peanut plant to the United States, where peanuts are still sometimes called "goober peas," from the Bantu (and Gullah dialect) term, "nguba." The chile peppers in the recipe had almost the same history. The oysters were locally cheap in Charleston, where the recipe was published by Sarah Rutledge in *The Carolina Housewife*. Peanut soup is also supposed to have been a favorite dish of George Washington, who had a substantial oyster fishery at Mount Vernon. Since slaves and free African-Americans were active in collecting oysters and peddling them door-to-door, this dish was probably invented entirely by African-Americans and taken up by white planters in places like Charleston, where slaves were the majority of the population. Significantly, Miss Rutledge's next recipe is a nearly identical soup substituting "Bennie" (sesame seeds)—another African import that retained its African name locally—for the groundnuts.

To a half a pint shelled ground-nuts, well beaten up, add two spoonsful of flour, and mix well. Put to them a pint of oysters, and a pint and a half of water. When boiling, throw on a seed pepper or two, if small.

Yield: Serves 6

1 cup peanuts

¼ cup flour

2 cups oysters

1–2 dried red chiles

Equipment: Food processor, spatula, soup pot

1. Process peanuts in short bursts about a minute to make a rough paste.

2. Add the flour and pulse a few more times to blend.

3. Heat up the peanut butter in a soup pot, and stir in 3 cups of water and the oysters with their liquor.

4. Add the dried pepper and bring to a boil.

5. Reduce heat to a simmer and cook 10 minutes, stirring frequently so soup does not stick and burn.

6. Remove pepper before serving.

Serve hot, perhaps with rice.

HOPPING JOHN (1847)

Also from *The Carolina Housewife* is this early recipe for Hoppin' John. Both the African field peas and the technique of cooking legumes and rice together in a pilaf mark this as an African-American dish, related to similar bean pilafs in every former-slave community in the Americas. The name is probably from the French, "pois de pigeon," as Huguenot French was widely spoken in Charleston and was later reinforced by the arrival of Haitian refugees and slaves after the Haitian revolution at the beginning of the eighteenth century. Food historian Karen Hess has proposed a combination of the Hindi "bahatta" (rice) and the Malay "kachang" (field peas) as the origin for "hoppin' John." This would imply that the earlier names stuck to the foodstuffs when they were introduced to Africa by early Malay and Arab traders. The times given are for black-eyed peas. If you can obtain cowpeas, or field peas, they cook more quickly.

One pound of bacon, one pint of red peas, one pint of rice. First put on the peas, and when half boiled, add the bacon. When the peas are well boiled, throw in the rice, which must be first washed and gravelled. When the rice has been boiling half an hour, take the pot off the fire and put it on coals to steam, as in boiling rice alone. Put a quart of water on the peas at first, and if it boils away too much, add a little more hot water. Season with salt and pepper, and, if liked, a sprig of green mint. In serving up, put the rice and peas first in the dish, and the bacon on top.

Yield: Serves 20

1 pound slab bacon

2 cups dried field peas or black-eyed peas

2 cups rice

Sprig fresh mint (optional)

Equipment: Large soup pot with cover

1. Soak the peas in cold water several hours or overnight.

2. Put the peas in a large soup pot with ½ teaspoon of pepper and a quart of water, and bring to a boil.

3. Cover pot and reduce heat to a simmer. Simmer ½ hour.

4. Add the slab bacon to the pot, and check if more water is needed. If so, heat it in teakettle and add boiling water to the pot. Cover and simmer another 20 minutes.

5. Taste the broth to see if you will need any more salt. Stir in the rice, cover the pot, and simmer on low heat for an additional 30 minutes.

6. Turn off the heat and let the pot sit covered for an additional 15 minutes.

Serve with the slab of bacon on top, garnished with the mint. At the table, a slice would be cut for each diner, with some of the rice and peas. At New Year's it was often served with greens and a fresh pork dish.

Aunt Lydia's Corn Cake (1854)

This is a rather rich and fancy cornbread, coming to us with the careful directions of Eliza Leslie (1787–1858). Miss Leslie says that the recipe comes from "a Southern colored woman, called Aunt Lydia" and claims, "This is the very best preparation of Indian cakes. If exactly followed, we believe there is none superior; as is the opinion of all persons who have eaten them." So we may assume that this kind of cornbread was served to the families of plantation owners. Aunt Lydia may have been a slave in 1854, but since Miss Leslie was living in a Philadelphia hotel at the time, it is more likely that Aunt Lydia was then working as a hired cook in the north. I have added some details from a more detailed version in *Miss Leslie's New Cookery Book* of 1858. Miss Leslie suggests baking these in tin pans four to five inches square and two to three inches deep. This is one of the earlier references to sheet-metal bake-ware, as early breads and cakes were baked in pottery or cast-iron pans. The closest thing to small tins we have today are baby loaf pans, and you will need seven or eight of them.

Yield: 16–24 muffins

1 quart yellow cornmeal (stone ground preferred)

1 teaspoon salt

3 cups whole milk

1 stick unsalted butter, plus some more to grease pans

5 small eggs or 4 large eggs

Equipment: 7–8 baby loaf pans, 2 muffin tins, 4 small loaf pans, 2 9-inch square layer-cake pans, or 3 9-inch round cake pans

1. Heat milk to boiling in a small saucepan or microwave oven.

2. Preheat oven to 400 degrees. Mix cornmeal and salt in a mixing bowl.

3. Pour on 2 cups of the milk, "sufficient to make a soft dough." Because modern cornmeal is degerminated and much drier than stone-ground cornmeal, you may need the rest of the milk, or even some additional cold milk.

4. Cut the butter into small pieces and stir into the dough.

5. Beat the eggs until creamy and light.

6. "Stir them gradually into the mixture, and set it to cool. All preparations of cornmeal require much beating and stirring."

7. Butter pans well.

8. "Fill the pans to the top with the above mixture, that the heat may immediately catch the surface, and cause it to puff up high above the edges of the pan. If properly mixed, and well beaten, there is no danger of it running over." You can try this with muffin tins or baby loaf pans. Fill larger pans ¾ full only.

9. Put cakes in oven and immediately reduce heat to 350 degrees. Bake muffins and baby loaf cakes 20–25 minutes, loaves and cake pans 45–55 minutes. Test frequently with wooden toothpicks or a wire cake tester. "Bake them brown. . . . Let them be well-baked; not scorched on the top, and raw at the bottom."

"[S]end them to the breakfast table hot. Split and butter them."

Okra a la Maulie (1857)

We cannot tell from the context if Maulie was a mistress or a slave, but the dish is a classic African-American okra gumbo. Both okra and gumbo derive from African names for a plant brought to the United States by African slaves and widely grown in their kitchen gardens when permitted. The recipe is recorded in the receipt book of Emily Wharton Sinkler, edited for publication by her great-great-grandaughter Anne Sinkler Whaley LeClerq. (*An Antebellum Plantation Household*, University of South Carolina Press, 1996.)

> With 2 tablespoons of butter, fry in a pot 3 slices of ham, 3 sliced onions, until onions are brown. Add 1 quart of young okra, 12 ripe tomatoes from which extract the juice and seeds. Add now the juice and a tumbler of water. Simmer over a slow fire for 3 hours. Thicken with flour and season with salt and pepper.

2–4 tablespoons butter

3 slices country ham

3 onions

1 quart fresh okra

12 ripe tomatoes

2 tablespoons flour

Equipment: Soup pot with cover, large sieve and bowl

1. Halve, peel, and slice the onions in thin half-rounds. Use swim goggles to avoid tears.

2. Melt the butter on low heat in the bottom of the soup pot.

3. Slice the ham, and put the 3 slices into the butter to brown.

4. Add the sliced onions, stir to coat with melted butter, and cover the pot for a few minutes.

5. Remove the cover when the onions have "sweated" out some liquid, and let the onions begin to brown before stirring.

6. Meanwhile trim the stems and tips of the okra, discarding any old, hard pods.

7. Halve the tomatoes at the equator. Put the sieve in the bowl and squeeze the tomato halves into the sieve so that it catches the seeds but lets the juice through.

8. Press some more tomato juice through the sieve with the back of a soup spoon.

9. Add the okra to the browned onions and stir-fry briefly to brown slightly.

10. Add the tomato juice from the bowl and 1 cup of water. Bring soup pot to a slight simmer and cook, half-covered, for 3 hours, adding more water if necessary.

11. Stir flour into a slurry with ½ cup water and stir into the soup pot. Let simmer for another 10 minutes to thicken and cook off the raw-flour taste.

Serve as a soup with rice, or as a side vegetable.

MISSISSIPPI CORN PONE (1859)

This recipe was in *The Graded Cookbook*, by Lavinia Hargis, published in Chicago in 1887, but is carefully attributed to "'Aunt Diddie' Colored Cook, Vicksburg, Miss., 1859." The recipe specifies cold water for making the batter, leaving us to wonder if "Aunt Diddie" was entirely forthcoming with Mrs. Hargis. Pone came directly from the Algonkian Indian languages of the East Coast from a word meaning baked. It was most usually applied to cornbreads shaped like elongated footballs, also called "Corn Dodgers."

> One quart of meal, sprinkle salt through it, then sift and put in three tablespoonfuls of bacon drippings,

pour in cold water sufficient to make a stiff batter; mould with the hands into three pones and then bake.

Yield: Serves about 20

4 cups white cornmeal

½ teaspoon salt

3–5 slices of bacon

Equipment: Frying pan, baking sheet

1. Fry bacon to obtain 3 tablespoons of drippings. Reserve bacon for another use.

2. Mix salt and cornmeal.

3. Use a little of the bacon drippings to grease baking sheet.

4. Stir the bacon drippings into the cornmeal thoroughly.

5. Add cold water to make a dough that can be molded.

6. Divide the dough in 3 and mold 3 oval "pones" on the baking sheet.

7. Bake at 375 degrees 40–50 minutes. Corn pones will be light brown and rather hard and crunchy.

Serve with greens so you can dip them in the "pot likker."

VIRGINIA STEW (1862)

This is one of the earliest published recipes for what is now called Brunswick Stew. It appeared in a Confederate newspaper, the *Southern Recorder*, of Milledgeville, Georgia, in the September 2, 1862, issue. It is reprinted in the outstanding collection, *The Confederate Housewife*, compiled by John Hammond Moore (Colombia, S.C.: Summerhouse Press, 1997). The attribution to Virginia would support the claim that Brunswick Stew was developed in Brunswick County, Virginia, in 1828 by "Uncle Jimmy" Matthews, the slave cook of Dr. Creed Haskins. Haskins was a Virginia

state legislator who had enjoyed the dish on hunting trips and asked his cook to produce a giant squirrel stew for a political rally for Andrew Jackson. In favor of this story is the Native American appearance of the original recipe: a slow stew of game, corn, and beans. As we have seen above, native cooking techniques were retained among African-American slaves. (They also persisted in hunting camps, where many Native Americans work as guides even today.) The negative argument is that Matthews's giant stew is sometimes described as made from squirrels, onions, and stale bread—no corn or beans. Also, there is some tendency in folklore to ascribe dishes dedicated to pro-slavery heroes to slaves, as Jefferson Davis Pie is attributed to a former slave cook in Texas.

Most subsequent recipes do have corn and beans, like the **Plymouth Succotash** recipe preserved among Anglo-Americans in Plymouth, Massachusetts. This recipe omits the beans, and substitutes chicken for squirrel, but most hungry Confederates would have substituted squirrel in a chicken dish. Removing the bones is another sign that this is a genteel version of the stew. All-male hunting parties or political rallies would not have minded bones in their stew.

Take two young chickens, cut them up, and parboil them; then peel and cook one quart of Irish potatoes; then peel and cut up one dozen large, ripe tomatoes; then cut the corn off one dozen soft roasting ears and mash it up; add to these one large onion, cut up fine. Put all in a stew pan and stew for two hours, stirring frequently to prevent burning. Extract the bones of the fowl; season with salt, butter and pepper, and serve hot. If, after a fair trial, you pronounce this an unpalatable dish, then your loyalty to the Southern Confederacy ought to be questioned.

Yield: Serves 12

2 broiler-fryer chickens

1 quart Irish (white) potatoes (2 pounds, about 6–8)

1 dozen tomatoes

1 dozen ears corn

1 onion

Salt, pepper, and butter to taste

Equipment: 2 large soup pots, kitchen tongs

1. Bring 2 quarts of water to a boil in each soup pot.

2. Cut the chickens into quarters.

3. When the water boils in the first pot, slide in the chicken pieces. Increase heat to bring back to a boil. Let boil for 1 minute, then pour off the water.

4. Return the chicken pieces to the empty pot, and cover with fresh water. Bring back to a boil as you add the other ingredients.

5. When the water boils in the second pot, dip each tomato for 1 minute, then cool it under cold running water. You can slide off the skins easily.

6. Quarter the skinned tomatoes and add to the chicken pot.

7. Peel the potatoes, and cut into half-inch slices. Add to the chicken pot.

8. With a sharp knife, cut the corn off the cobs. Run the back of the knife down the ears to "milk" out the remaining corn. Add to stew.

11

ORIGINS AND EARLY RECIPES OF POPULAR FOODS (1802–1876)

This chapter gives Early American recipes for several treats we still enjoy, such as macaroni and cheese, fried chicken, ham sandwiches, corn muffins, Eggs Benedict, two kinds of early soda pop, and strawberry shortcake. It may surprise you that the first printed American sandwich recipe was as late as 1837, or that something pretty close to Eggs Benedict was a popular brunch on the Kentucky frontier in 1839.

Written recipes often are behind what people are actually cooking, and some dishes seem so natural to us now that it is hard to believe they had to be invented. But in fact, although Early America had Pennsylvania Dutch noodles, macaroni had to be imported and the French version baked with cheese was all most Americans ever tasted until late in the nineteenth century. Sandwiches immediately suited the rapid pace of American life, but did not seem like a real meal to people accustomed to hot food and fresh bread only once a week. Strawberry shortcake probably didn't become very popular until north-south railroad lines extended the strawberry season.

Some inventions, like blueberry muffins, probably did arise naturally and weren't recorded until much later. (**Bran Muffins** weren't recorded until 1912, even though whole wheat "gems" and muffins had been eaten in the 1840s.) Potato chips were probably invented several times before the usual story of their invention by an angry chef in Saratoga, New York, in 1853. But American potato fryers did not work out the efficient stick-shape of French fries until the 1890s. Chapter 34 includes dishes created in a burst of creativity in 1880–1912, such as fudge, brownies, and hamburgers.

VERMICELLI PREPARED LIKE PUDDING (1802)

Here is the grandaddy of all American recipes for macaroni and cheese, as handed out with coiled cakes of noodles manufactured by Lewis Fresnaye of Philadelphia, possibly the first commercial pasta maker in the United States, and reprinted in *35 Receipts from "The Larder Invaded"* by William Woys Weaver, part of a 1986 exhibit by the Library Company of Philadelphia and the Pennsylvania Historical Society. Fresnaye, like a number of early chefs and caterers in the United States and Great Britain, was a refugee from the French Revolution. Imported pasta was viewed as a fancy French vegetable on the dinner table for much of the nineteenth century. Pasta with tomato sauce did not get into mainstream American kitchens until the last quarter of the nineteenth century. Plain macaroni and butter was known as "Irish Macaroni" by mid-century. Notice the similarity of the gravy option to **Potaje de Fideos**.

Take six pints of water and a sufficiency of salt, when boiling stir into it one pound of paste [pasta], let it boil as above ["about eight minutes. But if the paste is of larger size boil it more in proportion."], then strain the water well off, and put the paste in a large dish, mixing it therewith six ounces of grated parmisan or other good cheese; then take four ounces of good butter and melt it well in a saucer or small pot, and pour it over the paste while both are warm. It would be an improvement after all is done, to keep the dish a few minutes in the hot oven, till the butter and cheese have well penetrated the paste.

It may be rendered still more delicate by boiling the paste in milk instead of water, and putting on a little gravy of meat, or any other meat sauce thereon.

Yield: Serves 4, or more as a side dish

1 pound vermicelli

1 teaspoon salt

6 ounces Parmesan cheese

4 ounces (one stick) salted butter

Equipment: Large soup pot, casserole, colander, box grater or food processor, small saucepan

1. Bring 3 quarts water to a boil in a large soup pot.
2. Add 1 teaspoon of salt and break the vermicelli into the pot in 1–2 inch pieces.
3. Boil 8 minutes.
4. Grate Parmesan cheese.

5. Preheat oven to 350 degrees.
6. Melt butter in small saucepan, or in an ovenproof dish in the oven.
7. Drain vermicelli in the colander, and pour into the casserole.
8. Mix in the grated cheese.
9. Pour the melted butter over the vermicelli and cheese.
10. Put the casserole in the oven for "a few minutes."

Serve as a "side dish" or "corner dish" on a symmetrically arranged table with a roast at one end and a boiled meat at the other.

FRIED CHICKEN (1828)

This is the first written recipe for fried chicken as we know it today, from Mary Randolph's *The Virginia House-Wife*, third edition.

Although sixteenth- and seventeenth-century English cooking had fritters and some panfried foods, this kind of deep-fat frying was more characteristic of the Mediterranean and had already been brought to West Africa by Arab traders, and then by Spanish and Portuguese slavers and colonists. (Early fried-fish recipes in English cookbooks are generally attributed to Jewish people, who were coming from Spain.) Thus deep-fried food has generally followed the African American population, although fried chicken only became strongly identified with the African American community toward the end of the nineteenth century.

Mrs. Randolph's recipe also includes fried mush, the first documented **Hush Puppies**, and fried whole parsley—a fancy touch.

Cut them up as for fricassee, dredge them well with flour, sprinkle them with salt, put them into a good quantity of boiling lard, and fry them a light brown, fry small pieces of mush and a quantity of parsley nicely picked to be served in the dish with the chickens, take a half a pint of rich milk, add to it a small bit of butter with pepper, salt, and chopped parsley, stew it a little, and pour it over the chickens, and garnish with the fried parsley.

TO MAKE MUSH. Put a lump of butter the size of an egg into a quart of water, make it sufficiently thick with corn meal and a little salt; it must be mixed perfectly smooth, stir it constantly till done enough.

CAUTION: HOT OIL USED.

Yield: 24 pieces chicken

1–2 cups white cornmeal (stone ground preferred)

4 tablespoons butter

2 broiler-fryer chickens

2 cups all-purpose flour

1 bunch parsley

1½ pounds lard

1 cup light cream

Equipment: Soup pot, heavy skillet with high sides, cover for skillet (optional), tongs, slotted spoon or skimmer, waxed paper, slotted spoon or tongs, mixing bowl, deep-fry thermometer, wire racks, paper towels or clean newspapers

1. To make the mush, bring a quart of water to a boil in the soup pot.

2. Add 3 tablespoons of the butter and 1 teaspoon of salt.

3. Stirring constantly, add the cornmeal in a fine stream, stopping when it has the consistency of mush. One cup of modern cornmeal is usually enough; stone-ground cornmeal is a little moister.

4. Cover pot loosely and reduce heat to simmer mush for another 10–15 minutes, stirring thoroughly to get out all the lumps and avoid burning the bottom.

5. Remove pot from heat and let cool for the hush puppies.

6. Cut chickens at all the joints. Cut breasts away from the body across the ribs and at the collarbones. Cut breasts in two pieces. (Reserve wing tips, backbones, neck and giblets for soup stock.) Wash your hands, the knife, and the cutting board after handling raw chicken.

7. Mix the flour with 1 teaspoon salt.

8. Wash the parsley and dry with paper towels. Cut back the stems to make 10–12 nice sprigs for deep-frying.

9. Mince some of the smaller leaves of parsley to make 1 tablespoon minced parsley.

10. Spread out the flour mixture on a dinner plate or shallow bowl.

11. Roll the chicken pieces in the flour mixture, tap off the excess, and arrange them on waxed paper.

12. Heat up most of the lard in the heavy skillet with high sides. (I often use a soup pot for safety.)

13. Arrange the deep-fry thermometer so that the point is well in the lard but not touching the metal pot. Heat the oil to 350 degrees.

14. Using tongs or a slotted spoon dipped in the hot oil, add the pieces of chicken, skin side down, one by one so they don't splash hot oil. Let them bubble up and seal before moving them, and they won't stick. Brown each piece well and turn over to brown the other side. Larger pieces will cook more slowly, the thighs may need 15–20 minutes.

15. Arrange wire racks over newspapers or paper towels, well away from any open flames, for draining pieces of chicken as they are done.

16. Skim off any loose pieces of breading before they burn.

17. When all the chicken has been fried, add the parsley to the hot lard, just for a minute or less to crisp it.

18. Remove parsley and add the mush by teaspoonfuls. You can do with two teaspoons, or by wetting your hands and molding pieces up to the size of flattened golf balls. Fry these pieces three or four minutes to brown them.

19. To make the sauce, heat up the cream, the last tablespoon of butter, the minced parsley, a pinch of salt, and several grinds of black pepper.

Serve on a large platter, with the sauce poured over the chicken pieces, and garnished with fried parsley.

HAM SANDWICHES (1837)

Sandwiches were developed in England, quite possibly by the Earl of Sandwich. But they became much more important in the United States, where farm and factory work demanded foods that were easy to prepare and eat outside the home. Recipes were seldom written down, however, and when they were—in the 1890s—they were for dainty sandwiches served at the ladies' luncheons just coming into fashion. This is the earliest printed sandwich recipe I know, and it comes from *Directions for Cookery* by Eliza Leslie. Miss Leslie had lived in England for almost half her childhood, but had only learned to cook in her teens when the family had to take in boarders after the death of her father.

To get the really thin slices for these dainty sandwiches, try to find an unsliced loaf of bread that isn't too soft inside or too crusty outside. You may be able to find a loaf sliced "melba-thin" or "diet-thin," but the thin-slicing technique is what the recipe is about.

Cut some thin slices of bread very neatly, having slightly buttered them; and, if you choose, spread on a very little mustard. Have ready some very thin slices of cold boiled ham, and lay one between two slices of bread. You may either roll them up, or lay them flat on the plate.

. . . You may substitute for the ham, cold smoked tongue, shred or grated.

Yield: 6 sandwiches, easily multiplied

½ stick butter

1 loaf of white or whole wheat bread, unsliced

Cold boiled ham

Equipment: Ribbon to tie rolled sandwiches (optional)

1. Take butter out of refrigerator an hour before making sandwiches, to soften.

2. Cut the end piece from the bread and reserve for another use.

3. When butter is softened, butter the open end of the bread. (This helps hold the thin slices together, and is easier than buttering them after they are cut.)

4. Cut off a slice of bread about ¼-inch thick.

5. Repeat Steps 3 and 4 until you have 12 slices of bread.

6. Make very thin slices of boiled ham (or use 2 of the mechanically thin-sliced slices of ham).

7. Put a thin slice of ham between 2 buttered slices of bread.

8. For the rolled sandwiches, roll the long sides of a sandwich to make a long, thin roll, then tie with ribbon.

Serve "at supper or at luncheon."

POACHED EGGS (1839)

Although the name "Eggs Benedict" comes from New York restaurants in the 1890s, the general idea of this power breakfast was present in *The Kentucky Housewife* by Lettice Bryan, first published in 1839. It is a theme in American food history that a land-rich, labor-poor environment makes mealtime more efficient by combining foods on one platter. All they needed was the Hollandaise sauce.

Place a broad stew-pan of clean water over the fire till it boils, and set it level before the fire. Break the eggs separately into a plate or saucer, to ascertain if they are good, dropping them as you examine them into the boiling water. They must not be too much crowded, and there must be plenty of water to cover them well. Having put them all into the pan in this manner, let them remain till the whites become set; then place the pan again on the fire, and cook them as hard as you desire; they probably will be sufficiently hard by the time the water begins to boil. Raise them carefully from the water with an egg-slice, trimming the edges smoothly, and lay them separately upon small buttered toasts or broiled ham, arranging them neatly in the dish; sprinkle on a very little salt and black pepper; put on each a spoonful of melted butter, and send them up warm. They are eaten at breakfast. When prepared for the dinner table, omit the toasts or ham; serve them in a small deep dish, sprinkle on some salt and pepper, and pour over the same melted butter. They are sent as a side dish to accompany poultry and game."

Yield: Serves 6, but easily multiplied

6 small or medium eggs

6 small but thick slices of ham

6 thick slices of bread

1 stick butter

Equipment: Large soup pot, broiler pan, toaster, slotted spoon

1. Remove butter from refrigerator to soften.

2. Bring 3–4 inches of water to a boil in the soup pot. Cut slices of ham thick, but smaller than the slices of bread, and arrange them on broiler pan. Broil ham a few minutes to reheat and brown the edges.

3. Toast bread on a low setting. (In 1839, toast was made using large metal forks over an open fire, the way we toast marshmallows over a campfire now.)

4. Break eggs one at a time into a cup. (In 1839, people often broke eggs by hitting one egg with the small end of another egg.)

5. Turn off heat under boiling water, and drop in eggs one at a time.

6. When egg whites have firmed up, turn on heat and bring water back to a boil.

7. Butter toasts, then melt the rest of the butter.

8. Put a piece of buttered toast on each plate, top with a slice of ham.

9. When water boils, remove eggs from water with a slotted spoon, drain quickly, and put one on top of each slice of ham. Trim off any loose strings of egg white. Sprinkle on salt and pepper.

10. Spoon on a tablespoon of melted butter.

Serve hot for breakfast, or just the eggs to fill out a dinner of chicken or game birds.

INDIAN CUP CAKES (1846)

The first corn muffin we would recognize as such was developed by Philadelphia author Eliza Leslie for *The Indian Meal Book*, a pamphlet published in England and aimed at relieving the Irish potato famine. Leslie later added the recipe to editions of her best-selling *Directions for Cookery*. Most early American muffin recipes, such as the "Indian Muffins" in *The Kentucky Housewife*, 1839, were for flat cakes that we would now call English Muffins. What we now think of as muffins were called "soft cakes baked in cups" or "cup cakes," although there are also recipes for "cup cake" that simply measured the ingredients in cups, and were baked in loaves. (That was also the case with "tumbler cake" and "pint cake.") Just to make things more complicated, Mrs. A.L. Webster included a recipe for **Whig Cakes** to be baked in cups in her 1845 *The Improved Housewife*. By the mid-nineteenth century, some muffin recipes were thought to be interchangeable and could be baked in muffin rings to make "muffins," in the new "gem pans" to make gems (which we would now call mini-muffins), or in tall cups to make laplanders (see **Sally's Laplanders**), popovers, muffins, or cup cakes. Gems grew into muffins over the late nineteenth century, and from the mid-twentieth century became the larger and larger muffins we see today.

Yield: About 24 muffins

3 cups yellow cornmeal (stone ground preferred)

1 cup flour

3 cups whole milk, plus a little more to dissolve baking soda

1 tablespoon vinegar

1 level teaspoon baking soda (for "salaratus . . . or pearl-ash")

2 small or medium eggs

Salted butter to grease muffin tins or cups

Equipment: 20 ovenproof tea cups or 2 muffin pans, 2 good oven mitts, wire racks

1. The original recipe required sour milk, but today's pasteurized milk doesn't sour without getting really gross. Miss Leslie, as usual, had the answer: "If you have no sour milk, turn some sweet milk sour by setting a pan of it in the sun, or stirring in a spoonful of vinegar." Keep a little sweet milk to dissolve the baking soda, and in case today's drier cornmeal requires more liquid.

2. Grease tea cups or muffin pans. Miss Leslie's tea cups were 6-ounce cups.

3. Sift together the cornmeal, wheat flour, and ¼ teaspoon salt. Preheat oven to 425 degrees.

4. "Beat two eggs very light in a basin, and then stir them gradually into the pan of milk, alternately with the meal, a little at a time with each." You may have to add more milk or water to get the batter "as thick as that for a pound-cake"—a stiff batter.

5. Dissolve the baking soda in milk.

6. "Stir it at the last into the mixture, which, while foaming, must be put into buttered cups, or little tin pans, and set immediately into an oven, brisk but not too hot." Fill each cup or muffin cup ¾ full.

7. Bake 20 minutes.

8. Set on wire racks to cool.

"When done turn them out on large plates, and send them hot to the breakfast table. Split them into three pieces, and eat them with butter."

EFFERVESCING FRUIT DRINKS (1854)

The original carbonated beverage was natural spring water, bottled tightly at the source, and sold as health tonic in the early nineteenth century. People began flavoring mixing these mineral waters with flavored syrups and vinegars. At the same time, homemade, slightly alcoholic drinks like "ginger pop," "spruce beer," and "root beer" were being commercialized. This recipe, which works sort of like fruit-flavored Alka Seltzer, was intended to be a thriftier substitute. Catherine Beecher, always on the lookout for nonalcoholic beverage ideas, put this into the later editions of her *Domestic Receipt Book*. To keep this simple, find **Raspberry Vinegar** in a gourmet section. In the 1850s, families made fruit vinegars from wild fruits and used them for summer drinks without carbonation. I've adjusted her quantities for the smaller teaspoons of the 1850s, which were, however, rounded teaspoons for measuring purposes. It is likely that vinegar was somewhat weaker in the 1850s, so you may want to use a little less.

Very fine drinks for summer are prepared by putting strawberries, raspberries, or blackberries into good vinegar and then straining it off, and adding a new supply of fruit till enough flavor is secured, as directed in Strawberry Vinegar [Put four pounds very ripe strawberries, nicely dressed to three quarts of the best vinegar, and let them stand three or four days. Then drain the vinegar through a jelly bag, and pour it onto the same quantity of fruit. Repeat the process in three days a third time.] Keep the vinegar bottled, and in hot weather use it thus: Dissolve half a teaspoonful or less of saleratus [potassium bicarbonate], or [baking] soda in a tumbler, very little water till the lumps are all out. Then fill the tumbler two-thirds full of water, and then add the fruit vinegar. If several are to drink, put the soda, or saleratus into the pitcher, and then put the fruit vinegar into each tumbler, and pour

the alkali water from the pitcher into each tumbler, as each person is all ready to drink, as delay spoils it.

Yield: 1 glass

½ teaspoon baking soda

2½ ounces raspberry or blackberry vinegar

Equipment: 2 8-ounce drinking glasses

1. Dissolve baking soda in a little cold water in one of the drinking glasses.
2. Fill the glass with the baking soda ⅔ full with water.
3. Fill the other glass ¼ full with raspberry vinegar.
4. Drink quickly.
5. If you want to multiply the recipe, measure the right amount of water and baking soda into a pitcher and stir well. (Our baking soda is purer than it was in the 1850s, and dissolves better.) Fill each glass with ¼ cup of raspberry vinegar and pour away.

CHOCOLATE SYRUP (1857–1872)

This recipe is one of eleven for "Syrups for Soda and Mineral Water" given in *The New Encyclopedia of Domestic Economy* edited by Mrs. E.F. Ellet in 1872.

Baker's Chocolate, four ounces; dissolve in 20 ounces of boiling water, and dissolve in this one pound of granulated sugar.

Yield: Makes soda for 20–30

4 ounces unsweetened chocolate

1 pound (2 cups) granulated sugar

Unflavored sparkling water or seltzer

Equipment: Box grater of food processor with grating disk

1. Bring 2½ cups of water to a boil.

2. Break chocolate into small pieces, or grate on a box grater or food processor with a grating disk.

3. Add chocolate to boiling water, and remove from heat.

4. Stir well to dissolve chocolate, and add sugar.

5. Continue stirring until all the sugar is dissolved.

6. Cool and bottle in glass canning jars.

7. To make an easy chocolate soda, put two or three tablespoons of the syrup into a tall glass, and fill with soda water. Stir.

STRAWBERRY CAKE (1859–1876)

It is difficult to date the first modern-style strawberry shortcake. The general idea of mixing strawberries with cake probably goes back to the Indian **Strawberry Bread**, as the European strawberries (now called "Alpine strawberries") were seldom large or plentiful enough for cooked desserts until crossed with native American strawberries. Strawberries had too short a season for people to need many recipes, until the early north-south railroads (1840–1860) began to extend the season in urban markets. With the railroads, farmers hundreds of miles north and south could send berries to a city, so some quality of strawberries were available for months instead of weeks. Notice that strawberries needed sugar even in 1859. This is another sign that fruit was being picked before full ripeness so it would ship better.

Before the Civil War, "short cake" implied a flaky pastry, often served on top of a fruit cobbler or fruit tart. These recipes for "strawberry cake" and "strawberry biscuit" use easier, leaner, baking powder breads, and are fancied into layered sandwiches.

I have taken the "strawberry cake" recipe from the 1870 manuscript cookbook of Mrs.

Augusta (Haley) Bassett of Newton Corner, Massachusetts (the same woman who, a few years earlier and before her marriage, wrote her friend Clara's recipe for **Union Cake** in Chapter 24), because it is less buttery, and more like a modern shortcake than other early recipes. Mrs. Bassett's was a conventional sandwich. I have added steps to make a shortcake with two layers of strawberries and shortcake, as described under "strawberry biscuit" in the 1859 *Breakfast, Dinner, and Tea, viewed classically, poetically, and practically*, by Julia C. Andrews. And I have also given the steps to make one with four layers of biscuit and three layers of strawberries, as described in the greatly popular *Centennial Buckeye Cookbook* of 1876. The Buckeye recipe is almost exactly like Mrs. Bassett's, but rolls out the dough into thin layers, butters them, and then bakes the four layers in one cake pan. Although most people measured rounded spoonfuls in the nineteenth century, their teaspoons were smaller, holding about three-fourths of the present teaspoon. So I have specified level teaspoons in this recipe.

> Strawberry Biscuit.—Bake a soda biscuit after the first of the preceding rules, cutting it as large as a dining plate; open it while hot, and butter each half well; spread strawberries upon the lower half, sprinkling them thickly with sugar; lay the upper half on, and butter the upper side; cover it with strawberries, finishing it nicely with white sugar, and eat it while warm.—1859
>
> One quart of flour, two teaspoonsful cream of tartar, two tablespoonsful butter, one teaspoonful soda, one pint of milk, bake in a hot oven, when done split and butter it, have the berries ready mashed with warm water and sugar to spread on.—1870

Yield: Serves 24

4 cups flour

2 level teaspoons cream of tartar

2 tablespoons butter, plus another stick to butter baked layers

1 level teaspoon baking soda

2 cups milk

3 quarts ripe strawberries

2 cups sugar

Equipment: Food processor (optional) or pastry blender, mixing bowl, wood cutting board, 9-by-13-inch baking pan, wire rack to cool cake, long spatula or slicing knife to split layers, skimmer or slotted spoon to remove strawberries

1. Preheat oven to 400 degrees. Cut up butter into small cubes, and work into flour with pastry blender, or by whirling in food processor with metal blade. Leave rest of butter out to soften as cake bakes.

2. Mix cream of tartar with flour.

3. Add baking soda to milk and stir well.

4. Mix milk gradually into dry ingredients. (If using food processor, pour milk into the feed tube until the dough comes together and stop quickly.) You may not need all the milk.

5. Flour a board and turn out the dough. Flour the top of the dough and work just a little. It should be a very soft dough.

6. Butter the baking pan, and pat in the dough somewhat evenly.

7. Put in oven. After 15 minutes reduce to 350 degrees.

8. Hull and slice strawberries.

9. Put sugar in a pot with $\frac{1}{4}$ cup water and heat while stirring to make a syrup. Add strawberries to warm through.

10. Check cake at a thick part with wire cake tester or toothpick at 20 or 25 minutes. If the toothpick comes out clean, remove cake from oven. It will not brown very much on top.

11. After a few minutes, cut around cake to make sure it is not stuck to sides. (It will probably have pulled away from all four sides.) Flip onto wire rack to cool.

12. After a few minutes, put cake on a cutting board.

13. For Mrs. Haley's strawberry cake, cut cake into four long strips and then across the strips to make 24 small squares. Split each one, butter both layers with softened butter, and skim up enough strawberries to cover the bottom layer. Put on the top layer to make a sandwich and serve.

14. For the 1860 Julia C. Andrews version, slice the entire cake into 2 layers with a long spatula or slicing knife, butter the bottom, skim up enough strawberries to cover, then butter the top layer, and turn it upside down upon the lower layer and the strawberries, finally topping it with another layer of strawberries.

15. For a 4-layer cake in the style of the *Buckeye Cookbook*, half the original cake, then split layers and butter all 4 pieces. Build the cake on a butter-side-up bottom, a layer of strawberries, the other bottom piece butter-side-up, a layer of strawberries, the more even of the 2 tops butter-side-up, a last layer of strawberries, and the final topper butter-side-down.

"Eat it while warm."—Julia C. Andrews, 1859

12

PIONEERS
(1803–1850s)

This section includes five recipes widely used by American explorers, traders, "emigrants," prospectors, or pioneers. Except for **St. Jacob's Soup**, they are essentially older English recipes that became useful in remote places. Early pioneers west of the Mississippi relied heavily on game and nearly exterminated the buffalo, but were wary of Western plants for several generations. For much of this period, the goal was the central states around the Mississippi River system, but in the 1840s the United States acquired the West Coast and Southwest by war and purchase, and perhaps 350,000 Americans took the Overland and Oregon trails to settle there. The Mormon trek to Utah in 1847 is unusual only in that the group settled in mid-route and then became suppliers to other emigrants.

It is interesting that this group had a lot of contact with Indians, and traded foodstuffs with them, but does not seem to have been much influenced by the foods of the Plains Indians. (They were much more likely to pick up the foods of the settled Indians of the Southwest at the end of the Santa Fe trail, or the fishing tribes of the Pacific Northwest.) One food that may have started going back and forth in this period was fry bread, as pioneers were often reduced to

"baking" in frying pans, and the Plains Indians had always collected and traded buffalo tallow. (For more about fry bread, see the Navajo and Sioux chapters of *The American Ethnic Cookbook for Students*.) For later foods of the pioneers, see the settlers and homesteader recipes in Chapter 28.

PORTABLE SOUP (1803)

Portable Soup (or "pocket soup") was a boiled-down reduction of stock that made a kind of bouillon cube. Lewis and Clark started on their exploration of the Louisiana Territory with 193 pounds, which cost the government $289.50—the most expensive item in outfitting the thirty-three-person Corps of Discovery. Depending on the quality, that would have been enough to make 3–15,000 cups of soup! Captain Lewis obtained this large quantity of portable soup from military supplies. Because of the expense, portable soup was usually reserved for wealthy travelers, spies, explorers, and surveyors. For example, the wealthy planter William Byrd of Virginia took some on a trip across the Smoky Mountains in the early eighteenth century to survey the boundary between Virginia and North Carolina. It could be made in great houses, usually as a product of fall slaughtering. There are a number of recipes in early printed cookbooks, but they seem overly precise. The lengthy treatment in Mrs. Hill's *New Cook Book* (1867) suggests that she had actually made portable soup a few times, and it is the one used here. Mrs. Hill's soup is not so concentrated and more jellylike than the most portable kind of portable soup, but less likely to burn in the process of making it. (Miss Beecher's cookbook in the 1850s suggests a portable soup about thirty times stronger.) This kind of portable soup is still probably close to what Lewis and Clark had and might have been taken West by any of the better-funded explorers, traders, migrants, prospectors, or pioneers. The recipe is lengthy, but only difficult in the final stages of boiling down, where burning the reduction will spoil the whole effort.

NOTE: RECIPE TAKES SEVERAL DAYS.

Yield: 12 quarts of reconstituted soup

10 pounds beef shin, oxtails, feet, "or any scraps of fresh meat which are not choice"

1–2 ham hocks (optional)

5 pound fowl (optional)

4 onions or 6 cloves of garlic

1 bunch parsley

Equipment: 2 large soup pots with covers; clear measuring cup and turkey baster; stoneware dinner plates; 4 very wide, shallow, stoneware soup bowls; oven thermometer

1. Distribute the meat between the 2 soup pots.
2. Add enough cold water to keep the meat from burning, and set over low heat to "stew very gradually."
3. "When of a rich brown color, pour over the meat boiling water enough to cover the meat and two or three inches over."
4. Quarter the onions or garlic without peeling, and add to the two pots of soup.
5. Remove any wilted stems of parsley, then distribute it between the two pots without cutting it up.
6. Cover the pots and "boil slowly and steadily until the meat is done" (about 2 hours).
7. Strain off the broth. ("Use the meat to pot or hash.")
8. Refrigerate the broth overnight.
9. In the morning you should be able to take off all the fat with a fork. (If not, reheat the stock and skim into a clear measuring cup. Let the fat float to the surface, and use a turkey baster to remove the clear stock underneath. Repeat until there are no bubbles of fat on the surface of the stock.) Mrs. Hill suggested saving the fat "to add to gravies or soups."
10. Reheat the stock, uncovered, to a rolling boil. Season with "salt to taste and plenty of black and cayenne pepper." Put the stoneware dinner plate in the refrigerator to cool.
11. "The stew-pan must remain uncovered, and the water watched constantly at this stage of the boiling to prevent its burning." The liquid will be reduced to a small fraction of its former volume. You can combine the stock into one pot when it gets quite small.
12. "Drop a little [stock] on a cold plate; when it begins to jelly, pour it into shallow dishes and set it away to cool." If you use all four soup bowls, and the stock is more than an inch deep, you probably need to boil it down some more.
13. "Set it away to cool." This is really a drying step. Some older recipes re-

duced the jelly to a thick, gluelike consistency by putting it in cups, and setting the cups in a pan of boiling water. Another recipe sun-dried the soup. I think you could use a dehydrator, or put the bowls into the oven at its lowest possible heat. You may have to prop the oven door open to get something under 150 degrees. Old recipes then advise drying the discs or cut squares of portable soup with flannel cloths.

14. Cut the hardening soup into squares. "When dry, pack the cakes away in tin canisters; it is best to cut the pieces small; put a piece of letter paper between each layer of the jelly cakes; if there is any appearance of mold, wipe it off carefully with a dry cloth; if it cannot be removed with a cloth, use a little warm water, and expose them to the sun occasionally."

15. "With this portable broth, gravies and soups may be made with very little trouble, using to each pint of boiling water, four square inches of the jelly, an inch thick; and when the soup is made, add vegetables and seasoning as is necessary."

Serve remade into a simple bouillon as explorers might have used it in an emergency. According to Byrd, "If you should be faint with fasting or fatigue, let a small piece of this Glue melt in your mouth, and you will find yourself surprisingly refreshed."

WINTER SAUSAGE (1845)

The Farmer's and Emigrant's Hand-Book, by Josiah T. Marshall, was intended as a guidebook for pioneers, and homesteaders. This recipe was originally designed for one hundred pounds of pork, as would have been available at winter slaughtering time, when homesteaders could preserve sausage without curing or smoking. This adaptation of Marshall's recipe was reduced in size by

William Woys Weaver in his 1989 book, *America Eats*, but is still the authentic flavor of early America, especially in New England, where people still like a lot of sage. This can be cooked as patties, or stuffed into casings, or used in **A Very Economical Dish**. I have taken the directions from a similar recipe for a beef-pork sausage meat in the 1854, *The New Family Book, or Ladies' Indispensable Companion*, also published in New York. Probably the cheapest way to get a mixture of lean and fatty pork today is to cut up a pork shoulder.

Yield: Serves 12

> 1½ pounds lean pork
> 1½ pounds fatty pork
> 1 tablespoon pickling salt
> 2½ tablespoons powdered sage
> 1½ tablespoons fresh-ground pepper

Equipment: Meat grinder (optional)

1. Chop meat by hand, as they did in the 1840s, or in a meat grinder or food processor.
2. Sprinkle on the salt and spices, and mix well.
3. "To make this into small cakes, and fry in the same manner as sausages is very good for breakfast."

The New Family Book fries sausages in fat rendered from two or three slices of salt pork, but today we don't like to eat so much fat, so we would fry the sausages like hamburgers (which were originally thought of as sausages), in their own fat.

Serve two patties each as part of an enormous breakfast.

SALT RISING BREAD (1846)

It's interesting to think about how Early American housewives kept a yeast culture going before they know that yeast was a living collection of single-celled animals. Louis Pasteur proved that yeast were microorganisms in 1859, but this was not widely understood for at least another twenty years. People knew that the same stuff fermented bread, beer, wine, and cider. They knew that bread would rise if made with a frothing batter (which they called yeast) that included some dregs from the beer barrel or cider keg, or dregs obtained from a brewery, or a little dough kept over from a previous batch of bread. They also knew that dried yeast could be made into an effective batter and that sometimes frozen dough would thaw out and work, but that baked bread would not start yeast.

But they didn't know *why*, and it doesn't seem to have bothered anyone so long as they knew *how*. They also knew how to capture wild yeast to make "Bread Without Yeast," although they didn't exactly understand what they were doing. Housewives had no idea that yeast cells were present all over the environment—and especially in kitchens where bread had been made many times before. Some people evidently thought that the salt in the warmed batter was making the bread rise, hence the name salt-rising bread. Although recipes vary, they generally start with cornmeal (which makes very good yeast food and often had a little yeast on it) and always include a period where the batter is kept warm, which we now understand was to incubate the culture. Most of the recipes also included milk, which would sour over the incubation process, and begin to smell like ripened cheese, and worse. But as the bread was baked, the bacteria spoiling the milk were killed along with the yeast, and the bad smell went away. So salt-rising bread always smelled bad but ended up tasting good, a little like toasted cheese. (There may have been a little yeast in Early American milk; today's pasteurized milk arrives without any bacterial content.) The sour milk retains

moisture, so salt-rising bread has a somewhat dense crumb and makes good toast.

This recipe was set down toward the end of the eighteenth century by Mary Merrill Horton, an early settler of Kent County, Texas, who lived to be ninety-one. She and her husband James were given land there as payment for his service to the Republic of Texas in its war of independence from Mexico in 1835–1836. The Republic lasted ten years, and then became part of the United States in 1845. Mary Horton remembered making salt-rising bread for one hundred guests at the first Texas Fourth of July celebration in 1846. Her recipe was published in 1988 by her great-great-granddaughter Mary Lauderdale Kearns in *The Puddin Hill Cookbook; Recollections & Recipes*. The use of egg in her recipe is unusual, as is the small amount of salt. I have added techniques from Mrs. Kearns's modern comments and from pre–Civil War cookbooks. If you can obtain unpasteurized milk, it will sour more and not smell so bad. You can hurry things up with a pinch of dry yeast, but that's a cheat the pioneers often couldn't use. There are lots of ways to rig up 90- to 100-degree bowls of starter and dough, such as heating pads, electric blankets, electric ovens on the lowest setting, the pilot lights in gas ovens, and so on. If you can't provide constant warmth, your salt-rising bread will develop, but it may take a day or two longer.

> Break one egg into a teacup, and beat with a rotary beater [which was not available until the 1870s] until light. Add 1 rounded tablespoon cornmeal and 1 even tablespoon of sugar and beat again. Fill cup with boiling water and stir well. Set in a pan of warm water, cover and place in a warm place until morning. This needs to work at least 10 hours. In the morning, to one cup warm milk and 1 cup lukewarm

water, add enough flour to make a stiff batter. Stir into this the cornmeal and egg mixture to which you have just added ½ teaspoon salt—no more. Set in a warm place and let rise again. When light and bubbly add more flour and knead to make a smooth dough. Make into loaves. Brush with butter and let rise again. Bake in a moderate oven for 40–45 minutes."

NOTE: RECIPE TAKES TWO DAYS OR MORE.

Yield: 2 small loaves; serves 12–16

1 large egg

1 rounded tablespoon white cornmeal (stone ground preferred)

1 tablespoon sugar

1 cup whole milk

6 cups flour

1 cup whole wheat flour

¼ cup wheat germ

1 tablespoon butter

Solid shortening to grease pans

Equipment: Yogurt maker (optional), teakettle, 1-cup Pyrex measuring cup, flat whisk or very small whisk, kitchen towel, mixing bowls, wooden breadboard, 2 small bread pans, instant-read meat thermometer, microwave oven (optional), pastry brush or small clean nylon-bristle paintbrush

1. Bring 2 cups of water to a boil in a teakettle.

2. Break the egg into the 1-cup measuring cup. Beat the egg until light with a small whisk or a flat whisk.

3. Add sugar and cornmeal and beat again.

4. Dribble in boiling water while whisking the egg mixture until the liquid (not just the froth) reaches the six-ounce marker.

5. Put the small measuring cup into a larger pan or bowl. Pour the boiling water carefully into the larger pan to surround the small tea cup. Put the whole thing somewhere warm, such as over a pilot light or in a gas oven that is warmed by a pilot light. Cover with the kitchen towel. Leave overnight. The idea is to keep it about 95 degrees—"a warm place" in Texas in July. (A yogurt maker keeps the culture a little too warm, about 110–115 degrees, but you could try one with the lid ajar.)

6. Mix the flour with the whole wheat flour and wheat germ, and set aside.

7. In the morning, check the egg mixture for a topping of bubbles or froth and a "yeasty smell." If it seems ready, heat up the milk to nearly boiling. Pour it into a mixing bowl, and stir in enough of the flour mixture to make a stiff batter, about 3 cups. Check the temperature, you may need to let it cool to around 90–95 degrees.

8. Add ½ teaspoon salt to the egg mixture, and stir it into the batter.

9. Set this mixing bowl of warm batter in a warm place, cover, and let rise until light and bubbly, 6–8 hours or overnight or even 2 days. Don't rush it, and don't throw it out just because it smells putrid. (Throw it out if it turns colors or grows mold, however.)

10. When it bubbles and smells like yeast, add more flour, another 3 cups or so, to make a dough.

11. Flour the board and your hands, and knead until the dough is smooth and elastic.

12. Grease the bread pans.

13. Cut the dough in half and work each half into a loaf shape.

14. Melt the butter in a microwave or on the stove in a small saucepan.

15. Pat each loaf into the bread pans. Brush with melted butter and let rise until they look doubled in bulk, about 3 hours if you have a good strong yeast culture going, but possibly overnight or longer.

16. Bake at 375 degrees for 35–45 minutes. Bread is done when browned on top and the bottom sounds hollow when tapped. If it doesn't sound hollow, you can put the bread right back into the oven without the pan to finish.

Serve as toast, which the pioneers would have made over the fire as we toast marshmallows, but more slowly and carefully.

OVERLAND TRAIL LEMONADE (1849)

This recipe was recalled by Catherine Haun in a later diary after her trip from Iowa to Sacramento. The acid she mentions was citric acid, part of a medical kit to fight scurvy (which we now know was a vitamin C deficiency). It is now sold in the spice section of supermarkets as "sour salt." Since there are no proportions given, you may fiddle with the recipe, probably in the direction of making it weaker and less sweet.

A little of the [citric acid "—an antidote for scurvy"] acid mixed with sugar and water and a few drops of essence of lemon made a fine substitute for lemonade.—Catherine Haun, "A Woman's Trip Across the Plains, 1849," manuscript diary The Huntington Library, San Marino, California, quoted in *Women's Diaries of the Westward Journey,* by Lillian Schlissel, 1982.

Yield: 1 cup

2 tablespoons sugar

½ teaspoon sour salt

¼ teaspoon lemon extract

Equipment: Measuring cup, measuring spoons

1. To 1 measuring cup of cold water, add the sugar, sour salt, and lemon extract.

2. Stir well to dissolve everything.

Serve when very tired and hungry.

ST. JACOB'S SOUP (1850S)

This thrifty soup recipe came down in the family of Benjamin Morgan Roberts, an 1847 Utah pioneer and early settler of Southern Utah who was part of the "Mormon Battalion" that fought for the United States in the Mexican War of 1845–1846. Tradition holds that the soup was used by Roberts and his sons when working distant parts of the ranch. It was gathered by Winnifred Jardine for *Famous Mormon Recipes,* and reprinted in *Recipes from America's Restored Villages* (1975) by Jean Anderson. The battalion was more like an alliance between countries than volunteering, as relations between the federal government and the Mormons continued to be difficult until Utah statehood (on the seventh application) in 1896.

Yield: Serves 4–6

½ pound lean salt pork

2 large potatoes

2 large yellow onions

4 large ripe tomatoes (or a 14-ounce can of whole tomatoes)

2–3 tablespoons sugar (optional)

Equipment: Soup pot, heavy frying pan

1. Cut the salt pork in small dice. (This is easier if it is partially frozen first.)

2. Fry the salt pork slowly in a heavy pan until all the fat cooks out.

3. Meanwhile, peel potatoes and cut into ½-inch cubes.

4. Boil potatoes in 2 cups of water.

5. Halve and peel onions, and slice thin. (Wear swim goggles to avoid tears.)

6. Add onions to potatoes and simmer until potatoes are almost tender.

7. When salt pork is down to crispy bits, reserve them and 2 tablespoons of the fat. (The Roberts family would have saved the rest of the fat for cooking or soap, even when out on the range.)

8. Add the bits of salt pork, the fat, the tomatoes, 2 teaspoons salt, and $\frac{1}{8}$ teaspoon pepper to the potatoes and onions. Bring back to a simmer and cook uncovered for about 45 minutes.

9. Stir occasionally to break up tomatoes. You may need to add a little water if the soup starts to stick and burn.

10. Taste and add sugar if necessary to mellow not-so-ripe tomatoes (not necessary with canned tomatoes).

Serve in tin bowls.

13

EARLY AMERICAN HEALTH FOOD (1827–1857)

Health food reform really begins in the 1830s and 1840s with the lectures of Rev. Sylvester Graham (1794–1851). Prior to Graham, all cookbooks had health food recipes for curing the sick, but Americans ate what they could afford or what they liked. The food for sick people was bland and easy to digest, such as beef broth or oatmeal gruel. Lydia Maria Child's cure for chronic diarrhea was an "Egg Gruel," which was basically hot egg nog. In a time when all kinds of reform ideas were in the air, Graham began lecturing on temperance (see Chapter 18), but became well known when his lectures moved on to criticize the heavy lard-crust pies and puddings most people enjoyed, white bread, and mass market milk—some of which came from malnourished cows fed on brewery mash. Graham became a vegetarian, and also opposed leavened bread because yeast produced alcohol. He thought hot bread was bad and suggested baking it twice. In addition to alcohol, he opposed coffee, tea, chocolate, and spices as stimulants.

What lasted was the whole wheat flour. It certainly helped a lot of people with stomach problems, and it was eventually sweetened with cheap molasses to make the graham crackers we know today. Many Grahamites were also abolitionists (see Chapter 14), however, and would not eat sugar or molasses made by slaves. Temperance boarding houses became Graham boarding houses, with vegetarian food to go along with the no-alcohol policy.

Graham's criticisms of white flour and animal fats are still part of the health food movement, and there is a direct chain of association between the Early American Grahamites and much of health food since. The Seventh-Day Adventist church, founded in the 1840s, has been an important promoter of vegetarian foods and meat substitutes. As we will taste with the late Victorian health foods in Chapter 29, the Adventist Sanitarium under the Kellogg brothers became the leading American promoter of health food and vegetarianism. Doctors who worked with Graham developed forms of alternative medicine that were patronized by reformers, Adventists, and early followers of Christian Science. It is likely that Graham's ideas influenced his contemporary Joseph Smith in the diet regulations of the Mormon church and possible that they reached Fard Mohammed's regulations for the Nation of Islam. During Graham's lifetime and immediately after, some Shaker communities instituted vegetarian diets.

Terminology in early American health food was not always clear. For example, the "Homeopathic Molasses Cakes" in the 1856 [Hannah] *Widdifield's New Cookbook*, are made with graham flour, but aren't intended to cure by the homeopathic theory of like-cures-like—unless the cookies were intended to give you a stomachache to cure your stomach problems!

DYSPEPSIA BREAD (AND CRACKERS) (1827)

Graham bread and graham crackers existed before Sylvester Graham, as you can see in this recipe from *The Frugal Housewife*, by Lydia Maria Child. Twelve years later, Sarah Josepha Hale, an opponent of strict vegetarianism, confirmed that "Brown or Dyspepsia Bread . . . is now best known as 'Graham Bread' not that Doctor Graham invented or discovered the manner of its preparation, but that he has been unwearied and successful in recommending it to the public. It is an excellent article of diet for the dyspeptic and costive and, for most persons of sedentary habits, would be beneficial. It agrees well with children; and, in short, I think it should be used in every family, though not to the exclusion of fine bread." Strict Grahamites would not use the yeast. I have also used some details from a no-leaven 1870 recipe in *What to Eat and How to Cook It* by John Cowan, M.D. You can reduce the proportions of the recipe. Early American baking recipes are all very large because families ate a lot of bread and only fired up brick ovens once or twice a week.

The American Farmer publishes the following receipt for making bread, which has proved highly salutary to persons afflicted with that complaint, viz:—Three quarts unbolted wheat meal; one quart soft water, warm, not hot; one gill of fresh yeast; one gill of molasses, or not, as may suite the taste; 1 teas-spoonful of saleratus.

This will make two loaves and should remain in the oven at least one hour; and when taken out, placed where they will cool gradually. Dyspepsia crackers can be made with unbolted flour, water, and saleratus.

Yield: Serves about 20

11¼ cups whole wheat flour, and some for kneading

¾ cup wheat germ

1 tablespoon dry yeast (or ½ cup **Potato Yeast**)

½ cup molasses (optional)

1 teaspoon baking soda

Salted butter to grease pans

Equipment: Oversize mixing bowl, 2 large loaf pans or 4 small loaf pans, breadboard, wire racks, clean kitchen towel

1. If using dry yeast, dissolve it in ½ cup warm water with a pinch of sugar.

2. Mix wheat germ and flour thoroughly in the large mixing bowl.

3. Dissolve the baking soda in a little water. Warm 4 cups of cold water to lukewarm.

4. Once yeast has a foam of bubbles on the surface, pour it into the center of the flour mixture, then stir in the baking soda mixture, and the warm water, with the molasses if using.

5. Work the whole mixture into a dough that holds together. (You may need a little more water.)

6. Flour the board and your hands, and knead the dough until it is smooth and no longer sticky.

7. Set in a covered bowl to rise. (If you want to try graham crackers from before Graham, heat the oven to 400 degrees. Roll out the dough ¾-inch

thick, and cut large squares or rounds. Prick holes with a fork. Flour a baking sheet, and arrange the crackers not touching. Bake about 20 minutes. Cool on wire racks.)

8. When dough is visibly larger (it won't "double in bulk"), punch down the large bubbles, and give it a few more kneads. Divide dough in 4 pieces and put into bread pans.

9. Cover pans with a kitchen towel and let rise until visibly bigger.

10. Preheat oven to 450 degrees.

11. Bake 15 minutes, then reduce heat to 375 degrees for another 15 minutes.

12. Reduce heat to 330 degrees for 15 minutes, or 20–25 minutes for large loaves. Bread is done when it sounds hollow when tapped on the bottom.

13. Cool bread on wire racks.

Serve when cold with jam or fresh fruit.

GRAHAM BISCUIT OR ROLL (1845)

These heavy whole wheat muffins were the most popular health food of the early American period and were generally known as Graham gems. You will find a description of the childhood fare of Louisa May Alcott with the **Unleavened Bread and Apples** recipe in Chapter 20. Here is another, in the recollection of an Alcott family friend, Mrs. C.M. Severance for the 1894 book, *How We Cook in Los Angeles*, by the Ladies Social Circle, Simpson M.E. Church. "The usual 'cuts and joints' were being replaced by deliciously-cooked breads, by 'crushed wheat' molded into the appetizing and artistic forms of corn, melons, and other pretty fruits, and smothered to genuine cream; or by pears and apples baked to a luscious tenderness and rich brown." She adds directions "somewhat modified by later experiment," but clearly based on her taste

memory of enjoying Grahamite cooking in the Alcott home. The modifications on the original are probably the use of milk and butter. An 1856 recipe book kept by Abigail Alcott has a recipe for "Biscuit without Milk," which does use an early form of baking powder.

Take of this modern meal (which includes all the nutritious elements of the grain, leaving out only the harsh outer husk), 1 cupful, 1½ cups of fresh milk, or of cold water a trifle more or less, the former making the gem moister within and crisper and browner of crust. Beat the meal and milk together smartly, then pour the mixture into *very hot, iron,* gem pans and put these into a very hot oven. Twenty minutes, or less, [it] will take to give an even nut-brown color, and eaten with fresh butter they will give the full sweetness of the grain and of the well-baked crust.

Yield: 6–8 mini-muffins

1 cup minus 1 tablespoon whole wheat flour

1 tablespoon wheat germ

1½ cups of whole milk (optional)

Butter to grease pan, plus ½ stick for serving

Equipment: Muffin pan or mini-muffin pans, wire rack (optional), whisk

1. Butter pan(s) and preheat oven to 400 degrees.

2. Put pan(s) in oven to preheat.

3. Mix milk or water with flour and wheat germ, beating well to lighten them, since there is no leavening. You may need a little more milk or water because today's flour is drier.

4. Remove pan or pans from the oven, pour in batter, leaving regular muffin pans only half full.

5. Return to oven and bake 20 minutes, or until quite well browned.

6. Remove from oven and cool briefly on top of the stove or on a wire rack.

Serve hot with butter.

CORN CREAM CAKE (1854)

Russell T. Trall, M.D. was an associate of Graham whose clinic eventually specialized in the "Water Cure," a series of baths and treatments especially popular among women, who got little help from orthodox medicine in this period. (Trall also performed abortions, which were legal at the time.) In this recipe from *The Hydropathic Cook Book* (republished on <www.civilwarinteractive.com/cookbook.htm>), Trall uses the baking soda to neutralize the sour cream, rather than to lighten the cornbread without demon yeast. This large recipe can be divided in half or thirds.

> Take a pint of thick, sour, but not very old cream; one quart of milk or buttermilk; yellow corn-meal sufficient to thicken to the consistency of pound cake; and bicarbonate of soda enough to sweeten the cream; add the soda to the cream; stir in the meal; put it in floured pans, an inch thick, and bake in a quick oven.

Yield: 48 pieces

2 cups sour cream

4 cups milk or buttermilk

3 cups yellow cornmeal (stone ground preferred)

2 teaspoons to 2 tablespoons baking soda

Flour to flour pans

Equipment: 3 8-by-8-inch brownie pans, or 2 sheet cake pans 8 by 12 inches or larger, or 4 muffin tins

1. Mix sour cream with milk or buttermilk.

2. Sprinkle on 2 teaspoons of baking soda if using milk, 2 tablespoons if using buttermilk.

3. Mix in soda and cornmeal. You may not need all the cornmeal, or you may need a little more if using stone ground. You want a fairly stiff dough that won't stick to the pans.

4. Flour the pans.

5. Preheat the oven to 425 degrees.

6. Divide the dough, and pat it into the corners of the pans, but not hard enough so that it sticks. (For muffins, cut pieces that fill the cups entirely.)

7. Bake about 30 minutes, checking that they don't burn, and testing with a toothpick or wire cake tester. (Cornbread is always a little sticky, but the testers should come out almost clean.)

8. Let cool before serving; Grahamites did not eat hot bread.

Serve in 2-inch squares with fresh fruit and boiled vegetables.

MARLBOROUGH PUDDING (1857)

Marlborough Pudding (which was almost always a pie) is an old English recipe which became enormously useful in the American colonies because it makes a winter dessert out of stored apples or dried apples made into applesauce. It was probably the origin of pumpkin pie, which is also held together with custard. This recipe is from *Christianity in the Kitchen; A Physiological Cook Book*, by Mrs. Horace Mann. All Mrs. Mann meant by the title was that "Compounds like wedding cake, suet plum-puddings, and rich turtle soup, are masses of indigestible material, which should never find their way to any Christian table. ... If asked why I pronounce these and similar dishes *unchristian*,

I answer, that health is one of the indispensable conditions of the highest morality and beneficence." What is more Christian and healthful about her Marlborough Pudding is the use of mashed potatoes and cream instead of white flour and butter or lard in the crust. Mrs. Mann also opposed the use of spices. I have taken the crust recipe from elsewhere in her book.

> Stew and strain six large apples, add half a pint of rich cream, the rind of one lemon, and the juice of two, six eggs and six ounces of sugar. Line a deep baking dish with rich potato paste and bake it an hour.

Yield: Serves 12

2½ pounds potatoes (8 medium)

2 cups heavy cream

6 large apples

2 lemons

6 medium eggs (or 4 jumbo eggs)

¾ cup sugar

Equipment: 2 soup pots, mixing bowl, vegetable peeler, potato masher or ricer, lemon juicer, strainer or food mill, lemon zester or box grater (optional), large Pyrex or terracotta casserole or two pie plates

1. Peel and boil potatoes 20–30 minutes, or until a fork meets no resistance at the center.

2. Peel and slice the apples, discarding the cores.

3. Heat apples and a very little water in a covered pot over low heat. Stir and mash periodically.

4. When potatoes are done, drain and mash to get 1 quart of mashed potatoes.

5. Stir 1 cup of the cream into the potatoes, and chill for a few minutes while you make the filling.

6. When apples are done, mash thoroughly and push through a strainer with a wooden spoon (or use a food mill) to make a smooth applesauce.

7. Zest or grate or peel the peel from one of the lemons, and mince into fine bits (if you peeled it).

8. Juice both lemons.

9. Beat the eggs until creamy and light.

10. In a mixing bowl, combine the applesauce, lemon peel, the other cup of cream, the eggs, and the lemon juice.

11. Preheat oven to 425 degrees.

12. Take the potato mixture out of the refrigerator and mold it into the casserole or pie plates.

13. Fill with the apple mixture.

14. Bake 15 minutes, and reduce heat to 275 degrees.

15. Bake another 45 minutes (longer for deep dish casseroles), or until a knife blade poked into the center comes out clean.

Serve as dessert, or New England fashion, for breakfast.

14

ABOLITIONIST RECIPES (1827–c.1910)

As a cause, the abolition of slavery was initially part of a group of "reform" causes that also included women's rights, temperance (avoidance of alcohol), free public education, and a variety of other political and social reforms. As we will see in the recipes associated with women's suffrage in Chapter 23, some people embraced all these causes, some people divided up the reform agenda, and many Americans scoffed at the whole lot.

Thus, if you want to re-create a meal in an abolitionist home, you can draw on recipes in Chapters 13, 18, 24, and 32 as well as the recipes below and in Chapters 6 through 9.

From the mid-1830s, many abolitionists avoided sugar, molasses, and rum—products of slavery. There is no evidence that they attempted to boycott other plantation products such as rice, tobacco, or cotton, nor did they confront the role of the northern economy in providing salt cod and other foods to the slave system. As early as 1804, the *Old Farmer's Almanack* promoted maple sugar as a slavery-free sweetener: "[M]y poor maple stuff, as they call it, possesses no mingled tears of misery; no desponding slave

ever groaned over my cauldrons or fanned them with his sighs: No; this little lump in my hand is the reward of my own labour on my own farm." Honey production was also encouraged by abolitionists, and there were some experiments with beet sugar.

Although there were no cookbooks specifically dedicated to abolitionism, at least four committed abolitionists wrote full-length cookbooks. Three are discussed below. The fourth, Lydia Maria Child, author of the *American Frugal Housewife*, was among the first and most active abolitionists, and her husband lost much of her cookbook royalty money in a beet-sugar venture in western Massachusetts. It is possible that Mrs. Child deliberately omitted molasses and rum in her recipe for **Baked Beans** in Chapter 6. However, it is more likely that she was being as frugal as her title, and many early pork and beans recipes follow hers in omitting sweetener. This book was used in many abolitionist homes because of Mrs. Child's later work, although in most recipes, Mrs. Child uses all the products she would later boycott, as does Catherine E. Beecher, another early cookbook writer, reformer, and significant opponent of political abolitionism.

ANOTHER EXCELLENT LEMONADE (1827)

This recipe is in the 1827 *The House Servant's Directory*, by Robert Roberts, the first published book of recipes by an African-American. Roberts had been the chief butler for Massachusetts governor Christopher Gore and devotes much of his book to advising other African-Americans how to succeed as hired help. Roberts himself did well enough to buy several buildings in Boston and became an organizer of the Negro Conventions that took public stands on issues of civil rights. The amount of sugar is about half what we might use today, but Roberts was writing well before the abolitionist anti-sugar campaigns. Since the wealthy Gore could afford as much sugar as he wanted, this is evidence that the American sweet tooth developed mostly during the nineteenth century.

> Take one gallon of water, put to it the juice of ten good lemons, and the zeasts of six of them likewise, then add to this one pound of sugar, and mix it well together, strain it through a fine strainer, and put it in ice to cool; this will be a most delicious and fine lemonade.

Yield: Serves 18

1 pound sugar (4 cups)

10 lemons

Equipment: Lemon zester, manual or electric lemon juicer

1. Zest six of the lemons.
2. Halve and juice all the lemons.
3. In a large mixing bowl, add the lemon juice and zest to four quarts of water.
4. Add the sugar and stir until it is dissolved.
5. Strain into pitchers or another large mixing bowl.
6. Chill in a refrigerator, although the lemonade will be colder and taste somewhat different if you sink the pitchers into a large bowl or tub of ice, as Roberts did.

TO STEW GIBLETS (1847)

This is perhaps the first recipe for soul food written by an African-American for other African-Americans. Tunis G. Campbell was originally trained as a minister for missionary work in Liberia as part of one of the colonization schemes that were promoted as alternatives to either slavery or emancipation. About ten thousand African-Americans were resettled before the Civil War, but colonization came to be resented by free people of color like Tunis Campbell. As a student in an otherwise all-white seminary in New York in the 1820s, he decided to oppose colonization and began preaching antislavery and temperance among free African-American communities in New Jersey, Boston, and New York. Along the way, he supported himself as a waiter and hotel steward, and in 1847 published the *Hotel Keepers, Headwaiters, and Housekeeper's Guide*. By the 1840s, white immigrants and discrimination had pushed free African-Americans out of many occupations in northern cities. Food service remained an important career path, and self-employed black caterers were able to amass some wealth, employ others, and maintain contacts with white leaders. In most northern cities, the caterers were also stalwarts of the abolitionist movement and the "Underground Railroad" of escaped slaves seeking refuge in Canada. Tunis Campbell was thus not unusual as a politically active waiter, but he was remarkable in writing and publishing a cookbook and more remarkable for what he was able to do during and after the Civil War.

HARTWELL

Figure 9 Tunis G. Campbell. *Source: Reprinted from Tunis Campbell*, Hotel Keepers, Head Waiters, and House-keepers' Guide. *Boston: Coolidge and Wiley, 1848.*

Campbell's *Guide* describes how the black abolitionist organized African-American waiters into military-style squads to make their work more efficient. He advised waiters to learn some cooking so that they could substitute in the kitchen during emergencies. Most of the recipes in the book are for large quantities and for elaborate soups and sauces that might be featured in the fine hotels where Campbell worked, such as Howard's Hotel in New York or the Adams House in Boston. But this small recipe for spare poultry parts was probably never served to guests. Here we can cook along-

side Tunis Campbell as he makes an economical treat for himself and the men under his command.

Campbell was able to use his organizational talents during the Civil War, when he was put in charge of freed slaves farming cooperatively in the Carolina Sea Islands. This was both a support to the black and white troops massing on those islands and a test of emancipation. After the war, Campbell continued the same work in Northern Georgia, helping freed slaves resist the sharecropping schemes of their former owners as well as Northern speculators. He was elected justice of the peace and state senator, and apparently used these offices to support the rights of new African-American voters. Former slave-owners claimed to have been physically prevented from reclaiming plantations that were under cultivation by Campbell's supporters. The former waiter set up a political machine and retained considerable local power and a seat in the state legislature until 1876—four years after white political power was restored in Georgia. He was then jailed on a false charge and forced back North. He returned to preaching and wrote a second book justifying his work in Georgia.

The recipe does not specify whether the giblets came from a chicken, a turkey, a duck, a goose, or any of the various game birds served in urban hotels in the 1840s. Probably any of these could be combined into a larger stew for the whole crew. I have suggested substitutions based on chicken parts. For "sweet herbs," I have taken them in the older English sense of parsley, thyme and such. (I am indebted to Howard Paige's book, *Aspects of African-American Foodways*, for drawing my attention to Campbell's book. A recent biography of Campbell is *Freedom's Shore*, by Russell Duncan. *The Philadelphia Negro*, by W.E.B. Du Bois remains the best study of African-American communities in the north during the nineteenth century and has several pages on the role of cooks and caterers.)

To Stew Giblets—Let the giblets be clean picked and washed, the feet skinned, and the bill cut off, the head split in two, the pinion bones [wing tips] broken, the liver and the gizzard cut in four, and the neck in two pieces; put them in half a pint of water with pepper, salt, a small onion, and sweet herbs. Cover the sauce-pan close, and let them stew till enough, upon a slow fire. Then season them with salt, take out the onion and herbs and pour them into a dish with all the liquor.

Yield: Serves 1 tired headwaiter, but the recipe can easily be multiplied

2 chicken gizzards

2 chicken hearts

1 chicken liver

1 chicken neck

2 chicken feet (or substitute 2 more necks, or 4 wings)

2 chicken wing tips

1 small onion

1 sprig thyme (or a pinch of powdered thyme)

3 sprigs parsley

Equipment: Sharp chef's knife or cleaver, rubber mallet (optional), saucepan with tight cover.

1. Skin chicken feet if using. Remove any fat or membrane from chicken liver. Break wing tips (and wings if using) with a cleaver or chef's knife and a rubber mallet. (Set the cleaver on the chicken, hit with the mallet.)

2. Cut neck or necks in half.

3. Halve the hearts, liver, and gizzards. Cut the liver and gizzards again to make quarters.

4. Halve and peel the onion.

5. Tie the herbs into a bundle with one of the parsley stems.

6. Put everything in the saucepan with a cup of water, or a little more to cover.

7. Heat to boiling, then reduce heat so the pot will simmer when tightly covered.

8. Stew until gizzards are tender, about one hour.

9. Remove herb bundle and onion.

Serve in a bowl with a plate underneath for the bones.

AUNT LAURA'S BREAKFAST POTATOES (1875)

"Aunt" and "Uncle" were terms of both respect and condescension for older African-Americans throughout the nineteenth century. This recipe was recorded by Elizabeth Smith Miller for her 1875 book, *In the Kitchen*. Miller was the daughter of the prominent abolitionist Gerrit Smith and the cousin and lifelong associate of suffragist Elizabeth Cady Stanton. It was Miller who made and wore the first "Bloomer" costume, and demonstrated it for Amelia Bloomer, who published a pattern in her magazine. In the 1840s, the two Elizabeths were taken to an attic room in Smith's house and had a long talk with Harriet Powell, a recently escaped slave their own age who was on her way to Canada. It was said that in Gerrit Smith's house, even the servants were abolitionists.

So it is somewhat disappointing to see the racial stereotypes in Mrs. Miller's comment: "It requires no little time to cut the potatoes properly; it was 'Aunt Laura's' evening work, and instead of being additional *labor*, after her day's struggle in the kitchen, it seemed a recreation, as she sat, smiling and happy, while the delicate bits fell from her knife like snow-flakes into the basin below." Since the recipe requires four cups of potato pieces cut the size of a dime, Aunt Laura spent many dull hours making these potatoes. I would suggest doing this as a group project, and keeping track of time, so you can see how many person-hours this might take.

Many white abolitionists could not imagine African-Americans as their social equals, and this helps to explain why African-American rights were whittled away in the 1870s and 1880s.

This is a rich dish of scalloped potatoes. Mrs. Miller says that they were served in her childhood, so they may have been enjoyed by the fugitive slaves who stayed in the Smith mansion and by visitors such as John Brown.

Yield: Serves 8

2 pounds potatoes (new or waxy red potatoes preferred)

2 teaspoons salt

2 ounces butter (½ stick)

1 cup heavy cream

Equipment: 4–6-quart saucepan

1. Peel potatoes and boil until done (about 15 minutes, depending on size of potatoes) in salted water.

2. Cool potatoes in cold running water, or let cool overnight in refrigerator.

3. Melt butter.

4. "Take a small, sharp, thin-bladed knife and 'nip' the potatoes in bits about the size of dime, [1870s dimes were the same size as dimes are today] a little thinner on the edges than in the center." If you're not used to knife work, it is probably safer to cut the potatoes into sticks around the size of a dime (a little less than ¾-inch), and then cut those as thin as you can.

5. Collect the potatoes in a saucepan, in layers with the salt and melted butter.

6. When you have 2 quarts of potatoes (halfway up a 4-quart pan, ⅓ up a 6-quart pan), pour the cream on top.

7. "Cover, heat slowly, and let them stew gently for eight or ten minutes; stir as little as possible, and with a fork only."

8. "In taking them up, be careful not to break the pieces."

Serve as part of an enormous breakfast with eggs, pies, small steaks, and toast.

CHICKEN CROQUETTES (1874)

This dish was submitted by Mrs. J. Young Scammon to the *Home Cook Book*, published in Chicago in 1874 to raise funds for The Home for the Friendless. By 1874, Mr. Scammon was a wealthy lawyer, investor, and philanthropist leading the recovery from the Great Fire. But in the 1850s he was a stalwart of the Underground Railroad in Illinois. At one point he was called before the court and asked whether he, as a member of the bar, would be able to do his duty in a posse to capture a fugitive slave. His answer, "I would certainly obey the summons, but I should probably stub my toe and fall down before I reached him."

Chicken croquettes were a dish especially associated with African-American caterers in the nineteenth century and apparently quite popular with Chicago's upper crust: there are four other recipes in the book. Mrs. Scammon's are quite the best—meatier and more flavorful than any croquettes made today. If you can afford the optional truffles, you have the kind of dish enjoyed by America's first large group of millionaires in the late nineteenth century. One of Mrs. Scammon's other recipes in the book is taken from *In the Kitchen*, showing the circulation of Mrs. Miller's book in abolitionist homes. I have modernized the method with suggestions from *The Fearless Frying Cookbook*, by Hoppin' John Martin Taylor, the most historically minded of contemporary southern cooks (he suggests frying in peanut oil if you don't want to use lard). This recipe has a number of steps, and handling hot oil is always dangerous, but this makes a good team project, as it might have been at the affluent Scammon home.

The proportions that we give below are for half a good sized chicken. After

boiling, chop the meat fine, fry it with one ounce of butter; then add one half teaspoon of flour; stir for more than half a minute, adding the chopped meat and a little more than a gill of meat broth; salt, pepper and a pinch of nutmeg; stir for five minutes, then take it from the fire and mix the yolks of two eggs with it; put on the fire again, stirring the while. Lastly, you may or may not add four mushrooms chopped, or two truffles, or both, according to taste. Turn the mixture into a dish and set it away to cool. When perfectly cold mix it well, as the upper part is drier than the rest; put it in parts on the pasteboard, a tablespoon for each part. Have bread crumbs on the pasteboard, then make into any form required. Dip each croquette in beaten egg; roll in bread crumbs again and fry in hot fat. Garnish each croquette with a sprig of parsley.

NOTE: RECIPE MAY BE DONE OVER TWO DAYS.

CAUTION: HOT OIL USED.

Yield: About 25 croquettes

3-pound broiler-fryer chicken (free range preferred, or half a roaster chicken or roaster parts)

2 tablespoons butter (¼ stick)

½ teaspoon flour

pinch nutmeg

4 mushrooms (or two truffles)

4 large eggs

2 cups bread crumbs

1 bunch parsley

2 cups lard (or quantity that melts into 3 inches deep in a large, heavy pot)

Equipment: Heavy soup pot, large frying pan, cutting board, chef's knife or Chinese cleaver, large cutting board, heat-proof trivet to hold hot pan of chicken off the stove, waxed paper, deep-fry thermometer, wire skimmer or metal strainer, wire rack(s), and clean newspapers to drain fried croquettes

1. If using whole chicken, cut into quarters or serving pieces.

2. Put chicken in pot with water to cover. Bring to a boil, reduce heat to a simmer, and cook 15 minutes or until you can easily pull meat off the bone.

3. Remove chicken pieces from stock and cool them until you can handle them easily. Continue cooking stock uncovered until it is reduced to a cup or less.

4. When chicken is cool enough to handle, remove skin and fat from each piece, then take meat off the bones. Return the bones to the simmering stock. You should have 2 or 3 cups of meat.

5. Slice mushrooms (or truffles) into thin slices, then again into thin sticks, and a third time into fine dice.

6. Chop the meat very fine across the grain with a rocking motion, using a chef's knife or Chinese cleaver.

7. Melt butter in frying pan and sprinkle on the flour. Stir to make a light paste and cook for almost a minute so that it bubbles and browns the flour slightly.

8. Add chopped chicken meat and ½ cup of the reduced stock. Stir to blend well.

9. Season with salt and pepper and the pinch of nutmeg. Cover pan and simmer 5 minutes.

10. Separate 2 of the eggs by pouring them back and forth between shells over a cup to catch the whites. (Extra whites would have been saved for desserts.) Beat the yolks well in a small bowl.

11. Remove pan of chicken from heat, and stir in the egg yolks rapidly so they thicken the sauce rather than form clots of cooked yolk.

12. Continuing to stir, put the pan back on the stove and heat through. Stir in the finely diced mushrooms or truffles.

13. Remove the pan from heat, turn the chicken mixture into a clean bowl, and refrigerate at least an hour or until well chilled.

14. When ready to fry croquettes, break 2 eggs into a small bowl, add a tablespoon of water, and whisk them until creamy and light.

15. Pour out crumbs on a clean cutting board.

16. Cover part of counter with waxed paper. Cover part of the counter with clean newspaper and put wire racks on top. (This is for draining the fried croquettes.)

17. Remove chicken mixture from refrigerator and mix well. Spoon out tablespoons of the chicken mixture onto waxed paper.

18. Begin melting lard over low heat in a heavy pot with high sides, and set up deep-fry thermometer. The larger the pot, the more lard (or peanut oil) you will need, but the easier it is to maintain a high temperature and get good croquettes.

19. Wet your hands and begin forming croquettes into cones with flattened tops. (Some other popular shapes were balls, ovoid balls, cylinders, pears, and pointed cones. If you prefer to panfry, use half an inch of fat in a high-sided pan, and make flat patty shapes.)

20. Roll cones gently in crumbs, dip entire cone in egg, let extra egg drip back into the bowl, and roll the cones

in crumbs again. (You can do this step in advance, and refrigerate the completed croquettes on plates covered with waxed paper.) Place each cone on the waxed paper to dry a little, and repeat until all croquettes are dipped.

21. When all cones are dipped, increase heat so that lard reached 365 degrees, (390 degrees for peanut oil). It should not begin to smoke, however.

22. Dip a wire skimmer in the hot fat so the croquettes won't stick to it, and carefully lower them in, one at a time, to fill the pot without crowding. Fry them until golden brown, 2–4 minutes, turning if necessary.

23. Remove croquettes quickly to the wire racks. If you are making a lot, you can keep them in a warm oven, or reheat them in a 400-degree oven.

To serve, stand a sprig of parsley in the point of each cone.

"OUR 'AUNT HARRIET'S' FAVORITE DISH" (1910)

The most militant of all black abolitionists was Harriet Tubman (1820–1913), the great conductor of the Underground Railway who went on to further glory as a spy and guerrilla tactician in the Civil War. After the war, Mrs. Tubman brought her parents back from Canada to live with her in Aurora, New York. She made speeches for women's suffrage, took in orphans and former slaves, and won a government pension for her Civil War service. We may never be able to taste the exact rations she took on her nineteen trips back south to free more than four hundred slaves, or the meals she served in a canteen she ran in the Carolina Sea Islands during the Civil War, but we do have this northern-style corn-

bread that she enjoyed in her twilight years, visiting her pastor, the Reverend George Carter of Auburn. Florence Carter's recipe was contributed by daughter Vivian Carter Mason to the 1958 *The Historical Cookbook of the American Negro*, compiled by Sue Bailey Thurman for the National Council of Negro Women.

Yield: Serves 6 as a dinner with soup

6 slices lean salt pork

1 cup plain white flour

3 cups yellow cornmeal

1 heaping tablespoon baking powder

Pinch baking soda

1 teaspoon salt

2 tablespoons brown sugar

"Enough sour milk to moisten ingredients" (about 3 cups fresh milk plus 1 teaspoon lemon juice)

4 eggs

Solid shortening to grease pans

1 stick of butter

Equipment: Frying pan, mixing bowl, 9-by-13-inch sheet cake pan or 2 8-by-8-inch brownie pans, spatula, stoneware serving platter

1. Put salt pork in cold water to cover, bring to a boil for a minute.

2. Drain slices of salt pork, put into frying pan and fry crisp. Let cool.

3. Mix dry ingredients in a large bowl.

4. Beat the eggs well.

5. Stir eggs into dry ingredients with enough of the sour milk to make a stiff dough.

6. Cut the pork into small pieces and add to the cornmeal mixture, along with the drippings.

7. Grease pan or pans.

8. Pour in cornbread mix and level with a spatula.

9. Bake in a 350-degree oven "until done or bread shrinks from the sides and is a golden brown." Meanwhile remove butter from refrigerator to soften.

10. Heat an ovenproof platter, turn out the cornbread onto it, split open and butter generously.

11. Cut into squares.

Serve with soup. Listen to your elders.

15

THE FIRST AMERICAN CELEBRITIES (1827–1877)

Because the new United States had no royal family or hereditary aristocracy, it soon developed celebrities (recently defined cynically as people "famous for being famous"). One measure of celebrity as distinct from ordinary fame is that we take an interest in the personal lives of celebrities, including what they eat. Entire books have been published of recipes solicited from celebrities, as early as the 1900 *Favorite Food of Famous Folk*, published by the Ladies of the Guild of St. James Parish Church in Louisville, Kentucky. By 1857, Mary Peabody Mann accepted that her book, *Christianity in the Kitchen*, would sell a lot better if the author was listed as "Mrs. Horace Mann." After the Civil War, Catherine Beecher began listing her celebrity sister, the author Harriet Beecher Stowe, as coauthor of her cookbooks.

This book uses a few celebrity recipes where they reflect the participation of the celebrity cook in American history. This chapter, however, concentrates on four of the earliest celebrity recipes that illustrate the rise of celebrity itself in American life. Two later recipes show variations on the idea of celebrity recipes that arose in the early twentieth century.

LAFAYETTE GINGERBREAD (1827)

This recipe was published in *Seventy-Five Receipts for Pastry, Cakes, and Sweetmeats* by "A Lady of Philadelphia," who was in fact Eliza Leslie. The recipe was probably prompted by Lafayette's popular tour of the United States in 1824–1825, in which our French ally was greeted by crowds in the tens of thousands in major cities and feted at elaborate balls everywhere. This set off a revival of interest in the American Revolution, which had been neglected in the conservative atmosphere of the "Federal Period." Miss Leslie was then living at West Point, where her brother was treasurer, and may have met Lafayette. Later on, the story developed that Lafayette had been served gingerbread by George Washington's mother in Fredericksburg, Virginia, on a 1784 visit. The recipe is also called "Mary Ball Washington Gingerbread" in some later books. Miss Leslie in an 1850s book said it was also called "Franklin Gingerbread," suggesting that Lafayette's star was fading and that she and others in Philadelphia now thought more often of Benjamin Franklin, a friend of Leslie's father.

Lafayette Gingerbread is an American-style, cakelike "soft gingerbread" in contrast to the European gingerbreads, which were more like what we use to make gingerbread men and gingerbread houses. (The first printed recipe for soft gingerbread is in the 1796 first printed, American-written cookbook). As always, Miss Leslie's directions are so precise that we can still follow them with a few substitutions where ingredients have changed. Eggs and lemons were smaller; flour was heavier and usually had some bran and germ left in.

The cake gets all of its rise from the eggs and from stirring some air into the creamed butter and sugar, which is why the author emphasizes so much stirring. Some of Miss Leslie's readers could order a servant, slave, or daughter to do the stirring. Miss Leslie was aware of an early baking powder, pearl ash, but didn't like how it tasted: "It's lightness will be much improved by a small teaspoonful of pearl-ash [substitute baking soda] dissolved in a table-spoonful of milk, and stirred lightly in at the last. Too much pearl-ash will give it an unpleasant taste. If you use pearl-ash, you must omit the lemon, as its taste will be entirely destroyed by the pearl-ash. You may substitute for the lemon, some raisins and currants, well floured, to prevent their sinking." By the end of the nineteenth century, many American cakes were made with baking powders, and more sugar was added to cover the metallic flavor.

Yield: 3 loaves

Five eggs [medium]

Half a pound of brown sugar

Half a pound of fresh butter

A pint of sugar-house molasses

A pound and a half of flour, [about 4½ cups sifted white flour, 1 cup white whole wheat flour, and 6 tablespoons wheat germ]

Four table-spoonfuls of ginger—rounded

Two large sticks of cinnamon, powdered and sifted [1 level tablespoon]

Three dozen grains of allspice, powdered and sifted [1½ level teaspoons]

Three dozen of cloves, powdered and sifted [1 level teaspoon]

The juice and grated peel of two large lemons [average-size lemons today]

Equipment: 3 small loaf pans or 2 large loaf pans, or 1 sheet-cake pan (and/or small gingerbread molds)—Pyrex preferred, pastry blender, lemon zester, juicer, spice grinder or clean coffee mill if using whole spices; wire racks, cake tester

1. Take butter from refrigerator about an hour before starting. If using whole spices, grind and measure. Zest and juice the lemons.
2. "Beat the eggs very well."
3. "Stir the butter and sugar to a cream." (Miss Leslie used a wooden spoon to keep the butter cool; we can do it faster with a pastry blender or hand mixer.)
4. "Pour the molasses, at once, into the butter and sugar."
5. "Add the ginger and other spice, and stir all well together."
6. "Put in the egg and flour alternately, stirring all the time."
7. "Stir the whole very hard, and put in the lemon at the last. When the whole is mixed, stir it till very light."
8. "Butter an earthen pan, or a thick tin or iron one, and put the gingerbread in it. . . . Or you may bake it in small cakes, on little tins." I tried all three kinds of pan, and suggest terra cotta (or Pyrex) loaf pans as least likely to burn the cake.

9. "Bake in a moderate oven, an hour or more, according to its thickness. Take care that it does not burn." Bake in the middle rack of a 350-degree oven; test for doneness when a wooden toothpick or wire cake tester inserted in the middle of the loaf comes out clean.

"This is the finest of all gingerbread, but should not be kept long, as in a few days it becomes very hard and stale." (It freezes well, however.)

Jenny Lind Cake (1852)

There were performer celebrities before singer Jenny Lind's 1850 tour of the United States. But none of them were promoted by P.T. Barnum, the first great media manipulator. Advance stories about Miss Lind hyped her voice, appearance, religious commitments, and the delicate diet upon which such a creature must be fed. People traveled for days to see her in concert. Jenny Lind cakes followed, all based on quick mixing methods and newly popular baking powders, which pushed up the cakes as quick and light as Miss Lind's legendary soprano. This early version, from *Home Cookery* by Mrs. J. Chadwick, is listed with tea cakes and may have been baked in mini-muffin tins or French roll pans (sometimes sold as cast-iron "corn dodger" pans). In fact, the recipe is almost exactly the same as the basic recipe for muffins in the current Fannie Farmer cookbook by Marion Cunningham! Later Jenny Linds were made as round layer cakes. Although Mrs. Chadwick says not to vary the recipe, her baking powder ratio is clearly a typographical error. You can substitute a level tablespoon of baking powder for the soda and cream of tartar.

One quart of flour, two teaspoonfuls of cream of tartar put dry into the flour, about one third of a teaspoonful of soda [should be a third of a tablespoon], dissolved in a third of a cup of boiling water, a large teacupful of milk, half a teacupful of sugar, and three eggs. Mix all well together. Do not vary the receipt.

Yield: 24 muffins

4 cups sifted flour
2 level teaspoons cream of tartar
1 level teaspoon baking soda
1 cup light cream
3 ounces sugar
3 medium eggs or two large eggs
Butter to grease muffin pans

Equipment: 2 muffin pans, large mixing bowl, wood toothpicks or wire cake tester

1. Butter muffin pans. Preheat oven to 375 degrees.
2. Mix flour with cream of tartar or baking powder and sugar in a mixing bowl.
3. Dissolve baking soda (if using) in cream.
4. Beat eggs well.
5. Pour liquid ingredients into solid ingredients and mix quickly. It's okay if the batter is thick and lumpy. You may need a little more water or milk.
6. Spoon batter into muffin pans, filling each cup ⅔ full.
7. Bake 20–25 minutes, or until a toothpick or wire cake taster comes out clean.

Serve as dessert or tea cake. Mary Cornelius, author of The Young Housekeeper's Friend, *recommends this as a "nice cake for the basket," referring to the goody baskets exchanged among New England families during the winter.*

LAURA KEENE'S JELLY CAKE (1872)

"Laura Keene" (born Mary Francis Moss, 1826–1873) was a British-born actress and theater manager who helped make the American stage more respectable in the 1850s. She became a true celebrity, however, because she was onstage in her big hit, *Our American Cousin* when President Lincoln was shot by John Wilkes Booth. Laura Keene was able to identify Booth, whom she knew as a fellow actor. In 1869 and 1870 she had a theater in Philadelphia. The recipe appears in *The American House Wife Cook Book*, by Miss T.S. Shute, published in Philadelphia in 1878 by the George T. Lewis and Menzies Company. The Lewis and Menzies baking powder company made sure that their product was mentioned in the recipe, but it is possible that Ms. Keene had been paid while she was alive, making this a very early example of celebrity endorsement.

Jelly cakes were the original layer cakes, but at this time were still relatively flat, with thin layers like pancakes. This recipe shows a transition from the earlier use of pound-cake or sponge-cake layers to a cheaper and fluffier baking-powder recipe. The earlier style survived in Appalachian stack cakes like the two in *The American Ethnic Cookbook for Students*. Baking powder cakes soon led to the fluffier layers and taller cakes we know today. In the 1880s, cooks began making jelly cake one large layer, spreading it with jelly, and rolling it into a log-shaped "jelly roll."

The key to making jelly cakes was a set of three "jelly cake tins"—round baking pans with low sides. Some people had rings like muffin rings but the size of dinner plates and made jelly cake layers on a griddle, like pancakes. You can get away with two round cake pans (or even one), but it will take several quick bakings to get all the layers. I have used techniques from *Miss Leslie's New Cookbook* (1857) and *Six Little Cooks* (1877).

> One teacup of sugar, one of milk, one pint of flour, a teaspoonful of Lewis' Condensed Baking Powder, one egg, a tablespoonful of melted butter; flavor to suit and bake in thin sheets. When baked, spread jelly of any kind between the sheets.

Yield: 8–10 slices

¾ cup sugar

¾ cup half-and-half

½ cup milk (if needed)

2 cups flour

1 teaspoon baking powder

1 medium egg

1 tablespoon butter, plus ½ stick more to grease pans

8 ounces grape or other jelly

Equipment: Level, 2 or 3 round cake pans, stoneware plate larger than the cake pans, 2 oven mitts, brown paper or parchment paper, flexible spatula, microwave oven to warm jelly (optional)

1. Check that your cake pans have flat bottoms without dents and that the stove and oven shelves are level. If the cake layers come out uneven, you can compensate, but the cake will be neater if each layer is uniform.

2. Butter cake pans.

3. Preheat the oven to 350 degrees.

4. Melt 1 tablespoon of butter.

5. Measure flour, sugar, and baking powder into a mixing bowl and stir well to distribute baking powder.

6. Break egg into a cup. Use empty shell half to remove any bits of shell. Beat egg.

7. Add half-and-half, egg, and melted butter to dry ingredients and stir well.

You may need to add milk to get a thick batter.

8. Pour batter into pans to make layers ¼- to ⅜-inch thick. You may need to smooth it out with the spatula.

9. Bake layers 5 minutes and check if they are browning. Meanwhile, take the lid off the jelly and microwave 30 seconds on "warm" to soften the jelly (optional).

10. Cut enough brown paper or parchment paper to cover 1 layer, and arrange it on a stoneware plate.

11. When layers are lightly browned on top, remove from the oven. Put 1 pan on a heat-proof surface to cool. Run the spatula around the edges of the other pan to detach the layer, and invert that pan on the paper. The layer should fall out neatly.

12. Spread the jelly on the layer almost up to the edge.

13. Repeat Step 11 to invert the second layer upon the first. Adjust so the layers line up. (Here you can compensate for layers that are thicker on one side.)

14. Spread the jelly on the top of the second layer. Repeat this until all the layers are in place. Don't put jelly on the top layer.

15. Let the pans cool until they are safe to handle. Wipe them clean, and again butter them well.

16. Repeat Steps 8–14 until all the batter is used up.

17. Let cake cool before slicing.

Serve in pie-shaped wedges.

HENRY WARD BEECHER'S FAVORITE—TURTLE BEAN SOUP (1878)

The first general cookbook to have a chapter of "Favorite Dishes of Distinguished Persons" was *Jenny June's Cook Book* in 1878. "Jenny June" was the pseudonym of Jane Cunningham Croly, a full-time newspaper writer who also published sewing patterns and profiles and founded the women's club movement after she was excluded from an all-male press dinner. Most of her distinguished persons were women she knew (see **Susan B. Anthony's Apple Tapioca Pudding**), but she was able to start her chapter with Henry Ward Beecher, one of America's first national-celebrity ministers. Beecher, the son of an eminent conservative minister, and older brother of the authors Harriet Beecher Stowe and Catherine Beecher, had allied his Brooklyn pulpit to liberal causes like the abolition of slavery and votes for women. His sermons were widely reprinted and debated, in an era when touring ministers and revivalists still dominated popular culture. (Ironically, Beecher's career was eventually derailed by an adultery scandal and public trial.) This recipe also appeared the same year in *All Around the House*, by Mrs. H.W. Beecher, which could be viewed as the first single-celebrity cookbook, making the way for Oprah Winfrey and George Foreman. The Reverand Mr. Beecher's recipe is the type of slow-cooked stew many families started on Sunday morning to make a hot dinner after church, but it also uses new developments like canned tomatoes and commercial catsup. In 1878, some commercial ketchup was like ours, but some was still like the homemade catsups that had used more spices. If you want to approximate those, add ½ teaspoon each of allspice, mace, and black pepper. Since the beef stock is much of the flavor of this soup, you may want to make your own the day before from four pounds of shin beef and marrow bones.

NOTE: RECIPE TAKES TWO DAYS.

Yield: 15–20 servings

3 cups black beans

4 quarts beef stock

Soup-digester.   Ham-boiler.

Figure 10 The soup digester was an early form of pressure cooker. *Source:* Miss Parloa's Kitchen Companion, *1887.*

8 fresh tomatoes, or "half a can"

1 cup tomato catsup

1 onion (optional)

1 carrot (optional)

3 stalks celery (optional)

1 egg for each person to be served (optional)

Equipment: Large soup pot (the original mentions a "soup digester," an early pressure cooker), colander or food mill, serving ladle

1. Soak beans in cold water overnight.

2. "In the morning, drain off the water, wash the beans in fresh water, and put in the soup digester [an early form of pressure cooker], with four quarts of good beef stock, from which all fat has been removed."

3. "Set it where it will boil steadily but slowly, till dinner, or five hours, at the least—six is better."

4. Two hours before serving, peel and chop vegetables (if using) and add to soup, along with tomatoes and catsup. (Don't do this before the beans are tender, because the acidity of the tomatoes will keep the beans from softening.)

5. Just before serving, strain soup through a colander, "rubbing through enough of the beans to thicken the soup." You could also put some or all of the beans and cooked vegetables through a food mill.

6. Mrs. Beecher added, "After straining, I sometimes return the soup to the 'digester.' bring to a boil, and break in four or five eggs, and as soon as the whites have 'set'—a very little—dish the soup and bring to the table with the slightly cooked eggs floating on top. There should be eggs enough to take one out for every person at the table."

Serve hot, with bread and butter.

EMILY DICKINSON'S RICE CAKES (1851–1906)

Emily Dickinson's fame is unusual in that her poems were published only after her death in 1886, and much of her celebrity continues to rest on the contrast between her daring poems and allegedly reclusive lifestyle. This recipe was one of two published by her first cousin, Helen Bullard Wyman, in an article "Emily Dickinson as Cook and Poetess" in *The Boston Cooking-School Magazine* for June–July, 1906. Some details are based on the edited version of the recipe in the 1976 pamphlet, "Emily Dickinson: Profile of the Poet as Cook," by guides at the Dickinson Household in Amherst, Massachusetts. The pamphlet quotes a Dickinson letter showing that she was baking the rice cakes as early as 1851, when she was twenty. The spice is suggested on the basis of what Ms. Wyman wrote about the richer rice cakes in her family. In later years, when Emily was ill and really did stay in the house, she would lower a basket of ginger cookies from her window to her niece and her playmates. Maybe she included a few rice cakes.

> One cup of ground rice.
> One cup of powdered sugar.
> Two eggs.
> One-half a cup of butter.
> One spoonful of milk with a very little soda.
> Flavor to suit
>
> Cousin Emily

Yield: 16 brownie-like squares

1 cup of ground rice, or rice flour

1 cup sugar

2 medium eggs

½ cup (1 stick) salted butter, plus a little to grease pan

1 tablespoon milk

¼ teaspoon baking soda

1 teaspoon ground mace or nutmeg

Equipment: Pastry blender or large fork, whisk, 8-by-8-inch brownie pan, wire rack (optional)

1. Take out butter to soften 1 hour before starting recipe. Grease baking pan.

2. You can grind rice in a coffee grinder, by grinding a little to clean out the coffee, then grinding the rice you will use. Or you can use rice flour.

3. Cream butter and sugar together with pastry blender or large fork.

4. Beat eggs.

5. Add ground rice and eggs alternately to the butter-sugar mixture, beating as you go.

6. Dissolve baking soda in milk. Sprinkle spice on batter, then whisk in the milk/soda. You may need a little more milk with rice flour to make a stiff batter.

7. Bake at 350 degrees for 25–30 minutes. Cakes are done when a toothpick comes out clean.

8. Cool in the pan on a wire rack or cold stove top.

9. When cool, cut into squares.

Serve with afternoon tea. In Ms. Bullard's family, "Rice-cake was considered our very best 'company cake' in my childhood, being carefully placed in a large tin pail [round covered cookie tin], and only used when outside persons came to tea."

LEMON RICE PUDDING (1870s–1913)

Celebrity recipes took an unusual turn for the 1913, *The Economy Administration Cookbook*, edited by Susie Root Rhodes and Grace Porter Hopkins. The book is mostly a collection of recipes from the wives and daughters of President Wilson's cabinet members and Democratic Congressmen. However, it begins with the "Wilson Family Cook Book," recipes written by the president's mother at the time of his childhood. This marks the extension of our interest in celebrities to include their childhoods. The next time you find yourself looking at Britney Spears's baby pictures, consider that this trend was already beginning in 1913. The Wilson cookbook is transcribed with helpful penciled annotations, such as "Woodrow's Favorite." The future president's boyhood choice was a rather dull and difficult Charlotte Russe, so I am including the favorite of President Wilson's sister, Annie Wilson Howe. We have to imagine that the mother of the politically adroit President Wilson would be able to persuade her children to take turns, so young Woodrow also ate his share of Lemon Rice Pudding. His brother and his other sister also have favorites in the cookbook. This recipe is richer but lighter and less sweet than today's puddings. Lemon was a more prestigious flavor than cinnamon for most of the nineteenth century.

> Wash four tablespoons of rice and boil it until soft; one quart of milk sweetened to taste, butter size of an egg. When nearly cold add the beaten yolks of four eggs and the grated rind of one lemon. To the beaten whites of the eggs add the juice of the lemon and four spoons of powdered sugar. Pour the batter into a pudding dish and spread the whites upon the top and bake until brown. To be eaten cold.

Yield: Served all 6 Wilsons

¼ cup white rice

1 quart half-and-half

2 tablespoons sugar

4 tablespoons butter

4 medium eggs (or 3 extra large eggs; you can use pasteurized egg white products or powdered whites)

1 lemon

4 rounded tablespoons sugar

Equipment: 1½ quart baking dish, saucepan, lemon zester, juicer, whisk

1. Bring the rice and half-and-half to a boil. Reduce heat and simmer uncovered until rice is soft, about 20 minutes.

2. Butter baking dish, then add the rest of the butter to the simmering milk. (Don't add the sugar to the milk until the rice is done, or the rice will take much longer to soften.)

3. Zest the lemon, and add zest to rice.

4. Juice the lemon but reserve juice.

5. Separate the eggs by pouring each one back and forth between shells over a cup. Collect the yolks in a small bowl and the whites in a larger metal bowl.

6. Beat the yolks until creamy and light. When the cream and rice have cooled to warm, whisk in the egg yolks. Pour rice mixture into baking dish and let cool.

7. Clean whisk carefully, and beat whites until stiff, then add sugar and lemon juice and beat until it is a barely spreadable foam.

8. Spread whites over rice mixture.

9. Bake at 325 degrees for forty minutes. If meringue topping is browning too rapidly, reduce to 300 degrees.

Serve when cooled, but must be refrigerated after a few hours.

16

THE AGE OF JACKSON
(1820s–1852)

Once the American Constitution was in place, the culture of the new nation began a rather quiet and conservative period in which some of the democratic ideals of the Revolutionary period were forgotten. Americans concentrated on rebuilding, and political leaders wanted to avoid the disputes and bloodshed of the French revolutionary experience. All this changed with the presidency of Andrew Jackson (1829–1837). In addition to the obvious political changes that attended having nine states "west of the mountains," direct election of presidential electors, and the first mass political parties, there was a growing diversity of ideas and forces throughout the young country. Contending interests arose—partisan politicians aiming for political jobs, Western pioneers, Indians who didn't want to be relocated, abolitionists, slave owners who wanted to expand, traders, manufacturers, organizations of laborers and farmers, suffragists, prophets of new religions (both the Mormons and the Seventh-Day Adventists trace their beginnings to this period), utopians, canal builders. People took sides and changed sides through a rush of events: Indian wars, economic crises, slave revolts, the development of canals and railroads, the Texas Revolution, the Mexican War, the inventions of the McCormick reaper and the cotton gin, the rise of factories, and discoveries of gold. The first published works of Edgar Allen Poe, Hawthorne, Emerson, and Thoreau appeared. Reformers promoted free public education, prison reform, health food, women's rights, and abolitionism.

Although Jackson left office in 1836, he remained involved in many political questions until his death in 1845, and his supporters and their opponents dominated political debates into the early 1850s. Not all of these interest groups expressed themselves through food, but published cookbooks also began to show sectional differences, partisanship, and the growing diversity of the United States in the 1830s and '40s and '50s.

JACKSON JUMBLES (1830)

Jumbles are old English butter cookies, usually made in ring shapes. These easy drop cookies, using American-made pearlash [potassium carbonate] instead of yeast, convey something of the frontier spirit that came to Washington with President Andrew

Jackson. In sharp distinction to English Jumbles, these are plain cookies without spice, rosewater, or other flavorings. The recipe is from *The Cook Not Mad, or Rational Cookery*, published anonymously in Watertown, Massachusetts. You can also try baking these in the fireplace if you have a tin sheet that will fit inside a Dutch oven. Preheat the top and bottom of the Dutch oven, set over some hot coals, set the tin of jumbles inside on three pebbles, and heap coals on the lid, with the hottest coals at the sides.

> One cup of butter, one of cream, three of sugar, teaspoonful of pearlash, two eggs, five cups of flour, to be dropped on a tin with a spoon to bake.

Yield: 50–70 cookies

1 cup salted butter (two sticks), plus some to grease baking sheets.

1 cup heavy cream or sour cream

3 cups sugar

1 teaspoon baking soda

2 small or medium eggs

3½ cups flour

1 cup whole wheat flour

¼ cup wheat germ

Equipment: Pastry blender or food processor, baking sheets, wire racks, tight container

1. Remove butter from refrigerator one hour before starting.

2. Mix flour, wheat flour, and wheat germ to make an approximation of 1830s fine flour.

3. Cream butter and sugar in food processor or with pastry blender or a large fork.

4. Beat eggs until creamy and light.

5. Dissolve baking soda in a little water or milk.

6. Grease baking sheets with butter or shortening.

7. Preheat oven to 375 degrees.

8. Stir cream and eggs alternately with flour mixture into butter-sugar mixture to make a stiff batter. You may need a little more milk or water.

9. Stir in the baking soda.

10. Drop tablespoons onto the baking sheets in staggered rows. If batter is very stiff, you may need to press down the tops of the batter with the spoon.

11. Bake 10–12 minutes, or until slightly browned on the edges.

12. Remove cookies from baking sheets to cool on wire racks. If you overbake the cookies, they will soften a little bit in a tight container.

Serve with milk or buttermilk.

S-QUE-WI (CHEROKEE CABBAGE) (1830s)

President Jackson was elected in part on his record of fighting the Creek and Seminole Indians and spent much of his term in office arranging to move the five major tribes out of the southern states. The Cherokee were the most difficult to dislodge, in part because their educated leadership brought a legal case against the State of Georgia to the Supreme Court and won. Cherokees could follow the case in their own bilingual newspaper, with Cherokee-language columns in the alphabet devised by Sequoyah in 1821. Cherokees had adopted a Constitution similar to the U.S. Constitution, and many had taken a deliberate path of Americanization, becoming Christians, farming large plantations, living in wood houses. Some Cherokees even lived in mansions with white columns and owned African-American slaves.

This recipe is from Oconaluftee Indian Village in Cherokee, North Carolina, where a group of Cherokee were able to avoid "relocation" because they had established individual land titles and had a separate treaty with the United States. The recipe was printed in 1975 in *Recipes from America's Restored Villages*, by Jean Anderson, but likely represents a very typical dish of the settled Cherokee farmers throughout the Appalachians before they were forced out in 1838. The North Carolina Cherokees retain many old customs and recipes. None of the ingredients were available before contact with Europeans athrough there is some possibility of an early salt trade from the Gulf of Mexico up the Cherokee trail.

Yield: Serves 4–6

1 small cabbage

3–4 slices bacon or salt pork

1 small green pepper

1 teaspoon salt

⅛ teaspoon pepper

Equipment: Large, heavy kettle or Dutch oven with a tight lid

1. Cut the cabbage in quarters, cut out the core, and cut across the wedges to make bite-size chunks.

2. Fry the bacon or salt pork to make 3 tablespoons of drippings. Remove the bacon for another use.

3. Fry the cabbage in the drippings over moderately high heat until it begins to wilt and brown on some edges, about 8–10 minutes. Stir it once or twice.

4. Meanwhile, cut off the top and bottom of the green pepper.

5. Slit down one side of the pepper, and remove the core. Pare off any white pith.

6. Flatten the body of the pepper and cut into thin strips. Cut the bottom into thin strips. Remove the stem, and cut the top of the pepper into thin pieces.

7. Add the pepper strips to the cabbage and fry, stirring once in a while, until the green color of the pepper changes.

8. Put the lid on the kettle and turn down the heat, so the cabbage can "wilt" for 10–15 minutes. "It should be nicely glazed with meat drippings, touched with brown here and there, but still somewhat crisp."

9. Add salt and pepper, and stir well to mix.

Serve hot with **Hoe Cakes** *or* **Indian Bread**.

SOFKEE (1830S)

This recipe for a simple hot corn drink, related to the atole of Aztecan Mexico, is still widely used by Seminole, Creek, and other southern Indians. It was contributed by Nancy Osceola to *Favorite Food of Famous Folk*, published by the Ladies of the Guild of St. James Parish Church in Louisville, Kentucky, in 1900. I place it here because the recipe for Sofkee had not changed in more than a thousand years, and because Nancy Osceola was the sister-in-law of the great Seminole war chief Osceola (1804–1838), whose lieutenants successfully resisted the Indian removals of the Jacksonian era in the "Second Seminole War."

Quick grits are okay in this recipe. If your grits aren't very fine, you may need to cook the sofkee longer.

Yield: Serves 10

1 cup grits

Equipment: Soup pot, wooden spoon

1. Bring 2 quarts of water to a boil in the soup pot.

2. Stir in grits, pouring a fine stream to avoid lumps.

3. When all the grits are stirred in, reduce heat to a simmer, and let cook ten minutes.

Serve in mugs as a hot beverage. "No seasoning."

A VERY ECONOMICAL DISH (1837)

This kind of simple and relatively quick-cooking dish was suited to working families in the cities, but would not have been their first choice if they could afford more meat. It appears in *The Housekeeper's Book*, first published in Philadelphia in 1837 and was apparently written by Mrs. Francis Harriet (Whipple) McDougall. If Mrs. McDougall's married name is Scotch-Irish, this might be an early ethnic dish, as Scotch-Irish immigrants had introduced the white potato in most of the American colonies about hundred years earlier. (Mrs. McDougall's book has eight recipes for potatoes.) The Scotch-Irish were an important support for the American Revolution, the largest non-English ethnic group in the country and solidly anti-British. Andrew Jackson was the first of thirteen U.S. presidents of Scotch-Irish descent. The title of this recipe probably refers to the high prices of many foodstuffs in the runaway inflation of 1836, as the book was written before the resulting financial panic of 1837 that threw tens of thousands of city dwellers out of work.

> One pound of sausages, cut into pieces, with three pounds of potatoes, and a few onions, with about a tablespoonful of flour mixed in cold water, and added to it, will dine five or six persons. It must be well boiled.

Yield: Served a family of 5–6

1 pound pork sausages or **Winter Sausage**

3 pounds potatoes (9–10 medium potatoes)

2–3 medium onions

1 heaping tablespoon flour

Equipment: Large pot with loose cover

1. Slice the sausages into bite-size chunks.
2. Peel potatoes.
3. Halve and peel onions. Cut the halves one more time the long way to make quarters that will stay together.
4. Stir flour into a cup of water.
5. Combine ingredients in the pot, and add water to cover. If you aren't using salty sausages, add ¾ teaspoon salt.
6. Bring pot to a boil, covered, then reduce heat to simmer until potatoes and sausages are done, 20–40 minutes. We consider potatoes to be done when a fork goes to the center without resistance, but some Irish immigrants preferred a hard spot in the center, as discussed in the recipe for **Potatoes With the Bone In**.

Serve without dessert, because the price of flour has doubled since last year.

HAM OMELET (1839)

This omelet filled with tomatoes and ham we would now call a Spanish or Western or Denver Omelet. It may well derive from the Basque omelet called "Piperade." Its early appearance in *The Kentucky Housewife* by Lettice Bryan reminds us that there was still some French and Spanish colonial heritage in the Mississippi Valley states, reinforced by trade with Spanish Cuba, Santo Domingo, and Puerto Rico. Mrs. Bryan's book draws on Northern and Southern specialties and includes a few ethnic dishes as well: two kinds of Dutch-American "Oley Koeks" and a recipe for Pennsylvania Dutch noodles. She has some of the first written directions for "Cold Slaugh" and barbecue.

> Beat eight eggs till light, stir in four ounces of grated ham and as much ripe

tomatoes, that have been peeled and minced fine; add a little salt pepper, stir it well, and fry it as directed in the preceding recipe. [Have ready a pan of hot butter, pour in the omelet, and fry it till done, and the under side brown; then serve it up, . . . and fold it over, making a half moon.]

Yield: Serves 2–4

8 small eggs or six large eggs or 4 jumbo eggs

4 ounces ham, or ½ cup minced

1 medium tomato, or ½ cup canned, diced tomato

2 tablespoons butter

Equipment: Frying pan, pancake turner

1. If using fresh tomato, dip in boiling water to loosen skin, and remove skin. Halve tomato around the equator, over a sink, and squeeze out seeds from each half with your hand. Chop tomato into fine minced bits. If using canned tomato, drain and mince.

2. If you have some country ham, you can actually "grate" it. With cooked ham, mince fine, or pulse in a food processor.

3. Beat eggs in a small bowl.

4. Heat butter in the frying pan over low heat, and tilt the pan in all directions to distribute butter around.

5. Pour the beaten eggs into the frying pan and let the bottom set. If the eggs bubble up, open the bubbles with a corner of the pancake turner.

6. After some of the eggs have set, pick up one side with the pancake turner, and let the still-liquid eggs flow underneath. Repeat as necessary on the other side.

7. When eggs are nearly done, put the ham and tomatoes on one side of the omelet, leaving a ¾-inch margin at the edge. Season with salt and pepper.

8. Loosen half the edge, and flip the empty part of the omelet over to the filling to form a sealed "half moon."

9. Let the omelet cook a little longer to brown the underside, then loosen the edge, and flip the whole half moon over to brown the other side (and warm the filling a little more).

Serve immediately: "It is a breakfast dish, and should be eaten warm."

KUMBISH (1842)

This layered casserole is now called "Gumbis" in Pennsylvania Dutch. The recipe is originally from *Höchst nützliches Handbuch über Kochkunst*, by George Girardy, published in Cincinatti—the first cookbook by a Pennsylvania Dutch chef. The recipe was translated and adapted by William Woys Weaver in his 1989 *America Eats*. Weaver has traced the term "Gumbis" to Swiss German, and suggests it came originally from Latin "compositum," implying the composition of layers of food. Looking forward from 1842, we can see Kumbish as the ancestor of the many casseroles and convenient "hot dish" suppers of American food. The Pennsylvania Dutch were another non-English ethnic group that had cut all ties to Europe, supported the American Revolution, and with the Scotch-Irish, had settled and pioneered the Appalachian mountains and states west. Kumbish was then cooked in barrel-shaped pottery "bulge pots" that were heaped around with hot coals.

Yield: Serves 6–8

1 ham hock

4 large tart apples

½ head cabbage

4 medium onions

4–6 ounces slab bacon

2 6-inch bratwurst (optional)

Equipment: Small saucepan, tall covered casserole, ovenproof enamel pot, 2 Boston baked bean pots or 5-quart Dutch oven with cover, vegetable peeler

1. Bring 1 quart of water to a boil with the ham hock, reduce heat to a simmer, and cook 2 hours uncovered.

2. Halve, peel, and slice the onions. (Use swim goggles to avoid tears.)

3. Cut the cabbage into 4 wedges, remove core, and slice across the wedges to shred coarsely.

4. Peel and slice apples, discarding cores.

5. Cut bacon into small dice. (It is easier to do this if the bacon is partially frozen.)

6. Slice veal sausages.

7. When ham hock is falling off the bone, strain off the broth and reserve. (There should only be 2–3 cups left.)

8. Pick the meat off the bone, fat, and skin and cut into small pieces.

9. Make thin layers in the pot or casserole: sliced apple topped with cabbage topped with onion, followed by bacon, sausage, and ham hock meat. Repeat until all the ingredients are used up, but keep enough cabbage for the top layer.

10. Sprinkle on salt and pepper, and pour in ¾ cup of the ham hock broth.

11. Cover the pot and bake at 350 degrees for an hour, checking from time to time if the gumbis is drying out and needs more broth added. Weaver says that some people now make it soupier, or with a thickened gravy, or with more onions and cabbage.

12. Before serving, stir it with a wooden spoon.

Serve from the pot with pickles and relishes as a one-pot supper.

WHIG CAKES AND DEMOCRATIC TEA CAKES (1842)

This bipartisan ticket of afternoon dainties was devised by Mrs. T.J. Crowin in *Every Lady's Book* (1843). Whig (or wig) cakes had been part of English cookery since the 1300s. Their name had nothing to do with politics or hairpieces. "Wig" came from a Middle English spelling of "wedge" and they were originally round sweet breads of white flour cut into quarters. The political term "Whig" also came from Great Britain, applied first to Scottish Presbytarians who marched against an Episcopal king in the 1648 "Whiggemore Raid." The term was gradually picked up by the liberal party that developed in opposition to the monarchist "Tories" and by 1775 was generally used for the pro-independence American colonists, in contrast to our own Tories. The former Federalists and "anti-Jackson men" took the name Whigs from 1834 to 1856 because in England the Whigs had become advocates of an activist central government.

Mrs. Crowin seems to have invented the Democratic Tea Cakes, as a play on words for the previously apolitical Whig Cakes. As a New Yorker, she lived in a "swing state" and would have heard the debates between strong factions of each party. Her Democratic Tea Cakes are more plentiful but more expensive, although not so rich and sweet as later southern tea cakes.

There is a good discussion of English wigs, with a recipe used in many Colonial American homes, in Elizabeth David's *English Bread and Yeast Cookery*. For typical eighteenth-century Colonial wigs, add two tablespoons of caraway seeds and shape as four flat, round loaves divided into wedges, or divide the dough for thirty-two long buns or round or oval buns. For typical late nineteenth-century southern or African-American tea cakes, add a pound of sugar to the tea cakes recipe. These recipes can be halved.

> Whig Cakes—One pound and a half of fine flour; half a pint of warm milk; one gill of brewers' yeast; work this to a dough; set it in a warm place, to rise for an hour or two; then add one pound of sugar, rolled fine; half a pound of butter, and half a grated nutmeg; work them well into the risen dough; roll it thin, cut in small cakes, and bake in a quick oven.

Yield: Up to 200 cookies, depending on size of cutter

4½ cups all-purpose flour

1 teaspoon dry yeast

1½ cups whole milk

1 pound sugar

½ pound salted butter, plus more to grease baking sheets

Half nutmeg, or 1 teaspoon powdered nutmeg

Equipment: Baking sheets, mixing bowls, pastry blender, nutmeg grater if using whole nutmeg, rolling pin and board, biscuit cutter or glass tumbler

1. Warm milk to lukewarm and add yeast.
2. Measure out flour.
3. In a large mixing bowl, stir milk mixture and flour into a soft dough. You may need a little more milk or flour.
4. Take butter out of refrigerator.
5. Let dough rise until light and bubbly, 1 to 2 hours.
6. Use your hands or a pastry blender to beat in the softened butter.

7. Grate nutmeg or measure out powdered nutmeg, and mix into sugar.
8. Work sugar into dough.
9. Flour rolling pin and board; grease baking sheets.
10. Preheat oven to 450 degrees.
11. Roll out dough to ½ inch or thinner.
12. Cut out rounds with biscuit cutter or a glass tumbler.
13. Arrange rounds on baking sheets. Let rise 20 minutes.
14. Bake whigs about 12 minutes. They will brown at the edges a little, but still look white when done.

Serve at parties for Whig politicians such as Presidents Harrison, Tyler, Taylor, or Fillmore, or Senators Clay or Webster. Notice what that promising Lincoln from Illinois has to say.

> Democratic Tea Cakes—Take three quarts of fine flour; half a teacup of yeast, and half a pound of butter, dissolved in warm milk; the yolks of three eggs well beaten; a teaspoonful of salt, and a nutmeg grated; use enough warm milk to make a good dough; lay it in a buttered basin, and set it in a warm place for an hour to rise; then bake in a quick oven,—serve hot.

Yield: Up to 300 cookies

12 cups flour

1 tablespoon dry yeast

Half pound butter, plus more to grease bowl and baking sheets

About 3¼ cups whole milk

3 medium eggs, or 2 extra large

1 teaspoon salt

1 teaspoon sugar

1 heaping teaspoon nutmeg

Equipment: Baking sheets, mixing bowls, pastry blender, nutmeg grater if using whole nutmeg, rolling pin and board, biscuit cutter or glass tumbler

1. Remove butter from refrigerator 1 hour before starting.

2. Warm 1 cup of the milk to lukewarm and add yeast, sugar, and salt. Separate eggs and reserve whites for another use, such as **Apple Snow**.

3. In a large mixing bowl, cream butter and work in flour.

4. Sprinkle on the nutmeg. Stir milk mixture and egg yolks into flour to make a soft dough.

5. Let dough rise until light and bubbly, 1 to 2 hours.

6. Flour rolling pin and board; grease baking sheets.

7. Preheat oven to 450 degrees.

8. Roll out dough to ½ inch or thinner.

9. Cut out rounds with biscuit cutter or a glass tumbler.

10. Arrange rounds on baking sheets. Let rise 20 minutes.

11. Bake tea cakes about 12 minutes. They will hardly brown at all when done and will stiffen as they cool, but will become somewhat chewier if stored in an airtight container.

Serve at parties for Democratic politicians such as presidents Van Buren, Polk, or Pierce.

CAPIROTADA OR TORREJAS (1843)

With the annexation of Texas, the Mexican War, and the Gadsden Purchase, the United States added many Hispanic citizens and started a long-lasting interest in "Mexican food." This New Mexico recipe came into the family of Kit Carson with his 1843 marriage to Josefa Jaramillo at Taos. It was written down by his granddaughter, Leona

Wood, and published in the 1963 *Pioneer Potluck; Stories and Recipes of Early Colorado*, collected by the State Historical Society of Colorado. The Carsons died at Fort Lyon, Colorado. The deep-fat frying step is not how this bread pudding is usually made in New Mexico and probably represents the influence of army camp cooking.

CAUTION: HOT OIL USED.

Yield: Serves 6

1 loaf white or French bread, slightly stale

2 cups lard or shortening

1 egg

2¼ cups sugar

1½ teaspoons cinnamon

¾ cup pine nuts

½ cup citron

¼ teaspoon cream of tartar

Equipment: Baking sheets, ovenproof dish, heavy soup pot, deep-fry thermometer, paper towels, wire racks (optional), saucepan

1. Cut the bread into 1-inch cubes. You will need 2½ cups of cubes for the recipe.

2. Brown the cubes in a 300-degree oven.

3. Separate the egg by pouring between the shells over a cup.

4. Beat the white until it forms stiff peaks. Then beat in the yolk.

5. Heat lard or shortening in a large soup pot to 350 degrees.

6. Dip cubes of bread in egg, then put them on a skimmer or slotted spoon that has been dipped in the oil. Slide them into the hot oil without splashing, and fry briefly. Place fried cubes in ovenproof dish. (You can keep them warm in a 200-degree oven.)

7. When the cubes are all done, mix ¼ cup of sugar with 1 teaspoon of cinnamon, and sprinkle the mixture over the cubes. Stir in the pine nuts and citron.

8. To make the sauce, combine 2 cups of sugar, the cream of tartar, the other ½ teaspoon of cinnamon, and 1 cup of water in a saucepan.

9. Bring sauce mixture to a boil, stirring to dissolve all the sugar. Put in the candy/deep-fry thermometer. Boil until it makes threads from a spoon dipped in the mixture, or the thermometer reads 215 to 234 degrees at sea level.

10. Pour hot sauce over cubes in the ovenproof dish before serving.

Serve as dessert.

QUEEN ESTHER'S BREAD (1847)

This recipe for what we now call French toast appeared in the 1847 *The Carolina Housewife*, by Sarah Rutledge, and seems to be the first printed Jewish American recipe, although Miss Rutledge doesn't say so. Charleston's Sephardic Jewish community dates from the late seventeenth century and up to the 1840s was the largest in the United States. They would have been most visible around the late-winter holiday of Purim, "The Feast of Esther," then celebrated with Mardi Gras-like balls. Similar recipes, described as Jewish, appeared in New York and Philadelphia cookbooks of the 1870s. Today's Jewish Americans are mostly of northern European heritage, with different Purim treats, and have switched public celebrations to the winter festival, Hanukah. Meanwhile, the dish was known as "German Toast" for much of the nineteenth century. An 1866 recipe in *Godey's Lady's Book* is the earliest use of "French Toast" I could find. The dish became generally known as French Toast only around the turn of the twentieth century.

> Cut some slices of bread, and lay them in milk for some hours. Then beat two eggs; dip the slices in the egg, and fry them. When of a nice brown, pour over them any syrup you please, and serve up.

Yield: 6 pieces

6 slices bread
Whole milk to cover, about 1 cup
2 eggs
Butter to fry, about a tablespoon

Equipment: Bowl or square plastic container about the size of a slice of bread, frying pan, tongs, spatula

1. Slice bread if using an unsliced loaf. (Miss Rutledge's book has several recipes for dense white breads including rice.)

2. Soak in milk 1 hour, 30 minutes with today's sliced white bread.

3. Beat eggs in a bowl about the size of 1 slice of bread.

4. Melt butter in a frying pan over medium heat; tilt to coat the bottom of the pan.

5. Carefully remove bread from milk, dip in egg on both sides.

6. Arrange slices in frying pan.

7. Lift one corner with a spatula to see when one side is "of a nice brown." Turn toasts once to brown the other side.

Serve hot with syrup. Miss Rutledge had recipes for syrups flavored with almond, raspberry, orange flower, and lime, or might have used the syrups from preserved peaches or oranges.

GUMBO SOUP—A FOREIGN RECEIPT (1852)

This Boston publication seems to be the first recipe for a classic New Orleans Creole gumbo based on browned flour. The technique of cooking flour in fat ("roux") for thickening was well known to French cooks, but only in Southern "New France" did cooks decide to brown the flour until it lost much of its thickening power, with a distinctive smoky taste. I believe that this was done primarily by African slave cooks who wanted to reproduce the flavor of dendé palm oil, but today the technique is most identified with the white "Cajun" community.

Nothing is known about Mrs. J. Chadwick, author of *Home Cookery*, but on the basis of several election cakes and clam chowders, as well as references to Massachusetts politicians and place names, I believe she was a New Englander, perhaps related to the Civil War captain, Jonathan Chadwick of Salem, Massachusetts. Her book also has a recipe for "Charleston (S.C.) Method of Cooking Hominy" and recipes from France, Germany, England, Denmark, Norway, and Brazil. This would not be an unusual collection in an active port like Salem, and the gumbo recipe from New Orleans or Mobile may have reached her via a sea captain.

It is unlikely that Mrs. Chadwick actually made this gumbo herself, because there is a serious error right at the beginning. The amounts of lard and flour given make a crumbly dough that is impossible to brown. The proportion of lard to flour ought to be around fifty-fifty, which implies that the three heaping tablespoons of lard should be very large and that the pound of flour (three cups) should be a scant cup. I am suggesting the three-quarter cup each of lard and flour as a guess about Creole practice around 1850. The Cajun chef Paul Prudhomme uses about twice that much roux today.

The sassafras thickener, filé powder, was taken from Native Americans, but again suited an African taste for thick and oily soups, replacing the okra ("ochingombo" in Bantu languages of the Congo River Basin) that gives the soup its name. (It is possible that something like gumbo or "kombo" was an Indian name for sassafras.) The use of meat and seafood in the same stew is typical of both Native American and African cooking. Much American rice cookery likewise came from African sources, as slaves from rice-growing areas of Africa knew more about the grain than most British or French colonists. Mrs. Chadwick adds the filé powder too early. If you can get some, add it at the table.

> Three heaping tablespoonfuls of lard in a pot, and one pound of flour, browned in it; to do very slowly and be kept stirring all the time, to prevent its burning. Then add a few onions chopped very fine, a handful of parsley cut up, and stir together. Then a tender chicken, cut up small, the bones broken to get the marrow out; after that is browned, and eight or nine pints of hot water, red and black pepper (some use a tablespoon of both, which makes it very hot), a tablespoon of sassafras, and to this quantity, just before it is done, add one hundred oysters; a bunch of thyme to be tied and thrown in also. Boiled rice to be eaten with it.

CAUTION: HOT ROUX STICKS AND BURNS.

Yield: Serves 18–24

¾ cup lard

¾ cup flour

3 small onions

1 bunch parsley

1 teaspoon theme

3–4 pound broiler chicken

1 tablespoon cayenne pepper (optional)

1 tablespoon ground black pepper

1 tablespoon filé powder (if available)

100 oysters (3 16-ounce cans of small oysters)

3½ cups rice

Equipment: 2 large, heavy soup pots or 1 and a rice cooker, wooden spatula, kitchen mallet or cleaver (optional)

1. Halve, peel, and chop the onions. (Use swim goggles to avoid tears.)

2. Mince a handful of the parsley.

3. Cut the chicken at every joint, cut the breasts into 3 pieces, and the thighs into 2 pieces each. Cut the neck in half, and slice up the gizzard and heart. People in the 1850s would also get some meat off the cut-up backs. Reserve the liver for another use. If you have a kitchen mallet or cleaver, break the ends of the bones of the drumsticks, thighs, and wings.

4. Melt the lard in soup pot over low heat, and stir in the flour.

5. Brown the flour slowly, stirring constantly so that none of it sticks and burns. If you see black specks, you've burned it, and have to start over again. If you can get the flour to the color of peanut butter, you should probably throw in the onions. But if you are pa-

tient, you can get the roux to the dark brown color of barbecue sauce.

6. Stir in the onions and parsley. This will stop the roux from darkening, but you still have to stir it constantly. Cook a few minutes.

7. Add the chicken pieces except for the breast sections. Stir a few times to brown all sides at least a little.

8. Add 16–18 cups of water, stir well, and bring to a boil.

9. Add black pepper, and cayenne pepper if using, and simmer until the chicken pieces are done, about 30 minutes.

10. Meanwhile, bring 5 cups of water to a boil.

11. Add the rice and a tablespoon of salt to the boiling water. Cover tightly and cook on low heat (or in a rice cooker) for 15 minutes. Remove from heat and let steam until the soup is ready to serve.

12. Add oysters to soup and bring back to a boil.

13. Taste soup for salt (which will depend on the oysters), and add a tablespoon if necessary.

14. Just before serving, stir in the filé powder, if using.

Serve in bowls with rice.

17

COOKING FOR CHILDREN (1837–1861)

Children cooked in colonial and early America—it was part of their daily chores from the ages of seven or eight on and often part of their indentured work or apprenticeship outside the home from age eight through the teens. Very young children began with simple, tedious jobs (and dangerous) like hours of turning the spit before the open fire to roast meats, stirring the endless pots of **Hasty Pudding**, beating the biscuit dough, minding the fire under slow-cooking stews, and—as a matter of course—gathering, cutting, and splitting firewood. In early American history children above toddling age were regarded as small, inexperienced adults. They worked and ate as smaller, lower-status adults, and had surprisingly few toys.

Our present view of childhood and adolescence as separate and different stages of life, with different tastes than adults, did not really take hold until after the Civil War. It is not until the 1870s that cookbooks were published to be read and used by young people, as you will read in Chapter 31. This chapter collects some of the first recipes directed toward children. It is clear that children had a sweet tooth in Early America, although you will find that the amount of sugar necessary to make a sweet treat was quite a lot less than we use now. It is interesting that the recipes are described in terms of health rather than appeal. Children in early America had plenty of appetite unless they were sick and aren't described as picky eaters. It may be significant that some of these recipes were written by social reformers who did not have children of their own.

Lydia Maria Child (1802–1880) was the youngest child of five, but was sent from home at thirteen to help keep house for a married older sister. Her mother had died young, and she was somewhat neglected as a child. She was able to go to school in the summers until she was sixteen or seventeen, but always regretted her lack of formal education. She was a radical abolitionist and suffragist, but conventionally moralistic in her writing for and about children. However, the figure of the mischievous good boy, which later evolved into Tom Sawyer and Huck Finn, appears in her writing. And she did not include recipes in her *Girl's Handy Book*.

Catherine Beecher (1800–1878), the unmarried older sister of Harriet Beecher Stowe and other famous Beechers, was active in the movement to set up schools for girls. Although she opposed votes for women, her vision of enhanced family life was one of the first to consider children's food as distinct from servants', and she included recipes for "Good Child's Cake," "Child's Feather Cake," "Children's Boiled Fruit Pudding," "Children's Fruit Dumpling," "Little Girl's Pie," and "Little Boy's Pudding," as well as the temperance beverages below, in her 1846 *Domestic Receipt-Book*. This was the largest array of recipes for children in any American cookbook for another thirty years, and some of these may have been tested in the 1820s at her Hartford Female Seminary.

Sarah Josepha Hale was a widowed mother of five when she began fifty years of editing the popular magazine *Godey's Lady's Book*. It is significant that almost none of the recipes in her cookbooks or in *Godey's* were described as being children's favorites, since her magazine was substantially about family life.

MOLASSES WATER (1837)

This note, in *The Family Nurse*, by Lydia Maria Child, is one of the earliest American statements that children above toddler age were different from adults. Most of Child's readers served their children weak beer or hard cider, perhaps warmed. The admission that water might have to be sweetened with molasses shows that Child did not expect everyone to agree. I have suggested three levels of sweetening as a test of the 1837 sweet tooth versus the sodas we are accustomed to at the turn of the twenty-first century.

"Pure water, or molasses and water, is the only suitable drink for children. Much of moral, as well as bodily health, depends on the strict observance of this rule."

Yield: 3 somewhat varied servings

5 tablespoons molasses

Equipment: 3 drinking glasses

1. Stir 1 tablespoon of molasses into a 12-ounce glass of water.

2. Stir 2 tablespoons of molasses into another glass of water.

3. Stir 3 tablespoons of molasses into the third glass.

4. Which would you prefer with meals? (Based on the 1827 **Lemonade** recipe in Chapter 14, I suspect that Mrs. Child preferred the one-spoon version.)

BLACK BUTTER (1839)

Again, this recipe has about half the proportion of sugar as most jams and jellies today. It is from Mrs. Hale's *The Good Housekeeper*.

This is a very nice preserve to spread on bread for children, and much healthier in the winter than salt butter. Take any kind of berries, currants, of cherries, (the latter must be stoned;) to every pound of fruit allow half a pound of sugar, and boil till it is reduced one fourth.

CAUTION: HOT, JAMLIKE FRUIT BUTTER STICKS AND BURNS.

Yield: 3 cups light jam

1 pound currants, blueberries, blackberries, raspberries, or strawberries, or 1½ pounds sweet or sour cherries

1 cup sugar or 1¼ cups light brown sugar

Equipment: Cherry stoner (optional), heavy saucepan with lid

1. If you are using cherries or sour cherries, you should remove the pits. Today there are several kinds of mechanical cherry pitters, but in 1839 one cut the pits out of sweet cherries with a knife. Some sour cherry pits will pop out if you squeeze them between the fingers.

Hull strawberries and raspberries. Pick out any green blueberries or pink blackberries. Stem the currants.

2. Put the fruit in the saucepan. Pour the sugar over it.

3. Turn on low heat and stir to begin melting the sugar. You can mash some of the fruit to get things started.

4. Once the pot begins to bubble, stir once and cover tightly for a few minutes to melt the rest of the sugar.

5. Remove the lid and boil the mixture, stirring to prevent sticking, until it is reduced to ¾ its original height in the pot.

6. This can be canned while hot with 15 minutes in a boiling water bath. Or you can let it cool and refrigerate or freeze it. In Early American times such preserves were kept in tightly sealed jars, but sometimes developed mold.

Serve on bread or toast with meals or as a snack.

WHITE TEA (1840s)

This and the following recipe are from Miss Beecher's *Domestic Receipt Book*, first published in 1847. She wrote, "There are drinks easily prepared for children, which they love much better than tea or coffee, for no child at first loves these drinks till trained to it. As their older friends are served with *green* or *black* tea, there is a *white* tea to offer then, which they will always prefer, if properly trained, and it is *always* healthful." By 1869, in *The American Woman's Home*, cowritten with her sister Harriet Beecher Stowe, she had decided that, "Some constitutions can bear much less excitement than others; and in every family of children, there is usually one or more of delicate organization, and consequently peculiarly exposed to dangers from this source [hot coffee and tea]. It is this

child who ordinarily becomes the victim to stimulating drinks. The tea and coffee which the parents and the healthier children can use without immediate injury, gradually sap the energies of the feebler child, who proves either an early victim or a living martyr to all the sufferings that debilitated nerves inflict." Later in the same book there is a discussion of how to make tea and coffee as it was done in France and England, likely written by the better-traveled Mrs. Stowe. This apparently simple recipe changes a bit when you remember that Early American teaspoons were smaller but measures were rounded, milk was richer, and teacups held only six ounces.

Put two teaspoonfuls of sugar into half a cup of good milk, and fill it with boiling water.

Yield: Serves 1

3 ounces whole milk or light cream

2¼ level teaspoons of sugar

Equipment: Teakettle, measuring spoons, small teacup

1. Bring water to a boil in a teakettle.

2. Pour milk into teacup.

3. Add sugar.

4. Stir in boiling water.

Serve to children at breakfast or afternoon snack.

BOYS' COFFEE (1840s)

Miss Catherine Beecher had a complicated position about the differences between men and women, which included her opposition to women voting. But in practice she did a lot of the things that she wrote only men were supposed to do, such as write books about theology. Her cookbook has a few recipes specifically for boys or girls, but it is clear that these dishes were served to both. Calling this recipe "boys' coffee" did not prevent girls from having it. It seems to be based on a Pennsylvania Dutch breakfast dish of coffee served in a bowl with a lot of milk and toast or pie for dipping. Farm families substituted maple sugar or sorghum molasses for molasses.

Crumb bread, or dry toast, into a bowl. Put on plenty of sugar, or molasses. Put in one half milk and one half boiling water. To be eaten with a spoon, or drank if preferred. Molasses for sweetening is preferred by most children.

Yield: Serves 1

1 slice white or wheat bread, can be stale

1 tablespoon molasses

½ cup light cream

Equipment: Teakettle, toaster (optional)

1. Bring water to a boil in the teakettle.
2. If using toast, toast bread. Break up bread or toast into spoon-size pieces in a cereal bowl.
3. Pour on molasses.
4. Pour on water to about half the bowl.
5. Add the cream.

Serve for breakfast.

Molasses Toast (1861)

This recipe is from the 1861 *The House-keeper's Encyclopedia*, by Mrs. E.F. Haskell, as reprinted on the Civil War Interactive web site. Mrs. Haskell noted, "The author well remembers enjoying it much when a child." I have been unable to find out how old Mrs. Haskell was in 1861, but it is a good reminder that publication of recipes often lags behind their active use. So it is possible that parents made treats for at least the younger children from Colonial days. The point remains that hardly anyone considered such recipes important enough to publish for several decades after the Civil War.

Boil nice West India molasses; remove the scum, and strain it through a hair sieve or thin cloth strainer; let it boil five minutes slowly with a bit of butter to the pint, as large as half an egg. If the toast is dry and hard, dip it quickly in hot water, and then in the molasses; if fresh, in the molasses only; if the molasses has thickened, so that when not boiling the basin is not as full as when put to boil, add sufficient boiling water to make up the deficiency; some molasses thickens rapidly, while other does not. This dish is much better than would be supposed; resembling in taste a buckwheat cake with butter and molasses.

CAUTION: BOILING MOLASSES SPATTERS AND BURNS.

Yield: Serves 10

1 pint molasses

3 tablespoons butter

10 slices of bread, white or whole wheat

Equipment: Toaster, tongs

1. Bring molasses to a boil in a large skillet with the butter. Let it simmer slowly about 5 minutes.
2. If working with pre-made toast, bring a large pot of water to a boil, and keep uncovered at a slow boil.
3. Toast slices of bread to medium brown. Take slices of toast in tongs and dip in hot molasses on both sides. Bring plate near the skillet and transfer the molasses toast quickly.
4. If molasses becomes too thick, thin with water.

Serve as a special breakfast or afternoon snack.

18

TEMPERANCE AND PROHIBITION RECIPES (1837–1930)

One of the few real barriers to writing a book about American historical cooking for students is that there is no getting around the extensive use of alcoholic beverages by people of all ages and at every meal in Colonial and Early American times. Early explorers were surprised to see the Indians freely drinking water, since the water in most of Europe was so polluted that people who drank from rivers and lakes and even many wells almost always got sick. Wine had to be imported, but was widely used and added to soups, stews, and baked goods. Beer, some of it as weak or weaker than modern "light" beer, was the usual replacement, and poor farm families made do with cider or fermented drinks based on corn, molasses, or maple syrup. Public drunkenness and alcohol addiction were problems cited in all Colonial records, although things were much worse in eighteenth-century London and other European cities.

By the middle of the eighteenth century, though, some people switched to increasingly available tea, coffee, or chocolate, and some families stopped drinking alcoholic beverages altogether. Movements for temperance began before the Revolution, although temperance meant different things to different people. A temperance convention in Philadelphia in 1788 proclaimed the exclusive use of beer and cider, according to *Customs and Fashions in Old New England* by Alice Morse Earle, and proposed the slogan, "Despise Spiritous Liquors as Anti-Federal."

By the 1840s, Catherine Esther Beecher, the daughter of conservative evangelist Lyman Beecher, described three kinds of temperance: "One class consider it to be a sin *in itself*, to take anything that contains the intoxicating principle. Another class . . . engage not to use intoxicating drinks *as a beverage* . . . [and] to *avoid the appearance of evil*, they will not employ it in *cooking*, nor keep it in their houses. The third class . . . think it proper to use wine and brandy in cooking, and occasionally for medicinal purposes, and suppose that the cause of temperance will be best promoted by going no farther." Miss Beecher put herself in the third group, but also warns against coffee and tea.

The most common American substitution for alcoholic beverages in cooking was sweet cider. This alternative shows up as early as the first American cookbook, Amelia Simmons's *American Cookery of 1795*, where her "Minced Pie of Beef" includes, "one quart of wine or rich sweet cyder." Mincemeat was put up in the fall in many pots and jars and preserved by the brandy or rum added at the end. It is possible that some of the many early recipes for cider cake were made with sweet cider in ultra-temperate homes.

Temperance was considered a women's issue, because alcoholism was thought to strike hardest by disabling men, who were to support families. Before the Civil War, temperance was part of a constellation of issues under the general name of "reform." Reform included abolitionists, suffragists, health food reformers, opponents of the Mexican War, and others. Not everyone agreed with the entire program. Miss Beecher was opposed to women voting or working against slavery and quarreled with some of her activist brothers and sisters into the 1870s. But early reformers often promoted temperance as part of the path to freeing the slaves, or securing treaty rights for Native Americans, or improving public health.

In the same period, several of the religious denominations that formed in America also took up temperance or other health food regimes. It is striking that the largest surviving new denominations of that time, the Mormon church and Seventh-Day Adventism, both banned alcoholic beverages, as did later American denominations such as Christian Science and the Nation of Islam. In Early America, many Methodist groups arrived as nondrinkers.

After the Civil War, the old reform movement gradually broke up, but temperance and women's suffrage were still allied in the minds of most activists. The Women's Christian Temperance Union, founded in 1874, advanced the two issues together, especially in rural and conservative religious communities where more radical feminists had less support. The WCTU also favored the eight-hour day, an important labor issue, for much of the nineteenth century. Labor leaders like Mary "Mother" Jones, who worked with Catholic immigrants, were among the reformers who publicly broke with temperance principles. (For labor organizers, the saloon was an important meeting place. For the later generation of prohibitionists, such as Carrie Nation, the saloon was increasingly the focal point of attack.)

The later stages of temperance activism moved toward legal prohibition of the sale of alcoholic beverages. They did not abandon the earlier emphasis on individual and family temperance, circulating pledge cards in which young people signed an oath never to drink. The numbers of these pledge cards were communicated to politicians, and campaigns found themselves polarized between "wets" and "dries."

Despite some failed statewide measures as early as the 1840s, national prohibition did not take effect until 1919, a year before white women won the right to vote in every state. Prohibition had a few loopholes, and also marked the introduction of oversalted "cooking wine." Cookbooks of the 1920s have alcohol-free recipes for foods and drinks, but sometimes mention how much wine or brandy was used in the dish back in the old days. Prohibition was so widely violated that it was repealed in 1932. The effort to ban alcohol may have legitimized organized crime in the mind of the public. It certainly provided criminals with a profitable incentive to organize, since the import or manufacture of alcoholic beverages required an organization that could produce and distribute the product and bribe government officials.

After prohibition ended, some localities have kept restrictions on the sale of alcoholic beverages to the present day, but most of the effort to reduce drinking since Prohibition has been on the individual recovery model of Alcoholics Anonymous. Contemporary recipes where the usual alcohol has been removed are most often found in cookbooks published by the religious denominations where alcohol is not used.

TEMPERANCE CAKE, NO. 1 (1845)

The strictest New England style of temperance drew on the teachings of Sylvester Graham to avoid even yeast fermentation of bread, never mind the alcoholic beverages and flavorings that were permitted in cooking by more moderate reformers. This cake gets some rise from the eggs and the baking soda reacting with the natural acidity of milk, and comes out rather well for a plain cake without butter. I followed the general early New England pattern of making the cake in loaf pans, but Mrs. Howland may have made a flatter cake in a larger cake pan, since mine needed another thirteen minutes in the oven. The recipe is from *The New England Economical Housekeeper*, published in 1845 by S.A. Howland in Worcester, Mass.—a hotbed of reform. The author was his wife Esther, who also supplies "Temperance Cake, No. 2," which was rolled cookies rather like **Whig Cakes**.

Three eggs, two cups of sugar, one cup of milk, one tea-spoonful of saleratus [potassium carbonate, substitute baking soda], nutmeg, flour enough to make it pour into the pan; bake about 20 minutes. Allspice and raisins, instead of nutmeg, make a good plum cake.

Yield: 20 slices

3 small eggs or 2 large or extra large eggs

2 cups sugar

1 cup whole milk or half-and-half

¾ teaspoon baking soda

1 teaspoon nutmeg or allspice (with optional raisins)

1 cup raisins (optional)

2½ cups all purpose flour

Shortening to grease pans

Equipment: 2 loaf pans, mixing bowl, rubber spatula, wire rack to cool cakes

1. Preheat oven to 350 degrees. Beat eggs in a mixing bowl.
2. Stir in sugar and then milk.
3. Sprinkle on spice and baking soda and stir well.
4. If using raisins, toss them with a little of the flour.
5. Add most of the flour, whisking it in to get a smooth but stiff batter. Add the raisins if using.
6. Grease pans. Divide the batter between the pans, tapping them on the sides a few times to level the batter.
7. Bake about 30 minutes and test with a skewer or wire cake tester at the highest part of the loaf. (This cake will rise to make a low loaf from about an inch of batter.) If the cake isn't done, bake another 5 minutes at 325 degrees.
8. Remove from the oven and cool briefly in pans. Run a kitchen knife around the edges to detach any stuck parts and invert to turn the cakes out of the pans. Finish cooling on wire racks.

Serve with butter or jam and hot sweet cider.

MINCED PIE (1846)

"A good minced pie is a general favorite, and formerly brandy was deemed indispensable in giving them the right flavor. But we are happy to inform our temperance friends and others, that a mince pie can be made equally good without either wine or brandy." So announced Mrs. L.G. Abell in her *The Skillful Housewife's Book*. Since her substitute was molasses, which was cheaper than brandy, this method also saved money, although the preservative qualities of molasses are not so good. Molasses probably does preserve mincemeat better than the usual substitute, sweet cider. Mrs. Abell also removes the usual fat from the recipe. You should allow the meat to season for a week or more. Where the recipe is not specific, I have used proportions from Sandra L. Oliver's *Salt Water Foodways*. You can reduce the recipe proportionately.

Boil fresh beef perfectly tender, that will slip off the bone. The head and harslet [inner organs such as heart] are nice for this purpose. Take out all the hard gristle and bone and tough parts when hot. As soon as it is cold, chop it all very fine, and if you do not want it for immediate use, season it with pepper, salt, cloves and cinnamon, and press it closely into a stone jar, and pour molasses over the top, and when after a few days or weeks it has left the surface, pour on more to keep it nice. To every two quarts of chopped meat, a half a tea-cupful of ground cinnamon, a table spoon of ground cloves, a tea-spoonful of pepper and a table-spoonful of salt will keep it well with molasses poured over it, a year. It is far more convenient to have meat thus prepared for use through the winter than to boil every time it is needed. The proportions should be a third meat, and two thirds apple, chopped very fine, those a little sour are best. . . . Add a good quantity of box raisins, and season high with spices and molasses, adding water sufficient to keep them moist, made up in a rich nice paste, and there will be nothing wanting in flavor of quality. They should be baked one hour in a moderate oven.

NOTE: RECIPE TAKES ONE WEEK.

Yield: 6 quarts to make 6 large pies

4 pounds beef heart, or 8 pounds shin meat with bones, or a combination

4 ounces cinnamon ($\frac{1}{2}$ cup)

4$\frac{1}{2}$ tablespoons cloves

1 teaspoon black pepper

1 tablespoon salt

4 cups molasses

6 pounds apples (about 25 apples)

2–3 pounds raisins

6 9-inch pie crusts plus three more to make lattices

Equipment: Large soup pot, colander, meat grinder or food processor (optional), 6 glass quart jars or equivalent

1. If using beef heart, cut across the fiber into large chunks. Boil the beef heart and/or shin meat in water to cover until tender, about 3 hours.

2. Drain meat well in colander. You can use the broth as the basis of a stew.

3. Cut meat off bones (shin) and chop fine. Mrs. Abell did the chopping with a curved chopper in a wooden bowl, but you can use a meat grinder or food processor.

4. Mix in 3 ounces of the cinnamon, 1$\frac{1}{2}$ tablespoons of the cloves, 1 teaspoon of black pepper, and 1 tablespoon of salt. Work the mincemeat tightly into large glass jars or nonreactive crocks or bowls. Pour molasses over the top.

5. Put jars, uncovered, in refrigerator for a week to combine flavors. Add more molasses as needed to keep up level on jars.

6. When ready to make pies, peel apples and cut off chunks, discarding cores.

7. Chop apples fine and mix in raisins, another 2 ounces (3 tablespoons) of cinnamon, another 2 tablespoons of cloves, and another teaspoon of black pepper.

8. Mix apples with meat, adding a little water to make a pasty, marmalade-like consistency. You may need to add a little more molasses.

9. Preheat oven to 350 degrees.

10. Pour 2½ to 4 cups of mincemeat into each pie crust. Cover with a lattice crust. (Make the lattice on a flat board, starting from the central strips, and lifting up the edges to weave in the side strips, and lifting the entire crust onto the filled pie. The technique is illustrated with Austrian Linzer Torte in *The American Ethnic Cookbook for Students*.)

11. Bake about 45 minutes, a little longer if you are baking many pies in one oven.

Serve as a Thanksgiving, Christmas, or New Year's treat.

COUNTRY SYLLABUB (1851)

To satisfy traditional tastes, early temperance advocates generally recommended sweet apple cider as a substitute for beer or wine. This was only available in the fall, because it rapidly fermented into hard cider over the winter. (Many farm families drank this hard cider at every meal for most of the year.) Fall cider was good timing for mincemeat made from fall-slaughtered beef, but the only possible season for temperate families to enjoy syllabub, the widely popular English dessert of whipped cream and (usually) sweetened wine. This recipe is from *Eliza Leslie's Directions for Cookery, In Its Various Branches*, first published in 1837, and periodically updated by her. Milking the cow directly into the syllabub risked all kinds of contamination, and it is unlikely that Miss Leslie, a city dweller, often tested this recipe as written. I have taken details from her longer recipe for "Syllabub, or Whipt Cream," but used the simpler "country" recipe because it mentions that the dish can be made with fresh cider, a hint temperate readers would not have missed. Milk directly from a cow would have separated naturally into frothed cream and liquid milk.

Mix half a pound of white sugar with a pint of fine sweet cider, or of white wine; and grate in a nutmeg. Prepare them in a large bowl, just milking time. Then let it be taken to the cow, and have about three pints milked into it; stirring it occasionally with a spoon. Let it be before the froth subsides. If you use cider, a little brandy will improve it.

Yield: 16 6-ounce cups

1 cup sugar

1 pint sweet cider

1 pint heavy cream

1 quart light cream

2 teaspoons nutmeg

Equipment: Whisk or handheld electric beater, nutmeg grater (optional), cow (optional)

1. Dissolve the sugar in the cider.

2. Grate in 1 nutmeg, or stir in 2 teaspoons nutmeg.

3. Stir in the cream, and let it rise to the top.

4. "Then beat it with rods to a stiff froth . . ." You can use a whisk or electric mixer, keeping it up in the cream layer. You should have reasonably stiff whipped cream over sweet, milky liquid.

Serve in bowls or small glasses, with some of the cider and some of the whipped cream on top.

AN INNOCENT PLUM PUDDING (1857)

British plum puddings remained popular American dishes into the early twentieth century. In states where Christmas was not celebrated, plum pudding became a Thanksgiving dish. This one, from *Christianity in the Kitchen; A Physiological Cook Book*, by Mrs.

Horace Mann, is innocent even though it has wine cooked in, because it leaves out "the suet, cloves, nutmeg and brandy that render plum pudding so deleterious." Mrs. Mann was far more daring to oppose animal fats than distilled liquors in 1857, although brandy often went into the sauce.

> Ten or a dozen soft crackers may be broken into a quart of good milk or cream. Let it stand thus all night, and in the morning rub the whole through a cullender. Add eight eggs, a pound of sugar, a cup of molasses, a cup of wine, a table-spoonful of salt, the grated rind of a lemon, half a tea-spoonful of mace, a quarter of a pound of citron, a pound of currants, and a pound and a half of stoned raisins. Let it be boiled five hours, and served with a cold sauce of braided sugar and butter and white of egg.

NOTE: RECIPE TAKES TWO DAYS.

Yield: Serves 50, with sauce

10–12 large crackers such as Crown Pilot

1 quart whole milk or light cream, or a mixture

8 medium eggs, or 6 large or extra large eggs

2 cups sugar

1 cup molasses

1 cup wine (or sweet cider)

1 lemon

$\frac{1}{2}$ teaspoon mace

$\frac{1}{4}$ pound candied citron

1 pound currants

$1\frac{1}{2}$ pounds raisins

1 stick butter to butter cloth

$\frac{1}{2}$ cup flour to flour cloth

1 stick butter for sauce

1 cup sugar for sauce

1 egg or equivalent egg white product

Equipment: Clean old white sheet or pillow case, cotton twine, lemon zester or box grater, large nonreactive soup pot, plastic wrap or clean kitchen towel, colander or food mill, two mixing bowls, ovenproof plate that fits into soup pot

1. Tear out a 2-foot square of the sheet or pillow case. This will be "the pudding cloth." Bring a half pot of water to boil in the large soup pot, and soak the cloth and 2 feet of the cotton twine to remove any detergent flavors.

2. Break crackers into a bowl, and cover with the milk or cream. Cover with a clean kitchen towel or plastic wrap, and let stand overnight.

3. In the morning, bring a large pot of water ($\frac{1}{2}$ to $\frac{2}{3}$ full) to a boil. Drain milk and crackers into a food mill or colander. Press the softened crackers through the holes with a wooden spoon, or turn the handle of the food mill.

4. Grate the peel off the lemon and add to the mixture.

5. Beat the eggs well and add to the mixture.

6. Add the other ingredients and mix well.

7. Rinse out the cloth in hot water and wring out.

8. Flatten the cloth and butter the largest possible circle of the cloth. Getting butter to stick to wet cloth is not so easy, but stay with it.

9. Sprinkle flour over the butter circle so that butter is completely covered.

10. Put the cloth, flour side up, into one of the mixing bowls.

11. Pour the pudding into the cloth.

12. Take the string. Gather the pudding cloth into a pouch. Tie tightly with the string, leaving a little space

for the pudding to expand during cooking. If you also tie a strong loop with the ends of the string, it will make it easier to fish out the pudding at the end.

13. Slide the plate into the pot of boiling water.

14. Get the water up to a rolling boil, and carefully lower in the pudding, onto the plate so that it doesn't stick to the bottom of the pot and burn. It should be completely covered by boiling water at all times.

15. Heat more water in a second pot, so that you can add boiling water when the water comes below the pudding. Boil 5 hours.

16. To serve, lift the pudding carefully by the string with tongs or the end of a metal dipper, and place in a deep dish or bowl. Cut the string, and peel back the cloth. Turn the pudding out of the cloth, and trim loose "rags."

17. Mrs. Mann's sauce, again avoiding hard liquor, is somewhere between hard sauce and cake frosting. To make it, soften the butter for an hour (or quickly in the microwave), and cream it together with the sugar. Separate the egg and beat in the white. If you don't want to use uncooked egg white, use refrigerated egg whites from the supermarket, or powdered egg whites to make the equivalent of one egg white.

Serve hot, slicing ceremoniously at the table, with a spoonful of the sauce melting on top.

TEMPERANCE PUNCH (1890)

This recipe was submitted by Mrs. W.H.H. Miller to the 1890 *Statesmen's Dishes and How to Cook Them*, edited by Mrs. Benjamin Harrison. This was the first, and so far is the only, cookbook written in the White House by a First Lady. Mrs.

Miller's husband was attorney general, and most of the recipes came from the wives of cabinet members and Republican congressmen. The recipe was more than twenty-five years old in temperance circles, but its publication by Mrs. Miller shows the increasing respectability of temperance among the political elite. Only fourteen years earlier the temperate Mrs. President Hayes had been ridiculed as "Lemonade Lucy" for running an "ice-water regime" at the White House. I have taken some quantities and techniques from a similar recipe for American Temperance Beverage in the 1875 *Eating for Strength* by M.L. Holbrook, M.D.

Yield: Serves 25

12 lemons (or 2 cups juice)

6 oranges (or 3 cups juice)

2 cups cranberries

5 cups sugar

Equipment: Saucepan with lid, sieve, large mixing bowl or punchbowl, vegetable peeler or lemon zester, juicer

1. Peel thinly or zest the lemons and the oranges.

2. Juice the lemons and oranges and pour the juice over the peels. Discard the pith and seeds. Let stand an hour or more.

3. Heat cranberries with 2 cups of water to boiling. Lower heat and simmer until all the skins break and the cranberries are soft and easily mashed, about 20–30 minutes.

4. Let cranberry water cool, then strain into the punchbowl.

5. Strain the lemon and orange juice into the punchbowl.

6. Add "water and sugar to taste." Dr. Holbrook's recipe required more than 5 cups of sugar and 2 more quarts of water. (But he used no oranges, and

had raspberries and a pineapple instead of cranberries.)

Serve at a Washington party, perhaps with Mrs. Harrison's Sausage Rolls.

UNFERMENTED WINE (1897)

For the more religious membership of the Women's Christian Temperance Union, this was a crucial temperance recipe, providing communion wine that kept to the pledge. It was also used in place of wine in punches and cooking. It appears in the *White Ribbon Cook Book*, compiled by the WCTU of Clay County, Nebraska, in 1897. The canning was essential to preventing fermentation, but for modern use you can freeze the juice (a method used in some earlier temperance recipes from cold states), or refrigerate for up to a week.

8 pounds grapes, 1 pound sugar. Boil grapes and strain the juice. Put in sugar, boil and can.

Yield: About 28–30 4-ounce cups

5 quarts stemmed grapes (Concord preferred)

2 cups sugar

Equipment: Large pot with lid, potato masher, large ladle, large sieve or food mill, canning jars, lids, funnel, jar lifter, and tongs

1. Stem grapes to get 5 quarts.

2. Put grapes in large pot and mash some with potato masher to get a little juice.

3. Cover tightly and turn on heat slowly so that grapes begin to steam.

4. After about 5 minutes, lift lid and mash more grapes to get more juice. Cover again and increase heat to simmer juice, about 10 minutes in all.

5. Mash thoroughly with potato masher. Ladle juice and remaining berries into sieve or food mill, over a

large bowl. Press to extract more juice, or use food mill in batches. (Nebraska farm wives would have fed remaining skins and seeds to pigs or chickens.)

6. Return juice to large pot. Add sugar and bring to a simmer until sugar is dissolved.

7. If canning, boil 4 pint and 3 quart jars to sterilize and invert on wire racks. Follow directions with canning jars to fill, cap, and process 30 minutes in simmering water 1 inch above the lids. Otherwise refrigerate juice and serve or freeze.

8. As juice cools, you may see clear crystals of tartaric acid. These are harmless.

Serve as "wine" in religious ceremonies or festive dinners.

MINT JULEP (1930)

During the Prohibition period, some cookbooks helpfully suggested nonalcoholic punches and versions of cocktails like this mint julep, from the *Chicago Daily News Cook Book* of 1930, edited by Edith G. Shuck. Of course, Chicagoans with access to illegal liquor could simply add it back in.

Yield: Serves 1, can be multiplied

Several sprigs fresh mint

3 tablespoons lemon juice (from one large lemon)

2 tablespoons sugar

16 ounces ginger ale

1 cup cracked ice

Equipment: Strainer, juicer (optional), food processor (optional), 16-ounce glass

1. Juice the lemon, and add the juice to the sugar.

2. Crush most of the mint and stir it with the lemon juice and sugar.

3. Add the ginger ale.
4. Crack the ice in a food processor if available.
5. Half fill the glass with ice.
6. Strain the ginger ale mixture into the glass of ice.

Serve with a sprig of fresh mint.

GINGER ALE SODA (1930)

This refresher was one of a group of recipes for Memorial Day proposed in *The A&P News* for May 22–28, 1930. This flyer was sent to customers of the Boston-based supermarket chain. The other recipes suggest that many people traveled to the shore on the long weekend, or at least had a picnic, rather than cook a big meal at home. The "egg beater" required may have been a rotary eggbeater or a simple wire whisk.

Yield: Serves 1, can be repeated for any number

½ glass ginger ale
½ glass whole milk
1 heaping tablespoon vanilla ice cream

Equipment: Whisk or chocolate beater

1. "Beat ginger ale and milk with egg beater until it foams."
2. " . . . then add ice cream."

Serve with a light supper.

19

AMERICAN STEAK AND POTATOES (1841–1896)

Here we look at some nineteenth-century versions of the all-American meal, steak and potatoes. One thing to remember is that the meal was very often breakfast. The British taste for beef came directly to the English colonies, and roast beef is still a typical American dinner. The more rapid pace of American life pushed cooks toward steaks, even with beef that wasn't tender enough for rapid cooking. This was especially the case at breakfast, where Early Americans wanted meat and wouldn't wait for boiled beef. It was probably at the Early American breakfast that steaks were first linked with potatoes. Boiled potatoes or cold boiled potatoes fried were quicker breakfasts than most cereals or hot breads. In Early American times, steaks also required a lot of sawing, because beef was sold in large chunks. As late as the 1870s, a kitchen saw was standard home equipment. Many of the cuts steaked in the nineteenth century are now reserved for hamburger.

Beef fashions changed in regard to doneness. The first American cookbook, in 1796, said of roast beef, "Pricking with a fork will determine you whether done or not; rare done is the healthiest, and the taste of this Age." By 1841, Sarah Josepha Hale wrote of three-fourth inch steaks, "With a good fire

of coals, steaks will be thoroughly done in twelve or fifteen minutes. These are much healthier for delicate stomachs than *rare-done* steaks." Mrs. T.J. Crowin, a few years later, took a medium course: "Beefsteaks are generally preferred broiled so the middle will be slightly red; tomato catsup to be served with beefsteak." Miss Beecher, in the late 1840s, thought ten to twelve minutes was about right for steaks one-half to an inch thick. By 1852, Mrs. Hale, in her *New Cook Book*, had relented, "From 8 to 10 minutes will be sufficient to broil steaks for the generality of eaters, and more than enough for those who like them but partially done." It is also possible that beef had improved over ten years, or that general prosperity or Mrs. Hale's personal success as editor of *Godey's Lady's Book* had brought better cuts to her table. In her earlier book, she proposed much slower and more thorough cooking for cheap beef.

Most printed recipes for steaks have them grilled over hot coals (not flames) on a gridiron. There were differences of opinion about pounding them beforehand, about how many times to turn them, and about how to save the juices. Like every other food in Early American times, steaks were sauced with butter, but increasingly with sharp sauces and various ketchups; walnut, mushroom, and tomato being the most popular. The 1861 recipe for **Fried Beefsteak** probably records a common practice, as more people owned frying pans than gridirons. The potatoes with them would have been fried in slices, home-fried, hashed, or mashed. Baked potatoes were slow and tricky before stoves with reliable ovens—quite different from grilled steaks. Fried potatoes were sliced across the potato. The object was to get them as thin as possible so they would be crisp, and thus they were often what we would now call potato chips. Potato chips are usually dated from an especially thin batch served in 1853 at a resort hotel in Saratoga, New York, by a Native American chef named George Crum or George Speck. They were often called Saratoga chips. But the stick shape of french fries seems not to have been used in the nineteenth century, certainly not before the 1890s.

For the development of hamburgers, see the recipe for **Hamburger Steaks**. For some recipes in which vegetarians try to make substitutes for steaks and hamburgers, see the health food Chapters 29 and 41.

Steak and potatoes also became signifiers of patriotism, masculinity, and vigor. (See the recipe for **Sirloin Steak** from Mayor "Big Bill" Thompson of Chicago.)

POTATO SNOW (1839)

As discussed in Chapter 18, *The Kentucky Housewife* by Lettice Bryan is the first American cookbook from "west of the mountains" and records fully thirteen recipes for white potatoes. This is the more detailed of two recipes for riced mashed potatoes, more likely at mid-afternoon dinner than at breakfast, and possibly fancy enough to serve with Sunday chicken. "Very old" potatoes, perhaps by April, were better mashed with milk, butter, and sea-

soning before they got to the table. Mrs. Bryan's idea of drawn butter is given elsewhere as **To Melt Butter**.

Very old potatoes or very young ones are not fit for snow, the former being heavy and sodden, while preparing the latter for snow renders them insipid. Select large white, full grown potatoes, which are quite dry and farinaceous. Wash them clean, put them in a kettle with enough cold water to cover them little over an inch, as when boiled in too little water, they will not be so white. Boil them rather briskly till done, which you may tell by trying them with a fork, or by taking one out, and mashing it. Then turn off the remaining water immediately, set the kettle by the fire a few minutes, throwing over it a folded napkin or flannel, to absorb the superfluous moisture; after which peel them, rub them through a coarse wire sieve, letting the snow fall on the dish, forming a pyramidal heap: do not disturb it in any way, but send it immediately to the table with salt, pepper, and a boat of drawn butter, to be handed round with it to the company, that they may season it to suit their own tastes. Potato snow is very pretty when properly made, but if sent to the table without the seasonings, it is quite an insipid dish.

Yield: Serves 6

6 floury baking potatoes

1 recipe **To Melt Butter**

Equipment: Wire sieve and wooden spoon or food mill or potato ricer, clean kitchen towel, large gravy boat

1. Wash potatoes and put in the bottom of a soup pot. Cover them with water plus another inch.

2. Bring potatoes to a boil and cook until soft, testing with a fork in the thickest part.

3. When all the potatoes are ready, pour off the boiling water and put the pot back on the hot burner. Cover with a clean kitchen towel. Let the potatoes dry out and steam for another 15 minutes.

4. Take out the potatoes and peel them. The skins should come right off with a little help from a paring knife.

5. Push potatoes through sieve with a wooden spoon, or use a food mill or potato ricer. In any case, don't stir them out but just try to have them fall in an even way onto the serving platter. (Not stirring the potatoes keeps them soft and fluffy.)

Serve immediately with drawn butter, salt, and a pepper mill.

BEEF STEAKS STEWED (1841)

This recipe is one of a group of "Cheap Dishes" in Sarah Josepha Hale's *The Good Housekeeper*. Tougher cuts were pounded or stewed like this, and had been since the English and Colonial recipes for "Scotched Collops." Although the recipe may have been influenced by the high food prices of the 1837 depression, it is more likely that it reflects the general toughness of early American beef from free-range cattle, and the American tendency to reduce more and more of the carcass—including tough shin and leg muscles—to quick-cooking steaks. Through much of the nineteenth century, no kitchen was complete without a meat saw and a steak beater, and this recipe was eventually replaced by recipes for "Tomato steak" or "Swiss steak" stewed in tomato sauce. The optional pounding step reflects old English practice recorded in America as early as the 1720s in the recipe book kept by Isabella Morris Ashfield of New Jersey, which continued in widespread use into the 1880s.

> This is a very good and economical way of cooking steaks that are not very tender. Put the steaks in a stew-pan with a little butter, and fry them brown. Then add a little gravy or boiling water, some pepper, salt, and a table-spoonful of vinegar, and let them stew gently till tender. Thicken the gravy with a bit of butter rolled in flour.

Yield: Serves 4

2 large cheap steaks, or meat marked for "London broil" such as chuck or round

1 tablespoon butter, plus a half-tablespoon for thickening gravy

1 can of beef stock (optional)

1 tablespoon vinegar

1½ teaspoons flour

Equipment: Large, heavy frying pan with cover, tenderizing mallet (optional), ovenproof casserole with cover (optional)

1. Pound the steaks with the mallet or the side of a stoneware dinner plate. (optional)

2. Melt the tablespoon of butter in heavy frying pan. Increase heat and add steaks. Fry about 5 minutes to brown one side, then turn to brown the other side.

3. Add beef stock or water just to cover with the vinegar, and season well with salt and pepper. Bring to a boil and reduce heat to a simmer with the cover on or ajar. Simmer 45 minutes to 1 hour. (You can also do this step in a 350-degree oven, using an ovenproof casserole.)

4. Measure out flour and roll around with the rest of the butter. (In French

cooking, this was called "buerre manie.") As the steaks are about done, add this mixture to the simmering gravy and stir until it is well thickened and has lost the taste of uncooked flour (about three minutes).

Serve with potatoes.

TOMATO KETCHUP (1848)

It's hard to add anything to *Pure Ketchup*, Andrew Smith's 1996 study of the development of ketchup, but here is a recipe it doesn't have, one of the first fully quantified recipes, from *Godey's Lady's Book* of September 1848, as quoted in the 1957 *We Modernize Godey*, by the Foods II Class of Chillicothe [Ohio] High School. Like most early ketchup recipes, it is thinner, spicier and less sweet than modern ketchup, and was based on English recipes. Unlike modern ketchup, it has no added sweeteners or thickeners, which is why it had to be boiled for three hours. I have suggested quantities in brackets to make a one-twenty-fourth recipe, producing a one-quart bottle of ketchup. If you are making this at home, I would suggest cutting down to one-fourth or one-eighth of the total recipe, and borrowing four or five extra soup pots.

Yield: 6 gallons [1 quart]

The following, from our long experience, we know to be the best receipt extant for making tomato ketchup: Take one bushel of tomatoes and boil them until they are soft—squeeze them through a fine wire sieve, and add

Half a gallon of vinegar
Three half pints of salt,
Two ounces of cloves
Quarter of a pound of allspice
Three ounces of cayenne pepper
Three tablespoonfuls of black pepper, and

Five heads of garlic, skinned and separated.

Mix together, and boil about three hours, or until reduced to about one-half: then bottle without straining.

Yield: 6 gallons [1 quart]

50 pounds tomatoes [32 ounces canned]

2 quarts vinegar [⅓ cup]

7 cups salt [4 tablespoons and 2 teaspoons]

½ cup plus two tablespoons ground cloves [1¼ teaspoons]

1 cup plus 1 tablespoon ground allspice [2 teaspoons]

¾ cup cayenne pepper [1½ teaspoons]

¼ cup black pepper [½ teaspoon]

5 heads garlic [3 cloves]

Equipment: Food mill or wire sieve, 2 oversize stock pots, wooden spoons (one with a very long handle), commercial stove, enough canning jars or freezer containers for 6 gallons of sauce, rubber tube garlic skinner

1. If you are using canned whole tomatoes, start at Step 3. Wash fresh tomatoes and put in a pot or pots. Mash them a little to get some juice, and heat to boiling.

2. Reduce heat and cover pot so that tomatoes soften. Mash them some more so that the juice comes up to the top of the tomatoes. Uncover and cook over low heat until they are as soft as canned tomatoes, 15–30 minutes.

3. If you want to experience work in an 1848 farm kitchen, squeeze the tomatoes through a wire sieve with a wooden spoon. When too many seeds and skins get in the way, you can feed them to the pigs and chickens. If you want to experience Foods II at C.H.S.,

use a food mill. Discard seeds and skins. Of course, if you use canned whole tomatoes, they've already been skinned. (You could even use canned tomato puree and start at Step 4, but that is no longer historical cooking.)

4. Combine tomato pulp with vinegar, salt, and spices, and bring to a boil.

5. Rub skins off garlic with rubber tube device, and add to tomato pulp.

6. Boil tomato pulp uncovered about 3 hours, uncovered, stirring periodically with a long spoon to make sure it doesn't stick and burn. (I mention the commercial stove because some home stove burners do not put out enough heat to boil 12 gallons of tomato pulp. You can get around this at home by doing smaller batches on all the burners, and in two shifts.)

7. As the pulp boils down, it gets thicker and more likely to burn, so you have to stir more often, and possibly reduce the heat. Don't reduce the boil too much, though, since the ketchup isn't finished until it has reduced to one-half the original volume.

Serve with steak. Hamburger sandwiches won't be around for another sixty years. Some advanced thinkers are already trying tomato ketchup with fried potatoes.

FRIED BEEFSTEAK (1861)

This is still one of the best ways to make a steak, as recorded in *The Housekeeper's Encyclopedia* by Mrs. E.F. Haskell. A "spider" was a cast-iron frying pan with long legs that could be set above wood coals as a searing hot griddle.

Heat the spider before putting in the beef, cut off most of the fat, season the fat with pepper and salt, before frying; put the steak into the hot spider, and fry as quickly as possible; when the beef is turned, sprinkle on a little salt and pepper; mix a little flour and water together in the proportion of half a teacupful of water to a half teaspoonful of flour; take out the meat and scraps of fat, and stir in the flour and water; let the gravy brown a little, and pour it over the beef.

Yield: Serves 1, but can be multiplied, depending on the size of your frying pan

1 8–12-ounce steak of high quality, such as a rib-eye, sirloin, or tenderloin

½ teaspoon flour

Equipment: Cast-iron frying pan, pancake turner or tongs

1. Cut all the visible fat off the steak.

2. Heat the frying pan slowly, rubbing on some of the steak fat to make a nonstick coating. (Be careful not to burn your fingers doing this.) Throw in all the pieces of fat, so that the fat fries and melts.

3. Push the frying fat around in the frying pan to make a thin layer of liquid fat large enough for the steak. Sprinkle salt and pepper on this area.

4. Turn up the heat, and place the steak on the seasoned bed. Let it cook 3–4 minutes to sear well.

5. Meanwhile, stir the flour into 3 ounces of water for the gravy.

6. Salt and pepper the uncooked side of the steak, and put it on a dinner plate for a minute while you push the scraps of fat around to grease another area.

7. Set the steak back in the pan on the uncooked side, and let that side of the steak sear until the steak is a little less done than you want it (cut into a thick area to check). It will cook a little more while you make the gravy.

8. Put the steak on a dinner plate, remove all the scraps of fat, then stir the

flour-water mixture once more and pour into the frying pan.

9. Turn up the heat so the water boils, and stir around to loosen any caramelized juices that are stuck to the pan. When the gravy thickens, pour it over the steak and serve.

"Serve with fried potatoes, if convenient; if not, with mashed."

HASHED AND BROWNED POTATOES (1896)

There are two recipes for the dish in *The Chicago Record Cookbook*, contributed by readers. Both dishes are intended for breakfast, but to accompany meat. I will quote both, since they are very different from each other, and somewhat different from the way we make hashed browns now. These early recipes are more like early nineteenth-century recipes for hash, which were sliced meat reheated in gravy rather than fried. The modern recipe is for Miss Sloane's version.

Potatoes Hashed and Browned—Cut cold boiled potatoes into quarter-inch squares. Put into a three-pint greased pudding dish, pour over them a cup of warm milk seasoned with pepper and salt and a small piece of butter cut up in a tablespoonful of flour. Bake covered half an hour, then brown.—Mrs. C.B. Cannon, Peru, Indiana

Hashed and Browned Potatoes—One quart cooked potatoes, cut into pieces, two tablespoonfuls of butter, one tablespoonful of flour, one teaspoonful of salt, one-quarter teaspoonful of pepper, one teaspoonful of minced onion, one-half pint soup stock. Put the onion and half the butter into a frying-pan, and when the onion turns a light straw color, add the flour and stir until smooth and frothy. Gradually add the soup stock and stir until it boils, then add half the salt and pepper and cook five minutes; season the potatoes with the remainder of the salt and pepper and stir them into the sauce and cook five minutes without stirring. Put the remainder of the butter into another frying-pan and when it quite hot turn the potatoes into this pan and cook fifteen minutes, until browned thoroughly. Fold them over like an omelet, and turn on to a warm dish and serve at once, garnishing with a little parsley.—Miss Ella Sloane, Colorado Springs, Colorado

NOTE: RECIPE TAKES TWO DAYS.

Yield: Serves 4–5

6 medium potatoes

2 tablespoons butter

1 tablespoon flour

1 small onion

1 cup soup stock

Bunch parsley

Equipment: 2 large, heavy frying pans, wooden spoon, spatula, ovenproof plate

1. Peel potatoes and boil in salted water until a fork goes in without resistance. Drain and cool overnight.

2. Cut potatoes into half-inch dice.

3. Halve and peel onion. Cut slices into one of the ends, make a slice or two across and into the onion, then slice thinly across those slices to make a teaspoon of minced onion.

4. Melt 1 tablespoon of the butter in a frying pan, and use it to slightly brown the onions.

5. Add the flour and stir to combine. Let it froth and cook for a minute or two to lose the uncooked-flour taste.

6. Blend in the soup stock to make a cream sauce, and heat to boiling.

7. Add ½ teaspoon of salt and simmer for 5 minutes, stirring until it is somewhat thickened.

8. Season the potatoes with ½ teaspoon of salt and ¼ teaspoon pepper, and stir them into the cream sauce. Cook 5 minutes so the potatoes are heated through.

9. Melt the other tablespoon of butter in the second frying pan. Spread it around with a spatula.

10. Add the potato mixture and cook 15 minutes over medium heat without stirring. This allows the potato mixture to brown and loosen from the pot without burning.

11. Warm an ovenproof plate at the lowest oven setting.

12. You can turn up a little of the potatoes to see that they are browning. When they are ready, fold in half with the spatula. Loosen under the other half with the spatula, and move onto the warmed plate.

Serve sliced and garnished with sprigs of parsley for breakfast with "minced meat on toast, peaches, Graham muffins, and maple syrup."

20

COMMUNAL EXPERIMENTS (1842–1975)

American individualism has sometimes been expressed by communities pioneering in communal living, usually but not always in rural settings and with novel religious beliefs. In this chapter we look at some nineteenth-century communal experiments—by Shakers, transcendentalists, marriage reformers, and German-speaking Protestant sects—and also at the shorter-lived communal experiments by "hippies" and leftist activists in the 1960s and 1970s. Both waves of communal experimenters looked back to the Native American systems of holding farm and hunting land in common. (The Plymouth Pilgrims also intended to hold land, food, and clothing in common for seven years, but changed over to private ownership after 1622.)

While these groups vary considerably, they all use or used common meals to cement their sense of community and developed suitable dishes. In some groups, excellent cooking was a compensation for other sacrifices; in other groups dietary restrictions were part of the common ideology. Sometimes dietary restrictions led to culinary discoveries that influenced the wider culture. It is striking that almost all the religions founded in the United States—including the Church of Jesus Christ of Latter Day Saints, Christian Science, Seventh-Day Adventism, and the Nation of Islam—have special dietary rules or restrictions. Some of these groups are discussed in the *American Ethnic Cookbook for Students*, and some in the health and temperance foods chapters of this book, 13, 18, 29, and 41.

UNLEAVENED BREAD AND APPLES (1843)

Louisa May Alcott, author of *Little Women*, was part of an experiment in "consociate living" organized by her father at "Fruitlands" in Harvard, Massachusetts, in 1843. Louisa was ten and eleven, and wrote about the experience in a short story, "Transcendental Wild Oats," published thirty years later. She also kept a diary at the time, in which she recorded a dinner of "bread and water" and having frequently to wash the dishes for the almost all-male colony. In her story, she summarizes the principles of the transcendentalist-vegetarian colony in a speech by one character, "Neither sugar, molasses, milk, butter, cheese, nor flash are to be used among us,

Figure 11 Hutterite community meal for young women in Montana in 1968. *Source: Ted Streshinsky/CORBIS.*

for nothing is to be admitted which has caused wrong or death to man or beast." The meals, taken communally, were: "unleavened bread, porridge, and water for breakfast; bread, vegetables, and water for dinner; bread, fruit and water for supper."

The unleavened bread was one of the principles of Sylvester Graham, who is remembered for his advocacy of whole wheat flour, but also thought that yeast bread was partially putrefied. The argument was summarized by Louisa's cousin William Alcott, a close associate of Graham, in his 1846 *The Young House Keeper*, "My opinion is, that the best bread in the world is that which is made of recently and coarsely ground wheat meal, mixed with water and baked in thin cakes, not unlike the unfermented cakes so common in many parts of the east, and so much used by the ancient Israelites. My preference for unleavened bread arises, in part, from the consideration that leaven [sourdough yeast] is a foreign and partially decayed substance, which it were better to avoid."

Although no actual Fruitlands recipe has survived, you can serve an authentic Fruitlands meal if you can follow William Alcott's lead to a whole wheat pita bread, preferably one without salt. The colonists' main fruit was a supply of apples gathered from preexisting trees. They never developed an effective plan of work, and the colony broke up in the winter, with two members going on to join the Shakers.

Yield: Serves 1

1 whole wheat pita bread per person

1 or two apples per person

Serve with water and philosophical conversation.

CHEESE PUDDING (1880)

The longest-surviving communal experiment in the United States has been the Shakers, who reached New York in 1774 and established the first communal farm in New Lebanon, New York, in 1787. Although Shakers did not eat meat from 1837 to 1847 (and some Shakers remained vegetarians for life) and later dropped the use of stimulating and alcoholic beverages, Shaker food generally was good, plain, New England cooking, with some of the qualities of thrift, simplicity, and beauty expressed in Shaker furniture. The sect began supporting itself by selling surplus food products, vegetable seeds, herbs, and canned goods in the Early American period and sold inexpensive meals to visitors into the twentieth century. A Shaker cookbook was sold in the nineteenth century, and several fine books have revived Shaker cooking since the 1940s.

This meatless casserole, like a northern answer to cheese grits, was touted as a twelve-cent supper in an 1880 issue of *The Manifesto*, a Shaker magazine, and is reprinted in the 1970, *The Best of Shaker Cooking*, by Amy Bess Williams Miller and Persis Wellington Fuller.

Yield: Serves 8–12

2 cups yellow cornmeal

1 cup grated cheese (cheddar type)

Butter to grease casserole dish

Equipment: Soup pot, long-handled wooden spoon, ovenproof casserole dish

1. Bring 2 quarts of water to a boil in the soup pot.

2. Add 2 tablespoons salt.

3. Add the cornmeal and half the cheese, stirring well to break up lumps.

4. Reduce heat so that it just simmers and cook 20 minutes, stirring frequently so the mixture does not stick and burn.

5. Preheat oven to 400 degrees.

6. Grease casserole dish with butter and pour in cheese-corn mixture.

7. Top with the other half of the cheese.

8. Put in oven, uncovered, until cheese browns on top.

"Serve hot. If any remains, slice it cold and fry brown in good hot butter." The Shakers ate at long tables, one for the men and one for the women. They knelt for a minute of silent prayer before the meal, ate in silence, and knelt again to for a prayer of Thanksgiving. They left the table and returned directly to their many prayers and chores. Kitchen tasks were rotated.

CANNED TOMATOES (1850)

The Oneida community near the Canadian border with New York was founded in 1848 on a complex system including a form of group marriage, birth control, and vegetarianism. It grew to more than three hundred members with several other locations before breaking up in 1878–1881. One of the enterprises, a spoon factory, was then reconstituted as a corporation, with former communards as stockholders, and became the successful Oneida Silver company of the twentieth century.

Like the Shakers, the Oneida community went into food businesses, primarily preserves and pickles. They were also among the early canners of tomatoes. As the community was breaking up, some of their preserving recipes, including this one, were printed in *Jenny June's Cook Book* (1878). Students can use the directions in a modern canning book actually to can these tomatoes. The recipe here is to show the amounts of sugar and salt added to canned tomatoes and the way canned tomatoes tasted 150 years ago, so I have reduced proportions to make one quart of tomatoes, which the Oneida colony would have put into one large can.

Yield: 1 quart

12–16 medium tomatoes

3 tablespoons sugar

7 teaspoons salt

Equipment: Large soup pot, skimmer or slotted spoon, two mixing bowls

1. Bring soup pot half full of water to a boil.
2. Drop in tomatoes to scald for one minute.
3. Remove tomatoes and cool under running cold water.
4. Skin tomatoes (the skins should slip off easily after scalding) and put into one of the mixing bowls.
5. Cut each tomato in half along the equator.
6. Squeeze each half to expel seeds and juice. Collect the shells in a heavy pot.
7. In a small saucepan, heat 1 cup of water, and add the sugar and salt. Stir

until all the sugar and salt are dissolved.
8. Add 1 tablespoon of the salt-sugar syrup to the tomato shells.
9. Cook tomato shells 15 minutes in a covered pot, starting on medium heat so that they don't stick and burn.

Serve in any recipe calling for canned tomatoes, or have a tasting with a can of whole tomatoes from the supermarket.

TOMATENSALAT (1860S)

The Amana Colonies were German-speaking religious communes that were first established in the 1840s near Buffalo, New York, but ran out of room and moved to eastern Iowa. Their "Community of True Inspiration" had faced various persecutions in Europe from their foundation in 1714, but functioned reasonably well with communal kitchens, gardens, and craft shops from 1855 until 1932. As among the Shakers, the dining rooms were silent, but in the early twentieth century, families would eat at home with food from the communal kitchens. Soon after, paying guests were encouraged. This recipe by Erna Pitz is from the 1994 *Seasons of Plenty; Amana Communal Cooking* by Emilie Hoppe, but I have dated it in the 1860s because the simple sauce seems to be a German approach to a tomato salad and might well have been used early on in the communal era. It adds quite a lot of flavor to tomatoes slightly out of season.

Yield: Serves 6

6 tomatoes

1 large onion

1 green or red bell pepper

3 tablespoons sugar

3 tablespoons vinegar

½ teaspoon salt

Equipment: Non-reactive bowl

1. Chop or quarter tomatoes.

2. Peel onion and cut into rings.

3. Stem and core pepper, and chop into large pieces.

4. Stir together vinegar, sugar, salt, and some fresh ground pepper.

5. Combine vegetables, pour dressing over them, and toss well.

6. "Chill well before serving."

Cold Chow (1874)

The Hutterites are an Anabaptist group like the Amish and Mennonites, but had sought religious freedom in Eastern Europe while some other groups went to colonial Pennsylvania and joined the "Pennsylvania Dutch" community. The Hutterites took up the practice of living in a "community of goods" in 1528 in what is now the Czech Republic, but dropped it around 1690. The communal arrangement was revived in 1755 in Romania, but dropped again in Ukraine in 1819. Some Hutterite communities began sharing goods again in 1859, and most came to the prairie states in 1874, when the Russian government revoked their military exemption and their right to conduct schools in German. They thus became part of a large group of German-speaking Russians who moved to the center of the United States and the prairie provinces of Canada.

Hutterites are perhaps the most conservative communal groups in American history, and their communities have survived and thrived over more than 125 years. They split when they get too big, and one of the ceremonies when they do is to hand-copy the community recipes, as they have been hand-copying their German-language sermons since the sixteenth century. This recipe, for example, comes from *The Hutterite Community Cookbook*, edited by Joanita Kant in 1990 from the recipe book of the Sunset Colony of Britton, South Dakota, a granddaughter colony of the 1874 settlement at Bon Homme, then in the Dakota Territory before South Dakota statehood. The recipe makes a kind of cole slaw with a strong Ukrainian influence in the use of sour cream. Although a typical colony is about hundred people, men, women, and children eat at separate sittings, which may explain why this recipe only makes ten servings.

Yield: Serves 10

1 quart green cabbage [from about half a large cabbage]

1 cup sour cream

4 tablespoons sugar

2 teaspoons salt

½ teaspoon pepper

4 tablespoons cider vinegar

½ cup green pepper pieces [from 1 small green pepper]

Equipment: Non-reactive bowl

1. Halve the cabbage, cut out the core, and cut into wedges.

2. Cut thin slices across the wedges to shred the cabbage.

3. Core the green pepper, and remove any loose seeds and white pith.

4. Cut the green pepper into thin slices.

5. Combine cream, sugar, salt, pepper, and vinegar to make a dressing.

6. Toss cabbage and pepper with dressing, and refrigerate before serving.

Serve in a hearty meal of farm-grown meats and vegetables with many cookies for dessert.

Sweet-and-Sour Beet-Carrot Sauté (1972)

The combination of soy sauce and honey is the flavor I most associate with commune cooking. This example (one of commendably few) is from *Country Commune Cooking*, by Lucy Horton, a book collected from forty-seven hippy communes on a cross-country hitchhiking mission. This particular dish was from "The Motherlode" in Oregon. Ms. Horton then joined a rural commune in Vermont and has not published another cookbook.

Yield: Serves 4

3 tablespoons oil

2 beets

2 carrots

2 onions

¼ cup raisins

2 cloves garlic

2 tablespoons vinegar or lemon juice

2 tablespoons honey

2 tablespoons tamari [substitute Japanese soy sauce]

Equipment: Heavy skillet with tight cover, garlic press

1. Halve, peel, and chop onions. (Wear swim goggles to avoid tears.)

2. If the beets are smooth and well scrubbed, you don't have to peel them, but cut off the tops and roots, make a slice to get a flat base, and cut into thin slices.

3. Peel and slice the carrots.

4. Peel the garlic by rubbing back and forth in your hands or in a rolled piece of rubber.

5. Heat the oil in the skillet over medium high heat.

6. Add the beats, carrots, and onions and let brown on the bottom for a few minutes, then turn and stir-fry.

7. Add the raisins and crush the garlic cloves directly into the skillet.

8. Add the remaining ingredients and toss well to combine. Cover the pot and reduce heat to low.

9. Let the vegetables steam about 5 minutes, then uncover and scrape any browned areas off the bottom of the pot. (They should come up easily.) Cover again and steam until the vegetables are tender when tested with a fork, about 15–20 minutes total steaming time.

Serve on a low table or cloth laid out on the ground. Before eating, sit crosslegged, link hands, and chant "Om."

SOY WHIPPED CREAM (1975)

"The Farm" in Tennessee was the largest of all "longhair spiritual communities," and one that was strictly vegetarian. Led by Stephen Gaskin, it is still in existence. Sweets are very important to communal life, with even the Fruitlands group remembered best for baked apples. Here is a soy milk "whipped cream" used on soy milk chocolate pudding and other desserts, from *The Farm Vegetarian Cookbook*, edited by Louise Dotzler.

Yield: Serves 6–8, as a topping

¼ cup soy milk

½ cup oil

1 tablespoon sugar

Pinch salt

½ teaspoon vanilla

Equipment: Blender

1. Combine the soy milk and half the oil in the blender. Turn on to the highest speed.

2. "Slowly pour in the remaining ¼ cup oil."

3. Then blend in the remaining ingredients.

4. "Chill before serving, if possible."

21

EATING ON AMERICAN SHIPS (1854–1910)

Long sea voyages brought the European explorers, colonists, and immigrants to America. Once established, they built and supplied ships for still longer voyages of trade, slave running, and whaling. Even within the United States, long sea voyages were used to join the California gold rush and pioneer Alaska, and to trade Pacific Coast salmon for Hawaiian pineapples.

Shipboard food for much of American history was a crude ration designed to sustain life. Colorful names like plum duff, spotted dick, or dandyfunk concealed rather basic dishes, eternal variations on **Hardtack**, salt meat, salt cod, potatoes, molasses, **Peas Porridge**, and crude puddings. Thus sea pie, **Potato Bargain**, cracker hash, **Skillygalee**, and **Lobscouse** are all mixtures of salt meat, grease, and a simple starch. Dandyfunk was baked hardtack and molasses, and so was some of the plum duff, though usually with added fat and raisins. Land armies also ate these foods, and the recipes did not change from the seventeenth century into the twentieth century, nor between the ships of different countries. The recipe for Sea Pie in the 1824 *Virginia Housewife* is not very different from the one

provided by an active sea cook for the 1908 *Washington Women's Cook Book*. And the dish would not have been out of place on the Mayflower. Officers ate a little better, and unless they packed their own food, passengers often ate a little worse. Traders packed in some fruits and vegetables at landings, but the great majority of meals at sea would probably have been rejected under other circumstances.

Fishermen, who made shorter voyages in a more competitive labor market, ate better. According to Sandra Oliver, in *Saltwater Foodways*, the fisherman's three "P"s of the mid-nineteenth century were potpies, pancakes, and pudding. Of course, the potpies were sometimes sea pie and the pudding was often plum duff, but she records more fresh meat, fruits, and vegetables. Whalers sometimes had doughnuts as they filled their ships with oil. Chapter 4 of Ms. Oliver's book is the best account of shipboard American food, based on her sixteen years of food interpretation at Mystic Seaport Museum. Recipes for foods made every day are seldom written down, and a lot of what we know about eating at sea in American history is based on the writings of passengers.

SEA-VOYAGE GINGERBREAD (1854)

This recipe appeared in *Miss Leslie's New Cookery Book* and was reprinted in the [Martha's] *Vineyard Gazette* of August 28, 1857. This kind of hard, dry cookie was made in large batches by people preparing for long sea voyages such as going around South America to California. The recipe ends by noting "Many persons find highly spiced gingerbread a preventative to sea-sickness." This was scientifically confirmed only in the 1990s! As always, Miss Leslie's directions are full of interesting details. The recipe makes very, very spicy gingersnaps, like New Zealand gingernuts. One question is, how big was "the lid of a canister" in the 1850s? I'm guessing it was smaller than a "glass tumbler," as Miss Leslie would have called a drinking glass, because this dough is hard to handle.

> Sift two pounds of flour into a pan, and cut up in it a pound and a quarter of fresh butter; rub the butter well into the flour and them mix in a pint of *West India* molasses and a pound of the best brown sugar. Beat eight eggs till very light. Stir into the beaten egg two glasses or a gill of brandy. Add also to the egg a tea-cupful of ground ginger, and a table-spoonful of powdered cinnamon, with a tea-spoonful of soda melted in a little warm water. Wet the flour, &c. with this mixture until it becomes a soft dough. Sprinkle a little flour on your pasteboard, and with a broad knife spread portions of the mixture thickly and smoothly upon it. The thickness must be equal all through; therefore spread it carefully and evenly, as the dough will be too soft to roll out. Then with the edge of a tumbler dipped in flour, cut it out into round cakes. Have ready square pans, slightly buttered; lay the cakes in them sufficiently far apart to prevent their running into each other when baked. Set the pans into a brisk oven and bake the cakes well, seeing that they do not burn. You may cut them out small with a lid of a canister (or something similar) the usual size of gingerbread nuts.

Yield: 80–120 gingersnaps

6 cups flour, plus more for breadboard.

1¼ pounds salted butter (5 sticks) plus a little more to grease baking sheets

8 small eggs or 6 large eggs or 4 jumbo eggs

2 cups molasses

2 cups brown sugar

4–6 ounces brandy (optional)

¾ cup ground ginger

1 rounded tablespoon cinnamon

1 rounded teaspoon baking soda

Equipment: 2 baking sheets, pastry blender or standing mixer, breadboard, spatulas, pancake turner, wire racks

1. An hour before starting, remove butter from refrigerator to soften.
2. Cream butter with pastry blender or standing mixer, and then work in the flour to the consistency of kernels of corn.
3. Grease baking sheets.
4. Preheat oven to 375 degrees.
5. Mix in the sugar and molasses.
6. Dissolve baking soda in a little water.
7. Beat the eggs until creamy and light, then stir in the brandy or ¾ cup of water, the baking soda, and the spices.
8. Work this mixture into the flour mixture to get a soft dough. You may need to add more water or flour to get a dough that sticks together as much as it sticks to the spoon.

9. Flour breadboard and spread dough out as thinly and evenly as possible.

10. Cut round cookies with a 2-inch cookie cutter or a drinking glass dipped in flour. Use a pancake turner to space them out on the baking sheets. (Another approach would be to roll ¾-inch balls and let them melt in the oven.)

11. Bake about 12 minutes, checking that such a sweet dough does not burn. The cookies will flatten and crack on top.

12. Cool cookies on baking sheets 10–15 minutes, then lift onto wire racks.

Serve "on a long voyage" as needed.

LOBSCOUS (1857–1871)

Lobscouse is an old sailors' stew of hard-tack, salt beef, potatoes, and vegetables. This 'e'-less recipe is from *The New Encyclopedia of Domestic Economy* edited by Mrs. E.F. Ellet in 1872, but probably identical to her 1857 *Practical Housekeeper*. In either case, she has substituted fresh meat and dropped the hardtack. Lobscouse like this might have been made for sailors come ashore, or might have been served on coastal packets or steamers where fresh meat was roasted. Proportions are not too clear, but all accounts including this one portray lobscouse as more like gruel than like hash. The proportion of meat to starch was always variable according to the state of the ship's supplies, the temper of the cook, and the rank of the diners.

Mince, not too finely, some cold roast beef or mutton. Chop the bones and put them in a saucepan with six potatoes peeled and sliced, one onion, also sliced, some pepper and salt; of these make a gravy. When the potatoes are completely incorporated with the gravy, take out the bones and put in the meat; stew the whole together for an hour before it is served.

Yield: Serves 6

1 pound leftover roast beef, roast lamb, or corned beef (fresh or cooked)

6 medium potatoes

1 onion

1–2 Hardtacks or Crown Pilot crackers (optional)

Equipment: Soup pot with lid

1. Peel and slice potatoes.

2. Halve, peel, and slice the onion.

3. If using uncooked corned beef, cut it into small cubes.

4. Put potatoes, onion, and uncooked corn beef (if using) in a soup pot with 8 cups of water and bring to a boil. Reduce heat to simmer, covered, at least an hour, so that the potatoes are breaking up. Season with pepper and salt (if not using corned beef).

5. If using cooked meat, cut into small pieces and add the fat to the simmering soup.

6. When potatoes are done, add meat, and cook another 30–60 minutes, stirring occasionally to keep the lobscouse from burning and to break up more of the potatoes.

7. If soup seems too thin, you can break up a hardtack or two to thicken it.

Serve in tin cups.

POTATO BARGAIN (1880S)

This is an old recipe of the Tilton family, reprinted in the 1971 *Martha's Vineyard Cookbook* by Louise Tate King and Jean Stewart Wexler. The first Tiltons settled on Martha's Vineyard in 1674. The dish is also described in the 2001 *Cape Cod Wampanoag*

Cookbook by Earl Mills Sr. and Betty Breen, which draws on the traditions of a Cape Cod Indian tribe that was involved in English and American seafaring from about the same time. The dish was also known on shore as Poverty Hash or Necessity Mess. The technique is smothered potatoes, sometimes called "stifle" on Cape Cod, from the French "etouffée." This is a reduced recipe for eating on land. On ship the bargain would be reheated. A Tilton who crewed on the schooner *Alice S. Wentworth* (built in 1863, but active until 1953) is quoted as saying that it was "better after two of three days but tiresome after a week of being served up daily." If you add water and reheat, you have lobscouse.

Yield: Serves 4

4 slices of lean salt pork

4 medium onions

4 medium potatoes, pared and sliced thin

Equipment: Heavy pot with tight lid, teakettle

1. Cut salt pork into half-inch dice. (It is easier to do this if the pork is partially frozen.)

2. Heat salt pork in the pot until it begins to fry. Stir pork to render out fat until the cubes are crispy and brown.

3. Halve, peel, and slice the onions into thin half moons.

4. Sauté the onions in the salt pork fat until they are golden and translucent.

5. Meanwhile bring a teakettle of water to a boil. Peel potatoes and slice thin.

6. When onions are done, return the pork dice to the pan and add the sliced potatoes.

7. Add just enough boiling water to cover the ingredients. "The secret of a good Bargain is not too much water

but cook slowly and let the steam cook them."

8. Taste for salt, sprinkle on some pepper, and cover the pot tightly. Reduce heat to cook slowly.

9. Stir the food occasionally. The dish is done when the potatoes are tender and have absorbed most of the water.

Serve at any watch at sea, or for Sunday supper on land.

CURRIED SALT BEEF (1909)

This is one of an interesting group of recipes donated to the *Washington Women's Cook Book*, published by the Washington [State] Equal Suffrage Association, and compiled by Linda Deziah Jennings. (I am indebted to food historian Karen Hess for sending me these recipes from her copy of this rare book.) The author was Robert Carr, a member of Cook's Local 33 in Seattle and a popular cook on sailing vessels over the previous five years. The recipe has been reduced for the benefit of the suffragettes, but it shows the continuing use of salt meat on long sea voyages and the great popularity of curry powder on Pacific shipping, which has influenced cooking in ports of call from Malaysia to northern Alaska.

Yield: Serves 4

1 pound of cooked salt beef [corned beef]

2 small potatoes

2 dessertspoonfuls [4 teaspoons] curry powder

1 dessertspoonful [2 teaspoons] flour

1 tablespoon butter or dripping [fat from roast meat]

1 "good-sized" onion

1 teaspoon vinegar

1 "pinch" sugar

Equipment: Stew pot, stove with rail so pot won't fall off in high seas (optional)

1. Halve, peel, and chop the onion.
2. Make the dripping or butter hot in a stew pan.
3. Brown the onion, then add the curry powder and flour and mix to make a smooth paste.
4. Gradually stir in 1 cup water to make a thickened sauce.
5. Peel the potatoes and cut into small dice. Cut up the meat into similar pieces.
6. "If the meat is too salt, scald it and make it fresh before adding it to the curry."
7. Add the meat and potatoes to the sauce. Add the vinegar and sugar, and simmer 30 minutes.

Serve in tin cups.

22

CAMPING OUT (1856–1886)

American outdoor cookery started with the first Indians and has never ended. A Native American of ten thousand years ago might be surprised at the equipment at one of our twenty-first-century barbecues or chili contests, but she or he would quickly get the main idea. I was surprised, however, to find a recipe clearly intended for recreational campers in an 1856 cookbook. Many of the middle-class readers of that cookbook cooked over an open fire at home and remembered pioneering well. After the Civil War, disabled veterans, ex-Confederate raiders, and homeless ex-slaves formed a substantial body of homeless tramps—and we would not expect much romance about camping out while tens of thousands were living precariously on the road. Yet, as early as the 1870s and 1880s there is quite a lot published about cookouts, including directions for groups of boys and girls. We find these recipes from a time when many Americans were attempting to homestead the prairie and western states and were trading food uneasily with Indians who had always cooked out. The story of twentieth-century camping (Chapter 38) continues at hunting and fishing camps, and with the Boy Scouts and Girl Scouts.

A CAMP DISH (1857)

This dish appears among a number of mutton dishes in *Mrs. Hale's New Cookbook*, by Sara Josepha Hale, first published in 1852. This kind of pot roast worked at home or in camp.

> Take any joint of mutton, put it into a pot with a good many onions cut small, and as many vegetables as can be obtained to add to it; 2 tablespoonfuls of vinegar, 5 of port wine; season it with black and red pepper; add a spoonful of flour, and, if at hand, 4 dessert-spoonfuls of Harvey's sauce and essence of anchovies. Cover the meat with water, and let it stew one hour and a half; it should be stirred frequently to prevent it from burning, as there should be only water sufficient to cook it.

Yield: Serves 12

½ leg of lamb

2 large onions

4 small turnips

4 very large carrots

2 parsnips (optional)

12 small red potatoes (optional)

1 head celery (optional)

2 tablespoons cider vinegar

5 tablespoons port wine (optional)

1 rounded tablespoon flour

3 tablespoons Harvey's steak sauce, A-1, or Worcestershire (optional)

1 teaspoon anchovy paste (optional)

Equipment: Large stew pot (iron Dutch oven for campfire cooking), vegetable peeler, campfire (optional)

1. Halve, peel, and then quarter the onions.

2. Peel and halve the turnips.

3. Peel the carrots and cut into chunks of similar size.

4. Peel any of the optional vegetables and cut into chunks of similar size.

5. Put lamb and vegetables into the stew pot.

6. Add the flavorings and 1 teaspoon of salt, ½ teaspoon of pepper, and a few pinches of red pepper.

7. Stir the flour in a cup of water and add to the stew pot.

8. Add enough water to cover the lamb and set over heat.

9. Bring to a boil and cook 1½ hours. The trick is to add hot water, perhaps from a teakettle as needed to replace the water that boils away—while keeping the heat low enough to avoid too much burning.

Serve as a one-dish meal when the fish aren't biting.

FISH CHOWDER NO. 2 (1878)

Chowder began as a sailor's dish (see Chapter 3), then came ashore to mean both the stew and the event at which it was served. (The word "barbecue" has a similar dual meaning.) The event was often an outing on the shore. This recipe is from *Camp Cookery* by Maria Parloa and obtained from Mrs. T. Leighton. Miss Parloa was a former New England resort chef, and her idea of camping required fairly elaborate dishes produced in portable kitchens. This somewhat simplified chowder was designed for beach campfires, although the fish was purchased ahead of time.

> Four pounds of fish, half cod and half haddock, if you can get the two kinds, two onions, six potatoes, eight white browns [large soda crackers], one quarter of a pound of salt pork, salt, pepper. Prepare the chowder as directed in the preceding rule; split the crackers and lay on top, pour over the whole hot water enough to cover, and boil 15 minutes; then wet two tablespoons of flour with one-third of a cup of cream. Stir this into the boiling chowder, let it boil up once, and serve. When you cannot get the white browns, pilot bread will answer. When a very strong flavor of onion is desired, use four onions.

Yield: Serves 15–20

4 pounds cod and haddock fillets

2–4 onions

6 potatoes

8 Crown Pilot crackers (or 16 soda crackers)

¼ pound lean salt pork

2 rounded tablespoons flour

⅓ cup heavy cream

Equipment: Two large soup pots

1. Cut salt pork into small dice. Fry slowly in one of the soup pots until the pieces are crispy.

2. Bring 2 quarts of water to a boil in 1 of the soup pots.

3. Peel potatoes and slice thin.

4. Halve and peel onions, and slice into thin rounds.

5. "Cut your fish in small pieces, and wash in cold water."

6. When the salt pork is ready, remove the pieces and pour off some of the grease.

7. In the same pot, make a layer of potatoes and onions and one of fish. Season with salt and pepper.

8. Continue alternate layers, seasoning the fish, until all the fish and potatoes and onions are used up.

9. Now sprinkle on the salt pork, and top with the split crackers or Crown Pilot crackers.

10. Pour on hot water to cover, and simmer the whole thing 15 minutes.

11. Mix the flour with the cream, and stir this into the simmering chowder. Bring back to a brief boil and serve hot.

Serve as a one-pot meal.

CORNMEAL SLAPJACKS (1885)

Unlike Miss Parloa, the male author of *Canoe and Camp*, "Seneca" (H. Soule), seemed actually to have camped out in the modern sense. Cornmeal slapjacks were not much different from those made by Confederate soldiers in the Civil War, or from the "Indian Slapjack" in the first American cookbook of 1796, which may have mistaken "slapjack" for the then-usual flatjack. Because cornmeal varies so much, it is no easier to give precise directions now than it was in 1885, although it can be said that this recipe makes a lot of somewhat crispy pancakes.

One quart of cold water mixed with meal enough to make a thin batter, one teaspoon salt and one or two teaspoons of baking powder having been stirred into the latter. The addition of one or two well-beaten eggs will im-

prove it. Cook on a very hot pan, as above.

Yield: About 40 2-inch pancakes

2–4 cups cornmeal (stone ground preferred)

1–2 rounded teaspoons baking powder

1–2 eggs, optional

4 tablespoons butter

Equipment: Rag or brush for buttering pan; skillet, griddle, or cast-iron frying pan; pancake turner

1. Sift the baking powder and 1 teaspoon of salt with half the cornmeal.

2. Measure 4 cups of cold water, and stir in the cornmeal mixture.

3. If using eggs, beat well and add to the mixture.

4. Add more cornmeal, if necessary, to make a loose batter.

5. Melt 1 tablespoon of the butter in the pan and push around with the rag or brush to grease the pan evenly.

6. Stir the batter and spoon a test pancake onto the griddle. If the pancake seems too thick, add a little more water. If too thin, add a little more cornmeal. Test again.

7. When you have the batter right, stir it and spoon several pancakes onto the griddle. Cook until bubbles appear in the top, flip and cook until browned on the other side as well.

8. Between batches, brush or rub the pan with a little more butter. Keep stirring the batter, because the cornmeal settles to the bottom.

Serve with butter, jam, or syrup.

SWEET POTATOES (1886)

This recipe comes from a chapter called "Ho, For the Picnic" in the 1886 edition of

In the Kitchen by Elizabeth Smith Miller. The technique is based on a worldwide technique of earth-oven cooking best documented in Hawaii, but used by many Native American groups to cook wild roots and tubers. It may have been taken directly from the book, *Woodcraft*, by "Nessmuk" (George Sears), published in 1884, from which I have taken some details. You can try this in a large home fireplace if you collect a bucket of ashes or use builder's sand.

> Build a fire over a flat stone; when burned to coals, rake it off, wrap the potatoes in wet brown paper, cover them with sand, and rebuild the fire. Birds may be cooked in the same way.

Yield: Serves 6

6 medium sweet potatoes

A few tablespoons of cooking oil

Equipment: Campfire or home fireplace, brown paper bags, washed builder's sand (optional), fireplace tools, wood splinters or skewers

1. Find a flat rock quite a bit larger than all the sweet potatoes. Use it as the basis of a campfire, or brush off the bottom of a home fireplace to serve as a flat rock. Burn a few hardwood logs down to coals.

2. Clean off sweet potatoes if necessary. Poke a few holes in each one with a fork.

3. Rub oil all around the sweet potatoes.

4. If using builder's sand, heat it up in a 300-degree oven, or by stirring it in a heavy pot. Cut open the paper bags to make two sheets of brown paper. Soak the paper in cold water, and wrap several layers around each potato.

5. When fire is down to coals, shovel or rake them aside. Set the wrapped sweet potatoes on the hot stone or fireplace floor and cover immediately with ashes or hot sand.

6. Rake or shovel the coals back on top of the ashes or sand and add new wood to build a lively fire.

7. After 30 minutes, begin testing one of the larger potatoes with a splinter or wooden skewer. When the splinter goes right through, the potatoes are done. As Nessmuk advised for white potatoes, "Run the sliver through them from end to end, to let the steam escape, and use immediately, as a roast potato quickly becomes soggy and bitter."

Serve with butter, salt, and pepper.

23

IRISH IMMIGRATION (1859–1877)

The large-scale Irish Catholic immigration of the 1840s had an enormous influence on the development of American culture and democracy. The new immigrants spoke English, but had been regarded as an inferior race in Europe and were this country's first large minority of Roman Catholics. Earlier Irish Catholic immigrants had faced mob violence in the 1830s in Boston and other cities. Much of the later debate was played out in the kitchen, since Irish women became cooks and maids in large American cities, replacing the young white Protestant girls who had been indentured servants and could now attend public schools or work in factories. This section focuses on the interactions between Irish cooks and their Anglo-American mistresses. For some foods Irish Americans ate in their own homes, see *The American Ethnic Cookbook for Students*.

A large literature for housewives about how to work with hired servants focused on "Bridget" and "Nora." As early as 1841, Sarah Josepha Hale grandly generalized, "The great fault of the Irish help is, that they undertake to do what they have never learned." Miss Beecher's *Domestic Receipt Book*, in the third edition (first published

1847) noted, "In some portions of our country, the great influx of foreigners of another language and another faith, and the ready entrance they find as domestics into American families, impose peculiar trials and peculiar duties on American housekeepers." A reformer like Miss Beecher advised "kindness, patience and sympathy . . . Especially . . . in reference to their Religion." Other writers were not so kind. By 1881, Harriet Prescott Spofford wrote, "In the early days of our national existence, no one ever heard a word about servants; now, as one might almost say, nobody ever hears a word about anything else. If two matrons meet in the street, one cannot fail to catch the names of Bridget and Nora in their colloquy. . . . It is not upon nationality nor upon religion that the trouble hinges altogether, although these things have very much to do with it. You may think, for instance, that nothing could be worse than your Irish girl, till you get an African one; the Swede who takes the latter's place is only good while she is fresh—she needs to be in the country but six months before she knows all the 'tricks and manners;' the sprightliness of the French maid is as aggravating in its own way, and the stolidity of the German makes you long for the blarneying tongue of Bridget once again . . . you at last secure an American, her familiarity makes you wish you could do the work yourself" (*The Servant Girl Problem*, Boston: Houghton Mifflin, 1881).

It is surprisingly hard to trace Irish influence on American cooking. In part this is because earlier Protestant Irish immigrants (known since the 1840s as "Scotch-Irish") had already introduced potato dishes and milk-based soups that they had acquired in northern Ireland in the early 1700s. I suspect that the introduction of milk and potatoes to chowders, most of which took place in the 1840s and 1850s, was reinforced by Irish immigrant servants, since these changes made the chowder like a traditional Irish soup. (Clam chowder is on every Irish pub menu in Boston to this day.) But I have never found documentation for Irish cooks with a spoon in early American chowder.

BRIDGET'S BREAD CAKE (EXCELLENT) (1850S)

This recipe appears in my 1861 third edition (first published 1847) of *Miss Beecher's Domestic Receipt Book*, by Catherine Esther Beecher, and is one of the first explicitly Irish recipes printed in the United States. It starts with extra bread dough, which is not surprising, since Miss Beecher's basic bread recipes were for eight or sixteen loaves! But the result is something like an Irish soda bread. Although "Bridget" would have thought of a round loaf, Miss Beecher would have directed her to use a loaf pan. And since leftover dough is the basis of the recipe, you can use frozen bread dough! With both the pearlash (potassium carbonate, used like baking soda) and the yeast in the bread, this had two forms of leavening, which you can also see in **Bridget's Buckwheats**.

Yield: Two small loaves of cake

3 cups of dough, "very light"

3 cups of sugar

1 cup of butter, plus some to grease loaf pans

3 eggs

1 nutmeg (or 2 teaspoons powdered nutmeg)

1 cup raisins

1 teaspoon pearlash (substitute baking soda)

Equipment: Nutmeg grater, pastry blender or large fork, mixing bowl, 2 small loaf pans, wood toothpick or wire cake tester, wire racks to cool cakes

1. Take butter out of the refrigerator an hour before starting. If using frozen bread dough, follow package directions so that it is well risen ("very light") when you start.

2. If using whole nutmeg, grate on fine grater or nutmeg grater. Mind your fingers!

3. Butter the 2 pans.

4. Cream together butter and sugar with a pastry blender or a large fork.

5. Dissolve baking soda in a little hot water.

6. Beat eggs well and stir in spice, then blend into the butter-sugar mixture.

7. Mix the baking soda with the butter-sugar mixture.

8. Blend butter-sugar mixture and raisins into the bread dough. "*It is very important* that the ingredients should be thoroughly mixed with the dough."

9. Form the dough into loaves, and set into the pans. Cover with a kitchen towel and let rise 30–40 minutes or until doubled in bulk. "It will do to bake it immediately, but the cake will be lighter if it stands a short time to rise, before putting it into the oven."

10. Slash the top of the risen breads the long way.

11. Bake 15 minutes on the top shelf of a 425-degree oven.

12. Move breads to a lower shelf and reduce heat to 350 degrees. Bake another 15 minutes or until a wood toothpick or cake tester comes out clean. "Try whether cake is done by piercing it with a broom splinter, and if nothing adheres, it is done."

13. Cool on a wire rack for 10 minutes. Then pick up hot pan with pot holders, and turn each bread out to cool on wire racks.

Serve sliced with butter and jam.

POTATOES WITH THE BONE IN (1859)

We have all wondered why our Irish servants persist in bringing half-boiled potatoes to the table, notwithstanding our repeated orders to the contrary. Dr. James Johnson, in his tour in Ireland, discovered that it was almost a universal custom among the poor of that country, to only half boil their potatoes, leaving the center so hard, that it is called the bone of the potato.

When I first read this, in the 1859 *Breakfast, Dinner, and Tea, Viewed Classically, Poetically, and Practically*, by Julia C. Andrews, I thought it was a slur of some kind. For one thing, fully cooked boiled potatoes, dried in the empty pot over low heat, had been described as an Irish recipe in earlier books. However I have since read further descriptions of "potatoes with a bone" in Ireland, as early as 1812. The preference developed in hard times, for the undercooked potato was harder to digest, and seemed to stop hunger for a longer time. The name indicates also the lack of meat on many Irish tables in the early nineteenth century.

Yield: Serves 6

6 baking or all-purpose potatoes

Equipment: Potato peeler, large pot, fork for testing

1. Peel potatoes.
2. Put whole potatoes in pot with water to cover by an inch, and 1 tablespoon of salt.
3. Bring to a boil. Reduce heat to simmer with lid off or ajar.
4. After 15 minutes, begin testing by pushing fork into the center of a potato. When it goes in almost half the width of the potato, but meets a hard part—the "bone"—potatoes are ready.

Serve with butter. In the kitchen, Bridget eats her potato slowly with a cup of milk, thinking of home. She is interrupted by the bell, summoning her to the dining room where she is scolded for serving the potatoes undercooked.

BRIDGET'S BUCKWHEATS (1877)

Buckwheat was one of the first grains that grew well in New England and maritime Canada. Pancakes like these were widely popular in early America and remained important for pioneers, loggers, and prospectors in the northernmost states. There were some British buckwheat pancakes, and more from Normandy, which came over to French Canada and are still used as table bread in the Acadian communities of New Brunswick and northern Maine. (See Acadian "Ployes" in *The American Ethnic Cookbook for Students*.) Buckwheat pancakes became more popular after the Civil War when baking powder made it easier to leaven them.

Here "Bridget" lightens them first with yeast, then with baking soda, which reacts with the molasses and the sourdough. Her other trick was to mix the batter right in the pitcher, which I don't recommend. The source was *Mrs. Winslow's Domestic Receipt Book for 1877*, an almanac issued to promote home remedies.

Let the buckwheat be of the hulled sort (Platt's Mills) and fresh. Put into a two quart pitcher one and a half pints of tepid water: add four tablespoons of baker's yeast or as much 'compressed' yeast as will make one loaf of bread—other kinds in proportion—with a little salt. Then stir in buckwheat enough to make a thick batter; cover the pitcher and set away to rise overnight, after beating thoroughly. In the morning add three tablespoons of molasses, and a quarter of teaspoonful of soda, dissolved in about three tablespoons of milk. Beat all well together, and pour the cakes from the pitcher upon a well-heated griddle. A soapstone griddle needs no greasing; an iron griddle should be greased with a piece of rind of ham or fat salt pork on a fork. Butter and silver-drips syrup are best to eat with buckwheat cakes; maple syrup is also good.

NOTE: RECIPE TAKES TWO DAYS.

Yield: 30 small pancakes

1 package dried or compressed yeast

2 cups buckwheat flour

3 tablespoons molasses

¼ teaspoon baking soda

3 tablespoons milk

Piece of salt pork or fatback to grease griddle

Butter and maple syrup to serve

Equipment: Griddle or large frying pan, half-gallon or larger pitcher, kitchen towel to cover pitcher, wooden spoon, spatula or pancake turner, mixing bowl

1. The night before making pancakes, measure 3 cups of lukewarm water into a mixing bowl. Add a cake of yeast or a package of dried yeast. (The "three tablespoons" refers to a weaker liquid yeast; don't use 3 tablespoons of dry yeast!)

2. Stir in a teaspoon of salt, and enough of the buckwheat flour to make a fairly stiff but still pourable batter.

3. Get the batter into the pitcher and set in a warm place to rise overnight. Cover with the kitchen towel.

4. In the morning, dissolve the baking soda in the milk.

5. Add the molasses to the batter in the pitcher and stir well.

6. Heat up the griddle or frying pan. If it isn't a nonstick pan or griddle, take the piece of salt pork or fatback and rub on the hot pan so the pancakes won't stick.

7. Stir the milk mixture into the batter thoroughly. If the batter doesn't seem pourable, add a little more milk.

8. Pour out small pancakes and cook until the edges look done and there are bubbles throughout.

9. Flip over and cook on the other side until browned.

Serve with butter and maple syrup.

24

CIVIL WAR—NORTH (1860–1865)

The Civil War was fought almost entirely in the southern states and thus did not disrupt food supplies in the North very much. There are few if any civilian recipes especially associated with the war years in the northern states. During most of the war, the ration for Union soldiers was the most generous military ration in the world, although not all of it reached the soldiers. Especially in battle zones, however, they were dependent on crates of hard crackers (**Hardtack**), salt meat, beans, and poorly dried vegetables. Treats were mailed from home, purchased at high prices from peddlers called "suttlers," or "foraged" from southern farmers. Sometimes meals were shared or sold by African-American cooks, and for some northern recruits this was their first taste of African-American cooking.

In many ways the largest effect of the Civil War on northerners was what General Grant later described: "The war begot a spirit of independence and enterprise. The feeling now [1885] is, that a youth must cut loose from his old surroundings to enable him to get up in the world. There is now such a commingling of the people that particular idioms and pronunciation are no longer localized to any great extent." Regional cooking continued to evolve, and Southern cooking in some ways became more distinctive after the Civil War by dropping "Yankee dishes." But the war took many recruits out of the their hometowns for the first time and encouraged migration. The victorious North continued to invest in the heavy industry and railroads that had helped win the war. The northern troops that remained in some Southern states until 1877 were then sent west to remove Indians and make way for settlers.

HARDTACK (1860S)

These hard crackers were the universal ration of soldiers and sailors throughout the Civil War and generally for hundreds of years earlier. Union Army hardtack was made to precise specifications under contract, shipped by rail, and a pound per day (eight or nine hardtacks) issued to each soldier. According to *Hardtack and Coffee*, a memoir by John Billings (see excerpt in the *Readers Companion to the American Historical Cookbook for Students*), the system worked well enough that some soldiers did not draw their full ration, so others could often have extras. Confederate soldiers also ate cap-

Figure 12 "Weighing bread for the Union Army" in Virginia in 1864. Soft bread was available in permanent camps, and late in the war when the Union army developed a baker's oven on wagon wheels. *Source: The Photographic History of the Civil War, Vol. 8, New York, 1911.*

tured hardtacks, especially early in the war. They were baked hard to make them durable, and if kept dry would last for decades. More than a few soldiers kept one or two as souvenirs, and you can sometimes see them in Civil War museums. They were sometimes known as "Lincoln pies."

Because hardtack was produced in factories, there is no family-size recipe. But Civil War reenactors make them, generally to fit Billings's description. This recipe was posted by Danielle Jarest, of Peterborough, New Hampshire, at the Internet address ⟨http://www.conval.edu/schools/sms/www/diamond/cwfood.htm⟩. Hers are quite true to Billings's description, except somewhat thinner. I have added the drying step at the end to approximate the reported hardness of hardtack, which was sometimes too hard to chew. Mrs. Jarest, by contrast, writes that "Even my 4-year-old daughter fights for these!"

Yield: 10 hardtacks

2 cups flour

½ tablespoon salt (optional)

½ tablespoon sugar (optional)

Equipment: Food processor or blender, board and rolling pin, baking sheets

1. Mix with ½ cup water in a food processor or "electric blender medium speed until this has the consistency of playdough."

2. Flour board and rolling pin.

3. "I roll mine out with a rolling pin to about ⅓″ ± (the thinner the crisper), then cut it into 3″ × 3″ squares." Billings records his as "three and one-eighth by two and seven-eights inches, and are nearly half an inch thick."

4. "I use the barrel of a ball point pen to punch 16 holes (4 × 4) in each square." (This was done mechanically so that the crackers would not bubble up in baking.)

5. "Bake at 375 degrees on the first side for 20–25 minutes or until light brown."

6. "Then turn them over and bake for another 15–20 minutes."

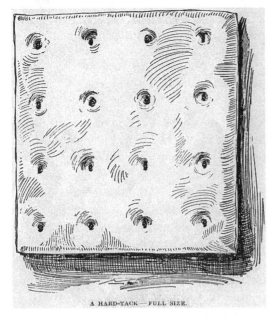

Figure 13 A full-size hardtack. *Source: John Davis Billings,* Hardtack and Coffee, *1901. Illustration by Charles W. Reed.*

7. Dry overnight at the lowest oven setting (optional).

Serve crumbled in coffee or soup, or toasted on a green stick with butter, or in the following recipe.

SKILLYGALEE (1863)

"Some crumbled them [hardtacks] in cold water, then fried the crumbs in the juice and fat of meat. A dish akin to this one, which was said to 'make the hair curl,' and certainly was indigestible enough to satisfy the cravings of the most ambitious dyspeptic, was prepared by soaking hardtack in cold water, then frying them brown in pork fat, salting to taste. Another name for this dish was 'skillygalee.' "—Billings.

I have taken quantities from the daily ration.
CAUTION: HOT OIL USED.

Yield: Serves 2 soldiers half their marching ration.

12 ounces lean salt pork

8–9 hardtacks (see previous recipe)

Equipment: Large pot for soaking hard tacks, cast-iron skillet, spatula

1. Soak hardtacks in a large pot of cold water.
2. Slice salt pork like bacon. (If you can't get thin slices, neither could the soldiers with pocket knives.)
3. Fry salt pork slowly in frying pan to extract as much fat as possible.
4. When salt pork is crisp, or you can't wait any longer, remove salt pork from frying pan.
5. Remove hardtacks from cold water.
6. Shake excess water from hardtacks and fry in the grease from the salt pork.
7. Turn hardtacks and brown on both sides.
8. Remove to a plate and finish the rest of the hardtacks.

Serve fried hardtacks and salt pork on a plate. See if that gives you enough energy to go out and attempt to forage vegetables or wild garlic.

DRIED BEEF (1862)

This may be the earliest official recipe for creamed chipped beef, which became the most famous American military dish of the twentieth century (see **My Not So Famous "S-O-S"** in Chapter 49.) It's interesting that the controversial dish may have entered military lore as a comfort food, since this recipe comes from *A Collection of Recipes for the Use of Special Diet Kitchens in Military Hospitals*, written by Mrs. Annie Wittenmyer and published by her U.S. Christian Commission. She had originally organized a charitable effort to help sick and wounded Iowa soldiers in Kansas and Mississippi, and by the end of the war, her recipes and recommendations were in use in a hundred military hospitals. Mrs. Wittenmyer went on to start a large orphanage in Iowa and to serve as first president of the Women's Christian Temperance Union. I have taken some proportions from the 1910 *Manual for Army Cooks*. Today's chipped beef probably doesn't need as much soaking and washing to be palatable, but since this was hospital food, it was intended to be bland.

> Shave down dried beef very thin; pour over cold water, and let it soak one hour; drain off the water, and pour over boiling water; let it stand a few minutes; drain off the water, and put it in a suitable vessel over the fire; add a little butter, pepper, and sweet milk, a very little flour; simmer a few minutes, stirring gently, and turn into a deep dish or pan serve with a little of the milk gravy.

Yield: Serves 8

2 pounds chipped beef

¼ stick butter

2 tablespoons flour

1 quart whole milk

Equipment: 2 large pots, colander

1. Soak beef in cold water 1 hour.

2. Bring half a pot of water to a boil.

3. Drain beef, put back into a pot, and pour on the boiling water.

4. After a few minutes, drain the hot water (or strain out the beef with a skimmer), and return the beef to the pot with the butter and a dash of pepper.

5. Melt the butter over low heat.

6. Stir the flour into the milk, and pour them both into the meat and butter.

7. Increase heat to medium and stir well until gravy thickens.

Serve in bowls. Apparently the toast wasn't part of the dish yet. Perhaps the men soaked hardtacks in the gravy.

UNION CAKE (1860s)

This recipe was pinned into a handwritten recipe book begun by Augusta A. Haley of South Dedham, Massachusetts, in June 1860. It is signed by "Clara." Miss Haley became Mrs. Charles W. Bassett and moved to Newton Corner sometime before starting a second culinary notebook in February 1867. She filled that one and returned to fill up her old book in 1870. The use of cornstarch to lighten the flour and give a finer crumb to the cake is quite early, and it is possible that this recipe was developed by a cornstarch manufacturer. (The *Nebraska Pioneer Cookbook* by Kay Graber reprints a similar recipe from a nineteenth-century Nebraska newspaper. Unfortunately she does not give a date or exact source, but this also suggests that the recipe was spread by suppliers.)

Miss Haley's copy of the recipe halves the quantities and substitutes nutmeg for lemon. Miss Haley does not give many directions, so I have borrowed some from Eliza Leslie that she might have learned, and some from the very similar recipe for "Classic Butter Cake" in *The Simple Art of Perfect Baking*, by Flo Braker (1985).

Yield: Serves 16–24

2 teacups sugar [1½ cups]

⅔ cup [salted] butter, plus more to grease pans

4 [medium] eggs [or 3 extra large eggs]

3 cups flour

½ cup cornstarch

1 [level] teaspoon cream tartar

½ teaspoon saleratus [substitute level measure of baking soda]

1 cup [whole] milk

1½ teaspoons lemon juice

AT THE TELEGRAPHERS' TENT, YORKTOWN—MAY, 1862

Figure 14 Union telegraphers at dinner in Virginia in 1862. The table is set with stew and hardtack. *Source: The Photographic History of the Civil War, Vol. 8, New York, 1911.*

Equipment: Pastry blender or food processor, whisk, lemon juicer, 2 large loaf pans, parchment paper or waxed paper, scissors, toothpick or wire cake tester

1. An hour before baking, remove butter from refrigerator to soften. Butter loaf pans. Cut out 2 rectangles of paper to fit the bottom and sides. Fold up 2 sides (or 2 ends). Butter paper on both sides and put into loaf pans.

2. Break each egg into a cup, remove any bits of shell with a half shell, and then put the eggs into a small bowl.

3. Beat eggs well. Mix dry ingredients except baking powder in a small bowl. Mix milk and baking powder.

4. Juice lemon to obtain lemon juice.

5. Cream butter and sugar together with pastry blender or in food processor. Work quickly so as not to overheat the butter.

COOKING PANCAKES.

Figure 15 Pancake flipping was already an American pastime. *Source: John Davis Billings,* Hardtack and Coffee, *1901. Illustration by Charles W. Reed.*

6. Whisk in flour mixture and milk mixture in alternate parts.

7. Whisk in lemon juice and divide batter into pans.

8. Bake at 350 degrees for 40 minutes and begin testing with wooden toothpick or wire cake tester.

9. Cool in pans on wire rack.

Serve in slices with butter and jam, or sell to raise funds for disabled Union veterans.

LOYAL BISCUITS (1860s)

These biscuits were loyal because they were southern cooking in the family of a union officer. They were copied from "Mrs. Billings—Alton, Illinois" by Alice Kirk Grierson, whose notebook has been published as *An Army Wife's Cookbook*, compiled and edited by Mary L. Williams of the Fort Davis [Texas] National Historic Site. Mrs. Grierson was married in 1856. After the Civil War, she followed her cavalry colonel husband in various western postings until her death in 1888. This recipe probably dates from her time in her in-laws' Illinois home during the Civil War or a visit there in the years immediately afterward. Although Mrs. Grierson's directions say to "bake as muffins," muffins in the nineteenth century were usually baked on a griddle in rings, like English muffins. Muffin rings would have been about an inch larger than a tuna fish can. You can remove both ends of a few tuna fish cans, file down any sharp areas, remove the labels, and put through a dishwasher a few times to make muffin rings. Or you can make the batter a little thicker, roll out the dough, and cut with a drinking glass into biscuits. I have reduced the amount of flour to compensate for the increased dryness of today's flour.

> 3 cups flour, 1 cup sweet milk, 3 eggs, little sugar, butter the size of an egg, 3 spoonfuls baking powder. Bake as muffins.

Yield: About 30 biscuits

2¾ cups flour

1 cup whole milk

3 small eggs or 2 large eggs

2 tablespoons sugar

3 tablespoons salted butter, a little more to grease griddle, and another stick to serve

1 tablespoon baking powder

Equipment: Muffin rings (optional), griddle or cast-iron skillet, muffin pans (optional)

1. Sift flour before measuring. Combine dry ingredients in a bowl and stir well.

2. Melt butter. Mix with milk. Beat eggs and add to milk.

3. Stir liquid ingredients into dry ingredients. You can leave a few lumps. You should have a soft dough or stiff batter. If you want to make biscuits without rings, add a little more flour so that you can pat it out ½ inch thick and cut with a drinking glass.

4. Butter muffin rings, if using. Heat griddle, grease if necessary, and set down muffin rings.

5. Pour about ½ inch of batter into each ring, and brown on both sides. If using biscuits without rings, brown on each side. (If using muffin pans, grease the pans, pour batter ½ full, and bake in a 375-degree oven for 20 minutes.) Batter should puff up considerably.

Serve hot, split and butter.

25

CIVIL WAR—SOUTH (1860S–1872)

Southern food was altered much more by the Civil War than the food of the northern states. Although the South was an agricultural region, some land was slow to convert from cotton and tobacco, transportation was limited and became worse, and the region was under naval blockade for almost all of the war. Food was diverted to the troops, and foraging Union soldiers took a lot in the later years of the war. If slaves ran away to the Union lines, there was a shortage of labor to plant or harvest. In addition, the hardships were increased in memory by the poor harvests and local food shortages in the five years after the war.

Thrown on their own resources, southern cooks substituted rice and corn for wheat flour. Once-wealthy plantation owners learned how their former slaves had been stretching the biscuits with sweet potato and getting by on field peas. Slave rations were often cut down.

Confederate soldiers began the war well supplied, and some of the officers were able to bring a slave to cook for them. Because the later parts of the war were fought on southern ground, packages could be sent from home. Some hardtacks were produced earlier in the war, but most Confederate rations were cornmeal and salt pork. The Confederates won most of the early battles, and sometimes seized northern supplies. Later in the war, even frying pans and mixing bowls were hard to find. The Confederate answer to **Skillygalee** was a similar hash of bacon grease, salt meat, and crumbled cornbread called "Cush" or "Slosh." Since the former name comes from the New Orleans Creole dish of refried cornmeal or cornbread, we can see that the many regional cuisines of the southern states were being combined into what was increasingly described after the war as "Southern Food."

LAPLANDS (1853)

On October 15, 1862, Confederate Col. Walter Herron Taylor, adjutant to Gen. Robert E. Lee, wrote to his family, "What would I not give for some of Sallie's Laplands, served up in the style I used to enjoy in her room, instead of the beef, flour and water which now constitute my breakfast, lunch, and dinner." The "Sallie" was family friend Sally Tompkins of Richmond, who organized a fine private hospital after the first Battle of Manassas. When Jefferson

Davis ordered all private hospitals closed to maintain military standards, he was persuaded to make Sally Tompkins a captain of cavalry so the "Robertson Hospital" could remain open. She thus became the only female officer in the CSA army.

Tompkins was the heiress of a prominent Virginia family and brought considerable resources to her hospital, including four of her own slaves. Captain Tompkins, according one recovered patient, was "a born forager," who obtained fresh ingredients for her patients and had an unusually good rate of recovery. She was much loved by survivors of her hospital and a popular figure at Confederate reunions for many decades after the war.

But what were Laplands? From postwar recipes, they were somewhere between muffins (then called "gems") and popovers. And how did Sally Tompkins make them so memorably? Probably the nearest written recipes are four collected by Mrs. Robert E. Lee in a kitchen book she and her daughters kept between 1860 and 1890. There are two recipes in *Housekeeping in Old Virginia*, edited by Mrs. Marion Cabell Tyree and published in 1879. Mrs. Tyree drew on the recipe books of many leading Virginians, including Mrs. Lee and one of her daughters, but does not name Captain Sally Tompkins, Walter Taylor, or anyone from their wartime circles as a source.

In the end, we have to guess that a "born forager" like Captain Sally Tompkins used better ingredients to make richer Laplands than other people, which brings us to an earlier Virginia recipe, recorded in 1853 in a manuscript cookbook then belonging to Mrs. Dr. Robert Fleming, and published in the 1957 *Virginia Cookery Past and Present*, by the Woman's Auxiliary of Olivet Episcopal Church, Franconia, Virginia. I have taken some details from a tested recipe in the same book.

4 eggs to a pint of the richest sweet cream, a teaspoonful of salt. Beat the eggs until they are very light then add the cream and mix the flour in it the consistency of muffins. Bake it in small pans. Beat the yolks and whites separately.

Yield: 6 muffins or 10–12 mini-muffins

4 small eggs or 3 large eggs

2 cups extra heavy cream

1½ cups flour

Butter to grease cups or muffin tins

Equipment: 3 metal mixing bowls, mini-muffin or muffin tins

1. Break the eggs and separate by pouring back and forth between shells over a cup to catch the whites. Gather the whites in a large metal bowl, and the yolks in another.
2. Beat the whites with a whisk or handheld mixer until they form soft peaks.
3. Beat the yolks until creamy and light.
4. Beat the cream until it forms soft peaks.
5. Add whipped cream and flour alternately to egg yolks.
6. "Fold in" egg whites with the whisk or one of the machine beaters.
7. Butter muffin tins or egg rolls.

CAUTION: FOR BEST RESULTS, YOU MUST HANDLE HOT MUFFIN PAN.

Yield: 6 muffins or 10–12 mini-muffins

1 cup flour

1 cup milk

1 egg

Butter to grease cups or muffin tin

Equipment: 2 good oven mitts, microwave oven (optional), ladle, mini-muffin pan (preferred), paper muffin cups, muffin pan or stoneware cups and baking sheet, whisk

1. Preheat oven to 400 degrees (375 degrees if using muffin pan or large cups). Measure out milk and warm to room temperature in microwave. (Without microwave, measure out milk an hour before making recipe.)
2. Beat egg in large mixing bowl until creamy and light.
3. Butter cups or muffin pan or mini-muffin pan.
4. Put empty pan or cups in oven to heat.
5. Quickly mix milk and flour into eggs to make a batter.
6. Put on both oven mitts. Remove hot pan from oven, place on heat-proof surface (top of stove) and—still wearing mitts—pour in batter. Return pan to oven.
7. For large muffin pans or cups, bake 20 minutes at 375 degrees. For mini-muffin pans or cups, 15 minutes at 400 degrees.

Serve hot.

SWEET POTATO WAFERS (1863)

This recipe for waffles first appeared in The *Edgefield (South Carolina) Adviser* of March 1, 1863, and is reprinted in *The Confederate Housewife*, by John Hammond Moore, an excellent collection of recipes from Confederate newspapers with extracts from diaries of the time. As you see in the recipe, the Dutch-American term "waffles" was used interchangeably with the Anglo-American "wafers." Genteel southerners had waffle irons, even if some of the slaves who held them in the fireplace had departed. Recipes substituted cornmeal or sweet potatoes to make quick waffles.

When flour is so high priced as at present, sweet potatoes can be used to great advantage in a variety of breads. Boil two large or four smaller sweet potatoes. Peel and mash them. Put in a large spoonful of lard, a little salt, and knead into them half a pound of wheat flour. Cut into small pieces and bake in a waffle iron, or roll out thin, cut into squares, and bake in an oven as biscuits. A little milk—an egg—or one or two tablespoons of sugar may be added—at will or possession, but simply made as above they are excellent tea cakes.

Yield: About 12 large waffles

2 medium sweet potatoes or "yams"
1 rounded tablespoon lard
½ teaspoon salt
½ pound flour (1¾ cups)
¾ cup half-and-half (optional)
1 medium egg (optional)
1–2 rounded tablespoons sugar (optional)

Equipment: Waffle iron

1. Boil sweet potatoes 25 minutes.
2. Peel and mash. Add the lard so it melts.
3. Sprinkle on salt. (Salt was often in short supply during the Civil War.)
4. Add the flour and work into a stiff batter. Adding any of the optional ingredients will make the batter more liquid, and the waffles will bake up crisper and more tender.
5. Heat waffle iron according to directions (if electric) or until hot but not smoking.
6. Spread ½ cup of the batter across the waffle iron and bake according to directions, or until waffle is golden

brown and comes off the waffle iron easily.

REPUBLICAN PUDDING (1863)

This Confederate rice pudding is named ironically, because rice was grown in South Carolina and Louisiana, but the war prevented imports of wheat. By the end of the war, eggs and sugar were very expensive in Richmond as well, and the sauce for this pudding might have been omitted, or made from molasses or sorghum molasses. This and the following recipe appeared in *Confederate Receipt Book; A Compilation of Over One Hundred Receipts, Adapted to the Times*, published in Richmond in 1863 and printed on polka-dot wallpaper, since paper was short in the Confederacy. Most of the *Confederate Receipt Book* is about substituting for foods the South could not grow or import because of the naval blockade. Rice or potatoes went into breads, cakes, pancakes, and pie crust. There are substitutes for coffee (acorns), fried oysters (corn), apples (crackers and tartaric acid), and beer (brewed from molasses).

> Take one cup of soft boiled rice, a pint of milk, a cup of sugar, three eggs, and piece of butter the size of an egg. Serve with sauce.

Yield: Serves 6

1 cup boiled rice (from ⅓ cup rice)

2 cups whole milk

1 cup sugar, plus ½ cup for sauce

3 small eggs or 2 extra large eggs

3 tablespoons butter, 2 tablespoons for sauce

Equipment: Saucepan, 1-quart pudding dish or soufflé dish

1. If you don't have leftover rice to work with, simmer ⅓ cup raw rice in ⅔ cup water, covered, until soft, about 20 minutes.

2. Beat eggs and combine with milk, 1 cup of the sugar, 3 tablespoons of the butter, and the rice in a saucepan. Heat, stirring until it is hot and thickened, about 20 minutes.

3. This pudding was probably served at room temperature, allowing the custard to set.

4. A typical sauce would be butter and sugar, brought to a boil together to make a light caramel syrup.

Serve.

INDIAN SAGAMITE (1863)

The idea is less like the **Sagamité** of the northern Indians, which was a dish of hominy, than like the universal Native American hunter's ration of parched corn. The result is very crunchy, probably too loud a food for serious spies, but its publication shows how the South was both highly mobilized for the war effort and suffering various shortages.

> Three parts of Indian meal and one of brown sugar, mixed and browned over the fire, will make the food known as "Sagamite." Used in small quantities, it not only appeases hunger but allays thirst, and is therefore useful to soldiers on a scout.

Yield: Serves 4 Confederate spies

¾ cup of white cornmeal

¼ cup brown sugar

Equipment: Cast-iron or other heavy frying pan, wooden spatula

1. Mix sugar and cornmeal in cold pan, breaking up lumps of sugar.

2. Turn on medium-low heat and stir constantly for 25 minutes so the sugar doesn't stick and burn. The result will

look like brown sugar with a few white spots.

3. Cool on a stoneware plate. Break up lumps with a spatula.

Serve three spoonfuls without water as an emergency ration.

POTATO SOUP (1864)

This hard-times recipe from South Carolina is described in a letter from Harriott Middleton of Flat Rock to her cousin Susan in Columbia, March 10, 1864. Harriott is exaggerating for comic effect, and a week later her cousin wrote back thanking her for the receipt and saying that her family had run out of potatoes months ago. The correspondence was published by descendant Isabella Middleton Leland in a historical journal in the 1960s. Excerpts were reprinted in *The Confederate Housewife*, compiled by John Hammond Moore. I have suggested herbs that might have been available in South Carolina in March and guessed at double the amount of water as was used in Virginia potato soups by the 1870s. Before the war, such soups had rich milk or cream, as well.

It is but disguised hot water, but like vice, though first abhorred on that account, its victims finally end by preferring it to any thing else. Alice dined out the other day and had all kinds of delicious things to eat, but she confessed to having given a sigh for potato soup, and she declared she had been so long debarred from luxuries she found she could not enjoy them! But to the receipt—a small piece of beef or a little piece of bacon two inches square— hot water—potatoes peeled and boiled in it, and then taken out and passed through the colander; and re-added— seasoned with herbs, pepper and salt, and scraps of vegetables I think should be an improvement.

Yield: As many bowlfuls as you need

2-inch square of corned beef or lean salt pork or slab bacon

4–6 potatoes (not new potatoes)

Bunch parsley

6 scallions

Equipment: Large soup pot, colander or potato ricer, skimmer or tongs to remove potatoes

1. Cut piece of meat and peel potatoes.

2. Bring to a boil in a full pot or water, 6–7 quarts.

3. Reduce heat to a slight boil and boil until potatoes are done when pierced by a fork, about 30–45 minutes.

4. Pare and slice scallions.

5. Wash and mince parsley.

6. When potatoes are done, remove them from the soup and let them cool slightly in the colander.

7. Mash the potatoes back into the soup with a potato ricer, or by pressing through the holes of the colander with the back of a ladle or large spoon. If this is too hard, you may need to cook the potatoes longer, or slice them up before pressing.

8. Add scallions and parsley to the soup.

9. Stir well to blend and cook a few minutes longer to reheat.

10. Add 1 teaspoon of salt and a ½ teaspoon of black pepper or red pepper sauce.

Serve in fancy bowls but without servants. Stretch with more hot water to serve visitors.

APPLEADE (1871)

The wartime adaptations to fewer foodstuffs and kitchen slaves in the Confederate states continued for many families for generations. *Mrs. Porter's New Southern Cookery Book* was the first cookbook to address these changes. This recipe might well have arisen during the blockade years as a way to stretch a rare lemon with apples grown in the Southern mountains. It continued useful in hard times when lemons were merely expensive, and paid servants were less willing to fuss over detailed preparations. I have taken quantities from Louis Szamarathy's version of the recipe in his 1974 *American Gastronomy*.

> Slice some apples, put them in a deep pan and pour enough boiling water over them to cover them; place the cover on the pan, and when cold, strain the liquid; sweeten it, and flavor with a little lemon.

NOTE: RECIPE TAKES TWO DAYS.

Yield: 2 quarts, serves 8

6 medium apples

½ to ¾ cup sugar

Large lemon

Equipment: Deep pot with tight lid, second pot to boil water, juicer, sieve

1. Bring 2 quarts of water to a boil.
2. Slice whole apples and put in the deep pot.
3. Pour water over the apples, cover, and let stand 2–3 hours.
4. Refrigerate apples and water in pot overnight.
5. The next day, strain the apples through the sieve. Press gently, but don't push any pulp into the clear liquid.
6. Juice lemon and strain juice into apple liquid.
7. Add sugar, depending on sweetness of apples.

Serve in glasses with a sprig of mint.

26

POLITICAL AND TOPICAL CAKES AND COOKIES (1865–1899)

This chapter documents a series of warring political cakes that commemorated Northern and Southern heroes and political positions after the Civil War and did not die out until 1900. Prior to the Civil War, it was rare to find cake recipes that referred to partisan politics, but quite common to find cakes that were generally patriotic, named after dead presidents or politicians respected as national leaders. The death of Lincoln was commemorated with **Lincoln Cakes**, like the **Harrison Cakes** and Taylor Cakes that had been named for previous presidents who had died in office.

Perhaps Mrs. Goodfellow, the veteran Philadelphia cooking teacher, seemed to be rubbing it in with her 1865 "Federal Cakes," "Federal Bread," "Yankee Cake," "Washington Breakfast Cake," and "Northern Ochra Soup" as well as "Southern Ochra Soup."

In any case, two years later Annabella P. Hill of Georgia, mother of two sons who were killed under the Stars and Bars, came back with a "Southern Rights Cake," "Secession Biscuit," and two cakes named for Georgia military leaders who were already moving back into politics: **General Gordon Cake** (see below), and [Nathan Bedford] **Forrest Cake**.

Another two years brought Mrs. Barringer's *Dixie Cookery* with [Jefferson] **Davis Jumbles**. Since Jefferson Davis was still under indictment for treason at the time the book was written, this was a serious gesture, although Mrs. Barringer also included her idea of "Washington Breakfast Cakes," [Andrew] **Jackson Jumbles**, and even [Henry] "Clay Jumbles," as a nod to border-state leaders of the Democrat and Whig parties who had opposed secession.

In 1871, *Mrs. Porter's New Southern Cook Book* was more clearly aimed at reconstruction households, including "Federal Cakes"; "Columbia Cake"; a typical prewar "Washington Cake"; a "Harrison Pudding" flavored like **Harrison Cake**, newly devised "Jefferson Cakes," "Plantation Cakes," and "Burgess Cakes"; a "Yankee Fruit Cake—Unrivaled"; and a sourly eggless, brandy-less "Confederate Fruit Cake." Mrs. Porter had plenty of desserts named for Southern places, a few for Northern places, no generals, and no active politicians. The only possible battlefield reference was "Spotsylvania Pudding," and Spotsylvania was a Confederate loss.

With the nation's Centennial looming, cookbook authors seemed to mute the regional rivalries. The aging abolitionist and suffragist Elizabeth Smith Miller restricted herself to a Harrison Cake and a Clay Cake in her 1875 *In the Kitchen*. Most cookbook authors were concentrating on old-fashioned recipes, a few of which you can try from Chapter 30 of this book. The Ohio *Centennial Buckeye Cookbook* of late 1876 had a **Hayes Cake** and a **Tilden Cake**, for both presidential candidates of what turned out to be the highly contested election of 1876, but they were similar lemon cakes. The Ohioans also put in a **Sheridan Cake** for the union cavalry general Philip Sheridan, disliked by Southerners for his destruction of crops in the Shenandoah Valley during the Civil War and for his military occupation of Texas and Louisiana afterward.

Sectional rivalry continued to simmer as cookbook authors revived old-fashioned recipes under the surface of the Colonial Revival. The 1879 *Housekeeping in Old Virginia* by Marion Cabell Tyree begins with a discussion of the sacrifices of Virginia housewives during the American Revolution, but the actual recipes include a Clay Cake, Jackson Jumbles, **Tyler Pudding** (for the only former U.S. president to serve in the Confederate legislature), and Washington Pudding. Mrs. Tyree also obtained two versions of Robert E. Lee cake, named for the one Confederate leader who was most admired in the north after the Civil War. Before his death in 1870, Robert E. Lee may have tasted the difficult orange-flavored layer cake that is named after him, although the recipe is not in his wife's kitchen notebook, republished in 1997 as *The Robert E. Lee Family Cooking and Housekeeping Book*, with very thorough notes by Lee descendant Anne Carter Zimmer. Zimmer believes that it was a family recipe that did not have to be written down. Mrs. Tyree sold her book with blurbs from the wives of politicians north and south, including those of President Hayes and Georgia Senator John B. Gordon, both of whom already had cakes named after them.

Northern writers kept churning out Harrison cakes and election cakes, and other old-fashioned if not exactly Colonial cakes of their regions, as well as the northern-style **Washington Pie**. Estelle Wilcox, editor of later editions of the *Buckeye Cook Book*, was a committed suffragist and temperance worker who changed the name of the original **Sheridan Cake** to the more intimate "Phil Sheridan Cake" by 1884. A few years later, she renamed the original "Buckeye Cake" after another Union cavalry general, John Buford.

In the 1890s, there was a last wave of political cakes. The 1893 Chicago World's Fair assembled a Board of Lady Managers from all over the United States, who produced a "Stonewall Jackson Pudding," and a **Gridley Cake**, dedicated to a man who had raised hundreds of thousands of dollars for medical care on the Union side. Two years later the Atlanta Cotton States Exposition, with a similar board of white Georgia ladies, produced a cookbook with "1776 Mincemeat," "Washington Fritters," a "Northen Cake" for then-governor William J. Northen, and two versions of Jeff Davis Pudding. Miss Lucy Cook Peel's was an improved **Tyler Pudding**. But Miss Carrie M. Merrill's was a real steamed pudding, with the raisins. Despite folklore that Jeff Davis Pie was created by a former slave who still admired the Confederate president, these are the earliest recipes I know for the custard pie, more usually with the raisins (and sometimes nuts) that has been Jeff Davis Pie ever since.

The 1898 *Key to the Pantry; Choice, Tried Recipes*, collected by The Ladies of the Church of the Epiphany, Danville, Virginia, summed up the Southern side of entire political-cake era with "Confederate Cake," "Mrs. Cleveland's Sunshine Cake," a "Jefferson Davis Cake," a "Stonewall Jackson Cake," two versions of "Gen. R.E. Lee cake," a "Confederate Cake," and **Bimetallist Cake**. This last item opened up a new front in the twenty-five year controversy over "hard money" versus the free coinage of silver, the rural, Democratic, and "Bimetallist" position.

Political cakes seem to end with the nineteenth century, as the new, college-educated and corporate-funded home economists who promoted new dessert ideas did not want to offend anyone politically. Women kept making Washington Pie, Harrison Cake, Jeff Davis Pie, Robert E. Lee Cake, or Tyler Pudding Pie, but new cakes did not arise for the contentious times leading up to World War I, Prohibition, and women voters. There was some revival of news-related desserts by the soda fountain industry in the 1920s and 1930s, but even political cookbooks published by Democrats and Republicans in the twentieth century did not usually want to offend voters of the other party with cakes named for candidates and causes.

LINCOLN CAKE (1865)

This recipe first appeared in *Godey's Lady's Book*, the highest circulating women's magazine of the time, in 1865. The influence of *Godey's*, edited by Sara Josepha Hale, can be seen by the way the recipe was reprinted verbatim in cookbooks from 1866 to 1888, written down by Mrs. Deyo of Kingston, New York, in manuscript cookbooks for her friends, and reprinted with minor changes by *Peterson's Magazine* in 1869. It was probably intended as a patriotic cake in the prewar sense, perhaps for the new national holiday of Thanksgiving that Mrs. Hale had championed. In 1871, the southern-born novelist Marion Harland included a Lincoln Cake with a Washington Cake in her *Common Sense in the Household*. But Marion Harland was a professional food writer with a national audience, planning a career that spanned another forty apolitical years. Southern cookbook authors still living in the South could not serve a Lincoln Cake and began to name cakes after Confederate heroes.

Yield: Serves 18

2 medium eggs

2 cups sugar

½ cup butter

1 cup sweet milk

3 cups flour

1 teaspoon cream of tartar

½ teaspoon baking soda

1 teaspoon lemon extract

Equipment: 2 large loaf pans, pastry blender, wooden toothpick or wire cake tester, wire racks

1. Take butter out of the refrigerator an hour before starting.
2. Combine flour, cream of tartar, and baking soda in a large mixing bowl
3. Butter the loaf pans. Preheat oven to 350 degrees.
4. Cream together butter and sugar in a large mixing bowl with a pastry blender or a large fork.
5. Break eggs 1 at a time into a cup. Remove any bits of shell with a half of shell.
6. Blend each egg into the butter-sugar mixture.
7. Add vanilla extract, then work in the dry ingredients to make a thick batter.
8. Divide batter between the loaf pans. Tap the sides of the pans to level the cakes.
9. Bake for 40 minutes and begin testing at the centers with wooden toothpick or wire cake tester.
10. Remove pans from oven and cool cakes in the pans for 15 minutes.
11. Remove cakes from pans and cool on wire racks.

Serve sliced with butter and jam.

FORREST CAKE (1867)

The effort to redeem the Southern states on the dessert table began in earnest with *Mrs. Hill's New Cook Book* by Annabella P. Hill of Georgia. This bread cake was named for General Nathan Bedford Forrest, a former plantation owner and slave dealer who joined the Confederate army as a private and turned out to be one of the greatest tacticians in military history. By 1867, Forrest had also helped found the original Ku Klux Klan, although he disavowed the group a year later. Forrest reached out to African-American voters before his death in 1877. His cake is based on bread dough, like **Bridget's Bread Cake**, but it is richer and has quite a lot of old-fashioned spice.

> After the dough for light bread or rolls has risen the first time, take from it about three teacupfuls. Beat three eggs thoroughly and add to them three cups of sugar, beating well. Cream one cup of butter and add to them the sugar and eggs, creaming all well together. Add the dough, and work well until you have made a smooth batter. Season with one nutmeg, a teaspoonful of coriander seed, powdered and sifted; the same of cinnamon, the same of allspice. Add last a small teaspoonful of soda dissolved in a tablespoonful of warm water. It is better to stand and rise about fifteen minutes before baking; but if fruit is added, it should be baked as soon as the fruit is worked in or it will sink to the bottom.

Yield: Serves 9–10

1½ cups bread dough (frozen will work, or any bread in this book)

1 cup butter (2 sticks)

3 medium eggs

3 cups sugar

1 nutmeg (or 1 rounded teaspoon powdered nutmeg)

1 level teaspoon coriander

1 level teaspoon cinnamon

1 level teaspoon allspice

1 level teaspoon baking soda

½ cup raisins (optional)

Equipment: Large loaf pan

1. Take butter out of the refrigerator an hour before starting. If using frozen bread dough, follow package directions so that is well risen when you start.

2. If using whole nutmeg, grate on fine grater or nutmeg grater. Mind your fingers!

3. Butter the loaf pan.

4. Cream together butter and sugar with a pastry blender or a large fork.

5. Dissolve baking soda in a little hot water.

6. Beat eggs well and stir in spice, then blend into the butter-sugar mixture.

7. Mix the baking soda with the butter-sugar mixture.

8. Blend butter-sugar mixture and raisins (if using) into the bread dough.

9. Form the dough into a loaf, and set into the pan. Cover with a kitchen towel and let rise 30–40 minutes or until doubled in bulk.

10. Slash the top of the risen bread the long way.

11. Bake 15 minutes on the top shelf of a 425-degree oven.

12. Move bread to a lower shelf and reduce heat to 350 degrees. Bake another 15 minutes or until a wood toothpick or cake tester comes out clean.

13. Cool on a wire rack for 10 minutes. Then pick up the hot pan with pot holders and turn the bread out to cool on wire racks.

Serve sliced with butter and jam.

GENERAL GORDON CAKE (1867)

Mrs. Hill's other Georgia confederate hero was John B. Gordon (1832–1904). Gordon was one of the most effective Confederate officers who came up through the ranks and went on to serve as a governor (1886–1890) and respected U.S. senator (1873–1880, 1891–1897), and even president of the U.S. Senate, always in the cause of restoring the power of Georgia's large landowners. In his early career, that placed him in opposition to radical Republicans and abolitionists like African-American State Senator Tunis Campbell (see his **To Stew Giblets**). Later on, Gordon opposed white populists who sought to rally north Georgia farmers, black and white, against the landowners.

The recipe makes a rich cornstarch cake of the kind being promoted by cornstarch manufacturers, making it a departure for the old-fashioned cookbook of Mrs. Hill, but perhaps appropriate for the young political aspirant, Gordon. Mrs. Hill's cake may have been used in his unsuccessful campaign for governor in 1868, when most Confederate veterans were not allowed to vote and some African Americans did. Gordon was also a member of the Ku Klux Klan.

> Three quarters of a pound of butter, one pound of sugar; cream them well together; break in one egg at a time until you have used ten; beat well and add a [half-pound] paper of corn starch; add a teaspoonful of yeast powder [baking powder]. Flavor with vanilla. Bake quickly.

Yield: 16 slices

3 sticks butter, plus some to grease pans

2¼ cups sugar

10 medium eggs or 8 large eggs

2 cups cornstarch

1 rounded teaspoon baking powder

1 teaspoon vanilla extract

Equipment: 2 large loaf pans, pastry blender or large fork

1. Take butter out of the refrigerator an hour before starting.
2. Combine cornstarch and baking powder in a bowl, stir well.
3. Butter the loaf pans.
4. Cream together butter and sugar in a large mixing bowl with a pastry blender or a large fork.
5. Break eggs one at a time into a cup. Remove any bits of shell with a half of shell.
6. Blend each egg into the butter-sugar mixture.
7. Add vanilla extract, then work in the dry ingredients to make a thick batter.
8. Form or pour into loaf pans.
9. Bake 25 minutes at 350 degrees, and begin testing with a toothpick or wire cake tester.

Serve with evening tea, or as part of a large mid-afternoon dinner.

DAVIS JUMBLES (VERY FINE) (1869)

Not much question who the Davis is in this recipe, which is right after [Henry] Clay Jumbles and [Andrew] Jackson Jumbles in Mrs. Barringer's 1869, *Dixie Cookery*. At the time the book was published, Jefferson Davis was still under indictment for treason. The president of the Confederate states had been jailed from 1865 to 1867, then was released on bail, much of it contributed by northern abolitionists who wanted to end the divisions. Davis spent much of 1867–1869 living in Canada and Europe. In 1869, charges were dropped against Davis, Robert E. Lee, and thirty-five other leading Confederates. Unlike many, Davis refused to sign an oath of allegiance to the United States and never regained citizenship or voting rights. He did travel freely in the United States, wrote his memoirs, and died in New Orleans in 1889. "Jumbals" go back to medieval times in Europe; the name seems to refer to gimbals, rings linked in pairs or more complicated arrangements. Old English Jumbles were heavier than these, and more exotically flavored. I have taken some details from a modern hearth recipe in *Hearthside Cooking* by Nancy Carter Crump, in turn based on an 1830s recipe of Eliza Leslie's. For Miss Leslie's jumbles, use two whole eggs, a tablespoon of rosewater, a rounded teaspoon of nutmeg, a teaspoon of mace, and a teaspoon of cinnamon.

> One teacupful of grated loaf-sugar, one cup of butter, and the white of one egg, beaten light. Mix to a tolerably stiff dough with flour, and if you like, add a tablespoonful of thick cream, and as much soda as will lie on a sixpence. Roll the dough in thin sheets, and cut in round cakes or rings. Dip the cakes in grated loaf sugar before baking.

Yield: About 24 cookies

1 cup salted butter (two sticks), plus some to grease baking sheets.

1 cup sugar

1 small egg or equivalent egg white product

1 tablespoon heavy cream or sour cream

1/4 teaspoon baking soda

3 cups sifted flour, plus more to flour rolling pin and board

Equipment: Pastry blender or food processor, whisk, rolling pin and breadboard, baking sheets, wire racks

1. Remove butter from refrigerator 1 hour before starting.
2. Sift flour before measuring.

3. Cream butter and 3/4 cup of the sugar in food processor or with pastry blender or a large fork.
4. Separate egg by pouring between shells, or make up one egg white from egg white product.
5. Whisk egg whites until you can cut the foam cleanly with a knife.
6. Dissolve baking soda in a little water or milk.
7. Grease baking sheets with butter or shortening.
8. Preheat oven to 375 degrees.
9. Stir cream and eggs alternately with flour mixture and baking soda into butter-sugar mixture to make a stiff dough.
10. Flour rolling pin and board and roll out dough from the center so that it is 1/4 inch thick.
11. Cut out rounds with a drinking glass or wineglass dipped in flour, or with a cookie cutter, biscuit cutter, or doughnut cutter. (You may cut out the centers with a knife to make the traditional loop shape.)
12. Spread out the rest of the sugar on a plate. Drop on the jumbles, then arrange the jumbles on the baking sheets. Gather the scraps of dough and re-roll them, or store in the refrigerator.
13. Bake 10–12 minutes, or until slightly browned on the edges.
14. Remove cookies from baking sheets to cool on wire racks.

Serve with dried fruits, nuts, ice cream, and other cookies as the third course of an enormous late lunch.

HAYES CAKE (1876)

This was submitted by nine-year-old Flora D. Ziegler of Columbus, Ohio, for the fall 1876 publication of the *Centennial Buckeye Cookbook*, compiled by the Women of the First Congregational Church of Marysville, Ohio, and recently reissued by Ohio State University Press with an introduction by food historian Andrew F. Smith. Ohio was a "swing state" in the Hayes-Tilden election of 1876, and the book also included a **Tilden Cake** (see below), and a "hard money cake" combining the common "gold" and "silver" cakes (see **Bimetallist Cake**). Both the Hayes and Tilden cakes are unfrosted lemon cakes. Voters also found little difference between the moderate Republican and the antislavery reformer Democrat, and it was an election so close it had to be resolved in Congress. New York Governor Tilden submitted a veal loaf (similar to today's meat loaf) to the same book and was countered by a green tomato pickle recipe from the wife of Ohio Governor Hayes.

The cake is between a 1-2-3-4 cake (see **Tilden Cake**) and the somewhat eggier versions that became today's yellow cake.

Yield: Serves 12

1 cup sugar

½ cup butter

3 medium or large eggs

1 "level teaspoon" baking soda

½ cup sour milk (or use ¼ cup buttermilk with ¼ cup whole milk, or use ½ cup whole milk with lemon juice below)

2 "small" cups flour (pre-sift flour for level measure, or use large eggs with unsifted flour)

½ teaspoon lemon extract (or juice of ½ lemon)

Equipment: "Small dripping pan" (use 8-by-8-inch brownie pan), pastry blender or food processor, lemon juicer, flexible spatula, toothpick or wire cake tester

1. An hour before baking, remove butter from refrigerator to soften. Butter brownie pan.

2. Break each egg into a cup, remove any bits of shell with a half shell, and then put the eggs into a small bowl. Preheat oven to 350 degrees.

3. Beat eggs well. Mix flour and baking powder. Mix sour milk substitutes if using.

4. Juice lemon to obtain lemon juice.

5. Cream butter and sugar together with pastry blender or in food processor. Work quickly so as not to overheat the butter.

6. Whisk in (or pulse to process) flour mixture and milk mixture in alternate parts.

7. Whisk in lemon juice or lemon extract.

8. Pour into brownie pan and level with spatula. Spread slightly from center to edges so cake will bake up more evenly.

9. "Bake half an hour and cut into squares." Test for doneness at the highest part of the cake with wooden toothpick or wire cake tester.

10. Cool in pan on wire rack.

Serve cut into squares, perhaps to children playing house, with the "mother" urging the "father" to vote for Governor Hayes for president.

TILDEN CAKE (1876)

Submitted by "Mrs. T.B." to the 1876 *Centennial Buckeye Cookbook*, compiled by the Women of the First Congregational Church of Marysville, Ohio, this is a typical "1-2-3-4 cake" with added cornstarch, possibly to offset the higher-protein flour from the western states that flooded eastern markets after the Civil War. Despite a growing interest in high layer cakes, this Tilden Cake was still listed with the loaf and sheet cakes, like the old election cakes discussed in Chapter 5. I have taken the standing-mixer directions from the "Basic 1-2-3-4 Cake" chapter of Susan G. Purdy's *A Piece of Cake* (1989) one of the most historically minded recent American baking books. Fine cooks in 1876 knew about beating the egg whites separately for airier cakes, but not everyone did this.

Yield: Serves 24

1 cup butter, plus some to grease pan

2 cups sugar

1 cup whole milk

3 cups flour

½ cup cornstarch

4 large eggs

2 [slightly rounded] teaspoons baking powder

2 teaspoons lemon extract

Equipment: Wax paper, 9-by-13-inch sheet-cake pan, pastry blender and whisk or standing mixer, wooden toothpicks or wire cake tester, wire rack

1. One hour before starting, remove butter from refrigerator to soften.

2. Butter sheet pan. Dust with flour. Tap out excess flour.

3. Preheat oven to 350 degrees.

4. If using standing mixer, beat butter in large bowl until smooth, and add sugar and beat until light and smooth. If using pastry blender, cream butter and sugar together.

5. In standing mixer method, separate eggs by pouring back and forth between shells over a clean cup; beat yolks and add 1 at a time to butter mixture, stopping to scrape down sides of bowl and mixers a few times. Oth-

erwise beat whole eggs in 1 at a time with whisk.

6. Sift together flour, cornstarch, and baking powder.

7. If using standing mixer, set to low speed, and alternately add milk and flour mixture. If not, whisk in milk and flour mixture alternately to make a soft batter.

8. Beat in lemon extract.

9. (If you are not using a standing mixer, you have already added whole eggs, and can skip to Step 11.) If using standing mixer, clean beaters and take a smaller mixing bowl to beat the separated egg whites until they begin forming stiff peaks.

10. (Standing mixer only). Stir about half a cup of the egg whites into the batter to lighten it. Then cut in parts of the remaining whites with the beaters or a whisk, just a few strokes each. This is called "folding in" and keeps the egg whites somewhat together for maximum rise.

11. Pour batter into sheet-cake pan. Level it with a spatula, and spread it slightly from the center to the edges of the pan so that it will rise more evenly.

12. Bake 30 to 45 minutes, testing the center with toothpick or wire cake tester.

13. Cool cake in pan on wire rack.

Serve at a rally for Democratic Governor Tilden, who won the popular vote but did not have an electoral college majority because of contested vote-counting in four southern states and lost the election in Congress. In compromise, the winning Republicans withdrew federal military forces from the southern states and permitted southern Democrats to force African-American voters off the rolls, paving the way for segregation laws.

Sheridan Cake (1876)

Although bipartisan on the Hayes-Tilden election, the ladies of Marysville, Ohio, editing the *Centennial Buckeye Cookbook* were solidly pro-Union and pleased to obtain this recipe from the sister of Union General Philip Sheridan. In later editions edited by the Minnesota suffragist Estelle Wilcox, the cake was slightly changed, and retitled "Phil Sheridan Cake." By the mid-1880s, she made her political position clear by adding a [John] Buford Cake named for another Union general. Sheridan was disliked by Southerners for his scorched-earth tactics in the Shenandoah Valley and had become the symbol of radical reconstruction when he sent troops into the Louisiana state assembly to arrest five white democrats who had been placed in disputed seats. By the time of his death, in 1886, he had become more widely accepted as general of the entire army and as an advocate for what became Yellowstone National Park.

The recipe makes a white sponge cake, and quite a lot of it. It would fill two of today's tube pans, but the recipe says, "This makes a cake for a six-quart pan," so this was intended to be an eleven by seventeen sheet cake. If General Sheridan ever tasted it, it was probably late in his life when taller and lighter cakes were coming into fashion. You can substitute one tablespoon of baking powder for the baking soda and cream of tartar. Mrs. Wilcox later reduced the butter to one cup, but she never did specify the flavoring.

Yield: Serves 30

16 large eggs (or equivalent amounts of egg white products to 16 whites)

4 cups sugar

5 cups sifted flour

1-1½ cups salted butter (2 sticks) plus some to grease pan

1½ cups whole milk or half-and-half

1 teaspoon baking soda

2 heaping teaspoons cream of tartar

2 teaspoons vanilla

Equipment: Standing mixer, handheld mixer, or two large bowls to whip egg whites; whisk; pastry blender; 11-by-17-inch sheet-cake pan, or 2 10- or 11-inch round springform pans; toothpick or wire cake tester, parchment paper or wax paper, rubber spatula, oven mitts, wire rack

1. Remove butter from refrigerator 1 hour before starting recipe.

2. If using whole eggs, separate by pouring back and forth between the shells over a cup. Collect the whites and yolks in separate bowls. If using powdered egg whites, reconstitute according to package directions. (You can use the yolks in custards or to make yellow cakes.)

3. Grease pan or pans. Cut out a piece of parchment paper or waxed paper to fit the bottom of the pan or pans. Dust a little flour around the pans, then put in the paper.

4. Butter the paper.

5. Sift flour with cream of tartar in a mixing bowl and stir well. Dissolve the baking soda in the milk.

6. Beat egg whites until quite stiff. If you are doing this recipe as a team project, you can make it the way it was done before electric mixers, by dividing the whites among two or more people.

7. Preheat oven to 350 degrees.

8. Cream butter and sugar together with a pastry blender, or using a standing mixer or hand beater.

9. With a whisk or electric beater, blend in the milk and egg whites and

flour mixture by turns. Add vanilla and mix well.

10. Pour batter in pans. Level off with a spatula, and work from the middle to raise a slight rim at the edges so the cake will bake more evenly.

11. Bake 35–45 minutes, until cake springs back when slightly indented and begins to pull away from sides.

12. Cool cake on wire rack for 10–15 minutes.

13. Tilt cake in pans to make sure it is loose on all sides. Detach any stuck points with spatula or wire cake tester.

14. Invert cake on platter, and carefully lift the pan away from it. (If using springform pans, unlatch the pans, and invert the cake onto a plate, peeling off the paper, then reinvert onto the cake platter.)

TYLER PUDDING (1879)

Just as **Washington Pie** has always been a cake, Tyler Pudding has always been a pie. It is an old Virginia "transparent pie" or "chess cake," a sweet custard pie that may well have been a Tyler family favorite. But the 1879 *Housekeeping in Old Virginia* by Marion Cabell Tyree seems to be the first publication. John Tyler was the only former U.S. president to serve in the Confederate legislature. Tyler died during the war years and was not a major target of northern wrath, but this is certainly a political pie.

Yield: 1 pie

"4 [medium] eggs

3 cupfuls sugar

1 cupful butter, washed and melted [unsalted butter]

1 cupful [heavy] cream seasoned with [1] lemon

Bake in a paste [unbaked 9-inch pie shell].—Mrs. C.N."

Equipment: Lemon juicer

1. Remove eggs from refrigerator an hour before starting.

2. Melt butter slowly in small saucepan or microwave oven.

3. Juice lemon to get about 2 tablespoons of juice.

4. Beat eggs until creamy and light. Stir in sugar.

5. Preheat oven to 325 degrees.

6. Stir in a thin stream of melted butter so that it neither cooks the eggs nor solidifies into lumps.

7. Beat in the cream, then 1 tablespoon of the lemon juice.

8. Pour filling into pie shell.

9. Bake 30 minutes or until custard is set. You can leave a small soft spot in the center of the pie which will cook as it cools.

GRIDLEY CAKE (1893)

Ruel C. Gridley (1829–1870) was a Nevada shopkeeper who lost a bet on a Democratic mayoral candidate and had to carry a fifty-pound bag of flour across town while the other bettor sang "John Brown's Body." Gridley then auctioned off the bag of flour for the benefit of The Sanitary Commission, a Red Cross-like charity aiding wounded Union soldiers. He purchased the bag himself, and donated it to be auctioned again, eventually netting $5,000 in a single day. Gridley then took the bag of flour on the road, and auctioned it hundreds of times across the Western mining towns to raise a reported $265,000. This cake in his honor was submitted by Theresa F. Cochrane of Groton, Vermont, to the 1893 *The Home Queen World's Fair Souvenir* edited by Mrs.

J.E. White. Mrs. Cochrane was one of hundreds of elected "lady managers" of the women's pavilion at the Colombian Exposition in Chicago, part of a complex and very political effort to present a moderate and respectable feminist position. She wasn't the only one with an opinion about the Civil War; an Arizona manager submitted an apple cobbler called "Stonewall Jackson Pudding."

The cake is made with volume measurements, similar to what was called "cup cake," "tumbler cake," or "pint cake" for more than a hundred years. You may have read that Fannie Farmer invented volume measurements in her 1896 book, but they had been in some use in American kitchens as time-savers since Colonial times. What was new in this cake was using the old formula to make thin layers for a layer cake. Earlier stack cakes and jelly cakes were made in layers, but the increasing use of refined flour and baking powders after the Civil War made possible lighter, higher cakes. To make up for the lack of flavor in these airier cakes, sweet icings began to define them.

Yield: Serves 12–16

2 cups sugar

2 cups flour

½ cup sweet milk

½ cup butter (1 stick), and more to butter cake pans

3 large eggs

1 teaspoon cream of tartar

½ teaspoon baking soda

1 lemon

2 apples

Equipment: Pastry blender or large fork, whisk, 3 round cake pans, spatula, wood toothpick or wire cake tester, wire racks to cool cake, lemon juicer, box grater, vegetable peeler, double boiler

1. One hour before starting, remove butter from refrigerator to soften. Butter cake pans.

2. In a mixing bowl, cream butter and 1 cup of sugar together with pastry blender or large fork.

3. Beat 2 of the eggs to a creamy, bright yellow.

4. Whisk eggs into butter-sugar mixture.

5. In another mixing bowl, combine flour, cream of tartar, baking soda, and a pinch of salt, and mix well.

6. Whisk flour mixture and milk alternately into butter mixture. You may need a little more milk to make a pourable batter.

7. Divide batter into 3 round cake pans. Use spatula to make the batter a little lower in the middle, a little higher on the sides, so it will bake up evenly.

8. Bake layers at 450 degrees for 10–15 minutes, testing at the thickest part.

9. Remove layers from oven and cool in pans on wire racks.

10. For filling, juice the lemon and grate the rind on a box grater.

11. Peel the apples, halve them and remove the cores.

12. Grate the apples with a box grater, or you can use the grating disk of a food processor.

13. Combine the apples, lemon zest, and lemon juice.

14. Beat the last egg well.

15. Bring water in the lower pot of the double boiler to a boil, reduce heat to a simmer.

16. Combine apple mixture and egg in top pan of double boiler and cook, stirring constantly, until mixture thickens.

17. When layers and filling are cool, place the ugliest (or most level) cake layer on a plate, and spread on one half of the filling. (Mrs. Cochrane doesn't tell us if her cake was frosted on top or not.)

18. Cover with the next-best-looking cake layer and a layer of filling.

19. Put the best-looking, or least level, cake layer on top. Trim with spatula to make an attractive cake.

Serve after auctioning off several times to raise money for charity.

BIMETALLIST CAKE (1898)

The hard money/free silver controversy of the last quarter of the nineteenth century pitted rural Democrats against urban Republicans, not exactly the map of the Civil War, but close enough for cakes, usually based on the Gold Cake and Silver Cake made from numerous egg yolks and whites, respectively. A free silver advocate in the health food business proposed a cake in 1898 made from shredded wheat that demonstrated the 16:1 coinage ratio suggested by soft money activists.

This recipe appeared in the 1898 *Key to the Pantry; Choice, Tried Recipes*, collected by The Ladies of the Church of the Epiphany, Danville, Virginia. The political reference is to the battle over fiscal policy in the 1896 presidential election. The Democratic nominee, William Jennings Bryan, favored widespread coinage of silver at a fixed ratio of value to gold, a "bimetallist" policy that might have benefited farmers and other debtors caught in the depression of the mid-'90s. The Republican nominee and most bankers favored a "gold standard" that prolonged the depression but helped restore fiscal stability. By layering the familiar gold and silver cakes, and decorating with yellow and white candy "coins" the anonymous au-

thor of this recipe produced a Bryan campaign cake. (Ironically, an 1876 Ohio combination of gold cake and silver cake by spoonfuls had the opposite political slant and was titled "Hard Money Cake.") The silver layers rise more than the gold layers, which showed the ratio of money the "free silver" side wanted to have, although not the 16:1 formula of some slogans. I have added a simple glaze for the top of the cakes.

Although this recipe is complicated, it makes a good group project, as once the eggs are separated, the batters can be made by two teams. Alternatively, you can illustrate the idea quickly with a box each of yellow cake mix and angel cake mix, white icing and purchased candies. In Danville, this cake was made in a huge mold, perhaps like a kugelhoff mold. I have given directions for loaf cakes, which can be inverted to look like gold and silver ingots, and for two tube cake pans.

Gold part: Yolks of 8 eggs, 1 cup of fine granulated sugar, scant ½ cup of butter, ½ cup sweet milk, 1½ cups of flour, 2 teaspoons of baking powder. Beat the yolks well; add the sugar, then butter, a little flour, the milk, balance of flour, and ½ teaspoon of essence of lemon.

Silver part: Whites of 8 eggs, 2 cups of pulverized sugar or 1½ of granulated, ½ cup of butter, ¾ cup of sweet milk, 3 cups of flour, 2 teaspoons of baking powders, ½ teaspoon of bitter almonds. Cream butter and sugar well; add milk, then beaten whites, flour. Stir hard and flavor. Have a mold greased and paper in the bottom. Put in a layer of gold, then silver; repeat and bake one and a half hours. Ice one and stick small yellow and white flat candies on the top.

Yield: Serves about 20

8 large eggs or 7 extra large eggs

2½ cups sugar, or one cup sugar and 2 cups confectioners sugar

1 cup salted butter

1¼ cups milk

4½ cups all-purpose flour

4 teaspoons baking powder

½ teaspoon lemon extract

1 teaspoon almond extract

2 cups confectioners sugar and ¼ cup cream for glaze, or commercial white frosting, gold butterscotch and silver mint hard candies for decoration

Equipment: Parchment paper or waxed paper, 2 large loaf pans and 1 small loaf pan or 2 tube pans, pastry blender or handheld electric mixer, whisk, standing mixer (optional), metal and rubber spatulas, wood toothpicks or wire cake tester

1. Remove butter from refrigerator 1 hour before starting recipe. Cut parchment paper to fit the bottoms of the pans. Butter pans, sprinkle a little flour over the butter, put in the paper, and butter the paper.

2. Separate eggs by pouring back and forth between the shells over a cup. Collect the whites and yolks in separate bowls. Preheat oven to 350 degrees.

3. For the gold cake, sift together 1½ cups of the flour and 2 teaspoons of the baking powder.

4. Cream together ½ cup (1 stick) of the butter with 1 cup of the sugar, using a pastry blender.

5. Beat the egg yolks until they are creamy and light.

6. Beat a thin stream of the egg yolks into the butter-sugar mixture.

7. Beat in flour mixture and ½ cup of milk alternately, ending with flour.

8. Stir in the lemon extract.

9. For the silver cake, sift together 3 cups of the flour and 2 teaspoons of the baking powder.

10. Cream together ½ cup (1 stick) of the butter with 1½ cups of the sugar or 2 cups of granulated sugar, using a pastry blender or handheld mixer.

11. Beat the egg with a whisk or handheld electric mixer or a standing mixer until they are stiff but not dry.

12. Whisk the remaining ¾ cup of milk little by little into the butter mixture.

13. Now whisk the egg whites into the batter, and then the flour.

14. Stir in the almond extract and beat hard for several minutes.

15. To build up the layers, start with a thin layer of gold batter in each pan. (It is less sticky when baked.)

16. Tap pans to level batter, and spread on a somewhat thicker layer of silver batter. Try to keep the layers as level as possible. Don't let your spatula touch the lower layer or it will catch and mix them.

17. Continue until pans are filled halfway. Level the top layer from center to the edges for a more even top. (If you have a lot of batter left, make a small "hard money cake" by greasing up another pan, and adding the batters by alternating spoonfuls.)

18. Bake small loaf cake or hard money cake 20–25 minutes, loaf cakes 30–40 minutes, and the tube-pan cakes 45 minutes to an hour, testing frequently at the deepest part of the cakes.

19. When cakes are done, remove from oven and cool briefly in the pans.

20. Cut around the edges of the pans with a knife, and remove from pans.

Peel off the paper from the bottom of the cakes.

21. Cool on wire racks.

22. To make the loaf cakes look like a large ingot, slice off the rounded tops of the cooled to make a level bottom. Invert cakes onto a long platter. Slice a little off the ends to make two sides meet cleanly so that it looks like one long cake. Slice a slanted piece off the outer ends to make it look more like a bar of precious metal.

23. For glaze, wet confectioners sugar with a little of cream until it is drippy but pours as a sheet.

24. Glaze tops of cakes, letting a little glaze drip down the sides, but let most of the gold-silver layering show.

25. Unwrap hard candy "coins" and stick them on top of the cakes.

Serve sliced across the layers to show gold and silver.

27

MILITARY OUTPOSTS DURING THE INDIAN WARS (1870s–1884)

Here are three recipes from the network of forts established by the United States Army before and after the Civil War, to expand the country and protect westward settlements, serve as bases for wars against the Western Indians, and control Alaska. For recipes from Indians and other groups outside the forts, dating from the same period, see the *American Ethnic Cookbook for Students* chapters on the Apache, Eskimos (Inuit) and Aleuts, Hopi, Navajo (Diné or Dineh), New Mexico Hispanics, Pueblo Indians (Eastern), Sioux (Dakota, Lakhota, and Nakota), Tlingit and Haida, and Zuni. For a recipe from the family of Kit Carson, the deadly foe of the Navajo, see **Capirotada** or **Torrejas**.

OXTAIL SOUP (1870s)

General George Armstrong Custer remains best known for losing the battle of Little Big Horn, but his wife Elizabeth wrote three books attempting to rebuild his reputation over her fifty years of widowhood. The last, *Following the Guidon*, contains a chapter about what army wives and their servants went through to provide meals in distant encampments. General Custer's favorite, we learn, was oxtail soup—an easy

taste to please in large forts where a steer was sacrificed daily, and most of the officers and men were too impatient to wait for oxtail soup. Mrs. Custer mentions the inadequacy of cookbooks on the frontier, and perhaps she had a copy of *The American Matron*, by "a housekeeper." More likely she let her African-American cook, Eliza, do what could be done with available produce, which sometimes included canned tomatoes. Bottled tomato ketchup was sometimes available and used in soups, and Mrs. Custer has a story about Eliza making ketchup from canned tomatoes in a Kansas outpost. I have taken some quantities from a second recipe for Shin of Beef Soup in *The American Matron* that is too long and fussy to quote. The recipe is quite large, but the soup would have been used over several days and served to guests.

> Oxtail soup may be made as a recipe for shin soup. Strain out vegetables; mix a pint of thickening and add it to soup. Add pepper, salt, allspice, and tomatoes.
> SHIN SOUP. Take a shin, put it in a pot with one gallon and a half of water. Let it stew gently for four hours. When cold, remove the fat. Put it on

the fire again with salt, pepper, onion, celery, and carrots. After it has browned some time, add a little browned flour; a glass of white wine. Let it simmer. Put toasted bread, cut in very small pieces, in the tureen.

Yield: Serves 20

½ cup flour

3–4 pounds oxtail

4 onions

2 carrots

1 teaspoon allspice berries

1 teaspoon pepper

2 cups canned tomatoes or 1 cup ketchup

¼ cup wine (optional)

½ loaf of crusty whole wheat bread

Equipment: Large soup pot, heavy frying pan or ovenproof dish or casserole, Pyrex measuring cup and turkey baster (optional)

1. Wash off oxtail pieces, and put in a large pot with 6 quarts of water and a teaspoon of salt. Bring to a boil and reduce heat to a simmer with the top of the pot ajar.

2. Brown flour to a golden color in skillet over low heat, stirring frequently so that it won't stick or burn. You can also use a 225-degree oven, again stirring frequently so it browns more evenly.

3. After 2–4 hours, remove soup from heat. In cold weather, you can chill pot outdoors overnight and remove the hardened fat with a fork in the morning. In warm weather, you can skim off the fat with a spoon. (You can recover the soup under the fat by skimming into a large Pyrex measuring cup, letting the fat come to the surface, and using a turkey baster to remove the soup from underneath.)

4. When the fat has been removed (Mrs. Custer or her cook saved it for cooking or making soap), return the meat to the soup and reheat slowly.

5. Halve and peel the onions. Peel the carrots. Add vegetables and spices to soup.

6. Mix the browned flour with the tomatoes or ketchup and wine (if using). Break up any lumps and stir this into the simmering soup.

7. Cut the bread into thick slices and toast. Cut warm toast into cubes.

8. The cookbook calls for straining out the vegetables before serving oxtail soup. Mrs. Custer's book describes vegetables as a treat in remote forts, so I think they were left in.

Serve soup with a piece of oxtail and toast cubes on top.

RICE AND BACON (1870s)

This recipe was written by Alice Kirk Grierson, whose notebook has been published as *An Army Wife's Cookbook*, compiled and edited in 1972 by Mary L. Williams of the Fort Davis (Texas) National Historic Site. Mrs. Grierson's husband was a cavalry colonel, and she followed him in various western postings from 1866 until her death in 1888. Wars with Western Indian tribes would be the major preoccupation of the U.S. military between the Civil War and the 1898 Spanish-American War. Mrs. Grierson collected several Mexican-American recipes, as well as recipes for fancy desserts requiring expensive canned supplies that were available only to the wives of officers. This gussied-up version of Spanish Rice was probably more typical of the make-do suppers available in remote forts, and may have been borrowed from another military wife from the American south or learned on a Texas or California post. Her directions are clearly aimed at poorly stored bacon and rice. I have specified beef stock because fresh army meat was almost exclusively beef, with some wild game including buffalo.

> Parboil ¾ cup of rice in boiling water 5 minutes. Drain on a sieve. Pour boiling water over ¼ pound bacon. Drain. Cut in inch pieces. Sautee to light yellow. Add rice, 3 cups stock or water, pepper. Simmer until tender, then add a cup of well reduced tomato purée—which means tomatoes passed through a sieve and simmered until thick. Mix thoroughly. Turn into a mound on a dish and arrange curls of fried bacon around it.

Yield: Serves 2

¾ cup rice

¼ pound bacon

3 cups canned beef stock (optional, or part stock and part water)

1 16-ounce can tomato puree

Equipment: Skillet, sieve, large pot, small saucepan

1. Bring a quart of water to a boil in the large pot. Add rice and boil 5 minutes. Drain rice on a sieve.

2. In small saucepan, simmer tomato puree until it thickens and reduces by at least a third. Stir often so that it does not stick and burn.

3. Cut bacon into 1-inch squares.

4. Fry bacon slowly until fat turns yellow but does not brown or crisp.

5. Put rice back into large pot with 3 cups stock or water (or a mixture) a teaspoon of salt (omit if using canned stock), ¼ teaspoon pepper. Bring to a boil, reduce heat to a simmer, cover pot and cook until tender, about 15 minutes.

6. When rice is ready, stir in 1 cup of the tomato puree.

7. Turn rice out and form a mound on serving platter.

8. Remove bacon from grease and arrange around the mound of rice. (Mrs. Grierson would have saved the fat for other cooking, or for making soap.)

Serve as a simple supper. It was often hard to get fresh vegetables in army posts.

CHICKEN SALAD (1884)

Chicken salad was something of a luxury lunch in the nineteenth century, when chicken was often more expensive than beef or pork. This recipe is from the manuscript cookbook of Elizabeth Burt, whose officer husband served two hitches at Fort Laramie in Wyoming. The recipe was reprinted by Sam Arnold in *Fryingpans West.* The mention of substituting cabbage and celery extract for celery reminds us of the quirks of military supplies.

> Mix 1 heaping teaspoon fine mustard, the yolk of a fresh egg and a teaspoon of fresh wine or cider vinegar into a smooth paste using a silver fork. Measure out 6 tablespoons pure salad oil and 1 tablespoon each of vinegar and lemon juice. Mix slowly, making a creamy paste. (Adding the oil last, stirring in a few drops at a time.) Take a cold boiled chicken, remove the skin, bones and fat, and chop . . . not too fine. Cut up an equal bulk of celery, mix with the chicken. Add a saltspoon [¼ teaspoon] salt and half of the dressing. Cover the bottom of the platter with the larger leaves of lettuce, and lay the smaller green leaves around the border. Place the salad in the dish and pour the remainder of the dressing over it. Garnish with parsley,

capers, olives and hard-boiled eggs. If celery cannot be found, use white tender cabbage mixed with a teaspoon of extract of celery.

Yield: Serves 8–10

3–4 pound broiler chicken

1 rounded teaspoon dry mustard powder

4 medium eggs, or three eggs and 1 tablespoon mayonnaise.

6 tablespoons salad oil

4 teaspoons red wine vinegar or cider vinegar

1 tablespoon fresh lemon juice

Large head celery

1 head romaine or Boston lettuce

Bunch parsley

$\frac{1}{2}$ cup green olives with pits

2 tablespoons capers

Equipment: Soup pot with cover, long metal tongs, paper towels, serving platter

1. Wash off chicken and put in a soup pot with water to cover. This measures the amount of water needed.

2. Remove chicken and bring water to a rolling boil.

3. Put in chicken with tongs, and without splashing boiling water. Bring the pot back to a boil, reduce heat to a simmer, covered loosely. Add 3 of the eggs and simmer 15 minutes, then remove them and chill.

4. After an hour, test chicken for doneness by inserting a knife at the thigh joint. Juices should run clear. Joints should be starting to loosen.

5. Remove chicken from pot, reserving stock for soup or another recipe. Let chicken cool, or refrigerate.

6. When chicken is cooled, cut into serving pieces, pull away skin, and cut meat off the bones.

7. Remove the last egg from refrigerator. Chop meat into $\frac{3}{4}$-inch pieces.

8. Break off celery ribs, wash, and cut them into similar-size pieces.

9. Mix celery with chicken meat, and sprinkle on $\frac{1}{4}$ teaspoon salt.

10. If you are concerned about eating raw egg yolk, substitute a tablespoon of mayonnaise. If not, separate the egg and reserve the white for another use.

11. Mix the yolk or the mayonnaise with the dry mustard powder in a small bowl. Beat in a teaspoon of the vinegar.

12. Now beat in a third of the oil, forming a creamy sauce.

13. Beat in the rest of the vinegar, which will make the sauce thinner.

14. Beat in another two tablespoons of the oil, which will make it thicker again.

15. Beat in the lemon juice, which will make it thinner again.

16. Beat in the rest of the oil. If at any point the mixture separates into oil and vinegar and gets thin and runny, start over again with a little more mayonnaise, and just beat everything into the mayonnaise, a little bit at a time.

17. Pour half the dressing over the chicken and celery, and toss to coat.

18. Wash the lettuce and dry with paper towels.

19. Line the platter with lettuce leaves, with some of the largest in the middle, and the smaller leaves fanned out around the edges.

20. Put the chicken and celery in the center, and pour the rest of the dressing over it.

21. Shell the hard-boiled eggs, and cut them in half or slice them to arrange around the salad.

22. Drain capers and olives and arrange around the salad.

23. Cut sprigs of parsley and arrange around the salad.

Serve with pride.

28

SETTLERS AND HOMESTEADERS (1873–1911)

Although historians believe the frontier days ended in the late 1890s, homesteading and settling continued substantially in remote areas for another fifteen years, and in parts of Alaska to the present day. (For recipes used by earlier pioneers and explorers, see Chapter 12.) In general, as the civilization got closer to the frontier, the period of identifiable "pioneer cooking" became shorter. Especially among prospectors, many of the cooks were men without cooking experience, and in the larger settlements and established mines they might eat food cooked by other men, often Chinese immigrants, with little more experience as cooks. In the mountains, inexperienced cooks were helped by the fact that baked goods and pancakes rise more rapidly at higher altitudes.

One American taste that was firmly fixed by the pioneering experience is for pancakes, biscuits, doughnuts, and quick breads. While meat, and especially beef, was still the most preferred food, the portability and durability of flour made pancakes and biscuits the staple food of prospectors as well as settlers and homesteaders. Even as Native Americans were being pushed off traditional hunting grounds and confined to reservations, they began to make fry bread from government-supplied flour and lard. (There is some scattered evidence of Indian fry bread prior to the Civil War, but most stories point to periods of government imprisonment in the 1860s and 1870s.)

PANCAKES (1873)

This untitled recipe is in a letter from Nebraska settler Mattie V. Oblinger to her parents and family, dated August 25, 1873, and now posted in the online collections of the Library of Congress exhibit: "Prairie Settlement: Nebraska Photographs and Family Letters, 1862–1912."

Nett you do not know how many things a person can do with out until they try Yesterday morning, I thought I would have some cakes for dinner I was going to make Jumbles but Giles had no rolling pin or cake cutter so I made a plate of pancakes as we always term it. Well, I had no eggs but I thought I would try it with out I tell you what, I used nearly a teacup of sugar about half teacup of cream filled up with water makeing teacupful of cream & water a small lump of butter and a little soda enough flour to make

[it] quite stiff and I never made any better pancake in my life try it some time I make Pancakes altogether without eggs We used to think if we had no eggs we could not make Pancakes but I have got bravely over that try some time take equal parts of sour & sweet milk soda and salt and see how nice and light they are it is my way of makeing them.

Yield: 7 4-inch pancakes

Scant 6 ounces sugar

3 ounces sour cream

2 tablespoons butter plus enough for frying pan

1 teaspoon baking soda

¾ cup flour (and some in reserve)

Equipment: Frying pan

1. Sift together dry ingredients.
2. Melt butter and mix with sour cream and 3 ounces water.
3. Mix sour cream mixture with dry ingredients to make a stiff dough, adding flour if necessary. Mix lightly, leaving a few small lumps. This is not a pourable dough. It will be spooned into the frying pan.
4. Heat a heavy frying pan or cast-iron skillet until a few drops of water skitter across the surface. Add butter if needed (well-seasoned cast-iron pans and nonstick pans do not need butter for these pancakes).
5. Reduce heat, and spoon tablespoonfuls into the pan. Flatten each disk with the back of the spoon.
6. Turn once to brown both sides. These thick pancakes will cook more slowly than most pancakes, so you have to reduce heat further to keep from burning them before they are done through.
7. When pancakes don't yield when poked, they are done.

Serve with butter and/or syrup or berry jam.

TOMATO SOUP (1881)

This recipe was submitted by Mrs. Emma Halvorson to the *Montana Cook Book*, edited by "The Ladies of Butte City" in 1881. It is one of the earliest printed recipes to mention the use of canned tomatoes in soup, which became much more widespread over the 1880s, as you can see in the **Rebel Soup** in Chapter 32. The instruction to use croutons suggests that Mrs. Halvorson got some of her recipe out of a book, possibly *Mrs. Parloa's New Cook Book* of 1880. If so, she simplified the recipe very nicely to make a quick supper dish suitable for company.

One quart can of tomatoes, two heaping tablespoonfuls of flour, one of butter, one teaspoonful salt, one of sugar, a pint of hot water. Let tomatoes and water come to a boil. Rub the butter

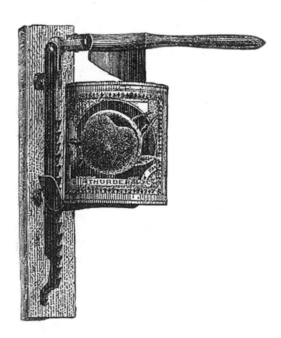

Figure 16 An early can opener. *Source:* The Latest and Best Cook Book, *1884*.

and flour together and add a table-spoonful of cold tomatoes; then stir into the boiling mixture and add seasoning. Boil fifteen minutes. Serve with croutons.

Yield: Serves 6

2 16-ounce cans whole tomatoes (or enough larger cans to make up the quart)

2 heaping tablespoons flour

1 tablespoon butter

1 teaspoon sugar

3–4 slices stale French bread

2 tablespoons vegetable oil, butter, or lard

Equipment: Heavy soup pot, frying pan

1. Cut the bread into cubes.

2. Rub the butter and flour together into a solid mass, then work in a tablespoonful of the juice from the tomatoes.

3. Measure the tomatoes and 2 cups of water into a large pot. Bring to a boil and reduce heat to simmer without a cover.

4. Stir in the butter-flour mixture and break it up with your spoon until it begins to thicken the soup.

5. Add a teaspoon of salt and the sugar. Simmer soup 15 minutes.

6. Heat butter, lard, or vegetable oil in a frying pan.

7. When it is hot but not smoking, put in the cubes of bread. Avoid adding in the crumbs.

8. Turn the bread cubes to brown on all sides without burning.

Serve in a tureen, adding croutons to each bowl.

CREAM PIE (1884)

Once settlers got established, they sometimes had more cream and eggs than they needed. This kind of simple custard pie has remained popular all over the United States. The recipe is that of Mrs. Martha Garland Fitch, submitted by Mrs. Earnest O'Mara, of Pender, Nebraska, to the *Nebraska Centennial First Ladies' Cookbook*, compiled by Maxine Morrison in 1966. Mrs. Fitch had moved to Nebraska by covered wagon from Derby, Iowa, in 1884, and moved three more times within her new state. You can skip separating the eggs and beating the whites, for a more solid pie.

Yield: Serves 4–6

1 pie shell

3 eggs

1 cup sugar

1½ tablespoons flour

1 pint cream

½ pint whole milk

Nutmeg

2 tablespoons butter

Equipment: Eggbeater or hand mixer, whisk, prepared pie shell, nutmeg grater (optional)

1. Take out butter to soften. Break each egg over a cup and separate the yolk by pouring between the shells. Place yolks in a small bowl.

2. Beat the yolks to a lemony-looking froth and stir in sugar, flour, and a pinch of nutmeg.

3. Beat the whites to the soft peak stage.

4. Stir the cream and milk into the yolks, then add the beaten egg whites. Don't overmix.

5. Spread the pie shell with softened butter.

6. Pour in the egg mixture.

7. Bake in a moderate (375 degree) oven until the outside of the pie is set, but the middle 2 inches still jiggle

when you tap the pan with a knife. (The middle will finish cooking as the rest of the pie cools.)

8. "Grate a little nutmeg on the top after it is done."

PINK PICKLED EGGS (1887)

Prospectors lived on beans and game for months, then came back to town and paid large prices in gold for more civilized foods. Unsuccessful prospectors could eat the "free lunch" in saloons, but it consisted of salted dishes like these pickled eggs, designed to make them thirsty for expensive drinks. This recipe is from the 1887 *The Nevada Cook Book*, reprinted in the 1950 *The Virginia City Cookbook* by Helen Evens Brown, Philip S. Brown, Katherine Best, and Katherine Hillyer. The modern recipe waters down the vinegar to approximate the weaker vinegar of earlier times. I have also reduced the amount of spice on the theory that Nevada saloonkeepers were making do with stale spices. (The full amount would be about two tablespoons of whole or ground allspice, and 3 tablespoons of broken mace or 2 tablespoons ground.)

Put a dozen shelled hard boiled eggs in a jar with ½ ounce of mace, ½ ounce of allspice, a whole pepper, 1 fresh boiled "blood" beet, and a little salt. Pour hot vinegar over to cover.

NOTE: RECIPE TAKES ONE WEEK.

Yield: 12 snacks

12 medium eggs

1 cooked beet

1 cup vinegar

½ ounce mace (1½ tablespoons ground or 2 tablespoons broken pieces)

½ ounce allspice (1½ tablespoons whole or ground)

1 "whole pepper" [chile, dried will work]

Equipment: Quart glass jar, pint glass jar (If you have a 2-quart jar, you can use bigger eggs.)

1. Place eggs in a pot. Cover with cold water and bring to a boil.

2. Simmer 15 minutes, and cool under cold running water.

3. When eggs are cold enough to handle, shell and put into a quart or larger jar. (If the eggs don't fit, you can squeeze a little, or use the second jar.)

4. Add the beet, spices, hot pepper, and a teaspoon of salt.

5. Mix vinegar with ½ cup of water. (You can heat the vinegar, but this step isn't really necessary with today's bottled vinegar.)

6. Fill the jar so that all the eggs are covered with the vinegar. (You may need a small, clean stone to weight leftover eggs in the other jar.)

7. Wait about a week before serving, so the eggs turn pink and spicy.

Serve with ham, sausages, cheeses, and salads, all salty and sharp.

SMULTBOLLER (1900s)

By the end of homesteading, homesteaders could have jobs off their farms. Carrine Gafkjen was born in Northern Minnesota, "proved up" a 160-acre homestead in William County, North Dakota, then rented out the land to a neighbor and worked winters as a housekeeper hundreds of miles away, and summers back on her homestead cooking for large threshing crews. She made enough to double her holdings in eight years. This recipe for sour cream doughnuts was popular with the Scandinavian farmworkers and had the advantage of filling them up faster than pancakes, biscuits, or pies. It is taken from *Prairie Cooks* by Carrine's daughter, Carrie Young.

CAUTION: HOT OIL USED.

Yield: 8–10 doughnuts and 12 doughnut holes

2 large eggs

¾ cup sugar, plus more for coating doughnuts (optional)

1 teaspoon vanilla

1 cup sour cream

3¼ cups all-purpose flour

1 teaspoon baking soda

1 teaspoon baking powder

½ teaspoon ground cardamom

Oil for deep-frying, at least 2 quarts

Equipment: Candy/deep frying thermometer, heavy deep pot, skimmer, rolling pin and wood board, pastry cloth (optional), 3-inch doughnut cutter or cookie cutter, 1¼-inch hole cutter (optional), waxed paper, wire racks for cooling doughnuts, newspaper or paper towels, slotted spoon or wire skimmer, small paper bag (optional) to shake doughnuts in sugar.

1. Mix 3 cups of the flour, ½ teaspoon salt, and the baking soda, baking powder, and cardamom.

2. In a large bowl, beat the eggs, sugar, and vanilla "until the mixture is thick and pale."

3. Add the sour cream to the egg mixture and beat well.

4. "Add all at once" to the flour mixture and stir until the dough is "just combined."

5. Use the remaining flour to flour the board and/or pastry cloth and rolling pin, and roll out the dough ⅝-inch thick, working from the center.

6. Cut out as many doughnuts as you can with the large cutter. "If neces-

sary," cut out the centers with the smaller cutter. "Flatten the doughnuts just a little with the rolling pin to make larger than ordinary doughnuts." Set them on waxed paper.

7. Gather up the scraps of dough, re-roll as needed, and cut out another doughnut or two, then make "holes" from the rest of the scraps.

8. Heat 3–4 inches of oil in a deep, heavy pot to 375 degrees.

9. Arrange wire racks over newspaper or paper towels for drying the fried doughnuts.

10. Dipping the skimmer in hot oil, carefully lower in three or four doughnuts at a time. Fry 1½ minutes on each side (or until golden brown) and turn only once.

11. Set the doughnuts to dry on the wire racks.

12. If you want to sugar the doughnuts, put ½ cup or more sugar in a small paper bar, and shake them while still warm, tapping the excess sugar off and back into the bag.

Serve warm or at room temperature.

SOURDOUGH AND SOURDOUGH HOTCAKES (1900s)

These recipes were published in the 1976 book, *Alaska Sourdough; The Real Stuff by a Real Alaskan*, by Ruth Allman. Mrs. Allman was brought up in the home of Judge James Wickersham (1857–1939), an Alaska pioneer and explorer, and her husband Jack Allman knew sourdough from mining camps. The concept of culturing yeast in an ongoing batter is nearly as old as bread. Sourdough became synonymous with prospectors of the far north during the Klondike Gold Rush of 1898.

NOTE: RECIPE TAKES THREE OR MORE DAYS.

Figure 17 Alaskan prospectors frying sourdough pancakes. *Source: ©Museum of History & Industry/CORBIS.*

Yield: About 20 four-inch pancakes

2 small-to-medium potatoes

2 tablespoons sugar, plus two more for the hotcakes

2 cups flour

½ teaspoon yeast (optional)

4 tablespoons oil

1 large egg

1 teaspoon baking soda

Equipment: Wooden spoon, crock with cover or mixing bowl and plastic wrap, non-stick griddle or well-seasoned cast-iron frying pan

1. Boil unpeeled potatoes in water to cover "until they fall to pieces."

2. Lift out skins, and mash potatoes "making a puree."

3. When cool, you may need more water to make it more liquid.

4. Put 2 cups (or more) of the potato water into the crock or mixing with sugar and flour, and beat into a "smooth, creamy batter."

5. You can use the yeast or some borrowed sourdough to speed up the development of a yeast culture, but wild yeast will find your starter if you set it aside uncovered "in a warm place." (A warm place in Alaska is 65–77 degrees, which used to be a special sourdough shelf behind the stove.)

6. Let sourdough rest, stirring occasionally with a wooden spoon, for at least 3 days, until it is full of bubbles and smells sour. One week would be typical, and up to a month not uncommon. If it thins down as the yeast works in it, add more flour. If it gets too thick, add a little water.

7. To make hotcakes, take 2 cups of the starter, and mix in 2 tablespoons of

sugar, the oil, the egg, and the salt. Mix well. You can let this mixture sit a little while for the yeast to develop.

8. Heat up griddle or frying pan.

9. Dissolve baking soda in a tablespoon of warm water. Use a little less if starter is fairly new, a full teaspoon if starter is quite sour. (Mrs. Allman suggests heating up the plates before serving.)

10. Just before cooking, "fold [baking soda mixture] gently into sourdough. Do not beat." Sourdough should expand rapidly as baking soda reacts with acidic sourdough.

11. Spoon or pour batter onto hot griddle to form thin pancakes. Turn when bubbles form on the top, and bake both sides "seal brown."

Serve hot for breakfast or with any meal.

BUTTERMILK BISCUITS (1909)

Pioneering continued in some areas after what most historians consider the end of the American frontier in the 1890s. Louise K. Nickey, author of *Cookery of the Prairie Homesteader* (1976) moved with her family from Indiana to quarter-section homesteads in northeast Montana in 1907. She arrived by "emigrant train" (a discount railroad coach to encourage settlement along railroads) at the age of five and began making biscuits two years later:

Picture a small serious girl standing on a small green box by the kitchen table, with her hands in a pan of flour. She wore a dark wool dress, with long sleeves and a high neck, that was practically covered by a full-length blue-checked apron that also had long sleeves. She wore black-ribbed stockings and black button shoes. Two big ribbon bows tied her plaited and rolled hair behind each ear. The kitchen was warm and cozy on those cold winter

days, when temperatures would dip to 60 degrees below zero. . . . A wall coal-oil lamp dimly lighted the room with a yellow glow.

Yield: Serves 4

2 cups flour plus ¼ cup to flour board

½ cup lard, plus a little to grease baking sheet

1 scant teaspoon salt

4 teaspoons baking powder

½ teaspoon baking soda

¾ cup buttermilk

Equipment: Pastry blender or large fork, food processor (optional), wooden board, rolling pin, biscuit cutter or large clean empty tunafish can with both ends removed, baking sheet

1. Mix dry ingredients in a bowl.

2. Cut in the lard with a pastry blender or large fork (or your fingers) until the flour mixture is in fine granules. (Or you could use a food processor with the steel knife.)

3. "Sprinkle buttermilk over the mixture." Mix to make a solid, soft dough. "If all the dry ingredients do not work in, gradually add a little more buttermilk."

4. Flour the board and rolling pin.

5. Work dough "lightly into a ball with the tips of fingers and roll out to approximately one-inch thick."

6. Lightly grease baking sheet (optional).

7. Preheat oven to 450 degrees.

8. Cut biscuits with cutter or tuna tin, arrange on baking sheet.

9. Bake "15 or 20 minutes or until they are a deep golden brown."

"Serve hot biscuits with butter and/or jelly, honey, or chokecherry syrup." Leftover biscuits

were eaten split and filled with butter and sugar, or reheated in a paper sack in a 325-degree oven, or crumbled into hot stewed tomatoes.

MILK GRAVY (1911)

Mrs. Nickey recalls light suppers of biscuits and milk gravy, still popular in both the Rocky Mountain states and the Ohio-Indiana region from which many homesteaders came. Milk gravy was also used on boiled potatoes, mashed potatoes, cornbread, and pancakes. "An instant milk made according to directions makes acceptable gravy."

Yield: Serves 4

4 tablespoons bacon grease

6 tablespoons flour

2 cups whole milk (or 1½ cups canned evaporated milk)

½ teaspoon salt

⅛ teaspoon pepper

Equipment: Large skillet, flat whisk

1. Melt bacon grease and stir in flour.

2. Keep stirring carefully until the flour is a golden brown (lighter than peanut butter). Don't burn the flour and don't burn yourself on the hot greasy mixture.

3. Remove from heat and stir in one cup of hot water and then the milk (or 1½ cups of water and the evaporated milk).

4. When well mixed, return to heat and cook, stirring constantly, until it is well thickened.

5. Season with the salt and pepper.

"I have seen some people take two of three biscuits at one time, break them open, place them on the plate, and then cover the biscuits liberally with milk gravy. It takes a big bowl of gravy to take care of a situation like that, so you might want to double the recipe."

29

LATE VICTORIAN HEALTH FOOD (1875–1904)

As early American health food revolved around Sylvester Graham, after the Civil War the center of health food moved to Battle Creek, Michigan, and to the family of Dr. J.H. Kellogg. Kellogg's parents were reformers interested in abolitionism, temperance, and the water cure and became converts to Seventh-Day Adventism. Their generous contributions encouraged the Seventh-Day Adventist movement to relocate its headquarters to Battle Creek and set up the Battle Creek Sanitarium. Dr. J.H. Kellogg grew up eating apples and Graham bread, trained as a surgeon, and returned to Battle Creek to enlarge and promote "The San." Kellogg was a tireless investigator of new foods and therapeutic machinery and invented the process to make corn flakes. He embraced new fad diets based on chewing or nuts as meat substitutes and added them to his system. He also attracted wealthy and celebrity patients. His wife Ella Eaton Kellogg ran the kitchens at The San, and developed a flavorful and varied vegetarian menu. Will Kellogg was his brother's tireless assistant, until he got tired of it in 1911 and set about building what became the giant Kellogg's cereal company. The Kellogg brothers stopped speaking and never reconciled, although they both lived into their eighties. Their story became a novel and movie titled *The Road to Wellville*.

There was also an un-Kellogg, Dr. J.H. Salisbury, a research physician whose Civil War experiences led him to the idea that a diet of shaved beef would restore the stomach. In contrast to the greasy bacon and moldy hardtack diet of the Civil War, Salisbury's simplified diet probably did cure a lot of people, but his theory was that vegetables and fiber made people sick. Salisbury steak was to be served medium-well done, but "seasoned to taste with butter, pepper, salt; also use either Worcestershire or Halford sauce, mustard, horseradish or lemon juice on the meat if desired."

The only serious rival to the Kelloggs was the movement of college-trained domestic scientists, whose activities are discussed in Chapter 33. Their works had recipes for bland, low-fiber diets for the sick. Their prescriptions for the well were mainstream food, modified more in the direction of "purity" and blandness. Purity was sometimes about getting the chemicals out of food, but sometimes about using factory-made foods in preference to natural foods.

Health goals have changed over time. As late as 1878, the *American House Wife Cook*

Book had five rules for "How to Grow Fat," including "Milk, butter, and sugar are very fattening, but everybody cannot take them with impunity, and to grow fat it is essential that digestion be almost perfect." And, "FIFTH—Sleep all you want, and take exercise in moderation."

OATMEAL MUSH (1875)

Even while Graham was alive, there were Graham boarding houses where travelers, students, or young men could eat fruits, vegetables, and grains. By 1875, they were "Hygienic Boarding Houses." This recipe comes directly from the New York Hygienic Hotel's Julia Coleman, who passed it to M.L. Holbrook, M.D., for the 1875 book, *Eating for Strength*. The book was published by Wood & Holbrook, at the same address as the hotel. The American breakfast, which then included steaks and chops as well as all the breakfast meats we might eat at Sunday brunch now, was a real challenge for health-food diets. Miss Coleman's answer was a very high quality of oatmeal. If you can obtain steel-cut oats from a health food store, or steel-cut McCann's Irish Oats, you will be quite impressed with this oatmeal even today. It is possible that Dr. J.H. Kellogg stayed at this hotel when in college. He ate mostly apples and crackers, and the experience inspired him to develop new foods as head of the Battle Creek Sanitarium.

> To three quarts of boiling water add one level teaspoonful of salt and one quart of good oatmeal, stirring while the latter is poured in slowly. Let it stand where it will boil gently and stir it occasionally for ten minutes, or until the meal is evenly diffused through the water. Then cover close, and place where it will barely simmer for one hour. Do not stir it during that time.

Yield: Serves 24

4 cups steel-cut oats

Equipment: Large pressure cooker or soup pot with a tight cover, long-handled spoon

1. Bring 4 quarts of water to a boil. (Present-day oats are better dried and require more water.)

2. If using pressure cooker at sea level, add oats and 1 teaspoonful of salt, cover, and bring pot up to full pressure for 20 minutes. Adjust heat to maintain pressure without over-pressuring. If using soup pot, add salt, and stir in the oats.

3. If using soup pot, let oats boil slowly for 10 minutes, stirring occasionally to heat the entire pot. Cover tightly and reduce heat so that the oats simmer but do not boil, for 1 hour.

4. With pressure cooker, after 20 minutes, remove from heat and allow pressure to come down naturally.

"Serve warm, messing it as little as possible." Dr. Holbrook had no objection to adding cream, maple syrup, or sugar.

GRANULA (A HYGIENIC DISH) (1883)

Granula was the first packaged health food cereal, trademarked in 1876 by Dr. Jackson, whose spa was visited by leaders of both Christian Science and Seventh-Day Adventism. Dr. Jackson's Granula apparently was not very convenient, since it had to cook almost half an hour to be soft enough to chew. In 1886, Dr. J.H. Kellogg of the Battle Creek Sanitarium, then an Adventist institution, developed a wheat-oat nugget cereal he wanted to call "Granula," but was forced by Jackson to change the name to "Granola." Amanda Whitmore of McPherson, Kansas, developed this recipe for Granula in 1883, apparently inspired by the Jackson product, and submit-

Figure 18 Advertisement for Battle Creek Sanitarium Health Food Company "Granola." *Source:* Every-Day Dishes and Every-Day Work *by Mrs. E.E. Kellogg, Battle Creek, Michigan, 1897.*

ted the recipe for the *Inglenook Cook Book* published by the Church of the Brethren in 1906 and enlarged in 1911. Ms. Whitmore's recipe is a classic Graham recipe for un-leavened crackers, complete with a second baking, which Graham considered neces-sary for avoiding indigestion. The contem-porary cereal that most resembles Granula, or early "Granola" is Grape-Nuts, developed by Harvey Post in 1898 after a stay at the Battle Creek Sanitarium. If you can find whole wheat flour that is not degerminated, that is, true Graham flour, you don't have to add the wheat germ. (You can get white whole wheat flour from the King Arthur Flour, online at <www.kingarthur-flour.com>.)

Get good graham flour, take pure spring of soft water, nothing else, and knead to a stiff dough. Roll and mould as for biscuit (not as thick). Bake thor-oughly in a hot oven. When well done, or over done, remove and cool, then cut each piece in halves and put back in a warm baker and dry to a crisp, not brown or burnt. A yellow brown will not hurt. Now crush or break in small bits and grind them as you would coffee. You now have one of the best health foods known. It can

be served in various ways. Soaked in a good rich milk is the best way to eat it. Some like to add a little sugar, some a little salt (but don't add salt when you bake it, it spoils the flavor). Some eat it with fruit. It makes a nice cold Sun-day dish and is always ready. It can be used in puddings and mixed with bread for dressings. We have made and used this hygienic food for 23 years, and know its merits. The biscuits, or graham crackers, warm from the oven, well baked, with crispy crust, make a delightful bread. We have a small hand mill to grind them. If you cannot get good graham flour, if it is too rough with bran, add a little white flour, or sift the coarsest bran out. Graham made of white wheat is best.

Yield: Serves 12

2 cups whole wheat flour, plus more for kneading and rolling and baking

2 tablespoons wheat germ

Equipment: Breadboard and rolling pin, bak-ing sheet, old-fashioned coffee grinder or food processor or paper bag

1. In a mixing bowl, mix the wheat germ with whole wheat flour, and stir

5. Cut dough into squares. Arrange the squares on baking sheets.

6. Bake 30 minutes at 375 degrees.

7. When cool, split and bake again at 200 degrees for 10 or 15 minutes to dry them out.

8. Cool once again and break into small pieces. To run them through a coffee grinder, clean it out by grinding some rice first. Pulse in a food processor, or just put the crackers in a paper bag and pummel the bag with a one-piece rolling pin. You want to get most of the pieces smaller than a kernel of corn.

9. Store in a recycled mayonnaise jar or other sealed container.

Serve with milk and a little sugar. You may need to let it soak for five or ten minutes before you can eat it.

VEGETABLE HASH (1892)

While Dr. J.H. Kellogg ran the Battle Creek Sanitarium and invented new food products, his wife Ella Eaton Kellogg actually ran the kitchens, gave lessons, and wrote on healthful and delicious cooking. Her 1892 book, *Science in the Kitchen*, even had a chapter about how to cook and eat meat in the least harmful ways, along with arguments against doing so. The heavy cream used would take this dish off the present-day health food menu, but in 1892 it gave recovering patients a dish that tasted like the old New England Red Flannel Hash, minus the corned beef.

Yield: Serves 4

3 large potatoes

1 carrot

1 beet

1 white turnip

1–2 stalks celery

Figure 19 Kneading bread dough. *Source:* Science in the Kitchen *by Ella Eaton Kellogg, Battle Creek, Michigan, 1910 edition.*

in ½ cup of water. You may need a little more water to make a dough that sticks together.

2. Flour the board and your hands, and knead the dough until it is smooth and elastic, and no longer sticky. You may need to add more flour to the board and your hands as you go, and it may take 15 minutes of kneading. The dough has to be well kneaded and stiff, so it won't stick to ungreased baking sheets when baked.

3. Roll out the dough from the center ½ inch thick, or a little thinner. Prick holes with a fork every inch or 2.

4. Flour the baking sheets so the wafers won't stick.

1 cup heavy cream

Equipment: Vegetable peeler, 1 large and 2 small pots, ovenproof dish or casserole

1. Bring a large pot and a small pot each half filled with water to a boil.
2. Peel potatoes, carrot, and turnip. Trim beet, leaving an inch of stalk.
3. Boil beet in the small pot 45 minutes, or until a fork goes in without resistance.
4. Boil potatoes, carrot, and turnip in large pot 30 minutes, or until a fork goes into a potato without resistance.
5. Heat up the cream to boiling.
6. When vegetables are done, slice potato into thin slices. Chop carrot and turnip.
7. Under cold running water, rub the skin, stem, and any remaining roots off the beet.
8. Chop the beet into small pieces.
9. Chop the celery.
10. Mix the vegetables and reheat in an ovenproof dish, at 350 degrees for 15 minutes.
11. Pour on the boiling cream, and stir well.

"Serve hot."

Nut and Bean Soup (1904)

By the 1904 fourth edition of *Science in the Kitchen*, Mrs. Kellogg had deleted the meat chapter but added some interesting uses of nut products and an appendix of recipes developed by others in the Sanitarium Kitchen and Cooking-School, including this "bean soup which may be enjoyed by those who still have a taste for the flavor of a ham bone in soup," attributed to "Cornforth."

Yield: Serves 8

1¾ cups dry lima beans

1 small potato

1 medium onion

½ cup nut butter (almond or peanut)

⅓ cup nut meal (from ½ cups peanuts or almonds)

Equipment: Food processor or meat grinder

1. "Wash the beans and put them to cook in cold water."
2. "Wash the potato with the skin on. [Peel off any green parts.] Slice it and the onion thin, and put them with the beans."
3. Grind nuts in meat grinder or pulse in food processor for a minute or 2 to get a coarse meal, but do not grind to butter.
4. After beans have been cooking ½ hour, add nut butter and nut meal to soup.
5. "When the beans are thoroughly cooked, rub the whole through a colander."
6. "Add water to make two quarts of soup." Add 2 teaspoons salt.
7. "Reheat and serve."

30

COLONIAL REVIVAL
(1876–1896)

The One Hundredth Anniversary of the Declaration of Independence in 1876 set off a Colonial Revival in architecture, home decorating, food, and even re-enactments. According to food historian Sandra L. Oliver, "'Martha Washington Teas' and 'New England Suppers' were offered for private and public entertainment" in coastal New England. In the southern states women from eminent families revived foods and customs of their Colonial forbears, with a subtext that many of the founding families were, after all, slaveholders. The 1879 *Housekeeping in Old Virginia* by Marion Cabell Tyree is introduced with a discussion of how Virginia women adjusted to the American Revolution but includes contemporary recipes for Robert E. Lee Cake. The meaning of the Centennial is discussed further in Chapters 26 and 33 of this book.

In fact, the United States is almost always having a colonial revival. Lincoln's Gettysburg Address revives the rhetoric of the Declaration of Independence (fourscore and seven years earlier) to make a unifying statement during the Civil War. Various ideas of Colonial architecture were being revived as early as the 1830s, and the idea of white houses with symmetrical columns (itself a style we now call "Greek Revival") never goes out of fashion—even as scholars point out that Colonial homes were often painted in bright colors, and Victorian homes were usually painted in pastel colors. Americans began to preserve historical houses as early as 1858 (Mount Vernon), but only recent years have a few restoration organizations realized that the kitchen fireplaces crowded with every possible cooking implement are not historically accurate. Estate inventories confirm that even wealthy people had many fewer pots and pans.

The difficulty for historians is that each colonial revival seems to add a layer of its own folklore to the original history. Some historians now write histories of how historic events were discussed at later times and describe periods like the Colonial Revival of the late nineteenth century in terms of "the construction of history."

Cookbook writers as early as Lydia Maria Child and Eliza Leslie in the 1820s were including deliberately old-fashioned recipes, but the Colonial revival in food writing began with the Centennial of 1876 and peaked in the 1890s. Northern cookbook authors like Evelyn Lincoln, Maria Parloa, and Sarah Tyson Rorer collected old-fashioned recipes, and early published recipes were reprinted verbatim with sources by Alice Morse Earle, and without sources by Gertrude Wilkinson. In their best work, the Colonial Revival of the late nineteenth century led to collecting, publishing, and preserving many traditional recipes and some early cooking manuscripts. Some writers changed recipes beyond recognition and falsified history. For example, in 1897, "several ladies" of the Deerfield [Massachusetts] Parish Guild, First Church of Deerfield, confected *The Pocumtuc Housewife; a Guide to Domestic Cookery*, alleging that it was based on a manuscript of advice to a daughter from 1805. Some of the recipes are from Early American cookbooks, especially that of Lydia Maria Child, and some are legitimate old family recipes of the Deerfield contributors. But some of the recipes were not used at all in Early America, and the made-up narrative of advice is bogus in a way that says more about 1897 than about 1805.

AUNT MOLLY'S GINGER BREAD (1876)

This recipe was described as "one hundred years old" by "Mrs. Woodworth of Springfield Mass." who contributed it to the 1876 *Centennial Buckeye Cookbook*, compiled by the Women of the First Congregational Church of Marysville, Ohio, and recently reissued by Ohio State University Press with an introduction by food historian Andrew F. Smith. The book reached print after the midsummer Centennial events but went on to become the best-selling cookbook of the nineteenth century. This recipe, which was deleted in later editions, is for the sort of cookie-like gingerbread that makes gingerbread men and gingerbread houses. It was going out of fashion after the American Revolution, being replaced by softer, cakey gingerbreads with more eggs. It is very unlikely that a 1776 recipe would

have used baking soda, but baking soda is a reasonable 1876 substitute for the pearlash (potassium carbonate) used in the similar recipe for Molasses Gingerbread in the 1796 *American Cookery* by Amelia Simmons.

This recipe also appeared in the 1897 *The Pocumtuc Housewife* as "Mollie Saunder's Upper Shelf Gingerbread," attributed to the owner of the best bake shop in Salem "about a hundred years ago." Since the recipe is always about a hundred years old, I've placed it in the Colonial Revival section of this book, as a recipe printed in Ohio 126 years ago.

Yield: About 50 square cookies

3½ pounds flour (10 cups)

1 pound butter, plus some to butter sheet pans

1 quart molasses

1 cup whole milk

1 rounded teaspoon baking soda

Equipment: 3 sheet-cake pans, wire racks

1. Melt butter over low heat

2. Dissolve soda in milk.

3. Preheat oven to 350 degrees.

4. In a large mixing bowl, work milk and molasses alternately into the flour.

5. Stir in melted butter to make a stiff dough.

6. Grease sheet-cake pans and roll or mold dough a little less than ½ inch thick on pans.

7. Bake 8–10 minutes. Test for doneness by denting the center of the cake with a wooden spoon. If it springs back, remove from oven and cut into squares while still warm. You can also cut them with a pattern for a gingerbread house. (To make gingerbread men or round cookies, chill the dough

at Step 6 to make it thicker, roll it out on a board, and cut or stamp the shapes you want.)

8. Cool squares on wire racks.

Serve to crowds assembled on July 4.

CENTENNIAL BISCUIT (MUSH ROLLS) (1870s)

This recipe appeared in a Nebraska newspaper, according to the 1974 study, *The Nebraska Pioneer Cookbook* by Kay Graber. Unfortunately, she does not give a date or exact source. The idea is similar to Benjamin Franklin's 1784 recipe, **To Make Bread with Maize Flour Mixed with Wheat Flour**, but without the yeast, so it makes a hard biscuit. Given the amount of baking going on in Nebraska kitchens of that time, there was probably enough wild yeast to leaven the biscuits overnight, so you could add a teaspoon of dry yeast with the flour.

> Make a good corn mush, just as if you were going to eat it with milk; when it is lukewarm take a quart of it, work in flour enough to make a stiff dough, make it into biscuits, put in your bake pan, and set it in a warm place over night. Bake in a very hot oven, and you have the best and sweetest biscuit you ever ate.

NOTE: RECIPE TAKES TWO DAYS.

Yield: About 50 1½-inch biscuits, or 16 3-inch biscuits

4 cups yellow cornmeal (stone ground preferred)

About 2 cups all-purpose flour, plus more for flouring baking sheets and boards

Equipment: Oven mitt, deep pot, wooden spoon, 2 baking sheets, wooden board, rolling pin (optional), drinking glass or biscuit cutter

1. Bring 4 cups water to a boil in a large pot.

2. Add 1 teaspoon salt to the boiling water.

3. Stirring with one hand, add the cornmeal a little bit at a time from the other hand.

4. When all the cornmeal is added, continue cooking and stirring the mush for another 15 minutes. Put an oven mitt on your stirring hand to avoid burns from sputtering mush.

5. Turn cooked mush into a large mixing bowl and let it cool somewhat, stirring occasionally. It will continue to thicken.

6. When the mush is lukewarm, work in the flour to make a stiff dough. Depending on the dryness of the original cornmeal, the dough will take more or less flour. Work with your hands (remove rings) or a wooden spoon until the dough will stick together in one ball.

7. Flour a wooden board. Turn the dough out onto the board.

8. Flour your hands and pat out the dough ½ inch thick, or flour a rolling pin and roll it that thick.

9. Scatter some flour on the baking sheets so the biscuits won't stick.

10. Cut biscuits with a drinking glass (dip the lip in flour so it won't stick) or biscuit cutter. Arrange them on the baking sheets without letting them touch.

11. Leave biscuits in a warm place overnight. (Modern kitchens are warm enough almost everywhere.)

12. In the morning, preheat oven to 425 degrees. Bake biscuits 10–12 minutes.

Serve "while hot for breakfast."

MARCH MEETING CAKE (1896)

This election cake from eastern Massachusetts may have been in continuous use from Colonial days, although by 1896 the *Hingham Journal* had to request recipes from subscribers. By the late nineteenth century, Election Day had become March Town Meeting, without the military drill, but still an all-day, all-male meeting to elect town officials and set policy. Over the century of democracy, the cake had lost all its eggs but kept the raisins that had been rare and imported luxuries in Colonial days. Some election cakes were frosted in Early America, and most were frosted in the Colonial revival recipes, but Hingham is a conservative town even now. The recipe is reprinted in *Out of the Ordinary*, a 1998 publication of the Hingham Historical Society. You can use a cup of the **Potato Yeast** recipe instead of the dry yeast, if you remember to reduce the milk by one cup.

> Three cups milk, 1 cup yeast, 1 cup sugar, flour enough to make a thick sponge. Make in morning. At night add 1 cup shortening—one-half butter, and one-half lard—½ cup sugar, salt, 2 cups currants, flour enough to make stiff. Rise over night. In the morning knead and put into pans to rise; then bake.

NOTE: RECIPE TAKES TWO DAYS.

Yield: Serves 24

4 cups whole milk

2 cups sugar

2 teaspoons dry yeast

10–12 cups flour, plus some for kneading

½ cup butter, plus some to grease pans

½ cup lard

1 pound currants

Equipment: 9-by-13-inch sheet-cake pan, 3 large bread pans, or 3 8-by-8-inch brownie pans; clean kitchen towel, large mixing bowl, wood board for kneading

1. Let the milk come to nearly room temperature. If using powdered yeast, dissolve in a cup of the milk with a little of the sugar. In about 10–15 minutes there should be lots of bubbles, even a foam on top. (If there isn't, check the dates on your yeast, and give it more time.)

2. In a large mixing bowl, combine the yeast, the rest of the milk, and a cup of the sugar.

3. Work in enough of the flour to make a stiff batter, but one that can still be stirred, about 6–8 cups (more if sifted first, less if you measure by dip-and-sweep). Cover with a clean kitchen towel and let rise all day (overnight if starting in the evening).

4. In the evening, mix together lard and butter. Stir the currants with a little of the flour. Mix 1 tablespoon of salt with 2 cups of the flour.

5. Stir the foamy batter in the mixing bowl to get rid of the large bubbles, and mix in the butter mixture, the currants, and about half of the remaining flour. Add more flour to make a dough that holds together.

6. Butter the pan or pans.

7. Flour the wood board, and turn out the cake dough. Knead in enough more flour to make a thick dough. It won't get as supple as bread dough, but it will be less sticky.

8. Pat the dough into the pan or divide among several pans, filling ⅔ full to allow for rising. (You may find you need more pans, or have a few cup cakes left over. Because of the varia-

tions of moisture in flour, this has always happened with yeast breads and cakes.

9. Cover pans with kitchen towel and let rise overnight, or until almost doubled in bulk. (If your kitchen is very warm, bread may over-rise overnight, and make a mess. Clean up, and re-knead the dough, put it back in the pan or pans, and let rise a third time for an hour or so, and it will be doubled in bulk and ready to bake.)

10. Bake at 425 degrees for 15 minutes, then reduce heat to 375 degrees, and bake another 15 minutes. Test with a toothpick or wire cake tester.

11. When cake is done, let cool in the pan. Or wait for a few minutes, then run a spatula around the edges, and take it out of the pan onto a wire rack to cool. (Or you can turn the original pan upside down, and cool the cake on that.)

Serve to town meeting goers with talk of how the old ways are best.

31

COOKING BY KIDS
(1877–1921)

The first cookbooks written for children and adolescents appeared in the 1870s. Prior to the Civil War, kids cooked and ate like miniature adults. This chapter traces the development of cook books for kids from their beginnings as Victorian storybooks to some early public school lessons in "home economics." What happened is not that children's cooking became more serious over that time. The shift is from an intended audience of upper-class families for whom cooking was a hobby on the cook's night off, to a captive audience of working-class girls for whom cooking would be an everyday task, or a possible profession. Cookbooks for children that are pretty and fun continue to be issued to the present day. However, the audiences generally are younger, and the recipes have become much, much easier. Public school courses in cooking were an attempt to instill what were thought of as scientific and healthful principles to improve the lives of the poor. It's a widely used joke to say that if you want teenagers to quit, say, listening to rap music, all you have to do is make rap music a mandatory subject in high school. Courses in home economics were not actually intended to make teenagers stop cooking, but

they were often intended to stop them from cooking like their mothers—and some immigrant mothers made much tastier food than what was in the textbooks.

Although none of these books were explicitly political, the early ones show a lot of casual ethnic prejudice, which their readers absorbed as the natural order of things. The school textbooks have a bland, white-sauce palate that corresponded to the "melting pot" ideology of this period of large-scale immigration. *Perfection Salad; Women and Cooking at the Turn of the Century*, by Laura Shapiro, is the best history of the "Domestic Science" movement that brought white sauce, jellied salads, and marshmallow garnishes to public school classrooms. As the late as the 1960s, Italo-American girls in New England were being taught to "cook everything white."

SOFT CANDY (1877)

Six Little Cooks, or Aunt Jane's Cooking Class, is written as a story with dialog and characters, and most of the cooking is done for adults to eat, although there are plenty of sweets. Aunt Jane is visiting for summer vacation, and the class is assembled of girls

Figure 20 Boston Public Schools home economics class. *Source:* The Boston Cooking-School Magazine, *Vol. XI, No. 3, October, 1906.*

nine to twelve years old. Each of fourteen chapters has the recipes and kitchen adventures of the day, which include dodging the family's African-American cook.

Candy making comes on the third day. This is a recipe for brown sugar fudge, although fudge is not supposed to have been invented for another eleven years! A number of 1870s recipes for candy and caramels are written so loosely that they are apt to make fudge, and so we have to assume that fudgy versions of harder candies were an acceptable result before the name "fudges" developed (see the **Fudges** recipe for more of the story). This one is explicitly titled "soft candy" and includes the instruction "when thick and ropy, take it from the fire and stir till it grains." I have added the candy ther-

mometer to clarify "thick and ropy," and some instructions from *Oh Fudge*, by Lee Edwards Benning.

CAUTION: BOILING CANDY STICKS AND BURNS.

Yield: 1 pound of fudge, 50 pieces

1 pound brown sugar (2 cups)

¼ pound butter, plus more to grease pan

½ cup chopped nuts (optional)

Equipment: Candy thermometer, 8-inch round cake pan, or 5-by-10-inch fudge pan, heavy 2-quart saucepan, wooden spoon, heat-proof spatula

1. Preheat thermometer in a cup of hot tap water.

"EACH EGG WAS TO BE BROKEN BY ITSELF IN A CUP FIRST, BEFORE GOING TO JOIN ITS COMPANIONS IN THE DISH."—PAGE 11.

Figure 21 The Victorian idea of girls learning to cook. *Source:* Six Little Cooks, or Aunt Jane's Cooking Class, *Chicago, 1877.*

2. Butter pan, and place on a heat-proof surface.

3. Melt brown sugar in the saucepan over low heat with 3 tablespoons water. Watch out that it does not boil over, because it can froth up quickly.

4. When sugar is melted, increase heat. When it begins to bubble, add the stick of butter.

5. Stir a little bit to melt the butter. Reduce heat and continue boiling. Add nuts if using.

6. Put candy thermometer in boiling candy. When it reaches nearly 238 degrees (at sea level), remove from heat and stir until it thickens noticeably. The original recipe says "until it grains." (Modern recipes delay this stirring until a skin forms so that the grains are finer. Aunt Jane did not do this.)

7. Pour into the buttered pan. The original recipe has you pour into "buttered plates."

Serve as a snack with milk.

WELSH RAREBIT NO. 2 (FOR TWELVE PERSONS) (1903)

This is listed under "Chafing Dish recipes" in *Three Hundred Things a Bright Girl Can Do*, by Lilla Elizabeth Kelley. The book has instructions for crafts, swimming, tennis, and forming girls' clubs, and seems to be directed toward teenagers, and college-bound girls at that. The chafing dish, a pan with an alcohol lamp underneath for tabletop cooking and reheating, was a popular gadget of the 1890s. Girls took them to the newly popular women's colleges and made fudge. Affluent families brought them out for Sunday night dinners when the servants had the day off. Bachelors and young singles used them in kitchenless rented rooms, as electric hot plates have been used since the 1920s. Ms. Kelley wrote: "Anything which may be made in an ordinary frying-pan, or boiled or broiled, may be cooked in a chafing dish. Delicious cream soups and oyster stews may be made for the Sunday evening meal. It may be carried on picnics, and is always a helpful friend." Welsh Rarebit was a genteel way of avoiding the ethnic slur "Welsh Rabbit" for this gooey Anglo-American comfort food.

Yield: Serves 12 teenagers of 1903

1 pound American cheese

2 cups whole milk

2 eggs

2 tablespoons flour

½ teaspoon prepared mustard

½ teaspoon salt

½ teaspoon paprika

12 slices of bread or 36 soda crackers

When you bake a small thing, have the oven hot,
But for baking big things cool it off a lot.

Figure 22 "When you bake a small thing, have the oven hot, / But for big things cool it off a lot." *Source:* When Mother Lets Us Cook, *New York, 1908.*

Equipment: Chafing dish or saucepan, whisk

1. Cut the cheese into small pieces.

2. With a fork, cream together butter, flour, mustard, salt, and paprika to form a paste.

3. Heat milk in a chafing dish or saucepan until quite hot but not boiling.

4. Meanwhile begin toasting slices of bread (if using).

5. Work the cream paste into the hot milk until thoroughly blended.

6. Add the cheese and stir into the milk.

7. Beat the eggs well, and add to the mixture when the cheese is melted.

8. Whisk in eggs and cook only 1 minute, then remove from heat (or shut off spirit lamp).

Serve on toast or crackers. "This is delicious when cold, and may be spread on sandwiches for picnics as you would spread butter or cream."

CURLYLOCKS PUDDING (1908)

By 1908, Constance Johnson's *When Mother Lets Us Cook,* could be illustrated with woodcuts on most pages. The age group is about the same as *Six Little Cooks,* "Well—ten or twelve years old," and the recipes are similar. What has changed is that there is no frame story, and the writing "talks down" more to child readers. The recipe is a clear cornstarch pudding, soon to be replaced by instant gelatin "jelly."

Yield: Serves 6

1 quart strawberries or raspberries

1 lemon

1 cup sugar

3 tablespoons cornstarch

Equipment: Strawberry huller (optional), juicer, double boiler, 1½-quart mold

1. "Pick over 1 quart of strawberries or raspberries, hull them [remove green sepals] and cut them in half. It is better to wipe the berries than wash them, but sometimes they have to be washed."

2. Half fill the bottom of a double boiler with water. Bring to a boil, reduce heat and simmer until needed.

3. "Cut a lemon in half and squeeze the juice into a cup with a lemon-squeezer."

4. "Measure 1 tablespoonful of the juice and put in the top pan of a double boiler or chafing dish. Add to this

Figure 23 Coffee Pot gets to go on the picnic. *Source:* Mary Francis Among the Kitchen People.

1 cup of granulated sugar, and 2 cups of cold water. Put the pan on a hot part of the stove." (Ms. Johnson is referring to a wood or coal stove; today we turn up the heat under the top of the double boiler.)

5. "Measure 3 [level] tablespoonfuls of cornstarch, and put it in a cup half full of cold water. Stir until the cornstarch is dissolved." (It doesn't ever dissolve, so you have to stir as you do the next step.)

6. "When the sugar water has come to a hard boil, add the dissolved cornstarch gradually."

7. "Stir until the mixture is thick and smooth."

8. "Now set the pan into the lower part of your chafing dish or double boiler containing boiling water."

9. "Put the berries into the cornstarch mixture, stir them in well, and put your double boiler on a hot part of the stove." (Increase the heat to boil the water in the lower part).

10. "The mixture should cook for 10 minutes." (And you should stir it to heat through.)

11. Rinse the jelly mold with very cold water.

12. "When [the pudding is] done, turn the pudding out into a jelly mold and put aside to cool."

13. Refrigerate until pudding is set.

14. Put a plate over jelly mold, and invert plate and mold to unmold the jelly.

"Serve cold with milk or cream."

STUFFED EGGS (1912)

The Mary Frances Cook Book, or Adventures Among the Kitchen People, by Jane Eayre Fryer, with illustrations by Margaret G. Hays and Jane Allen Boyer, reached a high point of whimsy, with a story featuring dialog with Tea Kettle and Auntie Rolling Pin. It was part of a series with a sewing book and others, all aimed at girls perhaps six to ten. The recipes are again easier, although it ends with baking powder cakes and a rather scary blackened steak. In 1912, making toast still required grilling it over a live fire. Mary Frances lives in a home without a servant, so stern Aunt Maria and a tramp with an Irish accent round out the human cast. A recipe for fudge contains what we would now regard as a racial slur. This recipe for stuffed eggs is for a picnic. At the last minute, Mary Frances decides that it could be scary, and brings Coffee Pot for protection.

Yield: 6 eggs

  6 large eggs
  1 tablespoon olive oil or butter
  ½ teaspoon prepared mustard
  ½ teaspoon salt
  Dash cayenne [red] pepper

Equipment: Saucepan, mixing bowl, waxed paper

1. Place eggs in cold water and bring to a boil. Boil 15 minutes.
2. Move the pot to the sink and run cold water onto the eggs to cool them.
3. Shell eggs carefully.
4. Cut each egg in half the long way, being careful to keep halves together.
5. Remove yolks and mash them together in the mixing bowl "with the back of a spoon."
6. If using butter, melt it. Add butter or oil, mustard, salt, and cayenne pepper to egg yolks and blend thoroughly.
7. Roll egg yolk mixture into six balls the size of the individual yolks.
8. "Fit one ball into each pair of whites."

Serve "with White Sauce poured around them" if used at table. "If used for picnic, wrap waxed paper around each until needed."

ORANGE JELLY (1912)

One of the first textbooks for high school cooking classes was *Household Science and Arts*, by Josephine S. Morris, first published in 1912 for use in the Boston public schools. It eventually was used in many other school systems. The recipes are practical, but very much of Yankee New England. In this dessert, jelly is not what we spread on peanut butter sandwiches, but a gelatin dessert we would now call Jell-O, after the trademarked instant gelatin desserts invented in 1897. For most of the nineteenth century, jellies were made from boiled down calves' feet or parts of large fish. They were hard to make and visually sensational. The school recipe takes advantage of commercial unflavored gelatin (a by-product of large-scale meatpacking) that had been available for about twenty years. This could be made into fresh fruit jellies in only one mixing bowl. In urban areas with year-round ice supplies, jellies became the easiest desserts. Manufacturers encouraged cooking teachers to develop recipes for jellies with embedded fruits and nuts, and for jellied salads. Now premixed gelatin desserts are so easy that no hostess would serve them for dinner parties. You may find this jelly made from natural fruit juice more interesting than packaged gelatin desserts.

Yield: Serves 5

  2 tablespoons granulated gelatin (unflavored)
  ⅔ cup sugar
  ½ cup orange juice
  2 tablespoons lemon juice

Equipment: Juicer, Pyrex or enameled metal bowl

1. Sprinkle the gelatin over ½ cup cold water to soften and swell for 5 minutes.
2. Bring 1½ cups of boiling water to a boil. Pour it over the gelatin and stir to dissolve.
3. Stir in the sugar until it, too, is dissolved.

4. Halve and juice oranges and a lemon to make the fruit juices, or measure prepared fruit juices. Add fruit juices to gelatin mixture, and sprinkle on a little salt. Stir well and put bowl in refrigerator for four hours to solidify.

Serve "with whipped cream or plain cream."

ONIONS WITH WHITE SAUCE (1921)

This recipe comes from the notebook of Janet Zanger (no relation to the author), from her eighth-grade cooking class, probably in Western Pennsylvania or Ohio. The effort to boil onions in two batches shows how determined early home economists were to avoid strong flavors. You can also see how many pots are required to do this, as opposed to the typical one-pot meals of American home cooking. I have taken the directions for "White Sauce (medium)" from the same notebook. White sauce, or "milk gravy," remains popular in the region, but was another bland, colorless favorite of home economics. Since this was also a period obsessed with hygiene, the whiteness of foods was a symbol of purity.

Select small or medium sized onions. Remove skins under water, cook in boiling water enough to cover five min. Drain and add fresher boiling water. Cook until tender in an uncovered kettle. Drain and sauce with white sauce.

Yield: Serves 6

12 small or 8 medium onions
1 cup whole milk
1–2 tablespoons butter
1½ tablespoon flour
⅛ teaspoon salt
Speck white pepper

Equipment: 2 large pots, colander, double boiler

1. Bring a large pot of water to a boil.

2. Fill a sink or a second large pot with cold water. Peel the onions under the water. (This works to avoid tears, although I prefer swim goggles. You can also peel the onions under running water, but it doesn't work as well.)

3. Put the onions in a second large pot, and cover with boiling water. (Keep the water going in the big pot.) Bring back to a simmer and cook 5 minutes.

4. Melt the butter over low heat in the top part of the double boiler or yet another sauce pan.

5. Add flour and stir until smooth. (It may bubble a little once it forms a golden paste.)

6. When onions have cooked 5 minutes, drain off the water in the colander. Return them to the pot and again cover with boiling water from the big pot. Bring back to a simmer and cook until a fork goes in easily.

7. Meanwhile, slowly stir the milk into the flour-butter paste over medium heat. Stir thoroughly until the mixture thickens, but don't let it boil.

8. When the mixture thickens, put some boiling water from the big pot into the bottom of the double boiler. Take the big pot off the heat, and put the bottom of the double boiler on the heat. Put the top on the double boiler, and stir in the salt and white pepper. Cook a few more minutes.

9. Drain onions once more. Put in serving dish and pour over white sauce.

Serve with roast meat and biscuits, or at Thanksgiving.

32

WOMEN'S SUFFRAGE (1878–1927)

In Early American times, the movement for women's rights was part of a group of issues that were known generally as "Reform"—including abolitionism, voting rights for men without property, some early ideas about health food, and temperance. Some people subscribed to the entire package, while others had differences. Among cookbook authors before the Civil War, Lydia Maria Child was a lifelong reformer and prominent abolitionist, while Catherine Beecher and Sarah Josepha Hale opposed suffrage but promoted women's rights to education and to be physicians. However, none of their cookbooks were openly political. Temperance recipes are the most apparent early reform recipes and were probably tried out on the tables of most abolitionists and suffragists. After the Civil War, political positions became more specialized. For example, religious temperance advocates such as Carrie Nation favored women's suffrage as a means to win votes to prohibit alcoholic beverages, while labor organizer Mary "Mother" Jones opposed temperance as an infringement on the rights of working men. Suffragists were briefly associated with "the reform costume for women," named after suffragist publisher Amelia Bloomer, but did not generally keep up the association with health food. Suffragists began to produce a few cookbooks, as did women's charities such as the Women's Exchange movement (see Chapter 37), but most active recipe publishers in the suffrage arena were local chapters of the Women's Christian Temperance Union, founded in 1874. The women's club movement was the other great expression of moderate feminism, but it did not take an official position on suffrage. Its founder, "Jenny June" Croly, published a cookbook with recipes from well-known suffragists, showing that women's clubs were forums for discussion of the suffrage issue.

SUSAN B. ANTHONY'S APPLE TAPIOCA PUDDING (1878)

This recipe was obtained by "Jenny June" (June Cunningham Croly) for a chapter of "Favorite Dishes of Distinguished Persons" in *Jennie June's Cook Book* (1878). By 1878, Miss Anthony was a veteran of the abolitionist and suffrage movements and a famous platform speaker—and not afraid to mix appeals for the vote with campaigns for women employees and criminals. Nevertheless, she is at pains to produce a recipe to convey the mixed messages that she is an ordinary woman who knows how to cook, a practical woman who can make a dessert in an hour, and a moral woman who likes plain food. Her apple tapioca pudding, possibly taken from her friend Elizabeth Smith Miller, is very plain, indeed. Modern eaters, even strongly committed feminists, will want to use quite a bit of cream and sugar. In the same book, an easy bread pudding is ascribed to suffragist Lucy Stone. By contrast, the abolitionist and suffragist platform speaker Anna Dickenson is associated with a just-like-men steak and mushroom dish. By 1900, Miss Anthony no longer felt she had to present herself as a homebody and responded to a recipe request with: "An Unfailing Recipe in Cookery. The best recipe for any possible compound is an ounce of good common sense."

"Jenny June" was a professional newspaper writer and the founder of both an early New York women's club and the National Association of Women's Clubs. She believed that suffrage was too divisive an issue for the clubs, which had already broken the taboo against women eating lunch together in public restaurants.

> Susan B. Anthony is an excellent cook and housekeeper, and it was a proverb at home that, when Susan did the housekeeping, the meals were always punctual and well served. She believes in a plain, simple diet, and the following is her favorite pudding. Peel and core eight apples, fill them with sugar in which a little nutmeg has been grated. Take a cupful of tapioca, which all night been soaking in water, add to it a little milk or water if needed, and pour it round the apples, which have been laid in a buttered dish. Bake slowly one hour, and serve with cream and powdered sugar. It is good hot or cold, the tapioca forming a jelly round the apples.

Yield: Serves 8

Butter to grease baking dish

8 baking apples, such as Northern Spy or Cortland

1 teaspoon nutmeg

¾ cup sugar

1 cup pearl tapioca

1 cup whole milk

Heavy cream and additional sugar for serving

Equipment: Ovenproof baking dish, vegetable peeler, apple corer

1. Soak tapioca overnight in a cup of cold water.

2. Core and peel the apples. If you can, slice a plug of pure apple from the lower part of the core, and use it to stop up the holes on the bottom of the apples.

3. Butter the baking dish, and arrange the apples.

4. Mix nutmeg and sugar, and fill the apples with the mixture.

5. Drain tapioca, mix with the milk, and pour around (but not over) the apples. Sprinkle on any leftover sugar.

6. Bake at 350 degrees for 20–30 minutes, depending on the size of the apples.

Serve with cream and sugar.

REBEL SOUP (1886)

This quick supper was contributed by Mrs. Mary F. Curtis of Boston to the 1886 *Women's Suffrage Cookbook* by Hattie A. Burr. Cream of tomato soup was rebellious less for its red color than for providing a hot meal while liberating the cook from hours at the stove. Tomato soup had been popular for more than a hundred years, but recipes in books usually called for lengthy boiling of meat stocks and such fillers as rice, browned onions, and strained stewed tomatoes. Mrs. Curtis does not specify canned tomatoes, but they were widely available and sometimes quite cheap in the late 1880s, and ideal for this kind of fast food.

Yield: Serves 4

1 quart whole milk

1 large soda cracker (Nabisco Crown Pilot size), or 2 or 3 regular crackers

1 cup canned tomatoes

$\frac{1}{4}$ teaspoon baking soda

4 tablespoons butter

Equipment: Saucepan, rolling pin and board, small bowl

1. "Heat one quart milk to the boiling point."
2. Roll out the cracker to make fine crumbs.
3. Add crumbs to near-boiling milk.
4. Mix tomatoes and baking soda.
5. " . . . while foaming, add it to the boiling milk."

To serve, *"Put butter, salt, and pepper in the dish and pour the soup on them."*

CHARLOTTE RUSSE (1900)

This recipe was submitted by Laura Clay (1849–1941) to *Favorite Food of Famous Folk*, published in 1900 by the Guild of St. James' Parish in Pewee Valley, Kentucky. Laura Clay had founded the Kentucky Equal Rights Association in 1888. Her father, Cassius Marcellus Clay (1810–1903), was a controversial abolitionist who had freed his own slaves despite pressure from other Kentucky leaders and who later was President Lincoln's minister to Russia. While in Russia, Cassius Clay had an open

extramarital affair with a ballerina, and Laura Clay dated her interest in women's rights from seeing her mother's weak position in the subsequent divorce. Charlotte Russe was a popular and elaborate southern dessert, but a deliberately ironic choice by Laura Clay given the role of Russia in her political education. The recipe fills two charlotte molds, but also works well in nine-inch springform pans and can be halved.

One-half ounce of isinglass (or an equivalent amount of gelatine), boiled in a half-pint of water until reduced to one-half teacupful barely; set it away to get lukewarm. Whip a pint of rich cream until you have a half-gallon bowlful. Save the cream you have left. Beat the yolks of two eggs light, and stir in two and two-thirds ounces of sugar. Season with what you like. Stir in the remaining cream, then the melted isinglass. Stir until it begins to thicken. Then immediately and quickly stir in the whipped cream. This quantity fills two ordinary sized blanc mange moulds.

Yield: Serves 16–20

4 dozen ladyfingers

2 tablespoons unflavored gelatin

1 pint heavy cream

2 large eggs

$\frac{1}{3}$ cup sugar

1 tablespoon vanilla

Equipment: 2 charlotte molds or 9-inch springform pans; whisk, eggbeater, or hand-held electric mixer to whip the cream; cooking thermometer (optional); double boiler (optional)

1. Bring a cup of water to a boil on a stove or in a microwave oven.
2. Dissolve the gelatin in 3 ounces of the water.

Figure 24 Lining a charlotte mold with lady fingers. *Source:* The Boston Cooking-School Magazine, *Vol. VIII, No. 7, February 1904.*

3. Separate the eggs, and beat the yolks until light and creamy. (You can save the whites for **Prune Soufflé.**)

4. Beat the sugar and vanilla into the egg yolks.

5. Beat the heavy cream until it forms soft peaks. Refrigerate until ready to use.

6. Pour any cream that doesn't froth into the egg mixture. (This isn't as likely with the added emulsifiers and stabilizers in today's cream, so you can add ½ cup of whole milk instead.) Beat in the gelatin as well.

7. Ms. Clay was not concerned about eating uncooked egg yolks. If you are, heat the egg-gelatin mixture in a double boiler or over low heat, stirring constantly, to 170–180 degrees. The mixture will thicken and steam a little but should not be allowed to boil.

8. Chill the mixture, perhaps in a larger bowl of ice water, stirring so that it doesn't set at the edges.

9. Split the ladyfingers and line the bottoms of the pans, crust side facing the pan surfaces (out). To get the round

shape, you can either trim the ladyfingers to petal shapes and cut a round for the center, or you can trim the ladyfingers and use a spiral arrangement. Don't worry if there are spaces between them. Some people in the nineteenth century preferred ½-inch spaces between ladyfingers for the filling to show through. You'll need the same trimming to line the sides of charlotte molds, which are somewhat conical. You can line the rims of springform pans with ladyfingers up and down, or the long way and bent around. Again, spaces are okay. Women will get the vote and keep the respect of the community, even if your charlotte isn't perfectly neat. (This is the advantage of knowing how history comes out.)

10. When the egg mixture is cool, fold in the whipped cream, and spoon the mixture into the lined molds. Stir and press a little to release any bubbles, and level the tops of the molds.

11. Refrigerate at least 4 hours to set the filling well.

12. To unmold, set plates on top of the molds, and invert. Undo the spring-

form pans and remove the sides, patching any areas that stick with a wet spoon, then take off the tops (bottom of the springform pans). With charlotte molds, tap the inverted mold and try to spin it a little before lifting off. If it seems stuck, invert again and run a thin knife around the edge to free all the sides, then redo the previous step.

Serve sliced with a knife dipped in water between slices.

CANDIED POTATOES (1895)

This recipe was submitted by "Mrs. W. H. Felton, Cartersville, Ga." to the *Tested Recipe Cook Book*, edited by Mrs. H. L. Wilson for the 1895 Atlanta Exposition. Rebecca Latimer Felton (1855–1931) was a longtime suffragist, prohibitionist, and political gadfly in Georgia, one of a faction of North Georgians who often opposed the planter interests of central Georgia. She was the particular enemy of Senator Gordon, whose **General Gordon Cake** was one of the first political cakes named after Confederate heroes. Her husband had served in the U.S. Congress, and in 1922 she was appointed to serve one day in the United States Senate after the death of Senator Thomas Watson and before the new senator would be sworn in. The eighty-seven-year-old Felton was thus the first female United States senator and marked her brief tenure with a policy speech, but no votes.

Her simple recipe for baked sweet potatoes was a subtle rebuke to the genteel recipes of the "lady managers" of the exposition, who were imitating the handiwork exhibits and upper-class feminism (no mention of the suffrage issue) of the lady managers of the 1893 Chicago World's Fair.

Boil your sweet potatoes, then slice and put in layers in your baking pan. Add sugar, butter and seasoning to taste, and pour on a half cupful of boiling water before you place in the oven to brown.

Yield: Serves 4

5 medium sweet potatoes

½ cup sugar

2 tablespoons butter

A pinch of cinnamon or nutmeg

Equipment: Large soup pot, tongs or slotted spoon, ovenproof baking dish

1. Bring 3 quarts of water to boil in a large soup pot.

2. Add sweet potatoes to water, bring back to boiling, reduce heat and simmer 20 minutes.

3. Remove sweet potatoes from boiling water with tongs or a skimmer.

4. Let potatoes cool. Remove skins, and cut into ½-inch slices.

5. Butter ovenproof baking dish and add sweet potatoes, sugar, spice, and the remaining butter. Sprinkle on salt.

6. Bake uncovered at 375 degrees for 20 minutes.

Serve with pride that you are not like those women in Atlanta.

PRUNE SOUFFLÉ (1916)

By 1916, with the twentieth Amendment in sight, the Equal Suffrage League of Wayne County (Michigan) was at pains with their *Suffrage Cook Book* that it "may help to show again what has been so often demonstrated before, that an interest in politics is not incompatible with an interest in cooking." This selection from their "desserts for children" section suggests a combination of the luxurious soufflé and the medicinal (if not political) prune purée.

Yield: Serves 2–4

1 cup stewed prunes

2 eggs (or equivalent egg white product)

1 teaspoon "vanilla or lemon juice"

Butter and powdered sugar for dish

Equipment: Colander, 9-inch straight-sided soufflé dish, baking sheet

1. "Mash the prunes through a colander with a spoon or wooden potato masher [the kind that looks a little like a bowling pin] and to this add flavoring."

2. Separate the eggs by pouring between shells over a cup. (You can save the yolks for **Charlotte Russe**, above.)

3. "Beat the whites of the eggs very stiff and mix lightly but thoroughly with the prunes."

4. Butter the straight-sided soufflé dish and dust with powdered sugar. Put the dish on the baking sheet.

5. "Turn into a buttered baking dish and bake 20 minutes in a moderate [350 degree] oven."

"Serve immediately [soufflés fall down in about 10 minutes] with plain or whipped cream."

EVER-READY BISCUIT DOUGH (1927)

This very practical refrigerator biscuit was submitted by "Mrs. Katherine Langley, Member of Congress (Ky.)" to the 1927 *The Congressional [Club] Cook Book*. Mrs. Langley, a Republican, was the eighth woman elected to the House of Representatives, and only the fourth to serve more than one term, representing her Kentucky district from 1927 to 1937. (Jeanette Rankin, the first woman elected, in 1917, returned for a second term, but not until 1941–1943.) The recipe shows that women elected to office were still expected to keep house, and that Representative Langley, for one, thought it

could be done with modern inventions and clever shortcuts, such as using baking powder *and* yeast *and* baking soda.

NOTE: RECIPE TAKES TWO DAYS.

Yield: Serves 25

1 quart whole milk

1 cup mashed potatoes

2 teaspoons salt

1 teaspoon baking soda

1 cake "magic yeast" (or 1 teaspoon dry yeast powder)

1 cup sugar

1 cup "melted fat"

3 pounds all-purpose flour (about 12 cups sifted, or 10 cups unsifted)

2 teaspoons baking powder

Equipment: Large mixing bowl, 2 baking sheets, board and rolling pin, biscuit cutter, refrigerator, kitchen towel

1. Dissolve yeast in ½ cup water with a pinch of the sugar.

2. When yeast has a froth of bubbles on top, mix with milk, mashed potatoes, salt, baking soda, and baking powder.

3. Melt fat. Add fat and sugar to yeast mixture, then enough flour "to make a soft sponge" (medium batter), about 4 cups.

4. Cover bowl with a kitchen towel and let sponge rise for about 2 hours in a warm kitchen.

5. Stir in enough flour to make a "stiff dough."

6. Flour the board and your hands, and knead the dough—not too much, or the biscuits will be tough.

7. "Set in refrigerator or some place where the temperature is low enough to keep the yeast and baking powder from acting, and not cold enough to destroy their action."

8. "Ever-ready biscuit dough is the best from 24 hours to a week after it is prepared."

9. When you want to make biscuits, flour the board and rolling pin.

10. Remove as much dough as you want from the refrigerator, and roll out ¾ inch thick.

11. Cut dough with a biscuit cutter dipped in flour. (Don't twist the cutter.) Gather scraps and return to the refrigerator, or roll out with the next batch.

12. Place biscuits on ungreased baking sheets, just touching at the edges.

13. Preheat the oven to 425 degrees while the biscuits warm and rise.

14. When biscuits have risen somewhat, bake for 15 minutes.

Serve hot with butter.

33

NATIONAL UNITY VERSUS DIVERSITY (1878–1902)

The last quarter of the nineteenth century was a difficult period in American history as the one hundred-year-old nation struggled to define itself. On the surface, it was "The Gilded Age," a time when millionaires built great mansions along Fifth Avenue in New York City. But underneath the surface, people struggled with two depressions, high food prices, and low wages. Unlimited European immigration brought many foreign immigrants to fill the cities and the increasingly dangerous mines and factories. Waves of strikes sometimes ended in gun battles with hired guards or state militias, sometimes in ethnic fighting among the workers. Federal compromises made after the deadlocked election of 1876 allowed southern states to repeal African American rights and set up a new system of racial segregation.

Industrialization also changed the food system as improved machinery, refrigeration, and railroads provided a more constant and nationally uniform supply of meat, flour, and dairy products. These products were often cheaper but less fresh than the local ones they replaced and sometimes adulterated with dangerous chemicals.

Mass-circulation newspapers reported on the elaborate dishes eaten by millionaires, as they would later publish investigative reports about conditions in the meat industry and poisonous additives in milk and flour. A new group of college-educated "domestic scientists" and home economists bounced between trying to create new and popular foods and a felt need to help poor families economize and immigrants give up their old food preferences. From the 1870s on, this movement sought to "improve" the diets of immigrants, working families, and the poor, as well as provide lessons for servants and middle-class housewives. This kind of culinary "Americanism" can be seen in early recipes for school lunch in Chapter 39, home economics and domestic science texts, and the cooking taught at settlement houses for immigrants. As late as the 1960s, an Italian American recalls taking home economics in a Boston school where "They made all this white food, everything white. All the food I knew from home was red."

By the end of the period, many of the domestic scientists had hired out to food corporations to promote particular brands of baking powder, vegetable shortening, flavoring extracts, flour, or canned foods. A few hired out to the producers of branded health foods and promoted cereals and

WEST HILLS COLLEGE
LEMOORE LIBRARY/LRC

Figure 25 Home economics class taught at Carlisle Indian School in 1900. *Source:* © CORBIS.

high-fiber crackers to repair the damage of the other commercial food products.

At the same, the nation's centennial celebrations set off a Colonial Revival (see Chapter 30) that included an interest in old-fashioned cooking and also a revival of interest in regional and ethnic cooking. With French cuisine popular among the very rich, there was national as well as regional interest in the Creole food of New Orleans. The post-Civil War wave of cookbooks sold to benefit local charities—including disabled veterans or war widows—recorded many regional dishes and the openly political cakes and cookies of Chapter 26. At the same time, regional cuisines were being mixed together by settlers of the prairie and Western states and the many individual relocations and migrations after the war.

These many contradictory trends can be seen more coherently as a national debate about what kind of a country we would have and what "American Food" was going to be. Toward the end of this period, in the 1890s, the debate became explicitly political as the United States began a foreign empire, annexing Hawaii and taking control of Puerto Rico, the Philippines, and Cuba in the Spanish-American War. The immediate effect of this empire on food was an increasing promotion of tropical products and inexpensive sugar. Domestic economists went to work for pineapple and banana importers, and solid shortenings included less cottonseed oil and more coconut oil. Domestic scientists also helped originate and spread some original treats and faster foods that have remained popular, as noted in Chapter 34.

While domestic scientists were working toward white food for immigrants in the Eastern states, emigrants to the western states were taking up the local "Spanish" foods, sometimes making them blander and more suitable for Victorian tables. Enchiladas reached English-language readers in 1876. Tortillas and tamales appeared in 1880s cookbooks by Anglo-Americans, joined by a recognizable "salza" and "chili con carna" in the 1890s.

The best book about the Domestic Science movement is the 1986 *Perfection Salad; Women and Cooking at the Turn of the Century*, by Laura Shapiro. Although the book has no recipes, it is very good at placing the efforts of the domestic scientists in context of the social conflicts of the time. Recipes in this section let you taste along as middle-class Americans tried to assimilate the growing diversity of this period. For foods eaten by immigrants and Hispanics immune to domestic science, see *The American Ethnic Cookbook for Students*. For the Gilded Age dining rooms of the super-rich, find facsimiles of cookbooks written by chefs of the time, such as the fancy dishes in *The White House Cook Book*, or *The Cook Book by "Oscar" of the Waldorf*.

JAM BOLAYA (1878)

This is not the earliest printed recipe for jambalaya—a sketchy one appeared in *Mrs. Hale's New Household Receipt-Book* in the 1853 edition—but it is the first reasonably accurate one and is not from New Orleans, but from the *Gulf City Cook Book*, compiled by the Ladies of the St. Francis Street Methodist Episcopal Church, in Mobile, Alabama. Mobile had a French Colonial and Creole tradition of its own, and the book also had early recipes for gumbo as a soup ("gumbo" as a term for okra had appeared in cookbooks since 1824), for court-bouillon, and for an etouffée—all dishes associated with New Orleans Creoles. However, the New Orleans white Creoles were Roman Catholics and had French or Spanish last names. "The Ladies" of Mobile were Protestant and almost entirely from Anglo-American or German American backgrounds. Dishes like this jambalaya had been preserved in Mobile through slavery times by their African American cooks. But by including recipes like this one, and attaching the words "Dixie," "Confederate," and "Rebel" to various desserts, "the Ladies" were asserting that their city had an independent culinary culture while they shared favorite dishes.

Although oysters are now an expensive treat, they were local and cheap in Mobile. George H. Daniels, who edited the 1990 University of Alabama Press reprint of the *Gulf City Cook Book*, points out that this dish could be made for a few cents in 1878, as Mobile was entering a disastrous depression in which it defaulted on bonds and lost its city charter. I have added quantities to make what is clearly an economy pilaf, perhaps for Sunday night supper after a lunch of roast or boiled or fricasseed chicken. "The Ladies" could buy oysters shucked to order from African American street vendors. I have added a safe method of opening them if you can buy whole oysters for this dish.

Have the lard hot, put in flour, cook to a light brown, with a medium-sized onion. Take the giblets, neck, small part of the wings and feet of your chicken, and put in the lard; add half a tea-cup of prepared tomatoes, two dozen oysters, with their liquor, pepper and salt to taste; put in nearly a pint of rice, one table-spoonful of butter; stir frequently when nearly done; set back on the stove and let steam.

CAUTION: HOT ROUX STICKS AND BURNS.

Yield: Serves 6

1 medium onion

3 tablespoons lard

2 tablespoons flour

Giblets and wing tips of a roasting chicken

2 chicken feet, or 2 wings

⅓ cup tomato puree

24 oysters (or 2 cans oysters and liquid)

2 cups rice

1 tablespoon butter

Equipment: Heavy pot with a tight cover, second pot with cover (if using whole oysters) wooden spoon or spatula or flat whisk, large measuring cup

1. Halve, peel, and chop the onion.

2. If using whole oysters, place in pot with ¼ cup water. Cover tightly and steam for a few minutes, until the shells open. Keeping the oyster liquor in the pot, pick out the oysters and cut them out of the shells with a paring knife. Pour liquid carefully off any sand or bits of shell into large measuring cup.

3. Cut the gizzard and liver and heart of the chicken into small pieces. Cut off the wing tips, and cut the wings or feet into several pieces.

4. Heat lard in the large pot. Reduce heat. Stir in flour to form a bubbling paste, the "roux."

5. Add the onion, stirring constantly until the paste is golden brown to the color of peanut butter. Go slowly, so as not to burn the roux and have to start over. Slow cooking is the key to many Creole and African American dishes.

6. When onion is transparent and the roux is about done, stir in chicken parts to brown a little.

7. If using canned oysters, pour off oyster liquor into measuring cup. Add enough water to make 3 cups.

8. Add tomatoes and the 3 cups of water/oyster liquor to pot.

9. Add butter and rice, and stir well. Bring pot to a boil.

10. When pot is boiling, reduce heat and stir in oysters.

11. Cover tightly and cook 10–12 minutes, until rice is almost done but still soupy.

12. Stir well, and cover to cook for another 2 or 3 minutes.

13. Without lifting cover, remove pot from heat and allow to steam another 15 minutes.

Serve hot in soup bowls.

CRÉOLE SOUP (1879)

This recipe is from the 1879 *Cooking School Text Book* by Juliet Corson, principal of the New York Cooking School. As you can see, this 12-cent soup (exotic accent in the name provided free), represented a 20 percent improvement in thrift over Miss Corson's previous work, *Fifteen Cent Dinners for Workingmen's Families*. This was no laughing matter in 1879, when the average nonfarm employee made $1.12 a day, or $386 a year for a six-day week. A wage-earning family spent about 60 percent of its income on food, as compared to less than 11 percent in 1997. So getting the daily food budget down from 58 cents to 40 or 45 cents could make a real difference, if only in the quality of Sunday dinner. Miss Corson trained some of the next generation of home economists and "domestic scientists," but they abandoned her liberal use of herbs and spices, which were thought to arouse passions and encourage the consumption of alcoholic beverages. With or without spices, working families were often aroused to strikes in this period of two major depressions and frequent industrial accidents. This is still an economical soup. See if you can make it for under $2.50. (Hint: Miss Corson advised her readers to grow herbs in window boxes.)

Yield: 6 large bowls

1 quart tomatoes [32 ounces canned or 6–8 medium]	5 cents
1 ounce butter [¼ stick]	2 cents
2 ounces rice [¼ cup]	2 cents
1 carrot	1 cent
1 turnip	1 cent
1 onion, parsley, and seasonings [thyme, marjoram, 2 bay leaves, 1 blade mace, 6 whole cloves]	1 cent
Total	12 cents

Equipment: 2 soup pots, vegetable peeler

1. Halve, peel, and chop onion.

2. Melt butter in soup pot, and brown onion. (This is the "Créole" part.)

3. Wash tomatoes. "Break in the hand," squeezing out seeds, and add to pot.

4. Peel and slice carrot and turnip, and add to pot.

5. Add 2 quarts of water and bring to a boil.

6. Miss Corson suggested a "bouquet" of a sprig of parsley, one of thyme, and one of marjoram tied together. This could be removed at the end. If you do not have fresh herbs, add a pinch each of powdered thyme and marjoram, and the sprig of parsley by itself.

7. The bay leaves, cloves, and blade of mace might have been sewed into a little cheesecloth bag, again so they could be removed. You can add them loose and remember to take them out at the end.

8. Reduce heat to a simmer and cook soup uncovered 2 hours.

9. Bring a quart of water to a boil in a separate pot.

10. Add ½ teaspoon salt and the rice to the plain boiling water. Boil 15 minutes, and drain rice.

11. Before serving, remove parsley, cloves, bay leaves, and mace (if you can find it) from soup.

12. Add rice, and season with salt and pepper.

Serve for supper. If the children ask for bread, offer them more soup.

BEEF LOAF (1883)

Meat loaf is a dish nearly as old as cookery, but earlier American meat loaves were almost always veal loaves, since veal was very cheap in the spring, when bull calves are culled from dairy herds. Very young veal, called "monkey veal" was particularly flavorless and hard to sell. (Ironically, milk-fed veal is now an expensive luxury.) This is one of the earliest American recipes for a meat loaf we would recognize, made primarily from beef. Two changes in the food system made beef loaf recipes appear at the end of the nineteenth century. One was the reorganization of the meatpacking industry by Armour and Swift, such that quantities of stringy range beef and the fattier parts of prime steers could be combined into salable "hamburger." The other was the availability of small, hand-crank meat grinders for home use. This recipe actually mentions grinding the meats "on a sausage-grinder." It was contributed by Mrs. Lizzie Bailey of Monticello, Arkansas, to *The Housekeeper's New Cookbook*, compiled by Mrs. T.J. Kirkpatrick of Springfield, Ohio.

Yield: Serves 12–16

3 pounds lean beef (or extra lean ground beef)

½ pound [lean] salt pork

1 cup cracker crumbs

3 medium eggs

1 tablespoon butter

Sage "to taste" (1 teaspoon to start)

Shortening to grease loaf pan

Equipment: Loaf pan, meat grinder or food processor, basting brush

1. Cut beef and salt pork into cubes and run several times through meat grinder, or pulse-process in small batches in food processor until it has the consistency of ground beef.

2. Mix in eggs, ¼ cup of the cracker crumbs, 2 teaspoons salt, and 1 teaspoon pepper. Pick out any pieces of gristle.

3. Grease loaf pan, and put in beef loaf mix.

4. Sprinkle the rest of the crumbs over the top.

5. "Bake two and one half hours." (An hour at 350 degrees should do the job.)

6. Melt a tablespoonful of butter in ¾ cup of boiling water. Use this to baste the meat loaf while baking.

Serve hot, sliced with gravy or ketchup, or cold in sandwiches with mustard.

Dried Bean Soup (1887)

This recipe illustrates the "melting pot" school of culinary Americanism. It comes from *The White House Cook Book*, the million-copy best-seller by chef Hugo Ziemann and Mrs. F.L. Gillette. This book was the culinary bible for more than a million American women, including many striving immigrants. Here the authors have started from the typical long-cooked bean soup that would be made on the back of the stove as it boiled huge pots of water for Monday laundry. They have removed individual or ethnic seasonings but added the extra refinement of pureeing the beans. (To taste what the authors were reacting against, try the Creole Red Beans in *The American Ethnic Cookbook for Students*.) I have halved the proportions to make a recipe that fits our modern soup pots.

Put two quarts of dried white beans to soak the night before you make the soup, which should be put on as early in the day as possible.

Take two pounds of the lean of fresh beef—the coarse pieces will do. Cut them up and put them in your soup-pot with the bones belonging to them, (which should be broken in pieces,) and a pound of lean bacon, cut very small. If you have the remains of a piece of beef that has been roasted the day before, and so much under-done that the juices remain in it, you may put it into the pot and its bones along with it. Season the meat with pepper only, and pour on it six quarts of water. As soon as it boils, take off the scum, and put in the beans (having first drained them) and a head of celery cut small, or a tablespoonful of pounded celery seed. Boil it slowly till the meat is done to shreds, and the beans all dissolved. Then strain it through a colander into the tureen, and put into it small squares of toasted bread with the crust cut off.

NOTE: REQUIRES SOAKING BEANS OVERNIGHT.

Yield: 6–8 hearty servings

1 pound dried white beans

1 pound lean beef [shin], or 2 pounds bone-in shin

¼ pound lean bacon

Leftover roast beef or steak bones (optional)

1 head celery (or 1 tablespoon celery seed)

8 slices bread

Equipment: Colander, 2 large soup pots, mortar and pestle (optional if using celery seed), long wooden spoon, tongs, skimmer, toaster, board to cut bread, ladle

1. Soak beans overnight in 4 quarts of water.

2. Drain beans.

3. Slice bacon if it is not already sliced.

4. Put meats and bones in soup pot with 3 quarts of fresh water. Sprinkle with black pepper. (Mrs. Gillette believed that beans would not soften in salted water, which is not the case.)

5. Bring to a boil. Skim off any scum or froth, and add beans to pot.

6. If using celery seed, bruise in mortar and pestle and add to soup. If using fresh celery, break off stalks to clean dirt from base, chop fine with any leaves, and add to soup.

7. When soup returns to a boil, reduce heat to a simmer, with lid ajar. Simmer 3–4 hours, stirring occasionally to make sure beans do not stick and burn. If you need more water, heat it separately in a teakettle, and add boiling water so soup does not stop simmering.

8. When meats are shredded and beans are very soft, soup is done. Pour it through colander into second soup pot.

9. Remove bones from colander with tongs. Press bean solids through colander to puree them. When process is complete, press any large pieces of meat to get all juices.

10. Stir pureed bean soup well and reheat over low heat, as pureed beans are more likely to burn.

11. Add salt to taste.

12. Toast slices of bread and let cool and dry.

13. Cut crusts off toast, and cut into small triangles.

14. Float toasts on top of soup in tureen, if you have one; or add the toast "sippits" to each bowl.

Serve from a soup tureen if you have one, or in bowls. At last washday is done for another week!

BROWN BETTY (1890)

This recipe was part of the winning essay for the $500 American Public Health Association Lomb Prize on *Practical, Sanitary, and Economic Cooking Adapted to Persons of Moderate and Small Means*, which became a book of the same title by Mrs. Mary Hinman Abel. It was part of a series of menus to feed a family on thirteen cents a day. Mrs. Abel may have carried the recipe into use in The New England Kitchen, an experimental Boston restaurant aimed at "improving" the food choices of the poor. According to *Perfection Salad; Women and Cooking at the Turn of the Century* by Laura Shapiro, The New England Kitchen eventually failed because the food was too plain for immigrant tastes. You may notice that the recipe is similar to but plainer than the 1862 Jenny Lind's Cake from *Godey's Lady's Book* modernized as **Apple Brown Betty** as made by the 1957 Chillicothe Ohio Foods II class. Although we imagine Early American food or 1950s food as plain, either was highly spiced by comparison with the late Victorian sanitary ideal.

Yield: Serves 4–6

2 cups bread crumbs, or dry bread moistened

4–5 sour apples

1 cup sugar

2 teaspoons cinnamon

4 tablespoons butter or suet

Equipment: 1½ quart casserole or ovenproof bowl with cover or aluminum foil

1. If possible, leave bread out for a day or two to make it easier to crumb. Make 2 cups of soft crumbs from the bread by pulling apart with 2 forks (so it doesn't compress).
2. Peel and slice the apples (discarding cores) to make 4 cups of sliced apples.
3. Arrange a layer of the crumbs in the bottom of the casserole.
4. Follow with a layer of the apples.
5. Mix cinnamon and sugar, and sprinkle on the apple layer.
6. Continue until all the apples and crumbs are used up, but end with a layer of bread crumbs.
7. Cut the butter into small pieces, and sprinkle them on top.
8. Cover with lid or aluminum foil and bake at 350 degrees ½ hour, or until "the apples are soft."
9. Uncover and brown at 400 degrees.

TOMALES (1899)

In *Mrs. Gillette's Cookbook; Fifty Years of Practical Housekeeping*, the author declared: "Ten years have elapsed since *The White House Cook Book* was placed in the principal households of the country; since which time the author has greatly simplified and improved upon past efforts. . . . The idea of presenting this new work is to confine its teachings strictly to the American way of cooking, rejecting foreign recipes, which are not adaptable in most of American homes." This apparently did not exclude English or French dishes, nor such foreign recipes as finnan haddie, a Spanish omelette, Irish stew, "Welsh rarebit," Swedish pudding, spaghetti and tomato sauce, a page of chutneys, nor a Canadian blueberry fungy. But Mrs. Gillette did cut down on the fashionable French and French-named dishes from the White House.

She also included this recipe, correctly spelled in the index as "chicken tamales." While Mrs. Gillette may have realized that Native Americans were eating tamales more than a thousand years before Amerigo Vespucci, she probably thought of the dish as one of the Mexican American foods that had come into the American mainstream in the last decade. One of the more authentic early recipes had been relayed from San Francisco to Chicago for the 1887 *The Graded Cook Book*, by Mrs. Lavinia Hargis. Street vendors—many of them African American youth—were shouting out "hot tamales" in cities across the southeast. Those tamales, like these were not spicy hot, but they were kept at a warm temperature in covered baskets. You can make them more authentic by using a chile pepper in the stuffing, or having hot sauce on the table. A recipe for Chicken Tamales in the 1894 *How We Cook in Los Angeles* used three *dozen* red chiles and "almost a whole head" of garlic for about twice as many tamales.

Yield: 15–20 tamales

4 cups white cornmeal

1 chicken

1 onion

1 "Spanish pepper" [red bell pepper or jalapeño or other chile]

3 whole cloves

1 bay leaf

6-ounce or larger package dried corn husks (or 3 dozen fresh corn husks)

1 bunch parsley

Equipment: Soup pot with cover, long metal tongs, paper towels, serving platter, cutting board, aluminum foil

1. Wash off chicken and put in a soup pot with water to cover. This is to measure the water.

2. Remove chicken and bring water to a rolling boil.

3. Put in chicken with tongs, and without splashing boiling water. Bring the pot back to a boil, reduce heat to a simmer, covered loosely, for an hour.

4. Soak corn husks in a pot of hot water until they are soft, about 30 minutes.

5. Test chicken for doneness by inserting a knife at the thigh joint. Juices should run clear. Joins should be well loosened.

6. Remove chicken from pot, reserving stock for scalding cornmeal at Step 8, or for another recipe. Let chicken cool, or refrigerate.

7. When chicken is cooled, cut into serving pieces, pull away skin, and cut meat off the bones. Reserve the bones. Chop into small pieces and shred the pieces. Season with salt and pepper.

8. Bring a quart of hot water to a boil (or add some or all of the chicken stock).

9. Separate the corn husks and wash away any dirt or corn silk under warm running water. Pile up the good ones, and "tear narrow strips like ribbons" from the torn or smaller husks. Cover with plastic wrap while you get the other ingredients ready.

10. Pour 2½ cups of boiling water or chicken stock on the cornmeal. "It should not be too soft, only moist." Add more water or stock as needed.

11. Slit the "Spanish pepper" down one side. Remove all the pith and seeds with a spoon. Cut off the stem and mince the pepper very small. If it is a hot chile pepper, wash your hands carefully with soap and water, and don't touch your eyes or sensitive areas even after that. Mix minced pepper with chicken.

12. Make tamales by spreading out 2 wide corn husks.

13. "Take in your hand enough corn meal to spread a quarter of an inch thick over them" in a square, in the middle of the corn husks.

14. "Put into this two tablespoonfuls of the seasoned chicken."

15. "Now roll the husks and the corn meal over with the chicken inside. Fold the [empty] ends of the corn husks over, and tie them with the narrow strips made of the husks. Don't worry if your tamales aren't meat."

16. Stack up the completed tamales with the folded side down to hold them together. (If you run out of corn husks, you can finish the fillings by making a few tamales out of aluminum foil.)

17. Put the bones left from the chicken in the bottom of the soup pot.

18. Halve and slice the onion (you can leave on the skin), and add it to the chicken bones.

19. Add the bay leaf, 1 teaspoon salt, the cloves, and some more black pepper.

20. "Cover bones and onions with cold water, and bring to a boil."

21. "Now place the tomales [folded side down] over the top, the bones acting as a sort of rack to keep them out of the water. Boil them without ceasing for three hours." You are actually steaming the tamales with the

cover on tightly. (If the cover is loose, make a collar of aluminum foil to hold in the steam.)

To serve, "Cut the rolls in halves; dish them so the ends will be exposed. Decorate the dish with curled parsley."

CHILE CON CARNE (1902)

Some form of chili con carne was eaten by Anglo Americans throughout the old West from about the time of the 1845 Mexican War. Written recipes appeared in the 1890s, and entered the *Manual for Army Cooks* by 1896, in time for the Spanish-American War. This version, one of the first that tastes like the chili of today, was written down by Capt. James A. Moss in the 1909 *The Story of a Troop Mess*, and reprinted in the 1981 *The Great American Chili Book* by Bill Bridges. Chili became a mainstream American food after soldiers returned from World War I, with local variations like Bulgarian-American Cincinnati Chili, but the chili fad really started in the 1960s and 1970s. Army chili did not include beans until 1910. I'm dating this chili from the introduction of chili powder in 1902.

Yield: Serves 8–12

3 pounds chopped fresh [extra lean] beef (or lean cheap beef)

¼ pound butter

2 tablespoons Worcestershire sauce

3 tablespoons "best ground chili powder"

2 teaspoons black pepper

1 teaspoon cayenne [red pepper]

2 tablespoons olive oil

1 large onion or clove of garlic

½ cup flour

Equipment: Food processor or meat grinder (optional), large soup pot

1. If using fresh beef, remove all fat and run through a food processor or meat grinder to get minced lean beef somewhat chunkier than hamburger. You can also mince the beef with a sharp knife.

2. Put the beef in the soup pot with 2 quarts of water. Bring to a boil, and simmer 3 hours. (This direction was based on very tough army beef, one hour or less may be sufficient for today's supermarket beef or hamburger.)

3. Halve, peel, and chop onion, or peel and mince garlic.

4. When beef is done, add 1 teaspoon of salt and the rest of the ingredients except the flour.

5. Stir the flour into a slushy mix with a cup or 2 of water.

6. Increase heat under soup and stir in flour mixture. Keep stirring until it starts to thicken.

7. Reduce heat to a simmer, and cook another hour. Stir periodically so it doesn't stick and burn.

Serve hot in tin cups with **hardtack** *or Crown Pilot crackers.*

SLICED BANANAS (1902)

This recipe is one of a group of "Hawaiian Recipes" in *Mrs. Rorer's New Cook Book* of 1902. Mrs. Rorer, a Philadelphian, was perhaps the most open minded of the domestic scientists. We know she read the newspapers, because she had also published the first American recipe for "Baked Alaska" in an earlier book. By the time of the *New Cook Book* she had been teaching cooking for twenty years, and included chapters of Spanish, Creole, and Jewish recipes as well as the Hawaiian group. The Kingdom of Hawaii had been annexed by the United States in 1893, but did not become a state until 1959. This no-cook recipe could be made by East Coast readers from Central American bananas. I often had it with sour cream growing up in the 1950s. For real Hawaiian recipes of this period, see *The American Ethnic Cookbook for Students* chapters on Hawaiians and Japanese-Americans.

Yield: Serves 6

  6 ripe bananas
  ½ cup sugar
  1 cup heavy cream
  ½ teaspoon nutmeg

  2 cups heavy cream (or sour cream)

Equipment: Nutmeg grater (optional)

1. Peel and slice bananas.
2. Sprinkle on sugar and nutmeg. (Mrs. Rorer said to grate on the nutmeg. You can do this with a whole nutmeg and grater.)
3. Let stand in a cool place 1 hour.
4. "At serving time, cover them with thick cream and send to the table."

Serve for dessert or as a snack.

34

ORIGINS AND EARLY RECIPES OF POPULAR FOODS (1877–1936)

This chapter documents a period of creativity in cooking from 1880 to 1912, and one dish developed later. It may surprise you that so many of today's familiar foods are only a few generations old. Somehow the United States got through its first hundred years without hamburger sandwiches, fudge, PB & J, or spaghetti with tomato sauce. Nineteenth-century Americans had no clue about chocolate brownies, bran muffins, or chocolate chip cookies. It may also surprise you that such recent food history is not clearly settled.

Two reasons for so many changes in food were the rise of daily newspapers as a mass medium and the development of a group of professional home economists. Food marketing was accelerated by the national railroad system and by the increasing use of industrial methods. Food companies hired home economists to develop recipes to sell vegetable shortening, baking powder, shredded wheat, packaged gelatin, peanut butter, and packaged cereals. Home economists were also involved in efforts to improve society, usually by teaching economical cooking to the urban poor or to immigrants. Most of their creative work, however, was directed to enticing dishes for middle-class homes, from novel cakes and cookies to jel-

lied salads. This was also a time of large-scale immigration, although only the adaptation of spaghetti with tomato sauce in this chapter was obviously influenced by immigrant groups. There was also a rush of new household gadgets, as Americans were fascinated by machinery.

HERMITS (1877–1880)

Hermits appeared all over the United States in the 1880s. Present-day hermits are square, brown lumpy cookies that look like the brown robes of English friars or monks (thus hermits), but this very early recipe makes a round, white spice cookie. The recipe is from *Fish, Flesh and Fowl*, compiled by the Ladies of State Street Parish (Portland, Maine, 1877), with details from *Miss Parloa's New Cook Book* (1880). Hermits and similar cookies became more popular as more homes were equipped with stoves that maintained steadier oven temperatures.

Another possibility is that hermit cookies, like most early cookies, became softer after a few days cloistered in the cookie jar. It is possible that the name came from an immigrant cookie, such as the Dutch "hernhutters" which are named for Moravians. Since Moravian Americans are known for

WEST HILLS COLLEGE
LEMOORE LIBRARY/LRC

spice cookies, the cookies may have been adapted from Moravian cookies. Food historian Stephen Schmidt suggests that some early recipes had one raisin in the center of the cookie, and that raisin was the hermit! Not everything in food history is settled. This is a very large recipe that can be halved.

Yield: About 30 4-inch cookies

1 cup salted butter, and some to grease baking sheets

1½ cups sugar

1 cup raisins

3 medium eggs (or two jumbo eggs)

1 teaspoon baking soda

3 tablespoons whole milk

1 rounded teaspoon nutmeg

1 rounded teaspoon cloves

1 rounded teaspoon cinnamon

5 cups flour

Equipment: Rolling pin and board, round cookie cutter or glass tumbler, food processor, 2 or more baking sheets, standing mixer or pastry blender

1. Remove butter from refrigerator an hour before starting, unless using food processor.

2. Chop raisins in a food processor by pulsing briefly. Do not grind to a paste.

3. Cream together butter and sugar in food processor, or with a standing mixer, or with a pastry blender or a large fork.

4. Mix flour with spices. Grease baking sheets.

5. Dissolve baking soda in milk.

6. Beat eggs until creamy and light.

7. Work eggs into butter-sugar mixture; then add flour, raisins, and milk mixture in turns. You may not need all the flour.

8. Work into a dough but do not knead.

9. When dough sticks together well enough to roll, flour the board and rolling pin.

10. "Roll about one-quarter of an inch thick and cut with a round cake cutter." Arrange cookies on baking sheets.

11. Gather scraps and roll out with the next portion of dough until all the dough is used up. (You can also refrigerate or freeze dough and bake the rest another day.)

12. Bake about 12–15 minutes at 375 degrees.

Serve with milk or afternoon tea. By the 1880s, many kitchens had a cookie jar, but it would have been rude for kids to take cookies without Mother's permission.

HAMBURG STEAKS (1886)

The first printed recipe for hamburger in English was in a 1796 London edition of Hannah Glasse's *Art of Cookery Made Plain and Easy*; it was reprinted in the American edition of 1805. (This has been only recently pointed out by food historian Andrew Smith.) That recipe is for "Hamburgh Sausages," which were stuffed and smoked like today's Lebanon Bologna, but already had the crucial feature of combining chopped lean beef with added fat, and could be "roasted with toasted bread under it." Chopped beef was also breaded and fried into "Beef Cakes," and beef-based sausages like **Winter Sausage** were formed into patties and fried plain.

By the end of the nineteenth century, when Swift and Armour had developed a national network of refrigerator cars to deliver consistent sides of beef, local butchers were able to make a low-cost, salable product by grinding the stringy, lean meat of range-fed cattle with the excessively fat "steer bellies" of feedlot cattle. Although the name has always suggested a German origin, there is no association of Hamburg with chopped meat in Germany. An early German-American Cookbook, *Praktisches Koch-Buch fur die Deutschen in Amerika* by Henrietta Davidis (Milwaukee, 1897) has "Hamburg Steaks" only as the English translation of "*Gute Beefstakes von Gehackteh Fleisch.*"

It would be wonderful to find a description of the "Hamburger Steak" listed on a Delmonico's menu in the 1834, but all we know is that it cost ten cents, was placed between ham and eggs and roast chicken at the end of the menu, and that roast beef cost only five cents. A "Beef Sausage" recipe in the 1839, *The Kentucky Housewife by Mrs. Lettice Bryan*, is quite similar to the Hannah Glasse recipe. An 1854 recipe for "Sausage Meat" in *The New Family Book, or Ladies' Indispensable Companion* uses two parts beef and one of fat pork, fried in "small cakes." Except for the spices, these would taste just like today's cheap hamburgers.

We have to assume that early hamburger steaks were served with a mushroom sauce or a gravy as were these of 1886. Hamburger sandwiches on buns may have been developed in some places as early as the 1880s, but did not become nationally known until the 1904 Louisiana Purchase Exposition in St. Louis and were not widely available until the 'teens.

This recipe is from *Mrs. Rorer's Philadelphia Cook Book*, by Mrs. S.T. Rorer. Mrs. Rorer does not add beef fat, but uses butter with ground round. The directions for making onion juice are from the same book. Note that Mrs. Rorer's sauce was being thickened with barely cooked flour, a deterioration of technique from the egg-thickened sauces of Colonial times.

One pound of meat from the upper side of the round; chop it very fine, add to it a tablespoonful of onion juice, half a teaspoon of salt, and two dashes of black pepper; mix well together. Moisten the hands in cold water, take two tablespoons of this mixture and form with the hands into small round cakes or steaks. This quantity will make eight Hamburg steaks. Put two tablespoonfuls of butter into a frying-pan; when hot, put in the steaks, fry brown on one side, turn and brown the other. Now place them on a hot dish, add a tablespoonful of flour to the butter remaining in the pan, mix until smooth, add a half-pint of boiling water, stir constantly until it boils; add salt and pepper to taste, and pour it over the steaks.

Or they may be broiled the same as a plain steak, seasoned with salt and pepper, and spread with butter.

Yield: 8 2-ounce patties

1 large onion

1 pound top round roast, or extra lean ground round

2 tablespoons butter

1 tablespoon flour

Equipment: Box grater, frying pan, food processor or meat grinder (Mrs. Rorer used either a hand-crank meat grinder or a half-moon chopper with a wooden oval chopping tray), cup to catch onion juice, mixing bowl, tablespoon or soup spoon, ovenproof plate or platter, flat whisk

1. Peel onion and trim off bottom.

2. "Press the onion firmly against a large grater and quickly draw it up and down allowing the juice to drop from one corner of the grater" into a cup. Do this until you have about a tablespoon of thick liquid. It's okay if some solids get into the juice, and it may take half the onion, depending on juiciness.

3. If starting from top round, cut into 1-inch cubes. (If starting with extra-lean ground round, go on to Step 5.)

4. Put half the cubes in a food processor and whirl for 5–7 seconds. Move this hamburger to a mixing bowl, and process the other half of the cubes. If using a meat grinder, run the meat through with a fine chopping blade.

5. Mix in the onion juice, ½ teaspoon of salt, and 2 dashes of black pepper.

6. Moistening your hand with cold water, take 2 rounded tablespoons of meat, and form into a small hamburger. Repeat until you have used up the meat.

7. Melt the butter in a frying pan, and brown the patties on each side, about 4–5 minutes.

8. Meanwhile, heat water in a teakettle, and warm a stoneware plate in a 150-degree oven. When patties are done, put them on the plate in the oven.

9. When all the patties are done, add the flour to the butter in the pan, and stir thoroughly until it is a smooth paste. Cook for a minute or two to remove the "raw flour" taste.

10. Measure 1 cup of boiling water, and add a little at a time to the frying pan, stirring it into the flour paste. Whisk until the sauce boils and thickens. Taste a little of the sauce with a spoon, and add more salt and pepper if needed.

11. Remove platter of hamburg steaks from the oven. Pour on the sauce.

Serve with vegetable and potato as a light lunch or supper. In the 1880s, these were also served for breakfast with oatmeal, griddle cakes, hash-browned potatoes, and eggs on toast!

SPAGHETTI IN ITALIAN STYLE (1892)

Although recipes for macaroni and cheese, and the wide use of tomatoes both date from the early nineteenth century, it took a while for the tomato sauce to get together with pasta. This recipe, from the 1892 *Little Dinners*, by Christine Terhune Herrick (daughter of Marion Harland), has many modern features: the name "spaghetti," the shortened cooking time, and the tomato sauce. Only with the arrival of large numbers of Italian immigrants in the 1900–1924 period would most Americans stop breaking their spaghetti in little pieces, however. (A recipe for "Macaroni with Tomato Sauce" in Mrs. Rorer's Philadelphia Cook Book of 1886 does describe how to cook whole spaghetti by bending them into the pot, but the tomato sauce is very plain.)

Break a half pound of spaghetti into inch-long bits and cook it until tender in boiling salted water. Fifteen minutes should be long enough. Slice an onion and brown it in a frying-pan with two tablespoonfuls of butter. Add to this a cupful of tomato sauce and last of all stir in three ounces of grated Parmesan cheese. Drain the macaroni, place it in a dish, and pour this sauce over it, lifting the macaroni with a fork that the sauce may penetrate to every part. Serve very hot.

Yield: Mrs. Herrick considered this an appetizer or vegetable side dish in a book about how to give dinner parties for six to eight people. We would now use it as a main supper dish for two people.

½ pound [½ box] spaghetti

1 onion

2 tablespoons butter

8-ounce can tomato sauce

3 ounces Parmesan cheese

Equipment: Soup pot, frying pan, box grater, colander

1. Fill a soup pot about ⅓ full with cold water and bring to a boil.
2. When the water boils, add 1 teaspoon salt, and begin breaking in the inch-lengths of spaghetti.
3. Halve, peel, and slice the onion into half-moons.
4. Melt the butter in a heavy skillet, and brown the onions.
5. Add the tomato sauce.
6. Grate the Parmesan cheese and add to the sauce.
7. Drain the spaghetti after 15 minutes (Non-Italian Americans ate very soft spaghetti until the 1970s, and many still do.)
8. Flip the spaghetti into a heat-proof dish, and pour the sauce over it. Stir well with a fork.

Serve hot.

FUDGES (1893)

The name "fudge" for a soft chocolate candy has been traced to Vassar College in 1888 by Lee Edwards Bening, author of *Oh, Fudge*. "Fudge" was already an exclamation the girls used instead of swearing. The fudge recipes spread among the early women's colleges since the young women away from home had a taste for sweets and could make fudge in their dormitories over the gas lamps, or over alcohol lamps "borrowed" from the chemistry lab, or with a chafing dish. Many early recipes are for "fudges," since the individual square was "a fudge."

It is much harder to trace the recipe than the name, since fudge sometimes just happens when chocolate caramels or other hard candies are not cooked long enough to harden, or if they are stirred as they cool. A great many early candy recipes probably made fudge by accident, and some deliberately, such as the 1877 **Soft Candy** recipe. The inventor of Vassar fudge, Emelyn Hartridge, got the recipe from a friend after having soft chocolate caramels in a Baltimore candy store, so the original recipe was originally for a Baltimore style of soft caramels. There was also the influence of Mexican "Cajeta" (see **Mexican Milk Candy**) that led to early fudge recipes with nuts being called "panocha" or "penuchie," from Spanish-language terms for sugar.

The earliest printed recipe I know appeared in the *Home Queen World's Fair Souvenir Cook Book* (1893) edited by Mrs. J.E. White. It was submitted by Mrs. J. Montgomery Smith of Mineral Point, Wisconsin. I have added techniques from a similar manuscript recipe of the same period by Mrs. Ames, reprinted in the Easton, Massachusetts Historical Society's *Cookbook*, 1973. Mrs. Ames's husband was governor of Massachusetts from 1887 to 1890; she began her cookbook in 1860 but probably acquired the "Chocolate Candy or Fudge" recipe from one of her three daughters in the 1890s, as shown by the collegiate chafing-dish directions.

Four cups granulated sugar, 1 cup cream, 1 cup water, ½ [8-ounce] cake Baker's Chocolate, ½ cup butter. Cook until it just holds together and pour into pans not buttered; when cool enough to bear finger, stir it until it no longer runs; should not grain, but be smooth. Cut in squares.—1893

¼ lb Choc—Bakers

3 Coffee Cups White Sugar gran

½ Cup Butter

1 Cup milk

1 tablespoon Vanilla

Boil it in a chafing dish over Alcohol, 20 minutes, Counting from time it begins to boil. Take it off, Beat well with spoon to make smooth.

The vanilla should be added when the lights are put out & before beating. Put in two greased pans. When cool, cut in squares.—Ames manuscript.

CAUTION: BOILING HOT CANDY STICKS AND BURNS.

Yield: 80–100 pieces

4 cups sugar

1 cup heavy cream

1 cup (1 stick) butter

¼ pound (four ounces) unsweetened chocolate

Equipment: Candy/deep-fry thermometer, 3-quart or larger saucepan, oven mitt, wooden spoon, 2 large loaf pans, or 10- or 11-inch round cake pan

1. Butter a ring around the inside of the saucepan.

2. Combine all ingredients and 1 cup of water in the saucepan, and turn on low heat.

3. Stir to dissolve sugar and chocolate. When you don't feel any more sugar crystals, increase heat to medium and bring to a boil.

4. Attach candy/deep fry thermometer, and put the oven mitt on your stirring hand to avoid burns.

5. Once candy begins to boil, reduce heat to keep it boiling slowly. Don't stir too much.

6. Boil until the thermometer reads 234–238 degrees (at sea level). The mixture will be thick and noisy.

7. Divide the mixture between the two loaf pans (or pour into the cake pan).

Let cool until lukewarm. A skin may form on top.

8. When fudge is still warm, stir with a spoon. When the fudge changes color and thickens, you can stop stirring and smooth the top.

9. When fudge is a little cooler, score a pattern of 1-inch squares on the top.

10. Store covered.

Serve by breaking into squares and arranging them on a candy dish.

SWEET AND NUT SANDWICHES (1896)

Although nut butters had been a popular health food, they did not appear in sandwich recipes until the end of the nineteenth century. It took even longer before recipes were published for the peanut, butter, and jelly sandwich—even though dairy butter-and-jelly was a widely used sandwich combination. This early version is in the 1896 *Enterprising Housekeeper*, by Helen Louise Johnson, a pamphlet published by The Enterprise Manufacturing Company, which made hand-crank meat grinders—the multi-use food processor of the 1890s. Enterprise was beginning to sell a nut-grinding blade. I have added directions from Mrs. W.H. Davis's recipe for "Peanut Filling for Sandwiches" from the 1897 *White Ribbon Cook Book*, compiled by the Women's Christian Temperance Union of Clay County, Nebraska, where there was a lot of butter. You can omit the butter or use ready-made peanut butter.

These may be made with marmalade, jams, or jellies, anything which will spread without running. Boston brown bread is generally used for nut sandwiches. Chop the nuts very fine or pound them to a paste, and spread on thin slices of bread. Lemon juice or ex-

Enterprise Meat Chopper

Figure 26 If you wanted a peanut butter sandwich in the 1890s, you needed one of these meat choppers to grind the nuts. *Source:* The Enterprising Housekeeper, *Philadelphia, 1896.*

tract flavorings may be used if desired.—1896

Cream 1–3 cupful of butter and add 2–3 cupfuls of peanuts chopped or ground. Season with salt.—1897

Yield: 10 sandwiches

2 cups roasted peanuts

1 cup butter (optional)

1 tablespoon lemon juice or 1 teaspoon lemon extract (optional)

16-ounce jar jelly, currant or grape.

1 loaf sliced bread or **Boston Brown Bread**

Equipment: Hand-crank meat grinder or food processor (for making peanut butter)

1. Remove butter (if using) from refrigerator to soften, 1 hour before starting.

2. Put nuts through finest blade or nut-butter blade of meat grinder, or process in a food processor in short bursts until the paste begins to form (about 1 minute).

3. If using butter, cut into small cubes and distribute with peanut paste in second and third grindings. If using food processor, add the butter and continue processing, working the peanut paste back down to the blades with a spatula periodically.

4. Keep grinding or pulsing until the peanut butter forms a ball and seems like peanut butter. You can choose

Figure 27 Pre-chocolate brownie pans made fancy-shaped cakes. *Source:* The Boston Cooking-School Magazine, *Vol. 8, No. 10, May 1904.*

somewhat crunchy or smooth. (In a food processor, a ball may form above the blade and then drop down and get churned into an oilier smooth paste.)

5. If using lemon juice or extract, work it into the peanut butter. Taste and add more salt if necessary.

Serve at women's club meetings, or pack with school lunch.

LOWNEY'S BROWNIES (1907)

Quite a few things were named after the Brownies, cartoon elves featured in long, illustrated poems, books, and comic strips by Palmer Cox from the early 1880s to his death in 1924. Like Smurfs, there were a lot of different Brownies, working together on all-night pranks and good deeds, invisible to mortal eyes. They inspired elf-shaped chocolate candies, a pudding, Eastman Kodak's user-friendly box cameras, and later

the Brownie Scouts. The first edible brownies we would recognize as such were individual molasses cakes with a single pecan on top, in the 1896 *The Boston Cooking-School Cook Book*, by Fannie Merritt Farmer. Miss Farmer developed the chocolate brownie for her 1906 edition, probably by reducing the flour in her 1896 chocolate cookie recipe to match the chewy texture of her 1896 molasses brownies. (All early brownie recipes included chopped nuts.)

The next year Miss Farmer's former assistant Maria Willett Howard confused things by producing enriched recipes for "Lowney's Brownies" and "Bangor Brownies" in *Lowney's Cook Book,* published by the chocolate manufacturer, Walter M. Lowney Company. This started the idea that chocolate brownies had arisen in Bangor, Maine, which has been sustained by Maine food writer Mildred Brown "Brownie" Schrumpf, born in Bangor in 1903. However, the earliest published Bangor "Chocolate Brownies" recipe, contributed by Marion Oliver to the 1912 *Girl's Welfare Cook Book*, collated by Mabel Freese Dennett, is identical to the 1907 "Lowney's Brownies." Until people began using smaller pans, brownies were only ⅜ inch thick.

In Bangor and elsewhere in New England, most peoples' first brownies seem to have been "Lowney's Brownies." Want to try some?

Yield: About 30 squares

½ cup butter (1 stick), plus some to grease pan

1 cup sugar

2 squares [2 ounces] Lowney's premium [unsweetened] chocolate

2 eggs

½ cup nut meats

½ cup flour

¼ teaspoon salt

Equipment: Pastry blender, baking sheet or 9-by-13-inch cake pan, spatula, wipe rack.

1. Remove butter and eggs from refrigerator 1 hour before starting

2. Melt the chocolate in small pan in a bowl of hot tap water. Preheat oven to 350 degrees.

3. Cream butter and sugar. Mix flour and nuts.

4. Beat the eggs and stir into the butter-sugar mixture.

5. Stir in the melted chocolate and other ingredients to make a stiff batter.

6. Grease the baking sheet or pan.

7. Spread out the batter on the baking sheet or pan to make a square 8–9 inches on a side. Batter will spread almost double.

8. Bake 15 minutes, or until dry on top and almost firm. This makes fudgy brownies. Twenty minutes makes them chewier.

9. Cut into 2-inch squares as soon as they come out of the oven. Cool on wire rack.

BRAN MUFFINS (1912)

By 1912, muffins were muffins, but most were corn or blueberry or "Graham Gems" made from whole wheat flour. It took Fannie Farmer, usually a promoter of white-sauce food, to record a muffin using bran in her 1912 *A New Book of Cookery*. These are relatively heavy muffins, like Graham gems. Later bran muffins were promoted by the Kellogg's cereal company using All-Bran, introduced in 1919. Kellogg added the raisins. All Miss Farmer's measurements are level cups and teaspoons.

Yield: About 18 muffins

1 cup flour

2 cups bran

1 teaspoon [baking] soda

1 teaspoon salt

1¼ cups whole milk

½ cup molasses

1 [large] egg

Butter to grease tins

Equipment: Muffin pans or mini-muffin pans (Miss Farmer suggested "individual tins.")

1. Preheat oven to 350 degrees.

2. Beat egg until creamy and light.

3. Mix dry ingredients well.

4. Butter muffin tins or mini-muffin pans.

5. Quickly mix wet and dry ingredients.

6. Spoon to fill muffin tins ⅔ full, and bake about 20–25 minutes.

Serve hot or split and toasted with butter.

Toll-House Chocolate Crunch Cookies (1936)

It may surprise you that chocolate chip cookies were invented as recently as 1936 by Ruth Wakefield, or it may surprise you even more that such a recent date cannot be determined accurately. Mrs. Wakefield started The Toll House Inn in 1930, in a 1709 building in Whitman, Massachusetts. Sometime between 1930 and 1936 she added a cut-up Nestlé's semi-sweet chocolate bar to a batch of cookies, and learned that most of the chocolate did not melt in the baking process. What's interesting is that she did not immediately publish the recipe in her book, *Toll House Tried and True Recipes*, but apparently had it published in a newspaper. Nestlé began marketing "Semi-Sweet Chocolate Morsels" in 1939 with the recipe. When their contract with Mrs. Wakefield ran out in 1979, they simplified the recipe.

Yield: 100 2-inch cookies

1 cup butter

¾ cup brown sugar

¾ cup sugar

2 eggs

1 teaspoon baking soda

2½ cups flour

1 teaspoon salt

1 cup chopped nuts

1 pound bar "Nestles yellow label chocolate, semi sweet" (or one pound chocolate chips)

1 teaspoon vanilla

Solid shortening to grease cookie sheets

Equipment: Pastry blender, food processor, hand mixer or standing mixer, 2 baking sheets, oven thermometer (optional), spatula, plates for cooling cookies

1. Remove butter from refrigerator to soften 1 hour before starting.

2. If using whole chocolate bar, cut into pieces the size of a pea.

3. Beat whole eggs until light and creamy.

4. Cream together butter and both kinds of sugar, using food processor, pastry blender, or either kind of mixer.

5. Dissolve baking soda in a teaspoon of hot water, and mix into butter-sugar mixture.

6. Beat eggs into butter-sugar mixture.

7. Sift flour with salt. The cookies will be flatter and crisper if you sift the flour before measuring.

8. Work flour into butter-sugar-egg mixture. Don't beat too much.

9. Mix in chocolate, nuts, and vanilla.

10. Grease baking sheets.

11. Preheat oven to 375 degrees.

12. Drop half teaspoonfuls on the baking sheets to make 2-inch cookies. (Like bagels and muffins, chocolate chip cookies have gotten much bigger over the years.)

13. Bake 10–12 minutes.

14. Remove from baking sheets with a spatula to cool on dinner plates. Don't put them into a cookie jar until they are quite cold, or they won't be the crispy cookies Mrs. Wakefield invented.

Serve with milk.

35

TRAINS, CARS, AND TRAILERS (1882–1939)

Americans have always moved around a lot, and eventually developed special ways of eating on trips. Railroads initially offered stops for questionable meals in small towns, but by the late nineteenth century they were beginning to compete for chain restaurants like the Harvey Houses. For the wealthier travelers, the Pullman company began offering cooked meals in dining cars. Some lines became famous for high quality meals. This also provided job opportunities for African American chefs as well as waiters and porters. Automobile trips as early as the 1920s were planned around roadhouse restaurants, and with the national highway system of the 1930s came national chains such as Howard Johnson's and Kentucky Fried Chicken.

The rise of the automobile began a new kind of recreation in the 1920s and 1930s, in which families went for excursions in the country. Recipes began to appear for automobile picnics, and the better country inns and restaurants began to cater to automobile tourists. There was a revived interest in regional cooking, and even chains like Howard Johnson's developed a menu of New England specialties and served clam chowder everywhere. (The automobile

sparked similar revivals of regional cuisines in France and England.)

The Great Depression of the 1930s forced great migrations, from the midwest and southwest to California, and from the rural south to northern cities. Much of the nation changed from the large midday meal to a smaller lunch at the workplace or school, with the larger dinner or supper in the evening.

BOSTON BROWN BREAD (1882)

The first dining cars on railroads appeared during and just after the Civil War. They took on food at stops and reheated it for passengers to eat at table. The first real dining cars with cooking facilities were developed by the Pullman Sleeping Car Company in 1867. The menu consisted mostly of steaks, chops, oysters, omelets, and cold meats—things easily cooked to order on a small stove, and based on foodstuffs that were themselves shipped everywhere by rail. By 1882, a menu reproduced in *Dining by Rail* by James Porterfield, shows the addition of broiled dishes and a variety of breads, some baked on board. The menu also includes Boston Brown Bread, a sweetened steamed version of the early American

Figure 28 Railroad chefs at work in 1937. *Source: © Bettmann/CORBIS.*

corn-rye-wheat breads that had become popular for sandwiches. Since the bread is steamed, it could be made on a back burner, with almost no attention. Our recipe comes from the 1911 *Good Things to Eat as Suggested by Rufus*, by Rufus Estes. Mr. Estes was born a slave but had gone to work as a Pullman cook in 1883. He rose to prominence and cooked for a number of celebrity travelers, and then for ten years in private railroad cars. If you can find coarse rye meal in a health food store, it works better than rye flour. Estes's suggestion for a makeshift mold was "a five pound lard pail."

Yield: Serves 20 or more

1 cup cornmeal

1 cup rye meal

1 cup whole wheat flour

¾ cup molasses

1¾ cups whole milk

½ teaspoon baking soda

Butter to grease cans

Equipment: 1 2-pound metal coffee can, or 2 1-pound coffee cans, or 3 12-ounce cans, or 4 28-ounce tomato cans; aluminum foil; trivet or steaming insert for pot; pressure cooker (optional); unwaxed dental floss (optional); soup pot with lid

1. Dissolve baking soda "in a little warm water." Clean all traces of coffee out of the can(s), being careful not to cut your hand on the edge.

2. Stir the other dry ingredients together, then mix in the milk and molasses.

3. Butter the coffee can(s), being careful not to cut your hand on the edges.

4. Now stir the baking soda into the batter thoroughly, and pour the batter into the can(s). It (they) should be no more than ¾ full.

5. Set up the soup pot as a steamer with a steamer insert or a metal trivet, so there is water under the coffee cans.

6. Cover the can(s) tightly with the plastic lid(s), or with a double layer of aluminum foil. Put the cans in the steamer.

7. Add water to the steamer so that it goes halfway up the sides of the can(s).

8. Bring to a boil, cover the pot, and reduce heat so that the bread steams for 3½ hours (2-pound can). Steam 3 hours for the smaller cans. If using pressure cooker, cook small cans 20–25 minutes at high pressure, then turn off heat and let pressure go down naturally for another 15 minutes.

9. Check to make sure water does not boil away. If you need more water, bring it to a boil in a teakettle, and add boiling water.

10. Remove cans from the water bath when bread is done, and let it cool.

11. The easiest way to get the bread out of the cans is to open the bottoms with a can opener and push it out.

12. To slice it neatly, you can use unwaxed, unflavored dental floss. Take a length and wrap the ends around your index fingers as though you were going to floss. Hold the floss tight, and press it through the cylinder to cut. Another way is to wrap the floss around the bread, and pull it tight to cut.

Serve on a moving train in a basket with hot rolls, cornbread, French bread, and "dry dipped, cream toast."

FINNAN HADDIE, DEARBORN (1899)

Early railroads had periodic stops to take on water and coal, during which the passengers could rush to street vendors or makeshift restaurants in the station for food. Fred Harvey owned three such restaurants in the mid-1870s, then made a deal with the Atchison, Topeka and Santa Fe Railroad to operate railroad-owned eating houses. As their routes expanded, and other railroads opted in, "Harvey Houses" became known across the west for efficiency and reliability. Harvey insisted on a system that grew into the factory-like organization of today's fast-food chains. From 1883 Harvey recruited waitresses through Eastern newspapers, and provided dormitories with a 10 P.M. curfew. There was a one-year contract, after which many of the waitresses married and were replaced. The food was not very different from dining car food, but the larger facilities made for more roasted meats and baked goods. Harvey Houses reached Chicago in 1899. Although no early recipes survive, this one may have come from a Santa Fe Railroad magazine of 1913 and is consistent with how this old Scottish-American dish was made at the turn of the twentieth century. The recipe is from *The Harvey House Cookbook* by George H. Foster and Peter C. Weiglin.

Yield: Serves 2

1 pound finnan haddie (smoked cod or haddock fillet)

1½ cups whole milk

2 medium potatoes

2 tablespoons butter

1 cup cream

Paprika and parsley

Equipment: 2 shallow individual casserole dishes with cover or ovenproof bowls, pastry brush, cloth napkin

1. Boil potatoes 20 minutes in their skins.

2. Melt the butter in a microwave or small saucepan.

3. Preheat oven to 350 degrees.

4. Simmer fish in milk for 10 minutes. (Don't boil hard or the fish will be tough.)

5. Drain fish and divide between the two casserole dishes.

6. Run cold water over the potatoes and rub off the skins.

7. Slice the potatoes thickly, and place them at one end of each dish.

8. Brush the butter over potatoes, and sprinkle on a little salt.

9. Pour cream carefully in each dish.

10. Sprinkle with paprika.

11. Bake 15 minutes.

12. Mince parsley, and sprinkle on before serving.

Serve hot and warn the customer that the dish is hot as you remove the cover carefully with a folded napkin.

GREAT BIG BAKED POTATO (1909)

Railroad dining cars often promoted agricultural products of the region outside the windows, in part because the railroad was trying to develop more freight business. This was how the Great Northern Railroad introduced oversized baked potatoes on the "North Coast Limited" to build up a market for Yakima Valley russet potatoes, which had been coming in at a size that resisted conventional recipes. The story and the recipe are from James Porterfield's 1993 *Dining by Rail*. I have added the step of rubbing in oil.

Yield: Serves 1 but can be multiplied

2-pound russet (rough skinned) baking potato

Oil to rub potato

Large pat of butter

Equipment: Ice pick or wood or metal skewer, cake pan (optional), oven mitts, cutting board, vegetable brush

1. Preheat oven to 350 degrees. Scrub potato thoroughly.

2. Pierce each end deeply with ice pick or skewer.

3. Rub potato with cooking oil (this keeps in moisture and helps it cook more rapidly).

4. Place potato on wire oven rack in the center and higher part of the oven. "In spring and summer it is recommended you place a pan of water in the oven with the potato to compensate for the loss of natural moisture that occurs during storage in this warmer time of the year." Bake spring and fall potatoes 1½ hours, fall and winter potatoes 2 hours.

5. Turn potato over one-quarter turn every 15 minutes.

6. Remove potato from oven with oven mitts and roll it gently against the board to loosen the skin.

7. Cut open end to end "on the top (flat side)."

8. "Fluff potato pulp with a fork."

"Serve steaming hot with a large pat of butter in the center."

PENNSYLVANIA CLUB SANDWICH (1910S)

The three-decker sandwich was developed in men's social clubs in the 1890s, but quickly took to the rails as an elegant looking and filling cold meal that could be quickly assembled. This recipe is from the 1965 *Dinner in the Diner; Great Railroad Recipes of All Time*, by Will C. Hollister and was probably taken from the Pennsylvania Railroad's cooking manual. The level of detail is typical of railroad cooking. Notice that the toast doesn't get soggy because it never touches mayonnaise or bacon or chicken, just dry lettuce. The usual tomato is held out of the sandwich for the same reason.

Yield: Serves 1

1 roaster chicken breast, or sliced chicken breast

3 slices white bread

3 slices bacon

4 inner leaves romaine lettuce

2 pickle chips

1 branch parsley

2 slices ripe tomato

Equipment: Instant-read meat thermometer (optional), paper towels, long wooden toothpicks

1. The railroad's recipe calls for "sliced breast of chicken from 4 lb. chicken." This was probably part of a whole chicken poached in water to cover (to an internal temperature of 170 degrees), with the rest of the chicken going into chicken salad or chicken a la king, and the water reduced for soup stock. The sliced chicken breast we buy in the supermarket tends to cut too thin, and dries out, but will work in the recipe.

2. Railroad bacon was broiled, or cooked on a griddle with a metal weight on top to keep it flat. For this sandwich, it should be about ¾ cooked, so the meat isn't crispy but some of the fat is.

3. Make toast from the white bread. Wash the lettuce leaves and dry carefully with paper towels.

4. "Spread a lettuce leaf with mayonnaise, lay three slices of broiled bacon on the lettuce, cover with another lettuce leaf, and place on slice of toast."

5. "Put the second piece of toast on top and cover with another lettuce leaf spread with mayonnaise."

6. "Next put the slices of white meat of chicken on the lettuce and cover with the last leaf of lettuce and then the third slice of toast."

7. You should have no mayonnaise touching toast, from the bottom: toast, lettuce, mayonnaise, bacon, lettuce, toast, lettuce, mayonnaise, chicken, lettuce, toast.

8. "Cut in four triangular sections [corner-to-corner cuts], each section to be pierced with a wooden toothpick to hold it together."

9. "Garnish with a leaf of lettuce in the center of the dinner plate; place the slices of tomato and pickle chips on top of the lettuce."

10. Arrange the four triangular shaped sections in stand-up position [i.e., standing on their long sides] around the tomato slices.

Serve wearing a white jacket and black bow-tie.

GOLD MEDAL CRANBERRY ROLY POLY (1920s)

This recipe is typical of those suggested for automobile-based picnics in the early days of recreational motoring. It is one of a group of recipe cards entitled "Motor Lunches" issued by the Washburn Crosby Company of Minnesota, probably around 1927, but before 1928, when Washburn Crosby was merged into General Mills. The cranberry roll could be assembled at home and steamed on a portable stove or campfire.

Figure 29 Motor lunch recipe cards from the 1920s. *Source: Author's collection.*

Yield: Serves 10

"2 cups GOLD MEDAL Flour" plus a little more for rolling and sauce.

4 teaspoons baking powder

2 tablespoons butter

¾ cup whole milk

4 cups cranberries

2½ cups sugar

Equipment: Rolling pin and wooden board, slotted spoon, steamer pot or steaming tray for soup pot

1. Stew cranberries, sugar, and 1 cup of water until cranberries have all burst and formed a sauce.

2. Combine flour baking powder, ½ teaspoon of salt, butter, and milk into a biscuit dough.

3. Flour board and rolling pin.

4. Roll out biscuit dough from the middle to the sides to make a ¾-inch rectangle.

5. Using a slotted spoon, spread ¾ of the cranberries (and as little of the juice as possible) on the dough, leaving an inch margin on all sides. Reserve about 1 cup of cranberries and 1 cup of juice for the sauce.

6. Roll up the dough, and tuck in the ends to make a neat log.

7. Bring an inch or more of water to a boil in a soup pot or steamer.

8. Put the roll on the steamer. (You can improvise a steaming set-up with 3 clean rocks and an ovenproof plate.)

9. Cover tightly and steam ½ hour.

10. Make a sauce by adding one table-spoon of "GOLD MEDAL Flour" to the leftover cranberries, stirring well, and cooking until thickened.

Serve sliced with sauce on top.

ORANGE REFRIGERATOR COOKIES (1937)

These easy cookies come from *Meals on Wheels; A Cook Book for Trailers and Kitch-enettes*, a paperback cookbook by Lou Mill-son and Olive Hoover. The recipe reflects at least four trends: (1) the national experi-ment with mobile homes both for vacation-ing, and as a lifestyle for the families of construction workers and engineers who had to move often to follow job opportunities; (2) the increasing availability of electricity in rural areas and the popularity of electric refrigerators; (3) the popularity of quickly as-sembled snacks and desserts as more women went to work; and (4) an increased use of citrus fruit in recipes as Florida and Califor-nia became leading agricultural producers (and trailer vacation destinations).

Although much of this cookbook de-pends on canned foods, trailer cooks were urged to seek "Fresh food on every roadside stand," since "Some of the same spirit of ad-venture that prompted the pioneer home-maker to feed her family well as she swayed across the continent in her covered wagon may still be required of today's trailer home-maker." As with most "refrigerator cookies," you can mix the dough ahead, keep it in the refrigerator, slice off as many cookies to bake as you want, and store the rest for several more days until you want more.

Yield: Approximately 40 cookies

½ cup butter

1 cup sugar

1 egg

¼ teaspoon salt

½ teaspoon baking soda

½ teaspoon baking powder

1 orange

2½ cups flour

Equipment: "1 small cooking sheet, 1 biscuit cutter, 1 cup flour sifter," and, if you are not avoiding clutter in a trailer: a juicer, strainer, lemon zester or grater, pastry blender or large fork, or a food processor, plastic wrap or "tin foil"

1. Take out butter an hour before start-ing so that it can soften.

2. Using a pastry blender or large fork or a food processor (or your fingers if you have a grandmother who knows how), blend together butter and sugar.

3. Beat the egg until creamy and light in a small cup, then work into the butter-sugar mixture.

4. Using the zester or grater, take the peel off the orange, and add it to the mixture.

5. Squeeze 2 tablespoons of orange juice into the mixture (through a strainer to catch seeds).

6. Sift the dry ingredients together, and stir into the mixture.

7. Chill the dough in a refrigerator until stiff, then work into a roll 2 inches in diameter. (You can wrap this roll in plastic wrap or aluminum foil and refrigerate for up to one week.)

8. Preheat oven to 400 degrees.

9. Slice dough into thin wafers and arrange on the ungreased cookie sheet.

10. Bake "for eight to ten minutes, or until a light golden brown."

11. Remove from cookie sheet as soon as done and cool on a plate.

12. Rewrap surplus dough in plastic wrap or aluminum foil and refrigerate

until needed. Baked cookies may be kept in an airtight tin.

Serve with milk.

SCRAMBLED EGGS (1939)

Duncan Hines, a former salesman, began issuing national guidebooks to hotels and restaurants in the 1930s. In his 1939 *Adventures in Good Cooking*, he collected recipes from the roadside restaurants and tourist attractions that were thriving on customers who arrived by car. Slow-cooking and plenty of fresh butter and cream are the key to these notable eggs from the McDonald Tea Room in Gallatin, Missouri. As Duncan Hines wrote in his guidebook, "This is a very small town about 70 miles from St. Joe—79 from Kansas City, around 200 from St. Louis and Omaha, but it is from there and other distant places that hundreds of people come to enjoy their very unusual food."

Yield: Serves 3

2 tablespoons butter

6 tablespoons cream

6 large eggs

Equipment: Double boiler

1. Heat water to boiling in the bottom of the double boiler.
2. Put in the top of the double boiler, and melt the butter.
3. Stir in the cream.
4. Break each egg into a cup, remove any bits of shell with a broken shell, and slide into the top of the double boiler.
5. When the eggs become hot, "start breaking them up."
6. Add salt and pepper and let the eggs cook to the "the consistency you like—either soft of hard scrambled."

Serve with buttered toast, breakfast meats, and perhaps hashed and browned potatoes.

36

LABOR VERSUS CAPITAL (1892–1983)

The first European colonists brought indentured servants with them, and a class of wage workers began to form in Colonial times in industries that supported shipping and trade. Some labor organizations began to form before the Civil War, and there were significant actions in the depression of the 1870s and thereafter. Although groups of working women were organized in all periods of American history, there are few printed recipes associated with the labor movement, perhaps because recipes are made at home, and organized labor has generally focused on the workplace. This chapter gathers a few recipes published as union recipes, touches upon the labor history of the steel industry, and notes the tricky role of ethnicity in published recipes from the families of two early union members who won election to Congress and also served as secretaries of labor.

Since industrial and mine workers often were immigrants over much of U.S. history, their identifiable cooking was often ethnic cooking. To reconstruct the foods of workers in particular industries and times, see *The American Ethnic Cookbook for Students*. This method was used in the 1993 book, *Out of This Kitchen; a History of the Ethnic Groups and Their Foods in the Steel Valley*, edited by Dan Karaczun.

This chapter also includes a recipe from the National Cash Register company cafeteria, part of a scheme of labor management cooperation called "welfare work" in the last years of the nineteenth century. That was also a peak period of the 160-year-old Women's Exchange (see Chapter 37) movement, which provided an outlet for the craft and food production of individual women working at home. A recipe submitted by a union cook to a Suffrage cookbook illustrates an alliance of those two movements.

OLD-FASHIONED POTATO SOUP (1892)

The 1892 Homestead Steel Strike lasted 143 days and set a tone of bitter relations between industrial workers and employers for more than forty years to come. Andrew Carnegie had built the Homestead Works near Pittsburgh as a fortified mini-city with an eye to resisting union demands. Nevertheless, the union fought an armed battle to defeat three hundred hired security guards (four guards and seven workers were killed) and stayed out of work almost five months.

Eighty-five hundred National Guard troops were called up to recapture the mills and re-open production. In the end, the unions lost, and workers accepted lower wages and longer hours. The steel industry was not again unionized in Pennsylvania until the late 1930s.

By 1907, more than half the steelworkers in Pittsburgh were Slovak-American immigrants. At the time of the Homestead Strike they were recent hires with little accumulated money and were among the first group of strikers to give up and reapply for their jobs after 143 days on strike. This recipe was submitted by Mary Kundravi to the 1993 *Out of This Kitchen; a History of the Ethnic Groups and Their Foods in the Steel Valley,* edited by Dan Karaczun, a former steel worker. But the same recipe might well have been used by union steelworkers and their families in hard times before or during the 1892 strike. The only ingredients the strikers would not have used was margarine, which was not widely available. Potatoes had been a cheap food in Europe and were a welcome meal-stretcher in the United States. The flavoring methods are typical of many ways of making soups without meat stocks in central Europe.

Yield: Serves as many as necessary with more water added

5–6 medium or large potatoes

1 tablespoon caraway seeds

1 stick margarine (or butter for 1890s reconstruction)

Equipment: Large soup pot and heavy skillet or saucepan

1. Peel and quarter potatoes.
2. Put potatoes and caraway seeds in soup pot. Add water to cover (or more in hard times) and bring to a boil.
3. Reduce heat to a simmer. Cook until a fork goes into a potato easily.
4. In heavy skillet, heat margarine or butter until it melts and then browns. Do not let it burn.
5. When potatoes are done, add browned margarine or butter to soup. Add 2 teaspoons salt, and taste to see if you need more.

Serve by itself as a weeknight supper.

GERMAN HOLIDAY BREAD (1894)

Although no written recipes are known from the actual strike period, this one for an Americanized *stollen* appeared in the January 29, 1894, issue of the *Homestead Local News*, a paper read by English-speaking steelworkers. (It is reprinted in *Out of This Kitchen.*) German-Americans were a large ethnic group among the workers, but a few German Americans had become executives in the steel industry, including Henry Clay Frick, Carnegie's manager at the time of the strike. This recipe, then, might have been read as a post-Christmas appeal for peace in the community, and for social acceptance of German Americans as they were being replaced by newer immigrants in the steel mills. (For ethnic foods enjoyed by later groups of steelworkers, see *The American Ethnic Cookbook for Students.*) The recipe is somewhat like **Bridget's Bread Cake**, so I have taken a bread recipe from *Mrs. Rorer's Philadelphia Cook Book* because Mrs. Rorer's recipes were sometimes reprinted in the *Homestead Local News*, and some details from modern recipes for stollen. You can also use frozen bread dough.

In the evening set a sponge as usual for bread, in quantity enough for three loaves. In the morning, when fully risen, add one pound of brown sugar, one pint of dried apples or pears, minced fine, one pint of broken hickory or walnut meats, three tablespoonfuls of caraway and one of coriander seeds. Mix thoroughly, mold into loaves and bake when light. Wrap each loaf in a towel and put in a cool place. It will keep for several weeks.

NOTE: RECIPE TAKES TWO DAYS.

Yield: 4–6 loaves, serves 25

12 cups flour

4 cups whole milk

1 tablespoon butter

1 tablespoon dry yeast

1 pound brown sugar

2 cups dried apples or pears

2 cups broken walnut meats

3 tablespoons caraway seeds

1 tablespoon coriander seeds

Shortening to grease baking sheets

Equipment: 2 baking sheets, large mixing bowl, kitchen towel, wooden board for kneading

1. Melt butter and combine with milk, yeast, and 1½ teaspoons salt in the large mixing bowl.

2. Stir in enough of the flour to make a thick batter. There should be room in the bowl for the batter to bubble up and expand without overflowing. Cover and leave overnight in a warm place.

3. The next day, grease baking sheets and flour board.

4. Stir down batter to release large air bubbles. Stir in remaining ingredients and as much of the rest of the flour as will make a dough.

5. Turn the dough out onto the board. Remove rings, flour your hands, and knead it together, adding as much flour as you need to keep it from sticking. (If you don't know how to knead, see Appendix I of *The American Ethnic Cookbook for Students*.) You may

need to work with half the dough at one time.

6. Knead, adding flour, until the dough is smooth and elastic and no longer sticks to your hands or the board.

7. Divide dough into 4 to 6 pieces.

8. Pat each piece into an oval flatbread about 7 inches wide and 10 inches long.

9. Fold over the long way, and press the edges together a few times so that the bread looks like a crude, long turnover, but won't open up.

10. Place breads on baking sheets, cover with kitchen towel, and let rise until almost doubled in bulk. This may take an hour or two.

11. Preheat an oven to 350 degrees.

12. When breads are fully risen, put in oven and bake for 30 minutes.

13. Check for doneness by picking up brownest loaf and tapping bottom. If it sounds hollow at the thickest part, it is done. If you have made only 4 loaves, and they are larger, baking will take longer, and you will have to keep checking.

Serve as dessert or coffeecake, or tuck a slice into a lunch bucket for school or work.

COCONUT MACAROONS (1903)

In the atmosphere of widespread industrial accidents and labor strife of the late nineteenth century, some employers tried to improve working conditions. John H. Patterson of the National Cash Register Company, in Dayton, Ohio, began in 1894 to provide coffee for three hundred female assemblers to go with cold lunches they brought from home. He added soup in 1895 and dining rooms the next year. These coconut cookies were a feature of the dining rooms after a men's dining room opened in

Figure 30 Kitchen workers below decks on a luxury liner. *Source:* The Boston Cooking-School Magazine, *Vol. 8, No. 10, May 1904.*

1903. All the dining rooms had instructive mottoes hung from the ceilings. Patterson also shortened the women's workday to just under nine hours and gave them a fifteen-minute break for calisthenics in the afternoon. He explained these reforms as both moral acts and sound investments in productivity.

Patterson called his scheme "Welfare Work," and by 1905, about two hundred other companies had taken up various welfare programs in their factories or surrounding communities. Welfare work did not spread to most of American workplaces, nor did it end all labor strife even in Dayton, but it did provide some positive examples for labor reformers of the 1930s. The story and recipe are from *Delicious*

Recipes & Food for Thought from the NCR Archive, edited by Curt Dalton and published by him in 2000.

Yield: About 90 cookies

> 1 cup egg whites (from 8–10 eggs)
>
> 2 cups sugar
>
> 5 cups granulated coconut (12 ounces bagged or one pound canned)
>
> ½ teaspoon vanilla

Equipment: Standing mixer, handheld mixer, egg beater or wire whisk, parchment paper, 2 baking sheets, tablespoons

1. "Beat egg whites until stiff."

2. Add sugar slowly.

3. With beater in hand, or using wire whisk, "fold" in coconut, by stirring it gently into the mounds of egg white.

4. Cut parchment paper to fit baking sheets. (Baked-on macaroons are the stickiest food known to kitchen science.)

5. Drop by tablespoons into rounded or conical shapes. (Don't try to shape them because unbaked macaroons are the second stickiest food known to kitchen science.)

6. Bake at 325 degrees until "golden color" (15 minutes).

PEA SOUP (1909)

This is one of an interesting group of recipes donated to the *Washington Women's Cook Book*, published by the Washington [State] Equal Suffrage Association and compiled by Linda Deziah Jennings. (I am indebted to food historian Karen Hess for sending me these recipes from her copy of this rare book.) The author was Robert Carr, a member of Cook's Local 33 in Seattle, but a popular cook on sailing vessels over the previous five years. The open identification of the author as a union member and the inclusion of the chapter shows the growing strength of the labor movement in Seattle. Ten years later, Seattle shipyard workers called a general strike in which organized labor shut down all industry and commerce and ran the city for several days. Carr's recipe shows that the jobsite feeding of working men had not changed very much since Colonial "pease porridge." It may well have been served at the barricades of the general strike.

Yield: About 50 cups of soup

6 cups split peas

2 large carrots "or piece of turnip the same size"

2 tablespoons celery seed

2 tablespoons flour

2 tablespoons dripping [fat from roast meat, substitute lard or margarine]

"4 pound piece of half-cooked salt pork"

"or sufficient salt stock to cover" [see below]

1 teaspoon sugar

6 leaves of mint [1 tablespoon dried mint]

Equipment: 1 oversized soup pot, second soup pot (optional), large wire sieve

1. Melt dripping or substitute in one of the soup pots.

2. Stir in the flour and cook over medium heat for 4 or 5 minutes to "brown slightly."

3. Add the celery seed and stir in a little water to thin the flour mixture.

4. Gradually stir in 8 quarts of water and bring to a boil.

5. Peel and chop carrots or turnip.

6. Add peas, carrots, mint and sugar, and simmer 2 hours with pan loosely covered.

7. If using salt pork, simmer in water to cover $\frac{1}{2}$ hour. (You can omit this step if you have salt stock from cooking a corned beef or boiled ham.)

8. After the pea soup has simmered 2 hours, add the pork or its cooking water, or the salt stock, and simmer another half hour.

9. "Rub all [except salt pork] through a wire sieve and warm up again before serving."

SCOTCH SCONES (1913)

This was submitted by Miss Agnes Hart Wilson to the 1913 *Economy Administration Cook Book*, edited by Susie Root Rhodes and Grace Porter Hopkins. Miss Wilson was the daughter of and Washington hostess for William B. Williams, a founder of the United Mine Workers, Pennsylvania congressman, and the first secretary of labor, under President Woodrow Wilson (no relation). Miss Wilson herself was a proud member of the Stenographers and Bookkeeper's Union and had worked as a secretary for the mineworkers. Both her parents were born in Scotland. Since early labor solidarity was along ethnic lines, but union organizers were stigmatized as foreign immigrants, the Wilsons are at pains to present themselves as ethnic, and yet members of an acceptable British Isles immigrant group. You can see how this brand of ethnic image politics continued to develop in the recipe for **Welsh Fruit Cake** below. The American-born Miss Wilson has turned these traditionally wedge-shaped breads into round biscuits, by the way.

Yield: Serves about 20

8 cups flour

pinch salt

3 cups sour milk (or whole milk with $\frac{1}{2}$ teaspoon cream of tartar)

1 teaspoon baking soda

Butter for griddle

Equipment: Griddle or cast-iron frying pan, biscuit cutter or cookie cutter, rolling pin and board, waxed paper

1. Sift a pinch of salt into the flour in a large mixing bowl.

2. Add baking soda and cream of tartar (if necessary) to milk, and stir into the flour to make a soft dough.

3. Flour rolling pin and board, and roll dough from the center ½ inch thick.

4. Cut into rounds, and arrange on waxed paper.

5. Heat up the griddle and spread on a little butter. Reduce heat to low-medium. Put on the scones and brown slowly on both sides, perhaps 5–7 minutes.

"Serve hot with butter."

WELSH FRUIT CAKE (1927)

Continuing in the path of the Wilsons, the wife of 1920s Secretary of Labor James J. Davis submitted this dish to *The Congressional Club Cook Book* published in 1927. What's Welsh (actually Welsh Methodist) about the fruitcake is the absence of liquor, which suited the Prohibition era. This is less like a heavy fruitcake and more like the raisin bread called "bara brith" in Wales. Mrs. Davis has Americanized the cake somewhat by adding more sugar, and omitting a glaze of honey at the end.

Born in Wales, James Davis came to America at the age of eight and immediately (or in another story at the age of eleven) became a puddler's assistant in a steel mill. As labor secretary to three Republican presidents, Davis was instrumental in persuading the steel industry to give up the twelve-hour workday, but also in getting the support of organized labor to reduce im-migration from non-English speaking countries. This was supposed to increase wages, but also split labor unions on ethnic lines and did not avert a wave of strikes and unionization in the 1930s. Davis left the Hoover cabinet to become a Republican senator from Pennsylvania and was the author of the Davis-Bacon Act, which mandates "prevailing [union-scale] wage" levels on government construction jobs. This law also had ethnic overtones, as many construction unions excluded minority members; nonunion construction companies who hired minorities could not compete on price under Davis-Bacon.

Yield: Serves 24 slices

1 pound self-rising flour (or 4 cups sifted flour plus 2 tablespoons baking powder)

1 pound bread flour (or about 4 cups sifted) plus another cup or so for flouring board.

½ pound butter (two sticks), plus a little more to grease two cake pans

2 cakes compressed yeast (or 2 teaspoons powdered yeast)

1 tablespoon orange peel

1 tablespoon lemon peel

salt "to taste" (try 2 teaspoons)

spice "to taste" (start with a teaspoon of mixed cinnamon and cloves)

2 large eggs

1 pound currants

1 pound raisins

¾ pound brown sugar (about 3½ cups packed)

2 cups milk

Equipment: Pastry blender, large mixing bowl, lemon zester, 2 round cake pans or cookie sheets, wire cake taster, wire racks to cool cakes

1. Remove butter from refrigerator an hour before starting. Zest an orange

and a lemon to get a tablespoon of peel from each.

2. If using cake yeast, crumble into the flour and mix well. If using dry yeast, whisk into flour in a large bowl.

3. When butter is soft but not melting, blend into flour until the texture of fine sand

4. Measure in dry ingredients and stir well.

5. Break the eggs into a small bowl, beat well, and pour into the flour mixture, but don't mix yet.

6. Warm milk in pot or microwave, and stir into the eggs, adding flour until all the flour is part of a soft dough. You may need a little more or less milk than the 2 cups.

7. Let rise in a warm place for about 2 hours.

8. Flour board, and turn out dough onto the board.

9. Flour your hands and knead the dough until smooth and elastic. It will still be somewhat sticky.

10. Butter 2 round cake pans or 2 cookie sheets.

11. Divide the dough in half and pat each half into one of the cake pans. (You can also make free-form round loaves and set them on the cookie sheets.)

12. Cover dough with an inverted bowl or paper towels. Let rise half an hour. It doesn't have to "double in bulk" since the baking powder or self-rising flour will provide extra lift.

13. Preheat oven to 325 degrees.

14. Bake fruitcakes for an hour and a half, then test with a wire cake tester, or turn out of pans onto wire racks and test by tapping the bottom at the center (which will sound hollow when cake is done).

15. If necessary, put cakes back on the oven racks and cook another 15 to 30 minutes. Let cool on wire racks before slicing.

Serve slices with butter.

SPAGHETTI À LA PROGRESSIVE (1933)

This recipe was submitted by former Republican Congressman Fiorello La Guardia to the 1933 *Congressional Cook Book*. (For La Guardia's 1927 recipe, see **Chicken Cornmeal À La Farm Relief** in Chapter 42.) By the 1930s, La Guardia was mayor of New York, running as the nominee of the American Labor Party, a coalition of unions and progressive reformers unique to New York state. The American Labor Party fell apart around 1940 in political disputes among the leftist and liberal factions, but this kind of spaghetti dinner remained a mainstay of informal dinner parties in the labor movement, the Civil Rights movement, and the anti-Vietnam War movement well into the 1980s. La Guardia's original recipe specified "spaghetti made of American Durum wheat" because of the plight of American farmers in 1933. La Guardia does not mention what to do with the discarded bacon and onions.

Yield: Serves 4–6

1 pound spaghetti, not imported

1 slice fatty bacon "for each person to be served"

1 onion

1 28-ounce can whole tomatoes

2 tablespoons butter

¼ teaspoon paprika

½ small can tomato paste

¼ cup Parmesan cheese

Equipment: Heavy saucepan, large soup pot

1. In a heavy saucepan slowly cook bacon to render out grease.

2. Halve and peel onion. Cut into thick slices.

3. When all grease is out of bacon, remove the crisp slices and stir in the onions.

4. Cook onions until brown, then remove onions from grease as well.

5. Carefully add the canned tomatoes to the hot grease, stir well.

6. Add the butter. Season with salt and pepper and add the paprika. Bring to a boil, reduce heat and simmer 10 minutes.

7. Dissolve the tomato sauce in a little water, and add to the sauce. Simmer an additional 20 minutes.

8. In a large pot, bring half a pot of water to a boil.

9. Add 2 teaspoons salt and the spaghetti.

10. Boil spaghetti 12 minutes. Drain through colander and return to pot.

11. Add sauce to spaghetti and stir to blend well.

12. Sprinkle on Parmesan cheese.

Serve in bowls, followed by salad.

MEXICAN MILK CANDY (1972)

Influenced by the Civil Rights movement, the drive to unionize farm workers began among Filipino-American and Mexican-American pickers and reached national attention with the table-grape boycotts beginning in 1968. The United Farmworkers Organizing Committee put out *A Farmworkers Cookbook; Recipes from the People Who Bring Food to Your Table.* Among them was this simple caramelized milk sweet, handy to make on a migrant family's hotplate, perhaps using the empty can of evaporated milk as a measuring cup for the sugar. Like picking fruit, this recipe looks simple but requires an expert touch. If you are making

these for the first time, use the fudge test of 238 degrees on a candy thermometer.

This recipe derives from a traditional Mexican sweet spread made of boiled-down goat's milk called *cajeta*, because it used to be made up with fruits and nuts into little boxes (*cajas*) of fudgelike confection. (An early form of **Fudge** was called *panocha*, a Mexican Spanish term for raw sugar, and was probably influenced by *cajeta*.) This Mexican Milk Candy is dropped like cookies and resembles New Orleans Pralines (which may also have taken this form under the Spanish empire.)

CAUTION: HOT CANDY STICKS TO SKIN AND BURNS.

Yield: 16 praline-like cookies

1 8-ounce can evaporated milk

1 cup sugar

1 tablespoon butter or margarine, plus a little more to butter plate

$1/2$ cup pecans or walnuts (optional)

Equipment: Candy thermometer, saucepan, wooden spoon or flat whisk, plate or cookie sheet for dropping, teaspoon for dropping

1. Bring evaporated milk and sugar to a boil in the saucepan. Watch out that it does not boil over, because it can froth up quickly.

2. Reduce heat and continue boiling, stirring continuously, for a half hour, or until it turns caramel brown. The idea is to use medium heat and boil off the liquid quickly. You can lower the heat and stir every so often—still watching out for boil-ups—but it will take longer.

3. Butter plate or cookie sheet.

4. Test boiling candy periodically with candy thermometer. When it gets just under 238 degrees (at sea level), remove from heat, and stir in butter or margarine.

Figure 31 Soup kitchen for strikers in Seattle in 1937. *Seattle Post-Intelligencer Collection. Source: © Museum of History & Industry/CORBIS.*

5. Stir in nuts if using. Stir as it cools until considerably thickened.

6. Drop by teaspoonfuls onto plate or cookie sheet. You will find that the candy sticks to the teaspoon.

7. You can speed up hardening by putting plate or cookie sheet in a refrigerator.

Serve when cool and hardened.

DEPRESSION SOUP (1983)

This recipe comes from *Cooking on Extended Benefits; The Unemployed Cookbook*, published by the Mon Valley Food Bank [Monongahela], then running food distribution centers for seventeen hundred families from fourteen United Steel Workers of America Locals at three sites in Pennsylvania. The globalization of steel production and recession within the United States ended many jobs in the steel industry in the early 1980s. Despite the glum name of this soup, the book includes many comforting treats, and resourceful recipes for wild game and home canning. The recipe was submitted by Norma Swanger and Patty Sullinger and is big enough for two families, or to last one family two or three meals.

Yield: Serves 12

1½ pounds ground beef

½ cup macaroni

½ cup onion (from 1 small onion)

½ cup celery (from 2–3 stalks celery)

1 "large can" (28 ounces) tomatoes

Equipment: Large soup pot

1. Bring 3½ quarts of water to a boil.
2. "Drop ground beef into boiling water, bit by bit."
3. Halve, peel, and chop a small onion and add to soup.
4. Cut up 2 or 3 stalks of celery and add to soup.
5. Add tomatoes and 2 teaspoons of salt.
6. "Cook until vegetables are almost tender," (about 15 minutes).
7. Add macaroni and cook until it is done (10–12 minutes).

Serve as cheerfully as you can.

37

THE WOMEN'S EXCHANGE MOVEMENT (1895–1972)

Women's rights were a subject of debate from the first colonial settlements, as life on the frontier required women to perform in many roles regarded as male in Europe. After the Civil War, attention shifted toward legal rights, voting rights, and temperance. There was still debate over the issue of women's workplace rights, with radical suffragists like Susan B. Anthony actively supporting working women, while many others held to a vision of women remaining at home. (Rights in the workplace did not became a unifying issue for feminists until the 1970s.) The Women's Exchange movement began in Philadelphia in 1837 as a means for society women who had become poor to sell off their household treasures (still their only legal property in some places). The "Women's Depositories" and "Art Leagues" quickly evolved into a marketplace for needlework produced at home, again anonymously. Although keeping women from employment outside the home was a conservative program, finding them an independent cash income was a move toward their financial independence. By the 1870s, many of the exchanges were providing full-time careers for the store managers, and consignors were moving into the production of foodstuffs such as pickles, preserves, home-canned goods, and fancy cakes. Mrs. Robert E. Lee's kitchen notebook has a list of 1870s prices of foods at the Richmond, Virginia, exchange. By the 1890s, there were more than seventy Women's Exchanges, with more than fifteen thousand active consignors, and all the larger exchanges were running restaurants. The Cincinnati exchange sold picnic baskets and box lunches. Milwaukee had an active "tearoom." Baltimore had a room for businessmen to have club meetings as well as a tearoom for women's clubs.

The Boston group, the Women's Industrial and Educational Union, was founded by pioneer physician Dr. Harriet Clisby and such notable female writers as Louisa May Alcott (see her recipe in Chapter 20) and Julia Ward Howe, author of "Battle Hymn of the Republic." Boston had baked goods as early as 1878 and contracted to provide hot lunches in the Boston public schools from 1907 to 1944. For more information on the Women's Exchange movement, see *The Business of Charity 1837–1900*, by Kathleen Waters Sander (1998).

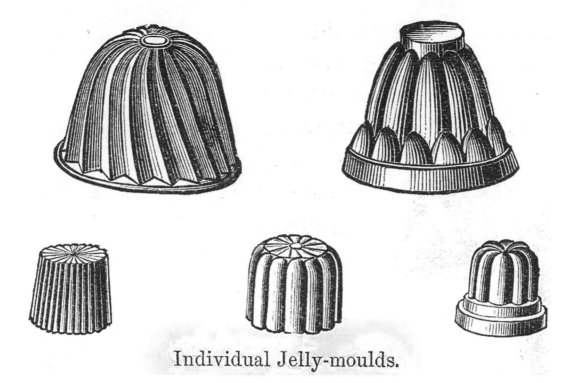

Individual Jelly-moulds.

Figure 32 Assorted jelly molds. *Source:* Miss Parloa's Kitchen Companion, *1887.*

PYRAMID JELLIES (1895)

The *Women's Exchange Cook Book* was written by Mrs. Minnie Palmer for the Chicago exchange in 1895. The United States was in a depression in 1895, and the book was probably intended to be sold as a fund-raiser, although it contains some instruction in basic and economical cooking. There are recipes for the kinds of preserves and pickles that could be sold at exchange "edible departments" and instructions for making vegetable dyes to make the jellies more attractive. Some dishes are clearly intended for an audience of middle-class women aspiring to entertain in the upper-class manner of the directors of the women's exchange. This recipe shows how to make a fancy dessert out of such jellies and would have been used proudly by women of means who could confide, if asked for the recipe, that they were doing good as well as saving time and money by purchasing the jellies at the women's exchange. I have suggested a recipe using the fruits and colors included in the book and the book's recipe for a whipped cream pie filling. The key to this dish is to remember that you are eating jelly, so it is very sweet. Use small glasses and make rounded cones about an inch and a half tall. You can save time by using aerosol whipped cream.

Mould various colored jellies, the more the better, in wine glasses pointed in shape. Warm a little of each enough to run, fill the glasses, and cool. Turn out on an ornamental plate, arrange prettily and heap whipped cream around the base. Serve one pyramid to each person in a sauce dish with a portion of cream. Lemon and orange jellies may be moulded and served in the same way. A dainty dish for a company tea. Takes the place of fruits.

Yield: 6 desserts

½ cup whipping cream

2 tablespoons sugar

Jars of three or more of the following jellies: apple, raspberry, blackberry, currant, grape, lemon.

Equipment: 6 or more 2-ounce liqueur glasses with tall but not recurved sides, whisk or handheld beater, small saucepan or microwave oven

1. Wash out liqueur glasses with hot water.

2. Melt some of the darkest-colored jelly in a sauce pan, or in the microwave oven in a microwave-safe dish.

3. Spoon in enough jelly to fill the glasses ⅓ full. Let it cool and harden a little before adding the next layer.

4. Melt some of the lightest-colored jelly.

5. Spoon in enough jelly to fill the glasses ⅔ full, making a middle layer.

6. Melt some of a jelly in a contrasting color.

7. Spoon in the jelly to fill the glasses near the rim.

8. Refrigerate so that the jellies harden again.

9. Whip cream with sugar in a metal bowl with whisk of handheld beater until stiff.

10. When ready to serve jellies, remove from refrigerator. Run a little warm (not hot) water around the outside of the glasses.

11. Invert each glass onto a dessert plate. The jelly cones should plop right out. If not, let them sit there for a while to warm up, and let gravity do the work.

Serve with whipped cream arranged around the cone.

CORN SALAD (1913)

This is the sort of canned relish that was commonly marketed through Women's Exchanges. While all poor women could not compete with Heinz, as many as sixteen to twenty thousand were employed in a given week making food to sell at women's exchanges, with many more engaged in needlework. The recipe is from the 1913 *Portland (Oregon) Women's Exchange Cookbook* and was submitted by Mrs. Henry B. Joy. The recipe can be reduced, or the excess frozen or—as the women would have done in Portland—canned for ten minutes in a hot water bath.

Yield: About 8 pint jars

24 ears fresh corn

1 medium-sized head cabbage

6 onions

3 large red peppers

2 bunches celery

½ cup salt

4 cups of sugar

2 quarts of vinegar

½ pound dried mustard

Equipment: Corn cutter (optional), nonreactive oversized pot or pots, canning jars and lids (optional)

1. Husk the corn and cut the kernels off the ears with a sharp knife or corn cutter.

2. Cut the cabbage into wedges, remove core, and shred by cutting thin slices across the wedges.

3. Halve, peel, and chop the onions.

4. Remove cores and seeds of peppers, and cut into dice.

5. Wash and chop celery, including leaves.

6. Combine all ingredients in large, nonreactive pots, and bring to a boil.

7. Reduce heat to a simmer and cook 1 hour.

8. If canning, spoon into hot, sterilized jars and process 15 minutes under boiling water.

CHICKEN HAMBURGERS (1910S)

In Detroit, the Women's Exchange was founded in 1891, with the usual needlework, prepared foods, and lunchroom, but it became an important caterer of society parties. These chicken hamburgers were served at a board meeting, and probably at catered events, as they would have been more difficult and expensive to make than beef hamburgers. The recipe is from the 1946 *Women's Exchange Recipes; Fifty Years of Good Cooking*, by Stella V. Hough, in collaboration with Kay Kopera. Miss Hough was the manager of the Detroit Women's Exchange from 1909 until it closed in 1942. I have set the date in the 1910s, because Miss Hough explains in the book that the Exchange recipes were typical of what she thought of as upper-class food of the 1890s "and several decades thereafter."

Yield: Serves 12

3–4 pound roaster chicken (or 2 pounds ground chicken)

½ pound fat pork (or ground pork)

½ pound veal (or ground veal)

¼ pound white bread

1½ cups heavy cream

1 small onion

4 large eggs

½ pound sliced mushrooms

1 tablespoon sherry (optional)

1 stick butter (for frying)

Equipment: Meat grinder or food processor, heavy frying pan, ovenproof platter

1. If using whole chicken, as the Detroit staff did, remove skin and breast meat, cut off legs and strip meat from bones, cut scallops of meat from back, and reserve frame for chicken soup. ("Clear Soup" was another Detroit Women's Exchange specialty.) Grind or process meat together, or mix ground meats well.

2. Soak bread in half a cup of the cream.

3. Halve, peel, and chop the onion.

4. Beat eggs lightly.

5. Mix eggs, onion, and soaked bread with meat. Season with salt and pepper. Miss Hough also suggested "a dash of meat sauce," but I don't know what she meant—possibly steak sauce, which would be very good.

6. Heat butter in heavy frying pan.

7. "Form [meat] into cakes, and fry in [half the] butter until brown."

8. Put browned cakes on the platter in a 350-degree oven to cook through.

9. To make sauce, sauté the mushrooms in the other half of the butter.

10. Add the rest of the cream and cook a few more minutes.

"Serve sauce over hamburger."

CUCUMBER SANDWICHES (1962)

The Memphis Women's Exchange was a comparative latecomer, organized as a crafts exchange by women of means who had organized community kitchens during the Great Depression. By their 1962 *Women's Exchange Cook Book*, the Memphis exchange had a crafts shop with the inevitable tearoom, featuring such delicate fare as cucumber sandwiches.

Yield: 3 to 4 dozen tiny sandwiches

1 loaf white bread

3 large-diameter cucumbers

3-ounce package cream cheese

1 tablespoon heavy cream

1 small onion

"Dash Tobasco"

½ teaspoon Worcestershire sauce

1 teaspoon lemon juice

1 bunch parsley

Equipment: Box grater, cucumber-caliber round cookie cutter or fluted biscuit cutter, food processor (optional), vegetable peeler

1. Mash (or use food processor to process) cream cheese with cream, Tobasco, Worcestershire sauce, and lemon juice.

2. Grate a teaspoon of the onion and work into cheese mixture.

3. Cut bread into cucumber-size rounds with biscuit cutter or cookie cutter, avoiding the crusts. (You can save the crusts and leftover scraps for bread crumbs or bread pudding.)

4. Peel cucumbers and cut into rounds about the size of the bread rounds. If you have unwaxed cucumbers you can wash them and cut the peel in patterns with a lemon zester. (You can save the ends and other parts for salads.)

5. Mince the parsley very fine.

6. "Spread [each bread round] with cheese, place cucumber slice on top, sprinkle lightly with chopped parsley."

Serve with shrimp mousse and lemon sponge pudding.

38

CAMPING IN THE TWENTIETH CENTURY (1906–1963)

As discussed in Chapter 22, Americans began recreational camping while other Americans were still camping out all the time. By the early twentieth century, most of the frontiers had closed, and camping became a nostalgic look back at "Indian lore" and "Woodcraft." The Boy Scouts of America was founded in 1910, combining the ideals of the British youth movement with Earnest Thompson Seton's American woodcraft. It was soon joined by Campfire Girls, Girl Scouts, Brownie Scouts, and Cub Scouts. Hunting and fishing camps were upper-class vacations at the beginning of the century, but became universal American pastimes in the 1950s. Family camping also grew throughout the twentieth century, with trailers, recreational vehicles, and SUVs gradually replacing snowshoes and canoes. The Civil War centennial and the nation's bicentennial stimulated reenactments, and reenacting became a weekend camping hobby for some families.

Conservation regulations now prohibit many aspects of the old woodcraft, and campfires may not be available everywhere, but the American urge to reexperience pioneering—if only with propane stoves and Gore-Tex sleeping bags—is ever stronger.

CORKSCREW BREAD (1906)

This is a Native American cooking technique, used by many tribes for cooking buffalo and deer meat in long strips. The Ojibway (Chippewa) adapted the technique for biscuit dough, possibly in collaboration with French fur traders. Stick bread may have moved into the mainstream culture via Ojibway fishing guides. The recipe is taken from *The Book of Camping and Woodcraft*, by Horace Kephart. This kind of dough was used for all kinds of biscuits, breads, and even doughnuts by early campers. For example, Earnest Thompson Seton's personal recipe for "sinkers" (camp doughnuts) used less baking powder and lard, but was otherwise identical.

NOTE: RECIPE REQUIRES ACTUAL CAMPFIRE.

Yield: Serves 20 or more, eventually

6 cups flour

3 "heaping teaspoonfuls" baking powder

1 heaping teaspoonful salt

4 heaping tablespoonfuls cold grease ("lard, cold pork fat, dripping, or bear's grease")

Butter for serving

Equipment: Hatchet, scout knife, four or more green hardwood saplings 2 feet long and 3 inches thick, or 2 broomstick-like lengths or both, campfire, large mixing pan, wooden spoon

1. Peel the bark from the thicker ⅔ of each stick, and sharpen the thinner end. (If using the broomstick method, peel the bark from the central 2 feet of each "broomstick.")

2. When fire is down to glowing smokeless embers, thrust thin end of sticks into the ground, leaning slightly toward the fire. Rotate sticks once or twice to heat them evenly.

3. Combine dry ingredients, then rub in grease "until there are no lumps left and no grease adhering to the bottom of pan. This is a little tedious, but don't shirk it."

4. Stir in a little less than two cups water to make a stiff dough.

5. "Work dough into a ribbon two inches wide."

6. Wind the dough in a spiral around the heated ends of the sticks, sealing it back to itself at each end so that it won't unroll as it bakes.

7. Thrust stick back into the ground near hot coals, and bake 12–15 minutes, turning stick occasionally so as to brown the bread evenly. You can bake several sticks at a time. "Bread for one man's meal can be quickly baked on a peeled stick as thick as a broomstick, holding over fire and turning."

Serve by removing bread from stick as soon as it is done and spreading with butter.

ROLLED OAT COOKIES (1918)

A very early book dedicated to scouts was *Camp Cookery; A Cookery and Equipment Handbook for Boy Scouts and Other Campers*, by Ava B. Milam, A. Grace Johnson, and Ruth McNary Smith, published in Portland, Oregon. These oatmeal cookies are designed to be cooked on a grill, over an open fire, but also work well at home.

Yield: About 42 2½ inch cookies

2 cups rolled oats

2 cups flour, plus some to flour board and rolling pin

⅔ cup sugar

1 teaspoon cinnamon

1 cup butter

1 teaspoon of baking soda

Equipment: Rolling pin and board (optional), empty condensed soup can (optional), skillet or griddle

1. Remove butter from any refrigeration one hour before starting. Heat up a cup of water.

2. Stir together oats, flour, sugar, and cinnamon.

3. Work in ¾ cup of the butter with fingers or a knife until the mixture is even and granular.

4. Dissolve the baking soda in ¾ cup hot water.

5. Stir the water into the mixture to form a dough.

6. Flour the board and rolling pin, and roll out dough to ¼ inch thick. Cut with a clean, empty soup can, and plop into a hot, greased pan, "or thin a little and drop from a spoon onto a greased pan."

7. Brown cookies on both sides over a low fire (or bake on greased cookie sheets at 350 degrees for 12 minutes). Re-grease pans as needed, although these cookies should have enough butter in them to cook in a well-seasoned

pan or griddle without much additional fat.

Serve with hot cocoa.

Fried Trout (1920)

This recipe was written up by Ernest Hemingway in article for the *Toronto Star*, "Camping Out: When You Camp Out, Do It Right," rediscovered and quantified by Craig Boreth for *The Hemingway Cookbook* (1998). The cornmeal is still used by Midwestern fishing guides, although a thicker coating of egg and cornflake crumbs has come to replace it.

> The proper way to cook is over coals. Have several cans of Crisco or Cotosuet or one of the vegetable shortenings along that are as good as lard and excellent for all kinds of shortening. Put the bacon in and when it is about half-cooked lay the trout in hot grease, dipping them in cornmeal first. Then put the bacon on top of the trout and it will baste them as it slowly cooks. . . . The trout are crisp outside and firm and pink inside and the bacon is well done but not too done.

CAUTION: HOT OIL USED.

Yield: Serves 1 or 2

4 whole trout

1 cup of Crisco or vegetable shortening

1 cup fine yellow cornmeal

8 slices bacon

Equipment: Cast-iron skillet or any heavy frying pan or soup pot, tongs or skimmer to handle frying trout, campfire (optional), paper towels or newspapers to drain fried trout.

1. If you have caught your own trout, gut them and remove the gills. You may remove the head, but the fish hold together better if you don't.

2. Cook bacon in skillet or soup pot over medium heat until about half done (not crisp).

3. Pour out cornmeal on a plate, or put into a paper bag.

4. Coat each trout with cornmeal by rolling on the plate or shaking lightly in the paper bag.

5. When bacon is half done, remove from skillet and add a cup of vegetable shortening.

6. When shortening is hot, carefully add trout. Don't splash the hot oil.

7. After a few minutes, tip the smallest fish to check for browning. When one side is browned (up to 5 minutes for large trout), turn each fish with tongs or spatula, again being careful not to splash the oil.

8. Put 2 strips of bacon on each trout.

9. Lower heat or move pan on campfire to reduce heat, and cook another 5–15 minutes, depending on thickness of fish. (You can test this by breaking into a thick part. If the fish flakes almost down to the bone, it is done.)

Serve on a camping trip with canned beans.

Slumgullion (1935)

Slumgullion has been the name for an American mixed stew associated with sailors, hobos, and army camps for more than one hundred years. The term may be related to salmagundi or Mulligan stew, which are similar mixtures. This rather precise recipe comes from the *Girl Scout Recipe Book*, compiled in 1935 by members of the Pocatello, Idaho, Council of Girl Scouts. The presence of cheese and absence of potatoes suggests that the contributor may have been thinking about Welsh Rabbit; the same chapter has a "Hobo Dish" of potatoes, onions, and canned corned beef that is closer to a typical slumgullion—if such a thing exists.

Yield: "Serves four to six."

4 slices bacon

1 onion

1 can tomatoes

¼ pound cheese

½ pound meat

8 slices bread

Equipment: Frying pan (cast iron preferred)

1. Halve, peel, and slice onion.

2. Fry bacon and sliced onion together.

3. Meanwhile cut meat into small pieces.

4. Being careful not to splash hot grease, add meat and tomatoes to frying pan. Cook 20 minutes.

5. "Season to taste." Cut cheese into small pieces and add to pan. "Let it melt."

6. Toast bread (in camp, use green sticks).

Serve on toasted bread.

HEAVENLY CRISP (ALSO KNOWN AS "S'MORES") (1940)

Originally published in *The Outdoor Book*, by the Campfire Girls (edited by Frances Loomis and Gladys Snyder) and picked up in the 1940 *Outdoor Cooking* by Cora, Rose, and Bob Brown, these treats are still popular and have not changed.

Yield: Serves 8, if they don't have "s'more"

8 bars of plain chocolate

16 graham crackers

16 marshmallows

Equipment: Open wood camp fire and green sticks to toast marshmallows

1. Whittle the bark off one end of a green wood stick.

2. Toast two marshmallows at a time until crisp and gooey, but do not let them catch fire.

3. Assemble a graham cracker and chocolate bar sandwich.

4. Remove top graham cracker, put marshmallows inside, and press down (removing stick). "The heat of the marshmallows between the halves of chocolate bar will melt the chocolate just enough, and the graham crackers on the outside are nice to hold on to, as well as tasty."

Serve after dark with ghost stories.

HAMBURGER A LA FOIL (1963)

The Boy Scouts didn't invent cooking in aluminum foil packages, but this staple of 1950s cookouts was codified for the next generation in *The Boy Scout Handbook*, sixth edition.

Yield: Serves 1, can be multiplied

¼ pound hamburger meat

1 large potato

1 medium carrot

Equipment: Aluminum foil, campfire, fireproof shovel or tongs

1. Let your campfire burn down to a solid bed of coals.

2. Cut off 3 to 4 feet of foil to make into a rectangular package 2 layers thick.

3. Form hamburger into a ¾-inch patty, put on foil.

4. Peel potato and "cut into strips as for French fries."

5. Scrape carrot and cut into sticks.

6. Arrange carrot sticks and sliced potatoes side by side around hamburger. The idea is to have 1 layer of food for even cooking.

7. Close aluminum foil package and fold over the ends to seal.

8. Rake some of the coal in the center to the sides. Place your foil package at the center and push the coals back over it.

9. Cook 15 minutes, then remove foil package from the coals.

Serve by opening the foil and eating right out of the package, as soon as the foil is cool enough to handle.

39

SCHOOL LUNCH (1912–1960s)

In colonial and Early American schools, students (usually boys) generally came home for the mid-afternoon dinner, the largest meal of the day. They might bring snacks to school. Families often rotated boarding the teacher. As free public schools developed, the school day also got longer, and—especially in more settled areas—lunch became a smaller meal. Students carried lunches to school, sometimes cold dishes like sandwiches, pickles, or leftovers. In places with cold winters, students would carry food to school in a metal bucket that could be heated on top of the schoolroom woodstove, or in a glass jar that could be heated in a kettle of water boiling on that stove.

The first in-school lunch experiment may have been an 1853 charitable lunch in a New York City vocational school. A few more cities piloted programs in a high school or two in the 1890s, the lunches being served by outside charities. These lunches sold for one to three cents, and not all students could afford them. There was a stronger push for food in schools after the turn of the twentieth century, as muckraking journalists published exposes about malnourished children failing in urban schools. School systems began setting up their own

programs in 1908–1910, but by 1921 there were still only about thirty-one thousand lunches being sold, mostly in the large cities. School lunch became part of federal government employment programs in the 1930s, and a permanent federal program of subsidies in 1946, when the price was up to nine cents. In the 1970s, a subsidized lunch could not cost more than twenty cents.

Like military food, school lunch food has always been compromised by the necessary blandness of volume feeding, the use of government surplus food, and industry lobbying about which foods to promote. But, again like military food, the uniformity of school lunch food makes it part of our national culture, a common experience that holds us together even as we complain about it.

Lunches brought from home got little attention in published cookbooks until the 1920s and 1930s. Undoubtedly, the same magazine articles and books about undernourished school children pushed cookbook writers to make up menus for school lunch boxes. Prior to that time, lunches brought from home were probably smaller versions of "lunch buckets" taken to work by mine and factory employees. The first commercial metal lunch box for children seems to be a 1902 tin box in the shape of a picnic basket.

FOR THE SCHOOL LUNCHEON

Figure 33 1911 school lunch as envisioned in *The Butterick Cook Book*, by Helena Johnson.

The first metal lunch box with the handle on a narrow side was a Mickey Mouse model in 1935. Metal lunch boxes were no longer sold after 1985.

CORN CHOWDER (1912)

A very early school system to set up its own division of school lunch was Philadelphia, in 1912, with Emma Smedley as superintendent. The same year, Ms. Smedley updated her 1904 book, *Institution Recipes*, with a full description of her plans and menus. (See the *Reader's Companion* to this volume for the full text of some of this material.) The chowder, which became a white-sauce mainstay of school lunch menus across the country, was sold with a small roll to high schoolers (and their teachers) for five cents. That was the top price for a soup-and-roll, or a hot-dish-and-

roll. Philadelphia lunches also had fruits and snacks intended to supplement cold lunches from home, for a penny or three. With only one soup, one hot dish, and a couple of sandwiches daily, Smedley juggled her menus to have fish on Fridays for Catholic students and a non-pork item every day for Jewish students. This recipe is easily reduced in size, or you can do it as a group project. If you have access to the school cafeteria, you may find the eight-quart double boilers Ms. Smedley used to heat the milk and white sauce. If you are working at home, it takes a long time to get these large volumes of milk and water heated up on home stoves.

Yield: 150 portions

2 No. 10 cans corn [12 16-ounce cans or 13 15½ ounce cans]

4 quarts diced potatoes [from 5 pounds potatoes]

3 large onions

¾ pound "butterine" [margarine]

14 quarts whole milk

1 pound flour [4 cups]

3 ounces salt [4½ tablespoons]

½ teaspoon red pepper

1 bunch parsley

Equipment: 2 oversized soup pots (1 40-quart), 2 heavy soup pots, roasting pan, very long-handled spoons

1. Heat a covered soup pot ¾ full of water to boiling.

2. Warm corn and half the milk in a roasting pan in a 175-degree oven. (Here's where one of those double boilers would be handy.)

3. Start warming the other half of the milk over medium heat in one of the large soup pots. Uncover and stir often so it won't stick to the pot or burn. (Here's where the other double boiler would be used.)

4. Peel potatoes and cut into ½-inch dice.

5. Halve, peel, and chop onions. (Wear swim goggles to avoid tears.)

6. Put potatoes and onions in the 40-quart soup pot. Ladle in boiling water to cover potatoes and onions, bring to a simmer, and cook until potatoes are tender.

7. Melt margarine in an oversized soup pot.

8. Stir in flour to form a bubbling paste. Cook a few minutes.

9. Ladle hot milk into the paste. Every 2 or 3 ladles, stop and stir mixture until it thickens to make a white sauce. Gradually increase the heat and stir often so it won't stick to the pot or burn.

10. Wash and mince parsley.

11. When potatoes are ready, and white sauce has absorbed the 7 quarts of milk, stir the white sauce into the potato pot.

12. Add parsley, salt, and a sprinkling of red pepper, and stir again.

13. Carefully remove roasting pan from oven, and add hot milk and corn to potato-milk mixture to assemble soup.

14. Heat carefully, stirring often to prevent sticking and burning. (Here is where Mrs. Smedley might have turned to a large, insulated tank called the "Seeley Fireless Cooker.")

Serve an 8-ounce portion with a soft roll the size of a child's fist for five cents.

EGG SANDWICHES (1913)

Sandwiches are poorly documented in early cookbooks, and the ones that began appearing after the 1870s were fancy sandwiches for ladies' luncheons. There is no reason to doubt that sandwiches had been carried to schools and workplaces since the early nineteenth century. Of the most common sandwiches by the time I was carrying a Hoppalong Cassidy (TV cowboy) lunch box in the early 1950s, egg salad may have been the first in print. Peanut butter and jelly was published as early as the 1890s, but may not have been widely used until the 1950s. Cream cheese and jelly—perhaps based on some of the ladies' lunch sandwiches—may date only from the 1920s. Tuna salad (my second favorite after PB & J) may have been a quite recent development. **Ham Sandwiches** may be the first sandwiches in American print (1837), but the ham-and-pickle salad sandwiches my friends had have little recorded history. Perhaps readers can fill in this chapter. This egg salad was recommended for school sandwiches in *The Institute Cook Book* by Helen Crump. My copy was used as a textbook for immigrants by the International Institute of Philadelphia, where the importance of healthful school lunches would have been emphasized.

> Mix hard-boiled egg, finely chopped, with mayonnaise dressing and spread on slices of buttered bread, preferably graham [whole wheat]. Chopped olives may be added to the egg mixture if desired.

Yield: 4 sandwiches

3 large eggs

¼ cup mayonnaise

½ cup stuffed green olives (optional)

8 slices bread (whole wheat preferred)

½ cup (1 stick) salted butter

Equipment: Egg slicer (optional), waxed paper

1. Remove butter from refrigerator to soften.

2. Bring eggs to a boil in water to cover, lower heat to a simmer, and cook 15 minutes.

3. If using olives, drain and chop.

4. When eggs are cooked, pour off water and run cold water over them to cool.

5. Shell eggs. If using egg slicer, slice, turn, and slice again to mince eggs. If using knife, mince fine.

6. In a mixing bowl, stir together eggs, olives (if using), and mayonnaise.

7. Butter each slice of bread. Spread with ¼ egg-salad mixture.

8. Wrap in waxed paper.

Serve packed with cocoa in a vacuum bottle, one whole raw tomato, salt on the side, one raisin cup cake—Better Homes Recipe Book, by Marjorie Mills (1926).

PEANUT BUTTER COOKIES (1961)

The 1946 National School Lunch Act set up standards for school lunch programs entitled to receive government aid, including surplus food. By the 1961 fourth edition of *Food for Fifty*, by Sina Faye Fowler, Bessie Brooks West, and Grace Severance Shugart, the requirements included that eight-ounce carton of milk, two teaspoons of butter or fortified margarine, and a protein requirement that could be satisfied by four tablespoons of peanut butter. I was sure my school cafeteria put peanut butter in the baked beans, but I've never found such a recipe. "In addition to meeting the nutritive requirements, the school lunch should provide satisfaction and pleasure to the pupil and help in the development of good eating habits."

Well, the *Food for Fifty* recipe for peanut butter cookies takes care of half the butter and a little of that surplus peanut butter, and I suppose a lifelong aversion to peanut butter cookies is sort of a "good eating habit."

Yield: About 90–100 cookies

1 cup sugar

¾ cup brown sugar, loosely packed

1 cup "fat" (butter or fortified margarine preferred)

2 eggs

1 cup creamy peanut butter

1 cup flour

1 teaspoon baking soda

½ teaspoon salt

1 teaspoon vanilla

Equipment: 2 baking sheets, standing mixer or handheld beater, mixing bowls

1. Remove butter or margarine from refrigerator ½ hour before starting.
2. Cream together butter or margarine, sugar, and brown sugar until light and fluffy.
3. Beat eggs and add with peanut butter to butter-sugar mixture.
4. Sift together flour, baking soda, and salt.
5. Beat flour mixture into peanut butter mixture.
6. Add vanilla to batter.
7. Divide batter into 8 dozen small balls (¾ inch in diameter).
8. Flatten balls on ungreased baking sheets with the tines of a fork. Press down a second time to make a criss-cross pattern.
9. Bake 8 minutes at 375 degrees.

Serve two cookies on a green plastic plate to each student.

PEANUT BUTTER BROWNIES (1960s)

One of the hardest things to understand about school lunch is that it used to be a lot worse than it is now. I tried to match my own memories of school lunches of the 1960s with a book called *School Lunch Menu Magic*, published by General Foods to promote their brands, such as Calumet Baking Powder. Besides these brownies, the only thing in the book I remember is a tuna chop suey so dreadful I will not even add the recipe for historical interest. I was surprised to see that General Foods recommended a smaller portion of tuna chop suey than I remember, but I suppose everything bad looked bigger when I was twelve or thirteen.

This recipe for brownies uses some government-surplus peanut butter as well as the company's chocolate and baking powder. If you can borrow the school cafeteria or a home economics classroom, you can make the whole recipe for sixty brownies. If not, you can do the math to reduce it. My high school cafeteria would have used about six hundred of these.

Yield: 60 brownies

8 ounces of "Baker's chocolate naps" (unsweetened chocolate)

½ cup shortening, plus more to grease pans

1⅓ cups (13 ounces) peanut butter

2⅔ cups flour

2 teaspoons baking powder

½ teaspoon salt

1¾ cups eggs (6 extra large eggs, or 1 cup "dried eggs with 1¼ cups water")

4 cups sugar

4 teaspoons vanilla

3 cups chopped nuts (12 ounces)

Equipment: 13-by-9-by-2-inch sheet-cake pans, double boiler, two mixing bowls, spatula

1. Bring water to a boil in the bottom of a large double boiler.
2. Add top pan and melt together shortening, chocolate, and peanut butter.
3. In the mixing bowl, sift together flour, baking powder, and salt.
4. In a second mixing bowl, beat the eggs and gradually beat in the sugar.
5. Beat the chocolate mixture into the eggs and sugar.
6. Mix in the flour mixture.
7. Mix in the vanilla and nuts.
8. Grease the pans.

9. Work batter into the 2 pans and level with a spatula.

10. Bake at 350 degrees 20 minutes.

11. Cool before cutting into squares.

Serve on a green plastic plate, with another green plate of formless stew, and an eight-ounce carton of milk. Carry them to your table on a brown plastic tray. Eat the brownie first.

40

WORLD WAR I
(1916–1919)

Although the United States only entered "The Great War" in 1917–1918, the impact on food habits was important and long lasting. This is all the more remarkable because the official food restrictions were entirely voluntary. They were quite effective and continued to be effective after the Armistice ended the war, when Americans were urged to continue restrictions so that food could be sent for European reconstruction. There had been considerable dissent before and during the war. About one-ninth of the U.S. population were immigrants or the children of immigrants from Germany and Austria-Hungary. Only a few years earlier there had been more students in German-language or bilingual schools as a percentage of all students than were in any bilingual education in the mid-1990s.

One effect of World War I was the temporary suppression of German culture generally and public German ethnic food in particular. However this is often overstated. Many history texts say that sauerkraut was renamed "Liberty Cabbage," and a few add that hamburger became known as "Salisbury steak" or that liverwurst was called "liberty sausage." However the only contemporary source for "Liberty Cabbage" I can find is in H.L. Mencken's 1921 *The American Language*, where he says the renaming was a short-lived failure.

One reason for the success of food restrictions was that there had been a buildup over several decades of public debate about the safety of the food supply, healthier diets, and more economical cooking. There had been food shortages and proposals about voluntary rationing in the winter of 1916–1917. The United States Food Administration, under future president Herbert Hoover, hired food writers and home economists to promote substitutions for meat, sugar, and butter. Food processors saw an opportunity to promote baking powders as a substitute for eggs, vegetable and cottonseed oil shortenings as substitutes for butter and lard, and branded molasses and corn syrup as substitutes for sugar. Canneries and home economists united to promote commercial canned salmon and vegetables as well as home canning. Health food promoters suggested peanuts, beans, and legume loaves as meat substitutes.

One device that rallied Americans around giving up wheat and red meat was a door-to-door campaign of pledge cards like those that had been used by the prohibition and temperance movements. The cards

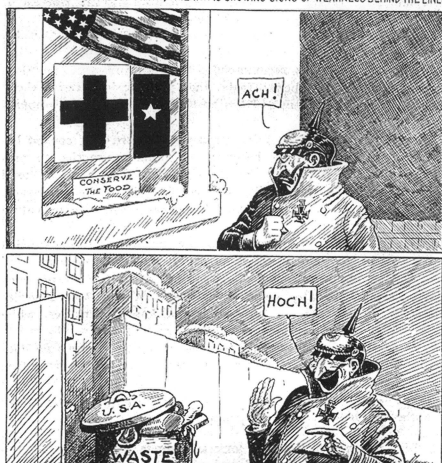

BERLIN, JAN. 15,
WHILE PUTTING ON A BOLD FRONT, AMERICA IS SHOWING SIGNS OF WEAKNESS BEHIND THE LINES

COURTESY DONNELL ST.LOUIS GLOBE DEMOCRAT

Figure 34 This World War I anti-waste cartoon from a St. Louis newspaper caricatures German soldiers. In heavily German-American St. Louis, the cartoonist could presume that readers knew what "Ach" and "Hoch" meant. *Source: Donnell cartoon in* St. Louis Globe-Democrat, *reprinted in* "Win the War" Cook Book, *published in 1918 by the St. Louis County Unit of the Women's Council of National Defense.*

were circulated by Scouts and other voluntary organizations. By the end of 1917, one half of all American families had signed these cards. They agreed to eat no wheat on Wednesdays, no red meat on Tuesdays (or Thursdays in areas where a lot of fish was made available for Roman Catholic families on Fridays), no pork on Saturdays either, and one meatless meal every day. People also were urged to cut down on white bread, butter, and sugar. The usual substitutes were corn and beans; chicken, eggs, cottage cheese, nuts, and fish; vegetable and cottonseed oils; and molasses, honey, and syrups. The restricted foods were supposed to go to U.S. and allied troops, and later to civilian populations. Anticipating the question of why the foreigners couldn't eat corn, beans, cottonseed oil, corn syrup, and peanut butter, the Food Administration said first that wheat, beef, dairy products and sugar were "the most concentrated nutritive value in the least shipping space." Later Hoover changed his argument, "[O]f the countries allied with us only Italy raises corn and is accustomed to its use. War time is not a good time to try to introduce a new product. Besides, there is practically no corn-milling machinery in Europe except in Italy, and corn meal can not be shipped in large quantities owing to the fact that it spoils readily. . . . We all like corn; a very trifling change in our diet will release for our Allies millions of bushels of wheat."

One immediate casualty of the meatless-meal rule was the traditional American breakfast steak. Millions of draftees developed a taste for novel army foods like chili con carne, "American chop suey," and Spanish rice. Processed cheese (patented in 1916) became "American Cheese" as Kraft won a contract to supply the armed services with six million pounds.

The U.S. Food Administration made a household name of the millionaire mining engineer Herbert Hoover, who had previously organized food relief in Belgium and other war-torn countries. His name became a synonym for voluntary "cooperative individualism." Compliant hostesses said that their households were "Hoovered." It is likely that President Hoover was personally blamed for the Great Depression, with its "Hooverville" shantytowns, when the same kind of voluntary schemes failed to relieve the massive unemployment of 1929–1932.

Canadian War Cake (1916)

Allied Cookery, "arranged by" Grace Clergue Harrison and Gertrude Clergue, was published as a fund-raiser for the reconstruction of rural France in 1916—before the United States had entered the war. Most of the recipes in the book are foreign foods from the countries then allied against Germany and Austria—Great Britain, France, Italy, Belgium, and Russia, but also

Serbia and Canada. Some eager Americans had already volunteered with Canadian forces. This eggless, butterless Canadian cake was a preview of the voluntary food restrictions that were soon used in the United States.

Yield: 2 loaves, serve 15

2 cups brown sugar
2 tablespoons lard, plus more to grease pans
1 pound raisins
1 teaspoon cinnamon
1 teaspoon cloves
1 teaspoon baking soda
3 cups flour

Equipment: 2 loaf pans or 1 baking sheet, wood toothpick or wire cake tester, wire rack

1. Bring 2 cups of water to a boil with the first 5 ingredients and a teaspoon of salt. Boil 5 minutes and remove from heat.

2. When sugar mixture is cool, dissolve the baking soda in another teaspoon of water and stir it in.

3. Grease 2 loaf pans or a baking sheet (for round loaves).

4. Work flour into sugar mixture to make a dough. You may need a little more water or flour.

5. Divide dough into 2 parts. Work each part into a ball and flatten for round loaves on a baking sheet, or pull into a long oval and pat into 2 loaf pans for loaf cakes.

6. Bake 45 minutes at 350 degrees. Test for doneness with a wood toothpick or wire cake tester.

7. Cool on wire racks.

Serve with hot cocoa.

Chop Suey Stew (1916)

This dish, from the 1916 *Manual for Army Cooks* compiled by Captain L.L. Deitrick, isn't much like Chinese food, but it is a lot like the "American chop suey" that appeared mysteriously at about the same time, according the Jean Anderson in the *American Century Cookbook*. I believe that World War I, with the first real military draft in American history, had an unusually strong effect on civilian food thereafter. After the war, veterans expected some of the same foods they had eaten together in the war, and former army cooks filled the ranks of short-order, restaurant, and institutional kitchens. The army's recipe is supposed to feed "60 men." You can make some or all of the recipe as a group project, or use the ingredients in brackets to make a dish for six, to get an idea of the size of army garrison rations at the beginning of the war. I have also used the army's rice recipe.

Yield: Serves 60 soldiers

15 pounds meat [1½ pounds beef round or pork shoulder]

10 pounds onions [about three large onions]

4 stalks of celery [½ stalk celery]

½ pint barbecue sauce [2 tablespoons]

2 gallons beef stock [3½ cups]

5 pounds rice [1 cup]

2 ounces salt [¾ teaspoon]

Lard to brown meat [3 tablespoons lard]

Equipment: Large soup pot with lid, second pot to make rice (large pot for 6-soldier version; oversized stock pot for 60-soldier version), colander.

1. Cut meat into "strips one-fourth inch thick and 1 inch long."

2. Melt lard in pot. Add meat and increase heat to brown.

3. After a few minutes turn over meat to brown another side.

4. After a few more minutes, stir to break up meat and brown a little more if possible.

5. Add beef stock and simmer "from one-half to two hours." (This must have depended on the quality of the meat.)

6. Meanwhile order soldiers assigned to K.P. duty to halve, peel, and chop onions.

7. For 5 pounds of rice, put 3 gallons of water in an oversized pot and bring to a boil. Remember that it takes the same burner on "high" twice as long to boil twice as much water, so allow more time for large quantities. To speed the process when necessary, heat rice in a sheet-cake pan in a 150-degree oven. When water boils, add 3 tablespoons salt and the rice. Return to a simmer and cover pot loosely. When rice "may be mashed in the fingers," drain rice into a colander, "after which each grain should be whole and separate."

8. Slice celery into thin cross sections.

9. Thirty minutes before serving add onions, celery, and barbecue sauce to stew pot.

10. If making 1 cup of rice, put 5 cups of water in a pot and bring to a boil. Add ¾ teaspoon salt and the rice. Return to a simmer and cover pot loosely. When rice "may be mashed in the fingers," drain rice into a colander, "after which each grain should be whole and separate."

Serve chop suey over rice with bread and butter as a light supper, with stewed prunes, coffee, tea, or cocoa. In the 1916 manual, the army planned supper as a lighter meal than "dinner" and served bread at every meal. Every breakfast included meat, and hamburger steaks were still considered a breakfast meal for soldiers, even as civilians were giving up meat at breakfast.

ANNIE ST. JOHN'S WAR COOKIES, OR GINGER DROPS (1917)

This recipe is from a handmade notebook of older recipes. It is penciled in at the end, initialed "A.B.F." and dated September 13, 1917. It uses flour and butter, but saves sugar.

Yield: About 80 2-inch cookies

"4 cups flour

¾ cup butter

3 eggs (Hen)

1 cup baking syrup [light corn syrup]

[½ teaspoon] Nutmeg

1 teaspoonful [baking] soda

1 tablespoon ginger"

[Solid shortening to grease baking sheets]

Equipment: Baking sheets, pastry blender or large fork

1. About an hour before beginning recipe, remove butter from refrigerator.

2. Cream the butter in a large mixing bowl with pastry blender or large fork.

3. Beat the eggs until creamy and light, then stir into the butter.

4. Stir in the syrup.

5. Mix the spices and flour.

6. Combine all ingredients to make a medium batter. You may need a little more water or milk.

7. Grease baking sheets and preheat oven to 350 degrees.

8. Drop teaspoonfuls of the batter a few inches apart on the baking sheets. If the batter is thicker, you may need a second spoon to release each spoonful.

9. Bake 15–20 minutes, or until cookies brown at the edges.

RYZON HOOVER PANCAKES (1918)

The General Chemical Company, makers of Ryzon Baking Powder, hired home economist Marion Harris Neil to solicit cooking experts for the best recipes to be published in the *Ryzon Baking Book*. This recipe, showing the increasing importance of Herbert Hoover as a public symbol of the wartime food restrictions, was submitted by Mrs. E.D. Cole of Brooklyn, New York.

Yield: 20 pancakes

2 cups buttermilk or sour milk

1 cup "stale bread crumbs" or leftover hot cereal

¾ cup cornmeal

2 level teaspoons RYZON [baking powder]

1 level teaspoon salt

½ level teaspoon baking soda

1 tablespoon molasses

Solid shortening to grease griddle.

Equipment: Teakettle, heavy skillet or griddle, pancake turner

1. Soak crumbs in milk or buttermilk for ½ hour.

2. Bring water to a boil in teakettle, measure out 1 cup boiling water and pour on the cornmeal.

3. When cornmeal is cool, mix in the crumbs and milk.

4. Dissolve baking soda in a teaspoon of hot water.

5. Sprinkle baking powder, salt, and molasses on cornmeal mixture. Add baking soda mixture and stir everything together.

6. Heat griddle or skillet with a little grease.

7. Pour out batter to form pancakes.

8. When edges of pancakes look done, turn once to brown both sides.

Serve hot with "syrup, honey, jam, or fruit butters."

MACARONI AND SALMON [OR TUNA] (1918)

This recipe appears in *Conservation Cook Book*, written by Kathryn Romig McMurray of the Illinois Farmers' Institute for the Lincoln, Illinois, *Star*. Mrs. McMurray's "patriotic, economical, good cooking" still used the terms "wiener" and "hamburg," although she does have a recipe for "Egyptian Rolls," which seems to be her way of attributing stuffed cabbage to Gypsies from Hungary, then an enemy nation. If you use the tuna substitution, you have a very early example of a tuna-noodle casserole. (Another of her recipes makes a tuna-rice casserole with a thicker white sauce.) Canned tuna was just beginning to rival salmon during World War I. "Gray fish" was a market term for the meat of small Pacific sharks, available fresh or canned at that time.

Yield: Serves 4–6

3 cups cooked macaroni (from 2⅓ cups uncooked elbows)

1 tablespoon "butter substitute," plus more to grease casserole

1 tablespoon flour

1 cup milk

½ teaspoon salt

⅓ cup crumbs

1 cup salmon, tuna, or gray fish

Equipment: Large soup pot, ovenproof casserole, 2 saucepans

1. Heat a half pot of water to boiling.

2. Add 2 teaspoons of salt and the macaroni. Return to a boil, and cook uncovered for 30 minutes. (Like many non-Italian Americans early in the twentieth century, Mrs. McMurray cooked macaroni quite soft by today's standards. Her general advice was to save fuel by cooking a lot of it for one meal and serving a different version the next day. She also advised saving the water for soups and gravies.)

3. Heat milk in small saucepan or microwave oven.

4. Melt margarine or other "butter substitute" in a saucepan.

5. Sprinkle on flour and mix well. Let mixture bubble and cook a few minutes.

6. Slowly work hot milk into butter-flour mixture to make a thin white sauce.

7. Add ½ teaspoon salt to the white sauce.

8. Grease casserole dish.

9. When macaroni is done, drain off water and wash macaroni in cold water.

10. Combine macaroni in the casserole dish with tuna or salmon. Pour white sauce over all.

11. Bake in a 350-degree oven until "slightly browned," about 30–35 minutes. (The book also suggests heating everything on top of the stove.)

Serve for "meatless Tuesday" supper.

OATMEAL PUDDING (1918)

One way to substitute other grains for wheat was to cover up the taste with chocolate. In a pamphlet on "Sugarless Sweets" published by the New York State Food Commission, Cornell Home Economist Lucile Brewer used chocolate in buckwheat cookies and in this nutritious pudding sweetened with "corn sirup." You can multiply the recipe by using a larger dish or a cake pan.

Yield: Serves 2

¼ cup "pinhead oatmeal [steel cut oats] or rolled oats"

1½ cups [whole] milk

2 tablespoons "grated chocolate" (from bittersweet chocolate bar)

5 tablespoons "corn sirup"

1 tablespoon salted butter

1 teaspoon vanilla

Equipment: Teakettle, 2 saucepans, box grater, ovenproof bowl

1. Bring water to a boil in a teakettle.
2. If using rolled oats, pour ¾ cup of hot water over the oats in the saucepan and let them stand for 15 minutes. If using steel-cut oats, use 1 cup of hot water and simmer the oats 20 minutes.
3. Heat the milk in another saucepan or in a microwave oven.
4. Use the butter to grease the ovenproof bowl and add the rest to the milk.
5. Grate the chocolate on the box grater, measure and combine with all the other ingredients in the ovenproof bowl.
6. Bake the bowl in a 350-degree oven for one hour.

"Serve it with or without cream."

BAILEY CHOCOLATE CAKE (1918)

Barley flour doesn't add any rise to breads or cakes but holds moisture well, so it made a good substitute for wheat flour in cakes. Clara Bailey Worthen, a Newbury, Vermont, neighbor of Frances Parkinson Keyes, used it in a chocolate cake in this "World War I 'substitute' cake," remembered as "one of our most successful experiments" for the 1955 publication of *The Frances Parkinson Keyes Cookbook*. You can obtain barley flour at a health food store or in the baking goods sections of some supermarkets. You can use a commercial white frosting for the "boiled frosting" (now called Italian meringue) Mrs. Worthen made.

CAUTION: HOT SYRUP FOR FROSTING STICKS AND BURNS.

Yield: Serves 10

1½ squares [ounces] bitter chocolate

2 tablespoons fat, plus some to grease cake pan

1½ cups barley flour

3 teaspoons baking powder

¼ teaspoon baking soda

2 large eggs, or one egg and equivalent egg white powder

1 cup corn syrup

1 teaspoon vanilla

1 cup sugar

Equipment: 9-inch round cake pan or springform pan; double boiler; whisk, eggbeater, or handheld electric mixer; 3 mixing bowls; wire cake rack, toothpick or wire cake tester; candy/deep fry thermometer, spatula for applying frosting

1. Run the hot water tap until the water feels hot. Use this water to half fill the lower half of a double boiler.
2. Put the chocolate and fat in the top of the double boiler and let it melt.
3. Whisk well the flour, baking soda, and baking powder.
4. Separate 1 egg by pouring back and forth between the shells over a cup.

5. Beat the yolk with the corn syrup and ¼ cup water.

6. Beat the white until it forms stiff peaks.

7. Combine the dry ingredients with the corn syrup mixture, then stir in the chocolate.

8. Grease the cake pan.

9. Stir the vanilla into the batter, then "fold in" the egg whites with a whisk or one of the beaters.

10. Bake 30 minutes at 350 degrees, or until a cake tester comes out clean.

11. Let cake cool a few minutes.

12. Start the frosting by dissolving the sugar in ¼ cup of water and bringing the syrup to a boil.

13. Boil the syrup to 230–234 degrees on the candy thermometer, the "thread" stage.

14. Separate the second egg (or use one egg white's worth of all whites or powdered egg white product). Beat the egg white until the foam is stiff but not dry.

15. Beating the egg white constantly, pour the hot syrup down the side of the bowl (so it doesn't splatter on the whisk or beaters) into the egg white "until the frosting stands in peaks."

16. Set the cooled cake on a plate. Frost the sides, being careful not to touch the cake with the spatula. (Some people like to do this holding up the cake plate with one hand.)

17. Frost the top of the cake. (This is easier with the cake on the table.)

Serve for dessert.

LIBERTY BREAD (1918)

"Better eat war bread now than the black bread of Germany later," advised the *Official Recipe Book* issued by the State Council of Defense of Illinois, perhaps the most militant World War I cookbook. "America and her Allies must not run out of Wheat, Meat, or Fats. If we let that happen, Germany will win the war." Some versions of liberty bread used barley flour. The effort to lighten this bread by tripling the usual amount of baking powder leaves a strong mineral aftertaste. Given the large German-American population in Chicago, some people might have preferred black bread.

Yield: 10–12 slices

1½ cups white flour

1 cup cornmeal

½ cup bran

6 teaspoons baking powder

1 teaspoon salt

1½ cups liquid ("water, milk or other liquid")

2 tablespoons fat [margarine or solid shortening], plus some to grease the loaf pan

1 egg

Equipment: Mixing bowl, large loaf pan, toothpick or wire cake tester

1. Mix all the dry ingredients.

2. Beat in the egg and "liquid," then the fat.

3. Preheat the oven to 350 degrees.

4. Grease the loaf pan.

5. Turn the batter into the loaf pan.

6. Bake about 40 minutes, testing for doneness with a toothpick or wire cake tester.

Serve with **War Butter.**

WAR BUTTER (1918)

Because Americans were so accustomed to bread and butter on the table with every meal, there were a number of recipes for stretching butter with gelatin and milk or cream, making something with the texture of today's tub margarines. War butter was not very stable even when refrigerated and could not be used in cooking or baking. This recipe comes from the *"Win the War" Cook Book*, compiled by Reah Jeannette Lynch and published by the St. Louis Unit, Woman's Committee, Council of National Defense, Missouri Division. I have taken some details from other recipes of the time, especially one in "Food Economy" by Mrs. Charles B. Knox, published by the Knox Gelatine Company. This kind of war butter was not made after 1919. For World War II, more stable oleomargarine was available.

Yield: "2¼ pounds of butter out of 1 pound"

1 pound butter

2 cups "rich milk" [the cream that gathered on top of un-homogenized milk: substitute light or medium cream]

1 tablespoon unflavored gelatin

Equipment: Saucepan, whisk or rotary egg-beater, several stoneware platters, ice cream freezer (optional)

1. Remove butter from refrigerator 1 hour early so that it softens.
2. Cream butter with a fork. Heat up a few inches of water in the bottom of the double boiler.
3. Use 2 tablespoons of the cream to soak the gelatin in a large mixing bowl.
4. Heat the rest of the cream in a small saucepan or microwave oven.
5. Pour the hot cream over the soaked gelatin. Stir well.
6. Beat the cooling cream mixture into the creamed butter. Salt to taste.
7. "As long as any milk is seen keep on beating until all is mixed in," suggested Mrs. Knox, "Place on ice or in a cool place until hard."
8. Ms. Lynch suggested "Place on platter[s] by spoonful to thicken." This would make about 100 1-tablespoon pats of war butter. Another method was to churn for a few minutes in an ice cream freezer.

Serve with **Liberty Bread.**

41

HEALTH FOOD IN THE TWENTIETH CENTURY (1912–1973)

As Early American health food revolved about Sylvester Graham and late Victorian health food centered on the Kellogg family, health food in the twentieth century has been primarily responsive to the zigzag progress of nutritional science. At their best, health food promoters have criticized the dangerous features of mass-market foods and kept wholesome fruits, vegetables, and whole grains on the American table. Graham and the Kelloggs had emphasized high-fiber diets and opposed animal foods, and science has proven them right.

At their worst, health food promoters have harmed people with extreme suggestions, sometimes based on partial truths. This has been especially true in the case of reducing diets. Even now, at the start of the twenty-first century, there is still no consensus on successful reducing diets, and Americans seem to have more obesity and more anorexia than ever. In the 1890s, as William Atwater was establishing the calorie values of common foods, Dr. J.H. Salisbury was promoting his cures based on an all-beef diet. A few years later Horace Fletcher described how he had lost weight by eating all kinds of food, so long as he chewed each mouthful thirty-two times.

This at least did no harm, but Fletcher then promoted an all-potato diet. In the 1920s, as scientists began isolating the major vitamins, trained nutritionists developed diets organized entirely around the known vitamins and calories and ignoring other aspects of a balanced diet. In the 1930s, Henry Ford forced inedible soybean concoctions on his engineers and staff. An important strain of 1960s–1980s health food was introduced by the "Macrobiotic Diet" of Michio and Aveline Kushi. The Kushis introduced many traditional Japanese flavors and organized a network to farm and distribute "organic" produce that still exists. Like traditional Japanese food, the diet could be very high in sodium, and it also permitted smoking cigarettes.

One of the most contradictory health food writers was the late Adele Davis, who in a 1970 revision of her book, *Let's Cook It Right*, removed some of the saturated fat, warned against the chemicals in stainless steel and nonstick cooking pots, and suggested, "Since radioactive fallout appears to be particularly dangerous to persons whose calcium intake is inadequate, it has become especially important to use calcium-rich ingredients in cooking. To show how this calcium need can be supplied, hundreds of ordinary recipes have been fortified with non-instant powdered milk." Thirty years later, saturated fat is still considered unhealthful, but none of the other points have been upheld.

Some health food promoters actually enjoyed good cooking, and this chapter is focused on some successful health-food recipes. The Adventist influence remained strong, and this chapter begins and ends with Adventist meat substitutes. Over the twentieth century the most important Kellogg proved to be little brother Will, who in rivalry with former Battle Creek patient C.W. Post founded the packaged breakfast cereal business. Much of the cereal aisle today is filled with sugary junk food, but the whole-grain cereals invented early in the twentieth century kept people eating milk and fiber for decades. This chapter does not attempt to summarize the explosion of new and old health food ideas in the 1960s and 1970s. You can get some of those recipes in Chapters 20 and 50.

VEGETARIAN BEEFSTEAK (1914)

The stockyard scandals of the early twentieth century sent new converts to vegetarianism and set off a century-long struggle to develop the vegetarian hamburger. Today you can buy frozen vegetarian patties that do quite well in a bun with ketchup, but in 1914, you were on your own. The recipe is from *The Vegetarian Cook Book*, by E.G. Fulton, a book that makes early reference to mock-meat products developed by the Seventh-Day Adventists. Although you could serve this on buns, real hamburger sandwiches were just getting popular, and most health food eaters were looking for a substitute for steaks.

CAUTION: CHECK COFFEE CANS FOR SHARP EDGES AT TIME AND FILE DOWN BEFORE USING.

Yield: 12–16 patties

2 cups of cooked lentils, from ½ cup dried lentils

3 cups coarse bread crumbs

¼ cup vegetable oil, plus more to fry completed patties

½ cup heavy cream

2 teaspoons salt

½ teaspoon sage

Equipment: Sieve or food mill, 2 1-pound coffee cans or similar molds, large soup pot, aluminum foil, a few feet of cotton twine, hand can opener

1. Check that the soup pot is deep enough to cover most of the coffee cans with water.

2. If you don't have leftover lentils, bring 3 cups of water to a boil and add the ½ cup of dried lentils. Simmer covered for 35 minutes. Remove cover and pour lentils into sieve or food mill to remove remaining water.

3. "Add the oil, sage, [1½ teaspoons] salt, and cream to the bread crumbs, and allow to soak for a few minutes."

4. Put the sieve or food mill full of lentils over a large bowl, and push the lentils through the sieve or turn the food mill to puree them into the bowl.

5. Mix lentils and bread crumbs to make a smooth paste.

6. Pack mixture into coffee cans. Put on lids, or cover tightly with aluminum foil (and tie on with kitchen string). It's okay that cans aren't completely filled.

7. Put coffee cans in the deep kettle, and pour boiling water up to half the height of the cans.

8. Cover kettle and simmer-steam for 2 hours.

9. Remove steamed cans from kettle and let cool to handle.

10. Use hand can opener to open a little of the bottom of the cans, and remove the steamed loaves. If you have trouble, you can use the can opener to open the entire bottom of the can, and push the loaves out, being careful of sharp edges.

11. Allow to cool.

12. Slice into ½-inch rounds.

13. Heat oil in heavy skillet. Brown vegetable beefsteaks on both sides.

Serve with a lot of ketchup or Worcestershire sauce, potatoes, and peas.

PEANUT MACARONI AND CHEESE (1925)

Nuts became increasingly important in early twentieth-century health food, both as meat substitutes and sources of flavor in vegetarian diets. George Washington Carver, born a slave, came at the question from a different angle, as his main concern was to provide a profitable crop for African American sharecroppers, and then to improve their diets in hard times. Many of his peanut recipes were for sweets, but this one is a simple attempt to sneak a little more protein into a southern favorite. He may have been inspired by one of Ella Kellogg's recipes for baked macaroni and "granola." The recipe is from Carver's *How to Grow the Peanut and 105 Ways of Preparing It for Human Consumption* (Bulletin No. 31, Experimental Station, Tuskegee Institute), first published in 1925.

Yield: Serves 4 or 6 as a side dish

1 cup broken [or elbow] macaroni

1 cup rich milk [or light cream]

2 tablespoons flour

2 quarts boiling salted water

1 cup coarsely ground peanuts

¼ to ½ pound cheese

½ teaspoon salt

A dash of cayenne pepper

2 tablespoons butter, plus some to grease casserole

¼ cup bread crumbs

Equipment: Colander or strainer, small frying pan, food processor or meat grinder, ovenproof casserole

1. Bring 2 quarts of water to a boil.

2. Add 1 teaspoon of salt and the macaroni.

3. Cook 10–12 minutes or until almost tender.

4. Butter casserole.

5. Melt butter in a small frying pan and mix in bread crumbs. Turn off heat.

6. Grind peanuts in meat grinder or by pulsing for a minute or 2 in a food processor.

7. Drain macaroni and "pour cold water over it to keep the pieces from sticking together."

8. "Mince cheese, and mix with all other ingredients except the macaroni." Add ½ teaspoon salt.

9. "Put sauce and macaroni in alternate layers in a well buttered baking dish."

10. "Cover with buttered crumbs, and bake slowly [at 350 degrees] until crumbs are brown [20–40 minutes]."

Serve as a light supper, or as a side dish with Sunday dinner.

CARROT LOAF (1927)

Mrs. John Robison frankly identifies this as a "Substitute for meat" in her recipe for the 1927 *Congressional Club Cook Book.* (Her husband was a Republican congressman from Kentucky.)

Yield: Serves 6

1 pound carrots

½ cup bread crumbs

½ cup chopped nuts

1 tablespoon sugar

2 large eggs

1 cup milk

1 "small cup" flour

1 tablespoon butter, plus some to grease pudding mold.

Equipment: Pudding mold or metal bowl that fits inside a soup pot, aluminum foil, soup pot, vegetable peeler, box grater or food processor with grating dish, teakettle

1. Remove butter from refrigerator to soften 1 hour before making recipe.
2. Peel carrots.
3. Grate carrots with box grater or food processor to get 1½ cups grated carrots.
4. Beat eggs.
5. Grease pudding mold or metal bowl.
6. Combine all ingredients with 1 teaspoon of salt and a sprinkling of black pepper.
7. Pack into pudding mold or bowl, tapping the sides to get rid of any bubbles. If using bowl, cover tightly with the aluminum foil.
8. Set up steamer insert, or crumple aluminum foil balls to make a stand to keep the bowl or pudding mold out of contact with the bottom of the pot, so water can circulate around it.
9. Set up mold or bowl on stand and surround with hot tap water.
10. Bring water to a boil, cover the soup pot, and cook carrot loaf 1 hour.
11. Bring more water to a boil in teakettle, so you can add hot water to keep up the level.

"Serve with Drawn Butter."

POTASSIUM BROTH (1934)

One of the more unusual dietary theories of the 1920s and 1930s was the Hay system, which suggested that proteins and carbohydrates are digested differently and should not be eaten together at the same meal. Hay dieters also tried to eat 80 percent "alkaline-forming" foods (vegetables) and avoid vinegar and hot pepper as well as the usual white flour, white sugar, and salt. Since non-starchy vegetables were encouraged at all meals, many of the recipes in *The Official Cookbook of the Hay System* by Esther L. Smith were, like this one, rather good, except for lack of salt. It is unclear if the "vegetable salt" called for was an all-potassium salt substitute or an herbal seasoning like "Mrs. Dash" or today.

Yield: Serves 8–12

1 pound celery and tops

¼ pound spinach

1 pound kale

1 large onion

1 pound carrots

Small bunch parsley

1 head lettuce

3 red beets

Vegetable salt (herbal salt substitute)

Equipment: 2 large pots, vegetable peeler, large strainer

1. Break off celery stalks and wash out any sand. Chop celery including inner leaves and put in a large pot.
2. Chop spinach and put in the pot.
3. Wash and chop kale, including stems and add to pot.
4. Halve, peel, and chop onion. Add to pot.
5. Peel and chop carrots. Add to pot.
6. Wash and chop parsley, including stems. Add to pot.

7. Wash and chop lettuce. Add to pot.

8. Wash or peel beets. Take 1 slice off to make a flat bottom, then slice thinly. Chop slices and add to pot.

9. Add fresh water to cover the vegetables in the pot.

10. Bring to a boil, then reduce heat to a simmer, and cook 2 hours with the lid ajar. Heat some more water in a teakettle and add boiling water if needed.

11. After 2 hours, strain broth into the other large pot.

12. "Season with vegetable salt. Vegetable paste may be added for additional flavor."

Serve hot as a snack or with either protein foods and vegetables, or carbohydrate foods and vegetables.

CORNELL "WHITE" BREAD (1955)

This popular health bread was developed by Clive M. McCay, professor of Animal Nutrition at Cornell University, in the 1930s, originally for the New York state mental hospitals, because some patients ate only bread. It spread around to other institutions and was widely recommended during World War II rationing because the soy flour and dry milk powder add protein. Unlike most American health breads, it was made from white flour and not whole wheat, because McCay was trying to win over white-bread eaters. You can refrigerate the dough after Step 6, Step 10, or Step 12 and freeze the baked bread.

Yield: 3 loaves

2 packages or 2 tablespoons dry yeast

2 tablespoons brown sugar or honey

3 teaspoons sea salt

2 tablespoons salad oil (plus a little more to oil mixing bowl)

6 cups unbleached flour (plus 1–3 cups more for kneading)

3 tablespoons wheat germ

½ cup "full-fat soy flour"

¾ cup nonfat dry milk

Equipment: 2 large mixing bowls, wood breadboard, standing mixer (optional), kitchen towel, 3 loaf pans

1. Combine first 4 ingredients with 3 cups of warm (105 to 115 degrees) water. Let stand until bubbles form on the surface.

2. In second mixing bowl, stir together the 4 dry ingredients.

3. Stir the liquid ingredients and work in half to ¾ of the flour mixture.

4. "Beat vigorously about 75 strokes by hand, or two minutes with the electric mixer."

5. Work in the rest of the flour mixture. "At first the dough will be sticky as you grasp it. Beat it, turning it round and round in the bowl. At the end of this time you'll feel it change and become firmer."

6. Flour the board, and turn out the dough onto it. Knead until the dough is smooth and no longer sticky.

7. Oil bowl, put ball of dough in and turn to cover with oil.

8. Cover with a kitchen towel and let rise until double in size, about 1 hour.

9. "Punch dough down" to remove air bubbles. Fold over the edges and turn it over to rise another 20 minutes, or until double again.

10. Turn back onto the board, and divide into 3 equal portions. "Fold each into the center to make smooth, tight balls." Cover and let stand 10 minutes on the board.

11. Oil the loaf pans.

12. Shape the balls into 3 loaves "or 2 loaves and a pan of rolls." (In *The Cornell Bread Book*, Mrs. McCay describes how to flatten each ball out into a rectangle, fold each long side to the center, and roll this smaller rectangle to make a loaf. She shapes her rolls like golf balls and puts them together in a large pie plate or round cake pan.)

13. Let rise in pans, again covered with the towel, until double in size, about 45 minutes.

14. Bake at 350 degrees for 50–60 minutes, about 30 minutes for rolls. "Bread is done if it sounds hollow when tapped."

15. Cool on wire racks. "Brush with oil if a thin, tender crust is desired."

Serve as white bread; they'll never know the difference.

WALNUT OAT BURGERS (1968)

We return to Seventh-Day Adventist authors for another approach to satisfying American meat hunger, this one a vegetarian hamburger, from the 1968 *Ten Talents*, by Frank J. Hurd and Rosalie Hurd.

Yield: Serves 6–10

1 cup quick oats

1 cup seasoned bread crumbs

1 cup onion from 1 large onion

2 tablespoons vegetable oil

1 cup chopped walnuts

¼ cup soy flour

2 tablespoons cashew nut butter (optional, or substitute natural peanut butter)

¼ teaspoon sage

¼ teaspoon Accent (MSG, optional)

Equipment: Teakettle or small saucepan, skillet with cover, large mixing bowl, waxed paper, pancake turner or spatula

1. Heat three cups of water in a teakettle or small saucepan.

2. Halve, peel, and chop onion to get one cup.

3. Heat 1 tablespoon of the oil in skillet over medium heat briefly. Add chopped onion and stir well. Cover for 2 minutes to "sweat" onions.

4. Uncover skillet and stir onions. When they are starting to brown, remove from heat.

5. Mix onions and all other listed ingredients in large mixing bowl.

6. "Add just enough hot water to hold together. Mix well."

7. Form in hamburger-size patties. Arrange on waxed paper.

8. Again heat skillet (which should still have some oil in it).

9. Add burgers and brown on both sides, adding a little more oil as needed.

"Serve in burger buns or with [meatless] gravy as meatless main dish."

LEMONAISE (1973)

The comedian and civil rights activist Dick Gregory became a vegetarian as part of the philosophy of nonviolent direct action and took up fasting to protest the Vietnam War. He eventually settled on a diet primarily of fruits, with raw vegetables and nuts and annual water fasts of a month or more. Gregory's diet was too extreme for many people, but helped spread a revived interest in more healthful foods, especially among African-Americans. Some of his combinations are really delicious! This "natural" dressing went onto all kinds of

Figure 35 Dick Gregory and co-author Alvenia Fulton examining a soybean "meat" skewer as Gregory ends his anti-war protest fast in 1967. *Source: © Bettmann/CORBIS.*

garden salads in Gregory's 1973 book, *Dick Gregory's Natural Diet for Folks Who Eat; Cookin' with Mother Nature*, edited by James R. McGraw with Alvenia M. Fulton.

Yield: Serves 1 as salad dressing or dip

 2 teaspoons almond or pecan flakes

 1 tablespoon lemon juice

 2 tablespoons olive oil

 ½ teaspoon caraway seed, aniseed, or mustard seed (optional)

Equipment: Lemon juicer, blender

1. Squeeze out the lemon juice and put in the blender with the almond or pecan flakes.

2. Pulse briefly to mix well, and let the mixture sit for 15 minutes.

3. Add the olive oil and beat to a cream.

4. If flavoring with the optional seeds, add them and blend another 30 seconds to spread them around.

Serve on a salad of shredded cabbage and carrot with minced onion and parsley.

42

CITIES AND CITY POLITICS (1922–1931)

For most of the nineteenth century, one-fourth or less of the American population lived in cities. The Constitution favored rural areas and low-population states through the composition of the U.S. Senate and the Electoral College. And most states deliberately set their state capital in a rural area away from the largest city. The 1920 census suddenly revealed that 51 percent of Americans lived in cities. By 1960 it was 70 percent. The demographic change scrambled the programs of both major parties. The Republicans, who had been the urban and northern party, found their strongholds given over to immigrant voters and migrants from the Democratic south, where the Great Depression really began in the early 1920s. The Democrats were unable to reconcile their progressive but anti-immigrant (and prohibitionist) rural wing, symbolized by three-time presidential candidate William Jennings Bryan, with their increasing urban base, which was progressive about different issues. Because cities have both mass media and public eating, the political issues of an increasingly urban America are reflected in recipes published by political leaders and their families.

For more recipes from the "roaring twenties" in American cities, see <www.historycook.com/urban>. On the web site,

you can trace the shifting alliances of Chicago politics in the 1920s and early 1930s, as reform-minded Republicans allied with ethnic Democrats to unseat a corrupt Republican mayor. Recipes from the families of leading participants show the kind of image politics that were expressed even in recipes as the country shifted from the "roaring twenties" to "The Great Depression." The boom had been most extreme in cities, and the crash was most abrupt in cities. We also look at some other aspects of urbanized cooking that developed in this period.

SIRLOIN STEAK (1922)

This recipe was submitted by Mayor William Thompson of Chicago to the 1922 *The Stag Cook Book; Written by Men for Men*, edited by C. Mac Sheridan. "Big Bill" Thompson was a Republican who built an urban machine around an unusually open alliance with organized crime. His raffish image included publishing this recipe for a rich man's dinner of steak, in a book that also included recipes from entertainers.

My favorite food is Roast Beef, rare, or a good American sirloin steak, which, I take it, are so simple to prepare that they need no recipe. Suggestions . . .

If your steak looks a bit fresh, rub with lemon juice (both sides) and allow to stand several hours before broiling or frying. Don't be frightened if it turns a bit black—be glad. 4. Pan may be rubbed with garlic. 5. Steaks should be *thick*, particularly if you broil.

Yield: Serves 1 "roaring twenties" mayor or 2 voters

16-ounce sirloin steak

1 lemon

1 clove garlic

Equipment: Lemon juicer, cast-iron griddle or frying pan, or broiling pan

1. Several hours before cooking, juice lemon.

2. Set steak to marinate in lemon juice, turning over several times to coat all surfaces.

3. Peel clove of garlic and cut off 1 end.

4. When ready to cook, trim any surface fat off steak.

5. Heat pan and rub with cut end of garlic clove. As it heats up, rub griddle or frying pan with fat cut from steak to grease it. (If using broiler pan, rub garlic directly on steak.)

6. Shake a layer of salt onto griddle or pan. (For broiled steak, salt both sides before cooking)

7. Add steak and sear for 3 or 4 minutes.

8. Salt top of steak and turn over. Steak is "rare" when both sides are thoroughly browned, but steak is still flexible in the middle when poked.

Serve with baked potatoes and peas. Mayor Thompson's table probably included illegal liquor.

SUB GUM FRIED RICE (1928)

This recipe appeared in the *Mandarin Chop Suey Cook Book* published by The Pacific Trading Company of Chicago, one of the first Chinese cookbooks published in English in the United States. Chinese restaurants appeared during the California gold rush. By the 1920s, Chinese restaurants had become so popular with Anglo-Americans in many cities that elaborately decorated ones began to open outside the segregated "Chinatowns." The first cookbooks were aimed at non-Chinese Americans who wanted to make the dishes they had enjoyed in the restaurants. The words "Sub Gum" means "eight treasure" and were widely used on early restaurant menus. Although cooked with butter in a frying pan, this attempt at Chinese food would have been the height of urban sophistication in the "roaring twenties." The recipe adds, "Chicken, lobster, and crab meat can be fried with rice in the same manner."

Yield: Serves 3–5

3 cups cold cooked rice (from ¾ cup dry rice)

1 cup leftover meat "(roast beef or pork)"

5 slices bacon

5 [large] eggs

1 green pepper

1 stalk celery

1 small onion or 2 green onions [scallions]

1 tomato

3 tablespoons "Chinese sauce" [soy sauce]

6 white mushrooms

5 tablespoons butter or olive oil

Equipment: Large frying pan (no one had woks), spatula, large fork

1. If you aren't starting from leftover rice, begin several hours ahead by making ¾ cup of rice by package directions. Do not refrigerate rice, which dries it out and makes it too hard.

2. Cut off the top and bottom of the green pepper, remove core and stem, open the cylinder of the middle and pare off any white pith or remaining seeds. Cut pepper into thin strips.

3. Halve, peel, and chop onion. Cut onion or scallions the long way into thin shreds.

4. Wash celery stalk and cut into 2-inch lengths and thin slices the long way.

5. Halve the tomato at the equator. Over a sink, squeeze tomato in your hand to remove some seeds and juice. Cut tomato into small, thin pieces.

6. Cut bacon into squares. Slice leftover meat into thin strips perhaps 2 inches long. Break each egg into a cup, remove any bits of shell, and add to a medium bowl. When all eggs are broken, beat thoroughly.

7. Heat butter or oil in large frying pan. Add bacon and fry until brown and almost crisp.

8. Add celery, onion, and green pepper. "Fry for five minutes."

9. Add the leftover meat and stir well to warm it up.

10. Increase heat and add the rice, "stirring well with a big fork" to break up any lumps and warm it with the hot oil.

11. "Last of all, break the eggs into the rice, mix well until eggs are cooked." (A Chinese chef would have fried the egg first in the oil, then cut them up and added them to the rice.)

"Serve with tea."

CHICKEN CORN MEAL À LA FARM RELIEF (1927)

This recipe was submitted by Republican Congressman Fiorello H. La Guardia of New York to the 1927 *Congressional Club Cook Book*. The recipe is for an Italian immigrant dish, polenta, which La Guardia calls cornmeal mush and turns into a joke about urban-rural coalition building because "Once corn meal served in this fashion is tasted, there will be such a demand for corn meal we will not have any more farm problems in the Middle West." La Guardia's political fluency (the Congressional Club did not permit partisanship, and La Guardia's are almost the only recipes with political titles in their book!) would soon make him mayor of New York City, where he cleverly balanced reform and patronage policies, as well as his own mixed Italian-Jewish heritage. See **Spaghetti À La Progressive** in Chapter 36 for another La Guardia recipe. Since La Guardia did not give a method for cooking the cornmeal mush, I have used modern descriptions of the traditional Italian method and an easy microwave method.

Yield: Serves a family of 4, possibly on Sunday when no one is at work.

2 cups yellow cornmeal

1 broiler-fryer chicken (3 pounds)

¼ pound (1 stick) salted butter

1 onion

Center leaves of celery

Pinch sage

½ teaspoon paprika

1 bunch fresh parsley

1 "large can" (28 ounces) whole tomatoes

Equipment: 2 large pots with covers, long-handled wooden spoon, oven mitt, slotted spoon, microwave oven and microwave-safe casserole and paper towels (optional), clean wooden board, string or unwaxed dental floss

1. Cut chicken into small pieces.

2. Halve and peel the onion and slice into thin half-rounds.

3. Slowly melt the butter in a heavy pot.

4. Add the onions, stir to coat with butter, and cover the pot for a few minutes.

5. Remove the cover and stir the onions frequently until golden brown.

6. Remove onions from the pan and add chicken pieces.

7. Mince celery leaves, and add to chicken with sage, paprika, 1 teaspoon of salt, and pepper to taste.

8. Turn chicken pieces to brown on all sides, but do not let anything burn.

9. Mince enough parsley for at least 2 tablespoons, more "according to taste."

10. Add parsley, stir once or twice, and add tomatoes. Return onions to the pot. Cover pot and simmer 40 minutes. Plan to remove top of pot after 30 minutes and increase heat to thicken sauce.

11. If you want to make polenta as La Guardia did, bring 6½ cups of water to a boil in the other pot. (For easier microwave method, skip to Step 15.)

12. Add a tablespoon of salt. (The water may boil up for a moment.) Reduce heat to a simmer.

13. Stirring constantly, add cornmeal to the water in a thin stream. (Traditional Italian-American cooks did this by taking handfuls of cornmeal.)

14. After all the cornmeal is added, stir for another 20 minutes, or until the mush begins to pull away from the sides of the pan. (Hot mush bubbles can spit up burning drops, so wear an oven mitt or wrap your stirring hand in a kitchen towel for this step.) Skip to Step 16.

15. Microwave method: Combine water and salt as in Step 11 with cornmeal in microwave-safe casserole. Stir thoroughly to eliminate lumps. Microwave 9–12 minutes on "high." (Use longer cooking times with smaller ovens). Stir thoroughly, cover with paper towels, and microwave another 9–12 minutes.

16. Pour polenta out onto a clean wooden board. (It should be thick enough to stay in a round, breadlike shape.) After 3–5 minutes it will cool enough to be sliced with 18 inches of string or unwaxed dental floss wound onto a finger of either hand.

17. Ladle chicken and sauce over slices of polenta.

Serve with a green salad.

43

RECENT COOKING BY KIDS (1922–1957)

These recipes catch up to the cooking our parents and grandparents learned as children and historians are just beginning to sift such periods. Although I associate the recipes below with specific trends, one way to read the section is to look at what adult food writers *thought* kids would be interested in cooking over the thirty-five-year period. Sugar is certainly a common denominator, and kids still like all the foods in this chapter, but none of these recipes are still cooked by kids despite contemporary kids' mastery of the microwave oven. Even chocolate milk shakes now emphasize thickness rather than froth or chill and are more often purchased than made at home.

AN EARLY GIRL SCOUT COOKIE RECIPE (1922)

Before the Girl Scouts contracted out to cookie bakers, they had to bake their own cookies for fund-raising sales. The earliest recorded sale was in 1917 in Oklahoma. In July 1922, *American Girl* magazine ran this recipe by Florence E. Neil, a Chicago district leader. Miss Neil estimated that the recipe could be made for 26–36 cents, and the cookies could be sold for 25–30 cents per dozen. (Source: <http://www.girlscouts.org/about/cookie_hist.html>.)

Yield: 6–7 dozen cookies

1 cup butter

1 cup sugar plus additional amount for topping (optional)

2 large eggs

2 tablespoons whole milk

1 teaspoon vanilla

2 cups flour

1 teaspoon salt

2 teaspoons baking powder

Shortening to grease baking sheets

Equipment: 2 baking sheets, pastry blender or large fork, breadboard and rolling pin, spatula, cake pans or wire racks for cooling cookies

1. Remove butter from refrigerator 1 hour before starting, to soften.

2. Cream butter and sugar with pastry blender or large fork.

3. Beat eggs until light and creamy, then stir into butter mixture.

4. Blend together flour, baking powder, and 1 teaspoon salt.

5. Stir vanilla into milk, and add alternately with the flour mixture to the butter-egg mixture.

6. Refrigerate dough at least 1 hour.

7. Flour board and rolling pin, and roll dough out into a thin sheet.

8. Cut into small rounds with a cookie cutter or the top of a small glass dipped in flour. (It is unclear if early cookies were cut into the trefoil [3-leaf clover] shapes now used.)

9. Grease baking sheets and arrange cookies in rows.

10. Preheat oven to 375 degrees and bake cookies 8–10 minutes, or until a little brown shows at the edges.

11. Sprinkle sugar on top of hot cookies (optional).

12. Remove from baking sheets with spatula and cool on wire racks or upside-down cake pans. Don't eat too many before selling, or the Girl Scouts won't make enough money to pay for camp this summer!

Sell in waxed paper packages of one dozen, or bundles tied with string.

ORANGE SHERBERT (1929)

By 1929, home economics had brightened up a little bit, but the forty-year-old theme of Americanizing immigrants was still strong. This recipe comes from *Americanization Through Homemaking*, a 1929 pamphlet by Pearl Idelia Ellis, who openly explains her prejudices about how Mexican-Americans in Cavina City, California, cooked and ate. "The noon lunch of the Mexican child quite often consists of a folded tortilla with no filling. There is no milk or fruit to whet the appetite. Such a lunch is not conducive to learning. The child becomes lazy. His hunger unappeased, he watches for an opportunity to take food

from the lunch boxes of more fortunate children. Thus the initial step in a life of thieving is taken." Ms. Ellis was determined to change this with recipes that, at least in this case, took advantage of local fruits. Sherbert goes well with Mexican American meals, but it requires access to ice or a home freezer, which would have been a problem.

Yield: 12 scoops

1 quart orange juice (or 8–10 oranges)

1 cup lemon juice (or 4–5 lemons)

1½ cups sugar

2 tablespoons gelatin

Equipment: Ice cream freezer with 1½ quart capacity (optional), juicer (optional), heat-proof 2 quart mixing bowl, 1½ quart mold

1. If using whole fruit, juice and measure. (Orange juice not-from-concentrate is the better substitute if you only have time to use one fresh fruit.)

2. Soak gelatin in ¼ cup lemon juice in heat-proof dish.

3. Heat orange juice near boiling. Pour on gelatin mixture and stir well to dissolve. Add sugar and the rest of the lemon juice and stir well.

4. Rinse out mold, and pour gelatin mixture in mold. Refrigerate at least 4 hours.

5. Unmold on a platter larger than the mold.

Serve in slices.

TOASTED CHOCOLATE SANDWICH (1938)

This recipe appears in *International Recipes*, published in 1938 by the Ladies Auxiliary No. 119 Fraternal Order of Eagles, of Pocatello, Idaho. Because the recipe specifies Hershey's milk chocolate, it may have come from a company handout. The recipe also appears right about the time as the first **S'mores** (see Chapter 38).

Yield: 1 sandwich, recipe may be multiplied

Two slices bread
Bar of "Hershey's Milk Chocolate (sweet) or Hershey's Almond Bar"

Equipment: Broiler pan, toaster, spatula, cutting board

1. "Toast two slices of bread on one side [each]."
2. "Between the toasted sides place a few squares" of either chocolate bar.
3. Set sandwich on broiler pan and toast under the broiler for a few minutes.
4. Remove from oven, turn sandwich over with spatula, and toast the other side.
5. Remove from oven again and put sandwich on cutting board to cut into four strips.

"Serve with fruit salad. This is also a good sandwich for children's parties."

CHOCOLATE MILK SHAKE (1946)

It's sometimes easier to imagine American colonists eating with their knives and no forks than to realize that grandmother and grandfather had no canned chocolate milk shakes. "First we must make our sirup," begins this recipe from *A Cookbook for Girls and Boys*, by Irma S. Rombauer. Canned chocolate syrup was soon available, and powdered chocolate milk mixes would be prominent advertisers on early television shows for kids. But this book was dedicated to teaching children self-reliance by showing them how to make foods that would be expensive at the soda fountain (a teenage hangout).

Yield: 4 cups milk shake (enough syrup for 25)

7 ounces (squares) unsweetened chocolate
1 can (1⅓ cups) sweetened condensed milk
½ cup sugar
4 cups whole milk

Equipment: Recycled 1-quart jar with cover, "egg beater" or recycled 2-quart glass jar with cover, clean tea towel, hammer to crack ice, double boiler.

1. Put hot tap water into the bottom pot of the double boiler and insert the top part. Put the chocolate in the top part to melt.
2. Heat double boiler over high heat until the water boils, then reduce heat.
3. When chocolate is melted, remove top of double boiler to a cool, heat-proof surface. Bring some cold water to a boil in a teakettle.
4. Stir condensed milk and 1 cup of boiling water into the melted chocolate.
5. Cool the syrup and put it in a clean jar. Cover tightly and refrigerate. "It will keep for a week or 10 days."
6. To make a chocolate milk shake, measure ½ cup of the syrup into a mixing bowl, add the milk, and beat with an eggbeater until uniformly brown and frothy. Or, measure the syrup into the large jar, add the milk, and shake the jar.
7. Take ice cubes from the freezer and wrap them in the tea towel. Place on a hard surface and hit the towel with a hammer to make cracked ice. (Some people in 1946 still had ice boxes cooled by a large block of ice, and would have had to split off some of the block ice with an ice pick.)

Serve by dividing milk shake between four tall glasses and topping with cracked ice.

Apple Brown Betty (1957)

In 1957, eleven high school home economics students in Chillicothe, Ohio, taught by Miss Dorothy Stewart, won a *Seventeen Magazine* contest with a book of recipes modernized from 1860s issues of *Godey's Lady's Book*, which they called "We Modernize Mr. Godey." Each girl took a section. This recipe is Godey's 1862 Jenny Lind's Pudding, modernized by Nancy Bucy, seventeen, who wrote, "[T]he boy I am going to marry likes fancy rich desserts, and he doesn't get very many at home. Many of the recipes I have chosen are ones we use at our home." Miss Bucy's recognition that this pudding was actually a brown betty, and her additions of spice and lemon juice, show that she had read many other Early American recipes. The students included the original text with each modernized recipe, just as this book often does. For more about the many recipes named after Jenny Lind, see **Jenny Lind Cake**.

> Grate the crums of half a loaf, butter a dish well, and lay in a thick layer of the crums; pare ten or twelve apples, cut them down, and put a layer of the and sugar; then crums alternately, until the dish is full; Put a bit of butter on the top, and bake it in an oven or American reflector. An excellent and economical pudding. (1862)

Yield: Serves 6

4 slices white bread

$\frac{1}{3}$ cup butter or margarine

6–8 apples

$\frac{1}{2}$ cup white or brown sugar

$\frac{1}{2}$ teaspoon nutmeg or mace

$\frac{1}{4}$ teaspoon cinnamon

$1\frac{1}{2}$ tablespoons lemon juice

1 lemon

Solid shortening to grease casserole

Equipment: $1\frac{1}{2}$ quart casserole, lemon zester or box grater, juicer

1. If possible, leave bread out for a day or two to make it easier to crumb. Make 2 cups of soft crumbs from the bread by pulling apart with 2 forks (so it doesn't compress).
2. Melt butter or margarine and combine with bread crumbs.
3. Grease casserole and arrange one third of the crumbs in the bottom.
4. Peel and slice the apples (discarding cores) to make 6 cups of sliced apples.
5. Put half the apples in the casserole dish.
6. Zest lemon to obtain 1 tablespoon of grated lemon rind.
7. Juice lemon to get the $1\frac{1}{2}$ tablespoons lemon juice.
8. Mix sugar, spices, and lemon zest, and sprinkle half over the apples in the dish.
9. Sprinkle half the lemon juice over the apples in the dish.
10. Add another one third of the crumbs, then the rest of the apples, and the rest of the spice mixture.
11. Sprinkle on the rest of the lemon juice.
12. Top with the rest of the crumbs.
13. Cover and bake at 375 degrees for $\frac{1}{2}$ hour.
14. Uncover and bake until the apples are tender and the crumbs on top are browned. (Miss Bucy estimated 1 more hour.)

"Serve with cream or milk."

4-H Peanut Candy Squares (1963)

This no-cook recipe was suitable for young 4-H groups, and submitted by Edna

Jones of the Dow's Prairie Grange No. 505 to *Our Favorite Grange Recipes*, compiled by the Home Economics Committee of the California State Grange. It does take some hard stirring and kneading toward the end.

Yield: 16 small squares

½ cup peanut butter

½ cup honey

¾ to 1 cup dry milk powder

½ cup coconut (or small peanuts)

1 teaspoon vanilla

Equipment: Mixing bowl

1. Stir just the peanut butter in the mixing bowl until it is creamy and light.
2. Stir in the honey and vanilla.
3. Add the coconut or peanuts and stir well.
4. "[A]dd the powdered milk a little at a time. This will be stiff. You will have to knead the mixture toward the last."
5. Roll out or pat into a square brownie pan.

Serve cut into squares.

BANANA SMOOTHIE (1947)

The Waring Blendor—that's not a typo, bandleader Fred Waring registered that spelling for his "Miracle Mixer" in 1938—opened up several interesting possibilities, as shown by this selection from "340 Recipes for the New Waring Blendor." Although the machine was inspired by large soda-fountain mixers, Waring (who didn't drink) thought it would catch on as a way to mix bar drinks and didn't include any recipes for home milk shakes. Another Waring pamphlet of the same period tells how to make alcoholic smoothies for adults. The following smoothie was apparently aimed at babies and toddlers, since the portion is rather small, and some of the other flavors would be hard to pass off on a child who could talk back: liver and chocolate, tomato, yellow turnip, prune, and spinach! When I got my hands on one of these units about ten years after this recipe, the first thing I made was a banana milk shake with chocolate syrup. (Molasses was not much used at my house.) I don't know if Waring overlooked milk shakes for some marketing reason, or if it was a quirk of inventive genius not to see what was obvious.

Yield: Serves 2 small children

1 cup whole milk (or evaporated milk)

1 medium-sized ripe banana

2 teaspoons molasses

Equipment: Blendor or blender

1. "Put milk in blendor container."
2. "Add other ingredients."
3. "Put cover on container."
4. "Turn on WARING and run until contents are thoroughly blended, from 20 seconds to 3 minutes."

Serve to a small child. While the child is eating this, make yourself a chocolate one.

44

RADIO RECIPES
(1928–1936)

Radio was the high-tech mass medium of the 1920s, '30s, and '40s. As with the Internet, the sudden rush to fill hours and hours of air time opened the new medium to public access as well as polished entertainment. Despite the limitations of sound-only, the intimacy of radio worked well for recipe programs. This chapter traces radio recipes from the formal instruction of some of the early experiments to locally popular shows that were important parts of the culture of rural areas, alongside some interesting commercial and government experiments. If you want to read more about the role of radio recipes in rural areas, Evelyn Birkby's wonderful 1991 book *Neighboring on the Air; Cooking with the KMA Radio Homemakers*, covers the life stories, recipes, and descendants of semi-professional recipe broadcasters over sixty-five years. Mrs. Birkby herself began at KMA in 1950. Early television presented many of the same opportunities to performers, but the visual emphasis of television quickly turned TV cooking shows away from home cooking toward newly made star "chefs" who could present elaborate dishes or were themselves attractive entertainers. With the important exception of Julia Child, television chefs did not often reconnect any style of home cooking until the 1990s. For early television food history, see Chapter 3 of *American Gourmet*, by Jane and Michael Stern.

The effect of Internet recipes on American cooking is still to be determined, but one apparent trend is the lively exchanges of ethnic recipes among small groups of immigrants, speeding up the usual process by which immigrant cooking adjusts to American lifestyles and then contributes to the mainstream.

CANDLE SALAD (1928)

One of the first radio cooking programs was the Gretchen McMullen Radio Cooking School, broadcast in early 1928 over WEEI in Boston, which is now a religious AM station. Her show was sponsored by processed-food companies, and most of her recipes make "white food" in the manner of Boston-based home economists from Fannie Farmer on. This no-cook "salad" is more like what we would eat as a dessert. It uses newly popular prepared foods and bananas to make a strong visual statement, although one we now find funny.

Yield: Serves 6

6 large leaves of lettuce

6 canned pineapple rounds

3 bananas

6 maraschino cherries

2 tablespoons marshmallow creme or fluff

1 cup mayonnaise

Equipment: Six dessert dishes

1. Blend marshmallow with mayonnaise to make "Marshmallow Mayonnaise."

2. Place a lettuce leaf on each plate, and center a slice of pineapple on each lettuce leaf.

3. Peel bananas and cut in half the short way. Stand a half banana in each pineapple slice.

4. "Top the banana with a cherry for the flame."

"Serve with marshmallow mayonnaise."

LAZY DAISY CAKE (1930s)

KMA radio in Shenandoah, Iowa, was started in 1925 by Earl May to promote his Earl May Seed and Nursery Company. Although recipes were broadcast by various people in the early days, Jessie Young was the first regularly scheduled "radio homemaker" and the first of many to broadcast from her own kitchen as her children wandered in and out. She continued broadcasting for thirty years and published a homemaking magazine for her listeners until 1980. The Lazy Daisy cake is so called because it is made much more simply than a "real cake," without creaming butter and sugar, whipping egg whites, or making a complicated frosting.

Yield: 12 small servings

1 cup whole milk

1/3 cup butter, plus 1 tablespoon, and some to grease cake pan

2 large eggs

1 cup sugar

1 cup flour

1 teaspoon baking powder

1/2 teaspoon salt

1 teaspoon vanilla

2/3 cup brown sugar

2 tablespoons "thick cream"

1/2 cup sweetened coconut

Equipment: 8-by-8-inch brownie pan

1. Heat the milk and the tablespoon of butter in a saucepan. Grease the cake pan.

2. Beat the eggs until light and creamy.

3. Beat 1 cup of sugar into the eggs.

4. Stir together the flour, baking powder, and salt.

5. Stir the flour mixture into the egg mixture, and add the vanilla.

6. Add the milk mixture "stirring carefully." The batter will be very pourable.

7. Bake 25 minutes at 350 degrees.

8. To make the frosting, melt the 1/3 cup of butter, and stir in the brown sugar, coconut, and cream.

9. Spread frosting on the warm cake, and put under the broiler (or in a hot oven) for a minute or two to caramelize, but not burn.

Serve with milk when the kids are home from school.

SPICED PRUNES (1931)

From 1926 through 1935, the United States Department of Agriculture produced broadcast recipes, with situation comedy written by Ruth Van Deman and Fanny Walker Yeatman for an imaginary "Aunt Sammy," the wife of "Uncle Sam." *Aunt Sammy's Radio Recipes* was published in 1927, *Aunt Sammy's Radio Recipes Revised* in

1931. The program was most popular in rural areas, which were already feeling the Great Depression in the late 1920s. The recipes were plain economical cooking without frills or ethnic references, and sometimes used inexpensive farm produce like prunes, which could be spiced up to please even children like Finicky Florine. (Information from the 1975 reprint edited by Martin Grief.) In making this recipe, remember that prunes used to always have pits, and they were a lot drier than they are now, so if you have a fresh box of soft prunes, skip the soaking step and reduce the simmering period.

Yield: Serves 4–6

  1 pound dried prunes

  1 cup sugar

  8 whole allspice

  8 whole cloves

  3 small pieces stick cinnamon

  ¼ cup vinegar

Equipment: Mixing bowl, saucepan, cheesecloth, and kitchen string

  1. "Select large prunes, wash well, and soak overnight in [1 quart] water."

  2. Make a small cheesecloth bag or bundle of the whole spices, and tie with kitchen string.

  3. Add the bag and the sugar to the prunes and their soaking water, and bring to a boil.

  4. Simmer 15 to 20 minutes.

  5. "Add the vinegar and cook about 10 minutes longer, or until the sirup is fairly thick."

Serve as a relish with roast or boiled meat.

SPANISH RICE (1932)

Network radio programs required sponsors. Winifred S. Carter was both the pro-

gram and the sponsor. She worked for Proctor & Gamble, makers of Crisco™ and had a regular feature on "Mrs. Blake's Radio Column," on WEAF and NBC affiliates nationally. Proctor & Gamble hedged its bets by also sponsoring "Sisters of the Skillet," a parody of radio cooking shows with "Ed" and "Ralph" pretending to be women. This recipe for what was already a depression favorite, is from "Good Things to Eat From Out of the Air; 136 Tested Radio Recipes," a P&G promotional pamphlet with Crisco™ in everything. Her directions are suitable for the brown rice; for white rice, skip the 15 minutes of frying in Step 3 and cut down the simmering in Step 11 to 12 minutes.

Yield: Serves 8

  ¼ cup Crisco™

  1 cup white or brown rice

  1 teaspoon salt

  ¼ teaspoon paprika

  1 cup meat stock or water

  1 small clove of garlic

  1 small onion

  2 green peppers

  2 stalks celery

  1 cup tomatoes

Equipment: Heavy skillet with cover

  1. Rub skillet with garlic clove.

  2. Melt shortening, add rice and fry over medium heat for 5 minutes.

  3. Add 1 teaspoon salt, paprika, and black pepper to taste, then fry over lower heat for another 15 minutes. Stir frequently so the rice browns without burning.

  4. Meanwhile, halve, peel, and chop the onion.

  5. Cut the top and bottom from the green peppers. Cut the stems out of

the tops. Core the cylinders of the middle of the peppers, cut down one side to open each one up, and slice off the white pith.

6. Cut the pepper pieces into strips, then crosswise into dice.

7. Chop the celery, including leaves.

8. Add the vegetables to the rice and sauté for five minutes.

9. Heat up stock or water.

10. Carefully, so that the hot shortening does not splash, add stock or water, and tomatoes.

11. Lower heat to a simmer, cover and cook until rice is tender, about 25 minutes.

Serve as a one-dish supper with cheese or bacon, or by itself.

CABBAGE (1934)

"The Mystery Chef," John Macpherson, claimed that he didn't use his name on the radio because his mother was embarrassed that her son had made even a hobby of cooking, much less broadcast recipes on the radio. This recipe for cabbage with no "back-talk," from *The Mystery Chef's Own Cook Book*, is typically technical, although his motto was, "Always be an artist at the stove, not just somebody who cooks." In taking the pose of a food authority, Macpherson was looking back to the early radio cooking teachers and forward to the "expert" television chefs like James Beard. Although this technique for cooking cabbage in two pots of water probably destroys some of the vitamins, the result has a brilliant green color and is light and well seasoned by all the salt in the second boiling.

Yield: Serves 6 as a side dish

1 head green cabbage

1 teaspoon baking soda

4 tablespoons salt

Equipment: Large mixing bowl, 2 8-quart soup pots (1 enamelware or stainless steel), colander

1. Bring 2 soup pots half full of water to a boil.

2. Wash cabbage and cut into quarters.

3. "Now cut the stalk right out, leaving all the leaves free. The outside of the stalk is fibrous, so throw it away."

4. If water isn't boiling yet, put leaves in a bowl of cold water.

5. Add baking soda to enamelware or stainless steel pot, and put in the cabbage. "Let it boil in this for 3 minutes, no longer." [If you count from when the water comes back to a boil, use the shorter boiling time in the second boiling.]

6. "Then strain the water off and refill the pot with the fresh boiling water from the other pot or kettle."

7. Add the salt and allow the cabbage to cook "till tender. A young cabbage will cook in 10–15 minutes."

8. Drain off the water and cut cabbage into small pieces.

9. To reheat cabbage, steam in a wire sieve over boiling water in the bottom of a double boiler.

To serve, "DO NOT add butter or fat of any kind, but serve exactly as it is, and you will find it will have a delicate, delicious flavor, and will be the most easily digested of all vegetables."

SHREDDED CARROT SALAD (1936)

"Sara and Aggie's Party Line" broadcast recipes along with gossip on an imaginary rural phone line where neighbors shared the line and had to identify their own ring, and could easily eavesdrop. Like "Aunt Sammy's" broadcasts, the cast eventually enlarged to include husbands, courting couples, kids, and curmudgeons. Also as with Aunt Sammy, listener requests led to several pamphlet cookbooks. The patter for this sweet carrot slaw went, "It's hard to get the family to eat the raw vegetables they ought to have, we know that from our experience with Clem and Curley. But even these two gentlemen who growl at the sight or mention of raw vegetables do eat this salad like they had especially asked for it." If the raw vegetables didn't restore regularity, the broadcasts were also infomercials for the sponsor's liquid laxative, Dr. W. B. Caldwell's Syrup Pepsin.

Yield: Serves 2

3–4 raw carrots

Small can sliced pineapple

"[S]alad dressing or mayonnaise"

½ cup cream

"[F]resh lettuce leaves (if you happen to have them)"

1 lemon

Equipment: Box grater or food processor with grating disk, vegetable peeler, whisk or handheld electric beater

1. Whip cream until it forms soft peaks when you remove the whisk or beaters.
2. Peel the carrots and shred "on your grater."
3. "Place a ring of pineapple on each dish, or if you have the lettuce, use that as the first thing on the plate, then put a slice of pineapple on the lettuce."
4. "Now heap a nice mound of the shredded raw carrot on top of that."
5. Make salad dressing or mayonnaise "fluffy" by beating the whipped cream into it.
6. "Add a dash of fresh lemon juice to it, too."
7. Pour fluffy salad dressing or mayonnaise "over the whole thing."

Serve as an appetizer.

45

THE GREAT DEPRESSION
(1930–1940)

In rural areas, the Great Depression began before the 1929 stock market crash. The ecological disaster of the "Dust Bowl" was already starting what would become an enormous migration out of the farm states. As millions more lost factory and service jobs, families hunkered down to share hard times, while many individuals became homeless.

President Herbert Hoover responded with voluntary programs like the World War I U.S. Food Administration he had headed, but the extent of the economic collapse overwhelmed his intentions. Shantytowns were called "Hoovervilles," and his name was vilified. (Mrs. Hoover tried to soften his conservative image with recipes. Coming up to the 1932 election, the First Lady sent a Chicago Republican fundraising cookbook an economical recipe for broiled tomatoes.)

The great migrations of the 1920s and 1930s mixed regional tastes into a new, more rapid, urban cuisine, which also had to be economical. People had time to cook and eat, and developed some interest in food fads along with radio programs, movies, board games, spectator sports, celebrity gossip, crime news, and technological progress. The federal make-work program for writers

had a project of collecting old-fashioned and regional and ethnic foods for a never-published series of books. Some of the drafts are now being published and give us a portrait of the variety of American foodways in the 1930s.

Unemployed people also had time to explore extreme political ideas, most of which had a core of economic populism. But food extremism, such as the fad diets of the 1920s, generally abated as many families were reduced to eating a very simplified diet in hard times. Economy-oriented cookbooks and magazine articles were published during the Great Depression, but many people were more interested in treats to cheer themselves up. Occasional luxury foods broke up the monotony of "Beans, bacon, and gravy/They almost drive me crazy," to quote a folk song. Here are some samples of what people ate in the 1930s, both when times were hardest, and when they could afford something special.

DEPRESSION COFFEE (1930S)

This was remembered by Peggy Nelson for the 1975 *Hill Country Historic Cook Book* of Kerrville, Texas, published by the Women's Division of the Kerr County Chamber of Commerce. Kerr County is the same area that was pioneered with **Salt-Rising Bread**, but was hard hit by the dust bowl and the depression. The general idea is like coffee substitutes that have been used in every American war including the Revolution, widely in the Civil War South, and as health foods since the 1890s. In the 1930s wheat bran was often free at the mill. Buy it now in bulk at the health food store. You can reduce the size of this recipe.

Yield: Whole recipe serves 40–50

   2 quarts wheat bran

   2 cups yellow cornmeal

   3 large eggs

   1 cup molasses

Equipment: Jelly-roll pan or baking sheet or pan with raised edges, long-handled spatula or spoon, recycled glass quart jars

1. Mix wheat bran and cornmeal.

2. Beat eggs and add to cornmeal with molasses.

3. Stir mixture thoroughly.

4. Spread in a shallow pan, and place in 250-degree oven. This is more to dry than to brown it quickly, although the mixture will eventually toast.

5. "Stir often while browning to prevent burning or scorching."

6. Remove from the oven when browned, and let cool. Store in a recycled glass jar or two.

7. To brew, bring two handfuls to a boil with 5 cups of water.

8. Simmer for a few minutes, then carefully pour off 4 cups of coffee.

Serve with milk or cream to help disguise the taste.

TRAMP COOKIES (1934)

This recipe was contributed by Mrs. Harry Telander to *Cookery Secrets*, published by the Girls Guild of Emmanuel Lutheran Church, Rockford, Illinois. The cookies are a lot like the old rolled style of **Hermits**, and perhaps Mrs. Telander thought of the many homeless hobos and tramps in the depression years as modern-day hermits. More likely these were good, cheap cookies that could be shared with the many tramps coming through this railroad town, itself hard hit by the depression. Mrs. Telander gave very few directions; probably every female member of this Scandinavian-American church knew how to make cookies.

Yield: 100 cookies or more

   ½ cup butter, plus some to grease baking sheets

   1 cup sugar

   1 egg

   1 cup raisins

   ¼ teaspoon [each] ginger and cloves

   1 teaspoon cinnamon

   ¼ cup "strong coffee" (or decaf)

   1 teaspoon baking soda

   "[A]bout 4 cups flour"

Equipment: Meat grinder or food processor, baking sheets, pastry blender or large fork, rolling pin and board, cookie cutter or glass tumbler

1. Remove butter from refrigerator 1 hour before starting.

2. Preheat oven to 350 degrees. Grease baking sheets.

3. Grind or pulse-process the raisins until granular. Make coffee if using brewed coffee.

4. Cream butter and sugar together with pastry blender or large fork (or in food processor).

5. Beat egg and work into butter-sugar mixture.

6. Stir spices into flour thoroughly.

7. Dissolve baking soda in hot coffee.

8. Alternately add flour and coffee to the butter mixture to make a firm dough.

9. Flour board and rolling pin. Roll out dough to about ¼ inch thick.

10. With a cookie cutter or glass tumbler dipped in flour, cut out rounds and place on the baking sheets. (Gather scraps and roll again.)

11. Bake 8–10 minutes.

12. Cool cookies on wire racks.

Serve with a hot drink, perhaps **Depression Coffee**, *or a full meal if the man chops wood for the stove.*

THE BANANA SKYSCRAPER (1936)

One symbol of hope during the Great Depression were skyscrapers, such as the Empire State Building, which opened in 1931. This variation of a banana split was devised at the Penn Pharmacy near the University of Pennsylvania, and popularized in *The Ice Cream Review*, July 1936 (and reprinted in the 1978 *The Great American Ice Cream Book*, by Paul Dickson).

Yield: Serves 1

½ ounce syrup, "any flavor"

1 scoop vanilla ice cream

1 banana, quartered

1 scoop chocolate ice cream

1 ounce syrup, "any flavor"

Whipped cream

½ maraschino cherry

Equipment: Ice cream scoop, tall sundae dish

1. Place ½ ounce of syrup at the bottom of the sundae dish.

2. Add the scoop of vanilla ice cream.

3. Peel the banana and halve it the long way, then the short way, to get long quarters.

4. Place the quarter slices of banana pointing upward (and cut side in) on 4 sides of the ice cream.

5. Put the chocolate scoop on top of the vanilla scoop, and between the banana slices.

6. Cover ice cream with one ounce of syrup, then top with whipped cream, and then the cherry.

SWEET POTATO BISCUITS (1937)

Dr. George Washington Carver spent much of his long career working with poor African American farmers to increase their income and nutrition. In times of depression his work reached some southern white farmers as well. This recipe is from his *How the Farmer Can Save His Sweet Potatoes and Ways of Preparing Them for the Table*, Bulletin No. 38 (4th edition) published in 1937 by the Tuskegee Institute Press, as quoted in *The African-American Heritage Cookbook*, by Carolyn Quick Tillery.

Yield: 12–16 biscuits

1 cup boiled and "finely mashed" sweet potatoes

2 eggs

2 cups flour, plus some for rolling out biscuits

2 teaspoons baking powder

1 teaspoon salt

2 "scant teaspoons melted butter or lard"

1 tablespoon sugar "(if desired)"

2 cups milk

Equipment: Biscuit cutter, baking sheet or 2 8-inch cake pans, food mill or potato ricer (optional), rolling pin and breadboard.

1. Preheat oven to 450 degrees.
2. "Mix together all the dry ingredients."
3. To get the sweet potatoes mashed "finely" put them through a food mill or potato ricer.
4. Beat eggs and beat together with potatoes and milk.
5. Combine potato mixture with dry ingredients and melted butter or lard to make a soft dough. "If the mixture is too soft, add sufficient flour to make a soft dough."
6. Flour rolling pin and board.
7. "Roll out lightly" from the center, to about ½ inch thick. Biscuits should not be handled too much, or they become tough.
8. "Cut with a biscuit cutter."
9. Arrange biscuits on ungreased baking sheets so they are just touching each other, and bake about 15 minutes.

Serve hot with butter at any meal.

GREEN TOMATO MINCEMEAT (1940)

The Great Depression began in the 1920s for farmworkers in the "dust bowl" states, and continued into the 1940s and 1950s as people from that region migrated westward, seeking work. This recipe was submitted by Opal Wyckoff to the July 20, 1940, issue of *The Covered Wagon News*, published by the Shafter Farm Workers Community at a federal Farm Services Agency camp for migrant workers at Shafter, California. The same issue notes that the camp infirmary had seen several children who had eaten too much green fruit, suggesting that hunger was still a problem at the camp. This recipe turns green tomatoes and apples into a more digestible mock mince pie, and also points a

way to preserve some vitamin-rich foods for the winter.

Yield: Cans 5 pint jars, serves about 40 as a condiment

2 cups chopped green tomatoes

3 cups chopped green apples

1 pound raisins

3 cups sugar

1 teaspoon cinnamon

1 teaspoon salt

1 teaspoon allspice

1 teaspoon cloves

¼ cup vinegar

Equipment: Heavy non-reactive pot (optional for canning: second large soup pot, tongs, jars, lids, grate that fits into pot)

1. Chop tomatoes and apples.
2. "Mix all together, bring to a boil and simmer till thick, seal."
3. If canning, process 15 minutes in water bath, using cans according to their directions.

Serve as a chutney, or as a filling for one-crust "mince" pies.

SKYSCRAPER SPECIAL (DAGWOOD SANDWICH)

In the 1930s, people escaped the depression with radio and comic strips, but the humor had qualities we now can see as depression-related. "Blondie," one of the most popular newspaper comic strips, made fun of misunderstandings between husband and wife, which often ended with Dagwood (the husband) repairing dinner with a giant sandwich. Most of the humor was about how Dagwood didn't know how to cook and hungrily included nonfood items in the sandwiches, but with many readers hungry at night, that was also a depression subtheme. Italian-style submarine sandwiches were renamed "Dagwoods" in some parts of the United States, but the real Dagwood sandwich was a multilayer club sandwich, such as the one described here by cartoonist Chic Young in *Blondie's Soups, Salads, Sandwiches Cookbook* (1948).

Yield: Serves 1 cartoon husband

2 slices bread

2 or more leaves crisp lettuce

2 tablespoons butter

2 ounces cold sliced chicken "(or ham or veal or pork or pot roast or turkey or cold cuts or bacon or sausage or almost anything)"

1 egg

Slice of American cheese "(or cottage or Swiss or cream cheese)"

1 tomato

1 can sardines "(or anchovies or smoked salmon)"

1 slice onion

Cold baked beans (small can)

Equipment: Egg slicer (optional)

1. Put egg in a small pot of hot water and bring to a boil.
2. Cook 15 minutes. Run cold water over egg to cool.
3. Shell egg and slice with knife or egg slicer.
4. Butter both slices of bread.
5. "Start building with crisp lettuce, continue with sliced chicken, egg, cheese, tomato, etc. Additions which may be inserted to taste are: sliced pineapple, chopped or sliced pickle, pickled beets, olives, cucumbers, Russian dressing, ketchup, mayonnaise, horseradish, salt and pepper."
6. Top with another layer of lettuce and the other piece of buttered bread.

Serve in kitchen late at night, taking one mouth-filling bite just before wife demands explanation.

46

WORLD WAR II
(1941–1945)

As in World War I, the United States had already begun to adapt its economy and food system before it formally entered the war. Many of the World War I measures were easily resumed after December 7, 1941. Victory Gardens were planted the following spring, and government relief agencies moved smoothly from helping people get through the Great Depression to smoothing over food and farm labor shortages.

Formal food rationing began in April 1942 with sugar. Six months later, coffee was rationed. But it was spring 1943 before full-scale ration books were issued, with stamps that could be torn out and handed in with the purchase of rationed goods. The first books had 48 blue points (for canned fruit and vegetables) and 64 red points (for meat and cheese). The system eventually applied to canned meats and fish, fresh fish, butter, and fresh milk as well. In contrast to World War I's voluntary food restrictions, the ration-stamp system was the law. Local authorities could grant a variety of exemptions, and there was some evasion of the rules and an informal "black market" in many places. Fluctuating prices also affected how home front families cooked and ate,

but the mobilization of women to work in war industries meant that many families had ready cash, and some were doing better than they had in the depression years. Rationing was part of a wider system of government economic controls that included freezes on wages, prices, and strikes; rationing of gasoline, tires, and shoes.

World War II rationing was enough similar to World War I's voluntary controls that many of the old recipes for **War Butter** and **War Cake** came back out. In addition, families saved cooking fats, tin cans, and aluminum foil to recycle for war production. A pound of fat could be sold back to a butcher for four cents and two ration points. Chicken and milk were rationed, in contrast to World War I, but were generally low-point bargains and widely available. Pork production was kept up, and Spam (introduced 1936) figures in many wartime memories. Cheese, eggs, soybeans, and peanuts were promoted as meat substitutes. Government food propaganda was generally more positive about helping the war effort and less directed to stereotypes of Germans or Japanese than had been the case during the World War I. Again, there was some renaming of hamburger as "Salisbury Steak,"

Figure 36 Woman shopping with ration coupons in the 1940s. *Source: © Bettmann/CORBIS.*

but less than in World War I, especially since hamburger was by now one of the more typical foods of the home front. For a brief period in early 1943 the government proposed to ban pre-sliced bread (the machines wasted power), but quickly gave up.

By 1943 there were an estimated 20 million Victory Gardens, providing almost one-third of the nation's vegetables. Home and group canning was widely promoted. There was a record crop of peanuts. Cooking pamphlets promoted organ meats and less popular cuts that required fewer ration points.

As in all previous American wars, mobilization meant migration for millions of people. War industries and the military draft took from their family farms many young people who became city dwellers (and then suburbanites) after the war.

At the end of the war, women workers were sent home almost immediately, and shortages of meat and flour quickly replaced rationing. As with the post-World War I period, food aid for reconstruction, especially of Europe, meant that American families continued to work with wartime recipes for a few years afterward.

Food in the armed services was plain but plentiful. Scientifically preserved rations were introduced at the front lines and were safer than, if just as widely despised as, the hardtack and salt beef of earlier wars. U.S. forces were overseas much longer in World War II and developed an interest in European and Asian foods that came back to the United States. The great postwar popularity of pizza and spaghetti came from tastes developed by American soldiers over the long campaign through Italy. Suburban Chinese restaurants took on a "Polynesian" theme to remind veterans of their postings in Hawaii and the South Pacific. Postwar military occupations were lengthened by the emerging Cold War, and one result was marriages between U.S. servicemen and women from Germany, Japan, England, France, and Italy. This brought foreign foods to America, not necessarily in the old immigrant pattern centered on city neighborhoods, but also in the often semirural areas around U.S. military bases.

A recent book, *Grandma's Wartime Kitchen*, by Joanne Lamb Hayes, gives some feel for cooking under rationing in the United States, but unfortunately most of the recipes are adapted for modern kitchens, and none are fully sourced. A much better job is the "Victory Dinner" chapter of *Square Meals*, by Jane and Michael Stern. Many older Americans recall the World War II period well, and much food history of the time can still be collected. A wonderful recent effort is the 1992 *Cooking Behind the Fence; Recipes and Recollections from the Oak Ridge '43 Club*, collecting the experiences of ordinary people caught up in the enormous secret effort to build the first atomic bombs.

EGGS FERRER (1941)

Much of military life, even during wartime, consists of training and waiting. Admiral T.L. Sprague captures the drabness of waiting for action in the early part of World War II, both in his story and in his relish of a rather simple egg dish that cheered him on. He contributed both to *Favorite Recipes of the Navy and Marine Corps*, compiled in 1950 by Volunteer Women of the Navy Relief Society, San Diego Auxiliary.

I spent the winter of 1941–42 in Argentia, Newfoundland. Breakfast was looked forward to with great relish after several pre-breakfast hours of lowering boats and manning planes in the bitter cold darkness of the North Atlantic winter. The eggs and the toast were usually cold by the time we got a chance to grab them. If there is anything worse than cold toast, it's a cold fried egg. The steward, Ferrer, finally introduced us to what I call "Eggs Ferrer" to honor a great and versatile Navy steward. His recipe intermingles felicitously the eggs and the toast.

Yield: Recipe serves 1, but you can make any number.

1 slice bread
½ tablespoon butter
1 egg

Equipment: Pancake turner, frying pan

1. "You first make a piece of toast, trimming the edges if you desire."
2. "A hole, about an inch and half, round or square, is cut in the center of each piece of toast."
3. "Next, take your trusty frying pan and put in a small piece of butter, being careful not to let it burn."
4. "Put the toast in the pan, and break an egg so that the yolk falls into the hole."
5. "After the toast has cooked on the bottom, turn it over with a pancake turner and let it brown on the other side. Perfectly done, the center will be a little runny."
6. "'Eggs Ferrer' can be put in a warm oven and kept for a considerable period without any serious deterioration in the quality of the delicacy."

"Serve with large cups of hot coffee and very crisp bacon."

SAUSAGE, BOLOGNA, FRIED (1942)

This is a dish my father remembered from "the service" and reproduced at home with Jewish salami. This recipe is from TM 10-405 *Technical Manual of the Army Cook* April 24, 1942. You can easily reduce the recipe for fewer servings.

Remove sausage casing and slice about one-half inch thick and dip in batter made by beating eggs and adding milk. Fry in deep fat. Serve hot. Bologna sausage may also be served cold with salad, made into sandwiches.

CAUTION: HOT OIL USED.

Yield: Serves 100 men

30 pounds bologna sausage

12 large eggs

2 [pint] cans milk, evaporated, or 2 quarts fresh milk

3 pounds "fat"

Equipment: Heavy kettle for frying, deep-fry thermometer, fry basket or long-handled skimmer or slotted spoon

1. Peel bolognas and cut into ½-inch slices.
2. Break eggs and whip briefly.
3. If using evaporated milk, dilute with 1 quart water to make 2 quarts. Stir milk into eggs.
4. Dip sausages into egg mixture.
5. Heat fat in kettle to 350 degrees.
6. Fry bologna slices in batches so that the oil keeps bubbling.

Serve buffet style with overcooked scrambled eggs and stale buttered toast.

APPLE SAUCE CAKE (1940s)

"This keeps a long time and is ideal to send to the boys or girls in the Service," wrote Rena Sherman, in submitting this recipe to *Favorite Recipes*, published by the Ladies' Benevolent Society, Second Congregational Church, Palmer, Massachusetts. Food packages from home have reached soldiers in all American wars, but during World War II the postal service made a special effort to reach GIs in the field. Arrangements were made for mailable books. Ms. Sherman suggested mailing this cake, in which applesauce replaces some of the fat, in coffee cans for "less drying and damage." Moist, chewy cookies also were more likely to reach the front lines in good condition.

Yield: Serves 12

1 cup unsweetened apple sauce

¼ cup molasses

½ cup soft shortening

2 eggs

2½ cups pastry flour

1 level teaspoon baking soda

1 teaspoon cinnamon

1 cup sugar

¼ teaspoon ginger

½ teaspoon nutmeg

1 teaspoon salt

1 cup raisins (or half raisins, half currants)

Nut meats or orange peel (optional)

Equipment: Electric mixer (optional); mixing bowl; large loaf pan or 2 small loaf pans; skewer, toothpick, or wire cake tester; wire rack to cool cake

1. Preheat oven to 350 degrees. "Sift all dry ingredients into mixing bowl."
2. "Now pour entire contents of liquids and shortening into flour and beat about 3 minutes with electric mixer or 4 minutes by hand, or until smooth. Do not over beat. Stir from sides and

bottom if electric mixer is used. Batter should be medium stiff."

3. Then fold in raisins. "Nut meats or orange peel may be added for variety."

4. Grease pan or pans.

5. Bake 45–60 minutes, or until a skewer, toothpick, or wire cake tester comes out clean, and cake pulls away from sides of pan.

6. Cool cake a few minutes in the pan, then remove from pan and cool on wire rack.

7. To mail to the front, wrap tightly in waxed paper.

Serve to best buddies or shipmates.

THE ALL-AMERICAN SUNDAE (1942)

This red-white-and-blue dessert was promoted by the Ice Cream Merchandising Institute in a "Victory Sundae" campaign in which each sundae was sold along with a ten-cent Defense Savings Stamp. Students were encouraged to collect $18.75 worth of the stamps in an album, which could then be exchanged for a $25 war bond. The stamp program continued until 1970. The recipe is from the 1978 *The Great American Ice Cream Book*, by Paul Dickson.

Yield: Serves 1

¼ cup white marshmallow topping

2 scoops vanilla ice cream

4 maraschino cherries

1 tablespoon fresh or frozen blueberries

Equipment: Scoop, ice cream sundae dish

1. Mince cherries.

2. Pour half the marshmallow sauce into the sundae dish.

3. Put two scoops of vanilla ice cream on top of the marshmallow sauce.

4. Pour the other half of the marshmallow sauce over the ice cream.

5. On one side of the dish, put 2 soda spoons of the cherries.

6. On the other side of the dish, put 2 soda spoons of the blueberries.

Serve with one 10-cent Defense Savings Stamp, and charge an extra dime.

CALIFORNIA "CHICKEN" (1942)

This tuna vegetable casserole used a fish that was then canned in the United States, stretched with unrationed vegetables. The recipe is from *Victory Meal Planner*, issued by the New York State Bureau of Milk Publicity. I've also referred to a recipe for fifty in "Community Meals," by May E. Foley, issued around the same time by the Massachusetts State College Extension Service, and intended for groups, organizations, and Red Cross canteens. Tuna fish was packed in thirteen-ounce cans in the 1940s.

Yield: Serves 6

⅓ pound carrots (to make 1 cup diced)

1 medium potato (to make 1 cup diced)

1 small onion

1 can peas (or ⅔ cup fresh)

3 tablespoons butter, plus some to grease casserole dish.

¼ cup bread crumbs

3 tablespoons flour

1½ cups whole milk

"1 can tuna fish" [2 6-ounce cans packed in oil]

Equipment: 2-quart casserole dish, large saucepan, heavy skillet

1. Peel and dice carrots and potato.

2. Halve, peel, and chop onion to get ¼ cup of chopped onion.

3. "If canned peas are used, do not cook with vegetables but use the water from

peas as part of water for cooking other vegetables." In a saucepan, cover vegetables with water (including pea-packing liquid), add 1 teaspoon salt, and bring to a boil. Cook 15 minutes.

4. In a heavy skillet, melt butter, add flour, and cook for a few minutes to blend well.

5. Stir milk into butter-flour mixture, and ½ cup of the vegetable cooking water. Cook until the mixture thickens.

6. Butter casserole, and add half the vegetables and half the white sauce. (If using canned peas, add half of them at this point.)

7. Add the tuna fish as a middle layer.

8. Now add the rest of the vegetables and white sauce.

9. Sprinkle on crumbs.

10. Bake at 350 degrees "until crumbs are brown and sauce bubbles up around the edges," about 25 minutes.

Serve with cabbage slaw, bread or rolls, apple crisp, and milk.

VICTORY SPREAD (1943)

War Butter from World War I was revived in many recipes, including one from Knox Gelatin that used evaporated milk. This, however, is the one spread anyone remembered or used after the war, although generally without the milk. The recipe is from *Cooking on a Ration*, by Marjorie Mills, a Boston food editor.

Yield: 48 1-tablespoon servings

½ pound (2 sticks) butter

½ pound (2 sticks) "fortified margerine"

1 cup whole milk or light cream

Yellow or red food coloring (optional)

Equipment: Whisk or handheld electric mixer, or standing rotary mixer

1. One hour before starting, remove butter and margarine from refrigerator to soften.

2. Cream together butter and margerine "until soft but not oily, tinting to desired shade" by adding a few drops of food coloring at a time.

3. Heat the milk or cream to lukewarm in a saucepan or microwave oven.

4. "Gradually add 1 cup lukewarm milk, beating with a rotary beater or electric mixer until mixture is well blended. Add salt to taste."

Serve with whole grain bread or cornbread.

SARA ROWAN WATKINS' VEGETABLE MEAT LOAF SANDWICH (1944)

With cuts of meat rationed by their scarcity, hamburger "cost" fewer points, and was easily stretched. Probably the most typical dish of the home front in World War II was meat loaf, and cold meat loaf sandwiches were popular with war workers.

One of the more unusual home front situations, however, was a secret city in East Tennessee now called Oak Ridge, built by the U.S. Army to produce nuclear materials for the first atomic bombs. Civilian workers arrived by train at the Knoxville railroad station and dialed a secret number for an army truck to pick them up and take them to the "Clinton Engineer Works." Eventually it was a city of seventy-five thousand, quietly using one-seventh of all the electricity in the United States, and $300 million worth of silver borrowed from the U.S. Treasury, to refine uranium 235 and plutonium.

Sara Rowan was fifteen when she came to Oak Ridge with her parents and eight siblings. With both parents and the oldest brother and sister working at one of the plants, Sara was assigned to lunch box duty and developed this meat loaf based on a 1943 Westinghouse pamphlet, "How to Pack Lunches for War Workers." Most of the workers were not supposed to know exactly what they were working on, but the rumor was that it was a bomb that would end the war. This recipe made one sandwich for each family member to take to the factory or school. (In some classes at the high school, there were thirty or more students, each from a different state!) The recipe was remembered for *Cooking Behind the Fence; Recipes and Recollections from the Oak Ridge '43 Club*, published in 1992.

Yield: Serves 9

2½ cups cooked peas and diced carrots

1 pound hamburger

½ cup quick-cooking oats

1 cup canned milk

6 tablespoons chopped onion (from medium onion)

Solid shortening to grease loaf pan

18 slices of bread

Equipment: Large loaf pan, mixing bowl, stoneware platter

1. "Cook and drain vegetables, reserving liquids for soup." (You can use frozen or canned peas and carrots as well.)
2. Halve, peel, and chop onion very fine to make the 6 tablespoons of chopped onion.
3. Grease loaf pan, and preheat oven to 350 degrees.
4. Mix all ingredients together with 1 teaspoon of salt and ⅛ teaspoon pepper in a mixing bowl.
5. Press mixture into the loaf pan.
6. Bake 1½ hours.
7. Cool loaf, and turn out onto a platter. Refrigerate.
8. Slice when cold.
9. Make one sandwich for each lunch box.

Serve meat loaf sandwiches with carrot sticks, lemonade and cookies, advised "Your Share," by "Betty Crocker," published by General Mills.

47

THE COLD WAR
(1948–1973)

With the end of World War II, world politics became polarized between the "Communist Bloc" and the "Western Allies" (the United States, Great Britain, and France). It was a "cold" war because few direct shots were fired by the superpowers, but policies were based on a worldwide struggle first for control of governments between the two alliances, and then for influence in less developed countries. The period became known for "proxy wars" such as the Korean Conflict, the early U.S. intervention in Laos, the Vietnam War, civil wars in Cuba, Ethiopia, Congo, Angola, and Mozambique; the three wars in the Middle East; and—at the end—the Soviet invasion of Afghanistan. Public concerns in the United States were also organized around the perceived Soviet threat, from the "Red Scares" and blacklisting of former Communists in the 1950s, to the "Missile Gap" issue of the 1960 election, the "Space Race," and the widespread anxiety about imminent nuclear war that led some people to build and equip "fallout shelters," and to the beginnings of the survivalist movement. Even the Civil Rights Movement was widely discussed in terms of how American democracy would

be perceived by new nations of Africa and Asia as they chose sides in the Cold War.

Probably more advice was given about fallout shelters than followed, but much of it was contradictory, as is shown in a University of California at Davis online collection of quotations from government shelter manuals from 1960–1984:

> The following conditions will probably prevail in the event of a nuclear attack. Fresh milk will be impossible to obtain and canned evaporated or dry powdered milk must be substituted. . . . Since chickens have great tolerance for radiation, fresh eggs will probably be one of the first staples available after a nuclear attack. . . .
>
> Buy only foods that will be enjoyed because shelter occupants will be under emotional stress. When buying shelter food select proper size containers to eliminate left-overs that might be difficult to preserve. . . .
>
> Store, prepare, and serve the following inside shelter facilities: bacon; corned beef hash; sausage; meat balls; chili con carne; tamales; chipped beef; salmon steak; crab meat; shrimp;

Figure 37 A well-equipped fallout shelter in Seattle in 1962. *Seattle Post Intelligencer Collection. Source:* © Museum of History & Industry/CORBIS.

clams; oysters; smoked bologna; country cured ham; au gratin potatoes; spaghetti; macaroni; buckwheat mix; canned cheese; tomatoes; brown bread; flour; relish; maple syrup; oatmeal; hot cereals; baby foods as needed. . . . It might be sensible to keep a few packages of vegetable seeds in the shelter for a do-it-yourself postwar project.

One early form of the Cold War was extended military occupations of the nations defeated in World War II, Japan and Germany, and their wartime conquests. In 1948 the U.S., British, and French governments announced a common form of money in their zones of occupation of Germany, as a prelude to ending the postwar occupation.

The Soviets wanted to continue occupying Germany and stopped all shipments on the road through Soviet-occupied Germany to Berlin (which had zones of occupation by each of four war-time allies). The "Berlin Airlift" was a series of air drops in 1948 and 1949 by which the United States and Great Britain nonviolently resisted this pressure to withdraw from Berlin with more than 276,000 flights. The official price of the American effort alone was $300 million. The Cold War is variously dated as beginning with the differences of opinion between the United States and the Soviet Union at the 1944 Yalta conference during World War II, U.S. Diplomat George F. Kennan's "long telegram" advocating political "containment" of the USSR in February 1946, Sir Winston Churchill's "Iron

Curtain" speech a month later, or the Berlin Blockade of 1948–1949. The period is most often described as having ended with the Soviet withdrawal from Afghanistan and the end of the Berlin Wall in 1989, the re-unification of Germany the next year, the end of 1991 (used by the U.S. Congress in a resolution asking the secretary of defense to award a Cold War service ribbon), and the breakup of the Soviet Union in 1992.

While there are few American dishes associated with the Cold War itself, many living Americans recall the period, and historians are now beginning to see it as ending around 1990 and to study it as a distinct time. This chapter gathers some recipes identified with particular personalities and issues of the time.

HURRY-UP SUPPER DISH AND COTTAGE CHEESE (1949)

This recipe was submitted by Evelyn Panuch to *Operation Vittles; What's Cooking in Berlin*, published in Germany by American military wives during the Berlin Airlift. The book had probably been planned before the blockade, and much of it is about the difficulties of explaining American food to German servants. However this easy recipe was designed to use the ingredients provided by the airlift, which some German youngsters called "noodle bombers." The dish is a quicker version of a German or German-American noodle pudding. I believe Ms. Panuch's cinnamon had become stale during the blockade, as she suggests half-cinnamon, half-sugar. I have adjusted the quantities for supermarket cinnamon.

For the genuine flavor of the blockade, here's Edith Gangloff's recipe for two cups of cottage cheese from powdered milk.

Mix powdered milk with water to make three quarts milk. Add ⅓ more powder than required, to make light cream. [10 cups water to 5⅓ cups of

today's nonfat dry milk.] Let sour naturally. (Takes about 3 days.) To make sour faster add either ½ cup lemon juice or ¼ cup vinegar. When thick, let drip in cloth bag (sugar sack) [jelly bag] over-night. Makes about two cups cheese.

Yield: Serves 4 as a light supper

1 package noodles (1 pound)

½ cup butter

2 cups cottage cheese

⅓ cup sugar and cinnamon (start with 1 tablespoon cinnamon)

Equipment: Colander, serving platter, spatula

1. Cook noodles according to package directions.

2. Meanwhile melt butter and cook to golden brown.

3. Measure a tablespoon of cinnamon into a measuring cup. Fill with sugar to the ⅓ cup mark. Mix well with a fork.

4. Drain noodles in colander. Tip into mixing bowl and mix well with butter.

5. Put noodles on platter in a flat layer.

6. Layer on cottage cheese.

7. Sprinkle on sugar-cinnamon mixture.

Serve with a spatula.

UNDER THE SEA SALAD (1952)

This recipe is from *Dolphin Dishes; The Submarine Cookbook*, published for the benefit of the Navy Relief Society. It was submitted by navy wife Sylvia Barnes and is a typical jellied salad of the 1950s. The submarine service played a large role in the Cold War, secretly helping spies in their missions and operating in distant areas where it was vulnerable to Soviet attack.

Submarines were an area where American military superiority contributed to American security, especially after the development of submarine-based missiles. This superiority was costly, as was proved by the disastrous losses of the nuclear submarines Thresher (in 1963 with 129 on board) and Scorpion (carrying 99 in 1968). The Thresher seems to have lost power on a test dive. Because it was designed for greater depths than any other submarine, the crew could not be rescued, and it was quite difficult to locate the wreck. The Scorpion was lost while experimenting with a reduced-maintenance policy. At the time, nuclear submarines were spending more time in repairs than actually serving at sea. Improvements after these disasters have made U.S. submarines safe for more than thirty years, but perhaps you can feel some of the anxiety that would have gone onto the table with Under the Sea Salad.

Yield: Serves 8–12

1 package lime Jell-o

1 package red colored Jell-o (optional)

2 cups of canned pears

½ cups juice from the pears

2 small [3-ounce] packages cream cheese

1 teaspoon vinegar

Equipment: Pyrex loaf pan, whisk or hand-held electric mixer

1. Bring 1½ cups of water to a boil.
2. Dissolve the Jell-o in the boiling water, and add pear juice, ¼ teaspoon of salt, and the vinegar.
3. Pour a ½ layer of the green Jell-o into the loaf pan. Chill until firm. (Chill the rest of the Jell-o in a mixing bowl.)
4. Cut the pears into half-inch dice.
5. When the Jell-o in the mixing bowl is "syrupy," whip "until like whipped cream."
6. Mash creamed cheese with a fork and work into the whipped Jell-o.
7. Fold in the diced pears, and pour this mixture over the green Jell-o.
8. "Add layer of red Jello [make according to package directions] for color contrast if desired."

Serve for dessert, hopefully to men safe on shore leave.

BEEF WITH OYSTER SAUCE (1950S)

During the Cold War, the United States adopted some of the conspiratorial tactics of its Communist opponents. An early leader in this outlook was General Claire Lee Chennault (1893–1958) an air force pioneer of the 1930s who set up an American volunteer group of advisers to Chinese General Chiang Kai Shek in 1941 and went on to lead the 14th Air Force, known as "the flying tigers" in the China-Burma-India theater during World War II. Forced to retire from the Air Force in 1945, Chennault returned to China, married a younger Chinese journalist, Anna Chan (1925–), and organized Chiang's airborne resistance to the Chinese Communists before and after the Communist takeover in 1949. Chennault became head of a CIA-supported airline that supplied secret anti-Communist missions in Asia, and he was active in the United States "China Lobby" that encouraged the United States to support the "Nationalist" Chinese government on Taiwan and to boycott the mainland government.

After Chennault's death, Anna Chenault continued his political work. She had become a United States citizen in 1950. In 1968 she was the go-between for Republican campaign efforts to persuade the president of South Vietnam to withdraw from peace negotiations, perhaps aiding the election of President Nixon. As history turned out, President Nixon began a diplomatic alliance with Communist China in 1972. Mrs. Chennault continued propaganda broadcasts on the Voice of America. In recent years, she has visited China, endowed scholarships there, and met with leading officials, who praise her work for reconciliation with the Taiwan government she had supported in the 1950s and 1960s. With George F. Kennan, physicist Henry Teller, and Fidel Castro, Mrs. Chennault is one of the very few living Cold War figures whose activity spans the entire period.

This recipe was contributed to the 1978 *The Celebrity Cookbook*. Mrs. Chennault's recipe is probably from her childhood in Beijing, but also caters to the American taste for beef. The deep-fat frying is more typical of Taiwan-style cooking and may reflect her many visits to Taiwan.

CAUTION: HOT OIL USED.

Yield: Serves 4

1 pound beef tenderloin

3 tablespoons oyster sauce

6 pieces green onion (scallions)

1-inch piece of root ginger

¼ teaspoon soy sauce

1 teaspoon salt (omit if using salted "cooking sherry")

3 cups oil for deep frying (peanut, canola)

1 teaspoon sesame oil

4 tablespoons rice wine (substitute dry sherry, cooking sherry, or cider vinegar), plus 1 teaspoon for stir-fry step

2 tablespoons "stock" (may substitute canned bouillon or bouillon made up from cubes)

1 tablespoon cornstarch

Equipment: Large bowl to marinate steak, deep heavy pot for deep frying, deep-fat thermometer, metal skimmer or Chinese brass-wire skimmer, wok or frying pan to stir-fry, paper towels, Chinese or western spatula to fit wok or frying pan

1. An hour before beginning, put beef in freezer. It will cut more easily if half-frozen.

2. Slice beef into thin slices 2 inches long and 1 inch wide.

3. In large bowl, mix cornstarch, 4 tablespoons rice wine, and salt if using. Add beef strips and toss to coat. Let marinate for 1 hour.

4. Peel ginger and cut 6 thin slices across. Cut each into matchsticks, and then again across the sticks to make very fine dice.

5. Cut scallions into 1-inch lengths.

6. Measure out and combine the teaspoon of rice wine, the sesame oil, the oyster sauce, and the stock.

7. Just before deep-frying beef, add ½ tablespoon of the oil and mix. "This prevents beef from sticking together when deep fried." Set up paper towels far away from open flame and hot oil.

8. Heat the 3 cups of oil to 370 degrees.

9. Dip the skimmer in the hot oil, put in about ¼ of the beef slices, and lower them into the hot oil for a few seconds to brown them. Lift to drain, then carry over to the paper towels over a light metal pan or stoneware plate. Dry the slices on paper towels.

10. When all the beef has been browned, heat a tablespoon of the oil in the wok or large frying pan.

11. Add the ginger and scallions and stir-fry for a few seconds.

12. Turn up the heat, and add the beef. Let it brown on one side. Don't worry if it sticks a little.

13. Stir-fry the beef, and add the oyster-sauce mixture. Toss with the spatula to coat all the pieces.

"Serve with rice or noodles and green salad."

E PLURIBUS UNUM (1957)

One of the enduring legacies of the Cold War was that all Americans have taken a far greater interest in world affairs. Between the Korean Conflict and the Cuban Missile Crisis, Americans read of confrontations in Vietnam, Iran, Guatemala, Hungary, Lebanon, Egypt, Taiwan, Congo, and South Africa, among other "hotspots." The twenty-nine cuisines in *What's Cooking Around the World*, a 1957 publication of the Army Language School Women's Club of Monterey, California, reflect American foreign policy concerns of the time, from Communist influence in European democracies, to realignments in Asia and Middle East. They were: Albanian, Arabian, Bulgarian, Burmese, Chinese, Czechoslovakian, Finnish, French, German, Greek, Hungarian, Indonesian, Italian, Japanese, Korean, Lithuanian, Persian, Polish, Portuguese, Romanian, Russian, Scandinavian, Serbo-Croatian, Slovene, Spanish, Thai, Turkish, Ukrainian, and Vietnamese. U.S. immigration was severely limited from 1924 to 1965, so some of the language instructors had few resources for familiar foods.

The book also includes a section of American dishes, among them this hot dish submitted by faculty wife Mrs. Jean Sexton. The name is a Latin motto on the U.S. dollar bill, meaning "many into one," with the implication that the United States—or at least the Army Language School—was a melting pot, or in this case, a casserole. The rise of what are now called "identity politics" in the 1970s cast doubt on the "melting pot" theory, as ethnic Americans and new immigrants argued for cultural diversity within majority-rule democracy.

Yield: Serves 4

4 medium potatoes

2 onions

¾ cup rice

1 green pepper

1 large can whole tomatoes

8 slices bacon

½ cup bread crumbs

¼ cup grated cheese

Shortening to grease casserole

Equipment: Saucepan with cover, ovenproof casserole

1. Cook rice 15 minutes in covered pot with 1¼ cups water, about 15 minutes. Remove from heat and let stand covered.

2. Peel and slice potatoes.

3. Halve, peel, and slice onions. (Use swim goggles to avoid tears.)

4. Cut off top and bottom of green pepper. Remove core and pith, and cut into rings. Cut stem out of top to make another ring.

5. Grease casserole and layer in half the rice, potatoes, onions, green pepper, and bacon.

6. Season with salt and pepper, and layer on tomatoes.

7. Layer in the other half of the rice, potatoes, onions, pepper, and bacon.

8. Season again. Cover with bread crumbs and grated cheese.

9. Bake casserole uncovered at 350 degrees for 1 hour.

Serve as light supper, or at a potluck for the commandant with foods from Lebanon, Korea, Romania, China, Japan, Hungary, Sweden, and Denmark.

Maria Von Braun's "Glorified Hamburger" (1960s)

Among the first skirmishes of the Cold War was the competition to recruit German military scientists in the last days of World War II. The United States kept missile-designer Wernher Von Braun (1912–1977) and his group in hiding on U.S. military bases for several years. He had to propose marriage to a cousin in Germany by mail. Eventually the Von Brauns settled in Huntsville, Alabama, where he led the U.S. intercontinental ballistic missile program, and the exploration of space through a landing on the moon. This scientifically precise version of Sloppy Joes was passed to a neighbor, Mrs. Alleda Coons, who recorded it in *Twickenham Receipts and Sketches*, published by the Twickenham Historic Preservation District Association, Inc., of Huntsville, Alabama, in 1978.

Yield: Serves 4

1 pound hamburger

1 medium onion

3 tablespoons vinegar

3 tablespoons sugar

$\frac{1}{2}$ teaspoon pepper

1 cup catsup

1 tablespoon Worcestershire sauce

1 teaspoon salt

4 hamburger rolls

Equipment: Skillet, Crock-Pot (optional)

1. Halve, peel, and chop the onion.

2. Brown onion and hamburger in skillet.

3. Add the other ingredients (except rolls) and mix well.

4. "The longer it cooks, the better it is. . . . This can be cooked in a crock pot after browning."

Serve spread quite thickly on rolls.

Savory Lemon Pats (1962)

This recipe was submitted by J. Edgar Hoover to the 1962 *Jango Mess Kit*, published by the Junior Army Navy Guild Organization of Washington D.C. Mr. Hoover was director of the Federal Bureau of Investigation from 1924 to his death in 1972, and the leading source of published and leaked information on alleged Communist activities as well as those of civil rights leaders, the presidents for whom he worked, and their political opponents. In the late 1960s it was learned that the FBI under Hoover had not only investigated and infiltrated radical and criminal organizations, it had also used "dirty tricks" and provocations to destroy them.

Some of the information Hoover held or leaked about political opponents and radicals was about nonconforming lifestyles such as homosexuality. Because of the atmosphere of fear during the Cold War, such accusations could ruin lives and careers. Ironically, rumors of homosexuality were also spread about Hoover, who never married and spent most of his nonworking hours with his assistant director of more than forty years, Clyde Tolson, also a bachelor. The two men socialized freely in Washington, D.C., and Hoover gave out several recipes for charitable cookbooks. In this recipe for herbed butter, he shows a gourmet sensibility, which might have been thought of as a homosexual trait in 1962, but of course the recipe is for something that goes on a hyper-masculine food, beefsteak.

Yield: "12 pats"

$\frac{1}{4}$ pound butter

1 lemon

1 teaspoon seasoned salt

2 tablespoons chopped parsley

$\frac{1}{8}$ teaspoon savory

¹⁄₈ teaspoon rosemary

¹⁄₈ teaspoon marjoram

Equipment: Juicer, lemon zester or grater

1. Remove butter from refrigerator 1 hour before making recipe.
2. Grate or zest off enough lemon peel to make 2 teaspoons finely minced.
3. Juice lemon to get 3 tablespoons juice. Mince parsley to get the 2 tablespoons required.
4. "Cream butter until soft."
5. "Add lemon peel and juice [and salt and parsley and herbs] gradually, mixing until butter has absorbed savory, rosemary, and marjoram."
6. "Place on waxed paper and mold into a roll."
7. "Chill until firm."
8. Slice to make 12 pats.

"Serve on broiled steaks."

ALMOND FLOAT (1960s)

This recipe was submitted by Claire Boothe Luce (1903–1987), another prominent member of the "China Lobby," to the 1978 *The Celebrity Cookbook*. Her husband, Henry Luce, was born in China of missionary parents and was publisher of *Time*, *Life*, and *Fortune* magazines, a powerful media combination over the middle of the twentieth century. Mrs. Luce was a Republican member of Congress (1943–1947), ambassador to Italy (1953–1957), and a member of the Foreign Interests Advisory Board under Presidents Ford and Reagan. She was also a playwright and novelist. This is an Americanized version of a Chinese dessert she must have encountered many times on visits to Taiwan and at China Lobby functions.

NOTE: DISH REQUIRES LENGTHY CHILLING.

Yield: Serves 8–12

¹⁄₂ cup sugar

1 envelope (1 tablespoon) Knox unflavored gelatin

1³⁄₄ cup milk

1 teaspoon almond extract

1 11-ounce can mandarin orange slices

1 cup fresh or canned pineapple cubes

Fresh mint leaves for garnish (optional)

Equipment: Small saucepan, 9-by-5-inch loaf pan

1. In a small saucepan, stir together ¹⁄₄ cup of the sugar, the gelatin, and a dash of salt. Add ¹⁄₂ cup of the milk and turn on low heat. Cook and stir until the gelatin is dissolved, approximately 5 minutes.
2. Add remaining milk and almond extract. Pour into the loaf pan and refrigerate until firm, 4–5 hours or overnight.
3. Combine the rest of the sugar and ¹⁄₄ cup water in the saucepan. Bring to a boil and cook about 3 minutes. Set aside to cool.
4. When the syrup is cool, refrigerate to chill thoroughly.
5. When ready to serve, cut gelatin on diagonals into 1-inch diamonds. Add to orange slices and pineapple cubes.
6. Pour chilled syrup over fruit and gelatin.

Serve garnished with mint leaves.

PERCOLATOR WASSAIL (1973)

The Cold War required a global military commitment, including many remote areas that had never before had strategic importance. Defense against nuclear bombs and missiles required a system of radar stations in the far north, and intelligence-gathering planes, ships, and remote bases. It's easy to envision this no-alcohol version of a traditional Christmas drink served up in the guard shack of a foreign base. The recipe was submitted by Michael Mello for *Something Special*, published by the Air Force Sergeants Association International Auxiliary.

Yield: 2 quarts, serves 16–24

2 quarts apple cider

½ cup brown sugar

½ teaspoon whole allspice

1 teaspoon whole cloves

1 cinnamon stick

Dash powdered nutmeg

¼ teaspoon salt

1 orange

Equipment: 10–12 cup electric coffee percolator

1. Cut orange in wedges, leaving on the peel.
2. Pour apple cider into the lower part of the coffeemaker.
3. Place basket in coffeemaker, put all remaining ingredients in basket.
4. "Cover and perk."

Serve with cookies from home.

48

THE CIVIL RIGHTS MOVEMENT AND ITS OPPONENTS (1950s–1970)

Neither the Civil Rights movement nor its opponents was famous for food, although a minor result of the struggle was the emergence of "soul food" restaurants and cookbooks in the early 1970s. Indirectly, the Civil Rights movement also fostered two health food movements that have attempted to reform soul food from within—the reducing diets and fasting promoted by activist and former comedian Dick Gregory and the special diet of the Black Muslims, which is discussed in *The American Ethnic Cookbook for Students*. This chapter gathers some recipes used by activists in the Civil Rights movement, some served at the tables of government officials committed to racial segregation and some published by politicians scrambling to position themselves.

CHICKEN & DUMPLINGS (1950s)

This recipe was contributed by "Rosa L. Parks, Civil Rights Activist" to *Celebrating Our Mothers' Kitchens: Treasured Memories And Tested Recipes*, published in 1994 by The National Council of Negro Women, Inc. It is a typical Sunday dinner and might even be served to family guests or the pastor and his family. Perhaps Mrs. Parks served this

dish to Rev. Martin Luther King Jr. when they worked together on the 1956 Montgomery, Alabama, bus boycott, the beginning of the modern Civil Rights movement.

Yield: Serves 6

1 3-pound broiler-fryer chicken

2 stalks celery, cut into 1-inch pieces

3 carrots, cut into 1-inch pieces

1 medium onion, quartered

½ cup flour, and more for rolling out dumplings

2 tablespoons cold water

1 egg white

Equipment: Large sauce pot, skimmer or slotted spoon, mixing bowl, rolling pin, board

1. Cut up chicken into serving pieces.

2. Wash celery and cut into 1-inch lengths.

3. Peel carrots and cut into 1-inch pieces.

4. Halve and peel onion, and halve again to make quarters.

5. Put chicken and vegetables into a large sauce pot with water to cover and bring to a boil.

6. Add 1½ teaspoons of salt and ¼ teaspoon pepper. Reduce heat and simmer 30 minutes or until chicken is tender.

7. Meanwhile, wash and dry cutting board.

8. Separate egg by pouring between shells over a cup (or use egg whites in cartons or powdered).

9. In a small bowl mix egg white and 2 tablespoons cold water, then work in the flour until you have a stiff dough. You may need to knead it a little bit until it is smooth.

10. Flour the cutting board and a rolling pin. Roll out the dough ⅛ inch thick. (Don't worry about the shape.)

11. Cut dough into 1-inch strips.

12. Remove chicken and vegetables with skimmer and set aside.

13. Bring broth to a full boil, and add the dumplings.

14. Return the vegetables and chicken to the pot, maintaining the boil. Cook without stirring on medium-high heat until the dumplings are tender.

Serve with greens or a green vegetable.

ANNE BRADEN'S SPAGHETTI (1960s)

Anne Braden and her husband Carl were introduced to civil rights activism when they agreed to purchase a home in a white neighborhood in Louisville, Kentucky, for an African-American couple in 1954. When the house was bombed, the Bradens themselves were charged with sedition. The prosecution's theory was that the bombing was a Communist plot to undermine the segregated basis of Kentucky society. Carl Braden served eight months of a fifteen-year sentence. The Bradens worked with Dr. King and later staffed the Southern Conference Educational Fund, which provided training and support for civil rights activists across the South. The recipe is from *SCEF Recipes; a Radical Cookbook*, edited by Ruth Goldberg and Lenore Hogan, and published in 1973. This kind of spaghetti was the universal dish of parties and suppers of the Civil Rights movement and the anti-Vietnam-War movement until vegetarianism became more prominent around 1970. (By 1973, Mrs. Braden wrote, "When you have vegetarian guests, do the meat balls separately.")

Yield: Serves 6–8 and could be multiplied

2 pounds hamburger

2–3 large green peppers "(when expensive, reduce amount)"

3–4 large onions

3 tablespoons cooking oil

2 medium cans tomatoes

2 small cans tomato sauce

2 small cans tomato paste

"a good bit" of garlic salt

"a good bit" of oregano

1 pound spaghetti

Grated cheese

Equipment: Large skillet, large spaghetti pot, large saucepan

1. Halve, peel, and chop onions "not particularly small."

2. Core and seed peppers, and cut into similar pieces.

3. Heat cooking oil in a large skillet, and fry onions and peppers until soft.

4. When vegetables are soft, crumble in hamburger.

5. While hamburger is cooking, put tomatoes, sauce, and paste in "a big cooker and season with a good bit of garlic salt, pepper, and oregano."

6. When hamburger is ready, drain off the grease, and dump the meat into the tomato sauce.

7. "Obviously, if it has time to simmer awhile it is better, but it can be served as soon as the spaghetti cooks."

8. Bring 4–6 quarts of water to a boil and cook spaghetti according to package directions. If you use more water to make more spaghetti, the cooking time will be the same, but it will take as much longer to bring to a boil as there is more water.

9. When spaghetti is done, but slightly chewy in the middle, drain and put back into the big pot. Pour the sauce over, and add grated cheese "in quantity desired."

Serve with salad and garlic bread.

LBJ Noche Specials (1964)

Were it not for the Vietnam War, Lyndon Johnson would be remembered as the first president who fully supported the Civil Rights movement and pushed Congress to pass legislation it had avoided for almost hundred years. Even as a Texas senator he had voted for the Civil Rights bills of 1957 and 1960. There is some evidence that President Johnson pursued the Vietnam war despite personal doubts because he felt that the Democrats—the traditional Southern white party—had to be seen as tough overseas if they embraced minority rights at home. The recipes the Johnson family released during his presidency were mostly, like this one, Texas versions of what most Americans view as "Mexican food." In the area of food politics, then, President Johnson was able to sidestep black-white stereotyping by favoring regional foods that were neither traditionally "white" nor "black." The recipe is in *Dining with Democrats*, by

Vera O'Lessker. These neat canapés were more usually called nachos, so the "Noche" in the title is a reference to President Johnson's late working hours. You can substitute fried tortilla chips for the tortillas and oil.

CAUTION: HOT OIL USED (unless you substitute chips).

Yield: About 40 snacks before you run out of cheese

   1 package corn tortillas
   ½ pound grated mild cheese
   1 small can sliced jalapeño peppers (or six whole pickled jalapeños)
   ½ cup oil

Equipment: Deep fry/candy thermometer, wire racks and paper towels, skimmer or tongs

1. Heat up ½ inch of the oil to 365 degrees in a deep pan.

2. "Cut tortillas into quarters and fry in deep hot fat until brown and crisp on both sides."

3. Drain triangles on wire racks over clean newspaper or paper towels.

4. Arrange triangles on baking sheets.

5. "Put about one teaspoon of grated cheese and a slice of jalapeno pepper on each quarter."

6. Place in a 350-degree oven until well heated and cheese begins to melt.

"Serve at once."

Cucumber Salad (1964)

Although some southern segregationists enjoyed African-American-style food and eagerly employed African-American cooks, others were at pains to present themselves differently, as seen is this neo-Victorian salad of processed foods contributed by Lurleen Wallace, the first wife of Alabama

Governor George C. Wallace, to the 1964 *Dining with Democrats*, by Vera O'Lessker. Not only are the salt and pepper kept strictly segregated from each other, the dish is completely unseasoned! By the mid-1970s Wallace was working with African-American politicians in Alabama, and beginning to appeal to African-American voters. The only tricky part is letting the Jell-o congeal a little bit to coat the mold, but not so much that you can't work in the salad filling.

Yield: Serves 6 as a side dish

1 carton (1 pint) cottage cheese
1 medium onion
1 medium cucumber
1 "scant cup" mayonnaise
1 package lime Jell-o

Equipment: Small round pudding mold or ring mold, colander

1. Rinse mold. "Dissolve Jello [*sic*] in one cup boiling water. [Pour into the mold and] set aside until partially congealed."
2. Drain the cottage cheese in a colander.
3. Halve, peel, and grate the onion (use swim goggles to avoid tears).
4. Grate the cucumber.
5. Mix together cottage cheese, onion, cucumber, and mayonnaise in a mixing bowl.
6. When Jell-o is partly set, fold in this mixture and put in refrigerator until firm.

Serve as a side dish or on a buffet table.

MISSISSIPPI CREOLE GUMBO (1960s)

Not all opponents of the Civil Rights movement had to give up "soul food." Lt. Governor Paul B. Johnson, Jr. (1916–1985)

of Mississippi stood in for Governor Ross Barnett opposing the registration of James Meredith as the first African-American student at the segregated University of Mississippi in 1962, was elected governor and served from 1964 to 1968 on the thinly disguised white supremacy slogan "Stand Tall with Paul." As governor, he opposed murder charges against the Klansmen alleged to have killed three civil rights workers, Goodwin, Schwerner, and Chaney, in 1964. Nevertheless, this African-influenced soup was "frequently served in the Governor's mansion in Jackson," according to Mrs. Paul B. Johnson (*Twickenham Receipts and Sketches*, published by the Twickenham Historic Preservation District Association, Inc., of Huntsville, Alabama, in 1978). This is a very large recipe suitable for large meetings, which might have included those of the Mississippi Sovereignty Commission (1957–1977) that spied on civil rights activists and may have leaked information about them to their murderers.

Yield: Serves 25–50

2 strips bacon
2 cups oil
2 cups flour
6 pounds okra
4 large onions
3 bunches green onions (scallions)
1 bunch parsley
2 bunches celery
6 bell peppers
Garlic powder
Oregano
1 large can and 1 small can Italian peeled tomatoes
½ can Ro-Tel tomatoes
½ can Ro-Tel green chile peppers
1 large can (46 ounces) tomato juice
1 can beef bouillon

6–8 pounds shrimp in the shell (fresh or frozen)

½ box (3 ounces) Zatarain crab boil

½ cup salt

1 to 1½ dozen crabs

1 pound lump crabmeat

1 quart shelled oysters

Kitchen Bouquet (optional)

2 pounds rice

Equipment: Whisk, two large soup pots, colander or food mill, rice cooker or third large pot

1. In a deep, heavy pot, fry bacon crisp.
2. Remove bacon, and add oil to the bacon grease.
3. Whisk in the flour and cook over medium heat, stirring frequently until the oil separates.
4. If using fresh okra, cut off stems and tips, and chop. If using frozen chopped okra, defrost.
5. Add okra to the browned flour oil (watch out for spatters) and "cook down."
6. Halve and peel the onions, and chop into dice.
7. Clean roots and dried parts off green onions and chop into half-inch lengths.
8. Chop celery including a few of the leaves.
9. Core, seed, and chop the green peppers.
10. Chop parsley, discarding most of the stems.
11. Add all the above and garlic powder "to taste" to the okra-flour mixture, and sauté slowly ("cook down") until vegetables are tender.
12. Mash canned tomatoes through colander or food mill into the pot, then wash out the colander or food mill with the tomato juice.
13. Add the can of beef bouillon and the ½ can of chile peppers and stir well.
14. Bring the second soup pot half full of water to a boil.
15. Add the shrimp boil and ½ cup salt to the water, and then the shrimp. Cook ten minutes and drain, reserving the cooking water.
16. Shell and clean the shrimp.
17. Divide the tomato soup mixture between the two pots, and add the shrimp water. Bring to a boil and reduce by ¼. Put on the rice with 1 tablespoon of salt and 1½ quarts of water in a rice cooker, or 2 quarts of water in a soup pot.
18. Clean and quarter the crabs, and remove the small claws.
19. Add the crabs to the soup, and cook 15 minutes.
20. Add the lump crab meat and the oysters to the two pots of soup, cooking only 5 more minutes, "then turn off the heat and your gumbo is ready to eat."
21. If the color is not dark enough, I add Kitchen Bouquet for desired effect.

"Serve over rice in large soup bowls."

PEACH COBBLER (1970)

Lester Maddox (1915–) jumped into national fame by chasing civil rights demonstrators out of his Atlanta cafeteria with a pick handle the day after Lyndon Johnson signed the 1964 Civil Rights Act that required eating places to desegregate. Two years later he was elected governor of Georgia. As governor he refused to attend the 1968 funeral of Dr. Martin Luther King Jr., but he did desegregate state agencies and appoint African-Americans to high positions. Maddox could not succeed himself as governor, but was elected lieutenant governor in 1970 on a ticket with Governor Jimmy Carter. Now in his late eighties, he continues to believe in separation of the races and remains a symbol of resistance to desegregation, along with the pick handle. The private Maddox and his record as governor are defended by some racial liberals, including Dr. King's associate, the late Hosea Williams. This recipe, submitted by Mrs. Lester Maddox to the 1970 *Congressional Club Cook Book*, would have been popular with Georgians of any race. At the Pickrick Restaurant, which the Maddoxes closed a few months after the pick handle incident to avoid desegregation, it might well have been served to African-American employees in the kitchen, or whites-only in the dining room. The specialty of the restaurant was fried chicken, and the pick handles were called "Pickrick drumsticks" in segregationist circles.

Yield: Serves 4–6

¾ cup flour

¾ cup milk

1½ cups sugar

2 teaspoons baking powder

½ cup butter

2 cups fresh peaches, sliced (4 medium peaches, about 1 pound)

Equipment: Vegetable peeler, Pyrex baking dish, microwave oven (optional), oven mitts

1. Sift together the flour, baking powder, 1 cup of the sugar, and a pinch of salt.

2. Peel and slice peaches. Mix with the remaining ½ cup of sugar.

3. Melt butter in the baking dish, either in a microwave on medium heat, or in a 300-degree oven.

4. Heat oven to 350 degrees.

5. Add milk to dry mixture to make a batter.

6. Spread butter around baking dish, and pour in the batter. "Do not stir."

7. Spread on the peaches. "Do not stir."

8. Bake 1 hour at 350 degrees.

   Serve hot or cold.

49

THE VIETNAM WAR
AND ITS OPPONENTS
(1962–1975)

Vietnam stands out among American wars because it was so widely opposed, because the United States and our allies lost decisively, and because there is still little agreement on the causes or meaning of that outcome. Every American military commitment since has been evaluated about whether it is "another Vietnam," but we have yet to agree on what that term means.

One difficulty of the Vietnam War acknowledged by all sides was that in waging a modern guerrilla war, it was important to win the "hearts and minds" of the Vietnamese people in ways that had not been so important even during the Korean Conflict, and certainly not during World War II.

HUSH PUPPIES (1962)

This traditional southern recipe suggests the cultural conservatism of the American military leadership forced to direct a new kind of war in Vietnam. The recipe was contributed by Air Force General Curtis E. LeMay to the 1962 *Jango Mess Kit*, published by the Junior Army-Navy Guild Organization in Washington, D.C. Over LeMay's long career he had originated aerial bombing tactics that were effective in

World War II, organized the Berlin Airlift, and reorganized America's nuclear bombing capability. During the war in Vietnam, LeMay is supposed to have threatened to bomb North Vietnam "back to the Stone Age." Massive bombing was an important part of the American war effort, and left Vietnam one of the world's poorest countries in the world after the war, but did not win it. LeMay was also associated with the use of napalm bombs in Vietnam, which he had pioneered in Japan. The 1972 news photo of a child burned by napalm, Phan Thi Kim Phuc, turned many Americans against the war. LeMay retired from the Joint Chiefs of Staff in 1965 and ran for vice president of the United States with third-party candidate George Wallace in 1968, criticizing limitations on the U.S. war effort. (Phan Thi Kim Phuc was rushed to the hospital by the photographer and survived. She now lives in Canada and is a activist for peace and Christianity.)

CAUTION: HOT OIL USED.

Yield: Serves 8

2 cups cornmeal

2 teaspoons baking powder

1 large onion

⅔ cup milk

1 egg

"[H]ot bacon fat in which fish has been fried"

Equipment: Heavy skillet with high sides, waxed paper, slotted spoon or tongs, mixing bowl, deep-fry thermometer, wire racks

1. Halve, peel, and chop the onion. Mince well. (Use swim goggles to avoid tears.)

2. Combine cornmeal, baking powder, a teaspoon of salt, and chopped onion in a bowl.

3. Beat egg, and add egg and milk to cornmeal.

4. Mold into round balls "about the size of a golf ball" and arrange on waxed paper.

5. Fry in an inch or a little more of hot bacon fat, browning well on both sides, about 3–4 minutes. If you haven't fried too many fish, or are using a more stable fat like peanut oil, you could use the fat at 375 degrees.

6. Drain hush puppies on wire racks.

Serve with fried fish.

MY NOT SO FAMOUS "S-O-S" (1968)

American soldiers went to Vietnam prepared for a more traditional kind of war. Many adjusted quickly, but army food was intended to sustain morale by being familiar. Of course, hardly anyone ate creamed beef at home, but it had been familiar U.S. military food for almost hundred years. (See **Dried Beef**.) Baker Bob Hersey recalls this field kitchen dish from his Vietnam service in 1968–1969 with the 11th Armored Cavalry on his website, ⟨www.ktroop.com⟩. Historically, S-O-S—Hersey suggests "Shucks-On-A-Shingle"—was a dish of creamed chipped beef or ground beef on

toast. Hersey's Vietnam version is based on hamburger, and in less military circumstances might have been called "Hamburger Stroganoff." Hersey writes, "Every GI since Hannibal crossed the Alps has eaten or at least encountered SOS. It is best described as a plate of mouse droppings in wallpaper paste served over burnt toast. It's actually quite good (but remember I lost my taste buds in the war)." I have added some details from the 1969 Armed Forces Recipe Service recipe for "creamed ground beef," posted with many others at ⟨www.seabeecook.com/cookery/recipes/⟩. One difference between Hersey's and the standard recipe of the time is that Hersey uses a lot less milk; the typical proportion would have been about two and a half cups of nonfat dry milk and one and a half gallons of water.

Start with 10 pounds of ground beef (hamburger). The fatty kind is best. Brown the beef in a large saucepan with salt, pepper, finely chopped onions and a splash or two of Worcestershire sauce. This next ingredient isn't in any of the Army's cookbooks but I always added a generous portion of cooking sherry. If I didn't have sherry I would add cognac. Once browned, add a cup of water, a cup of whole milk and bring to a boil. Slowly stir in 1/2 cup of bread flour. This thickens the mixture. Lower the heat and cook slowly for about 5 minutes. If the sauce is too thick add more milk. If it's too thin add more flour. Hint: It's best if the final product is a little on the "thin" side because as it sits in your marmite can, it will thicken up. Serve over toast or better yet, hot biscuits. Any leftovers may be used as brick mortar by the engineers.

Yield: Serves 40

10 pounds cheapest hamburger

3 medium onions

1 tablespoon Worcestershire sauce

1 cup cooking sherry (optional)

1 cup whole milk

½ cup bread flour

Equipment: Oversize stock pot or two large spaghetti pots, long-handled spoon or spatula

1. Halve, peel, and chop onions. Wear swim goggles to avoid tears.

2. Heat up pot or pots. Put 2 tablespoons of salt in the bottom of the pot or pots, and crumble in hamburger. (If using 2 pots, divide hamburger and other ingredients evenly between the pots.)

3. Let hamburger brown and stick for a few minutes before stirring. Add 1 teaspoon of ground black pepper.

4. When the hamburger has released some oil in the bottom of the pot, add the onions and stir well. Cover pot. Lift to stir now and then.

5. When hamburger has lost its red color and there is quite a bit of oil in the pot, add Worcestershire sauce and sherry. (If not using sherry, substitute water.)

6. Scrape bottom of pot to dissolve browned parts in liquid.

7. Add milk and 1 cup of water, and stir well.

8. When pot is again boiling, sprinkle on ½ cup bread flour and stir in thoroughly. Reduce heat and cook 5 minutes more until it thickens to a heavy soupy texture.

9. Adjust thickness with more milk or flour. Don't worry if there are some lumps or too much grease—this was combat comfort food made quickly for stressed-out soldiers.

Serve with toast or biscuits in tin camp bowls.

Do Xao Thap Cam—Buddhist Vegetable Dish (1969)

Unlike opponents of previous United States wars, parts of the anti-Vietnam war movement tried to take the point of view of Vietnamese civilians. Opponents of World War I did not distribute German cookbooks, but during the Vietnam war, the pacifist Committee of Responsibility sold a booklet called "Simple Vietnamese Cookery" to raise money for their project to bring medical aid to Vietnamese children injured in the war. Putting this recipe first was a reminder that the earlier Catholic leadership of Vietnam had alienated the Buddhist majority, engendering a Buddhist peace movement in Vietnam. It also catered to the vegetarians in the American peace movement. Almost the same recipe also appeared in the 1969 *The Powell House Cookbook*, a fund-raiser for a Quaker conference center in Old Chatham, New York, contributed by Nguyen Ngot Thoa and Julia Lyman of Purchase, New York. They were working on the COR project bringing injured Vietnamese children to the United States for treatment. It is unclear if they adapted the recipe from "Simple Vietnamese Cookery" or were among its authors. I have taken options from both recipes.

Yield: Serves 12

1 cucumber

2 carrots

½ green pepper

3 green onions or scallions

2 medium tomatoes

½ pound fresh mushrooms (or ¼ pound dried Chinese mushrooms)

2 cloves garlic (optional)

2 tablespoons "soy sauce (or fish sauce)"

3 tablespoons vegetable oil

Equipment: Heavy skillet with cover

1. If dried mushrooms are used, soak them in warm water for 10 minutes.

2. Slice the tomatoes into small chunks. Cut the other vegetables into thin slices.

3. "Heat oil in large heavy skillet until very hot but not burning."

4. "Drop in garlic cloves, if used, and stir quickly."

5. Add all the vegetables.

6. Add soy sauce—fish sauce was not available in the United States in 1969 except in Filipino groceries—and ¼ cup water, and a pinch each of salt and pepper.

7. Cover pan tightly and steam for 10 minutes.

Serve with rice.

AN EASY RECIPE FOR PROTEIN-ANXIOUS VEGETARIANS (1973)

This recipe was submitted by the well-known author and writing teacher Grace Paley to *Peacemeal; A Cookbook* from the Greenwich Village Peace Center, edited by a committee of five and published in 1973. You can gather something about the frustration of the opposition in the later stages of the war from the introduction, also by Ms. Paley:

> I have also gathered some hot [cooking] tips at the Resistance dinners which we served once a week at the Peace Center to about a hundred young men who were not going to be part of the US plan to torment and murder the Vietnamese people.

Yield: Serves 4–6

1 pint skim-milk ricotta cheese

1 or 2 eggs

2 or 3 heaping tablespoons Parmesan cheese

1½ pounds fresh spinach or 2 packages frozen leaf spinach

Equipment: Microwave oven (optional)

1. If using frozen spinach, defrost. (The microwave oven was not widely used in 1973, but will not change the flavor of the recipe.) Preheat an oven to 350 degrees.

2. Mix thoroughly the ricotta and egg(s), then add the Parmesan cheese.

3. "Add the spinach and mix to a nice green-and-ivory marble."

4. Season to taste with salt and pepper.

5. Bake for 45 minutes.

Serve on a buffet table with spaghetti, tabouli, four-bean salad, whole wheat bread, several more salads and casseroles, and oatmeal raisin cookies.

PHO (1975)

The war in Vietnam ended suddenly with the collapse of the American-supported government of South Vietnam in 1975. About 110,000 refugees were evacuated to the United States immediately and were kept in five relocation camps for processing. At Eglin Air Force Base in Florida, the YMCA was brought in to run recreation and classes in English and in American customs. A cookbook was produced, possibly as a language exercise, but it turned into a project to explain Vietnamese culture to Americans. "All the recipes were contributed by the Vietnamese refugees who were genuinely touched by the thought that Americans might care about their food and how to prepare it," wrote compiler Marjorie K. Doughty, about *Happy in My Stomach/Tôi Vui Trong Lòng; A Collection of Vietnamese/Chinese Cookery and Customs.*

If any reconciliation has been made out of the bitter disputes about the Vietnam War, it is in the warm reception of Vietnamese refugees and their wonderful food. This home-style recipe is for a beef noodle soup that has become popular with customers of many backgrounds in Vietnamese American restaurants. The original recipe has no quantities, so I have filled them in from other Vietnamese cookbooks. The ingredients were checked for availability with Asian groceries, but the typical restaurant condiments are now a slice of lime, fresh Asian basil, and cilantro along with hot chile sauce and hoisin sauce.

Yield: Serves 12

1 pound beef round or brisket

2 pounds beef short ribs or 3 pounds of oxtail

1 5-pound fowl

1 to 1½-inch piece of fresh ginger

1 onion

2 star anise

2 stalks lemon grass

1 tablespoon Accent or MSG (optional)

1½ cups *nuoc mam* (fish sauce)

12 tiny hot chile peppers, or 4 jalapeño chiles

¼ teaspoon 5-spice powder (available in Chinese groceries)

1 pound bean sprouts

2 pounds dried flat rice noodles

6 green onions or scallions

1 large romaine lettuce

4 stalks celery

2 inches of cucumber

1 carrot

4 tablespoons vinegar

1½ tablespoons sugar

Equipment: Oversized stock pot and large soup pot, or 3 large soup pots, ovenproof plate or dish, 12 very large soup bowls

1. Rub unpeeled onion and ginger with oil.

2. Bake onion and ginger 15–20 minutes at 375 degrees in an oven or toaster oven.

3. Cut chicken into serving pieces, reserving backs, neck, and gizzards.

4. Bring ⅓ pot of water to a boil.

5. Add chicken backs and neck, and the bony pieces of the beef, and simmer for 5 minutes.

6. Drain and discard the water.

7. Now add the rest of the chicken parts, fresh beef, the onion, and the ginger to the pot.

8. Cover with 5 quarts of water, and bring to a boil. Skim off any foam or scum that rises to the top.

9. Add the lemongrass, Accent, 1 cup of the fish sauce, the 5-spice powder, and the star anise.

10. Reduce heat to simmer, and cook about 2 hours uncovered.

11. Shred lettuce, chop green onions, slice celery thinly, and slice jalapeño peppers if using.

12. Put each item on a separate plate. Put the bean sprouts on a separate plate, with the chile peppers on one side.

13. Mix the other half cup of fish sauce with the vinegar, sugar, and 4 tablespoons of water.

14. Peel carrot and cucumber. Chop them into fine dice, and add to the fish sauce mixture.

15. Bring a large pot of water to boil and add the rice noodles. Cook 8–10 minutes, or until tender.

16. Strain everything out of the soup. Cut meat off the bones and chicken and slice as well as you can. Slice the boneless beef in very thin slices.

17. Drain rice noodles in a colander and wash under cold running water.

18. "Arrange slices of cooked meat on top of noodles."

19. "Dip out soup and [nearly] fill bowl."

20. Sprinkle on green onions, lettuce, and bean sprouts.

Serve hot with the rest of the salad vegetables, the chile peppers, and the fish sauce mixture for people to add as they go along. Let the bean sprouts cook a little in the hot soup before eating them. Pho is eaten with chopsticks in one hand and a Chinese-style soup spoon in the other hand. The noodles are picked up with chopsticks and put on the spoon.

50

THE 1970S
(1971–1975)

This book ends in 1975, not because that was the end of American history, but because it was the end of the Vietnam War, a clear point of demarcation. Many historical debates are never settled. But after about twenty-five years, people begin to agree on most of the basic facts. We include here some recipes that refer to political events of the 1970s. The next generation of historians will begin to decide which events were most important. The 1960s as they are now remembered really did not start until the late 1960s and continued well into the 1970s. Another way to look at the early 1970s is as a time when the political and cultural "center" or mainstream seemed very weak, and new ideas that had been viewed as extreme or unconventional were taken more seriously. Of the recipes in this section, two are from the political center, two from the cultural left, and two from emerging conservative activists.

FIVE CAN HOT DISH (1971)

To understand what the hippies were rebelling against, try this dish that was submitted to a commemorative cookbook by Mrs. Harold LeVander, wife of the Republican governor of Minnesota. She wrote,

"This is a good recipe for a career lady or one involved in community service. If the ingredients are in the kitchen, the recipe is quick and easy!" (Source: *Missouri 1821–1971 Sesquicentennial Edition Cookbook*.) It was this combination of good intentions and corporatized eating, that set off the urge to reform everyday life that was at the heart of the '70s protests. At the same time, we have to remember that convenience foods were long associated with women taking a larger role outside the home—and the hippie period was initially quite antifeminist. The revival of feminism in the mid-1970s was about the workplace, and home cooking was viewed part of the housework problem (and then opened up for sensitive men, especially if we would do the dishes as well). The 1980s revival of ethnic home cooking may have been a reaction to both canned cuisine and crunchy **Granola**.

Yield: Serves 4

1 can cream of mushroom soup

1 can chicken soup

1 can tuna fish

1 can evaporated milk

1 can chow mein noodles

1 cup chopped celery

Equipment: Soup pot, casserole dish and a larger pan that it fits inside

1. Preheat oven to 350 degrees. Heat a quart of water in the soup pot.
2. Wash celery stalks and chop enough for a cup of finely sliced celery.
3. Combine all ingredients in casserole dish.
4. Put hot water into the large pan, then put in the casserole dish so it is surrounded by water. This makes it cook more evenly.
5. Bake casserole 1 hour at 350 degrees.

Serve as a one-dish supper, or carry to a potluck political dinner.

FAMILIA (1972)

This uncooked granola mixture from Switzerland was promoted by the "Hog Farm" commune at political demonstrations, including the May 1970 New Haven demonstrations to support jailed members of the Black Panther Party. The recipe is from *Recipes for a Small Planet*, by Ellen Buchman Ewald, an organic food activist whose recipes are mostly intended to maximize the protein content of vegetarian diets. This bit of science was politicized with the theory that such diets would increase the world's food supply by reducing the inefficiency of feeding grain to meat animals. The amount of cheese and eggs in some recipes has since reduced the appeal of this book among health food eaters, although a politicized vegetarianism remains part of American life, as it has been since the 1830s. The Hog Farm recipe had only three ingredients: rolled oats, raisins, and sunflower seeds. You can obtain rolled wheat flakes from online suppliers, such as www.buttecreekmill.com and www.raymondhadley.com.

Yield: Serves 10, providing about $\frac{1}{3}$ of adult protein for one day, according to 1972 definitions

$2\frac{2}{3}$ cups rolled oats

$2\frac{2}{3}$ cups rolled wheat

2 cups raw wheat germ

$1\frac{1}{2}$ cups peanuts (raw or roasted)

1 cup sunflower seeds (raw or roasted)

1 cup (or more) raisins

1 cup dried apricots, peaches, or apples

Equipment: Meat grinder or food processor, 10-cup covered container

1. Grind or process half the peanuts to make about 1 cup of peanut meal.
2. Chop the dried fruit into bite-size pieces. (Apples were used in the original Swiss familia.)
3. Stir all the ingredients together and store in a covered container.

Serve one cup "with milk, yogurt or buttermilk, golden honey or pure maple syrup."

CRUNCHY DRY CEREAL (GRANOLA) (1972)

As crunchy granola has only gradually become the culinary symbol of the hippies of the 1960s, it will be up to future food historians to locate its actual origins. The term is very confusing, because for many years it was a trademark of J.L. Kellogg, older brother of Harvey Kellogg who started the famous cornflake company. Kellogg's version was a multigrain cereal so crunchy it had to be cooked for almost half an hour to be eaten. He had wanted to call it "Granula," but that name was in use by an older and even less edible health cereal. This recipe from the *Whole Earth Cook Book*, by Sharon Cadwallader and Judi Ohr, is typical of the latter-day granola cooked on communes and served in healthfood restaurants in the early 1970s.

Yield: Serves 9–12

3 cups rolled oats ("old-fashioned oat-meal")

1 cup wheat germ

1 cup sesame seeds

1 cup shredded, unsweetened coconut

¼ cup oil

¾ cup honey

1 teaspoon vanilla

Equipment: 2 baking sheets, long oven mitts, long-handled spatula or spoon for mixing, 2 wire racks for cooling

1. Mix all ingredients.
2. Spread ½-inch deep on cookie sheets.
3. Bake at 250 degrees "until golden brown."
4. Remove pans from oven and stir twice, "as sides brown first."
5. When browned, let cool on wire racks.
6. Break up with hands. Store in jars.

"Serve with milk."

BJH's New England Boiled Dinner (1973)

This is a more a braised beef stew than a traditional New England boiled dinner, but it shows that not everyone in the 1970s was a hippie, or ate like one, because this was submitted by Betty Jane Hargis, wife of the ultra-conservative evangelist Dr. Billy James Hargis, to *Christian Crusade Blue Ribbon Recipes*, compiled by Maxine Secrest, and "Dedicated to Christian Conservative Women." Although the leadership of what would become a powerful "Religious Right" movement presented a meat-and-potatoes recipe, some submissions from the rank and file specified organic produce and whole wheat flour. Hargis became disillusioned with Richard Nixon and also went through a sex scandal, but still preaches and sells anti-Communist books through an Internet web site. A *culinary* conservative might demand that a New England Boiled Dinner be boiled, where this is more like a Yankee Pot Roast. But it is certainly "Middle American" meat and potatoes.

Yield: Serves 6

4-pound chuck roast

½ cup flour

1 tablespoon fat

4 peppercorns

1 bay leaf

6 potatoes

6 onions

6 carrots

1 green cabbage

Equipment: Dutch oven or heavy soup pot, vegetable peeler

1. Add salt and pepper or seasoned salt to flour to make seasoned flour.
2. "Rub the roast lightly with seasoned flour."
3. Melt fat in Dutch oven or heavy soup pot.
4. Brown roast on all sides over medium-high heat.
5. Add 2 cups water, peppercorns and bay leaf. Reduce heat to simmer slowly, or put in the oven at 350 degrees. Cook 2 hours 15 minutes to 2 hours 45 minutes.
6. Meanwhile, peel carrots, onions, and potatoes.
7. Add potatoes, onions, and carrots and cook another 20 minutes.
8. Meanwhile, remove wilted cabbage leaves. Halve cabbage and cut out core. Cut each half into 3 wedges.

9. Add the cabbage wedges on top of the other ingredients and cook 20 more minutes.

"Serve with buttered corn muffins."

CHICANO CONVICT GUACAMOLE (MID-1970S)

This recipe was submitted by G. Gordon Liddy for the *Arizona Celebrity Cookbook* (1997). Liddy, a former FBI agent and presidential adviser, became a celebrity when he was caught among others breaking into a Democratic Party headquarters in the Watergate building of Washington, D.C. in 1971. Liddy refused to implicate higher officials and served five years in prison. But the scandal involved leaders of the Republican Party and government officials. President Nixon resigned in 1974, as he was about to be impeached by Congress. Liddy went on to become a popular conservative radio talk-show host and says of the recipe, "This I learned from the Chicanos in prison. These ingredients were used because they were what could be smuggled out of the mess hall."

The Watergate Scandal led to many new laws, but also produced a wave of conspiracy theories and an increase in public cynicism and apathy about politics and government. The new laws were invoked in a series of political scandals in the 1990s, President Clinton was impeached (but not convicted by the Senate), and the election of 2000 had a very high voter turnout. So it is still under debate whether Watergate was a turning point, part of a trend, or just another of the political scandals that are part of the culture of a free society. Liddy's post-prison career shows that many Americans agree that lawbreaking is sometimes justified in the name of political principles and loyalty, and his choice of recipe indicates a consistent pride over his role.

Yield: Serves 4 as an appetizer

6 ripe avocados

4 eggs

$^3/_4$ cup prepared salsa

1 bag tortilla chips, or

Sliced raw vegetables (celery, carrots, red and green bell peppers)

Equipment: Knife and fork smuggled from the prison mess hall, potato masher, egg slicer (optional)

1. Boil eggs 15 minutes. Cool in cold running water and shell.
2. Halve avocados and remove the large seed.
3. Mash the avocados in a large bowl.
4. Chop the hard-boiled eggs.
5. Mix in the eggs and salsa.

"Serve with chips or raw vegetables."

GARDEN SALAD (1975)

The first "oil shock" in 1974 brought gas lines and high prices to a nation that had not suffered major economic problems in twenty years. The National Federation of Republican Women responded with *The Energy Saving Cookbook*. Most of the recipes were about conserving the energy of busy Republican women, but some, like this no-cook salad, also cut down on the use of fossil fuels. It is a variation on the three-bean salad popular throughout the seventies and eighties. The book called it a "Can Opener Special." It was submitted by Mary Bell Shepherd of Forest Heights, Maryland.

NOTE: RECIPE TAKES TWO DAYS.

Yield: Serves 18–24

1 can green beans

1 can wax beans

1 can lima beans

1 can diced carrots

1 can kidney beans

$^1/_2$ bunch celery

1 large onion

1 red pepper

1 green pepper

$1^1/_2$ cups vinegar

$^1/_2$ cup peanut oil

2 cups sugar

1 teaspoon celery seed

Equipment: Can opener, colander, large mixing bowl

1. Halve, peel, and chop the onion. (Wear swim goggles to avoid tears.)

2. Cut of the tops and bottoms of the peppers, remove stems and cut out the cores. Cut into small dice.

3. Wash and chop celery.

4. Open and drain canned beans. Rinse off kidney beans and limas in colander.

5. Combine vegetables in large bowl.

6. Mix last 4 ingredients with $^1/_2$ cup water and 1 teaspoon salt.

7. Chill for 24 hours before serving.

Serve with a casserole, "Easy Popovers" (you've already got the oven hot), and "Strawberry and Pineapple Cocktail."

ANNOTATED SELECT BIBLIOGRAPHY

A more complete bibliography will appear in the *American History Cookbook Reference Companion*.

BOOKS ABOUT AMERICAN FOOD HISTORY

Andrews, Mrs. Lewis R., and Kelly, Mrs. J. Reaney. *Maryland's Way*. Annapolis, MD: The Hammond-Harwood House Association, 1963.

To raise funds to preserve a 1795 mansion, the authors collected two hundred years of traditional recipes from old Maryland families. It would be nice if they had put dates on all the recipes, and if the dates they do cite were explained better, and if some information were provided on the people who kept the kitchen books. But some people ate really well in Maryland, the recipes are wonderful, and the authors didn't make anything up.

Dillon, Clarissa. *So Serve It Up: Eighteenth Century Foodways in Eastern Pennsylvania*. Published by the author, 1999.

Brilliant research into food cooked around Philadelphia about the time of the American Revolution, with many period recipes given verbatim. The book is organized by months of the year and topics. For example, March is about what prisoners ate in the first "gaols." April is an attempt to reconstruct the dinner shared by botanist William Bartram with his visiting Swedish counterpart, Pehr Kalm.

Hess, John L., and Hess, Karen. *The Taste of America*. Urbana and Chicago: University of Illinois Press, 2000. (Updated edition with new introduction; first published 1976.)

This is the book that changed everything for food historians. He was an investigative reporter; she became the dean of American food historians. Some of the book exposes the falsified history promoted by popular food writers, some is a real history with examples from early cookbooks, and some is a devastating attack on corporate food producers and their allies in the press.

Hess, Karen. *The Carolina Rice Kitchen: The African Connection*. Columbia: University of South Carolina Press, 1992.

The book is built around a facsimile of a 1901 cookbook, but ranges over many centuries with the precision and accuracy demanded by Karen Hess in all things. This volume is her definitive statement on the making of American food, at least until the completion of her edition of the Jefferson family recipes that is now in progress.

Hooker, Richard J. *The Book of Chowder*. Boston: The Harvard Common Press, 1978.

The definitive work on chowder, with seventy-three recipes from 1751 to 1972. But it is still something of a mystery why potatoes and milk became part of most chowders around the 1840s.

———. *A History of Food and Drink in America*. Indianapolis: Bobbs Merrill, 1981.

Although dated, this is the best history survey of American food because Hooker read everything published up to that time and didn't invent as much to fill gaps as did other writers. No recipes.

Neithammer, Carolyn. *American Indian Food and Lore.* New York: Collier Macmillan, 1974. (Reissued in 1999 as *The Southwest Indian Cookbook.*)

Well researched and organized by plant species with many wild plants. Covers southwestern tribes exclusively.

Oliver, Sandra L. *Saltwater Foodways: New Englanders and Their Food at Sea and Ashore, in the Nineteenth Century.* Mystic, CT: Mystic Seaport Museum Inc., 1995.

Sandra Oliver was a historic interpreter at the Mystic Seaport Museum and is now editor of *Food History News.* This beautiful book is the state of the art in food history—all recipes sourced and given verbatim with separate modern interpretations. The starting point is specific people who lived and worked in six of the restored buildings at the museum.

Parker, Arthur C. *Iroquois Uses of Maize and Other Food Plants.* Ontario, Canada: Iroqcrafts Iroquois Reprints, 1983. (Originally published in the *New York State Museum Bulletin* 144, November 1, 1910. Reprinted with some additional material by William Guy Spittal.)

Classic source for Iroquois foodways and recipes, with one hundred named corn dishes and some quotation of early explorers.

Shapiro, Laura. *Perfection Salad: Women and Cooking at the Turn of the Century.* New York: Farrar, Straus, and Giroux, 1986.

No recipes, but a very readable and well-researched story of how food writers became "domestic scientists" and home economists, and what they did to American eating in the process.

Smith, Andrew F. *Popped Culture: A Social History of Popcorn in America.* Columbia: University of South Carolina Press, 1999.

Andrew Smith continues his myth-busting books on the history of popular foods. The Pilgrims did not have popcorn.

———. *Pure Ketchup: A History of America's National Condiment with Recipes.* Columbia: University of South Carolina Press, 1996.

Smith's narrowest subject, but perhaps the best of his books.

———. *Souper Tomatoes: The Story of America's Favorite Food.* Piscataway, NJ: Rutgers University Press, 2000.

Smith rounds out his tomato trilogy with tomato soup.

———. *The Tomato in America.* Columbia: University of South Carolina Press, 1994.

The first in what has become a series of detailed one-food surveys by Andrew Smith. Smith conveys a lot of American food history from such "micro studies" by reaching out to other kinds of social history for understanding.

Spaulding, Lily May, and Spaulding, John. *Civil War Recipes: Receipts from the Pages of* Godey's Lady's Book. Lexington: University Press of Kentucky, 1999.

This is not really a Civil War book, and *Godey's* was not a magazine that printed detailed recipes. However, *Godey's* was at its highest circulation in the Civil War years and collected lots of what Americans were eating, and its readers tried out what they read. The Spauldings contribute a useful introduction, although they are not fully up to speed on measurement issues, such as how much smaller eggs were in the 1860s.

Williams, Susan. *Savory Suppers and Fashionable Feasts: Dining in Victorian America.* New York: Pantheon Books, 1985.

This book offers many period recipes accurately sourced within a somewhat academic discussion of how dinner was served. Williams uses some of the earlier histories uncritically, and isn't rigorous enough about what came before what and when cookbooks were first published. Recipes aren't glossed, but they are verbatim. If you don't have access to a library with nineteenth-century cookbooks or facsimiles, there are a lot of recipes here.

EARLY COOKBOOKS REPRINTED OR REPUBLISHED IN FACSIMILE

Beecher, Catherine E. *Miss Beecher's Domestic Receipt-Book.* Third Edition. New York: Harper and Brothers, 1858. (Facsimile with introduction by Janice (Jan) Bluestein Langone; Mineola, NY: Dover Books, 2001.)

Miss Beecher was less interested in food than reform, although she was not a suffragist nor an abolitionist. She was an early educator of girls and one of the first American food writers to take an interest in what children were fed. Because she was the daughter and sister of ministers, she is often preaching, which makes her a useful cooking writer for modern readers, who also have to be *told what to do.*

Bryan, Mrs. Lettice. *The Kentucky Housewife.* Cincinnati: Shepard and Stearns, 1839. (Facsimile by Image Graphics, Inc, Paducah, KY, no date, and apparently out of print.)

Like all early cookbook writers, Mrs. Bryan stole recipes and recited some of her thirteen hundred without trying them; however, in the open-minded spirit of the Age of Jackson, she gathered many useful things for the first time.

Child, Lydia Maria. *The American Frugal Housewife.* Twelfth Edition. Boston: Carter, Hendee, 1832. (Facsimile published 1965 by Worthington, Ohio, Historical Society).

There are several other facsimiles of this popular early American cookbook. Mrs. Child was possibly the first American woman to support her family by writing and editing. She lost her mother when young and probably learned to cook by trial and error, and from relatives in Maine, so her food is practical and economical, both as a moral point and by necessity.

Estes, Rufus. *Good Things to Eat as Suggested by Rufus.* Chicago: Published by the author, 1911. (Facsimile of the first edition by D.J. Frienz; Jenks, OK: Howling at the Moon Press, 1999.)

A wonderful collection of plain and fancy dishes by a man born into slavery. Because Estes worked thirty years as a chef on Pullman dining and private railroad cars, the book is the best source for early railroad cooking.

Fisher, Abby. *What Mrs. Fisher Knows About Old Southern Cooking: Soups, Pickles, Preserves, etc.* San Francisco: Women's Co-operative Printing Office, 1881. (Facsimile with an introduction by Karen Hess; Bedford, MA: Applewood Books, 1995.)

African American cooking by a veteran caterer who learned many of her dishes during slavery times.

Hale, Sarah Josepha. *The Good Housekeeper.* Boston: Otis, Broaders, 1841. (Facsimile of the sixth edition with an introduction by Janice (Jan) Bluestein Langone; Mineola, NY: Dover, 1996.)

This very early book by the fifty-year editor of *Ladies' Magazine* and *Godey's Lady's Book* was first published in 1839.

Hill, Annabella P. *Mrs. Hill's Southern Practical Cookery and Receipt Book.* New York: Carlton Publisher, 1867. (Facsimile with historical commentary by Damon L. Fowler; Columbia: University of South Carolina Press, 1995.)

A huge authorititave collection of southern dishes by a prominent Georgia woman. Mrs. Hill had been cooking and directing kitchens for decades, and the book is full of details about how early recipes were actually turned into food.

"A Lady of Charleston" [Sarah Rutledge]. *The Carolina Housewife.* Charleston: W.R. Babcock, 1847. (Facsimile with introduction by Anna Wells Rutledge; Columbia: University of South Carolina Press, 1979.)

One of the most important sources of early American recipes, and vital to any reconstruction of the deeply Africanized cuisine of South Carolina.

"A Lady of Philadelphia" [Eliza Leslie]. *Seventy-Five Receipts for Pastry, Cakes, and Sweetmeats.* Boston: Monroe and Francis, 1828. (Facsimile published Cambridge, MA: Applewood Books, 1988.)

Enormously influential recipes with many important observations about cooking techniques that are invaluable to historical research. This book launched the thirty-year career of Miss Leslie, the most prolific and influential American food writer up to the 1870s.

Leslie, Eliza. *Directions for Cookery.* Philadelphia: Henry Carey Baird, 1854. (Facsimile with introduction by Jan Langone; Mineola, NY: Dover Books, 1999.)

Food historian Jan Langone wisely used one of the last editions of this book, first published in 1837, because Miss Leslie kept adding to it. This is arguably the best American cookbook published before the Civil War, and certainly the easiest to use because it is full of Miss Leslie's detailed instructions.

"A Married Lady" [Mrs. A.L. Webster]. *The Improved Housewife.* Hartford, CT: A.L. Webster, 1845. (Facsimile of the sixth edition, revised with introduction by Louis Szathmary; New York: Arno Press, 1973.)

A very interesting and somewhat neglected book with more than five hundred recipes from both North and South.

Randolph, Mary. *The Virginia House-Wife*. Washington, DC: Davis & Force, 1824. (Facsimile with notes and commentaries by Karen Hess; Columbia: University of South Carolina Press, 1984.)

The most important southern cookbook published before the Civil War and still the major text for what the founding fathers ate at home. Mrs. Randolph was acquainted with all the leading Virginia families, but was eventually reduced to running a boarding house. The book featured an early refrigerator and ice cream all summer! This cookbook has the first published recipe for almost everything that isn't in *The American Frugal Housewife*.

Simmons, Amelia. *American Cookery: Or,. . . .* Albany, NY: C.R. Webster, 1796. (Facsimile with an introduction by Karen Hess; 1996: Bedford, MA: Applewood Books, 1996.)

This is the second edition, with corrections and additions by the author, of the first American cookbook.

AMERICAN COOKBOOKS

The Congressional Club. *The Congressional Club Cook Book*. Washington, DC: The Congressional Club, 1927.

A wonderful survey of regional cooking with extracts from the Jefferson family cookbooks and a collection of early American baking recipes. Contributed by wives of officials. An enlarged edition was published in 1933, and seven more editions have appeared since.

Croly, Jane Cunningham. *Jenny June's Cook Book*. New York: The American News Company, 1978.

Pioneer journalist "Jenny June" was too busy to be a great cook, but she was a fine collector of many interesting items: celebrity recipes from the leading suffragists of the time, a selection of recipes from the notorious Oneida free-love commune, and a chapter of exotic "Jewish Receipts." I am indebted to Karen Hicks for introducing me to Jenny June.

Ellet, Mrs. E.F. *The New Encyclopedia of Domestic Economy*. Norwich, CT: Henry Hill, 1872.

(Probably identical to her 1857 *Practical Housekeeper*.)

An enormous and interesting compendium from many sources. If the earlier book was not much expanded in 1872, Mrs. Ellet published some of the earliest recipes for Jewish foods, strawberry shortcake, soda fountain syrups, and other popular foods of the day. If anyone knows where to read a copy, please let me know!

Leslie, Eliza. *Miss Leslie's New Cookery Book*. Philadelphia: T.B. Peterson and Brothers, 1857.

Miss Leslie added more recipes to her works every year or two. She also added details about her earlier recipes, going back to the thirty-year-old *Seventy-Five Receipts*. This is probably her last work, a 650-page summary of everything she knew about food, and thus the most important nineteenth-century cookbook that has never been issued in facsimile.

Lincoln, Mary J. *The Boston Cook Book*. Boston: Little Brown, 1904.

This book has been published in a facsimile of the 1883 first edition. But like Eliza Leslie, Mrs. Lincoln added new recipes every few years, so later editions are more complete. Like her mentor, Maria Parloa, Mrs. Lincoln was grounded in old New England cooking, but worked with the domestic science movement.

Mann, Mrs. Horace [Mary Tyler Peabody Mann]. *Christianity in the Kitchen: A Physiological Cook Book*. [Spine title: Mrs. Horace Mann's Health and Economy in Cooking.] Boston: Ticknor and Fields, 1857.

A moderate reform cookbook with many traditional New England foods by a woman at the center of the period's intellectual life. Despite the off-putting title, the recipes are good and the book deserves to be better known. Mrs. Mann included a chapter of un-Christian and un-physiological French recipes because she had to admit French food was delicious.

Parloa, Maria. *Miss Parloa's Kitchen Companion*. Boston: Estes and Lauriat, 1887.

Miss Parloa was the most experienced and fully grounded American cooking teacher of the second half of the nineteenth century, with many useful observations about older dishes, and a good eye for new developments. The *Kitchen Companion* is especially useful for its illustrations, many of which are reprinted in this book, and for the comments on how things were done in the kitchen at this time of transition.

————. *Miss Parloa's New Cookbook*. Boston: Estes and Lauriat, 1881.

Many useful comments on old dishes as Miss Parloa collected, often from named sources, a number of early American specialties as part of the colonial revival.

PUBLISHED MANUSCRIPTS

Eaton, Susan, ed. *A Quaker Lady's Cookbook: Recipes from the Parry Mansion*. The New Hope [Pennsylvania] Historical Society, 1998.

Actual transcriptions of four handwritten recipe books in the same family from 1787 to 1900.

Pinckney, Eliza Lucas. *Recipe Book of Eliza Lucas Pinckney*, 1756. South Carolina Society of the Colonial Dames of America, n.d.

Very important document showing African influences on rice and yam cookery. Mrs. Pinckney was an indigo planter near Charleston, and the mother of Eliza Pinckney Horry.

A Tryon Palace Trifle, or Eighteenth Century Cookery &C. Williamsburg, VA: The Tryon Palace Commission, 1960. (With introduction by Bess Hyman Guion and other historical materials relating to the Tryon family and their house at New Bern, North Carolina, built 1767–1770.)

Dated by the editors to between 1730 and 1760, this manuscript is in the kitchen of the historic mansion originally built by British Governor William Tryon. If the book did belong to the Tryons, it was probably written in England by or for previous generations and then brought to the colonies, since it contains no specifically American recipes.

UNPUBLISHED MANUSCRIPTS

Anonymous. Recipe Book. 1832. (Collection of Karen Hicks.)

A very attractive small booklet bound and lettered in various styles by two young people in northern New Hampshire or southern Maine. The authors copied about one-third of their recipes from *75 Receipts* by Eliza Leslie (1824), and another ten or twelve from *The Frugal Housewife* (1827) by Lydia Maria Child, but the rest seem to come from neighbors and probably from older kitchen manuscripts.

Haley, Anne Augusta. Recipe Book. South Dedham, Massachusetts, 1860. (Boston Public Library)

The library also has a later kitchen book by the same writer.

Hubbell, Anna Moore [?]. Loose collection of recipes, eight sheets, some numbered as though pages 84–89 were torn from a top-bound ledger, 1829 to 1849. (Author's collection)

Recipes signed by A.M.H., J.H., and J. Hubbell suggest that these may have been associated with Anna Moore Hubbell (1790–1861) of Bennington, Vermont, who married Julius C. Hubbell in 1812.

Zanger, Janet. Untitled. 1921. (Author's collection)

Notes taken in an eighth-grade cooking class, possibly in Ohio or western Pennsylvania, since the composition book used was made in Clearfield, Pennsylvania. Janet Zanger, no relation to the author of this book, wrote careful directions for muffins, ice cream, boiled salad dressing, and other dishes that became cooking basics for much of the twentieth century.

WORLD WIDE WEB SITES

Civil War Interactive, The CWi Civil War Cookbook. March 10, 2002 ⟨http:www.civilwarinteractive.com/cookbook.html⟩

A very good and large (five hundred-plus and growing) selection of verbatim recipes from 1795 into the 1880s, with a few thoughtful reconstructions by contemporary re-enactors. The sources include current facsimiles of early cookbooks, but also some that have not been reprinted.

Connor Prairie, History Online. March 13, 2002. ⟨http://www.connorprairie.org/historyonline/index.html⟩

Research articles on many subjects from the Ohio living history village, with six very good cooking articles offering period recipes verbatim.

Kitchenlink.com, Kitchenlink.com Food History. March 13, 2002. ⟨http://www.kitchenlink.com/cgi/public_frames?page=history⟩

Very good page of links to online cookbooks, including some full-text examples not otherwise listed here.

Michigan State University, Feeding America: This Historic American Cookbook Project. March 13, 2002. ⟨http://digital.lib.msu.edu/cookbooks⟩

A project that aims to put seventy-five historic cookbooks online from the Clements Library under the guidance of food historian and cookbook collector Janice Langone. They are in the form of large .gif images, which are slow to load and browse unless you have a broadband connection.

Morris County [New Jersey] Library, The Food Timeline. March 13, 2002. ⟨http://www.git.net.mocolib/kid/food.html⟩

Morris County [New Jersey] Library, The Culinary History Timeline. March 13, 2002. ⟨http://www.git.net.mocolib/kid/food1.html⟩

Amazing and frequently updated links to food history resources, not all equally reliable but worth constant checking, especially as whole cookbooks are coming online.

Skjöldebrand, Martin, The Olde Cookery Book. May 13, 2000. ⟨http://www.bahnhof.se/~chimbis/⟩ August 14, 2000.

Medieval and early modern recipes from many sources. Especially valuable for the author's translations of early Scandinavian cookbooks.

University of Michigan Humanities Text Initiative, Making of America. March 13, 2002. ⟨http://www.moa.umdl.umich.edu⟩

The largest online text collection, with eighty-five hundred books and long runs of some significant magazines. Searchable, but very slow and tricky to browse. Includes about six cookbooks that I have found, in the form of large images that are slow to load and browse. You can also download scans of the books, but they are unedited and messy. Nevertheless, a crucial resource.

CHRONOLOGICAL
INDEX OF RECIPES

The years given are usually the year the recipe was published. In some cases, dishes are dated from when they are known to have been used. Thus, most dishes actually were in use prior to the listed dates and almost all have been used since. For example, Sofkee, a hominy porridge beloved of Creek and Seminole Indians to this day, has been used in some parts of the United States for more than 1,000 years. The recipe in the book was first published in 1900, but it is dated 1830 because the printed recipe is associated with the Seminole war chief Osceola, who died in 1838.

INDEX OF RECIPES BY STATES

Soufflé (Suffrage), 295–96; Vegetable Hash
(Late Victorian Health Food), 274–75
Minnesota: Five Can Hot Dish (1970s), 427–28;
Gold Medal Cranberry Roly Poly (Trains,
Cars), 325–27; Walnut Oat Burgers (Twentieth
Century Health Food), 372
Mississippi: Mississippi Corn Pone (Masters and
Slaves), 132–33; Mississippi Creole Gumbo
(Civil Rights), 418–19
Missouri: Chocolate Milk Shake (Recent Cooking
by Kids), 381; Scrambled Eggs (Trains, Cars,
Movers), 329; War Butter (World War I),
364–65
Montana: Buttermilk Biscuits (Settlers and Home-
steaders), 269–70; Milk Gravy (Settlers and
Homesteaders), 270; Tomato Soup (Settlers
and Homesteaders), 264–64

Nebraska: Centennial Biscuit (Mush Rolls), 279;
Cream Pie (Settlers and Homesteaders),
265–66; Pancakes (Settlers and Homesteaders),
263–64; Sweet and Nut Sandwiches (Origins,
1880–1936), 316–18; Unfermented Wine
(Temperance), 200
Nevada: Overland Trail Lemonade (Pioneers), 150;
Pink Pickled Eggs (Settlers and Homesteaders),
266
New Hampshire: Hardtack, (Civil War—North),
231–33; Preble Cake (Patriotic Cakes), 62–63
New Jersey: Hamburger À la Foil (Camping in the
Twentieth Century), 348–49; Pork and Parsnip
Hash (Early American Winter Meals), 109;
Stuffed Eggs (Cooking by Kids), 287–88; To
make Chocolate Cream (The Twenty-One
Colonies), 37–38
New Mexico: Gisado de Trigo (The Twenty-One
Colonies), 28–29; Potaje de Fideos (Early
Colonial), 18–19
New York: An Easy Recipe for Protein-Anxious Veg-
etarians (Vietnam), 424–25; Aunt Laura's
Breakfast Potatoes (Abolitionist), 163–64; Ba-
nana Smoothie (Recent Cooking by Kids), 383;
Bridget's Buckwheats (Irish Immigration),
229–30; Brown Betty (National Unity versus
Diversity), 305–306; Cabbage (Radio), 388;
Canadian War Cake (World War I), 359;
Canned Tomatoes (Communal), 213–14;
Chicken Corn Meal À La Farm Relief (Cities,
Urban), 377–78; Codfish Toast (Early American
Winter Meals), 107–108; Cole Slaw (The
Twenty-One Colonies), 33; Corned Beef Hash
(Early American Spring Meals), 72–73; Cornell
"White" Bread, 371–72; Cornmeal Slapjacks
(Camping in the Twentieth Century), 225;
Créole Soup (National Unity versus Diversity),

302–303; Curlylocks Pudding (Cooking by
Kids), 286–87; Do Xao Thap Cam—Buddhist
Vegetable Dish (Vietnam), 423–24; Doed Koeks
(The Twenty-One Colonies), 45–46; Fried Beef-
steak, 207–208; Hard Bread (Revolution),
53–54; Harvest Drink (Early American Fall),
104–105; Henry Ward Beecher's Favorite—
Turtle Bean Soup (Celebrities), 173–74;
Knickerbocker Pickle (Early American Spring),
69–70; Lobscous (Eating on Ships), 219;
Minced Pie, 195–197; Molasses Toast, 192; Oat-
meal Mush (Late Victorian Health Food), 272;
Oatmeal Pudding (World War I), 362–63; Oly
Cooks, 44–45; Our Aunt Harriet's Favorite Dish
(Abolitionist), 166–67; Peanut Butter Brownies
(School Lunch), 355–56; Peas Pudding, 54;
Potassium Broth, 370–71; Potatoes with the
Bone In (Irish Immigration), 229; Ryzon
Hoover Pancakes (World War I), 361–62;
Spaghetti À La Progressive (Labor), 335–36;
Susan B. Anthony's Apple Tapioca Pudding,
291–92; Sweet Potatoes, 225–26; To Make a
Soupe Meagre, 29–30; To Make Cranberry Tarts
(Early American Fall), 99–101; To Prepare
Salad from Celery (Early Colonial), 20–21;
Whig Cakes and Democratic Tea Cakes (The
Age of Jackson), 182–84; Winter Sausage (Pio-
neers), 147
North Carolina: Corkscrew Bread (Camping in the
Twentieth Century), 345–46; Herb Tea (First
Nations), 4; S-Que-Wi (Cherokee Cabbage),
178–79; To Make Chocolet Puffs (The Twenty-
One Colonies), 33–35
North Dakota: Smultboller (Settlers and
Homesteaders), 266–67

Ohio: Apple Brown Betty (Recent Cooking by
Kids), 382; Boy's Coffee (Cooking for
Children), 191–92; Coconut Macaroons
(Labor), 331–32; Delightful Cakes (Early
American Spring Meals), 78–80; Effervescing
Fruit Drinks, 140; Hayes Cake (Political
Cakes), 250–51; Kumbish (Age of Jackson),
181–82; Onions with White Sauce (Cooking
by Kids), 289; Potato Yeast (Early American
Spring), 87–88; Sheridan Cake, 253–54; Span-
ish Rice (Radio), 387–88; Tilden Cake (Politi-
cal and Topical Cakes), 251–52; Wheat Bread
of Potato Yeast (Early American Meals),
88–89; White Tea (Cooking for Children), 191
Oklahoma: BJH's New England Boiled Dinner
(1970s), 429; Rice and Bacon (Military),
260–61
Oregon: Corn Salad (Women's Exchange
Movement), 341–42; Rolled Oat Cookies

SUBJECT AND RECIPE INDEX

WEST HILLS COLLEGE
LEMOORE LIBRARY/LRC

Fire safety, xxi

Firsts. *See* Original or early recipes of popular dishes

Fish dishes: California Chicken, 401–402; Codfish Toast, 107–108; Common Egg Sauce, 78; Directions for Making a Chouder, 35–36; Finnan Haddie, Dearborn, 323–24; Fish Chowder No. 2, 224–25; Fried Trout, 347; Macaroni and Salmon [or Tuna], 362; To Broil Cod, Salmon, Whiting, or Haddock, 77–78; To Pickle Salmon, 38–40

Fisher, Abby, 122–23

Five Can Hot Dish, 427–28

Floating Island, 94–95

Florida colonies, 16–18, 40–41, 179–180

Food, income spent on, xvii, 302–303; relative prices of, xvii, xix, 74, 160, 303–304

Food history, xix

Food-borne illness, xxi

Fool, Raspberry, 92

Ford, Henry, 367

Forrest, General Nathan Bedford, 248

4-H Peanut Candy Squares, 382–83

Franco-Americans, recipes associated with, 13–14, 135–36, 186–87, 301–302, 302–303

Franklin, Benjamin, recipes associated with, 49, 50–51, 169–171

French toast, original, 185

Fried Bologna Sausage, 400

Fried Chicken, original, 136–38

Fried Rice, Sub Gum, 376–77

Fromojadas, 16–18

Fruit Cake, Welsh, 334–35

Fruit dishes: Black Butter, 190–91; Under the Sea Salad, 407–408

Fudge. *See* Desserts, fudge

Funeral cookies, colonial, 45–46

German Holiday Bread, 330–31

"German Toast," 185

German-Americans, dishes associated with: Apisas, 110–11, Cold Chow, 215; German Holiday Bread, 330–31; Kumbish, 181–82; Ryzon Hoover Pancakes, 361–62; Snitz and Knep, 109–110; Tomatensalat, 214–15

Ginger: Ginger Drops, 361; Harvest Drink, 104–105. *See also* Desserts, gingerbreads

Ginger Ale Soda, 201

Gingerbread. *See* Desserts, gingerbreads

Girl Scout Cookie Recipe, An Early, 379. *See also* Scouting

Gordon, Senator and General John B., 249, 295

Graham boarding houses, 272

Graham, Sylvester, 154ff, 212, 271–2, 367; Graham boarding houses, 272; Graham Biscuit or Roll, 155–56; graham crackers, original, 154–55;

Oatmeal Mush, 272; Unleavened Bread and Apples, 211–13. *See also* Temperance

Granola, 272–74, 428–29

Gravy, 270, 289

Great Big Baked Potato, 324

Great Depression (1929–41). *See* Depression, Great

Green beans. *See* Beans, green

Green Tomato Mincemeat, 394

Gregory, Dick (comedian, civil rights and anti-war activist), 372–73

Gridley, Ruell, 254–56

Ground-Nut Soup, 129–30

Guacamole, 430

Gumbo: Gumbo Soup—A Foreign Receipt, 186–87; Mississippi Creole Gumbo, 418–19

Haddock: To Broil Cod, Salmon, Whiting, or, 77–78

Ham dishes: Boiled Ham, 25–26; Ham Omelet, 180; Ham Sandwiches, 138; Ham, Boiled, 25–26

Hamburger dishes: Maria von Braun's Glorified Hamburger, 411; My Not So Famous "S-O-S," 422–23

Hamburgers: Chicken Hamburgers, 342; Hamburg Steak (original Hamburgers), 312–14; Hamburger a la Foil, 348–49; Salisbury steak, 271; Vegetarian Beefsteak, 368–69; Walnut Oat Burgers, 372; Winter Sausage, 147

Hands-on history, x–xiii, xv–xvii

Hanson's Mode of Making Chicken Broth, 126–28

Hardtack, 53, 217, 231–32; Directions for Making a Chouder, 35–36

Hargis, Rev. Billy James, 429

Harrison, President William Henry, 63–64, 246

Harrison, President Benjamin, 199–200

Harvest Drink, 104–105

Hashed and Browned Potatoes, 208–209

Hashes, Corned Beef Hash, 72–73; Pork and Parsnip Hash, 109; Potato Bargain, 219–220; Skillygalee, 233; Vegetable Hash, 274–75

Hasty Pudding, 51–53

Hayes, Mrs. Rutherford B., 199

Hayes, President Rutherford, 250–51

Haymakers' Switchel, 104–105

Health food, dishes promoted as, 154–57, 272–275, 368–73; An Innocent Plum Pudding, 197–99; Shredded Carrot Salad, 388–89; Soy "Whipped Cream," 216; Sweet-and-Sour Beet-Carrot Sauté, 215–16; Unleavened Bread and Apples, 211–13; Hanson's Mode of Making Chicken Broth, 126–28

Hearth Cooking, Boiled Dish—Meat, 70–71. *See also* Dutch oven

Hemingway, Ernest, 347

Herb Tea, 4

Hermits, original, 311–12

Norwegian-Americans, recipe associated with: Smultboller, 266–67
Nuclear weapons, 402–403, 407–408, 410–413
Nut and Bean Soup, 275

Oatmeal: Another Standing Dish in New England, 23–25; Oatmeal Mush, 272; Oatmeal Pudding, 362–63; Rolled Oat Cookies, 347–48; Walnut Oat Burgers, 372
Okra: Gumbo Soup—A Foreign Receipt, 186–87; Mississippi Creole Gumbo, 418–19; Okra a la Maulie, 131–32
Oly Cooks, 44–45
Omelets. See Egg dishes
Oneida community, 213–14
Onions with White Sauce, 289
Orange Jelly, 288–89
Orange Refrigerator Cookies, 327–28
Orange Sherbert, 380
Original or early recipes of popular dishes, 135–43, 311–320; American Chop Suey, 360; Chili Con Carne, 308; Chipped Beef, 233–34; French Toast, 185; Fried Chicken, 136; Graham Crackers, 134–35; Jambalaya, 302; Ketchup, 206–207; Mashed Potatoes, 204–205; Meatloaf, 303–304; PB & J, 316–318; Pumpkin Pie, 11–13; Sandwiches, 138; S'mores, 348; Tuna Casserole, 362
Osceola (Seminole war chief): Sofkee, ix, 179–80
Oven, outdoor, 28
Overland Trail Lemonade, 150
Oxtail Soup, 259–60
Oysters: Ground-Nut Soup, 129–30; Gumbo Soup—A Foreign Receipt, 186–87; Jam Bolaya, 301–302; Oyster Soup Mr. Paca's Way, 76–77

Paca, Justice William, xvii, 76–77
Pancakes. See Breads, pancakes
Parks, Rosa L., 415–16
Pasta dishes: Anne Braden's Spaghetti, 416–17; Depression Soup, 337–38; Hurry-Up Supper Dish, 407; Peanut Macaroni and Cheese, 369; Potaje de Fideos, 18–19; Spaghetti À La Progressive, 335–36; Spaghetti in Italian Style, 314–15; Vermicelli Prepared Like Pudding, 135–36
Patriotism, 58–66. See also Cakes named after politicians; Cold War
Pausarawmena, 8–9
Peace movement. See Vietnam period
Peach Chips, Old Letty's, 128–29
Peach Cobbler, 419–20
Peanut Butter, 194; Peanut Butter Brownies, 355–56; Peanut Butter Cookies, 354–55; Sweet and Nut Sandwiches, 316–18

Peanuts: Familia, 428; Ground-Nut Soup, 129–30; Nut and Bean Soup, 275; Peanut Macaroni and Cheese, 369
Peas: Pea Soup, 332–33; Peas Pudding, 54; To Make a Soupe Meagre, 29–30
Percolator Wassail, 412–13
Pho, 425
Pickled Salmon, 38–40
Pies. See Desserts, pies
Pilau, Minorcan, 40–41
Pinckney, Eliza Lucas (Colonial Planter), 36–37
Pineapple: Candle Salad, 385–86
Pink Pickled Eggs, 266
Pioneer and explorers, recipes associated with, xvii, 145–150, 263–270
Pippins, Stewed Golden, 112–13
Plantation Corn Bread or Hoe Cake, 122–23
Plum Pudding, An Innocent, 197–99
Plymouth Colony, 11–13, 41–43
Politicians. See Cakes named after politicians; Democrats; Federalists; Republicans; Third-Party Candidates; Tories; Whigs
Ponce de León, 16–18
Pone, Mississippi Corn, 132–33
Pork Dishes, Knickerbocker Pickle, 69–70; Pork and Beans, 73–75; Pork and Parsnip Hash, 109; Potato Bargain, 219–220; Snitz and Knep, 109–110; Winter Sausage, 147
Portable Soup, 145–47
Potaje de Fideos, 18–19
Potassium Broth, 370–71
Potato dishes: A Very Economical Dish, 180; Aunt Laura's Breakfast Potatoes, 163–64; Hashed and Browned Potatoes, 208–209; Old Fashioned Potato Soup, 329–30; Potato Bargain, 219–220; Potato Snow, 204–205; Potatoes with the Bone In, 229; Virginia Stew, 133–34. See also Hashes
Potato masher, 80
Potatoes: Boiled Dish—Meat, 70–71; Corn Chowder, 352–53; E Pluribus Unum, 410; Potato Yeast, 87–88
Potatoes, sweet. See Sweet potatoes
Pottages by Col. Paynter, 54–55
Poverty Hash, 219–220
Preble, Senator William Pitt, 62–63
Present-day history, recipes, xix
Pressure cooker, early, 174
Prices of food, xvii. See also Food, relative prices of; Sugar
Prohibition, recipes of: Ginger Ale Soda, 201; Mint Julep, 200–201
Prunes: Prune Soufflé, 295–96; Spiced Prunes, 386–87
Puddings. See Desserts, puddings

Seventh-Day Adventists, 170, 194. *See also* Kellogg family
Shaker Cheese Pudding, 213
Sherbert, Orange, 380
Sheridan, General Phillip, 253–54
Ships, dishes carried on: Gumbo Soup—A Foreign Receipt, 186–87; dishes eaten on, 217–22; Pea Soup, 332–33; Stewed Beans and Pork, 74–75
Shnitz (dried apples). *See* Snitz and Knep; Apples, dried
Short cake, strawberry, 142–43
Shukey Beans, 3–4
Silpee, 23–25
Skillygalee, 233
Skyscraper Special (Dagwood Sandwich), 395
Skyscraper, Banana, 393
Slapjacks, Cornmeal, 225
Slavery, dishes of, 116–134; not to reenact, xviii. *See also* African-Americans
Slovak-Americans, dish identified with, 329–30
Slumgullion, 347–48
Smoothie, Banana, 383
Smultboller, 266–67
Snitz and Knep, 109–110
Sodas, original, 140
Sofkee, ix–x , 179–80
Soufflé, Omelette, 125–27
Soufflé, Prune, 295–96
Soup digester, 174
Soups, chowders: Corn Chowder, 352–53; Directions for Making a Chouder, 35–36; Fish Chowder No. 2, 224–25
Soups and stews: A Very Economical Dish, 180; Carrot Soup, 108–109; Chicken Broth, Hanson's Mode of Making, 126–28; Créole Soup, 302–303; Depression Soup, 337–38; Dried Bean Soup, 304–305; Ground-Nut Soup, 129–30; Gumbo Soup—A Foreign Receipt, 186–87; Lobscous, 219; Mississippi Creole Gumbo, 418–19; Nut and Bean Soup, 275; Okra a la Maulie, 131–32; Old Fashioned Potato Soup, 329–30; Ox-Tail Soup, 259–60; Oyster Soup Mr. Paca's Way, 76–77; Pausarawmena, 8–9; Pea Soup, 332–33; Pho, 425; Portable Soup, 145–47; Potassium Broth, 370–71; [Sweet] Potato Soup, 243; Pottages by Col. Paynter, 54–5; Rebel Soup, 292–93; St. Jacob's Soup, 150–51; To Make a Soupe Meagre, 29–30; Tomato Soup, 264–65; Turtle Bean Soup, 173–74
Sourdough and Sourdough Hotcakes, 267–69
Soy "Whipped Cream," 216
"Space Race," 411

Spaghetti: Anne Braden's Spaghetti, 416–17; Spaghetti À La Progressive, 335–36; Spaghetti in Italian Style, 314–15. *See also* Macaroni; Pasta dishes
Spanish Omelet, 180
Spanish Rice, 387–88
Spanish-American War, 308
St. Augustine colony, 16–18, 40–41
St. Jacob's Soup, 150–51
Steak, 203–210; Hamburg Steak, 312–14; Lemon Pats, 411–12; Mary Hunter's Stewed Beef, 98–99; Sirloin Steak, 375–76
Stollen, 330–31
Strawberries: Curlylocks Pudding, 286–87; Strawberry Bread, 10–11; Strawberry Cake, 142–43
Sub Gum Fried Rice, 376–77
Succotash, Plymouth, 41–43
Suffrage, women's, 163–64, 200, 220–21, 291–97, 332–33. *See also* Abolitionism; Communal experiments; Temperance; WCTU
Sugar, trends in use, 73–74, 160
Sundae, The All-American, 401
Suppawn, 13–14
Swedish Colonists, 19–20
Sweet potatoes: Candied Potatoes, 295; Potato Soup, 243; Sweet Potato Biscuits, 393–94; Sweet Potato Wafers, 241–42; Sweet Potatoes, 225–26
Syllabub, 197

Tamales. *See* Breads, tamales
Tapioca, 291–92
Tarts. *See* Desserts, pies
Tea, White, 191
Tea Cakes, Democratic, 182–84
Teaspoons, changes in size, 140
Teenagers. *See* Kids, dishes made for or by
Temperance, 154, 159,160, 190, 194–202, 211; and alcoholism, xviii; Cream Tartar Bread, 89–90; Harvest Drink, 104–105. *See also* Health food; Prohibition
Texas Independence, 147
Thanksgiving, 97, 99, 101, 108; An Innocent Plum Pudding, 197–99
Third party candidates, dishes identified with: Gregory (Freedom and Peace Party), 372–73; La Guardia (American Labor Party), 335–36, 377–78; Maddox (Independent American Party), 419–420; Wallace-LeMay (American Independent Party), 417–18, 421–22. *See also* Democrats; Republicans
Thirded Bread, 75–76
Thompson, Benjamin. *See* Rumford, Count
Tilden, Governor Samuel, 251–52

Whiting, Cod, Salmon, or Haddock, To Broil, 77–78

Whole Wheat, Gisado de Trigo (Whole Wheat Stew), 28–29

Williams, Roger: Nasaŭmp, 9–11

Wilson, President Woodrow, dish identified with: Lemon Rice Pudding, 175–76; dish of cabinet member, Scotch Scones, 333–34; World War I food restrictions, 360–364

Wine, Unfermented, 200

Women in the Civil War, 233–34, 239–41

Women's Exchange movement, 340–43

World War I, 359–64

World War II, xviii, 399–403, 411

Yam Puding, 36–37

Yams. *See* Sweet potatoes

Yeast, discovery of, 148; Temperance opposition to, 154ff; ways of making, 87–88, 147–50

About the Author

MARK H. ZANGER is a veteran Boston journalist and 20-year restaurant critic from the *Boston Phoenix*, under the name "Robert Nadeau." He is the author of *The American Ethnic Cookbook for Students* (2001) and the associate editor of the *Oxford Encyclopedia of American Food and Drink* (forthcoming).

79813z-3

16